PUZZLER'S GIANT BOOK OF CROSSWORDS

63

Penny Press is the publisher of a fine family of puzzle magazines and books renowned for their editorial excellence.

This delightful collection has been carefully selected by the editors of Penny Press for your special enjoyment and entertainment.

Puzzler's Giant Book of Crosswords, No. 63, August 2017. Published four times a year by Penny Press, Inc., 6 Prowitt Street, Norwalk, CT 06855-1220. On the web at PennyDellPuzzles.com. Copyright © 2017 by Penny Press, Inc. Penny Press is a trademark registered in the U.S. Patent Office. All rights reserved. No material from this publication may be reproduced or used without the written permission of the publisher.

ISBN-13: 978-1-59238-114-2

ISBN-10: 1-59238-114-6

Printed by LSC Communications, Dwight, IL, U.S.A. 7/11/17

PENNY PRESS PUZZLE PUBLICATIONS

✦ PUZZLE MAGAZINES ✦

All-Star Word Seeks
Approved Variety Puzzles
Classic Variety Puzzles
    Plus Crosswords
Easy & Fun Variety Puzzles
Easy Crossword Express
Family Variety Puzzles & Games
Famous Fill-In Puzzles
Fast & Easy Crosswords
Favorite Easy Crosswords
Favorite Fill-In
Favorite Variety Puzzles
Fill-In Puzzles
Garfield's Word Seeks
Good Time Crosswords
Good Time Easy Crosswords
Good Time Variety Puzzles

Large-Print Word Seek Puzzles
Master's Variety Puzzles
Merit Variety Puzzles & Games
Original Logic Problems
Penny's Finest Favorite Word Seeks
Penny's Finest Good Time Word Seeks
Penny's Finest Super Word Seeks
Quick & Easy Crosswords
Spotlight Celebrity Word Seek
Spotlight Movie & TV Word Seek
Spotlight Remember When Word Seek
Tournament Variety Puzzles
Variety Puzzles and Games
Variety Puzzles and Games
    Special Issue
Word Seek Puzzles
World's Finest Variety Puzzles

✦ SPECIAL SELECTED COLLECTIONS ✦

Alphabet Soup
Anagram Magic
    Square
Brick by Brick
Codewords
Cross Pairs Word Seeks
Crostics
Crypto-Families
Cryptograms
Diagramless
Double Trouble
England's Best
    Logic Puzzles

Flower Power
Frameworks
Large-Print Crosswords
Large-Print
    Cryptograms
Large-Print
    Missing Vowels
Letterboxes
Match-Up
Missing List Word Seeks
Missing Vowels
Number Fill-In
Number Seek

Patchwords
Places, Please
Quotefalls
Share-A-Letter
Simon Says
Stretch Letters
Syllacrostics
The Shadow
Three's Company
What's Left?
Word Games Puzzles
Zigzag

✦ PUZZLER'S GIANT BOOKS ✦

Crosswords   Sudoku   Word Games   Word Seeks

ACROSS

1. Cold
4. Neon, e.g.
7. Revel
11. Norse king
13. River plain
15. Gulf of ____
16. Yarn
17. Scott Adams's creation
19. Ice-cream holder
20. Chip in chips
21. Sub shop
22. On the summit
24. A woodwind
25. Jim Davis's creation
27. Al Capp's creation
29. Ethereal
30. What ____ is new?
31. Computer unit
32. Phases
35. Hole punch
37. Moray
39. Part of a lariat
42. Make happy
44. Hopeless case
45. Stocking stuffer?
46. Senior
47. People
48. Island necklace
49. Pipe joint
50. Stable sound
54. Probability
57. Air-show maneuver
59. ____ Rabbit
60. Jerry Siegel's/ Joe Shuster's creation
64. V.T. Hamlin's creation
68. Any
69. Bigfoot's kin
70. Condemn
71. Trudge
73. British subway
74. Dave Kellett's creation

76. Supporter
77. ____-friendly
78. Burn with water
79. Big pond
80. Prevents
81. Flock female
82. Cheerless

DOWN

1. Tad
2. Trolley's sound
3. 1945 conference site
4. Frigid
5. Cleric's vestment
6. Purloin
7. Pork strip
8. Sun-dried brick
9. Madrid mister
10. Leg joint
12. Swerve
13. Lollapalooza
14. Bandleader Shaw

17. Plow manufacturer
18. Road fees
21. Eat sparingly
23. Bygone
26. Fairy
28. Hive insect
31. Chic Young's creation
33. Charles Schulz's creation
34. Colonize
35. Broadway backer
36. Made of fleece
38. Tenant's contract
40. Observe
41. Slip up
42. Curvy letter
43. Thai language

51. ____ du Diable
52. Sensational
53. Dwellings
54. Acrylic fiber
55. Consider
56. Parched
58. Trails
59. Vital fluid
60. The March King
61. Reddish brown
62. Equals
63. Sister's daughter
64. Confuse
65. October's gem
66. Water jars
67. Bohemian dance
68. Hit, as a toe
72. Stained
75. Statute

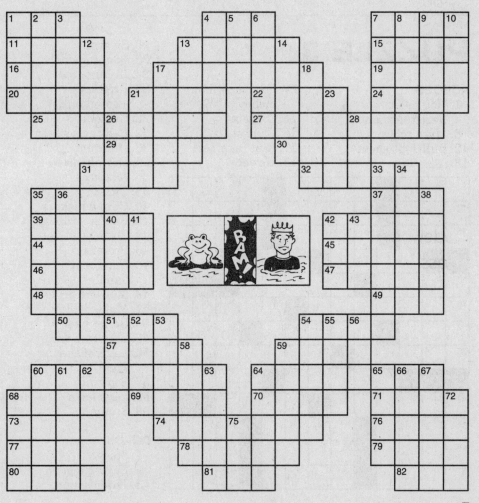

PUZZLE 2

ACROSS
1. Flower support
5. Father, in Dogpatch
8. Moistens, poetically
12. Bossa ____
13. Earlier than, in verse
14. Complain
15. Lyrical
16. A primary color
17. Speck on a map
18. Gaucho's tool
19. Obligated to repay
21. Cheered
23. In a foreign country
26. Scatter off
31. A Tarleton twin
32. British chap
33. More elementary
35. Scheduled
36. Dashes
38. Tries to find
42. Brick holders
46. Car's wheel shaft
47. Cold-weather virus
48. Pagan god
49. Hollow
50. Certain tennis shot
51. Beak
52. Garment fastener
53. Tee preceder
54. Raised

DOWN
1. Uppity person
2. Fuss
3. Sinful
4. Tubular pasta
5. Punctuation mark
6. "____ We All"
7. United
8. Small amount
9. Bridge position
10. Artifice
11. Musher's vehicle
20. Good to munch
22. Roy Rogers's films
23. Lincoln's nickname
24. Swimsuit part
25. Legal matter
27. Cutting drastically
28. Lobster ____
29. Add to
30. Directed
34. Disturb
35. Landscaper's greenery
37. Flies alone
38. Boys
39. Water buffaloes
40. Earthen jug
41. Seaweed variety
43. Skunk's defense
44. Medicinal portion
45. Heap

1	2	3	4		5	6	7		8	9	10	11
12					13				14			
15					16				17			
18					19		20					
			21	22								
23	24	25				26		27	28	29	30	
31						32						
33				34		35						
		36		37								
38	39	40	41				42	43	44	45		
46				47			48					
49				50			51					
52				53			54					

PUZZLE 3

ACROSS
1. Hog meat
4. Resistance units
8. Mass robes
12. Bullfight shout
13. ____ tide
14. Former Milan money
15. Canister
16. Candy ____
17. Rest (against)
18. Wowed
20. Swarm
22. Longing
24. Ill-humored
26. Brightly colored birds
28. Custom
32. Religious sister
33. Different
35. Downhearted
36. Auspices
38. Twist
40. Chin whiskers
42. Easter edibles
43. State positively
46. Promise
48. Impudent female
49. Mower's pride
51. Make doilies
54. Ballet bend
55. Like fine wine
56. "____ of the Tiger"
57. Soaks up
58. Lays lawn
59. Study

DOWN
1. Spicy
2. Boxing legend
3. Threatening
4. Without repetition
5. Earphones
6. Grown boy
7. Broccoli shoot
8. Metal mixtures
9. In ____ of
10. Wheat husk
11. Desert dirt
19. He's on first
21. Utter impulsively
22. Hebrides island
23. Loyal
25. Theater guide
27. Runner-up
29. Landed
30. Bell-like sound
31. Rams' mates
34. Gifted
37. Mountain goats
39. Drenched
41. Book of maps
43. Rock-concert blasters
44. Fodder storage
45. Quick cut
47. Ampersands
50. Earlier
52. Sailor's consent
53. Bo Derek's number

1	2	3		4	5	6	7		8	9	10	11
12				13					14			
15				16					17			
		18	19				20	21				
22	23				24	25						
26			27				28		29	30	31	
32			33		34				35			
36		37			38		39					
		40		41				42				
43	44	45				46	47					
48				49	50				51	52	53	
54				55					56			
57				58					59			

ACROSS

1. Song for Sills
5. Bridle strap
9. Detest
14. ___ a hand
15. Lofty hairstyle
16. Desire badly
17. Picks
18. Property right
19. Legends
20. Above, in poems
21. Kind of coffee
22. Refusal word
23. ___ and fauna
25. Church response
28. Fake
32. Owns
35. Daybreak
38. "Willard" pet
39. Crucial
41. Ah, me!
42. Verbal exams
44. Former
45. Scattered
47. "My country, ___ of thee . . ."
48. Correct copy
49. Very warm
50. And so forth
53. Matinee ___
54. Start
58. Box
61. Monastery figure
65. Limousine, e.g.
66. Three-dimensional
68. Withdraw gradually
69. Unmixed
70. Charm
71. Loosen
72. Having talent
73. Swim for pleasure
74. Lodge fees
75. Situates

DOWN

1. Standoffish
2. Fend off
3. Beginning
4. Newspaper spots
5. Dominate
6. "The Odyssey," e.g.
7. Mental flash
8. Like skim milk
9. Behave
10. Muscle
11. Saintly glow
12. Chef's need
13. Remainder
21. Block
24. Cleanse
26. Whipped dessert
27. Blow it
29. Right now!
30. Rowboat need
31. Declare
32. Noggin
33. Opposed to
34. Manuscript mark
35. Tiny amount
36. Low voice
37. Skin woe
40. Garner
43. Kindled
46. Got hitched
51. Scratched
52. Nonsense
53. Setter breed
55. Diving equipment
56. Ahead of schedule
57. Shade providers
58. Wound cover
59. Mountain cat
60. Border
62. Wooer
63. Diamond feature
64. Washington bills
67. So-so grade
69. Good buddy

Rhyme Time

The answers to the clues below are pairs of rhyming words. For example: "Plump feline" would be FAT CAT.

1. Temperate tot

2. Fast stompers

3. Reality detective

4. Cut-rate jerk

5. Pinnacle cry

7

PUZZLE 6

ACROSS

1. Pops
5. Garden flower
9. Pine substance
14. Depart
15. Midday
16. Wear down
17. Further
18. Greek cheese
19. Not as old
20. The '80s, for one
22. Staff member
24. Gloomy
25. Stink
26. NBC's peacock, e.g.
28. Stoppage
30. Chew
33. River embankment
36. Wagon track
37. Nursery decor
39. Canned
41. Scene of action
43. Hawaiian neckwear
44. Signal
45. Rational
46. Eliminate
48. Tonic partner
49. Ante
51. Trio minus one
52. Fetch
53. Split
55. Hurt
57. Tree's juice
60. Theater receipt
62. Use a credit card
65. African shrubs
67. Eat
69. Nerve
70. Tend the fire
71. Sailor's direction
72. Molecule component
73. Punctured
74. Take wing
75. Salesmen

DOWN

1. House document
2. Shaft
3. Unhappiness
4. Place
5. Hot spot
6. Fish beginnings
7. Whit
8. Slowpoke
9. Break a promise
10. Afore
11. Plants seed
12. Intention
13. Twerp
21. Belief
23. Allot
27. President's office
28. Swimsuit tops
29. Atmospheres
31. Apt
32. Manipulate
34. Magnify
35. Creepy
38. In ___ of
40. Car scar
42. Imminent
44. Bring
46. Adept
47. Instructor
50. Smooched
54. Albacore and bluefin
56. Cartoon Viking
57. Waist accessory
58. Female voice
59. Place for crawling
61. Western tie
63. Gooey stuff
64. Shade providers
66. ___ out (make do)
68. Abundance

[Crossword grid with numbered cells 1-75]

PUZZLE 7

Crossroads

Fill in the squares of each diagram to form a compound word or phrase. One part of the answer reads across, and the other part reads down. The first part may be in either the across or the down boxes. Use only the letters given above the diagram. The letter shown in the diagram is shared by both parts of the answer.

1. E F H I I L R V

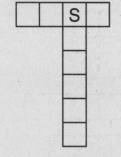

2. B G I I R R T T

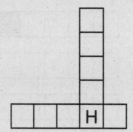

3. A A D F G H I O R S T T W

ACROSS

1. Shredded
5. Made a hole in one on
9. Tax agency: abbr.
12. Strider
13. Frozen-water mass
14. Darling
16. Mountain ridge
17. Speak wildly
18. Gumbo ingredient
19. Combat
20. Downhearted
21. Assistance
23. Kind of daisy
26. "Pygmalion" playwright
28. Mesh
29. Curve
31. Surrender
33. Rome's nation
36. Portent
38. Verve
41. PBS science series
42. Crazy birds
43. Of flight: pref.
44. Minute particle
45. "____ La Douce"
46. Beneath
47. Around
49. Purpose
51. Lingerie item
53. Spinning toy
55. Evolve
59. Message
61. Through
63. Gear
64. Pierre's friend
65. Infuriated
67. Office employee
69. Life stories
70. Remedy
71. Evergreens
72. Explosive initials
73. Comics-character Kett
74. Mimicked

DOWN

1. Jewish scriptures
2. "Carmen," e.g.
3. No longer working: abbr.
4. Before, to Keats
5. Hairstyle
6. Talons
7. Long time span
8. Disembarks
9. Pagan god
10. Reignited
11. Hindu garment
12. Ordinances
15. Flat boat
20. Natural resin
22. Wool provider
24. Spicy sausage
25. Hear legally
27. Laughing animals
30. Exultant shout
32. Skinnier
33. Actress Claire
34. Wee one
35. Hobby
37. Parent
39. Form of "to be"
40. Negative conjunction
42. Candy stick
46. Guitar's kin
48. Hearty bread
50. Nabokov heroine
51. Tattle
52. Send payment
54. Visible
56. Cara or Dunne
57. Covered with ivy
58. Ids' companions
60. Quiz
62. Imaginative thought
66. Furrow
67. Bottled-water source
68. Gratuity

Word Ways

Hidden in each diagram are five 5-letter words beginning with the same letter. Draw a continuous line through the letters as you spell each word by moving in any direction from letter to adjoining letter without crossing your line. Each puzzle has a different starting letter.

1.

```
R N V U G
I E A E O
S K R Y R
Y L H R M
R E I C E
```

2.

```
D Y L A D
R E I M A
O C I V G
D A D O O
R W L T D
```

3.

```
O F N I O
T E G W T
N O C B I
O S C R O
A S I U R
```

PUZZLE 10

ACROSS
1. Biological pouches
5. Powers of "Daniel Boone"
9. Salamander
12. Arch variety
13. Teen follower
14. "Who Slew Auntie ____?"
15. Mythology
16. Percolating
18. Mistaken
20. Informed of
21. Marvy
23. Real
25. Wear away
27. Extract
31. Barton or Bow
32. Dog's lead
33. Conger catchers
35. Move quickly
36. Fish hawk
38. Twilight, in verse
39. Canine sound
42. Not greater
44. Glue, e.g.
46. Caresses
49. Burr, to Hamilton
50. Lulu
51. Of a historic time
52. Endeavor
53. Swelling
54. Behold

DOWN
1. Fifth scale tone
2. Previously
3. Intellectual
4. Prophet
5. Spite
6. Ten-percenter
7. "A ____ of Their Own"
8. Joan of ____
9. Ms. Moran
10. Baptismal basin
11. West African republic
17. More sacred
19. Detecting devices
21. Coin side
22. Skilled
24. Alleviates
26. Small gap
28. Food providers
29. ____ of Man
30. Formerly
34. Wooden strip
35. Leave behind
37. Carouse
39. Dagger's handle
40. Polecat's defense
41. Curds and ____
43. Fencing sword
45. Piglet's mother
47. Knock gently
48. Cunning

PUZZLE 11

ACROSS
1. Player or grand
6. Seasoning
11. Sweater material
13. ____ staircase
14. Radio noise
15. Spuds
16. Cliff
17. Gaudy
19. More agreeable
20. Lawn
24. Terse
27. Vote of denial
28. Felled
29. Be indisposed
31. Dismiss
32. ____-advised
33. Equaled
35. Salami shop
37. Shine again
38. Paving machine
40. Doctrine
43. Type style
46. Artist's workroom
48. Brooding
49. Recipients
50. Kind of tea
51. Put back to zero

DOWN
1. Finished
2. ____ thin air
3. Seaweed extract
4. Forget-me-____
5. Beginning
6. Fitness resorts
7. Meaty
8. Bitter anger
9. Sedan, e.g.
10. Chicago transports
12. Locust tree
13. Mix with a swizzle stick
18. Read out loud
19. Wordless yes
21. Indigo
22. Scarce
23. Hid the gray in
24. Set down
25. Wheel rod
26. Prison pad
30. Nearest the ground
31. Office copy
34. ____ sauce
36. Arctic abode
37. Sprint, e.g.
39. Ascent
40. 15th of March
41. Beget
42. Lion's share
43. Gremlin
44. Tip of Italy
45. Deluge refuge
47. Molokai instrument

CODEWORD

Codeword is a special crossword puzzle in which conventional clues are omitted. Instead, answer words in the diagram are represented by numbers. Each number represents a different letter of the alphabet, and all of the letters of the alphabet are used. When you are sure of a letter, put it in the code key chart and cross it off in the alphabet box. A group of letters has been inserted to start you off.

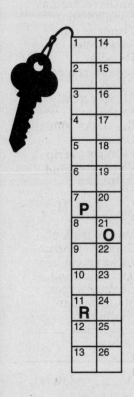

Code key chart:

#		#	
1		14	
2		15	
3		16	
4		17	
5		18	
6		19	
7	P	20	
8	O	21	
9		22	
10		23	
11	R	24	
12		25	
13		26	

Alphabet box:

A N
B Ø
C P̷
D Q
E R̷
F S
G T
H U
I V
J W
K X
L Y
M Z

Grid (top-left cells show P R O prefilled):

6	25	3		8	15	13		9	7(P)	24		11	21	16
25	11	15		24	22	15		15	11(R)	3		15	11	24
20	21	15		11	4	1		19	21(O)	21		15	24	11
25	3	23	15	15	23			9	3	25	10	10	13	15
			16	13	15	9	19		1	3	4			
		16	24	16	15		7	25	7		19	15	3	19	18
24	13	13		9	8	11	15	24	26		13	25	11	24
11	24	19		9	4	15		9	25	9		3	25	13
8	5	24	11		16	24	19	19	13	15		17	15	19
18	15	11	21	3		23	15	15		2	4	24	23	
		12	21	20		24	13	16	4	26			
20	25	11	15	19	24	7			11	15	7	24	25	11
21	23	15		24	23	15		10	25	3		8	21	21
13	15	25		19	15	15		11	15	8		25	19	9
10	24	3		15	11	11		21	11	15		23	24	14

LOVE CODEWORDS? Enjoy hours of fun with our special collections of Selected Codewords! See page 159 for details.

Pairs in Rhyme

Each of these pairs of words is a rhyme for a familiar phrase.

Example: Car and ride (**Answer:** Far and wide)

1. Tin and weather _____

2. Sappy and wealthy _____

3. Right and scary _____

4. Car and allay _____

5. Crow and stain _____

6. Joint and root _____

7. Brand and tight _____

8. Flit and plink _____

PUZZLE 14

• ON THE WATCH •

ACROSS
1. Brownies' parent organization: abbr.
4. Grime
8. Foundation
12. In the previous month: abbr.
13. Scent
14. Indigo
15. Elsie's comment
16. Employee record-keeper
18. Peter's ___ (old papal tax)
20. Soup veggies
21. 19th-century inventor
23. Cut, as wood
27. Kettles
29. Actress Thompson
32. Famed boxer
33. Give out
34. Ms. Farrow
35. B ___ boy
36. Roth or Curry
37. ___ tooth (baby tooth)
38. Without a date
39. Office worker
41. French suffix
43. Kind of type: abbr.
46. Despised
49. Noon, for many
53. Judge Lance ___
54. Frenzied
55. General Bradley
56. Pop's spouse
57. Excludes
58. Shave
59. Vane reading: abbr.

DOWN
1. Andy or Forrest
2. ___ gin
3. Formerly
4. Loved too much
5. Ugandan president Amin
6. Frolic
7. Birch, e.g.
8. Model wood
9. Year, to Pedro
10. "___ semper tyrannis"
11. Antlered animal
17. Spanish house
19. Throw of dice
22. 18-wheeler
24. Dawdle
25. Lamb's pen name
26. Small dent
27. Strokes gently
28. Exclude
30. Big bucks, slangily
31. Create
35. Film pooch
37. Wool eater
40. Nolte and Mancuso
42. "___ Goes My Baby"
44. On the peak of
45. Capital of Peru
47. Jacket style
48. Arched ceiling
49. Chemist's room
50. Ms. Thurman
51. Neither's companion
52. Deface

PUZZLE 15

• FORWARD THINKING •

ACROSS
1. High peak
4. Knock sharply
7. Faction
11. Train part
12. Region: abbr.
13. Tooth trouble
14. Duo number
15. Casino city
16. Slender
17. Careers
20. Bed linen
22. Omelet maker
23. Credit ___
24. Quarry
26. Layer
29. Model Carol ___
30. Charles S. Dutton series
31. "Norma ___"
32. Plaything
33. Maya Angelou, e.g.
34. Tumble
35. Wolf down
36. Sticker
37. Modern
42. Burrow
43. Leg front
44. Yale alumnus
47. Stare rudely
48. Carry
49. Actor Johnson
50. "___ Side Story"
51. Realize
52. Belt or bonnet

DOWN
1. Pretend to be
2. In-___ (relative)
3. Real estate
4. Coral ridge
5. British composer
6. Outlook
7. Silky fabric
8. Canyon sound
9. Goatee's locale
10. Wallet bills
12. Horse's gait
18. Footballer Grange
19. Assert
20. Go away!
21. Crown of light
24. Objects to
25. Fish eggs
26. Carries on
27. Tra follower
28. Scream
33. Average
34. Gun a motor
35. Wading bird
36. Have supper
37. Farm tool
38. Fury
39. Olive and corn
40. Sandal, e.g.
41. Position
45. Mary ___ Retton
46. Hostel

Rearrange this stack of bricks to form a crossword puzzle. The clues will help you fit the bricks into their correct places. Row 1 has been filled in for you. Use the bricks to fill in the remaining spaces.

ACROSS

1. Latch
   Small boat
   Glory
2. Notion
   Roll topping
   Summon forth
3. Filth
   Fix
   London length
4. For e'er and
   e'er
   Diver's goal
   Perused
5. Hops kiln
   Ultimate
6. Custodian
   Sack
7. Motor coach
   Liquid
   measure
   Comprehen-
   sive
8. Place
   Desert beast
   Church
   section
9. Sulfuric and
   nitric
   Purple flower
   Cliff
10. Rye fungus
    Huge
11. Vivacity
    Film
12. Ship's front
    Feather wrap
    Grow
    choppers
13. ___ lazuli
    French cheese
    Gateway
14. Czarist edict
    Cooking fat
    Mortgage
15. Skirmish
    To be, in old
    Rome
    Raison d'___

DOWN

1. Mask
   Youth gp.
   Purple fruit
2. Mine entrance
   Breakfast
   drink
   Perform a fall
   chore
3. Bone-dry
   Up and about
   Milky
   gemstone
4. Benefactor
   Sideways
5. Fingertip
   feature
   Costa del ___,
   Spain
   Observe
6. Home-oriented
   Computer key
7. Madrid cheer
   Sum
   Of high birth
8. Landlord's fee
   Pay
   Woeful word
9. Alpine music
   Artifact
   Vocalized
   pauses
10. Doze off
    Leeway
11. Skirt bottom
    Cry
    Candy ___
12. Upset
    Heckle
13. Brief message
    Raccoon's kin
    Whistle sound
14. Gumbo
    ingredient
    Chaos
    Frost
15. Cattail
    Bonn article
    Marine eagle

BRICKS

N I T / L I ■	E A D / ■ ■ ■	S E ■ / E E ■	A V E / T O R	E ■ C / D S ■
P R O / L A P	N ■ R / A S T	O K E / T R E	T H E / O O R	A ■ O / T ■ M
C H ■ / O A D	W ■ B / I S ■	U K A / M E L	■ J A / B U S	L ■ N / A C ■
I D E / D I R	R N E / O A S	T E E / U ■ D	L E O / E N D	S I T / A C I
E T E / ■ ■ ■	■ T I / N ■ C	■ E R / ■ ■ ■	O R ■ / T E R	P O U / ■ B R
G O T / E L A	I C ■ / ■ ■ ■	O A N / T R E	D ■ L / E ■ E	■ E V / ■ M E
L A R / E S S	O A ■ / B L E	■ T E / T ■ L	A M E / L I L	T A N / I N E

DIAGRAM

	1	2	3	4	5	6	7	8	9	10	11	12	13	14	15
1	H	A	S	P	■	D	O	R	Y	■	H	O	N	O	R
2															
3															
4															
5															
6															
7															
8															
9															
10															
11															
12															
13															
14															
15															

PUZZLE 17

ACROSS

1. Spending limit
4. Sector
8. Staff
12. Canola, e.g.
13. Important periods
14. Shampoo ingredient
15. Singleton
16. Implores
17. Come up
18. Step
20. Made a choice
21. Henpecked
25. Salary
28. Cover up
29. Geese formation
32. Cereal grain
33. Croons
34. Squid's squirt
35. Still
36. Poker term
37. Slosh through water
38. Sorcery
40. Jiggle
44. Capital of Japan
48. Small opening
49. Power unit
52. Eggy drink
53. Slender woodwind
54. To the sheltered side
55. Be human
56. Village's kin
57. Cogwheel
58. Willie Winkie's size

DOWN

1. Dove sounds
2. "___ No Sunshine"
3. Urgent request
4. Horse behind bars?
5. Lode yield
6. Badger
7. 19th of 26
8. Twist
9. Got down
10. Beak
11. Legal document
19. Freezer cube
20. Certain poems
22. African mammal, briefly
23. Type of bean
24. Approached
25. Twisted, as a grin
26. Yes, at sea
27. Reach
29. By way of
30. Football player
31. ___ out a living
33. Put aside
37. Seek to marry
39. Aquatic mammal
40. Splotch
41. Tramp
42. Lined up
43. Zealous
45. Was aware of
46. Long ago
47. Meany
49. Wiggle
50. Ginger ___
51. Pot or rose

14

ACROSS
1. City parcel
4. Mulligan or Irish
8. Pay
12. Before now
13. Came to
14. Warning sign
15. Paid athlete
16. Ogler
17. Chooses
18. Raise
20. Building wing
22. Process part
25. Edition
29. Out of danger
32. Teacher's helper
34. "Stand ___ Deliver"
35. Distinctive period
36. Fitness resort
37. Band's booking
38. Tire filler
39. Yard parts
40. Spouse
41. Caribbean dance
43. Test model
45. Circle segment
47. Superior to
51. Dirt stain
54. Plumber's concern
57. Naught
58. Hearty's companion
59. Egg on
60. Subways' cousins
61. Football linemen
62. Brewed drink
63. "___ No Evil"

DOWN
1. Track circuits
2. Grimm heavy
3. Beep
4. Broomed
5. Santa's gift
6. ___ out a living
7. Had been
8. Warm fabrics
9. Stereo component
10. Understand
11. Printers' concerns
19. Operate
21. Falsehood
23. Soothe
24. Uttered shrilly
26. Adventure story
27. Single thing
28. Rim
29. Stitching joint
30. Formal solo
31. Raise crops
33. Calendar entry
39. Supporting
40. Rowdy crowd
42. Actress Kathy ___
44. Creator
46. Soda or sandwich
48. Billfold bills
49. Base
50. Other than
51. Feminine pronoun
52. Cooking utensil
53. Ancient
55. Prior to, in verse
56. Ripen, as cheese

21

PUZZLE 25

ACROSS

1. Overthrow
6. Heifers
10. Running bill
13. Echo
15. Island feast
16. Mode or carte
17. Cave
18. Placed
20. Yet, to a poet
21. Gush
23. "___ Got to Be Me"
24. Church song
25. Slow, in music
28. Spicy stew
31. Strangely
34. Draw wages
36. Green legumes
37. Short-billed rail
38. Street, in Rome
39. Field cover
40. Current style
42. Pilsner or lager
43. Quiche ingredient
44. Japanese drink
45. Sea eagle
46. Sword fight
48. Truckers' rigs
49. Industrious insects
50. Gush lava
52. Formerly, of old
54. Unfriendly dog
55. Gator's kin
56. Female sheep
59. Historical tales
63. Indian religious leader
65. Chaos
66. Snow slider
67. Avoids
68. Badger
69. Additional
70. ___ tunes (crazy)

DOWN

1. Yearning
2. Bone-dry
3. Atop
4. Soak hemp
5. Sucker
6. Pincer
7. "___ Gang"
8. Cautiously
9. Debonair
10. Chasing game
11. Ginger drink
12. Precedes worse
14. Highest
19. Hawaiian goose
22. Support
24. Catch
26. Pub
27. Acquaint
28. Chose
29. Association
30. Bigger
32. Sleeper's vision
33. Leaner
35. Nostrils
41. Undress
42. Worn out
47. Fortune
48. Walk
51. Throb
53. Racing rowboat
55. Surrender
56. Edible root
57. At what time?
58. Chair or street
59. Air mover
60. Whoopi's "Ghost" role
61. Skipper's diary
62. Legal thing
64. Sonny and Cher, once

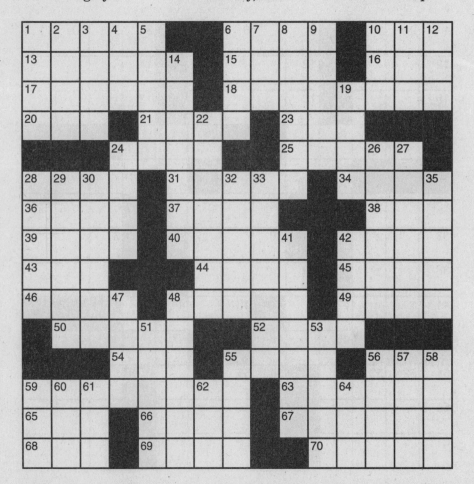

ACROSS

1. Winter flakes
5. Receded, as a tide
10. PBS science series
14. Knot
15. Writer Boothe Luce
16. Distinctive times
17. A Great Lake
18. Nathan and Alan
19. Building extensions
20. Queensland bird
21. Solitary
22. Verify
23. Brazilian dance
25. Swedish money
28. Household animal
29. Corduroy ridges
31. Haul
32. Kind of cat
35. Bookish
40. Pivot line
41. Flourish
43. Healing plant
44. Tot's game
46. Young American bird
48. Baby's smock
49. Fairy-tale brute
50. "___ Loves You"
53. Close by
55. Theater
59. Cato's dog
61. Adequate, to a bard
63. Desertlike
64. Touch on
65. Groucho's prop
67. Billboard, for one
68. Auto's spare
69. Join forces
70. Olive genus
71. Goblet part
72. Double curves
73. Snoozing sites

DOWN

1. Daggers
2. "___ Rae"
3. Antipathy
4. Tiny
5. Mimic
6. Spaces on a form
7. Hay bundler
8. Browning's before
9. Plaines preceder
10. Poetic contraction
11. Low ship deck
12. Flow-control device
13. Valuable thing
21. Secular
22. Messenger
24. Strong
26. Meat stew
27. Apple-pie spice
30. Thread holder
32. Beret or tam
33. Woodchopper's tool
34. Tell a whopper
35. Card game
36. Blew one's top
37. Every
38. Small European deer
39. Nonetheless
42. Earring site
45. Arabian garments
47. In line
49. Showy
50. Shoos
51. Nun's garb
52. Accustom
54. Protection
56. Roman judge
57. Persuaded
58. Talking birds
60. Bit of news
62. Raw metals
65. Stage prompt
66. Winners
67. Bawl

PUZZLE 30

PUZZLE 31

ACROSS

1. Wanes
5. Peat ——
9. Nearly all
13. Got down
14. Maple product
15. Engrave
16. "Swan Lake" costume
17. Opponent
18. Sky twinkler
19. Glimpsed
20. Price mark
21. In which place?
22. Large antelope
24. Cartridge-box contents
27. Cereal bread
28. Type of doll
31. View
33. Verbal exams
35. Auctioned off
36. Wanders about
40. Values
42. Misconduct mark
44. Loosen
45. Old instrument
47. Animated
48. Honeycomb material
50. Block
51. Geologic age
54. Foolhardy
55. Galahad's title
57. Share
59. Provoke
61. Desire
65. Till
66. Blender option
68. Kitten sound
69. King toppers
70. Daisy's kin
71. Expose
72. Smaller amount
73. Office furniture
74. Sweet drinks

DOWN

1. Devours
2. Azure or aqua
3. Mouthful
4. Pricked
5. Talking bird
6. Pizza herb
7. Amount of money
8. Secret watcher
9. Netting
10. Aquatic animal
11. Creepy
12. Trio number
14. Raise
21. Took the prize
23. Smeller
25. Fungus mold
26. Method
28. Kimono, e.g.
29. Place
30. Girls
32. Publishes
34. Fib
36. Hair goo
37. Waterless
38. Opera singer
39. Arise
41. Small bug
43. Long skirt
46. Casual pullovers
48. Bathing-suit part
49. Inquisitive one
51. Tied
52. Part of a pound
53. Records
56. Latin dance
58. Hurl
60. Terrible smell
62. Finished a book
63. Clinton's VP
64. Flock mamas
66. Paw part
67. Advantage

PUZZLE 32

ACROSS

1. Quarrel
5. Very dry
9. Female horses
14. Curve
15. "Of ___ and Men"
16. Separated
17. Attendee
18. Hymn finisher
19. Striped animal
20. Classify
22. ___ of passage
24. Swamp
25. Queen ___
26. Watched
27. Father
28. Approves
31. Bear's kid
33. Defeat
35. Coral structure
37. TKO caller
39. Tour leaders
43. Send cash
45. Pair
47. Ambition
48. Faucet
50. Uncooked
52. Birch, e.g.
53. Cow's foot
55. Certain evergreen
57. Halt
58. Unruly tot
61. ___-tac-toe
63. Pond barrier
65. Polish
66. Gibe
67. Develop
71. Wash away
73. Incline
75. Seized
76. Hip boot
77. Printer's mark
78. Aruban export
79. Smooth
80. Hurried
81. Grant use of

DOWN

1. Long tale
2. Masters
3. Serves perfectly
4. Ache
5. Beginner
6. Curb
7. Bakery workers
8. Refusal
9. Labyrinth
10. Gorilla
11. Synagogue official
12. Mistake
13. Platform
21. ___ room
23. Skinny branch
27. Kilt, e.g.
28. Hockey great's kin
29. Maintain
30. Teamster's rig
32. Bunk
34. Cow's chew
36. Conflict
38. Cat's coat
40. Drastic
41. Not odd
42. Pip
44. Overly
46. Clumsy one
49. Shopping bag
51. Broadened
54. Pastures
56. Thrust
58. Makes beer
59. Rustic
60. Domicile
62. Move slowly
64. Heavy ___
66. Tug
68. TV part
69. Hoodlum
70. ___ out a living
72. Barely passing grade
74. Ginger ___

29

PUZZLE 33

ACROSS

1. Snack
5. ____ Albert
8. Certainty
12. Singing voice
13. Parcel out
15. Doozie
16. Design
17. Cuts of meat
18. Manacle
19. Stuffing herb
20. Temperature tester
21. Reverence
23. Long
25. Freud's concerns
26. Ones who yield
28. Offered thanks
31. Ages
32. Baby fox
33. Unburden
35. Confesses
36. Entreat
37. Man of La Mancha
39. Photo
40. Small dog
41. Fast
42. Singing groups
45. Skimpy
46. Slangy chum
47. Raccoon's kin
48. Catching some z's
51. Varnish ingredient
52. Bump
56. Satiate
57. Summon
59. Black, to poets
60. Filly feature
61. Like notebook paper
62. Auctioned
63. Watched carefully
64. At any time, in poetry
65. Outfits

DOWN

1. Dozes off
2. Stewpot
3. Without a date
4. Winter melon
5. Astonishes
6. Stranger
7. Freight weight
8. Weak
9. Subtle air
10. Plug up
11. Melody
13. Mass tables
14. Summer garment
22. Sultan's room
24. Poetic twilights
26. Public
27. Period of history
28. Boar or sow
29. Sea raptors
30. Electron tube
31. Music or sheet
32. Kind of party
34. Dull
36. Commuter's vehicle
37. Lovers' quarrel
38. Uncanniness
40. Drive forward
41. Spread out
43. Heeded
44. Dander
45. One who drenches
47. Duplication
48. Pinnacle
49. Overwhelm with humor
50. Unshared
53. Clarinet kin
54. Dummy
55. Boundaries
58. Contend

DOUBLE CROSSER

When you fill in the correct missing letters in the crossword diagram, those letters, transferred to the correspondingly numbered dashes below the diagram, will reveal a quotation. Make sure no word is repeated in the diagram. Proper names, abbreviations, contractions, and foreign words are not allowed. There are different possibilities to fill the diagram, but only one way will give you the correct quotation.

$$\overline{1} \ \overline{2} \ \overline{3} \quad \overline{4} \ \overline{5} \ \overline{6} \ \overline{7} \ \overline{8} \ \overline{9} \quad \overline{10} \ \overline{11} \quad \overline{12} \ \overline{13} \quad \overline{14}$$

$$\overline{15} \ \overline{16} \ \overline{17} \ \overline{18} \quad \overline{19} \ \overline{20} \ \overline{21} \quad \overline{22} \quad \overline{23} \ \overline{24} \ \overline{25} \quad \overline{26} \ \overline{27} \ \overline{28} \ \overline{29}$$

$$\overline{30} \quad \overline{31} \ \overline{32} \ \overline{33} \ \overline{34} \ \overline{35} \quad \overline{36} \ \overline{37} \ \overline{38} \quad \overline{39} \ \overline{40} \ \overline{41} \ \overline{42}$$

$$\overline{43} \ \overline{44} \ \overline{45} \ \overline{46}$$

31

PUZZLE 35

ACROSS
1. Foamy brew
4. Furthermore
8. Thunderous noise
12. Term of respect
13. Silent
14. Paddy crop
15. Sailor
17. Hymn closer
18. Operator
19. Soft throw
20. Ties
23. Or ____ (threat)
26. Roundish
27. Snatched
28. Dollop
31. Dwarfed tree
33. Apt
35. Mama sheep
36. Movie spool
38. Newspaper item, shortly
39. Fiddlehead, e.g.
40. Class division
41. La Scala solo
44. Saw or hammer
46. Monastery dweller
47. Doubtful
51. Companion
52. Foyer
53. Hallow follower
54. Perfume
55. Accelerated
56. Accomplished

DOWN
1. Horse's kin
2. Falsehood
3. Notable time
4. Accumulate
5. Fishing decoy
6. Music system
7. Above, to bards
8. Shipping case
9. Exec's wheels
10. Highest cards
11. Ballpoints
16. Energy sources
20. Ear projection
21. State firmly
22. Walking stick
24. Lounge
25. Tackle moguls
27. Cake layer
28. Young society women
29. Got down
30. Group of computer bits
32. "You ____ Sixteen"
34. Australian "bear"
37. Snare
39. Impostor
40. "I ____ Go on Singing"
41. Bullets, to a GI
42. Lane
43. Hooked on
45. Gawk at
47. Checkup sounds
48. Bunk
49. Honolulu handout
50. Result

PUZZLE 36

ACROSS
1. Impersonator
5. Decades
9. To-and-____
12. Pigeon's kin
13. Fail to include
14. Cool, man!
15. Mysterious
16. Mobile or biography starter
17. "Bonnie ____ Clyde"
18. Leather bands
20. Fog plus smoke
22. Tad
24. Heavy jacket
27. Prince ____
31. Phoned
32. It floats on water
33. Flower feature
35. Surnamed at birth
36. Faded
38. Detours
40. Barber's sharpener
42. Whack
43. Lass
45. Respond
49. Hawaiian fare
51. Very bright, as colors
53. Bees' place
54. Vase
55. Dressed
56. Works by Keats
57. Beseech
58. Popular songs
59. Camper's dwelling

DOWN
1. Tallies up
2. Frost or Browning
3. Eternally
4. Fix
5. Warmer
6. Flightless bird
7. Insects' eggs
8. Trample
9. Pleasant-smelling
10. Dashed
11. Kooky
19. Splendor
21. Boat propeller
23. Feeds the kitty
25. Jerky joint
26. Gets older
27. Certain food fishes
28. Trumpeter Al ____
29. Disturbing
30. Wreaths
34. Advance money
37. Feathery wrap
39. Outcome
41. Squeeze
44. Salami seller
46. Vast
47. Divisible by two
48. Breather
49. British bar
50. Unpurified metal
52. Cereal grain

DOUBLE TROUBLE

Not really double trouble, but double fun! Solve this puzzle as you would a regular crossword, except place one, two, or three letters in each box. The number of letters in each answer is shown in parentheses after its clue.

ACROSS

1. Big (5)
3. Appearance (6)
6. Box a bit (4)
8. Barn toppers (5)
10. House of worship (6)
11. Private school (7)
12. Call it a day (6)
14. Dullness (6)
16. Declare (8)
19. Exhausted (5)
21. Creme de la creme (5)
23. Sea god (7)
25. Pay hike (5)
27. Bishop's hat (5)
28. Kitchen herb (4)
29. Chapter's partner (5)
30. Ashen (4)
31. Stool pigeon (3)
32. Precook (7)
34. Skinflint (5)
35. Accompany (6)
37. Unnecessary (8)
39. Mountain group (5)
41. Enmity (6)
43. Digestive organ (7)
45. Cozy corner (5)
48. Beginning (5)
50. Elect (3)
51. Slumber stopper (5)
52. Dodge (5)

DOWN

1. Insect stage (5)
2. Style (5)
3. Kismet (4)
4. Engine disk (3)
5. Use up (7)
6. Garden digger (5)
7. Military branch (4)
9. Guess (8)
11. Insight (6)
13. Bridle strap (4)
15. Scatter (8)
17. Scarlet bird (7)
18. Bumbling (5)
20. Walk aimlessly (7)
21. Muslim prince (4)
22. Well-read (8)
24. Revealed (8)
26. Paint undercoat (6)
28. Austere (7)
33. Skeletal piece (4)
34. Military operation (7)
36. Singe (6)
38. Low in fat (4)
40. Cordial (6)
42. Edible bivalve (6)
43. Small porch (5)
44. Gymnast's pad (3)
46. Freeway occupant (3)
47. Skirt border (3)
49. Practice piece (5)

Complete-A-Word

Fill in the dashes with the 4-letter answers to the clues to complete 7-letter words.

1. Judge's garb   P __ __ __ A T __

2. Relocate   I __ P R __ __ __

3. Story   S __ __ R T __ __

4. "Stop!"   A S P __ __ __ __

5. Wise   __ T __ G __ __ R

6. In person   B E __ __ E __ __

7. Long walk   T __ __ C __ __ T

8. Quote   __ __ __ I Z __ N

PUZZLE 39

ACROSS
1. Chances
5. Shop
9. Plains dwelling
14. Drawn tight
15. Bakery worker
16. Incensed
17. Proposal
18. Hand out
19. Copper, e.g.
20. Cotton fabric
22. Decrease
24. Highway curve
25. Part of CD
27. "Blessed ____ the meek . . ."
29. Top
32. Slangy refusals
34. Broadcast again
37. Make amends
39. Vehicle
41. Tiny fly
43. Covered walk
44. "Happy Days" actress
45. Fairy-tale beginning
46. Twitches
47. Patron
48. Inventory
49. Worthless matter
51. Frolic
53. Japanese monetary unit
54. Put a match to
55. Grass
57. Xenon, e.g.
60. Bite
62. Abundant
66. Remove pins from
68. Gyro meat
71. Killer whale
72. Acting platform
73. Skating maneuver
74. Bulblike base
75. Male singing voice
76. Hawaiian bird
77. On bended ____

DOWN
1. Of the ear
2. Art movement
3. Swordplay
4. Solemn
5. Brunch order
6. Expert
7. Steep
8. Redwood, e.g.
9. Pitch
10. Before, to Byron
11. Party spread
12. Athenian vowels
13. Snigglers' quarry
21. Theater
23. Noble title
26. Complete confusion
28. Rye fungus
29. Playbill listing
30. Garret
31. Dog
33. More definite
35. Rankle
36. Mother-of-pearl
38. Schnoz-related
40. Mystical deck
42. New driver, often
44. Civilian clothes
48. Peppy
50. Digit
52. Speak incoherently
56. Dress
57. Burst of wind
58. Poker opener
59. Extend
61. Prepare
63. Something to pump
64. Unit of land
65. Knight's wife
67. Easily bruised item?
69. Hewing tool
70. Chess pieces

PUZZLE 40   Triangle Sums

The two diagonals divide the diagram on the left into four large triangles. Place the nine squares on the right into the diagram so that the sums of the four numbers in those triangles are equal. If a square is divided, place it in the diagram in a square that is divided the same way.

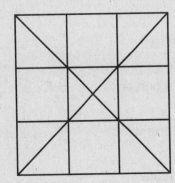

ACROSS

1. Does in a dragon
6. Marcel Marceau, e.g.
10. Recedes
14. Hot chocolate
15. Malicious
16. Applaud
17. Representative
18. Unhealthy
19. Regulation
20. "The ___ Squad"
21. Old anesthetic
23. Swear
24. Split ___ soup
25. Average
27. Smidgen
28. Makes butter
31. Pay dirt
33. Cable
34. Brownish gray
38. Chances
41. Does sums
42. Annoyed
43. Sticky stuff
44. Encounter
45. Correct
46. Canned fish
47. Paddles
49. More angry
51. TV breaks
53. Powerful particle
56. Pester
57. Packs of cards
59. Hold power
61. Mutt
64. Burn soother
65. Placid
66. Gander's mate
68. Actor Busey
69. Perched on
70. Bungled
71. Watches carefully
72. Hamilton bills
73. Divides

DOWN

1. Con game
2. Trademark
3. Served perfectly
4. Hither's partner
5. Glossy fabric
6. Net
7. Vines that climb
8. Minuscule
9. Lodge member
10. Tan shade
11. Spoke suddenly
12. Model wood
13. Accelerate
22. Most savory
23. Dove's murmur
24. Magician's word
26. Winter coasting
28. Steamer, e.g.
29. Conceal
30. Highlight
32. Soldier's identification
35. Provide with weapons
36. Guitar's kin
37. Ink stick
39. Complete
40. Boxers do it
48. No longer is
50. Park official
51. Proverb
52. Layover
54. Give a speech
55. Cantaloupe, e.g.
58. Lock openers
60. Bratty kids
61. ___ on the cob
62. Pre-owned
63. Beatty film of 1981
65. Garfield, e.g.
67. Prospector's quest

Crossblocks

Insert the letters and letter groups into each diagram to form words reading across that answer the clues on the left. In each diagram, a bonus word will read diagonally down in the tinted blocks.

1.

B CA EY HU I IS
IT L LOM NO OL
OR P PA TR V

Tourist

Cable car

Wheel cover

Kind of horse

2.

A AS AV DE E
ELE EMA EN K N
NOT OR R T TE Y

Intricate

Come forth

Effort

Let go

PUZZLE 43

BRICK BY BRICK

Rearrange this stack of bricks to form a crossword puzzle. The clues will help you fit the bricks into their correct places. Row 1 has been filled in for you. Use the bricks to fill in the remaining spaces.

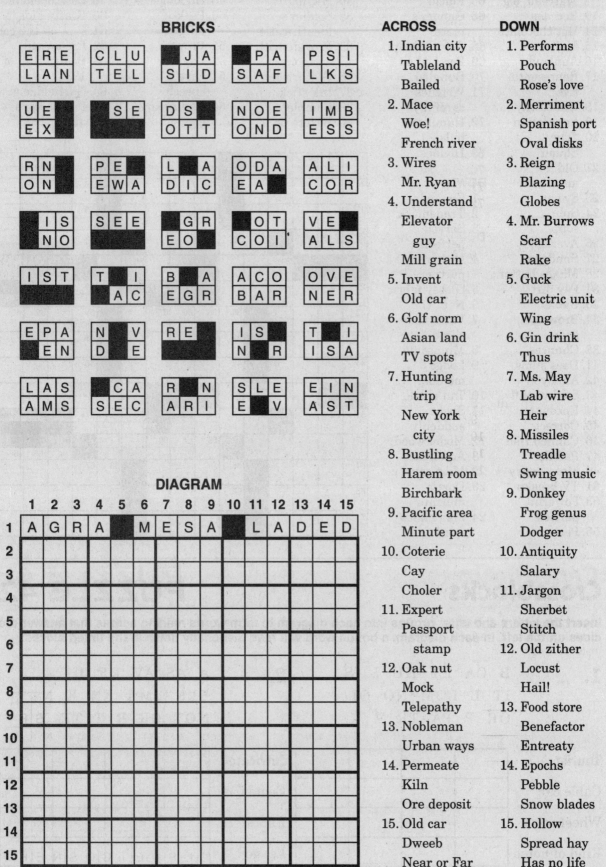

BRICKS

DIAGRAM

ACROSS

1. Indian city
   Tableland
   Bailed
2. Mace
   Woe!
   French river
3. Wires
   Mr. Ryan
4. Understand
   Elevator
   guy
   Mill grain
5. Invent
   Old car
6. Golf norm
   Asian land
   TV spots
7. Hunting
   trip
   New York
   city
8. Bustling
   Harem room
   Birchbark
9. Pacific area
   Minute part
10. Coterie
    Cay
    Choler
11. Expert
    Passport
    stamp
12. Oak nut
    Mock
    Telepathy
13. Nobleman
    Urban ways
14. Permeate
    Kiln
    Ore deposit
15. Old car
    Dweeb
    Near or Far

DOWN

1. Performs
   Pouch
   Rose's love
2. Merriment
   Spanish port
   Oval disks
3. Reign
   Blazing
   Globes
4. Mr. Burrows
   Scarf
   Rake
5. Guck
   Electric unit
   Wing
6. Gin drink
   Thus
7. Ms. May
   Lab wire
   Heir
8. Missiles
   Treadle
   Swing music
9. Donkey
   Frog genus
   Dodger
10. Antiquity
    Salary
11. Jargon
    Sherbet
    Stitch
12. Old zither
    Locust
    Hail!
13. Food store
    Benefactor
    Entreaty
14. Epochs
    Pebble
    Snow blades
15. Hollow
    Spread hay
    Has no life

PUZZLE 44

ACROSS

1. Bean variety
6. Location
10. Experts
14. Oak nut
15. Inhabit
16. Frenzy
17. Repatch the roof
18. Scored on a serve
19. Gumbo ingredient
20. Creamy dessert
22. Swarm
23. Most arid
26. Harp's relative
28. Sunset, in verse
29. Move quickly
32. Ventilates
35. Priest's robe
36. Fruit pastry
37. Ripe old age
39. Also
40. Football
42. Heckler's call
43. Dreadful
45. Muscle twitch
46. Noah's vessel
47. Half hitch, e.g.
48. Fall bloomer
50. Casual shirt
51. Small sailboat
53. Cuts off
55. Rowlands of "Gloria"
58. Disciple
61. October gem
62. Lemon's kin
63. Absurd
67. Astronaut Armstrong
68. On bended ___
69. Heals
70. Wriggly
71. Transmit
72. Factions

DOWN

1. Golf norm
2. Rink surface
3. Touch-me-___
4. Outline
5. Stampede
6. Mattress support
7. Type style
8. Excessively
9. Toy bear
10. Dietary need
11. Gather leaves
12. Fairy-tale giant
13. Fabric joint
21. Dull-witted
23. "___ on the Nile"
24. Peek again
25. Hereditary
27. Drizzle
30. Large truck
31. Musical pauses
33. Partial refund
34. Hoarder
37. Kindest
38. Harnesses
40. Pocket bread
41. Do-it-yourself set
44. In a regal manner
48. Mountainous
49. Ancient remains
52. Takes a hike
54. Scene of action
55. Missing
56. Fencer's weapon
57. Hammer's target
59. Sign of the future
60. Sesame or poppy
64. Circle section
65. Butterfly catcher
66. Snaky curve

Cancellations

PUZZLE 45

There are 12 names of garments and a quotation hidden in the diagram. Taking one letter from each box, cross off the 7-letter words from the across rows. Then cross off the 5-letter words from the down columns. The leftover letters, one in each box, will reveal the quotation, reading left to right, row by row.

ACROSS

1. _____
2. _____
3. _____
4. _____
5. _____

DOWN

1. _____
2. _____
3. _____
4. _____
5. _____
6. _____
7. _____

	1	2	3	4	5	6	7
1	S D	A A	E E	H			
1	T W E W E S R S J T A S R F						
2	A A	H D	O N	R			
2	C U R P S E H S A E C P D K						
3	N E	S O	I R	N			
3	C F A U A T H I F A F O O S						
4	I H	B M	N H	E			
4	E C S D E W Y R I W O S A C						
5	S W	I L	K V	R			
5	C T L S L E T C O S N E K E						

PUZZLE 46

OVERLAPS

Place the answer to each clue into the diagram beginning at the corresponding number. Words will overlap with other words.

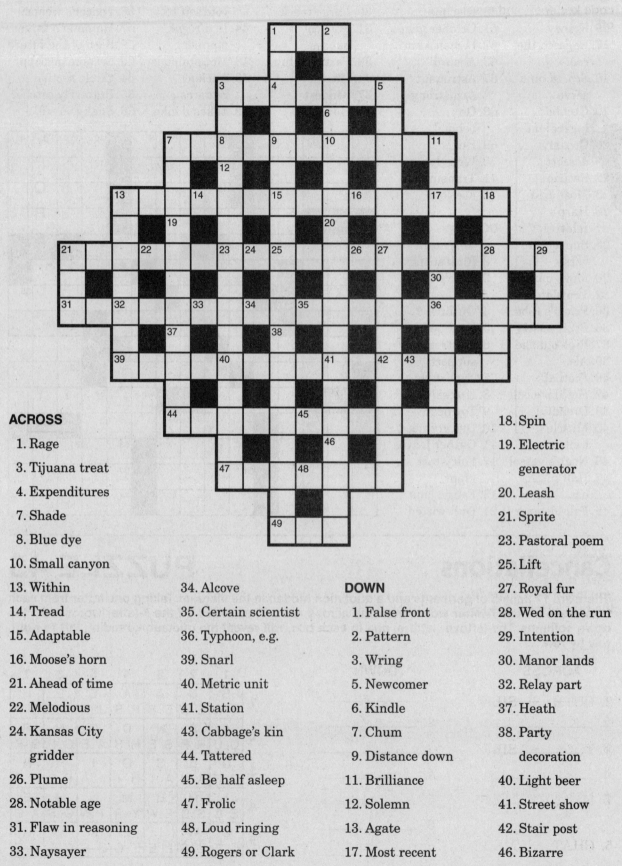

ACROSS

1. Rage
3. Tijuana treat
4. Expenditures
7. Shade
8. Blue dye
10. Small canyon
13. Within
14. Tread
15. Adaptable
16. Moose's horn
21. Ahead of time
22. Melodious
24. Kansas City gridder
26. Plume
28. Notable age
31. Flaw in reasoning
33. Naysayer
34. Alcove
35. Certain scientist
36. Typhoon, e.g.
39. Snarl
40. Metric unit
41. Station
43. Cabbage's kin
44. Tattered
45. Be half asleep
47. Frolic
48. Loud ringing
49. Rogers or Clark

DOWN

1. False front
2. Pattern
3. Wring
5. Newcomer
6. Kindle
7. Chum
9. Distance down
11. Brilliance
12. Solemn
13. Agate
17. Most recent
18. Spin
19. Electric generator
20. Leash
21. Sprite
23. Pastoral poem
25. Lift
27. Royal fur
28. Wed on the run
29. Intention
30. Manor lands
32. Relay part
37. Heath
38. Party decoration
40. Light beer
41. Street show
42. Stair post
46. Bizarre

CODEWORD

Codeword is a special crossword puzzle in which conventional clues are omitted. Instead, answer words in the diagram are represented by numbers. Each number represents a different letter of the alphabet, and all of the letters of the alphabet are used. When you are sure of a letter, put it in the code key chart and cross it off in the alphabet box. A group of letters has been inserted to start you off.

Code key chart:

1	14
2	15 (W)
3	16
4	17
5	18
6	19
7	20 (E)
8 (O)	21
9	22
10	23
11	24
12	25
13	26

Alphabet box: A B C D E̸ F G H I J K L M N Ø P Q R S T U V W̸ X Y Z

Crossword grid (numbered):

8	17	25	22	26			19	25	19		10	18	25	13
11	8	23	24	20	17		20	19	25		18	17	26	20
11	20	20	9	1	20		17	8	6		25	22	8	22
					6	25	15	4	3	8	17			
4	25	22		14	8	2			25	19	8	22	20
25	17	19		8	22	20	14	3	8	19		25	18	16
14	6	3	2	25		6	18	9		20	17	22	20
		8	4	20	17	25	19	24	12	20			
17	8	6	16		26	18	22			8	1	21	24	20
20	12	20		6	8	22	19	20	14	19		20	17	26
14	25	1	14	25			14	18	20		9	20	26
	4	17	8 (O)	2 (W)	20 (E)	14	14						
25	5	25	17	17	20	21		3	25	7	25	17	21
17	25	22	24	7	24	26		24	14	8	15	20	17
20	15	24	19	8	17	20		4	8	4	4	13

Successorgrams

Rearrange the letters in each pair of words below to make an 8-letter word. The last letter of the word you make will be the first letter of the following word. The last letter of the last word formed will be the first letter of the first word formed.

1. SLIP + RARE = _____

2. CUTE + SILK = _____

3. TOOT + SIRE = _____

4. MIME + POUR = _____

5. CHAT + MUSE = _____

6. DEER + NOVA = _____

7. ROAN + DRIP = _____

8. BOLT + REAP = _____

9. HOUR + EPIC = _____

10. CURT + POEM = _____

PUZZLE 49

ACROSS

1. Arrogant
5. Fight
9. Customary way
14. Knit one, ___ one
15. Grandmother
16. Surfaced
17. Seaweed
18. Parroted
19. Defeats
20. Look
21. Uncooked
22. Scale notes
23. Like some suntan lotion
25. Preface
28. Verb's subject, often
30. Prayer closer
33. Aspires
35. Cheer
37. Has an unpaid mortgage
39. Sign of triumph
40. Puzzling
41. Model
43. Bar drink
44. Stone or Bronze
45. Taunt
46. Bellowed
48. Stern
50. Be aware of
52. "___ of Eden"
53. Piece of bread
55. Merit
57. Chair cushion
58. Crone
59. Pier
63. Heron type
66. ___ Scotia
67. Certain golf club
68. Baking ingredient
69. Aid and ___
70. Neck area
71. Vacant
72. Days of old
73. Happiness

DOWN

1. Saratoga Springs et al.
2. Stubborn one
3. Advise
4. Beauty
5. Tangle, as of hair
6. Tropical fruit
7. Freshly
8. Tiny amount
9. Citified
10. Afternoon nap
11. Beast of burden
12. Realize
13. Some dashes
22. Showy dress
24. Not fitting
26. Foes
27. Breakfast order
28. Prompts
29. Difficult experience
31. Byword
32. Pasture mom
34. Parakeet's meal
35. Frost
36. Loudly peddled
38. Scornful smile
42. ___ Pan Alley
47. Wharf
49. Most ready
51. Cloth maker
54. Spiteful
56. Semiprecious stone
58. Vagabond
60. Uttered
61. Contend (with)
62. Jerky joint
63. Chart or contact
64. Valuable thing
65. Seance response
66. Vote of rejection

ACROSS

1. Kind
5. Showy
9. Bundle
14. Frayed
15. Is indebted to
16. Hawaiian welcome
17. Full of excitement
18. Authentic
19. "___ Eagles"
20. African trip
22. Detect
24. Broke a fast
25. Lass
26. Desire
28. Ladybug, e.g.
31. Trial prints
34. Hit the jackpot
35. One or more
37. "Moonlight ___"
39. Use eradicator
42. Small spot
44. Nitwit
45. Honest
47. Holiday beverage
49. Stomach
50. Rank
52. Whistling kettle
55. Prospector
57. Zero
58. Egyptian snake
61. Indy event
62. Occupations
66. Marine mammal
68. Roundish
70. Contribute
71. Coat fold
72. Without clothes
73. Branch
74. Cloudy
75. Forest creature
76. Snaky swimmers

DOWN

1. "___ the night before . . ."
2. Calming exercise
3. Instructor, for short
4. Involve
5. Magilla, e.g.
6. Deep respect
7. Covered in foliage
8. Gone to bed
9. Dance hall
10. Ginger drink
11. Cato's clothing
12. Casual talk
13. Healthy
21. Cheese eater
23. Jug handles
27. Taboo
28. Tiresome people
29. Make into law
30. Last word
32. North Dakota city
33. Portly
34. Get married
36. Hither and ___
38. Picnic pest
40. Baseball feature
41. Completely
43. Child
46. Sandwich fish
48. Softer
51. Moment
53. Tire's content
54. Torment
56. Variety show
58. Hole-punching tools
59. Persian ruler
60. "___ Don't Preach"
63. Have a meal
64. Wicked
65. Stage furnishings
67. Preceded
69. Orange drink

PUZZLE 51

ACROSS

1. Cuckoo
4. Substance
8. Brokers
14. Came in first
15. Official records
16. Art gallery
17. Bluegrass players
19. Mad
20. ___-friendly
21. Alike
23. Furry foot
24. Dictionary
27. Curved projection
30. Thrifty
32. Materialize
36. Like some garden gates
39. Palatable
40. Mouths
41. Done with
44. Phony story
45. Double quartet
47. Desk toppers
49. Scottish lord
50. Long way around
51. Farm wagon
53. Kind of boat motor
57. Snoop
60. Ship's wheel
62. Cypress, e.g.
63. Hairpiece
66. Headset part
69. Mistakes
70. Greek covered walk
71. Make weak
72. Foursome
73. ___ off (irate)
74. High tracks

DOWN

1. Horrible
2. Din
3. List in a book
4. Miss
5. Arctic sight
6. Foreigner
7. Assigned job
8. Acid type
9. Revolver, e.g.
10. 19th of 26
11. Lowest tide
12. Salad fish
13. Merganser
18. Float
22. Feeling bad
25. Varmint
26. Hurt sound
28. Washing place
29. Period in history
31. Certain brick house
33. Capri, e.g.
34. Awaken
35. "Bright ___ "
36. Swag
37. St. Louis sight
38. Cheerio
42. Last
43. Mobster's man
46. Termination
48. Loyalty
50. Go blond
52. Leading
54. "___ by any other name . . ."
55. Of the kidneys
56. Certain ocean areas
57. Printing term
58. Study steadily
59. Mongolian dwelling
61. For fear that
64. Golf norm
65. Greek vowel
67. Sturgeon eggs
68. Cushion

ACROSS

1. Rustle
5. Sal, for example
8. Move, as wings
12. Walk the floor
13. More inexperienced
15. Comparison word
16. Hit a hole in one
17. Dodge
18. Spring flower
19. Went fast
20. ___ your request
21. Renter
23. Pasture
25. Future chicken
26. Spins
28. Pleases a dentist
32. Acknowledges
33. Suffer
34. ___ and gown
35. Encourages
36. ___ conditioning
37. Big slipknot
39. Hive dweller
40. Vitality
41. Chatted
42. Won over
45. Small horses
46. Catholic sister
47. Sound of pain
48. Fearful
51. Disintegrate
52. Pinch
56. Gold fabric
57. Drab green color
59. Yield to commands
60. Tentacles
61. More mellow
62. Naught
63. Flower bed
64. Informal room
65. Arrays

DOWN

1. Quarrel
2. Mexican sandwich
3. Froster
4. Clarify again
5. Mallets
6. Trophy, e.g.
7. Conducted
8. Tosses
9. Money in Milan, once
10. Comparable
11. Pain in the neck
13. Turns back
14. Say again
22. ___ trip
24. Bothers
26. Midafternoon
27. Engaged in
28. Evergreen variety
29. Range of view
30. Relaxes
31. Went over the limit
32. Vats
33. Zero in
36. Give help to
37. Granny
38. Views
40. Merchant
41. Cheerleader
43. State of discontent
44. Ball or stick
45. Established
47. Squawk
48. Wallop
49. Poet Sandburg
50. Bullets, to a GI
53. Woodwind instrument
54. Camper's cover
55. Favorable votes
58. Slangy hat

PUZZLE 53

ACROSS

1. RBI, e.g.
5. Ailing
9. Like a city
14. Olympic sled
15. Light tan
16. Dorothy, to Em
17. Wild goat
18. Peruse
19. Flings
20. Fish sauce
22. Roll up
24. Make doilies
25. Clever
27. Sweet tuber
29. Kettle and Barker
32. Airport abbr.
33. Spanish coin, once
36. Appendage
37. Stairway support
39. Strips
41. Slangy affirmative
43. Trim meat
45. Colt's gait
46. Start
48. Enclosed in a pigpen
50. Greek letter
51. Tonsils' site
53. Daniel ___-Lewis
54. Kennel sound
55. Beseech
56. Beasts of burden
58. Cobra's cousin
61. Parka feature
63. Strut
67. Liberace's instrument
69. Newspaper section
71. Galosh
72. Bay window
73. The Stooges, e.g.
74. ___ von Bismarck
75. Erased
76. Envisioned
77. New driver, often

DOWN

1. Skirt opening
2. Large brass horn
3. Antiquing material
4. Writings
5. Like a bread knife
6. Bar rocks
7. Skill
8. Antelope
9. Release
10. Estuary
11. Finest
12. Deeds
13. Bird's abode
21. Prayer conclusion
23. Pastrami on ___
26. Most crude
28. Swimming event
29. BLT spread
30. "___ We All"
31. Shatter
33. Scottish fabrics
34. Towel fabric
35. Hawaiian hello
38. Newt
40. Whoa!
42. Seasoning
44. Kitchen measure
47. Progress-aiding advantage
49. Colorist
52. Before now
56. Revere
57. Wooden shoe
58. Limbless animal
59. Regal title
60. Bucket
62. Leftovers
64. Short letter
65. Sheep shelter
66. English school
68. Maiden-name preceder
70. Knot

ACROSS

1. Chewy candy
6. Took the bus
10. Talents
14. In flames
15. 24th letters
16. Outerwear
17. Quarries
18. "Body ___"
19. Nervous
20. Corn portion
21. Doghouses
23. Attack!
24. Obstruct a stream
25. Admit as a visitor
26. Selfish one
29. Furnishings
31. "___ Bovary"
33. Inglenook
37. Risk
38. Casual restaurant
41. Traffic jam
43. Leases
44. Delight
46. Notice
48. Cement
50. Seashore
53. Blue above
54. Brother's sib
56. Loft or ride
57. Tea server
59. Tropical storm
61. Rightful
62. Voice range
65. Teller's pal
66. Generals' helpers
68. Settled, as a bill
69. Certain parasites
70. Peak
71. Printed mistake
72. ___ out (barely made)
73. Circus coverings

DOWN

1. Records
2. Fearful
3. Hostile
4. Cook in fat
5. Proposal reply
6. Alter slacks
7. Farm animals
8. College officials
9. Admiration
10. Crack pilots
11. Angler's need
12. License plate
13. Pen
21. Gold purity measure
22. Jump
24. Bambi's mom
26. Bunny's kin
27. Leave out
28. Hairstyling products
30. Dresser
32. "___ Dawn"
34. Weed out
35. Fit to a ___
36. Crude shelter
38. Engine parts
39. Berserk
40. Wrath
42. Nut for pies
45. A snap
47. Bashful
49. Wavelet
51. Unexpected
52. Most reliable
55. Arab chief
56. Sharpened
58. Robins' retreats
59. Fuss
60. Story starter
62. Skillful
63. "Now I ___ me . . ."
64. Pointer
66. Work onstage
67. Ill humor

PUZZLE 55

ACROSS

1. Baby's food
4. Persian ruler
8. Health resorts
12. Notable age
13. Pinches
15. Foot part
16. Beast of burden
17. Least tanned
18. Silver finish?
19. Barracks item
20. Calamities
21. Heeded
23. Glossy paints
25. Nudged
26. Busy activity
27. Facts and figures
28. "A Tale of ___ Cities"
31. Acceptable
34. Sudden notion
36. Theater guide
38. Underneath
40. Had a pizza
41. Look steadily
42. Beginning part
43. Telegram word
45. Flock members
46. Likewise
47. Golden Rule word
49. Tantrum cause
51. Run away from
52. Trickled
56. Dwell
59. Type of history
60. Logger's tool
61. At all
62. Give
64. Break the tape
65. Ten-cent piece
66. Barked
67. Subways' kin
68. Skidded
69. Whiskey and bread
70. Alphabet's fourth

DOWN

1. Tranquillity
2. Flagrant felony
3. Italian staple
4. Gulp
5. Beverly ___
6. Copycats
7. "___ So Shy"
8. Cut, as wood
9. Entreat
10. Farm unit
11. Molt
13. Snooped
14. Portly
22. Boyfriends
24. Koch, once
25. Brief film role
27. Duplicate
28. Defrost
29. "___ No Angels"
30. Metal deposits
31. Newspaper item
32. Game of chance
33. Certain sax
35. Waste maker
37. Overpriced
39. Was willing
44. Buccaneers
48. Wanting
50. Angered
51. Discharged
52. Curtain
53. Handled roughly
54. Deport
55. Thick
56. Cincinnati players
57. Vile
58. Trucker's rig
59. "___ the Lonely"
63. Above, in poems

ACROSS

1. Falcon
5. Seashore
10. Go astray
13. Downwind, to Popeye
14. Duplicating machine
15. Bill and ___
16. Cut of meat
17. List of activities
18. Body joint
19. Hurled
21. Immature frog
23. Blue
24. Hastens
27. Once named
28. Coves
30. Popcorn seasoning
34. Wedge tightly
37. Complaint
38. Musical ensemble
39. Regions
41. Neckline style
42. Elevate
43. Delivery trucks
44. Door
46. Mock
47. Touch against
48. Song
49. Do lunch
51. Rough-cut
52. Bro's sib
55. Mysteries
59. Tilted
61. "___ Got You Under My Skin"
62. Writer's patron
65. Besides
66. Game cube
67. Put out
68. Web surfer
69. Certain railways
70. Anesthetic
71. Escort

DOWN

1. Interrupts
2. Hello, to Ho
3. Eerie
4. Gambling game
5. Gear part
6. Unlock, in poems
7. "___ Misbehavin'"
8. Family cars
9. Swap
10. Sonic feedback
11. Agitate
12. Heavy twine
14. Like Lassie
20. Licks
22. Basil sauce
25. Football team
26. In ___ heaven
29. Grow choppers
31. Opera singer's solo
32. Speech defect
33. Lug
34. Cup of joe
35. Egyptian, e.g.
36. Entree listing
40. Daisylike flower
42. Sacred songs
45. Recompense
48. Certify
50. Cliff home
52. Mexican sauce
53. Map feature
54. Mart
55. Street or walk
56. Vile
57. Passing grades
58. Cummerbund
60. Esteem
63. Unpaid
64. Always, to a bard

PUZZLE 57

ACROSS
1. Trudge
5. Spear
10. Noncoms: abbr.
14. Moon over Milan
15. Bounding main
16. High notes
17. Etching liquid
18. Written copy
20. TV's "F ___"
22. Danish money
23. Cathedral parts
24. Yet, in poetry
25. Insurgent
27. Soak in water
28. Gabor et al.
29. Bird's retreat
32. "___ Abner"
35. Spat
37. Lab burners
38. Bother
39. Yale man
40. Streets: abbr.
42. Greek vowel
43. Uncertainty
45. Plebe
47. German article
48. Nobelist Wiesel
49. Muck's partner
50. Briny deep
52. Lustrous velvet
53. Resort of sorts
56. Hoity-___
58. Actress Maris
59. Like a lion
61. Having a milky iridescence
64. Bye-bye, in London
65. Mr. Hackman
66. Gravy, e.g.
67. Authentic: abbr.
68. Collections
69. Maryland town
70. Rose or Sampras

DOWN
1. License or dinner
2. Money
3. Leek's kin
4. Pedestal part
5. Parking field
6. Like a gymnast's moves
7. ___ and dearest
8. Suez or Erie
9. Printing measures
10. Snake
11. Shimmered
12. Masking ___
13. JFK sights, once
19. Subway unit
21. Arranged in advance
26. Daredevil Knievel
30. Fully satisfy
31. Royal Russian
32. Take on cargo
33. Fan's favorite
34. Prudhomme's state
36. Decree
37. Regard
41. Bruce or Laura
44. Garden scourges
46. Tom Hulce film
51. Pirate's yes
52. Tropical rodents
53. Type of drum
54. Small
55. Old saw
56. Roman garb
57. Unrestricted
60. Overhead
62. Wind direction: abbr.
63. A Ritter

ACROSS

1. ___ to (cite)
6. Wound covering
10. River barge
14. Spry
15. Humdinger
16. Use a towel
17. Belief
18. Copycat
19. Earnest
20. Do needlepoint
22. Getting fed up?
24. Old refrigerator
28. Rise sharply
30. Tommy ___ Jones
31. Steep valley
32. Cookie-jar scrap
34. Was in arrears
35. Sidewalk edge
37. Crooned
40. Geek
41. Pub mug
43. Ilk
45. Colorer
47. So long!
48. Weeder
49. Alter slacks
51. Midday nap
53. Play section
56. Songs
57. Shining
58. Knight's protection
60. Winter ailment
61. Compassion
62. Tad
65. Water plants
70. At rest
71. City light
72. Wednesday, to Fester
73. High notes
74. Liquor
75. Promo producers

DOWN

1. Great, slangily
2. Self
3. Newton ingredient
4. Stately tree
5. Motive
6. Deli side order
7. Coffee container
8. Bar brew
9. Agency
10. Slap
11. Certain servant
12. Reckon
13. Pie piece
21. VIPs, often
23. "A Farewell to ___"
24. Hard metal
25. Made like a crow
26. ___ which way
27. Offer maker
28. Piercing cries
29. Flight path
33. Four pecks
36. Say
38. Lasso loop
39. Ms. Garbo
42. Of the nose
44. Trolley
46. Not imaginary
50. Concealing
52. Green lizard
53. Savory jelly
54. Scold
55. Sir or Lady, e.g.
59. Watches closely
60. Snake's tooth
63. Atop, to Tennyson
64. "A Bridge ___ Far"
66. Cap
67. Jewel
68. Score on a serve
69. Twilight, in verse

PUZZLE 59

MOVIES & TELEVISION

ACROSS
1. Ms. Leigh
6. Gluck or Kruger
10. Candice's dad
15. Dunne et al.
17. Hollywood's Norman ___
18. Actress Keaton
19. "___, My Lovely"
20. Caron film
21. "A Passage to ___"
22. Anna's post
24. Williams/ Montalban film
26. Director Zetterling
29. Seles stroke
31. CBS series
32. "___ Copy"
36. Ms. Taina ___
37. Film again
39. Famous collie
41. Star of "The Naked Truth"
43. "___ Fine Day"
44. Vereen or Affleck
45. Cable station letters, formerly

46. Actor's text
48. Rose ___ on "The Golden Girls"
50. "___ Pablo"
51. "___ of Two Cities"
53. Elroy's dog
55. House wing
58. Actress Merle ___
60. Daytime drama
64. Pinocchio's misdeed
65. ___ Tin Tin
66. Actress Maris
68. Benigni's home
69. Doug ___ of "Melrose Place"
71. "Once ___"(Dreyfuss film)
73. Menu words
74. Director Kusturica
75. Bugs's motion
77. Keanu in "The Matrix"
78. Kurosawa movie

79. Aidan Quinn film
82. Hollywood's Barrett
85. "Come Back, Little ___"
88. Oscar Madison, e.g.
90. Popeye, e.g.
94. "A Fish Called Wanda" actor
95. Ms. Lanchester
96. "Bewitched" role
97. Spy series
98. A Harrison
99. "Full House" star

DOWN
1. "Wind" prop
2. "Butterflies ___ Free"
3. Recently made
4. Hartmann et al.
5. TV's Copley
6. Everybody
7. Actor Erickson
8. "Absence of ___"
9. Brando's sign
10. Cut film
11. Shore and Manoff

12. Emulate a starlet
13. "Wheel of Fortune" buy
14. Actor Stephen ___
16. Douglas ___ of "Rags to Riches"
23. Mr. ___ (Lorre role)
25. Early movies
26. Gibson and Torme
27. A Baldwin
28. Pet bat on "The Munsters"
30. The Hulk's alter ego
33. Canine celebrity
34. "Ice Castles" site
35. Dietrich of "The Ropers"
37. "The Larry Sanders Show" actor
38. "___ Exchange"
40. C-3PO, e.g.
42. Ms. Long
44. Kramden's vehicle
47. Baby on "Bewitched"
49. "Bonanza" actor

50

52. Cariou of films

54. Bit for Flicka

55. "Anything ___"

56. Actor Neeson

57. Dolly ___ of "Hello, Dolly"

59. Dinghy blade

61. Carson's predecessor

62. Ms. Joyce

63. Actor O'Neal

67. Mischa ___

70. "Lawrence of ___"

71. Rocky's opponent

72. Western prop

76. Actor Merlin ___

80. Johnson and Cliburn

81. Cyrano's feature

83. Grey et al.

84. Ms. Turturro

85. Celeb hot spot

86. Actor Holbrook

87. Wallach of films

89. "Mr. Novak" star

91. Kirk's book

92. Mined metal

93. Muppet Rizzo, e.g.

PUZZLE 60

ACROSS

1. Plus
5. Rental props.
9. Large amount
13. Mower's pride
14. Slip-up
15. Bee house
16. Stats for Mets
17. Riding whips
18. Hymn closer
19. Lip
20. Exclamations
21. Separated
22. Drum lightly
23. Kite or ball
24. Beget
26. Printer's mistake
28. Digging tool
30. Direction aid
33. Ref's cousin
35. Hooter
36. Dipstick coating
37. Lump
40. Mistreat
42. Competently
43. Sped
44. Coffee server
45. Battering ___
47. Stun
48. Stage whisper
50. Informed about
53. Object
54. Yearning
56. Cap-gun sound
58. Duplicate
61. Warmth
62. Humble ___
63. Drag
64. Shoe parts
66. Stockings
67. Unit of land
68. Ghostly
69. Client
70. Examination
71. Proceed slowly
72. Clutter

DOWN

1. On the ball
2. Cowboy's rope
3. Boggy
4. Switch positions
5. Places in order
6. Masters
7. ___ banana
8. Jrs.' dads
9. Form
10. Certain bean
11. At all times
12. Exited
14. Mountain refrain
20. Powerful particle
21. Exist
24. Cuts wood
25. Loafer
27. British bar
29. Sixteen ounces
30. Disorderly crowd
31. Be troubled
32. Fabric layer
34. Interruption
37. Swimsuit component
38. Legal decree
39. "___ Fine Day"
41. Panama part
42. Electrical unit
46. Em or Clara
48. Grazed
49. Facial feature
51. Go against
52. Squeaks
53. Bayou
55. Let up
57. Colleagues
58. Conversation
59. Ornamental edge
60. Not theirs
61. Savior
64. With it
65. Elongated fish
66. Sing without words

ACROSS

1. Health club
4. Pause mark
9. Afternoon snoozes
13. Armed fight
14. Beat
15. Elaborate solo
16. Yes, matey!
17. Baby
18. Money drawer
19. Resident
21. Tall tale
22. Do nothing
23. Ocean plant
25. Bullets, for short
27. Cupid's missile
29. Rain gear
33. Yogi, for one
36. Sight
38. By what means?
39. Plumed wader
41. Clean-air gp.
42. Uproar
44. Foot part
45. Bowler's button
47. Frosted
48. Attack
50. Showed again
53. Drove over the limit
55. Most gloomy
59. Gator's relative
62. Hoodwink
64. Fellow lead
65. "All You Need Is ___"
66. Threads
68. Tinge
69. Shop sign
70. Audience's shout
71. Rest stop
72. Await judgment
73. Colorers
74. Louse

DOWN

1. Strikes
2. Name on a check
3. Sport spot
4. Core
5. Not quite right
6. Breakfast, e.g.
7. Craze
8. Endeavor
9. Country
10. Very dry
11. Tiresome one
12. Red-tag event
14. Restaurant patron
20. Informed
24. Birds of peace
26. Sound of woe
28. Squeegee
30. Stylish
31. Gardening aid
32. Was in debt
33. Greek letter
34. Personalities
35. Greek god
37. Satisfied
40. Journey
43. Sty cries
46. Voted in
49. Go up
51. Fast cars
52. Moved upward
54. Soft and fluffy
56. Moral standard
57. Steam bath
58. Fad
59. Dull sound
60. Clothesline
61. Cake baker
63. Agreeable
67. Negative link

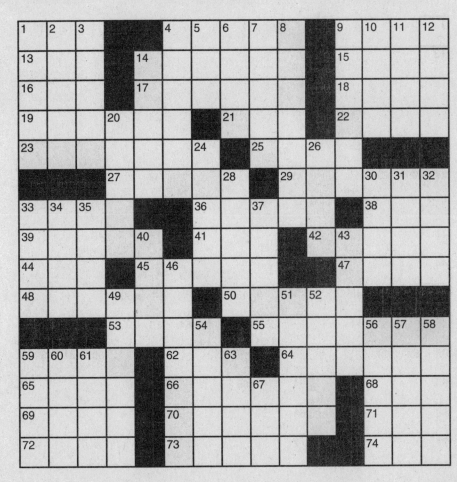

PUZZLE 62

ACROSS

1. Chinese mammal
6. Sword handle
10. Large amount
14. Improper
15. "___ the Rainbow"
16. Fast-food order
17. Door part
18. Give out
19. Advantage
20. Land measure
21. Unlatch, in poems
23. Fish hawks
25. Stare at
26. Result
27. Phi ___ Kappa
30. Certain vote
32. Plant's anchor
35. Sly look
36. Experimenter
39. To's mate
41. Swiss peak
42. Scallion
43. Belt or mail
44. Swarming insect
45. Put in
46. "The Seventh ___"
47. The Grateful ___
49. "___ No Evil"
50. Pretentious
51. Dynamite
54. Snitch
56. Examiner
59. Cleopatra's snake
60. Dinner roll
63. Imitate
64. Play group
66. Licorice-tasting seed
68. Chills
69. Potpourri
70. Mentions
71. Push in
72. Word
73. Put forth

DOWN

1. Dad
2. Off yonder
3. Zilch
4. Proper
5. Mix of two metals
6. Abode
7. "___ Gotta Be Me"
8. Drop a hint
9. Curl
10. Hi-fi
11. Ore vein
12. Like an omelet
13. Sorrows
22. "___ Place"
24. Contented sound
25. Tin ___
26. Least difficult
27. Tell all
28. Caught congers
29. Indian tent
31. Bards' sunsets
33. Bid
34. Characteristic
37. Slit
38. Logs
40. Merely
45. Leisurely
46. Dyer's tank
48. Most fit
52. Broad scarf
53. Trite
55. Quickly
56. During
57. Agreeable
58. Hymn conclusion
59. Tiny unit of matter
60. Morsel
61. Client
62. Sparrow's shelter
65. Man's title
67. Cancel

ACROSS

1. "___ in the Wind"
5. Wheeled vehicle
9. Old-style
14. Involved with
15. Curved molding
16. Like sea lions
17. Upon
18. Short message
19. Lieu
20. Kindest
22. Clever remark
24. Classified notices
25. Large deer
26. Upper limb
28. Sweater pulls
30. Heavy hammer
32. Plays a guitar
35. Imbued by a spirit
40. Ghostly
41. Radiate
42. Golfer Woods
44. Crooked
45. Tries the patience of one
47. Lunchroom
49. Main course
51. Tariff
52. Busybody
54. D.C. figure
55. Bad Ems, e.g.
58. ___-limits
60. Father
61. Curbed
63. Get up
65. Pot starter
68. African coin
69. Party gift
70. Intend
71. Coastal flier
72. Dance moves
73. Dress-shirt fastener
74. Clairvoyant

DOWN

1. Journalist Sawyer
2. "Wait ___ Dark"
3. Wall Street commodity
4. Tipple
5. TV brightness ratio
6. In the past
7. Soak flax
8. Abounds
9. Reiterate
10. Munch on
11. Financial officer
12. Peruse
13. Chances
21. Ditto
23. Light-switch positions
27. "The ___ Man"
29. Diving bird
31. Permissible
33. Skirt length
34. Bristle
35. Singer Seeger
36. Muscat's country
37. Three hundred ___ days a year
38. Cordwood measure
39. Postpone
43. Clergyman
46. Transmitters
48. Sort
50. LAX info
53. 2nd president
55. Trap
56. Tubular pasta
57. Common viper
58. Louts
59. College group
62. Angers greatly
64. Food for dipping
66. Angler's aid
67. Sorority letter

PUZZLE 64

ACROSS

1. Proverb
6. Manner of running
10. Stu Pickles, to Tommy
13. Fortify
16. Symbol
17. Sack
18. "___ to Billie Joe"
19. Prompt
20. Disregards
21. Future time
22. Grippe
23. Nothing
24. Hostess's handout
25. All of two
26. Capable
29. Fur
31. October birthstone
33. Gardener's place
34. Snacked
37. Road depression
38. Grade
39. Rich topsoil
43. Matched
46. Broadway's Harrison
47. Perspiring
49. The Kingston ___
50. London trolley
52. Below, to a poet
54. 20 hundred-weight
55. Discord
57. Cave denizen
59. Horrible
60. Evian, e.g.
61. Eccentric
63. Flit about
65. Disfigure
66. Public notices
69. Origin
71. Ruff's mate
73. ___ up (gushed)
78. Caribbean, e.g.
79. Instructor
81. Talk too much
83. Helper
84. Predicament
86. Vivacity
88. Lack of restrictions
90. Ledge
91. Thought
93. Emulate Niobe
94. Farm enclosure
95. Road bend
98. Chew the fat
99. Designated space
101. Thoroughbred
105. Neat
107. College figure, for short
111. "___ Been Lonely Too Long"
112. Have bills
113. Critical
115. Larceny, e.g.
116. Dirt
117. Conger, e.g.
118. Sandy hills
119. Applied grease
120. Meadow muncher
121. Withered
122. Emanate
123. Certain valleys

DOWN

1. Energy source
2. Arched ceiling
3. Analogous
4. Costume
5. Type spaces
6. Fall guy
7. Originator
8. Bar rocks
9. Menace
10. Remove
11. Improvise
12. Playing card
13. Adolescent's bane
14. Devastate
15. Liquefy
17. Schemer
25. Uttered suddenly
27. Showed off muscles
28. Dormant
30. The Roaring Twenties, e.g.
32. Average
34. Statutes
35. Civil wrong
36. Arab bigwig
40. Pony fare
41. At the peak
42. Talking bird
44. Luau dish
45. Tiny bit
47. Daiquiri fruit, sometimes
48. "___ the Sidewalk Ends"
51. Monthly, shortly
53. Purpose
56. Onward
58. Macadam mix-in
62. On the ___ (precisely)
64. Dr. Chen of "ER"

66. Deadly serpents

67. Pastrami purveyor

68. Jib, e.g.

70. Subjects

72. Brownie

74. Household spirit

75. "True ___"

76. Alter

77. Say no to

80. Lucille Ball and Sarah Ferguson

82. Galleries

85. Mirth

87. Garden veggie

89. Look at closely

92. Bring into harmony

96. Wearing sneakers

97. Planter

100. "___ Come She Will"

101. Float upward

102. Maintain

103. Surrender

104. Put trust (in)

106. Newspaper article

108. Bug

109. Prophetic sign

110. G-men

114. Snip

115. Gear

PUZZLE 65

ACROSS
1. Donkey
4. Fuse
8. Mail drop
12. Dog doc
13. Easter flowers
15. Quality of sound
16. Snacked
17. Acid's opposite
18. Frosts
19. Mug
21. Volunteer again
23. Sail supports
26. Drunkard
27. Toll road
28. Certain fly
32. Goes wrong
35. Below
38. Sketch
39. "Casper" cry
40. Also
41. Guitar's kin
42. Sow's mate
44. Shoulder gesture
46. Palmer's pegs
47. Zebra feature
49. Black-tie event
51. Dry, as wine
52. Bleaching agent
56. Capitalize
60. Shy
61. Kerghiz mountains
62. Sugar-paste candy
65. Crackerjack
66. Heavy cord
67. Game tile with dots
68. Ruby, e.g.
69. Polaris, e.g.
70. Shut in
71. Age

DOWN
1. Captain's command
2. Brawl
3. Sharply inclined
4. Diameter measure
5. Antlered animal
6. Fibbers
7. Remove
8. Stiffly formal
9. Places
10. Single units
11. School exam
13. Veranda
14. Midday snooze
20. Brats
22. Negative answers
24. Snow blade
25. Next after ninth
29. "___ Colors"
30. Welfare
31. Flock mothers
32. Subsides
33. Carrot or beet
34. Lion's yell
36. Pro
37. Cheek reddener
43. More hazardous
44. Instant
45. Needlefish
46. Hired car
48. ___ capita
50. Bingo-like game
52. Feather
53. Reflection
54. Chopper
55. Tomato-plant disease
56. Taverns
57. Very many
58. Chinese cabbage
59. Coil
63. Martini liquor
64. Red or army

58

PUZZLE 66

ACROSS

1. Luau offering
4. Gigantic
8. Old hat
13. "The King ___ I"
14. Invade
16. Districts
17. Once known as
18. Jeweled coronet
19. Skin on the head
20. Snatch
22. Short skirt
23. Pretentious
24. Slant
26. Bawdy
29. Ordinary
31. Readies for baking
35. Fall bloomer
36. Daft
37. Expensive eggs
38. Bumps
39. Soft-drink nuts
40. Remitted
41. Before now
42. Had supper
43. Regions
44. Lizards, e.g.
46. Shows to a chair
47. Revered person
48. Quayle, once
49. Title of respect
52. Cake decorator
54. Football measure
58. Vary
60. Bizarre
62. Golf implement
63. Tower or Coast
64. Imperial
65. Unclosed, in poems
66. Interruption
67. Peddle
68. Floor cleaner

DOWN

1. Ache
2. Unique being
3. Intention
4. Garfield's doc
5. "___ Farm" (Orwell book)
6. Blemish
7. Shorebird
8. Dads
9. Pinball place
10. Scorch
11. Lot's wife, ultimately
12. Behold
15. Monopoly purchase
21. Type of jazz
25. Spike of maize
27. Poetic twilights
28. How come?
29. Info from a dictionary
30. Sharpener
31. Ski sticks
32. "___ We All"
33. Sounds
34. Tennis-match units
35. Almost closed
36. More solitary
39. Metric weight
40. Covered with suds
42. Accomplished
43. Final letter
45. Second-hand items?
46. Consecutive
48. Brink
49. Post
50. Edison's middle name
51. Over
53. Average grades
55. Particle
56. "___ Man'"
57. Intense
59. Hearty bread
61. Addition shape

PUZZLE 67

ACROSS

1. Band's need
4. Had an obligation
8. Absorbed
12. Roadster, e.g.
13. Small piano
15. Curved molding
16. Increase
17. Shorter
18. Vatican dweller
19. Gun the engine
20. Raw metal
21. Fixed fee
23. Part of speech
26. Around
29. Map line
31. Out of the wind
33. Conveyed
35. Voucher
36. Linoleum square
38. British county
40. Relay ____
41. Improvise
43. "Iliad," e.g.
44. Cognizant
46. Soften
47. Mast or boom
48. Rock or peeve
49. Globule
51. Prudently
53. Furnishings
55. Tarantula, e.g.
57. In a short time
59. Completely
60. Farm enclosure
63. Out of
66. Mislead
68. Color
69. Burden
70. Pencil top
71. Small hotel
72. Lofty hairstyle
73. Tinter
74. Mas' mates

DOWN

1. Serving scorer
2. Create
3. Lie
4. Light musical work
5. Electrician, at times
6. Nanny has three
7. Hart, e.g.
8. Lassoer
9. Past
10. Rally or squad
11. Casual shirt
13. Potbelly, e.g.
14. Tiny amount
22. Fastens
24. Check
25. Romantic songs
27. Sailing vessel
28. ____ photograph
29. Junkyard fodder
30. Defrosted
32. Hilo garlands
34. Denounce
37. Theory
39. Author Hermann ____
42. Perplex
45. Black
50. Gnaw away
52. Lazy person
54. Granny's brooch
56. Short stop
58. Dull person
61. Yellowfin, e.g.
62. Inclinations
63. Winter illness
64. Sharp blow
65. Uneven
67. Deposit, as eggs

PUZZLE 68

ACROSS
1. Laser's kin
6. Thousand: pref.
10. Faction
14. Far-out
15. Salicylic, e.g.
16. Sore
17. Jargon
18. Dweeb
19. Applaud
20. Radial ___
21. Settled
23. Intense rage
24. Dry, as wine
25. Turkish officials
26. Play
28. Black eye
30. Gave a portion of medicine to
33. Legal body
35. Give up
36. Tablet
39. South American raccoon
41. Wafture
42. Zoo's bird house
44. Hillsides
46. Contour feather
47. Snoozing
50. Lyrical
52. Thrash
53. Take it on the ___
55. Slippery customer
57. Game tile with dots
59. Folder holder
60. Serving scorer
62. Transfer
63. Ticket
64. Factual
65. Fencer's need
66. Join forces
67. Totals
68. Refs' counts
69. River creature

DOWN
1. Vital things
2. Treaty members
3. Stiffen
4. Ocean bird
5. Scrap
6. Pouched animal
7. Bakery workers
8. Italian bread, once
9. More peculiar
10. Baglike structure
11. Surpassed
12. Scorch
13. Classify
21. Bureau
22. Dummy
25. Whichever
27. Brooding
29. Crete, e.g.
31. Self-conceit
32. June bug
34. Tiny amount
35. Flop
36. Infant's food
37. "___ Waited So Long"
38. Floor covering
40. Apprentices
43. Foray
45. Lodge member
48. Draw out
49. Taste
51. Halley's ___
52. Cheer up
54. Uniformed maid
55. Erodes
56. Neutral hue
58. Pine
59. TV's Allen ___
61. Legal matter
63. Musical twosome

61

PUZZLE 69

ACROSS
1. Frilly
5. Bill and ___
8. Feeds, as horses
12. Folklore giant
13. Fragment
15. Kind of tradition
16. ". . . maids all in ___"
17. Spud
18. Cable
19. Brand-___
20. Deep wound
21. Tahiti, e.g.
23. Guards
25. ___ out a living
26. Flock
27. Breakfast skillet
31. War groups
34. Car fuel
35. Above, to a poet
36. Minimal
37. English tavern
38. Cut
40. Jazz instrument, for short
41. Tin container
42. Hens
43. View
46. Bus fee
47. Plumbing joint
48. Move apart
52. Remember
55. Iditarod command
56. Ewe's mate
57. Anytime
58. Apart
60. Water barrier
61. Farmer's locale?
62. Angered
63. Customer
64. Nothing more than
65. Primary color
66. Refute

DOWN
1. Cash advances
2. Consent
3. Royal headgear
4. Spreading shrub
5. Ran after
6. Vows
7. Valuable mineral
8. Yelled
9. Opera solo
10. Knitting thread
11. Sleigh
13. Steps
14. Laundry machines
20. Welcome
22. Descend Mt. Snow
24. The thing here
27. Talk idly
28. Peace bird
29. Sly gaze
30. Goofs up
31. Likewise
32. Harvest
33. Long skirt
34. "Top ___"
37. Frying ___
38. Ms. Miles
39. Ogler
41. Shirt feature
42. Expired
44. Almost
45. Sick
46. Quarreled
48. Funt's directive
49. Stand up
50. Seized
51. Manicurist's board
52. Improve
53. Square
54. Prison unit
59. Address of respect
60. Faulty firecracker

CAMOUFLAGE

The answers to the clues can be found in the diagram, but they have been camouflaged. Their letters are in correct order, but sometimes they are separated by extra letters that have been inserted throughout the diagram. You must black out all the extra Camouflage letters. The remaining letters will be used in words reading across and down. Solve ACROSS and DOWN together to determine the correct letters where there is a choice. The number of answer words in a row or column is indicated by the number of clues.

	1	2	3	4	5	6	7	8	9	10	11	12	13
1	M	I	K	M	E	V	A	B	R	A	W	I	N
2	A	N	O	U	T	E	S	U	K	R	C	G	E
3	M	I	N	S	C	W	E	S	A	N	I	L	Y
4	B	T	E	A	L	C	I	H	S	E	B	U	A
5	M	I	Z	S	H	O	A	F	P	A	T	E	M
6	O	A	T	J	U	H	T	E	S	C	T	E	R
7	T	E	W	H	R	O	N	C	E	G	H	A	B
8	A	L	U	C	I	N	M	D	A	L	I	L	Y
9	H	A	P	R	P	E	A	L	N	E	Y	D	E
10	C	L	E	A	S	V	E	S	H	G	L	O	W
11	I	R	N	G	E	I	S	T	C	A	D	N	E
12	T	E	A	V	N	E	T	G	R	N	E	E	T
13	E	B	D	E	Y	N	D	Y	E	M	A	N	R

ACROSS

1. Imitate • Muscles
2. Kitty food • Gush
3. Chop • Boat canvas
4. Instruct • Ocean
5. Accident • Dined
6. Promise • Assayer
7. Royal perch • Prattle
8. Clear • Confederate
9. Occur • Ogle
10. Divide • Sluggish
11. Swallow • Walking aid
12. Doctrine • Born as
13. Paradise • Annum

DOWN

1. Huge • Refer
2. First • Pub quaff
3. Realize • Turn over
4. Press • Enclose
5. Engrave • Mature
6. Reverberate • Tied
7. Chair • Aerie
8. Tired • Pigpen
9. Grate • Medium's meeting
10. Region • Gather
11. Jocular • Meadow
12. Merriment • Solitary
13. Close • Jug

PUZZLE 71

ACROSS

1. Throb
5. Metric weight
9. Grow more mature
12. Tosses
17. Urge
18. Occasional
19. Mink's coat
20. Of the eye
21. Fine powder
22. Colony insects
23. Hairy spider
25. Drizzles frozen drops
27. Sorrowful
29. Line of seats
30. Rookie socialite
31. Mexican coin
33. Formal speech
37. List of books
40. Garden bloomer
41. Australian marsupial
45. High peak
46. Loaf
47. Bering, e.g.
48. Tinted
49. Dates
51. ___-do-well
53. Feed the pot
55. Short hellos
56. Endangered
58. Look to be
60. Cake froster
63. Result
64. Furry pets
66. More discourteous
70. Adhesive stuff
72. Accept
73. Photog's device
74. Prior to, in verse
77. Entree listing
79. Well-off
81. Sting
82. Horse's gait
85. Had a bite
87. Dramatist Coward
89. Deadly snake
90. Eyed
91. Beef dish
92. Tall animal
94. Loathe
96. Exec's auto
97. Beg
100. NHL athlete, e.g.
101. Clump of turf
104. Ranch
108. Keeps up
112. Track
114. Tempest
115. White house?
116. Opening
117. Healing plant
118. Flush
119. Fine and ___
120. Clever
121. Impart
122. Midterm, e.g.

DOWN

1. Biblical book
2. Ember
3. Hearty's mate
4. Excluding
5. Pasture
6. Fled
7. Music and painting, e.g.
8. Tableland
9. In the back
10. Protector
11. Blunders
12. Prisoner
13. Liable
14. Kind of poker
15. Clay square
16. Wound covering
24. Dazzle
26. Small duck
28. Raised platform
32. Trickle
34. More wonderful
35. Winter lodge
36. Dad's boy
37. Immaculate
38. Imitators
39. Honking fowl
42. Fire remnant
43. Hula wear
44. Commercials
45. Tennis great
48. Family room
50. Arrogant
52. Detours
54. Scale notes
57. Long fish
59. Fade away
61. Distinct period
62. Liquors
64. Golly!
65. Fibbing

67. Joltless joe

68. Wipe out

69. Boarding device

71. Ref's cousin

73. Treasured

74. Jung topic

75. Torn cloth

76. Building wing

78. Citizen

80. Curl

83. Escorted

84. Sonnet's kin

86. Wool sources

88. Lantern

91. Parsley portions

93. Blank out

95. Workout site

97. During

98. Epic tale

99. Brickmaker's oven

102. Milky gem

103. Valley

105. Chalet feature

106. Pub drinks

107. Depression

109. Show agreement

110. Yo-yo, e.g.

111. Snoop

113. Heavy weight

PUZZLE 72   CRISS-CROSSWORD

The answer words for Criss-Crossword are entered diagonally, reading downward, from upper left to lower right or from upper right to lower left. We have entered the words MALL and NAP as examples.

TO THE RIGHT

1. Shopping plaza
2. Shaving cut
3. Air duct
4. Valley
5. Self-respect
6. Steer
7. Tilling tool
9. Military unit
11. Put in order
14. Dutch cheese
15. Singer Campbell
16. More resolute
17. Stunt
18. Dine
20. Richer in content
22. Choose by ballot
25. Hermit
26. Tuck's partner
29. Colorized
31. Kiln
32. Tennis call
34. Ex-soldier

TO THE LEFT

2. Doze
3. Mansion
4. Announce
5. Damp and chilly
6. Gold leaf
7. Immense
8. Mint issue
10. Enlightened
12. Perpetual
13. Coal wagon
14. Pointy beard
15. Hoodlum
16. Tossed
19. Sweet potato
21. Joined wood
23. Whole
24. Royal command
27. Metal bolt
28. Run rampant
30. Atop
33. Thus far
35. According to

PUZZLE 73   Scrambled Up

Match up each group of letters in column A with one group each from columns B and C to form the names of European countries. Each letter group will be used once. Do not switch the order of a group of letters.

A	B	C	
GR	NG	NIA	_____
DE	NL	AL	_____
LIT	ED	CE	_____
HU	TUG	RK	_____
LA	EE	IA	_____
POR	HUA	ARY	_____
FI	TV	EN	_____
SW	NMA	AND	_____

PUZZLE 74

ACROSS
1. Scatter seed
4. Foundation
8. Up in ____ (indignant)
12. Japanese sash
13. Conform
14. China flaw
15. Easily carried
17. Tot
18. Foreteller
19. Pipe joints
21. Danson of "Becker"
22. Road bend
24. Prickly feeling
26. "The Green ____"
29. Serious plays
32. Crested ridge
33. Simian
34. Aplenty
36. Like a cinnamon bun
37. Pinnacle
38. Tabby, e.g.
39. Careless
41. Slick
43. Cry of woe
47. Show-stopper at the Met
49. Smallest
51. Biddies
52. Cave sound
53. Even score
54. Fabric scraps
55. Consider
56. Maple fluid

DOWN
1. Morsels for dipping
2. Clarinet's cousin
3. Cable
4. Feathered neckwear
5. Convent superior
6. Market
7. Place for shadow?
8. Behave
9. Lilting
10. Sleuth Hammer
11. Went too fast
16. Oak's summit
20. Levels
23. Music system
25. Austin or Albany, e.g.
26. Sack
27. Pitching stat
28. Taking a rest
30. Beg
31. Introverted
35. Deported
36. Reaper's tool
39. Cowardly Lion portrayer
40. Surface measure
42. Parasites
44. Permits
45. Largest continent
46. Footfall
48. Stubborn animal
50. Male turkey

PUZZLE 75

ACROSS
1. Plant stem
6. Hurrah
11. Suave
13. Applied the brake
14. Truck fuel
15. Bayed
16. Grass section
17. Mischievous
19. Sounded loudly
20. Health haven
23. Employee's take
26. Voter
28. Land unit
29. Jest
30. Lemieux's milieu
31. Party
33. Minerals
34. With it
35. Cultural
38. Say
39. Biology class, shortly
42. Origin
46. Cautiously
48. Invisible
49. Moe or Curly
50. Chirps
51. Alcohol burners

DOWN
1. Lather
2. Small ensemble
3. Not up yet
4. ____ Vegas, Nevada
5. Prepare to pray
6. Fair-haired woman
7. Squabble
8. Cobbler's tool
9. Geese formation
10. Bizarre
12. Actress Raines
13. Protect
18. Boxcar's contents
19. "I've ____ Lonely Too Long"
20. Blend
21. Johnnycake
22. Awkward vessels
23. Bathe
24. Twinge
25. Seize firmly
27. Gator's kin
29. Young cat
32. Cards with two pips
36. Dan Rather's delivery
37. Angry
39. Maned male
40. Water growth
41. Quick farewells
42. Eat late
43. Dollar
44. Consume
45. D.C. figure
47. Spoil

PUZZLE 76 CODEWORD

Codeword is a special crossword puzzle in which conventional clues are omitted. Instead, answer words in the diagram are represented by numbers. Each number represents a different letter of the alphabet, and all of the letters of the alphabet are used. When you are sure of a letter, put it in the code key chart and cross it off in the alphabet box. A group of letters has been inserted to start you off.

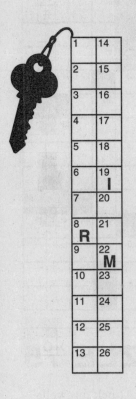

Code key chart:

1	14	14	
2	15	15	
3	16	16	
4	17	17	
5	18	18	
6	19 (I)	19	I
7	20	20	
8	21 (R)	21	R
9	22 (M)	22	M
10	23	23	
11	24	24	
12	25	25	
13	26	26	

Alphabet box:

A	N
B	O
C	P
D	Q̶
E	R̶
F	S
G	T
H	U
I̶	V
J	W
K	X
L	Y
M̶	Z

Grid (numbers):

14	19	6		18	13	19		13	19	26		8	20	11
26	25	25		8(R)	12	6		20	26	12		20	2	12
12	26	20		19(I)	1	3		19	14	22		24	19	1
22	20	7	19	22(M)		11	20	3		18	8	19	1	26
			2	25	4		14	10	1		19	15	12	20
6	20	14	3		25	8	26		25	21	21			
20	23	20		24	12	12	8		4	20	2	2	25	18
21	20	1	6	11		26	25	11		4	12	20	8	11
12	8	14	20	26	17		2	25	19	1		22	20	8
			6	12	12		25	10	8		5	20	2	12
13	12	21	26		12	23	23		3	25	19			
12	9	10	19	18		20	11	12		24	20	1	16	25
8	10	1		20	15	17		10	3	12		25	24	19
24	20	1		8	10	12		8	12	14		5	20	1
14	2	11		26	25	8		25	1	12		20	8	3

PUZZLE 77 Theme Words

Example:

S	OO	HE	SAW
L	AT	W	LATHE
T	A	L	TOOL

Four related words plus a fifth word describing their category are concealed in each diagram. Choose one square from each column, moving from left to right in order, to form a word. In the example the category is TOOL, and the related words are SAW and LATHE.

1.

T	O	T	A	SE
OA	OL	TB	I	R
C	T	E	OU	AD
SH	TM	LH	E	E
BU	OR	OK	RE	L

2.

B	AC	PC	A	W
MA	O	K	O	ER
J	L	A	NA	T
T	CK	R	E	K
A	NO	I	Z	AT

Rearrange this stack of bricks to form a crossword puzzle. The clues will help you fit the bricks into their correct places. Row 1 has been filled in for you. Use the bricks to fill in the remaining spaces.

ACROSS

1. Zany
   Ostrichlike animal
   Lapse
2. Aviator Earhart
   French negative
   Border on
3. Tape
   Wyatt's pal
   Epic tale
4. Snarl
   Faulty item
   Paving goo
5. Clutched
   Mitchum or De Niro
6. Sports official
   Ice mass
7. Paris summer
   Jewish cleric
   Ms. Adoree
8. Play division
   French money, once
   TV's Byrnes
9. Stage
   Potato type
   Help
10. Christmas contraction
    Freedom
11. Plea
    Send off
12. Crimson
    Fold father
    Wrestler Hogan
13. Orchestra member
    Ghostly greeting
    Miniature tree
14. Detective Wolfe
    Author Fleming
    Acquaint
15. Valley
    Chowed down
    Edict

DOWN

1. Swimmer Spitz
   Gather
   Tine
2. Hemsley series
   Engrave on glass
   Revolutionary
3. Art ___
   Greek cheese
   Idolize
4. Outfit
   Swine's enclosure
   Geological division
5. Make public
   Be wrong
   Widemouthed jug
6. Cushion
   Book page
   Saudi ___
7. Rubble
   Castle ditch
8. Cease
   "The ___ Seed"
   Single item
9. Disposition
   Conclusion
10. Straighten, as hair
    Word in a "Mary Poppins" song
    Physique, for short
11. Room opening
    Kimono closer
    Valuable mineral
12. Ballet step
    Honey-making insect
    Pertaining to a culture
13. Decrease
    Close
    Operator
14. Sweet stuff
    Correct copy
    Alley
15. Commence
    Circular current
    High-flying toy

BRICKS

A C T		D	R E F		O R I
P H A	D		E T E	N E E	D E C

| L O E | E D D | T | E N T | R E D |
| ■ R E | A I D | H E L | R E E | O B O |

| A M E | U D | L I A | A N | R A |
| R E C | R O B | O R D | T E | E B |

| B U T | U L K | N O | F | S L |
| A G A | S A I | D O | S E | E |

| H | E F | R T Y | C |
| B O N | B B I | P R A | H O |

| T A R | E R E | N E R | K N O | T W A |
| E R T | R A | G L E | | Y E R |

| I B E | R A N | O I | N | A | M |
| M I T | I D A | N A | C S | O O |

DIAGRAM

	1	2	3	4	5	6	7	8	9	10	11	12	13	14	15
1	M	A	D	C	A	P	■	E	M	U	■	P	A	S	S
2															
3															
4															
5															
6															
7															
8															
9															
10															
11															
12															
13															
14															
15															

PUZZLE 79

ACROSS

1. Jab
5. Killer whales
10. That boy
13. Fizzy drink
14. Skier's retreat
16. Munched
17. At a distance
18. Against
19. Authorize
20. Chest of drawers
22. Result
24. Drove fast
27. Impair
28. Dads
31. Kitchen wrap
33. Similar
36. Performance
37. Charm
39. Chunk
41. Shoves
43. Slight trace
45. "Body ____"
46. Pick
48. Gym pad
49. Enjoy a pool
51. Greasy spoon
52. Car protector
53. Pitcher spout
55. Cassette
56. Humorous
60. Enlaced
65. Ginza belt
66. Ristorante seafood
69. Missed by a ____
70. Muscle twitch
71. Matador
72. High point
73. Airport abbr.
74. Mortise filler
75. Clutter

DOWN

1. Strike-breaker
2. Health food
3. Wing-shaped
4. Like Hubbard's cupboard
5. Junk-mail addressees
6. Greek letter
7. Container
8. Voice range
9. Truth ____
10. Angel's crown
11. Bit of gossip
12. Distribute
15. Ipswich farewells
21. Burros
23. Pastry shell
25. Wiped clean
26. Hoover or Aswan, e.g.
28. Trail
29. Dull pains
30. Tube for sipping
32. Nine-day devotion
34. Scale
35. Comic-strip Viking
38. Wedding celebration
40. Alpha's follower
42. Being of service
44. Cast about
47. Set ablaze
50. Among
54. Edging loop
56. Sheepfold
57. Newspaper article
58. Lustrous mineral
59. Not a ____ in the world
61. Mosque official
62. Agreeable
63. Shady trees
64. Poor grades
67. "A Few Good ____"
68. Con's opposite

PUZZLE 80   Disco

Each numbered disc has a 5-letter answer (Clue A) and a 4-letter answer (Clue B) reading in a clockwise direction. Enter the first letter of each 5-letter answer in the circle in the preceding disc. For example, in disc 1: R + EMIT = REMIT.

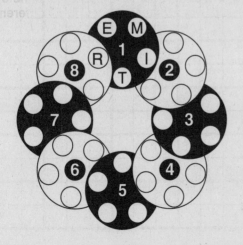

A

1. Send payment
2. Cross
3. Postpone
4. Rent
5. Range
6. Explore
7. Lively
8. Throng

B

1. Radiate
2. Speed
3. Competent
4. Soothe
5. Contend
6. Choir gown
7. Gamble
8. Heat up

ACROSS

1. Turkish rulers
5. Outbuilding
9. Pig's lunch
13. Unit of length
14. Motor vehicles
16. Company symbol
17. Doll's cry
18. Minimum amount
19. Gain income
20. Inflates
22. Avoided capture
24. Averse
27. ___ King Cole
28. Barbecue selection
31. Glancing rebound
35. Delight
36. Belittle
37. Coat sleeve
39. Deposit
40. Long-nosed fish
41. View
42. Paid athlete
43. Bread serving
45. "___ We All?"
47. Facial hair
49. Welshmen, e.g.
50. Cleaning tool
51. Immobile
53. Engrossed
56. Discuss again
60. Prevaricator
61. Short ape?
65. Land amid water
66. Temper tantrum
67. Terrace
68. In the vicinity of
69. Poetic twilights
70. Sobbed
71. Moon Mullins's brother

DOWN

1. Goals
2. Chew on, as a bone
3. Top
4. Onion's kin
5. Mexican condiment
6. Color
7. Greek letter
8. Counterparts for don'ts
9. Detective
10. Cargo
11. Fictional fiend
12. Walden, e.g.
15. Pool members
21. Earring's place
23. Lingerie trim
25. Disastrous
26. Portable grill
28. Iodine source
29. Frighten
30. "Blue ___"
32. Sway
33. Monet's stand
34. English river
38. New York athletes
43. Traffic sign
44. Compact computer
45. "God's Little ___"
46. Consider anew
48. Stings
52. Rye fungus
53. What ___ is new?
54. Innings number
55. Cloudburst
57. Adrift
58. Destroy
59. Big sandwich
62. Rarer than rare
63. Consumed food
64. Puppy's bite

Missing Trios

For each numbered group fill in the same three missing letters (not necessarily in the same order) to complete a 7-letter, 6-letter, 5-letter, 4-letter, and 3-letter word. The Missing Trio is different for each group.

1. C _ _ _ U L E   _ _ L E E _   L _ _ _ E   _ O _ _   _ _ _

2. H O _ _ _ O _ N   P O _ _ _ R   _ _ _ L L   _ _ _ Y   _ _ _ _

3. T _ _ L O I _   _ _ S U R _   _ R _ I _   _ _ U _   _ _ _ _

4. A D A _ _ _ _   R A S _ _ C _   _ _ M _ O K   _ _ _ _   _ _ _ _

5. R O _ _ _ I _ E   C I _ E _ _ _   _ S O _   _ _ _ _   _ _ _ _

PUZZLE 83 DOUBLE TROUBLE

Not really double trouble, but double fun! Solve this puzzle as you would a regular crossword, except place one, two, or three letters in each box. The number of letters in each answer is shown in parentheses after its clue.

ACROSS

1. Dirigible (5)
3. Thrive (7)
6. Repeat (5)
8. Assist a burglar (4)
9. Conclusion (6)
11. Guarantee (6)
12. Without worth (7)
14. Adaptation (10)
16. Attic window (6)
19. Flaky dessert (3)
20. Directive (6)
22. Food plan (4)
23. Future frog (7)
26. Cloak (4)
27. Moral strength (9)
29. Row of seats (4)
30. Car fixer (8)
32. Greenish blue (4)
33. Pal (5)
34. Throttle (5)
35. Give (6)
37. Alienate (8)
40. Peevish (5)
42. Relax (6)
43. Renowned (7)
46. Fossil resin (5)
48. Animal companion (3)
49. Wakeful (7)
50. Festive (5)

DOWN

1. Tell secrets (4)
2. Incentive (7)
3. "The Nutty ____" (9)
4. Twirl (4)
5. Baseball stat (3)
6. Begin again (6)
7. Most recent (7)
10. Precede (4)
11. Alternately (7)
13. Firstborn (6)
15. Largest planet (7)
17. The press (5)
18. Withdrew (9)
20. Turn into (6)
21. Deck opening (5)
24. Magical tonic (6)
25. Suspicious (5)
27. Coward (7)
28. Eagle's claw (5)
31. Alaskan port (9)
33. Ridge (5)
36. Watchful (9)
37. Flee to marry (5)
38. Risky feat (5)
39. ____ whiz! (3)
41. Prattle (6)
44. Bog (4)
45. Wren's home (4)
47. Jam fruit (5)

PUZZLE 84 Crackers

Test your safecracking skills by rotating the four lettered dials until a common 8-letter word can be read across the middle of the dials.

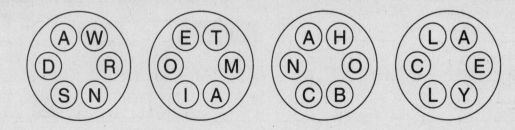

ACROSS

1. Get the point
4. Madras mister
7. Woman's title
11. Engine part
12. Hardware pro
14. Disconnect
15. Escort's offering
16. Burn balm
17. Recipe verb
18. Lacking color
21. Greeting word
22. Merry
23. Wise guys?
26. Embarrassed
27. Mr. Torme
30. McCartney/ Wonder song
34. Hanoi holiday
35. Eggs, to Ovid
36. Border
37. Birthday count
38. That lady
40. Common seasonings
47. Burglar's take
48. Put on a happy face
49. Byron product
50. "____ Karenina"
51. Merit
52. Cotton machine
53. Gaze
54. Herbal drink
55. Famous Giant

DOWN

1. Sign of healing
2. British noble
3. Madame Bovary
4. Pointed stick
5. Team race
6. Desktop symbol
7. Pulpy
8. Person opposed
9. Mine entrance
10. Additional
13. Avoided commitment
19. Jaw feature
20. Dry gully
23. Bumped into
24. Actor Vigoda
25. Procured
26. Genetic letters
27. Trendy
28. Unit of energy
29. Soap ingredient
31. Eastern discipline
32. Get even for
33. Prez's underling
37. Perfume essence
38. Church topper
39. Hair tint
40. Hit with the palm
41. Excellent
42. Solitary
43. Rats!
44. ____ stick
45. Prepare to publish
46. Landlady's due

PUZZLE 85
• CONTRASTS •

ACROSS

1. Posed
4. City in Iowa
8. Strong cord
12. Before today
13. Cookie favorite
14. Desertlike
15. "Rah!", said Tom ____
17. Clothes
18. Egyptian statesman
19. Former fast flier
21. Spanish appetizer
24. Chores
28. Atlas entries
31. "I love camping," said Tom ____
33. Here, to Henri
34. Hamburger extra
35. Dusk, poetically
36. "I've lost my penny," said Tom ____
38. Emancipate
39. Stern with a bow
40. Italian family surname
42. Dry, as wine
44. Mental picture
48. Pacific island
51. "I'll end the prayer," said Tom ____
54. Sheltered, at sea
55. Innocent one
56. Shoebox letters
57. Sugar substitute?
58. Blubbers
59. Senator Kennedy

DOWN

1. Biological pouches
2. Turkish title
3. Pigeon-____
4. Main artery
5. Hosp. test
6. Flexible fish
7. Some beans
8. Wicker material
9. Granada gold
10. Glutton
11. Mag. moguls
16. Diner sign
20. British gun
22. Two cups
23. Doddering
25. Road ending
26. Painter Paul ____
27. "Auld Lang ____"
28. Skirt length
29. Super serves
30. Type type
32. Items for play
34. A single time
37. Simpler
38. Disaster org.
41. Prongs
43. Hired vehicles
45. Aid in crime
46. Merriment
47. Gazed upon
48. Defective
49. London libation
50. Meadow
52. Chinese leader
53. Fade away

PUZZLE 86
• TOM SWIFTIES •

73

PUZZLE 87

Diagramless crosswords are solved by using the clues and their numbers to fill in the answer words and the arrangement of black squares. Insert the number of each clue with the first letter of its answer, across and down. Fill in a black square at the end of each answer. Every black square must have a corresponding black square on the opposite side of the diagram to form a diagonally symmetrical pattern. Puzzles 87 and 88 have been started for you.

ACROSS
1. Concealed
4. Glide down the slopes
7. Burro
10. "A Chorus Line" finale
11. Bowler's target
12. Sickly
13. Pipe joint
14. &
15. Meet the bet of
16. Some rodents
18. Ran in neutral
20. Graceful water bird
21. Wading birds
22. Pester
24. Smirked
27. Outskirts
31. Verbal exams
32. ___ estate
33. Trig. ratio
34. Small amount
37. Chicago baseballer
38. Lemon or lime drink
39. Tell a falsehood
40. Earlier than present
41. Played the first card
42. Before, in a poem
43. Evergreen plant

DOWN
1. Removers of weeds
2. Relative by marriage
3. River-mouth plain
4. Bath, e.g.
5. Nieces and uncles
6. Deep, violet-blue
7. Supermarket pathway
8. Winter forecast
9. Toboggans
17. Growl with bared teeth
19. Washer's companion
21. Terminal
23. Cuddle
24. Not the express
25. Eat away at
26. Slackened
28. Rot
29. Appraise
30. Macaroni shape
35. Tire input
36. Cee's follower

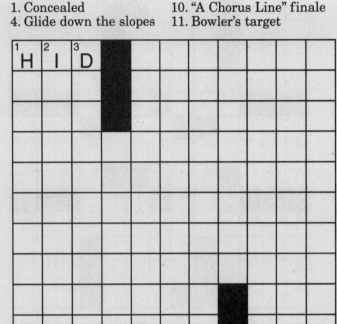

PUZZLE 88

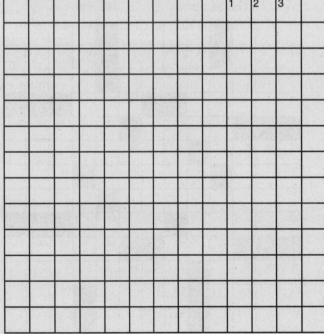

ACROSS
1. Cleo's serpent
4. Old womanish
6. Curbside garbage
7. Chilled
9. Coal distillate
10. Sweet wine
11. Tennis call
12. Aruban export
13. Card game
14. Strike lightly
15. Devotee
16. Chick's mom
17. "Black Velvet ___"
18. Crate
19. Employ
20. Neighbor of Miss.
21. Location
22. Lugged
24. Follow
25. Study

DOWN
1. Emmet
2. Baby minder
3. Fabric fold
4. Feel unwell
5. Make a mistake
6. Parking area
7. Aquatic bird
8. Mine find
10. Scheme
11. Alight
12. Peak
13. Ebb
15. Cab fee
16. Raspy
17. 1/8 byte
18. Tasteless
19. Secreted
20. Poker "bullet"
21. View
23. Large cask

PUZZLE 89

ACROSS
1. Suitable
4. Wrought ____
6. Slow, in music
8. Squeeze
9. Pecan, e.g.
11. Describe
12. Repeated sound
14. Goddess, e.g.
16. ____ Christian Andersen
18. Sea eagle
19. Juvenile
21. Took a chair
22. Pilfer
24. In case
27. Leap headfirst
28. Not clerical
30. Trim meat
31. Medicine
33. Shark film
34. Go wrong
35. Moral obligation
36. Yellow fruit
38. Soil
39. Small vegetable

DOWN
1. Actor Quinn
2. Baby buggy, for short
3. Garb
5. Diamond number
6. West Point team
7. Expression of pain
8. Refer to
10. "____ Darn Cat!"
11. Doorframe part
13. Undivided
14. ____ Moines, Iowa
15. Of a historic time
17. Letter strokes
20. Exploding star
23. Casino transaction
25. Blue
26. Fatigue
27. Having morning moisture
29. Sidewalk's edge
30. Statistics
32. Alumnus
33. Spanish council
35. Be bold enough
37. Bite

Starting box on page 562

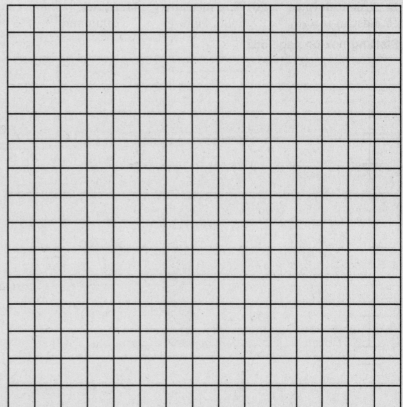

Face to Face

PUZZLE 90

Place the eight squares on the left into the diagram so that each number will match the number in the adjacent square. Do not turn the squares or rearrange the numbers within each square.

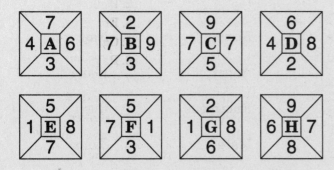

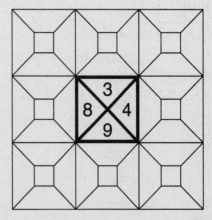

75

PUZZLE 91

ACROSS
1. Maple genus
5. British school
9. Bush
11. Clearing
12. Flower organ
14. Ardent devotee
15. Restful resort
16. Traipse
18. Hunting dogs
19. Porky's pad
21. Portable boat
23. Winners
24. Dash
26. Wire measure
27. Polka follower
28. Vivacity
30. Make tardy
32. Chafe
34. Outskirts
35. Develop
37. Mutt
39. Be ill
40. Baltic or Caspian
42. Gun, as an engine
44. Attack command
45. Sorority members
47. Siamese or Persian
49. Tumbler
51. Lone Ranger and Tonto, e.g.
53. Hawaiian handout
55. Enticer
56. Breed of sheep
58. Mountain crest
59. Darn again
60. Florence's evening
61. Second in a series

DOWN
1. Deadly snakes
2. Poker tokens
3. Phony
4. Boring routine
5. High spirits
6. Flair
7. Smells
8. Fishermen's tools
10. Large
11. Acquire
13. Resinous substance
14. Zorro's mark
17. Beaver's barrier
18. Type of power
20. Sharp bark
22. Nada
25. Danger
27. Take exception
29. Baby beagle
31. Personal quirk
33. Inebriate
35. Soft cheese
36. Named at birth
38. ___ room (family room)
39. More open
41. Total up
43. Suitcase
44. Spook
45. Train unit
46. Amount of money
48. Firm belief
49. Arabian garments
50. Flying stinger
52. Opposite of 'neath
54. Ames's locale
57. Yank's foe

Starting box on page 562

PUZZLE 92   Matchmaker

Fill in the missing first letter of each word in the column on the left. Next, look for a related word in the group at the right and put it in the blank in the second column. When the puzzle is completed, read the first letters of both columns in order, from top to bottom, to reveal the name of a vegetable dish.

___ arth   _____

___ uardian   _____

___ old   _____   Acorn   Nail

___ lay   _____

___ arge   _____   Angel   Planet

___ pple   _____   Enormous   Rush

___ ut   _____

___ oe   _____   Mate   Sauce

76

ACROSS

1. Possesses
4. Hilo garland
7. Taken by mouth
9. British noble
10. Bona fide
11. Smug grin
12. Adds (up)
13. Mongrel
14. Affirmative votes
15. Sticky stuff
17. Short notes
19. Tarnish
20. Actress Miles
21. Money at hand
26. Indigo
27. Prepared
29. Sandwich cookie
30. Tepid
32. Curved arch
33. At the apex of
34. Beauty parlor
36. Brown of renown
37. Yearn
38. Annoy
40. Among
41. Concentrate
43. Exec's car
44. Golf club
45. Norwegian king
46. Twice five
47. Pixie

DOWN

1. Cinnamon-flavored candy
2. Gulch
3. Fries
4. Hideaway
5. Miss the mark
6. Sort
8. Not as much
9. Rhea's kin
11. Dress down
15. Well-behaved
16. Greasy
17. Diner handout
18. Estrada of "CHiPs"
19. Imp
20. Actor Kilmer
22. Became calmer
23. Jason's ship
24. Viewed
25. Weeding tool
27. Evaluate
28. God of love
31. Goes on foot
34. Poetic comparison
35. Beast
37. ___ Alto
38. Image
39. Flee
41. In shape
42. Miner's harvest

PUZZLE 93

• TEMPERATURE •

Starting box on page 562

Whirly Words

PUZZLE 94

This diagram has been divided into sections, numbered 1 to 6, and each contains spaces for four letters. The answer to the clue for each section is a 4-letter word whose letters fit into the corresponding section so that the inner ring, middle ring, and outer ring all spell words reading clockwise beginning in section 1.

CLUES

Section 1: Future blooms

Section 2: Home plate, e.g.

Section 3: Wagon

Section 4: Talk wildly

Section 5: Notion

Section 6: Adolescent

Inner Ring: Desolate

Middle Ring: Ten years

Outer Ring: Verify

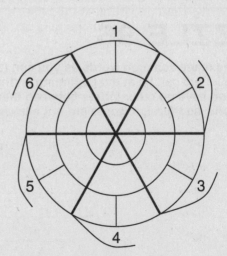

PUZZLE 95

ACROSS

1. Pouch
4. Feel concern
5. Compel
6. Press
7. Mast
11. Hero
12. Roof parts
14. Designer Cassini
15. Holler
16. Guys' companions
17. Beam
18. Cudgel
19. Barks
23. Dark or Middle
25. Enrage
26. Pub game
28. Do a lawn chore
29. Baseball call
31. Voyage
33. Iridescent gem
35. Podiatrist's concern
36. Danger
38. Thug
39. Whirl
40. Lament
41. Advantage
43. Primary
44. Hill builder

DOWN

1. Hayloft's place
2. Semicircle
3. Migratory fowl
4. Unflappable
5. Spring peeper
6. Roman date
8. Salary
9. Allege
10. Pass along
11. Under the weather
13. More foxy
14. Cowboy flick
16. Wildly enthusiastic
18. Faulty
20. Restriction
21. Plunk
22. Make a seam
24. Crouch
27. Terrific!
30. Weight allowance
31. Implement
32. Actor/director Howard
34. Falsify
35. Thwart
37. Camel's kin
38. Acquire
40. Tarry
42. Highway sight

Starting box on page 562

PUZZLE 96   These Three

Think of as many common words as you can (up to 7 letters) that contain the letters VAN consecutively. The letters can be at the beginning, at the end, or in the middle of the word, but they must be in order and have no other letters between them. Plurals ending in S, proper names, abbreviations, contractions, and foreign words are not allowed.

VAN

PUZZLE 97

ACROSS

1. Decimal base
4. Composer Khachaturian
6. Dolphins' home
7. Antiquity
10. Rang up
11. Rich earth
13. Crosby contemporary
14. Party prize
16. Find out
17. Canned
19. Young fellow
20. Bargain event
21. Throat tissue
24. Recline
25. Bad toupee
26. Limit
28. Pleat
30. Barely made
32. Summer cooler
33. Hunter's lure
35. Central part
37. Gluts
39. Operates
40. Orderly
41. Floral perfumes
44. Rap's Dr. ____
45. Cracks a book
46. Statuesque
47. Appomattox figure

DOWN

1. Suit sewer
2. Of a period
3. Designate
5. Central
6. Baby's cry
7. Gnome's kin
8. Bread unit
9. Trumpet great
10. Sorority members
12. Righteous
13. Modify
15. Ancient item
18. Forest creature
19. Scoundrel
21. Swaps
22. Frosted
23. Michigan and Ontario
27. Pie nut
29. Rakes in
31. Was overly fond
34. Calendar span
35. Nursery furniture
36. Yours and mine
38. Holy fem.
41. Gallery display
42. Bluish green
43. Yarn

Starting box on page 562

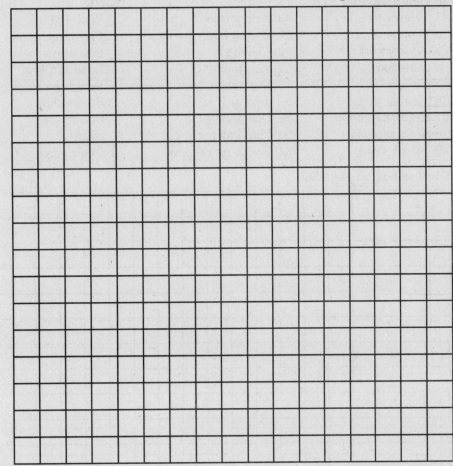

Miniatures

PUZZLE 98

Using each letter of the given words only once, fill in the small diagrams so that 3-letter words read across and down to form miniature crosswords.

1. DEITY

2. LOFTY

3. GRATE

4. COMET

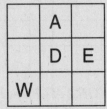

PUZZLE 99

ACROSS
1. Mental picture
6. Church sounds
7. Breeze
12. Violinist Stern
13. Streisand hit
14. Ship deserter
17. Summer shoes
20. Small warship
21. Cherry-tree chopper
22. Wickerwork material
24. Sidle
25. Kennel pest
27. Staircase shape
28. Take care of
29. Burnt wood
31. Indian coin
33. Worth
35. Sheer curtain fabric
37. Slanted
38. Breakfast fare
41. Perform onstage
42. Drift off
43. Ramble
48. Arm joints
51. Salary boost
52. Charter
53. ___ four
55. Vegetable drawer
56. Dog-paddle
60. Piano piece
62. Ocean movement
63. FDR's Scottie
67. Turns back
68. Corral
69. Smelly
71. Most profound
76. ___ de Cologne
77. Convert, as coupons
78. Book's name
79. Work dough
80. Arose
81. Serfs

DOWN
1. Wading bird
2. Flat-topped formation
3. Ladd of films
4. Delighted
5. Steep slope
7. Comfortable room
8. Choir gown
9. Footless animal
10. Pennant
11. Pierre's pate
13. Groaner
14. Huck Finn's transport
15. Wheel shaft
16. Adolescent
18. Lion's cave
19. High-___ (nervous)
20. Lead sulfide
23. South American mammal
26. Recommendation
27. Storage building
29. Computer key
30. "Curly ___"
32. Chunk of eternity
34. Sacred table
36. Forbidden things
37. Beret
39. Nearest the ground
40. Junk mail, usually
44. Brief sleep
45. Locomotive fuel
46. Hinder legally
47. Restrained
48. 1814 exile isle
49. Flower wreath
50. Prohibit
54. Fictitious story
57. Rub dry
58. Brainchild
59. Entree listing
61. African fly
63. Dining utensil
64. Yemeni port
65. Metal deposit
66. Length x width
67. Pirate's drink
70. Provided with food
72. Cherry seeds
73. Kind of jacket
74. Gin flavoring
75. Koppel and Kennedy

Starting box on page 562

Starting box on page 562

DIAGRAMLESS DEVOTEES! Delve into a special collection with loads of challenging puzzles in every volume of Selected Diagramless. To order, see page 159.

80

ACROSS

1. That's opposite
5. Ogre
10. Circle dance
11. Ahead
13. More difficult
15. Whistle cord
17. Identity
18. "____ Got to Be Me"
20. Computer message
22. Jewish cleric
25. Yelling
28. NHL athlete, e.g.
29. Anonymous
31. Foot parts
33. Await judgment
37. RBI, e.g.
38. Place
40. Steep ledge
43. Sufficient
45. Shrill barks
47. Tangle
49. Zilch
50. Sorbonne send-off
51. Coop
52. Greek vowel
53. Bawl
54. Lettuce variety
55. Pipe puffer
57. Coin side
60. Cote denizen
61. Rocky pinnacle
62. Drink chiller
63. French peak
66. Equine coloring
67. Spanish celebration
70. Old card game
71. Tarzan's friend
73. Energy unit
76. Indian nanny
77. Epic tales
79. Charged atom
80. Man-goat deity
81. Catch
82. Bun seed
83. Gaucho's rope
85. Battle of honor
87. Microbe
89. Clock winders
90. Flood wall
92. Soccer official
94. Stylish
95. Zeal
96. Live
100. Earlier
102. Skipper's OK
104. Gentle animal
105. Disgrace
108. Agree to
111. Medical sorting
112. Drill
113. Embroidered
114. Florence's evening

DOWN

1. Pulse
2. Coal scuttle
3. Exasperation
4. Calcutta clothing
5. Short jacket
6. Hartmann of Hollywood
7. Bristle
8. Speaker
9. Overhead railway
12. Fall in folds
13. Self starter?
14. Muslim leader
16. Supervise
19. Viewpoint
21. Laze
23. Jungle
24. Savings acct. gain
26. Night hooters
27. Tropical bird
30. Canoe's kin
31. Pursue prey
32. Inasmuch as
33. Serenity
34. Fund generously
35. Silence spoiler
36. Rightful
39. Gain with effort
41. Pine tree
42. Operate a plane
44. Zest
46. Miles ____ hour
48. Cloddish
51. Eye part
56. Grounded bird
58. Behave
59. Bring to a halt
63. Plankton
64. Earthy
65. Models
66. Kidney-related
67. Loyal admirer
68. Figurative description
69. Impatient
71. Gaseous mixture
72. Hawaiian staple
74. Disrespectful
75. Bearded antelope
78. Solicit
80. Prefers
81. Luge
82. Diving duck
84. Sub, e.g.
86. Miscalculate
88. "The ____ Baron"
91. Proclamation
93. Gave birth to a colt
95. Golfer Palmer, to pals
97. Plant swelling
98. Chop off
99. Court call
101. Paddles
103. Dumbo's wings
106. Small crow
107. Generation
109. Bee's follower
110. Honda, e.g.

Starting box on page 562

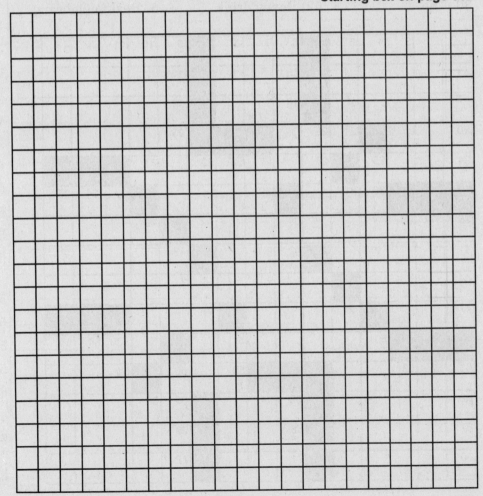

PUZZLE 101

ACROSS
1. ___ to my ears
6. Monk's title
9. Drive off
14. Rhone feeder
15. Floor covering
16. Sidestep
17. Airport device
18. "___ Life to Live"
19. Fastens securely
20. Hen's output
21. Consume
23. Margarines
24. Low in pitch
26. Little guys
30. The "I"
32. Maned male
33. Fancy resort
36. Wide-ranging scheme
40. Jai ___
41. At right angles, on a ship
42. Twilight, to Keats
43. Exercise
44. Small duck
45. Overwhelming wins
47. Loop trains
48. Western pal
49. Tumult
50. ___ energy
52. Honey drink
56. Fire a gun
59. ___ Vegas
61. Harem room
62. Gypsy's card
63. Spider's trap
65. Resource
67. Wipe out
68. Flightless bird
69. Deceit
70. Coal digger
71. Mr. Seaver
72. "Li'l ___"

DOWN
1. Bogged down
2. Custom
3. Rushlike plant
4. Pension-plan abbr.
5. Beak membrane
6. Foam
7. Dart
8. Era
9. Converted
10. Wrongs
11. Window unit
12. Taro root
13. Not so much
22. Hebrew lyre
25. Rose part
27. Novelist Isabel ___
28. Food item
29. Eternity
31. Jewel
33. Snow toy
34. Peel, as fruit
35. Islets
36. Husband or wife
37. Son of Adam
38. The Seven ___
39. Oyster find
40. Basic tenet
43. Antiquity
45. Fond du ___
46. Poet Teasdale
48. Golf club
50. Lasso part
51. Record
53. Red dye
54. Fred Astaire's sister
55. Library stamp
56. Flower stalk
57. Mata ___
58. Algerian city
60. Heroic narrative
63. Soaked
64. Comedian Philips
66. Stand-in

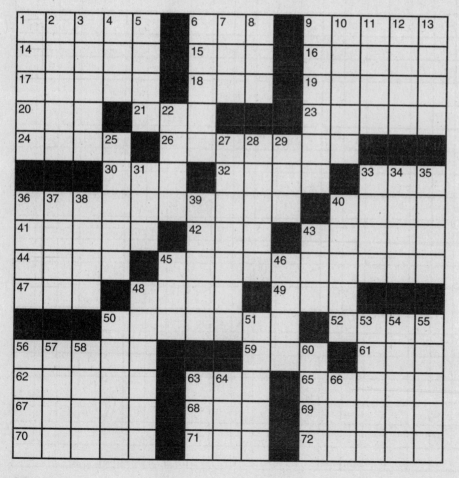

ACROSS

1. Felon's flight
4. Singer Meat ___
8. Hone
12. ___-man band
13. Sell
15. Frost
16. Had a knish
17. Used as transportation
18. Aquatic growth
19. Safecracker's soup
21. Calmly
23. Bridge seat
26. Jalopy
27. Certainly!
28. Actor Parker
31. Important
33. Wheel shaft
34. Guy's date
35. Revolve
40. Washer cycle
41. Delight
43. Greek vowels
44. Wobble
46. Cock an ___
47. "___ Free"
48. Smear
50. Church recess
51. Excitement
54. Frying vessel
55. Red-pencil
57. Hairdresser's item
60. Whinny
64. S-shaped molding
65. Untie
68. Lone Ranger and Tonto, e.g.
69. Float upward
70. Diplomatic agents
71. Dutch ___ disease
72. Minor
73. Mentally sound
74. British brew

DOWN

1. Give temporarily
2. Opponent
3. "___ the Press"
4. Hawaiian garland
5. Different
6. Does sums
7. Sheep's coat
8. Come again?
9. Full of openings
10. National symbol
11. Waiters' burdens
13. Malayan boat
14. ___ species
20. Begrudge
22. Bohemian
24. Syrup source
25. Streetcar, in London
28. Swiftly
29. Montreal player
30. Skirt feature
32. Joined
36. Mail-in refund
37. At the peak
38. Paves
39. Medieval slave
42. Wise seasoning?
45. View
49. Labor organizations
51. Scrub a space mission
52. "Git Along, Little ___"
53. Corpulent
56. Hostelries
58. ___ there, done that
59. Bossa ___
61. Notion
62. Seabird
63. Residence
66. "Sanford and ___"
67. Gaze at

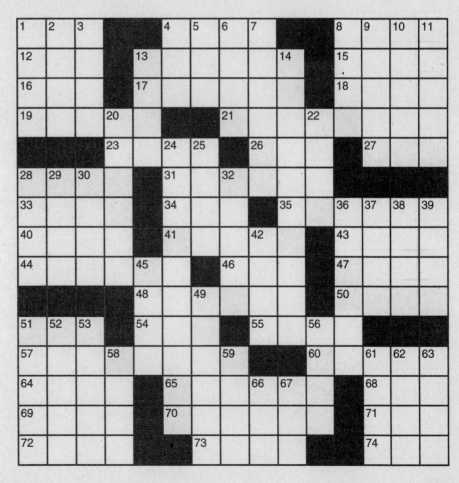

83

PUZZLE 103

ACROSS

1. Bush
6. Fall short
10. Cable car
14. Lasso part
15. "The ___ Duckling"
16. Type of hoop
17. Reed instruments
18. Part in a play
19. Discharge
20. Asian cookware
21. Taste
23. Chess action
24. Ghost's cry
25. Made changes
28. Remote
32. Fasten
33. Milky stone
34. Man's title
36. Feathered stole
39. Frolic
41. Get by
42. Poets' daybreaks
44. Browning's before
45. Wasting time
48. Hit with the foot
49. Commanded
50. Harms
52. Riots
56. Income
57. City light
58. Japanese coin
59. Pro
62. Outstanding loan
63. Destiny
66. Appraise
68. At all
69. Matinee star
70. Watchers
71. Decorate anew
72. Whirl
73. Rent again

DOWN

1. Falling flakes
2. Tramp
3. Chess castle
4. Employ
5. Give as a gift
6. Ire
7. Back in time
8. Unhealthy
9. Caustic material
10. Topic
11. Hearsay
12. Animated
13. Paired
22. Walk aimlessly
24. Bundle of hay
25. Be present at
26. Be untruthful
27. School semester
28. Aft's opposite
29. Impersonator
30. Rant and ___
31. Capitulates
35. Go down the slope
36. Ship's jail
37. Story starter
38. Begs
40. Diamond gal et al.
43. Approval word
46. Sandra or Ruby
47. Stare blankly
51. Trough
52. Beneath
53. Annoy
54. Dressed
55. Prelim
58. Cheer
59. Engine's need
60. Mythical monster
61. Pause
63. Pine
64. Summer cooler
65. Sock part
67. Pro vote

ACROSS

1. Bombay garment
5. Follow orders
9. "Red ___"
14. Terminated
15. Uncovered
16. Brawl
17. Sorts
18. Fastener
19. Bluish purple
20. Honolulu handout
21. Marries
22. Soaked
23. Loudest
26. Wriggly
27. Most unhappy
29. Midday
31. Actress Barkin
32. Satisfy
33. Fitness club
36. Had dinner
37. Turned outward
40. Jar top
41. Stylish
42. Decorate again
43. Exceed the limit
45. Secondhand
46. Is present at
48. Bridge length
51. Reuben ingredient
53. Pastry shells
55. ___ of duty
56. Fade away
59. Rascal
60. Hosiery shade
61. The Kingston ___
62. Asserts firmly
63. Cooling drinks
64. Dampens
65. Fathers, in France
66. Pain in the neck
67. Mine finds

DOWN

1. Put to sea
2. Shaft
3. Reignited
4. Freudian concerns
5. Think constantly (about)
6. One-armed ___
7. Eradicate
8. Slangy affirmative
9. Bullets and bombs
10. Heavy
11. Avoid capture
12. Make merry
13. Very little
21. Frankfurters
22. Fur piece
24. Poetic form
25. Agitated state
27. Row of stitches
28. Kind of saxophone
30. Senior citizen
32. To's partner
33. Thinner
34. ___ Piper
35. Totals
38. Changes direction
39. Circular current
44. Split ___ soup
45. Doubtful
46. Dwellings
47. Most loyal
48. Remnant
49. Verify
50. Hole-boring tool
52. Piano composition
54. "___ of the D'Urbervilles"
57. Nibble
58. Supervisor
60. Forty winks
61. Couple

PUZZLE 105

ACROSS

1. Deep breaths
6. Society newcomers
10. Early birds?
14. White heron
15. Farm team
16. Distinctive air
17. Detached
18. Awful
19. Raise
20. Oar
21. Alarm cluck
24. Fitness club
25. Sang singly
27. Menace
29. Dunce
31. Merchandise
32. Valises
35. Ditch
37. Cheek dent
41. Customer, after the sale
43. Met in session
45. Shows concern
46. Multiple
48. Scratch
50. Yuletide quaffs
51. Competes
53. Gyro bread
55. Stores of weapons
59. Amuse
63. One, when marching
64. Walked
66. Wimple wearer
67. Red-pencil
69. Long lunch
70. Inactive
72. Wordy birdie
73. Continuously
74. Sniggler
75. He gets what's coming
76. Stench
77. Attempt anew

DOWN

1. Chars
2. Blockhouse?
3. Bowwow gone mad
4. Biddy
5. Sound investment?
6. Ninny
7. Survive
8. Ship quarters
9. Scoffed (at)
10. Hearing device
11. Visitor
12. Raisin, once
13. It's a wrap
22. Stink
23. Artifact
26. Notice
28. Annual book
30. Clear tables
32. Jazz type
33. Pointed tool
34. Wildebeest
36. Kiltie's beret
38. Not amateur
39. Drumstick
40. Snaky curve
42. Pours
44. Dance or water
47. Deerskin
49. Ceremony
52. Garment arm
54. Neater
55. Throat-clearers
56. Tint again
57. Book back
58. Bout of indulgence
60. Prepared to propose
61. Tempter
62. Diary item
65. Ham, e.g.
68. Blacktop
71. By birth

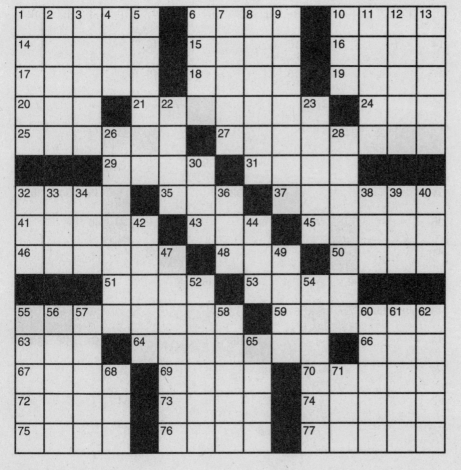

ACROSS

1. Violin holder
5. Japanese rice wine
9. Fairy-tale beast
13. Highest point
14. Henry and Cassius
16. Slow leak
17. Criminal, slangily
18. Sultan's ladies
19. Pedestal part
20. Spoken
21. Belief
22. Removed
24. Bouncers' requests
26. Rainbows
28. Before, to a bard
29. Fop
33. Tiny Tim's instrument
34. Strip of equipment
35. Fewer
37. Brother's sib
40. Vermont or Oregon
41. Cereal type
42. Nitwit
44. ___ sauce
45. Con
46. Actress Reed
47. Pea container
48. Most peaceful
50. Sit-up's target
53. District
55. Caustic liquid
56. ___ card
58. "Me and My ___"
60. Take flight on a peel
64. Sermon topic
65. Bicker
67. Mexican fare
68. Hawaiian honker
69. Taking to court
70. News flash
71. To boot
72. Allot
73. Yield

DOWN

1. Guitar adjunct
2. Impersonator
3. Watery fluids
4. Leaving nothing implied
5. Split
6. Alack!
7. Hindu's destiny
8. Look at
9. ___ and ends
10. Rub harshly
11. Passenger
12. Lyric poem
15. Loose overgarments
23. Apply
25. Venetian ruler
27. Bucolic
29. Swear
30. Aware of
31. Medical photo
32. Fair-haired woman
36. Dine
37. Trig term
38. Charged particles
39. At once, on "ER"
42. Lazily
43. Of the home
45. Main arteries
47. Golf norm
49. Assert
50. Gladiator's spot
51. Slanting edge
52. Rotates
54. Texas A & M athlete
57. Toast topper
59. Uncle's wife
61. Not prompt
62. Made cold
63. Apple or pear
66. Island drink

PUZZLE 107

CODEWORD

Codeword is a special crossword puzzle in which conventional clues are omitted. Instead, answer words in the diagram are represented by numbers. Each number represents a different letter of the alphabet, and all of the letters of the alphabet are used. When you are sure of a letter, put it in the code key chart and cross it off in the Alphabet Box. A group of letters has been inserted to start you off.

1	2 E	3 R	4	5	6	7	8	9	10	11	12	13
14	15	16	17	18	19	20	21	22	23	24	25	26 V

21	25	19		18	23	5		8	25	16		3	2	16
2	3	25		23	26	25		23	3	18		2	25	18
24	2	12		18	2	3	3	14	2	3		15	3	7
23	10	2			3	23	2			17	18	14	20	2
19	25	3	21		9	23	24	24		10	25	8		
		2	21	23	10		3	23	19	17	14	16	11
5	17	16	2	3		6	25	22			2	18	25
25	8	18		25	19	3	23	17	10	9		10	23	3
5	23	25			10	2	18			23	15	18	25	9
25	10	18	14	1	17	2		2	9	19	2			
		2	5	17		24	14	26	2		2	13	25	5
18	2	5	8	23			15	23	21			2	19	23
23	8	2		3 R	2 E	26 V	2	20	3	7		10	25	10
19	14	10		17	4	2		26	14	2		23	8	18
25	15	18		5	2	18		2	16	16		10	2	2

Alphabet Box

A B C D E F G H I J K L M N O P Q R S T U V W X Y Z

88

ACROSS

1. Havana export
6. Mall division
10. Bean curd
14. Ring
15. 60 minutes
16. Fusses
17. Kilmer and Keats
18. Conscious of
19. French mother
20. Printers' concerns
21. Put down asphalt
23. Ran after
25. Hearty breads
27. Performed nuptials
28. Grown grig
29. Impostor
31. Breakfast foods
35. Quite smart
38. It's a reel need
39. Neckwear
40. Allows to borrow
41. Prohibition
42. Solo
44. Feedbag morsel
45. ___ rally
46. Votes to accept
47. Struggle
50. Plane people
51. Fiddle
52. Earned
53. Old sailor
57. Distress
60. Quiet down
62. Saloon
63. A woodwind
64. Garlic feature
66. Leave by ladder
68. G-men
69. Unseat
70. Wake up
71. Yeas
72. Seurat trademarks
73. Made a choice

DOWN

1. Prank
2. Twist of fate
3. Silly birds
4. Tiny carpenter
5. Scrape
6. Pushy type?
7. Put an edge on
8. Not at home
9. Carry on
10. Mexican dish
11. Certain poems
12. Aft's opposite
13. Spent
22. On the road
24. That woman's
26. Slipped
30. Those elected
31. Against
32. Spin like ___
33. Bits of fiber
34. Notices
35. Emit air
36. Aft
37. Poker-pot stake
38. Talk over
41. Honey insect
42. Thirst quencher
43. Depressions
45. Lumber buy
46. Abilities
48. Emphasize
49. Excessively
50. Woos
52. Phantom
54. Regarding
55. Slight error
56. Wooded
57. Couch
58. Conform
59. Went by bus
61. Sub sandwich
65. Twosome
67. Cut

PUZZLE 109

ACROSS

1. Neck scarf
6. Tuna containers
10. Iota
14. Biscuit
15. In a short time
16. Stockings
17. March King
18. Stand up
19. Spanish pot
20. Go astray
21. Spunk
23. One who dodges
25. Establish
26. Become rusty
29. Bigfoot's cousin
31. Continuously
32. 23rd Greek letter
35. Smack
37. Places
39. Sailors' stories
41. Silver or glass follower
42. Heron
44. Froth
45. Appended
47. Remodel
48. Horned vipers
49. You bet!
50. To shelter
52. Waterproof cover
54. Distribute cards incorrectly
56. Chicago Loop trains
59. Concrete material
63. Type
64. Not cooked
65. Bear's den
66. Overwhelmed
69. Flaming
71. Puzzled
72. Memo
73. Sword thrust
74. Ballpoints
75. "___ of the Cat"
76. Metal bar

DOWN

1. Burros
2. Tally
3. Enclosed lawns
4. Switch positions
5. Tempest's spot?
6. Wrist bones
7. Cuckoo
8. Refusals
9. Allergic reaction
10. Halt!
11. Grip
12. Castaway's home
13. Salty drop
22. Outcast
24. Excessively
27. Mandated
28. Like some college walls
30. "En garde" weapon
32. Thriving
33. Break suddenly
34. Beliefs
35. Influence
36. Emulate a longshoreman
38. Fairy-tale monsters
40. At a distance
43. Complete
46. "___ Yankees"
51. Prayer
53. Acid's opposite
55. Sea duck
57. "Key ___"
58. Sugary
59. Thunder's sound
60. Relax
61. Demeanor
62. Historic ages
67. ___ is me!
68. JFK info
70. Amusing

90

ACROSS

1. Sourpuss
6. Rooster's crest
10. Heap of wood
14. Fasten again
15. Cactuslike plant
16. Coral shelf
17. Speak
18. Plod heavily
19. Bridge position
20. French coin
21. Sultans' wives
23. Tit ___ tat
24. Tavern order
26. ___ pole
29. Tilled
32. Forbidden items
34. Was merciful to
37. Fenway ___
39. Habit wearer
40. As well
41. Hollow stone
43. Atmosphere
44. Kind of feeling
45. Convey
46. Tearing
48. Organic compound
50. Deceive
52. Thin soup
54. ___ how!
55. Cleo's serpent
58. Neigh
61. Nobility
63. Promgoer
66. Chamber
67. Of the central point
68. S-shaped molding
69. Medieval slave
70. Resided
71. Good as ___
72. Noticed
73. Donkeys

DOWN

1. Brusque
2. Of an earlier time
3. ___ Pradesh
4. Air
5. Sheet fabric
6. Curved nut
7. Earthen vessel
8. Othello, e.g.
9. Father
10. Magician's word
11. Yes vote
12. Legal matter
13. Newt
22. Friar
25. Skier's inn
27. Boredom
28. Express grief
29. Debate side
30. Classical poem
31. Parent
33. Hosiery problem
34. Lengthy tale
35. Level
36. Moving about
38. TV repeat
42. To the bitter ___
43. Highest card
45. Clockmaker Thomas
47. Appendixes
49. Defeated
51. Nonprofessionals
53. Employs
55. Staffers
56. Not fresh
57. Animal skins
59. Win by a ___
60. Zero
62. Depressions
63. Dress up
64. Self-image
65. Wriggly fish

PUZZLE 111

ACROSS

1. Outlaw chasers
6. Of a time
10. Greek vowels
14. Made of a hardwood
15. Pie spice
16. Aerie
17. Dentist's tool
18. It gives you a trill
19. Editing mark
20. Town on the Rio Grande
22. Soft food
23. Preschooler?
26. Obnoxious male
27. Clear tables
30. Printing measures
31. Degrades
33. Fortification
35. News finder
36. Roofed porch
38. Ensemble
40. Luau food
41. Blackthorn fruits
45. It's golden
48. "Figaro" feature
49. Forbidding
51. Despot
53. Cozy lodging
54. Indeed, in Psalms
55. Book of sayings
56. "___ Miserables"
57. Cartoonist Browne
58. Facing
61. Between
63. La Scala singer
64. Present
68. Full house, e.g.
69. Maintain
70. Inventor Howe
71. Shoppe adjective
72. Twist
73. Small valleys

DOWN

1. Seed vessel
2. Thole insert
3. Go schussing
4. Hard or soft
5. Intertwine
6. Insert
7. Sortie
8. Like a gymnast's moves
9. Taken
10. Put a stop to
11. Wigwam's kin
12. Oblique
13. Measures
21. Grind
23. Pealed
24. Hautboy
25. Wrong way for Greeley
28. Psychic Geller
29. Pouches
32. Grinch creator
33. Lying flat
34. Pivotal
37. Running
39. Compassion
42. Like some vaccines
43. German article
44. Exams for H.S. seniors
46. Jackie's sister
47. Lab burner
49. Cracker type
50. Mean
52. Told a long tale
53. Spud state
55. Accolade
59. "Hansel and Gretel" prop
60. Apportion
62. Ike's monogram
63. Morsel
65. Diddly
66. Mr. Ripken
67. Sibilant sound

PUZZLE 112

ACROSS

1. Cowboy's chum
5. This ___ up
9. Thin board
13. Cake decorator
14. Hunger for
16. At a loss
17. Therefore
18. Strong guys
19. Doctrines
20. Harness strap
21. Snaky curve
22. Consent to
24. Bird food
26. Engrave
28. "___ Soldiers"
29. Fido or Fluffy
31. News flash
34. Constantly, to a bard
35. Sacred
36. Units of resistance
40. Passed
42. Oared vessel
45. Apollo's instrument
46. Tropical fruit
48. Guitar's cousin
49. Was present at
52. Female pig
53. "___ Not Unusual"
56. Sentence component
57. Prevalent
59. Woman officer
61. City trains
63. U.S. citizen
66. Donkey's comment
67. Come to terms
69. Dell
70. Prod
71. On the up and up
72. Of the ear
73. "Ebony ___"
74. Lichen's kin
75. Scan

DOWN

1. Wharf
2. Measure of farmland
3. College employee
4. Male bee
5. Timetable
6. Infuriates
7. Maidens
8. First lady
9. Secular
10. Good attribute
11. Rhythm
12. Rushed
15. Put into law
23. Fraternity letter
25. Lessens
27. Foursome
29. Banana skin
30. Squirmy
32. Record book
33. San Francisco's ___ Hill
37. Rent sharer
38. Powerful shark
39. Irish or beef
41. Pod resident
43. Turns upside down
44. Watercourse
47. Experience
50. Tango number
51. Of musical pitch
53. Permeate
54. Linger
55. "All the world's a ___"
58. Party prize
60. Hearty breads
62. Hilo garlands
64. Lamb's pen name
65. Shpt. stamp
68. Precious stone

PUZZLE 113

The answers to this petaled puzzle will go in a curve from the number on the outside to the center of the flower. Each number in the flower will have two 5-letter answers. One goes in a clockwise direction and the second in a counterclockwise direction. We have entered two answers to help you begin.

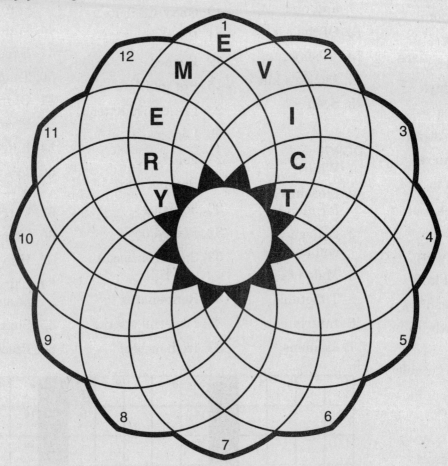

CLOCKWISE

1. Kick out
2. In advance
3. Store employee
4. Fire-starting stone
5. Sea jewel
6. Although
7. That location
8. Mentioned
9. Creepy
10. Dog's warning
11. Arab chief
12. Hit

COUNTERCLOCKWISE

1. Grinding substance
2. Profit
3. Baby bird
4. Speckle
5. Skirt feature
6. Bizarre
7. Express gratitude to
8. Top type
9. Hex
10. Point total
11. Python or boa
12. Stake

FLOWER POWER FANS! *Fun is always in full bloom with every volume of Selected Flower Power. To order, see page 159.*

ACROSS

1. Long narrative
5. Used a loom
9. Urban pall
13. Taboo
14. Dough nut?
15. Cassette
16. Mummy's place
17. Cross
18. Quiz
19. The Roaring Twenties
20. Skinny
21. Feels unwell
22. Patch the roof
24. Admiration
28. Register
30. Roadhouse
31. Shade of blond
34. Meadow mama
35. Alumnus
36. Small vegetable
37. September 13, e.g.
40. Wimp
42. Buck
43. Big truck
44. Eat less
45. Mouthpiece
47. Small barrel
48. Babble
49. Creepier
52. Punched
54. Enclosed
56. Child's toy
59. Falsehoods
61. Freud topic
62. Space
63. Decrease
65. Swimsuit tops
66. Canisters
67. Higgins, to Eliza
68. Stare at
69. Strong emotion
70. Watcher
71. Sailors' affirmatives

DOWN

1. Infiltrate
2. Not as good
3. Prisoner
4. Corn core
5. Alerted
6. Authorizes
7. Asta's doc
8. Before, before
9. Sauna feature
10. Long skirt
11. October stone
12. Some stones
14. Life story, for short
20. Head front
23. Experts
25. Auto's spare
26. Empower
27. Culmination
29. Phone again
31. Skillful
32. Abundance
33. Old witch
35. Acquire
37. Anger
38. ___ down
39. Horton hatched it
41. Cried
42. Make a web
44. Add color
46. Crocus's kin
49. "People" person
50. Strength
51. Entertain lavishly
52. Unimpressed
53. Please greatly
55. Romantic bouquet
56. Basin
57. Battle song?
58. Advanced, as money
60. Always, in poems
63. Pleased the chef
64. Ad verb?
65. Main squeeze?

PUZZLE 115

ACROSS
1. Gear teeth
5. ___ goodness
10. Doily fabric
14. Oblong
15. TV repeat
16. Milky stone
17. Sub shop
18. Legal excuse
19. Microbe
20. South American boa
22. Scandinavian bays
24. Chicago Loop trains
25. Black or Red
26. Stove fuel
29. Trench
32. Cuban dance
37. Lines
39. Blunder
41. Galahad and Lancelot
42. Press
43. Unsophisticated
44. Ratite birds
45. Greek portico
46. Clocked
47. Trigonometric function
48. Two to ___
50. Reveals
52. Camp bed
53. "Kilroy ___ Here"
55. Have a taco
57. Floating down the river
61. Building that puts up a fight?
66. Footless animal
67. Distribute
69. Potpourri
70. Hero
71. Path
72. Refusals
73. Solitary
74. Promise
75. Lady's man

DOWN
1. Musical conclusion
2. Bakery need
3. Grand party
4. Pie piece
5. Passing
6. Clutched
7. Met highlight
8. Gist
9. "Mack the ___"
10. Trademark
11. Copier
12. Report ___
13. Shady trees
21. Antique
23. Jelly holder
25. Dirt mover
26. Ground grain
27. Major artery
28. Faint
30. Characteristics
31. Wrongdoing
33. Operates
34. Imitate
35. Conductor Walter
36. Credit
38. Difficulty
40. Memorable for Hester Prynne?
49. Possess
51. Vocalize
54. Culture mediums
56. Beach sandal
57. Dog's wagger
58. Hairstyle
59. Benefit
60. At leisure
61. Sherlock's find
62. Minute amount
63. Burn soother
64. Property claim
65. "___ in Space"
68. Unhappy

ACROSS

1. Fresh talk
5. Break apart
10. Play parts
14. Thunderous sound
15. Pageant prize
16. Commandment start
17. Slippery
18. Major highway
20. Switch positions
21. Birth-name word
22. Squeegee
23. Pekoe portions
26. "___-Told Tales"
28. Wintry
29. Injure
30. Talk
33. Kind of tire
36. Stargazer's tool
38. Earsplitting
39. Nobleman
40. Over
41. Verbally frank
43. Toboggans
44. Con's foe
45. Billfold items
46. Vigor
47. Manufacturer
49. Prom wear
53. Motto
55. Cushion
56. Daily record
57. Poetry and prose
60. Wild swine
61. Equivalent
62. Runner-up
63. Chip in a chip
64. Faction
65. Water pitchers
66. Tree home

DOWN

1. Hurry
2. Type of dress
3. Mexican sauce
4. Snoop
5. Like Scrooge
6. Evergreens
7. Tardy
8. Intense anger
9. Gooey stuff
10. Garret
11. Prom overseer
12. Carry
13. Litigator
19. Does the crawl
24. Winged animals
25. Winning serve
26. Hawk's claw
27. British acronym
29. Toast word
31. Copied
32. Church benches
33. Splash
34. Rain hard
35. Mechanical
36. Giver's opposite
37. Quiets
39. Skeleton member
42. Fireplace tool
43. Guinness's title
46. Electors
48. Representative
49. Nurturer
50. Isolated
51. Nannies
52. White heron
53. Too bad!
54. Water barrier
55. Ruminate
58. Porter or stout
59. Haul
60. Forbid

PUZZLE 117

ACROSS

1. Insert
4. Aswan, e.g.
7. Big birds
11. Rollaways
15. Opponent
16. Clearances
18. Escapade
19. Monster
20. Grape drink
21. Doglike scavenger
22. Skittish
23. Got down
24. Lover
26. Slump
27. Passing grade
28. Agts.
29. Queer
31. Chap
33. Snakelike curve
35. Gull relative
38. Be indebted to
40. Branch
42. Required
46. Air hero
47. Cake decorator
48. Stab
50. Beam
51. Horned animal
53. Memoirs, briefly
55. Sing
56. Before, poetically
57. Musical form
59. Snack
61. Corn spike
62. Shoemaking tools
63. A or B
65. Pioneer Carson
67. Negotiate
69. Sport
72. Bro's sib
74. Convent figure
76. Gets points
80. RBI's kin
81. Reveals
83. Wow!
85. Whinny
86. Maui wreath
87. Aim
89. "We ___ Soldiers"
91. Fawn's mother
92. Deli meat
94. Misery
95. Shady
96. Eyesore
97. VCR button
98. Hornet
100. Just get by
102. Unaccompanied
105. Talk
107. Kitty
109. Restless
113. Party with poi
114. Old Bologna bread
115. Stain protector
117. Tint
118. Deeds
119. Cruel
120. Existence
121. Sick
122. Biblical pronoun
123. Greenish blue
124. Fish eggs
125. Buddy

DOWN

1. Remote
2. Dummy
3. Judge
4. Week part
5. Pub drinks
6. Zoo
7. Like some toothbrushes
8. Created
9. Advise
10. Firmament
11. Grating
12. Stare
13. Voyage
14. Solidifies
16. Booted
17. Scholar
25. Many, many years
30. Medic
32. Snooze
33. Repeated performances
34. Observed
35. Paves
36. Mimic
37. Curb
39. Network
41. Simple
43. Doodled
44. Aristocrat
45. Recolors
47. Jot
49. Path
52. Designate
54. Hardwood tree
58. "___ and Old Lace"
60. Canister
62. Healing plant
64. Scot's skirt

66. Harbor vessel

68. Skin problem

69. Firms up

70. Vicinity

71. Post

73. Large amount

75. Daily publication

77. Motor

78. Freudian terms

79. Women

81. 12:00, e.g.

82. Develop quickly

84. Moray, e.g.

88. Afternoon social

90. Deli loaf

93. Incite

96. Faced

99. Wound covering

101. Part of MLK

102. Bed support

103. "That smarts!"

104. Tardy

105. Donate

106. Opera part

108. Group of three

110. Potato snack

111. Island dance

112. Scream

114. Allow

116. Unity

PUZZLE 117

PUZZLE 118

ACROSS

1. Alack's partner
5. Hidden supply
10. Holds
14. Comic Kaplan
15. English horns
16. ___-biter
17. Inspiration
18. Most terrible
19. Sherry, e.g.
20. Sit still for
21. Not subtract
22. Ecstatic
24. Tangle up
27. Milwaukee brew
28. Close
29. Shtick figure?
33. Small hooter
36. Hopeless case
37. Verse type
38. Attendee
39. Beat
40. Stash
41. Lumberjack's product
42. Daft
43. It also rises
44. Nonfiction writer
46. Writing tool
47. Desire
48. Apprehend
52. Increase
55. Time span
56. Egg drink
57. Hose shade
58. Semiprecious stone
60. Skunk's defense
61. Beat this
62. Lint trap?
63. Show anger
64. Viewed
65. Lock of hair
66. Prove

DOWN

1. Spry
2. Encumbered
3. Assists
4. Bering, e.g.
5. Fearful one
6. Home
7. Strong twine
8. Drakes and stags
9. Prized
10. Ahead
11. Bide
12. Baseball team
13. Tundra taxi
23. Malicious look
25. At no time, in verse
26. Aardvark's prey
27. Pretty, in Glasgow
29. Tally
30. Tad
31. Commotions
32. Colorful salamander
33. Flirty look
34. Dates
35. Table supports
36. Silly bird
39. Touching
40. Used the mail
42. Old harp
43. Sure 'nuff
45. Fall
46. Wall sections
48. Doves' homes
49. Unnecessary
50. Chambers
51. Wading bird
52. G-men
53. Farm fraction
54. Faithful
55. Mansard feature
59. Slender fish
60. Frequently, in poems

ACROSS

1. Deuces
5. Amino or lactic
9. Rush
13. ___-and-go-seek
14. Hums along
16. Knowledgeable about
17. Tiny thing
18. Black brew
19. Call it quits
20. Excite
22. Ex-soldier
24. "___ Got a Secret"
25. Pirate's domain
26. Goes back over
28. Gathered
31. Deceive
33. Old witch
34. Decorates a cake
36. Hoover or Aswan, e.g.
37. Time periods
41. Softens
43. Stir-fry pan
45. Be nosy
46. Ketchup base
48. Gear
50. "Forever ___ Girl"
51. Trim the lawn
52. Like a bug in a rug
54. Undertake
55. Reply
59. Tai's preceder
61. Bend
62. Morning moisture
63. Powerhouse
67. Afternoon events
69. Beard cutter
72. ". . . maids all in ___"
73. Old lace shade
74. Exec's scribe
75. Ring
76. Goblet part
77. Drip
78. Cures leather

DOWN

1. Not this
2. Among
3. Stench
4. Highway sights
5. Clap
6. Inkling
7. Tick off
8. Herd
9. Parts of wedding vows
10. Caper
11. Potbellied ___
12. Expects
15. Churn
21. Ushered
23. Pitfalls
26. Guilt
27. Pain
28. Catcher's catcher
29. Resonate
30. Sports unit
32. Fido's foot
35. Marsh
38. Water bird
39. Clock cycle
40. Lively
42. Waited in line
44. Family
47. Title holders
49. Chewy candy
53. Joyful
55. Scales of prices
56. Upright
57. Unnerve
58. Strikes
60. Not fitting
64. Telephone code
65. Bewail
66. Night fliers
68. Entirety
70. Final letter
71. United

PUZZLE 120

ACROSS
1. Alone
5. Smack
9. Pedestal
13. Mimicker
14. Narrow boat
16. Excited
17. Flora
19. Two of a kind
20. Printers' measures
21. Crafts' partner
22. Snitch
24. Legendary shoemaker
25. First to arrive
27. Leading lady
31. D.C. figures
32. Singer Adams
33. On a voyage
35. Short note
39. Prune
40. Occupants
43. Uncooked
44. Decorative vessel
46. Greek cheese
47. Waste maker
49. Dunces
51. Angled
53. Amusing story
57. Trailing vine
58. TV host Bob ___
59. Roof part
61. Weep
64. Employ
65. Paint solvent
68. Completed
69. Salesman's pitch
70. Bright thought
71. Cincinnati team
72. Alluring
73. Dweeb

DOWN
1. Economize
2. Store sign
3. Centipede's pride
4. Lode's load
5. Mufflers
6. Electrical unit
7. Licorice-tasting seed
8. Also
9. Immersion ceremony
10. Semiprecious stone
11. Gets dirty
12. White-plumed bird
15. Beseech
18. Natural gift
23. Heidi's mountain
24. Important age
26. Coliseums
27. Proficient
28. Raven's kin
29. Sort
30. Most sensible
34. Took a seat
36. Formerly, formerly
37. Australian fellow
38. Had a debt
41. Endeavors
42. Like a whisker-less face
45. Relaxing chairs
48. ___ port in a storm
50. Refreshing drink
52. Energetic
53. Despise
54. Innocent
55. Did wrong
56. Unearthly
60. Pinnacle
61. Faction
62. Unique being
63. Bauble
66. Prosperous periods
67. ___ Pan Alley

ACROSS

1. Beach shade
4. Arabian prince
8. Distributes
13. Guitar's kin
14. Trademark
15. Separate
16. Secure
17. Ump's call
18. Come out
19. Destroy
21. Mexican dip
23. Liotta et al.
24. A timely question?
26. Pagan god
28. Long hair
30. Breeze
32. Stained
35. Peaceful
37. Monopoly card
39. Expel
41. Utility patron
42. Part of a play
44. Oxen's harness
45. Boo, from Ebert
46. On a cruise
47. Heavy
49. Stash
51. The whole amount
53. Passed easily
54. River bottoms
56. Voir dire
58. Thin opening
61. Spy mission, for short
63. Poise
67. Fiesta novelty
69. Probes
71. Cast
72. Declare
73. Thaw
74. Metallic dirt
75. Full of rocks
76. Quarry
77. Longing

DOWN

1. "Swan Lake" costume
2. Comparable
3. Require
4. Northern toymaker
5. Bullwinkle, e.g
6. Tropical lizard
7. Burger bread
8. Dull
9. Too
10. Capri cabbage, once
11. Anxious
12. Understands
15. The Grateful ___
20. Possessor
22. Seductress
25. Lobster female
27. Strange
28. Tablelands
29. Don't exist
31. Perfect
33. Wash away
34. Put up a barrier
35. Dine at night
36. Curve shape
38. Slippery fish
40. Bear's hideout
43. Wrap up
44. Pleasure boat
46. Fearful respect
48. Break bread
50. Acquire
52. Less restricted
55. Liquid measure
57. Bracelet locale
58. Fashionable resorts
59. Raise
60. Data
62. A summer place
64. Nautical shout
65. Remedy
66. Adolescent
68. Go for it
70. Boar's home

PUZZLE 122

ACROSS
1. Not up yet
5. Rowing items
9. Bizarre
12. Impose, as a tax
13. Sales pitches
15. Tiny
16. Arch type
17. Allow
18. Sprite
19. "The Last ___"
21. In a holy way
23. Whatever
24. Bro or sis
26. Scan a book
27. Creep about
29. Splitting device
33. Attach to
36. Figure-skating jump
37. Coal source
38. Like a marsh
40. Shriner's hat
42. Hackneyed
43. Scoop
44. "The ___ of Spring"
46. Attempt
47. Toys' location?
49. Perfume
50. Void's partner
52. Building vine
53. Appear onstage
56. Some shoes
60. Runaway groom
62. Metallic rock
63. More wicked
65. Ill temper
66. Soak flax
67. Acclaim
68. "For Your Eyes ___"
69. Curve
70. Neural plexus
71. Freudian concerns

DOWN
1. Hilo howdy
2. Started
3. ___ which way
4. Colorist
5. Unlock, to a poet
6. Ventilates
7. Comment
8. Bread piece
9. Due
10. Farmer's place?
11. Disobey
13. Mythological riddler
14. Scarecrow material
20. Analyze
22. Plant disease
25. Steak, e.g.
28. Watchful
30. Sheer force
31. Snarl
32. Slippery
33. Solo for Sills
34. Bumper damage
35. Nimble
39. Performing
41. Tubular pasta
42. "The Adventure of the ___ Coronet"
45. Pub
48. Prettier
49. Olympic skiing category
51. ___ and onions
53. Impersonating
54. Violin's kin
55. They top deuces
56. Became frayed
57. Angers
58. Hair holders
59. Reno machine
61. Hautboy
64. Ram's dam

ACROSS

1. Long cut
5. Big monkey
8. Coast or Indies
12. Band instrument
13. Skating jumps
15. Point of ___
16. Ram's coat
17. Recently
18. Voice range
19. Aromatic spice
21. Sample
23. Farm pen
24. Jar tops
27. Honks
30. Athletic event
31. Add value to
33. Chewing and bubble
36. Not windy
38. Sunburn soother
39. Candy ___
40. Bubbly drinks
41. Gull-like bird
42. Spirited
43. Expedition
44. Feathery plant
45. Turn in
47. Employer
49. Ease off
50. Short letter
51. Large tub
54. Electric unit
55. Domain
57. Clenched hand
60. Lawn tool
64. Poems of praise
65. Hurt
66. Murky
67. Church season
68. Hollow plant
69. Shoveled
70. House sites

DOWN

1. Robes
2. Roughly
3. Like a chimney
4. Ship's tiller
5. Chopper
6. Cathedral bench
7. Addition to a house
8. Disappear
9. Be unwell
10. Adjust, as a clock
11. Duo number
13. Actress Dickinson
14. Procedures
20. Stately trees
22. Charged atom
25. Room theme
26. Wrigley Field, e.g.
28. Mosaic maker
29. Disdain
32. Chick's mama
33. Judge's mallet
34. Become one
35. Contemplated
37. Failure
39. Convertible, e.g.
40. Walked
44. Out of
46. Sailor's drink
48. Type of board
51. Home movie
52. "___ We All"
53. Orals
56. Survey
57. A long way off
58. Water or milk
59. "___-Devil"
61. Performed
62. Type of antelope
63. Omelet necessity

PUZZLE 124

ACROSS
1. Went too fast
5. Modify
9. Key group
14. Fish story
15. Out of the wind
16. Edible bulb
17. Fervor
18. Breaches
19. Man, for one
20. European peak
21. Regretful person
22. Motor disk
23. Renter
25. Quarantines
30. Afternoon socials
31. Not moving
32. Hearth residue
33. Come back in
35. Skin problem
36. Largest
39. Honored
41. Doing nothing
42. Rode a bike
44. Digit
45. Cupid's weapon
46. Main point
49. Choosing
51. Sodium compounds
53. Decompose
54. Hit, as a fly
56. Dupe
57. Colorado resort
60. Dismounted
61. Long narrative
62. Jeweler's glass
63. Hiker's abode
64. Exclude
65. Declined
66. Whirling current
67. Chest muscles, shortly

DOWN
1. Pilfer
2. Portable platform
3. Pass by
4. Family room
5. Not specific
6. Winglike parts
7. Publish again
8. Absolutely!
9. Shade of blue
10. Soul
11. Brief swim
12. Shad ___
13. Football position
21. Witness again
22. Stockade
24. Beetle Bailey's nemesis
26. Playground toy
27. Diplomacy
28. Feudal serf
29. Storage building
31. Trainee
34. ___ de corps
35. Examine the books
36. Nip
37. Fan's favorite
38. Great joy
40. Legal
43. Iditarod vehicle
45. Made amends
47. Open, ___!
48. Disastrous
50. French pancake
51. Dapper
52. Tiffs
55. Breeze
57. "Cakes and ___"
58. Bawl
59. Saloon
60. Consumed
61. Drench

ACROSS

1. Enjoys a pool
6. Teases
10. Facts
14. Deck
15. Tan
16. Brewery brews
17. Adversary
18. By 'n' by
19. Friar
20. Test model
21. Hamlet-like?
23. Weed
24. Spit out
26. Panther's kin
28. Reach
31. In addition
32. Put
33. Courteous
37. Scuba enthusiast
41. Swiss mountain
42. Bogged down
44. Gorilla
45. Jeer
48. Olympian's goal
50. Husbands
51. Electric particle
53. Scraped
55. Saloon
59. Info from Willard Scott
60. Gone by
61. Extinguished
63. Kimono, e.g.
67. Near
69. Trickle
70. Caught
71. Stickum
72. Some comers
73. Expressed
74. Appear
75. Word in a threat
76. Biting bugs

DOWN

1. Ran
2. Subside
3. News flash
4. Brunch punch
5. ___ sauce
6. Recut wood
7. Church display
8. Grill
9. Nightfall
10. Beaver project
11. Maui howdy
12. Male singer
13. Invited
21. Jeans material
22. Parka's feature
25. Photo
27. Hawaiian fare
28. Woe is me!
29. After-bath sprinkle
30. Mistake in print
34. ___ and vigor
35. Hot temper
36. Escorted
38. Flirt
39. Weapon for fencing
40. Split
43. Provoked
46. Pine
47. Thought's fuel?
49. Getaway
52. Soup pasta
54. Ankle mishap
55. Forehead fringe
56. Spry
57. Scoundrel
58. Wall art
59. Plains dwelling
62. Settles back
64. Gumbo pod
65. Borscht veggie
66. Make ___ meet
68. Haw's partner
70. Price ticket

PUZZLE 126

ACROSS
1. Flower wreath
4. Earring's location
8. Doodler's art
12. Hold title to
13. Self-images
14. Bread baker
15. Cowboy movies
17. Swinging cadence
18. Mined minerals
19. Dated ditty
20. Regretful
23. Viper
25. Down-under birds
26. Observance
27. Water barrier
30. Brunch cocktail
32. Soft wool
34. Common contraction
35. Cake decorator
37. Folk dance
38. Topaz or opal
39. Wall painting
40. Chart's kin
44. Method
46. Let up
47. Warning
51. Perpetually
52. Electrified atoms
53. Through
54. Quantity of paper
55. Legendary story
56. Building section

DOWN
1. Unworthy
2. Fleecy female
3. Outs' opposites
4. Cautious
5. Fairy-tale beast
6. Dwarfed tree
7. 19th letter
8. Barbie or Ken
9. Enthusiastic
10. Sandwich shop
11. Initial wager
16. Body
19. Unlocked
20. Trailer truck
21. Fail to mention
22. Liquors
24. Headliner
26. Track event
27. Active one
28. Domain
29. Shopper's paradise
31. Sound of relief
33. Emulate a hog
36. Hire
39. Swamp
40. Grandpa Walton's portrayer
41. Babble wildly
42. On the Pacific
43. Beauty-parlor treatment
45. Fasting season
47. Draw a bead
48. "____ Always Loved You"
49. None
50. Miss

PUZZLE 127

ACROSS
1. Nasty mutt
4. Fashionable
8. ____ goes nothing!
12. Unclose, in verse
13. Make over
14. Eons
15. Pale gray
16. Rich Little, e.g.
17. Forest-floor plant
18. Ravine
20. At least one
22. Chill
23. Party thrower
24. Population count
26. Vicious criminal
28. Civil
29. Long-lasting
31. Popeye, e.g.
33. Wound reminder
36. Awning
37. Meadow mamas
39. BPOE member
40. Grabbed a chair
42. Abraham's son
43. Artist Salvador ____
45. Cuckoo
47. "Rhoda" role
48. So be it!
49. Fox's dance?
50. Number of toes
51. Dangerous chance
52. Type of exercise
53. Soon-to-be-grads

DOWN
1. Bus
2. Outcome
3. Discuss again
4. Stuff full
5. In the know
6. Brainchild
7. Pipe material
8. Sunday dinner entree
9. Self-centered person
10. Save
11. Road curves
19. Photographer's workplace
21. Hollers
25. Nephews' sisters
27. Guzzles
28. ____ for the course
30. Aristocracy
31. Spicy sausage
32. Leg parts
34. Expects
35. Bookworm
36. Fragrant lumber
38. Browses through
41. Bull, in Barcelona
42. Particle
44. Squid's fluid
46. Metal tooth

ACROSS

1. "____ Fear"
5. Hoofbeats
10. Bridge feats
15. Upper-stage rocket
17. "Clara's ____"
18. "Test ____"
19. "____ and Bess"
20. Cosmetics queen Lauder
21. Actress Massey
22. "____ Bowlers' Tour"
23. David Schwimmer role on "Friends"
25. Tizzy
27. Sea, in Paris
28. "Charlie's ____"
30. "A Yank at ____"
31. "Knight & ____"
32. "Captain Carey, ____"
33. Yoko ____
34. "____ Ventura, Pet Detective"
36. "More ____ Friends"
39. Idi ____
40. "The ____ On"
44. "____ of Bright Water"
45. "One ____ Soldiers"
46. Actress in "Nine to Five"
47. Actress Taina ____
48. Prop for Julia Child
49. Conrad or Barbara
51. "Grand ____ Opry"
52. "____ Fideles"
54. Thaw
55. Growl
56. Fortune-teller's card
57. TV serial
58. Give for a time
59. A Stooge
61. "____ Jackson"
62. "Car 54, Where ____ You?"
64. Carp's cousin
67. Movie plantation
69. Danson series
72. According to
73. "She ____ Him Wrong"
74. Dull
75. Tool on "Home Improvement"
77. Locale
79. Nora Ephron's screenwriter sister
81. Fisher or Cantor
83. Actor Jeremy ____
84. Column bits
85. Rainer of "The Good Earth"
86. T-bone or porterhouse
87. Hazardous curves
88. "She Married Her ____"

DOWN

1. Cartoonist Al ____
2. Greek marketplace
3. "Evita ____"
4. Brother to Chang
5. Game in "Searching for Bobby Fischer"
6. Smaller amount
7. Cereal grain
8. Robert ____ of "The Music Man"
9. Office worker
10. Skewer
11. "____ Abner"
12. "____ of the South Seas"
13. "Easy ____"
14. Gawk
16. Actor Lew ____
24. Spanish wave
26. Claire or Balin
29. "____ Ho"
30. Ms. Markey of "Tarzan of the Apes"
31. "The ____ Hunter"
33. Peck film, with "The"
35. Charlie ____
36. Williams of "Good Advice"
37. "____ Crane"
38. "Look Back in ____"
39. Yes, to Popeye
41. Do penance
42. Michael ____ of TV's "The Senator"
43. Bergen's Mortimer ____
45. "All About ____"
46. "The Snake ____"
48. Director Preminger
49. "Sunset ____"
50. Tyrolean mountain
53. "____ Like It Hot"
54. "____ Lisa"
55. Joy
57. "Mean ____"
60. DDE's command
62. Cry of discovery
63. "____ Without a Cause"
64. Bette or Brad
65. "Red ____"
66. Paddled boat
68. MacDowell of "Green Card"
69. Crude
70. "____ Days"
71. "____ Family Robinson"
73. Prop on "Murphy Brown"
74. "____ With a Halo"
76. Spike and Ruta
78. Actress Merkel
80. "____ Girls"
82. Copy, as a tape

PUZZLE 129

ACROSS

1. Darn again
6. Travel document
10. Hats
14. Restaurant patron
15. Showy flower
16. Island dance
17. Terrify
18. Without
19. Certain golf club
20. Old pronoun
21. 100%
23. "____ from Alcatraz"
25. Wheeled table
28. First Greek letter
31. Atop
32. Boar or sow
35. Sincere appeal
36. City haze
38. Straggly
40. Bellow
41. Howdy!
43. Date source
44. Concluded
46. Scallion's kin
47. Sorbets
48. Okey-doke
49. Diminishes
51. Indy 500 participant
53. Rower
55. Conforms
59. Request
60. Backdrop
63. Birthmark
64. Whirled
67. In a while
69. Cat's call
70. Choice word
71. Banish
72. Mine finds
73. Tinted
74. Abrupt

DOWN

1. Coffee break
2. Every individual
3. Don't leave!
4. At any time, to a bard
5. Garland
6. Country house
7. Ill will
8. Brother's sib
9. Proclaim
10. Stylish
11. Radiance
12. Fall heavily
13. Of sound mind
22. Fido's line
24. Load cargo
26. Most refreshing
27. Sharp corner
28. Solitary
29. Is winning
30. Whittle down
32. Harmony
33. Loafer
34. Sports facilities
35. Hunted animal
37. Kind of toast
39. Saga
42. Gumbo veggies
45. Something owed
50. Ordered around
52. Sock type
54. Like a lion
55. Bullets, to a GI
56. Achiever
57. Sunburn soother
58. Benches
60. Move slightly
61. Slippery fish
62. Poplar or spruce
65. Tissue layer
66. Capitalize on
68. Bunyan's tool

PUZZLE 130   Mind Boggler

Each of the symbols in the diagram represents one of the numbers given. Replace each of the four symbols with one of the numbers in order to make this addition problem work.

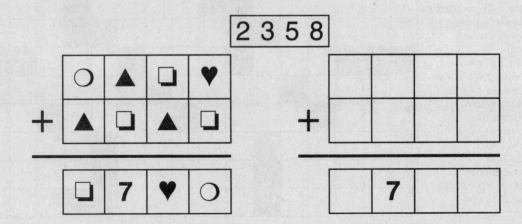

110

DOUBLE TROUBLE

Not really double trouble, but double fun! Solve this puzzle as you would a regular crossword, except place one, two, or three letters in each box. The number of letters in each answer is shown in parentheses after its clue.

ACROSS

1. Gravy dish (4)
3. Coffee variety (5)
5. Pay dirt (4)
7. Morse ____ (4)
9. Poet Thomas (5)
10. Bearing (9)
12. Nearby (5)
13. Clock sound (4)
15. Lanky (4)
16. Twist of fate (5)
18. Prepare (7)
20. Buy stocks (6)
21. Guess (8)
23. Correct text (4)
24. Greek muse (5)
27. Approached (4)
28. Vital (7)
29. Debatable (4)
30. Bike part (5)
32. Devoured (3)
33. Smashed (7)
35. Executive (7)
37. Starving (8)
38. Sermonize (6)
39. Go by ship (4)
40. Canyon reply (4)
42. Margin (4)
43. Colleague (9)
46. Fury (3)
48. Spring up (5)
49. Paving stuff (3)
50. "Stand" band (3)
51. Penny (4)

DOWN

1. Physique (4)
2. East Coast ocean (8)
3. Further (4)
4. Dare (9)
5. Bank deal (4)
6. Trick (7)
7. Settlement (6)
8. Sticker (5)
11. Author Hunter (4)
14. Hindu concept (5)
17. Name list (6)
19. Tempo (4)
20. Monogram part (7)
21. Sneak away (6)
22. Scheduled (5)
23. Bring forth (5)
25. Haywire (4)
26. Whistled (6)
28. Moon feature (6)
31. Reference work (7)
33. Hope (4)
34. Withdraw (6)
36. Shocked (6)
37. Well-known (8)
38. Proposition (7)
39. Cul-de-____ (3)
41. Option (6)
42. Thorny shrub (5)
44. Skyrocket (4)
45. Abound (4)
47. Lease money (4)

Tie-In

Place a 3-letter word on the dashes to complete a word on the left and to begin another word on the right. For example, HEN between EART and NA would complete EARTHEN and begin HENNA.

SC __ __ __ END   ARM __ __ __ CHER

ACRO __ __ __ HE   AZA __ __ __ GUE

ORI __ __ __ GER   STIF __ __ __ CE

OP __ __ __ SE   DI __ __ __ ISH

MATI __ __ __ DLE   HIP __ __ __ RCE

111

PUZZLE 133

BRICK BY BRICK

Rearrange this stack of bricks to form a crossword puzzle. The clues will help you fit the bricks into their correct places. Row 1 has been filled in for you. Use the bricks to fill in the remaining spaces.

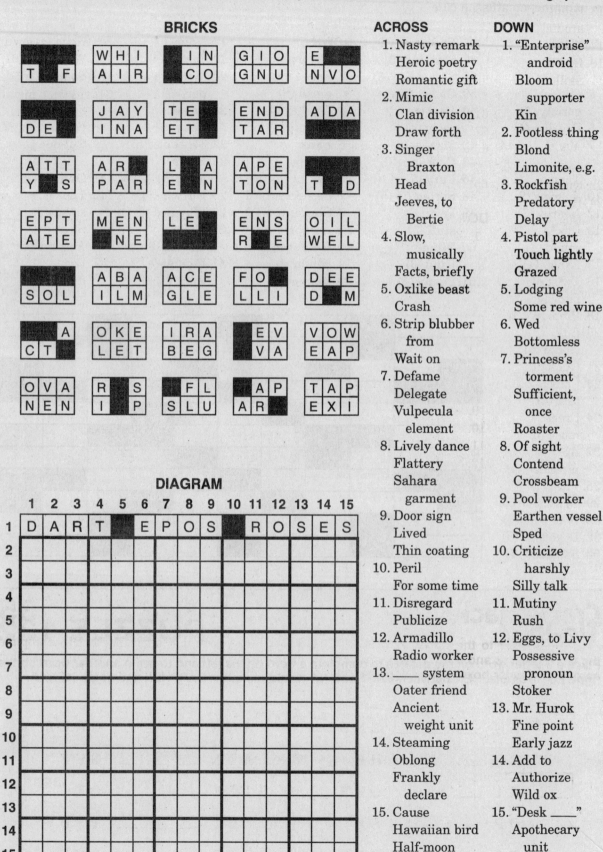

BRICKS

DIAGRAM

ACROSS

1. Nasty remark
   Heroic poetry
   Romantic gift
2. Mimic
   Clan division
   Draw forth
3. Singer
   Braxton
   Head
   Jeeves, to
   Bertie
4. Slow,
   musically
   Facts, briefly
5. Oxlike beast
   Crash
6. Strip blubber
   from
   Wait on
7. Defame
   Delegate
   Vulpecula
   element
8. Lively dance
   Flattery
   Sahara
   garment
9. Door sign
   Lived
   Thin coating
10. Peril
    For some time
11. Disregard
    Publicize
12. Armadillo
    Radio worker
13. ____ system
    Oater friend
    Ancient
    weight unit
14. Steaming
    Oblong
    Frankly
    declare
15. Cause
    Hawaiian bird
    Half-moon
    tide

DOWN

1. "Enterprise"
   android
   Bloom
   supporter
   Kin
2. Footless thing
   Blond
   Limonite, e.g.
3. Rockfish
   Predatory
   Delay
4. Pistol part
   Touch lightly
   Grazed
5. Lodging
   Some red wine
6. Wed
   Bottomless
7. Princess's
   torment
   Sufficient,
   once
   Roaster
8. Of sight
   Contend
   Crossbeam
9. Pool worker
   Earthen vessel
   Sped
10. Criticize
    harshly
    Silly talk
11. Mutiny
    Rush
12. Eggs, to Livy
    Possessive
    pronoun
    Stoker
13. Mr. Hurok
    Fine point
    Early jazz
14. Add to
    Authorize
    Wild ox
15. "Desk ____"
    Apothecary
    unit
    Harsh cry

PUZZLE 134

ACROSS

1. Export
5. Commotion
9. Realty unit
13. Lounge around
14. Cougars
16. Hinted
17. Skillfully
18. "___ Nest"
19. Rocky cliff
20. Not me
21. Heavy hammer
22. Quick
24. Humbly
26. Blouse
27. Frying pan
29. A, B, or C, e.g.
32. Harbor sight
33. Ruby or diamond
34. Kind of neckline
36. Put down
37. Through
38. Hiatus
40. Acquired
41. Canister
42. Engaged male
43. Confusion
46. Painters, e.g.
47. Gobble up
48. Customer
49. "___ Street"
52. Brewed drinks
53. The self
56. Like tea, sometimes
57. Violinist's need
59. Admit openly
60. On the house
61. Located
62. Jail part
63. Swivel
64. Minus
65. Wraps up

DOWN

1. Kill, as a dragon
2. Vagabond
3. Brighten
4. Tissue thickness
5. Orator
6. Uproar
7. Suggest
8. Pier rodent
9. Receive
10. Fix
11. Interpret
12. Nervous
15. Procedure
21. Skirmish
23. Cook's vessel
25. Lodge members
27. Doe's partner
28. Barbecue selection
29. Actress Thompson
30. Equal
31. Reply
33. Rummy game
35. ___ out (barely makes)
37. Energy
38. Small samples
39. April shower
41. Spuds
42. Pals
44. Numb
45. Getaway
46. Treaty members
48. Social class
49. Filter, as flour
50. Wedding-gown shade
51. Predictor
54. Valuable metal
55. Hooting birds
58. Vinegar's mate
59. King beater

Crackerjacks

PUZZLE 135

Find the answer to the riddle by filling in the center boxes with the letters needed to complete the words across and down. When you have correctly filled in the Crackerjacks, the letters reading across the center boxes from left to right will spell out the riddle answer.

RIDDLE: What do you call a traffic tie-up at the shore?

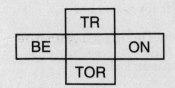

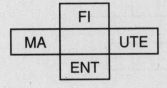

ANSWER: _____

113

PUZZLE 136   CODEWORD

Codeword is a special crossword puzzle in which conventional clues are omitted. Instead, answer words in the diagram are represented by numbers. Each number represents a different letter of the alphabet, and all of the letters of the alphabet are used. When you are sure of a letter, put it in the code key chart and cross it off in the alphabet box. A group of letters has been inserted to start you off.

Code key chart:

1	14
2	15
3	16
4 **L**	17
5	18 **I**
6	19
7	20
8	21 **T**
9	22
10	23
11	24
12	25
13	26

Alphabet box:

A	N
B	O
C	P
D	Q
E	R
F	S
G	~~T~~
H	U
~~I~~	V
J	W
K	X
~~L~~	Y
M	Z

Grid numbers:

Row: 15 24 26 · 26 3 26 · 14 3 23 24 2
3 7 9 3 · 3 5 24 · 3 2 24 14 3 15
11 9 21 15 · 5 13 13 · 2 13 21 18 2 13
21 18 16 · 1 3 11 21 3 14 · 21 13 3
13 2 2 · 13 11 20 · 4 3 17
14 17 11 3 · 3 5 18 4 13 · 10 13 13
24 9 2 · 4 13 3 11 · 13 4 25
19 4 18 21 · 13 14 13 11 20 · 3 12 4 13
13 3 2 · 3 14 13 11 · 13 4 19
13 22 13 · 15 3 4 15 3 · 3 21 24 26
6 18 13 · 19 13 8 · 19 13 20
6 24 1 · 11 13 3 2 1 17 · 19 4 17
24 25 3 17 13 20 · 4 3 1 · 16 18 21 13
5 2 18 13 10 13 · 21 18 13 · 3 16 13 15
3 4 21 13 2 · 24 20 20 · 22 13 20

PUZZLE 137   Fore 'n' Aft

Enter the answers to the clues into their correspondingly numbered boxes. The words will begin or end with a letter in CONTAINER. When finished, the first letters of the words on the left side and the last letters of the words on the right side will spell out two related words.

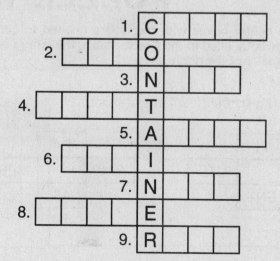

1. C _ _ _ _
2. _ _ O _
3. N _ _ _
4. _ _ _ T
5. A _ _ _ _
6. _ _ _ I
7. N _ _
8. _ _ _ E _
9. R _ _ _

1. Stand-up performer

2. Disapprove

3. Lexicographer Webster

4. Representative

5. Gift for a teacher

6. New Delhi garb

7. Famous loch

8. Highflying bird

9. Public disturbance

114

ACROSS

1. Roman dress
5. Jolt
9. Details
14. Self-images
15. To the ocean
16. On the left, matey
17. Angled additions
18. Kind of duck
19. Erode
20. Vanquish
22. Tone down
24. Cooking liquid
25. Whiskey blend
26. Pen for swine
27. Walking aid
28. State-run raffle
32. Engrave on glass
34. In history
35. Evergreen plant
37. Saves
41. Verity
44. Naught
46. Grill
47. Male leads
49. Piece of advice
51. Health hot spot
52. Had creditors
54. Least messy
57. Computer perch
60. Authorize
62. "___ Town"
63. Bedridden
64. Huffed and puffed
65. Stable sounds
69. Nearby
71. Correspond
73. Bath need
74. Angler's objective
75. Real-estate measure
76. Icicle's spot
77. Looks to be
78. Four seasons
79. Santa's transport

DOWN

1. ___ off (annoyed)
2. Rubberneck
3. Go clubbing?
4. Declare
5. Power source
6. Function
7. Butchers' wares
8. Roof of the mouth
9. Get lighter
10. Parody
11. Winter drink
12. Teach
13. Mode
21. Nay's opposite
23. Fable
27. Burn
28. Thin board
29. Grimm villain
30. ___ of duty
31. Yearning
33. Corn unit
36. Sense of humor
38. American Beauty, e.g.
39. Slopes down
40. Strip of wood
42. Stole
43. Chop down
45. Kindled
48. Merchandise
50. Settler
53. Imus, e.g.
55. Unpaid
56. Spring flowers
57. Makes a phone call
58. Borden's cow
59. Ooze
61. Double
64. Risks money
66. Soccer score
67. ___ it coming
68. Ran
70. Cloudy
72. Car protector

PUZZLE 139

ACROSS

1. Lingers
5. Notable act
9. Slightly wet
13. Fitness place
16. Fairy-tale villain
17. Because
18. Hunch
19. Catch 40 winks
20. Liberate
21. More aged
22. Deliver
23. ___-way street
24. Fellow player
26. Bath rug
28. Bureau part
30. Until now
31. Sectors
33. Showy blooms
35. Comedian Seinfeld
36. Gathered
37. Horse's foot
41. Not on
44. Work by Keats
45. Assembled
48. Days gone by
49. Pantry staple
51. Amount owed
53. Pollution
55. Final letter
56. Yanks
57. Obtained
58. Quickest
60. Winding curve
63. Green shade
66. Lobster eggs
67. Sound systems
71. Fracas
72. Partly closed
76. Memorable period
77. Distantly
79. Watched carefully
81. Twist of fate
82. Vapor
84. Schedule
86. ___ a girl!
88. See ya!
89. Tiny bit
90. Pub order
91. Small mallet
93. For men and women
96. Wed on the run
97. Baby's apron
100. Caressed
103. Chowed down
105. Keep safe
107. Drink cubes
108. Hairpieces
110. "___-Told Tales"
112. Self-centered
113. Hitch
114. Sound pitch
115. Traffic barriers
116. ___ out (barely made)
117. Calculate
118. Earring
119. Did a garden chore
120. Beatty film

DOWN

1. High
2. Consent
3. Terrific!
4. Look to be
5. Purified
6. Make beloved
7. King beater
8. Duration
9. Trouble
10. Tangy refresher
11. Repairs
12. Priest
13. Skier's need
14. Glass unit
15. Imitator
17. Flew
25. Army rank
27. Goals
29. Pale
32. Sign
34. Details
38. Drip
39. Metal-bearing rocks
40. Length measures
41. Frequently, to Keats
42. Winter ailment
43. Haze
46. Clothed
47. Room opening
50. Customer
52. Kind of maniac
54. Icky stuff
59. Close
61. Briny expanse
62. Davenport
64. Sailor's trip
65. Pasture mother

67. 18-wheeler

68. Group of three

69. Opposite of west

70. Legends

73. Chore

74. "___ Wednesday"

75. Bread grain

78. Discharged

80. Like Bruce and Demi, e.g.

81. The British ___

83. Rigid

85. Subsequent

87. Wigwams' cousins

92. Mountainous

94. Salamanders

95. Nitwit

97. Auto pedal

98. Covered with vines

99. Kneels

100. Pocket bread

101. Lab fluid

102. Prepared a golf ball

104. Inscribe

106. Eternity

109. Type of antelope

111. Court romantically

PUZZLE 140

ACROSS

1. Gather in
5. Stop, to Dobbin
9. Part of the leg
13. Wheel rod
14. Oozes
15. Mexican food
16. Store away
17. Prunes
18. Dollar bills
19. Debate side
20. Fallacy
21. Teed-off
22. African trip
24. Governess
26. Glass unit
28. Break a commandment
29. Expert person
32. Mouse catcher
35. Mountain pass
37. Flower spores
39. Our planet
41. Stood for office
43. Road sign
44. Followed orders
46. Traveler's aid
48. Hair tamers
49. Baltic or Bering
50. Criminal gang
52. Slangy assent
54. Phony
56. Property
60. Compare
63. Barren
65. Chafe
66. Brainchild
67. No longer fresh
68. Drifter
69. Escaped
70. Exercised
71. Forewarning
72. Elongated fishes
73. Wishes
74. Not hard

DOWN

1. Scrapes
2. Spare
3. Unsociable
4. Chapel seat
5. Have on
6. Long-legged bird
7. Met offerings
8. Horse's kin
9. Rocky
10. Dangle
11. Bakery worker
12. Prying
14. Water source
20. Period of time
21. Aggravate
23. Put in for a job
25. Tuck's companion
27. Organ of hearing
29. Out of the wind
30. Jail part
31. Odds and ___
32. Deuces
33. Lounging garment
34. Telephone code
36. Actress Dawber
38. Illuminate
40. Villain
42. Negative vote
45. Collie
47. Stared intently
51. Rush around
53. Request
54. Sweat bullets
55. Tarnish
57. Pleasing smell
58. Ointment holders
59. Hard wood
60. ___ preserver
61. Dormant
62. Ship bottom
64. Bar brews
67. Snoop
68. Weed

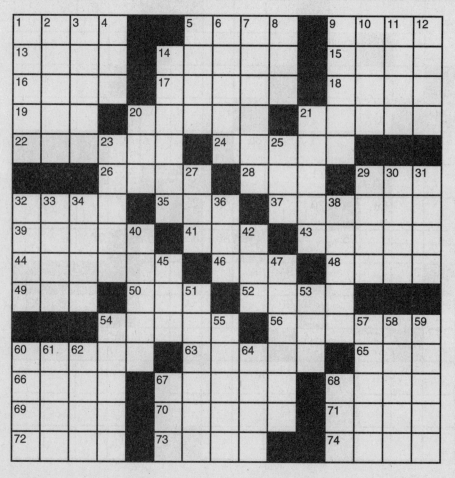

118

ACROSS

1. Skinny one
6. Wanes
10. Nail
14. Perfume
15. Fido's bane
16. Sedan, e.g.
17. Parking timer
18. Small duck
19. At the top of
20. Entities
22. Go downhill
23. Moniker
24. Classifieds
25. Place for a kiss
27. By means of
29. Whiff
31. Machine part
32. Weaken
35. "Of ___ I Sing"
37. Buddhist monk
39. Dignity
41. Cornucopia
42. Pointed end
43. Skater's jump
44. Intense antipathy
46. Verve
48. ERA or RBI
49. Consume
50. Slugger Mel ___
52. Under, in poems
54. Hair gel
55. Wheelbarrow
56. Fitness spot
59. Tuning knob
62. Hostilities
64. Adorers
66. Actress Swenson
67. Winglike
69. Taboos
70. Dumbfound
71. Nerve network
72. Follow
73. Female pupil
74. Judge
75. Legal papers

DOWN

1. Brazilian dance
2. "Rocky" character Apollo ___
3. Barbecue spit
4. Hymn finisher
5. Employ mouthwash
6. Young newt
7. Consecrate
8. Crow's bill
9. Digestion need
10. Steam bath
11. Insect stage
12. Mighty mite
13. Fully cooked
21. Window frame
26. Mars, e.g.
28. Little rascal
30. Entree list
31. Beach changing-room
32. ESP
33. Floating
34. Animal hide
35. Archaic pronoun
36. Coal scuttles
38. Wire measure
40. Brewer's kiln
45. Cow's cry
47. Dull person
51. In the direction of
53. Made amends
54. Secreting organ
55. Packing box
57. "___ Mary"
58. Burros
59. Record
60. Preposition
61. Malaria symptom
63. Nautical term
65. Musical sound
68. Unit of radiation

PUZZLE 142

ACROSS

1. Fido's feet
5. Sight organs
9. Medicate
13. In a line
14. Legal tender
16. Psychology topics
17. Turkish coin
18. Sam or Remus
19. Firm grasp
20. Heavenly dish
22. Many times, poetically
23. Depend
24. Leave a mark
27. Break the ___
29. Pavement pit
32. Enjoy a book
35. Grape plant
36. Small cafe
39. Booster
41. Trap
43. Welcome
45. ___ out (barely make)
46. Paddled
48. A Great Lake
49. Goblet part
51. Rifle attachment
53. Zip
55. Footfall
56. Large sandwich
59. "Look ___ ye leap"
61. Confidence
66. Saga
67. Gall
70. Opponent
71. Intertwine
72. Wicked person
73. Kind of poker
74. Goes out with
75. Drip
76. Child's steed

DOWN

1. Inner hand
2. Opera show-stopper
3. Shabby
4. Graceful waterfowl
5. Australian bird
6. Hither and ___
7. Repeat performances
8. ___-evident
9. Unit of heat
10. Monster
11. Stain
12. View
15. Bigfoot's kin
21. Cigar residue
25. Hooded viper
26. Little green man
28. Gator's relative
29. Pastel colors
30. Beginning
31. ___-gallon hat
33. Blazing
34. Lifeboat support
35. Victory sign
37. Trick or ___
38. Tint again
40. Formerly known as
42. Zenith
44. Still, to Keats
47. Regard closely
50. Geologic divisions
52. Choose
54. Remain undecided
56. Skirt edges
57. Dueling sword
58. Ascent
60. Rod's partner
62. Coarse file
63. Biblical preposition
64. Shock
65. In order
68. Through
69. Lodge member

ACROSS

1. Smarted
6. The full amount of
9. Chooses
14. Blend to a pulp
15. Commit perjury
16. Dark
17. Heavenly cake
19. Ice or roller
20. Mounted on a peg
21. Duration
23. Cheerleader's virtue
24. Indeed, in Psalms
26. Truth ___
28. Get 'em, Fido
31. Charcoal residue
33. Phantom's domain
36. Summer drink
37. Badge
40. Pesters
42. Nutty
44. To's opposite
45. Woolly
46. Diva's aria
47. Disaster
49. Hallow suffix
50. Honorable
52. Bungle
53. Cook's dir.
54. Choose
57. State further
59. Gremlin
62. Export duty
64. Boring tools
68. Rental contract
70. Opinion piece
72. Light beer
73. Duffer's dream
74. Accomplice
75. One-dish dinners
76. Shady tree
77. Released

DOWN

1. Small quarrel
2. Lullaby
3. Impulse
4. Requiring
5. Solidify
6. African lily
7. Columbia's team
8. Rock shelf
9. Exercise
10. It's in a pen
11. Applaud
12. Go fly this
13. Walk
18. Glimmer
22. Trampled
25. Effortless
27. Vittle statistics
28. Talk back
29. Jargon
30. Ma's instrument
32. 45 player
34. More unique
35. Coincide
38. Generation
39. Come in last
41. Out of ___
43. Myth
45. A president
47. Kennel pest
48. Special skill
51. Changes
55. French pancake
56. Basin or wave
58. Challenger
59. Woes
60. Pork chops, e.g.
61. Court attendant
63. Unshaken
65. Grape drink
66. Mechlin, e.g.
67. Winter coaster
69. Make a seam
71. Wide of the mark

PUZZLE 143

121

The answers to this petaled puzzle will go in a curve from the number on the outside to the center of the flower. Each number in the flower will have two 5-letter answers. One goes in a clockwise direction and the second in a counterclockwise direction. We have entered two answers to help you begin.

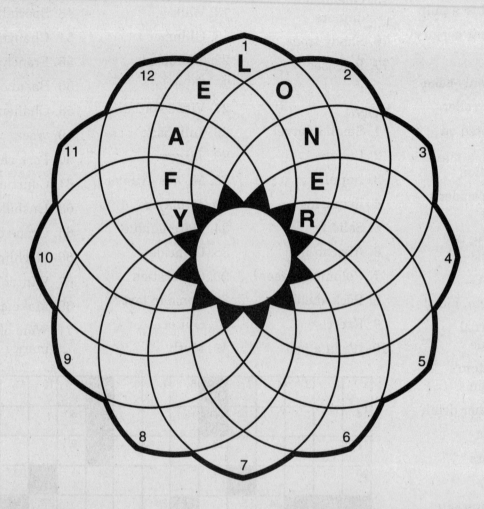

CLOCKWISE

1. Hermit, e.g.
2. Cheapskate
3. In the future
4. Jacket flap
5. Telegram
6. Durable
7. Glide on ice
8. Have a cigar
9. Twist of fate
10. Frank
11. Intellect
12. Actor Falk

COUNTERCLOCKWISE

1. Full of foliage
2. Theme
3. Woven fabric
4. Type of printer
5. Provide service for
6. Slender candle
7. Levelheaded
8. —— and crossbones
9. Reflection
10. Soup base
11. Fellow
12. Dried plum

ACROSS

1. Battery fluid
5. Bubbles
9. Some vipers
13. Footwear
14. Jeweled crown
15. Imperfection
16. Wind-borne toy
17. Major highway
19. Beetle
21. Fireplace find
22. Puppy's bite
23. Traces
26. Specialized vocabulary
28. Antlered animal
31. "Into ___ life some rain. . ."
32. Color
33. Water nymph
35. Indian princess
37. Feats
41. Pickle herb
42. Expressed
43. Trim
44. Highbrow
45. Sail pole
46. Layered rock
47. Increases
49. Track shape
51. Archer's wood
52. Point the finger at
55. ___ or reason
56. Diamond ___
57. Lyric verse
59. Most indolent
64. Dumbfounded
68. Concert solo
69. Swine's meal
70. Unpleasant sound
71. Tropical tree
72. Big quiz
73. Flock females
74. Purple plum

DOWN

1. Inquires
2. Fashionable
3. Whit
4. Doe
5. Five-spot
6. Breakfast grain
7. Vicinities
8. Red planet
9. Rearward, nautically
10. Informal language
11. Barbecue site
12. Used a broom
14. Leg bone
18. One-horse carriage
20. Dazzled
24. Paper currency
25. Egyptian king
27. Range
28. Completes
29. Reposed
30. Metric weight
32. Performed
34. Scrapbook
36. Presumptuous
38. Feet of ___
39. Scrabble piece
40. Spit out
42. Mule's father
46. Husky's load
48. Laborer
50. Organic compound
52. Use dynamite
53. Cotton fabric
54. High voices
55. Plant again
58. Eat in style
60. Race sections
61. Of a time
62. Farm building
63. Unexciting
65. Select
66. Hurry
67. Curvy turn

PUZZLE 146

ACROSS

1. Texas fare
6. Suggestive
10. Milky jewel
14. Violinist's need
15. Wind instrument
16. Base
17. Opening
18. Paint the ___ red
19. Shade providers
20. Quilting party
21. Arab chief
23. Salad green
24. Corrode
25. "___ City"
26. Pick
29. City trains
30. Craftsman
34. Mongrel
35. Suitable
37. Bethlehem trio
38. Moved gradually
40. Tire mark
41. Macho type
42. ___-friendly
43. Orange juice and champagne
45. Storage place
46. Remains
48. Pistol
49. Several
50. At the center of
51. Dull person
52. Combination of notes
55. Ledger entry
56. Vague
59. Corporate symbol
60. Affluent
62. Linger
64. Lobes' sites
65. Throb painfully
66. Fights
67. Release
68. Poetic contraction
69. Snaky curves

DOWN

1. Nursery bed
2. Sharpen
3. The Emerald ___
4. Mislead
5. Intrigue
6. Barbecue spit
7. Scrub a space mission
8. Elsie's mom
9. Itch
10. Extra work period
11. Carpet's surface
12. Gifts to charity
13. Subtraction term
22. Stubborn sort
23. House pet
25. Sizzle
26. Happen
27. Prize money
28. Pine and cedar
30. Utterly
31. Brazilian dance
32. Another time
33. Fool
36. Silent
39. Evening ___
41. Self-crafted
43. Kiddie pie ingredient
44. Bound to happen
47. Caused
51. Suitable spot
52. Musical staff sign
53. Frost
54. Grimm villain
56. Conks out
57. Do nothing
58. Untidy heap
60. Sought office
61. Break the ___
63. Mass transit vehicle

ACROSS

1. Distantly
5. Miami, e.g.
9. Curtsies
13. Impolite
14. Reel life
15. Over again
16. Granny ___
17. Care for an orphan
18. Exultant joy
19. Affirm
21. Apart
22. Refrain
25. Cry in distress
27. Fishing device
28. Polish
29. Spelling ___
31. Deteriorated
33. "... maids all in ___"
35. Decimal point
37. Second person
38. Barnyard sound
40. Habit wearer
42. Flu symptom
46. Watery juice
48. Jazz type
50. Tempo
51. Willow's kin
54. Canine beast
56. Cow's chew
57. Mister
58. Musical symbol
60. Except
62. Sheets
64. Purity
66. Burn soother
67. Riot
68. Came to ground
72. Tumble
73. Like an octopus
74. Peel, as fruit
75. Wool sources
76. Office table
77. Tot

DOWN

1. Noah's vessel
2. Recreation
3. Hoopla
4. Repair the roof
5. System of laws
6. Creamy white
7. Walk cautiously
8. Up until now
9. Satchels
10. Connected to a computer
11. Hoed
12. Pleasing
14. Assembled
20. Pinch hitter
21. Unsociable
22. Complainer
23. Fling
24. Clarinet's kin
26. Twisted
30. Eternity
32. Trio less one
34. Stinging insect
36. Bucket
39. Powders
41. Signal yes
43. "Miami ___"
44. Outback birds
45. Cerise and scarlet
47. Buddy
49. Sulked
51. Headquarters?
52. Baltimore player
53. Worship
55. Stocky antelope
57. Certain tire
59. Flicks
61. Vaulted
63. Slippery fellows
65. Terrible smell
67. Ticked off
69. Place
70. Anger
71. There's one in it

PUZZLE 148

ACROSS

1. Church part
5. A woodwind
9. Pointed comment
13. Gift paper
14. In the know
15. Of an epoch
16. Actor Rob ___
17. Emphasize
19. Most rational
21. Made like a crow
22. Meet defeat
25. Buddy
26. Hawaiian welcome
30. Council member
34. Chocolate substitute
35. Raid
36. Sever
38. Correct copy
39. Escapade
40. Not home
41. Poor grade
42. Sensational
43. Playing card
44. Dormant
46. Of yore
47. Musical notes
48. Microbe
50. Grain husks
53. Creepier
58. Postnuptial vacations
63. Perimeter
64. Newspaper notice
65. Expect
66. One billion years
67. Sit for a photo
68. Saucy
69. History

DOWN

1. Piercing tools
2. Malayan boat
3. Hewn
4. Fencing sword
5. Possess
6. Naughty
7. Natural mineral
8. At any time, to Blake
9. Pacify
10. Lined up
11. Burger order
12. Extorted money from
14. Sedan, e.g.
18. Frightening
20. Thick piece
23. "Surfin' ___"
24. Marrying secretly
25. Bosc or Anjou
26. Got a hole in one
27. Puts on cargo
28. Bay window
29. Scalding
31. Drag the bottom of
32. Vocally
33. Present
37. Hammerhead end
39. Mugs
40. Hair product
42. Covered in foliage
43. Curved roof
45. Lacking vitality
49. Pause
50. ___ suey
51. Vagabond
52. Black cuckoos
54. Gather in
55. Intention
56. Selves
57. Leaser's expense
59. Tourist guide
60. Be in arrears
61. Rowing device
62. Young bug

ACROSS

1. Fall ___ grace
5. PDQ, in the ER
9. Shocked responses
14. Former Italian currency
15. Launder
16. Allow
17. Imitator
18. Montreal pro, once
19. Travel course
20. Next to
22. Make free (of)
24. Cavity
25. Pecan, e.g.
26. Break in
28. Scurry
31. Insulting
34. Honey insect
35. Foot lever
37. Long skirt
39. Night hooter
40. Wilt
41. Pro vote
44. Toy soldier metal
45. Bark
47. Tales
49. Forest creature
50. Uncertainty
53. Portion
55. Stout
57. Husbands
58. Livelihood
61. Kind of maniac
62. Engraver
66. Overhead
68. Metal bar
71. Buddhist monk
72. Made a cow sound
73. Pimples
74. Touched ground
75. Parks and Lahr
76. Extend credit
77. Care for

DOWN

1. Extra weight
2. Fully developed
3. Miners' quests
4. Boat basin
5. Climbing flower
6. Sales ___
7. Egyptian cobra
8. Rose spike
9. Veggie bed
10. Busy activity
11. Conceited
12. Pocket bread
13. Pedometer unit
21. Despair
23. "___ My Party"
26. RBI's kin
27. Border
28. Needled a bit
29. Casals's instrument
30. Uneasy
32. Library stamp
33. Deport
34. Young fellow
36. Old Greek harp
38. Printing fluid
42. Glazed
43. Valuable possession
46. Baby poodle
48. Stereo component
51. Runs, as dye
52. Harbor vessel
54. Naked
56. Upstanding
58. Door part
59. Double-reed instrument
60. Clod
63. Circle of light
64. Shoot forth
65. Rank
67. Former GI
69. ___ in the hole
70. Tourist's stop

PUZZLE 150

ACROSS

1. Takes up the slacks?
5. Faction
9. Broad scarf
14. Sermon closer
15. Barren wasteland
16. Baby grand, e.g.
17. Exec's auto
18. Urgency
20. Mason's tool
22. Moreover
23. Witnesses
24. Guns
26. Bumped into
28. Buzzing insect
31. Beauty's love
34. Central point
35. More willing
38. Beret
40. Boric ___
41. More unkind
42. Tart
43. Salmon beginnings
44. Caller
45. Old-fashioned
46. Fire crime
48. Sum
50. This minute!
51. Not busy
52. Bullets and bombs
55. Bonfire residue
57. At hand
62. Enclosed lawns
65. Lump of soil
66. Enemy of
67. Fellows
68. Boxing site
69. Way in
70. Baseballer Tommie ___
71. Fencing blade

DOWN

1. Pause
2. Arab chieftain
3. Office note
4. Blizzard stuff
5. Beamed
6. Geologic timespan
7. Charges
8. Quartet with an absentee
9. Skillful
10. Midday snooze
11. Walking stick
12. Thrice minus twice
13. Low digits
19. Gloomy
21. Ages
25. Not specific
27. Racket ending
28. Winter beverage
29. Colder
30. Chew the ___
32. Contempt
33. Jeer
34. Not near
36. Bus posters
37. Steel or iron
39. Use a lever
41. Model's path
42. Old French coin
44. Infant's sound
45. Dairy animals
47. A sound sleeper?
49. Styling foam
51. Shoulder gesture
52. Pain
53. Bewail
54. Kennel Club reject
56. Long narrative
58. Land tract
59. Radar spot
60. Solitary
61. "Jagged ___"
63. Strive
64. Coloring agent

ACROSS

1. Electrical units
5. Meaning
9. Cider fruit
14. Shade of red
15. Teen skin problem
16. Reef substance
17. Client
18. Slant
19. Potent particles
20. Excite
22. Business ___
24. Poor grade
25. Lincoln center?
26. Bow
28. Fortified place
32. Mexican dish
35. Large coffeepot
36. Commandment word
38. Bedding
40. Piece of land
43. Clump
45. Stop
46. Distress
48. Burst
50. Manage
51. Importance
53. Wished for
56. Pilsner and lager
58. Crusty dessert
59. Ship's stern
62. Tease
63. Earth or Venus
67. Fabric
69. Ride cost
71. Fly high
72. Uncanny
73. Teller of tales
74. Wise about
75. More normal
76. Tense
77. Cozy abode

DOWN

1. Border on
2. Screen
3. Nobleman
4. Tough
5. Spanish treasure ship
6. Skating surface
7. Quick bite
8. Lessee
9. Educational
10. Cook's item
11. Cattle stick
12. Kind of excuse
13. Differently
21. Hilo garland
23. Genuine
27. Bowling alley
28. No ifs, ands, or ___
29. Direction sign
30. Two-headed drum
31. Egg drink
33. Discover
34. Develop
37. Peak
39. Fax
41. Baby's bed
42. United
44. Mama's ___
47. Cry of relief
49. Hot-tasting
52. Minor thing
54. Be ill
55. Cause
57. Solemn
59. Mavens
60. Dog's woe
61. Shredded
64. Zilch
65. Gobbles
66. Fox's dance?
68. Make a knot
70. Remnant

129

PUZZLE 152

ACROSS

1. False front
4. Criticize
8. Quick taste
11. Time gone by
15. Put down
16. Matador's foe
17. Slouch
19. Choir member
20. Question
21. Consumer
22. Metric unit
23. Wander
24. Wool source
26. Instruct
28. "___ Dance"
29. Entry permit
32. Provokes
33. Besides
35. Monotony
38. Austin Powers, e.g.
39. Pined
43. Brewery specialty
44. ___ and tired
46. Bump
47. Fill with wonder
48. Carriage
49. Dimwit
50. Ages
51. Golly!
52. Avoid
54. "We try harder," e.g.
57. Ostrich kin
60. Artifact
61. Virginia crop
63. Manicure board
67. Clump
69. Ground squirrel
70. Buying frenzy
71. "___, two, three, four"
74. Unaccompanied
76. Leaning Tower site
78. NATO member
79. Utah Indian
80. Green gemstone
81. Molecule part
82. Eddie, to Martin
83. Festoon of blooms
85. Bolted
87. Finds
90. Biblical craft
91. Monthly payment
92. Selves
93. Party dealmakers
96. Expelled
99. "Carmen," e.g.
103. Blue-pencil
104. Hauls
105. Milky jewel
108. Shapely leg
109. Domino piece
110. Bright
111. Snout
112. ___ Maria
113. Writer Bagnold
114. Mesh fabric
115. Zoomed
116. Hideaway

DOWN

1. Woeful word
2. ___ register
3. Elmo fan
4. Dull-witted
5. Part of UCLA
6. "We ___ Family"
7. In addition
8. Like glue
9. Very small quantities
10. Emily Dickinson, e.g.
11. Drawing room
12. Burn soother
13. Immediately, in medicine
14. Male turkeys
17. Drink noisily
18. Sham
25. December 24 or 31
27. Floppy ___
30. Just fair
31. Surrounded by
34. Wine-barrel wood
35. Less adorned
36. ___ branch
37. Imperial
39. In the distance
40. Broken-down horse
41. Meadow mama
42. "Look at Me, I'm Sandra ___"
45. Perfume's kin
46. Idea
49. Certain art
50. Every individual
53. Burrow
55. Slender instrument
56. Empty space

58. Flat formation

59. Ref's cousin

62. Ripken was one

64. Burst

65. Watch again

66. Irish dramatist

68. Covers

71. Embrace

72. Timetable info

73. Apiece

75. Puzzling

77. City haze

80. Preserves container

81. Poker word

84. Survived

85. Modern

86. Restless

88. Iced

89. Nile biter

91. Double a knot

93. Mr. Sampras

94. Scandinavian deity

95. "___ Marlene"

97. Pilgrim Alden

98. Wears

100. Gosh!

101. Good review

102. Blessing close

106. Weasel sound?

107. Enzyme suffix

PUZZLE 153

ACROSS
1. Potato ___
6. Asian legume
9. Zenith
13. Antenna
15. Tint
16. Say the rosary
17. Right now!
18. "___ a Wonderful Life"
19. Audition prize
20. "Sanford and ___"
21. Onion holders
23. Jogger
24. Look like
26. Central
28. Winter coat
31. Sunday song
33. Adapted
36. Spinning
38. Bolster
39. First digit
40. Blithe
41. Teed off
43. Like Methuselah
44. Upper limb
45. Scored well
46. Smoothed
49. Formerly named
50. Cuban Castro
52. Powdery
53. Counterpart
54. Aide to a pres.
56. Enthusiasm
59. Per
61. Truck type
64. Bound
65. Flightless bird
66. Guarantee
69. Labyrinth
70. Put in curlers
71. Distressed
72. Drove fast
73. Tokyo, formerly
74. Ringlet

DOWN
1. Bottle tops
2. Long sandwich
3. Club for Lopez
4. Wrestling coup
5. Made a lap
6. Tibia front
7. Get the better of
8. Sure!
9. Kitchen garment
10. Field yield
11. Gander or drake
12. Observer
14. Lung section
22. Rascal
23. Not rigid
24. Do the slalom
25. A receiver
27. Herbal healers
28. Idol worshiper
29. Mindful
30. Limerick
32. Deck member
33. Victuals
34. Bay
35. Kind of bear
37. Lawful
42. Used coupons
45. Not nearby
47. Sponsors' words
48. Fanatic
51. Varnish resin
53. Motorbike
55. Freighter
56. Offering
57. Gather in
58. Fog
60. Biography starter
61. Lullaby
62. Raw deposits
63. Marries
65. Opposite of WNW
67. Turner or Cole
68. Title

132

ACROSS

1. Twig
6. Powerful shark
10. Pledges
14. Palaestras
15. Pig's sound
16. Inspiration
17. Oven-cook
18. Fragrance
19. Shortcoming
20. Little demon
21. Not hers
23. Uneven
25. River embankment
27. Common trees
30. Yarn
32. Mislaid
35. Unlock, in poems
37. Chisel
38. Army vehicle
39. Bark at the moon
40. Loose
41. Radical
44. Great rage
45. Lode yield
46. Sedan
47. Greased
49. Combine
50. Opponent
51. Curtin and Fonda
52. Busy person
54. Butter maker
56. Between
59. "___ a Small World"
60. Ignited
63. Senseless
66. Substitute worker
68. Slip away from
70. Mythical monster
71. Applaud
72. Dark fur
73. Thug
74. Guy in white
75. Suit fabric

DOWN

1. Bombay dress
2. School formal
3. Sow's opposite
4. Winners
5. Collected
6. Bullwinkle, e.g.
7. Relief
8. Recognize
9. Southern veggie
10. Record plastic
11. "___ to Joy"
12. Miniscule
13. Gloomy
22. College vine
24. Garfield's doc
25. Jam ingredient
26. Springy
28. Crib toy
29. Certain tires
30. Flew high
31. Dinner jacket
33. Informed of
34. Go down the slopes
36. Gazed at
37. Flush
38. Stiff
42. Scurried
43. Most grating
48. Lodging place
50. Sleeve filler
51. Stick out
53. Consumed
55. African animal
57. Scratch provoker
58. Pressroom mark
60. Grease job
61. Doing nothing
62. ___ off (angry)
63. Pound prisoner
64. Before now
65. To's partner
67. Damage
69. Rule

PUZZLE 155

WATERWAYS

ACROSS

1. Oozes
6. Speaker
12. Berry or board
17. Up, in baseball
18. Longed for
20. Printing technique, for short
21. It divides Maryland
23. Well-founded
24. Dray
25. Bolt remnant
26. Reeves film
28. Celestial altar
29. Aboard
30. Indian state
33. Id ___
34. Toll-payer's rd.
35. Ploy
37. Furtado's "I'm Like a ___"
39. Division
41. "The Nutcracker" girl
43. Youth gp.
44. Heavy fabric
46. Negotiating
48. Tag-sale warning
50. Breakfast server
52. Kind
53. Fr. holy women
55. Old Peruvians
57. Hernando De ___
58. Brewery product
59. Pogo, e.g.
61. Train part
62. Scratch
64. Criticizes
65. Rocky hills
68. Letter add.
69. On land
71. Constraint
73. Beach activity
75. Seer's deck
76. Cert. mail facility
77. Demeanors
78. Run into
79. Guitar gadget
80. Bandstand gear
81. Pop
83. Tokyo, once
85. Within: pref.
87. Mouse catcher
91. Wing
92. Mining transports
94. Crone
95. Infrequent
96. Wide open
98. It borders New Jersey
102. Parent
103. Fortitude
104. Inventor's fodder
105. Vladimir Ulyanov
106. Piano type
107. Solid

DOWN

1. ___ & Vanzetti
2. Denzel costar
3. Movie touter
4. Certain poem
5. RR stop
6. Danish seaport
7. Pores over
8. Solicit
9. Hitch
10. Mercury and Jupiter
11. Gained
12. Wide st.
13. ___ Fail
14. Columbus crossed it
15. Nest sound
16. Film maker
19. Hues
22. Common man
27. Music compositions
31. Swedish pop group
32. It passes by Hannibal
34. Metallic sounds
36. "Trinity" writer
38. Pours
40. Opp. of affirmative
41. Yo-Yo Ma, for one
42. It borders Vermont
45. X-Men, e.g.
46. Forest goddess
47. Rock sci.

49. Bunny tail

51. Piazza

54. Shadowbox

56. Joel follower

60. Last of a series

63. '88 Olympics site

64. Irish or English dog

66. Certain sale

67. Cut off

70. Salmon beginnings

72. Midday

74. Straddle

79. Sky sights

80. Genesis landfall

81. Singer Bailey

82. Pond scum

84. Some forebears

86. Scottish noble

88. Rook's relative

89. Spots

90. By itself

92. Number suffix

93. Wallop

97. Fraternity letter

99. French pal

100. Prevail

101. Unburden

PUZZLE 156

ACROSS
1. Window base
5. Actress Moore
9. ___ and crafts
13. Three-spot
14. Muggy
15. Messy stuff
16. Icicle's spot
17. Ted, to Caroline
18. Fox's home
19. Gobbled
20. Set loose
21. "___ the Lonely"
22. Union
24. ___ macaroni
27. Type of year
29. Hither's partner
30. Evergreen
33. Long narrative
36. That guy
38. Tool
40. Jeweled headwear
42. Nasty mutt
44. Temptress
45. Part of speech
47. Cumberland ___
49. Dweeb
50. Nectar seeker
51. Toothed wheel
53. Entreat
55. Pointy
57. Least occupied
61. Cease
64. Hall's partner
66. Lounge
67. Egg on
68. Reward
69. Quiet
70. Invalid
71. Kick out
72. On the peak of
73. Hull feature
74. Pack of cards
75. Bother

DOWN
1. Water vapor
2. Incensed
3. Crowbar, e.g.
4. Caustic stuff
5. Desert hill
6. Host
7. Moderately
8. Chemical-compound suffix
9. Radiant
10. Horse color
11. Labor
12. Lively
14. Three cheers!
20. Greens charge
23. Fierce look
25. Gym word
26. Smallest bills
28. Photo
30. Inferno
31. Cake froster
32. Split
33. Wild attempt
34. Camp worker
35. Provided
37. Kisser
39. Strong plastic
41. Building curve
43. Music type
46. Feathery wrap
48. Clergyman
52. Furrow
54. Consumer lures
55. Incantation
56. Terror
58. Overjoy
59. Rural sights
60. Entice
61. Scuttled
62. Honest
63. Gape
65. Sherwood Forest friar
68. Crib
69. Maximum limit

PUZZLE 157

ACROSS

1. Thicken
5. Brother's sib
8. Part played
12. Sprint
13. Rub clean
15. Worshiped object
16. Lemon coolers
17. Fireplace tool
18. Wooden pins
19. Motoring nuisance
21. King beater
23. Half of twenty
24. Notice
25. Picnic crashers
28. Papas
29. Fish flipper
31. First baseman?
33. Slender
35. Small parrot
37. The ___ and wherefores
38. Daily journal
40. Glazed
41. Constructing
43. Asked urgently
44. Reader's retreat
45. "___ So Shy"
46. Comet part
48. Baseball's Boggs
50. Shopper's delight
51. Sun's path
54. Printing fluid
56. Moviemaker
58. Epic tale
61. Reflection
63. PBS science show
64. Yaks
65. Artists' subjects
66. Beat this
67. Remove from print
68. Shinjo, e.g.
69. Bucks

DOWN

1. Skill
2. Dipper
3. Abundance
4. Exam
5. Kicks a field goal
6. Bothered
7. Bring legal action
8. Age
9. Poet's output
10. Ship's record
11. Subways' cousins
13. Watched secretly
14. Car protector
20. Comparative word
22. Hiker's aid
26. Once too often?
27. Tear
28. Part of CD
29. Pro
30. Trailing vine
32. Different
33. Hurled
34. Zoo giggler
35. Loiter
36. Beak
37. Elope
38. "___ Hard"
39. Those elected
42. At the time
43. Hamelin piper
46. Objective
47. Hand-cream ingredients
49. Ms. Keaton
50. Deck suit member
51. Squirrel's tidbit
52. Variety show
53. Stuffs
55. Relatives
57. Destroy
58. Lay turf
59. Hatchet
60. Hair product
62. Quiet

137

PUZZLE 158

ACROSS
1. Cigar remnant
5. Tortilla dish
9. Strong male
14. Swab
15. Customer
16. Deport
17. Compass point
18. Harvest
19. Liquefy
20. Prior to, in verse
21. Great success
22. Stag or fawn
23. Skin art
25. National symbol
28. Highway sign
30. Opposite of yea
31. Beagle or boxer
34. Guilty, e.g.
37. Little boy
39. Feel sorrow
41. Washer cycle
43. Wheel part
45. Game-show host
46. Eager
48. Dad
50. Ham or bacon
51. Sure!
52. Storage tank
54. Ring
56. Talking birds
58. Burdensome
62. Bullets, to a GI
65. Joke teller
67. Damage
68. Manipulate
70. Cable-stitch
71. Tibetan holy man
72. Composition
73. Fancy trim
74. Elderly
75. Gaze intently
76. Pitching stats
77. Fourposters

DOWN
1. Lovely
2. Royal headwear
3. Agitated
4. Play the ponies
5. Uproar
6. On the water
7. Leave off
8. "Little ___ Annie"
9. With it
10. Ooze out
11. Muck's partner
12. Opposite of aweather
13. Poetic contraction
21. Boston Red ___
24. Mock
26. Quip
27. Old instrument
29. Roofing goo
31. Art ___
32. Concluded
33. Nerd
34. Say grace
35. Italian money, once
36. Concludes
38. Slope down
40. Suggest
42. Green with ___
44. Broom's kin
47. Catch some rays
49. Small sizes
53. Fishing gear
55. Curved line
56. Back tooth
57. Sub device
59. Portrayal
60. Dubbed
61. Alums
62. Astonishes
63. Light rain
64. Flat-topped hill
66. Certain mineral
69. Hair tint
71. Research place

ACROSS

1. Pop
4. Flirt
8. "Home ___"
13. Freud topic
14. Scene of action
15. Quitter's prop
16. Jet effect
17. Articles
18. Stories
19. Vitality
20. Not loud
21. ___ the line
23. Empower
25. Remove stitches
28. Relieve
30. Call it quits
31. Male child
33. Mild
36. Quickly
38. Lingerie buy
39. Tavern beverage
40. Called it a day
42. Deer's kin
43. Supporting
44. Pick
45. Gamblers' numbers
46. Pull
47. Impair
48. 45 player
51. Trim meat
53. Explain
57. Told a falsehood
59. By what means
60. Huge
61. Couch
64. Atmosphere layer
66. Pouch
67. Similar
68. Sculler
69. Mine yield
70. Run
71. Gelatin form
72. Small child

DOWN

1. Dig
2. Another time
3. Belief
4. Rejects, to the President
5. Once more
6. It's the word!
7. Nuisance
8. Served
9. Heavy burdens
10. Night person
11. Social register word
12. Raised RRs
14. Country home
22. Unit of weight
24. Honey source
26. Waned
27. Universe
29. Child pleaser?
30. Globe
32. Shaggy oxen
33. 27th president
34. Verbally
35. Fuse
37. Photo
40. Stayed
41. Overjoy
45. Castor or olive
49. Smoothed
50. Not as many
52. Peel
54. Monastery superior
55. Royal headpiece
56. ___ on (urged)
58. Frosh's home
59. Yell
61. Pat gently
62. ___-advised
63. Compete
65. Chaotic place

PUZZLE 159

PUZZLE 160

ACROSS
1. Subside
4. ___ India Company
8. Transmits
13. Hawaiian dish
14. Sales pitch
16. Dated ditty
17. Type
18. Plains tent
19. Dig
20. Role for Liz
22. Back of the neck
24. Not nope
25. Adept
29. Unit of current
31. Encumbered
35. Choose
38. Petite
39. Land parcel
40. Prophets
42. Always, to a poet
43. Link
46. Fitting
47. Enjoy soda
49. Excitement
50. Drama part
51. Aegean, e.g.
52. Striking sights
55. Make bread
57. Promotion
58. Sorry
61. Computer unit
63. Malevolent
67. Ascend
69. Coliseum
73. Wrath
74. Be in harmony
75. Beam emitter
76. Niles, to Martin
77. Loony
78. Track down
79. Cessation

DOWN
1. Long tale
2. ___ weevil
3. Two-wheeler
4. NY hours
5. Mock
6. Sample
7. Number suffix
8. Mannequin
9. Bitter brew
10. Lazily
11. In person
12. Leak slowly
15. Furlough
21. Boat blade
23. Pea's container
26. Ebony
27. Starter for motion
28. Make, as money
30. Piggy
31. Had a debt
32. Turns aside
33. Supernatural
34. Thickly populated
36. Organ part
37. Cease-fire
40. Subway loop
41. Passes below the horizon
44. Inscribe
45. New York ___
48. Grab hold of
52. The limit?
53. Daisy segment
54. Average mark
56. Beatles' road
58. Picket-line crosser
59. Ocean plant
60. ___-cheap
62. Historic ages
64. Gripper
65. Golf club
66. Advance
68. Came together
70. Chemical suffix
71. Once known as
72. ___ of the covenant

ACROSS

1. Edible fish
5. Grouchy one
9. Coarse files
14. Dorothy's pet
15. Aesop racer
16. WWII craft
17. Moved to another country
19. News sources
20. Elongated fish
21. Reduced in price
23. Sharp flavor
24. Large snake
26. Jazz instruments
28. Portent
30. Be sociable
31. Lid
34. Lobby
37. Fugitive's flight
39. Mexican food
41. Coldly
43. Risk cash
45. Insignificant
46. Duller
48. Baby bug
50. Nerd
51. Personal pronoun
52. Jerk
54. Walkway
56. Traffic jam
58. Sample again
62. Wool eater
65. Clear of silt
67. Future fish
68. Monstrous giants
70. Novice
72. Ooze
73. Sprightly tune
74. Sweet drinks
75. Plains tent
76. House additions
77. "The Way We ___"

DOWN

1. Brew
2. Cozy
3. Cocked
4. Pooch
5. Furrow
6. Rodents
7. Locales
8. Confusion
9. Island liquor
10. Assists a felon
11. Carbonated drink
12. Hurt
13. Doe's beau
18. Motel offering
22. Theater sign
25. Christmas shrub
27. Checkup
29. Catch
31. Sugar source
32. Shampoo ingredient
33. Bonus
34. "___ Noon"
35. Property unit
36. Deceiver
38. Big boys
40. Strength
42. Sasquatch's cousin
44. Gratuity
47. Was sorry for
49. Bull's-eyes, e.g.
53. Baby's sound
55. Adolescent
56. Subject
57. Danger
59. Wash away
60. More achy
61. Keyed up
62. Lion's share
63. Stare
64. Journey
66. Vale
69. Visualize
71. Hem's partner

PUZZLE 161

141

PUZZLE 162

ACROSS

1. Healing sign
5. Squash
9. Beat cream
13. Detest
14. Moisten the bird
15. Bunny's kin
16. Auth. unknown
17. Bleacher feature
18. At all
19. Mr. Howard
20. Steamship
21. Musical pause
22. Glimpsed
24. Strained
27. Come closer
29. Kind of paneling
30. Head cover
33. Entry permit
36. Haul
38. Captain Hook, e.g.
40. Proclamation
42. Arthur or Lillie
44. Orange type
45. Figure out
47. Airport abbr.
49. Exercise places
50. Tibetan beast
51. Succeeded
53. Otherwise
55. Caper
57. Shine
61. Baseball's Musial
64. Synthetic fabric
66. Mature
67. Skirt type
68. Duck, e.g.
69. Ignite
70. Canola and olive
71. Geography book
72. Made like
73. Club type
74. Stained
75. Retrieves

DOWN

1. Clever
2. Outrigger
3. Do penance
4. Affleck or Stiller
5. Bounding ___
6. Attribute
7. Sound system
8. The lady's
9. In what place?
10. ___ a field day
11. Outrages
12. Impudent
14. Bouquet or gown
20. Grant's foe
23. Talent
25. Quick snooze
26. Peel
28. Chafe
30. Squiggly
31. List entry
32. Hardens
33. Considerably
34. Scheme
35. Unwell
37. Gosh!
39. Latest fads
41. Crier or house
43. Noshed
46. Negative
48. Metal mixtures
52. Fourscore plus ten
54. Daystar
55. Liqueur herb
56. Go by bike
58. Brownish gray
59. Plumed bird
60. Divides
61. Unhealthy air
62. Turn ___ (flee)
63. Spindle
65. Burden
68. Pop
69. Entrap

CODEWORD

Codeword is a special crossword puzzle in which conventional clues are omitted. Instead, answer words in the diagram are represented by numbers. Each number represents a different letter of the alphabet, and all of the letters of the alphabet are used. When you are sure of a letter, put it in the code key chart and cross it off in the Alphabet Box. A group of letters has been inserted to start you off.

1	2	3 U	4	5 R	6	7	8	9	10	11	12 O	13
14	15	16	17	18	19	20	21	22	23	24	25	26

5	20	2	17			15	23	9		23	19	20	9
12	12	22	25		26	20	19	12	9		19	12	5	25
7	9	23	5		5	12	1	25	12		3	26	12	13
8	23	5	1	7	23	19	25		6	12	6	25	13	9
			9	20	25	5		2	23	13				
	14	5	25	23	7	9		6	23	5	23	2	23	
14	12	12	24	20	25		11	25	9			20	13	13
23	3	21	25	5		4	3	13		2	23	5	21	12
21	13	3			26	20	9		7	12	2	2	25	5
	1	25	26	12	5	9		7	10	3	25	23	19	
		25	16	25			7	26	3	5				
14	25	17	23	19	4		2	5	20	9	20	2	23	19
5	23	20	13		23	21	23	20	13		9	23	18	20
25	2	5	3		14	3	5	13	9		25	15	25	13
16	17	25	9			8	25	9			6	25	19	9

Alphabet Box

A B C D E F G H I J K L M N Ø P Q Ŗ S T Ų V W X Y Z

143

PUZZLE 164

ACROSS

1. Froth
5. Lyrical
9. Consumed
13. "___ Twist Again"
17. Jug
18. PBS science series
19. Full-strength
20. Fail to mention
21. Hunting dog
23. Lass
24. Parisian priest
25. Plus
26. Be in arrears
27. Heart conduit
29. Complimentary
30. Tiny pests
32. Construction adhesive
35. Hockey legend
36. Church nook
39. Jabbered
41. Arcade name
43. Electrical units
45. Laundry worker
47. Piano pieces
50. Stretch
51. Sea anemone
53. Belief
55. Utah lily
56. Baggage handler
58. New cadet
61. Stomped
62. "Beetle Bailey" pooch
64. A reel shocker?
65. Whimper
68. Clerical robes
71. Police identifier
73. Cravat accessory
77. Skiff
78. Repair
79. ___ cords
82. Opposite of WSW
83. Spicy sausage
85. Inspire affection
88. Eggs' centers
90. Metallic waste
92. Grunted like swine
94. Bulletproof garment
95. Rail-splitter Lincoln
97. Dissertation
99. Finnish bathhouse
101. Scratch
103. Japanese fare
105. London libation
106. Golf gadget
109. Angry frenzy
110. Palm starch
111. Rodin and Bernini
114. Perry's creator
115. Mosque official
116. Folk wisdom
117. Cape
118. Finch food
119. Shriveled
120. Washstand pitcher
121. "___ the Lonely"

DOWN

1. ___ Knox
2. Buttery spread
3. Choral member
4. Disfigure
5. Moving in a single direction
6. Interlocking joint
7. "___ Got a Secret"
8. Williams of "Doctors' Wives"
9. Incline
10. Spades and clubs
11. Boo-boo list
12. Neighbor of Md.
13. Bread shape
14. Decorate with needlework
15. Rome's river
16. Take the helm
22. Obsess ender
28. Premonition
30. Fetch
31. Peppy
33. Collector's ___
34. Tabby
36. Profess
37. Prod
38. Santa's transport
40. Exploded
42. Stir
44. Petty quarrel
46. Chest bone
48. Freudian topic
49. Grassy patch
52. Select
54. Religious sch.
57. Share top billing
59. Chair support
60. Football team
63. Ginza sash
66. Airport abbr.
67. Foxy
68. Car-stopping sys.
69. Mauna ___
70. American symbol
72. Wood cutter
74. Brazilian soccer great
75. Readies the press
76. Hatchling's home
78. Tuna, e.g.
80. Acorn bearers
81. Beast
84. Clever remark
86. Noxious
87. Deep-___ pie
89. Roe
91. Big Bird's street
93. Fencer
95. Land tracts
96. Trumpet sound
98. Sweet stuff
100. Short sleep
102. Gardener's bane
104. Capri, e.g.
106. Tattered
107. Epochal
108. Glimpse
110. Bro's sibling
112. Dairy animal
113. Tango requirement

ACROSS

1. Hired vehicles
5. Legal matter
8. Sheriff's gang
13. Hawaiian dance
14. Climbing vine
15. "Harper ___ P.T.A."
16. Correct a manuscript
17. Writing tool
18. Compose, as a poem
19. Goal
20. Admit grudgingly
22. Mom's guy
23. Highest
25. Counterfeit
27. Sculptor, e.g.
29. Herring
32. Runaway herd
35. Gigantic
36. Salon treatments
37. Shoemaker's helper
39. Confused fight
40. Caisson's contents
41. Workers
43. Sputters
45. Sneak away
46. Frauds
48. Railroad bridge
52. Competent
54. Ministers
56. Pale
57. Venom
59. Lode's load
60. Back
61. Theater call
62. Toothpaste form
63. ___ in a lifetime
64. Staggers
65. Words from sponsors
66. Tidy a garden

DOWN

1. Swindle
2. Of sound
3. Dirigible
4. Day after Fri.
5. Retort
6. Twilight
7. In ___ (together)
8. Wall sections
9. ___ Glory (U.S. flag)
10. Calculating device
11. Bristle
12. Ogled
15. Pitcher Blue
20. Drum and bugle ___
21. Immature salamander
24. Extinct hairy mammal
26. Orbs
28. Hawks
30. Golden ___ (retiree)
31. Kickers' gadgets
32. Hot tubs
33. Secretary's sub
34. Truce
38. Planned, with "in"
39. Sulks
42. Casks
44. Flavors
45. Snaky letter
47. Filly feature
49. Heavy string
50. Jousting spear
51. Concluded
52. Mimic
53. Southern corn bread
55. Cato's clothing
58. Fifth scale tone
60. In what manner?

Step by Step

In five steps change each word one letter at a time into a new 5-letter word so that by the fifth step each letter has been changed. Do not rearrange the order of the letters. You do not have to change the letters in order.

Example: Rouge, Rough, Cough, Couch, Conch, Cinch

1. STORY

2. CHEAT

3. GRAND

4. STOLE

PUZZLE 167

ACROSS

1. Church part
5. Shady trees
9. Disney mule
12. Sports group
16. Trendy
17. Chicken and veal
19. Volcano dust
20. Great review
21. Cash register
22. Edging loop
23. ___ culpa
24. Currier and ___
25. Ingested
27. "Chances ___"
28. Waterways
30. Rouse
33. Paper amount
35. Kind of skirt
36. Be obliged to
37. Extinct bird
39. Skirt style
41. Small nails
45. Relay portion
46. Steel element
47. Pace
49. "___ More Night"
50. Serrated
52. Thin tuft
55. Bog fuel
56. "___ Abner"
57. Great times
59. Evict
61. Fall asleep
63. Life-saving tech.
65. Hexed
68. Before, in poems
69. Natural sponge
71. Choir voice
72. Bothers
74. Heidi's mountain
75. Frosh's senior
77. "___ Lake"
79. Gumbo veggies
83. Early jazz form
84. TV's "F ___"
86. Pecans, e.g.
88. 12 months, in Seville
89. Foul-up
91. Terrier talk
93. Affected manner
94. RR depot
95. Athenian vowels
97. Part of D.J.
99. Or's partner
101. Debater
104. "Alice" waitress
105. Copycat
106. Freight
107. Large
110. Fit
112. Hard candy
116. Not taped
117. Egg cells
118. Swiss song
119. Fully cooked
120. Rosebud, e.g.
121. Loser at Vicksburg
122. Window unit
123. Leap ___

DOWN

1. "Sister ___"
2. Greek letter
3. ___ vous plait
4. Brilliance
5. Penguin variety
6. Wahine's wear
7. Pasta type
8. Retail outlet
9. Lower limb
10. Function
11. Lewis or Belafonte
12. Minor details
13. Icicle's perch
14. Assert
15. Hodgepodge
18. Hot vapor
26. Neater
29. Entirely
30. Tree trunk
31. Slender jug
32. Western lily
34. Cambridge univ.
35. Marceau, e.g.
38. Search for water
40. Distance down
42. Hue
43. Cutting implement
44. ___-control
48. Chinese mammal
51. Menial worker
53. Stain
54. Golf strokes
58. Hate
60. Flat-bottomed boat
62. Escritoire
63. List starter
64. Momma's partner
66. Mackerel
67. Malaise
69. Science rooms
70. Intelligent
73. Type of columnist
76. Hard blows
78. South American boa
80. Hasty
81. Initial bet
82. Glide high
85. Seed coat
87. Foot lever
90. Quarreled
92. Half of a hundred
96. Leafy bower
98. Sailboat
100. Kind of bear
101. "___ Fair"
102. Stir up
103. Contributed
108. "___ Always Loved You"
109. Prattle
111. Yet, in verse
113. Future fish
114. Stop ___ dime
115. Part of mpg

DOUBLE TROUBLE

Not really double trouble, but double fun! Solve this puzzle as you would a regular crossword, except place one, two, or three letters in each box. The number of letters in each answer is shown in parentheses after its clue.

ACROSS

1. Give a leg up (5)
3. Dance club (5)
5. Spotless (5)
7. Trapshooting (5)
9. At that time (4)
10. Vend (4)
11. Clothes (6)
13. Cringe (6)
14. Hairy spider (9)
17. Blunder (7)
19. Gesture (6)
20. Take a chair (3)
21. Sermon (7)
22. Health clubs (4)
24. Responsibility (4)
25. Coolly unconcerned (10)
27. Property agent (7)
28. Whip (4)
29. Evening affair (6)
31. Of first importance (6)
32. Astound (11)
35. Small reed organ (8)
37. Thread holder (5)
38. Brazilian dance (5)
40. Enter a swimming pool (4)
41. Lobe ornament (7)
42. Contrariness (10)
45. Cotton bundle (4)
47. Warble (4)
48. Supply (7)
50. Decimal unit (3)
51. Ooze deposit (6)
52. Bug (6)
53. Wrist ornaments (9)
55. Unimaginative (7)
57. Grove (7)
60. Bridle strap (4)
61. Vestige (5)
63. Shout of encouragement (5)
64. Suit of mail (5)
65. Bee wound (5)
66. Fender damage (4)

DOWN

1. The two (4)
2. Very showy (12)
3. Question the court's ruling (7)
4. Connivance (9)
5. Sports shoe spike (5)
6. Opposed (4)
7. Yarn bundle (5)
8. Engrave (4)
12. Careless (6)
13. Piece of snow (5)
15. Sprinted (3)
16. Cupboard hook (5)
18. Theater platform (5)
19. Earth's satellite (4)
21. Interim (8)
22. Food fish (6)
23. Rustic (8)
25. Less disorganized (6)
26. Too (4)
27. Delay of punishment (8)
28. Like brook sound (8)
30. Scottish dance (4)
32. Parquet, e.g. (8)
33. Car fuel (3)
34. Cattle panic (8)
36. Strangeness (6)
37. Lances (6)
39. Cocktail lounge (3)
43. Spine segment (8)
44. Most genuine (9)
45. Railing (10)
46. Shelf (5)
48. Ordinary writing (5)
49. Champion (6)
51. Coterie (3)
52. Senseless (5)
54. Inner layer of a jacket (6)
55. Snack on (5)
56. Antlered animal (4)
58. Amulet (5)
59. Zeal (5)
62. Penny (4)

PUZZLE 169

BRICK BY BRICK

Rearrange this stack of bricks to form a crossword puzzle. The clues will help you fit the bricks into their correct places. Row 1 has been filled in for you. Use the bricks to fill in the remaining spaces.

BRICKS

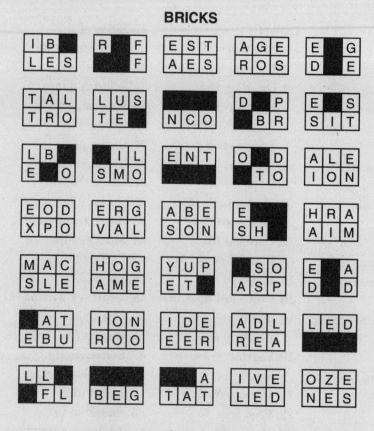

ACROSS

1. Wing-shaped
   Do in, as a dragon
   Once, once
2. Fable
   Hollow stone
   Bargain event
3. Walked
   Exhibit
4. Historic period
   Had food
   Fixed a shoe
5. Flowering shrub
   European viper
6. Slangy affirmative
   Hallucination
7. Sire
   Struck
   Kanga's baby
8. Slumbering
   Green sauce
   Catnap
9. Male heir
   Highland hills
   Sounds
10. Captivate
    Sty dweller
11. Point
    Spanish dance
12. Improvise
    Priest's garment
    Energy unit
13. Land
    Face shape
14. Nutmeglike spice
    Supporter
    "___ Easy Pieces"
15. Musher's vehicle
    Whitetail
    Ran

DOWN

1. Fragrant oil
   Home plate, e.g.
   Appendages
2. Slow, in music
   Poet's black
   Wheel's partner
3. Healing plants
   Polite chap
   Decorative material
4. Beet's color
   Watched carefully
   Summoned
5. Adjoin
   Tempt
6. Ensemble
   Baby buggy
   Gloomy
7. Genders
   Close securely
   Make a knot
8. Cut
   "The Man Who Haunted ___"
   Citrus cooler
9. Big fuss
   Tons
   By and by
10. Of course!
    Female voice
    More healthy
11. Edition
    Tut's place
12. Legally bars
    Genoa ruler
    Not at work
13. Rant
    Golf club
    Author Shute
14. Blackthorn
    Flow out slowly
    Want urgently
15. Take care of
    Negatives
    Stared at

DIAGRAM

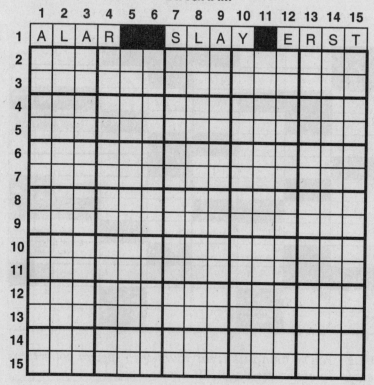

ACROSS

1. Clear the windshield
5. Emcee
9. Pronounce
12. Average
16. Mideast gulf
17. Netman Nastase
18. Ballet move
19. Ambiance
20. Down-to-earth
21. Spanakopita ingredient
22. Pinch
23. Field yield
24. Spite
27. Jingle
28. Mr. Strauss
29. A pop
30. Avril follower
31. Art deco artist
34. Quilting party
35. Rococo
39. 15th-century Italian painter
44. Hot headline
46. Undisciplined
47. Praises
49. Foaming at the mouth
50. Spring bulb
52. Bit of info
54. Wine region
55. Soft mineral
56. Space Shuttle attachments
59. Arch type
63. ____ Bator
65. Actress Russo
66. Stem joint
67. Overwhelm
70. Most ready
74. It floats on water
75. Bird brain?
77. Hopefuls
79. Set
80. Arctic abundance
83. Genesis gent
84. Crete peak
85. Oat eater
87. Long-jawed fish
90. Hooray!
93. Investing with sentiment
98. Soil sweetener
99. Locale
100. Verdi opus
101. Movie hero
102. Solemnly swear
103. Sound return
104. Ball of yarn
105. Caligula's nephew
106. Mrs. Truman
107. Child's question
108. "Dick Tracy" girl
109. Sprouted

DOWN

1. Luke's follower?
2. Model
3. American painter
4. Perk up
5. 45 player
6. Soft spread
7. In ____ (undisturbed)
8. Tantalize
9. Spills
10. Small islands
11. Indeed!
12. Cabal
13. Continental currency
14. Actor Kincaid
15. Scruff
18. Portion
25. Men are pigs around her
26. Collar
27. Mom or pop
30. Quagmire
32. Hinton novel
33. NYC hours
36. Pau pal
37. Down yards
38. Joule's kin
39. Float like a butterfly
40. Unusual, for Caesar
41. Botanist's angle
42. Make money
43. Temple table
45. Stuff
48. Passover feast
51. Coral reef visitors
53. Obsession
56. Canopus constellation
57. Common conjunctions
58. Agts.
60. Thug
61. Censor
62. Slippery swimmers
64. Rio Grande city
67. Scrooge's scoff
68. Egg cells
69. Troubled space station
71. Pollution control grp.
72. Baseball's Fernandez
73. Ear cartilage
76. Disciple of Paul
78. Wondrous
81. Walk-on
82. Important time
86. Make law
88. Bus passenger
89. Saw wood
90. Spill the beans
91. Tear asunder
92. Singing brothers
93. Fattening
94. Tessera
95. March time
96. Cornfield sounds
97. Shine
99. Darn it

• COUNTRY CODED •

PUZZLE 171

FOUR-MOST

The 4-letter entries in this crossword puzzle are listed separately and are in alphabetical order. Use the answers to the numbered clues to help you determine where each 4-letter entry goes in the diagram.

4 LETTERS

ABIE	OBEY
ABLE	OFFS
DENT	OWES
DYES	SAND
ELAN	SEER
EPIC	SETS
ERAL	STEW
FALK	SYNC
FELL	TALE
FRAY	TIKI
GELS	TOWS
GORY	WARY
LADD	
LIMO	
NEAT	
NINE	

ACROSS

9. Young newt
13. Engrossed
15. Podded veggie
17. Mutter
18. "____ Be Seeing You"
19. Baggage handler
21. Brawn
23. Most slender
27. Large parrot
35. Spam source
37. Connecting device
39. Foot lever
41. Nostalgia-inducing
46. Be where you shouldn't
48. Jam knife
50. Tenant
53. Hosiery
58. Mr. Gershwin
59. Count (on)
64. Boy, someday
65. Green fruits
67. The good ____ days

DOWN

5. Wildebeest
6. Goof
7. On the ____
8. Froth
13. Board, as a 747
14. Administrator
20. Inquire
22. Plant mouths
24. Restate
25. Kiwi's kin
26. Blotchy
27. ZIP and Morse
28. Proclaim
29. Swamp tree
31. Dry African streams
32. Lingerie fabrics
33. Long-jawed fish
36. Aloha gift
38. Sub's weapon
40. Dispatches again
43. Bathing-suit part
47. Jimmy
49. Spins
60. Excavation hole
61. First lady
62. Modern

ACROSS

1. Miss
4. Sash
7. Released
13. Future groom
19. Southern st.
20. Campaign
21. Partake of drink
22. Temper
23. Kiddie cars
25. Principal plunges?
27. Leak
28. Mjollnir's wielder
30. Siam governess
31. "Duino Elegies" poet
32. Stowe character
35. Black bird
36. Wharton grads
38. ___ Paulo
40. Concord
43. Cylinder
45. Mr. Linden
48. Pull tighter
50. Postwar Korean leader
51. Exude
52. Wimpy
53. Celestial hunter
54. Daze
55. Bookish
57. ___ Rica
58. Once existed
59. Dawn's personification
62. Clear
63. Patella's site
64. Moccasin
65. Account for
69. Named at birth
70. Raye's grapevines?
74. Inflationary meas.
77. Bonding
78. Charged particle
79. Notice
83. TV's Winfrey
85. Fork out
86. MSNBC rival
87. Ogle
88. Spot celebrities?
92. Clods
93. Nairobi's land
94. Descended
95. Bait fish
97. Faux pas
98. Monsieur's menus
99. Barely get by
100. City-related prefix
101. Because of that
103. Cunning
104. Detail
106. Humbug preceder
108. Photog's need
110. "Semper Fidelis" composer
113. Has-___
115. Aid a felon
117. "Diana" singer
120. Wine named for a Bronte?
123. Growing rapidly
126. Flowering shrub
127. Appointed relation
128. Prefix meaning "up"
129. Pullover
130. Rents again
131. Semi-arid plain
132. Cartoon cat
133. Wonderment

DOWN

1. Chokes
2. Burn reliever
3. Body of water owned by Brooks?
4. Bruin great
5. Except
6. Foot part
7. Lively, to musicians
8. Arab bigwig
9. CBS rival
10. Prometheus, e.g.
11. Inelastic rubber
12. "Jurassic Park" actress
13. Air traffic agcy.
14. Red start?
15. Diarist Nin
16. Foster film
17. Horseshoe extension
18. Choice word
24. Chimp
26. ___ pentameter
29. Sorrow
33. Ms. Davis
34. LBJ's successor
35. Salty assent?
37. Alpha follower
38. Soup base
39. Brother of Moses
41. In this way
42. Biddy
44. Ms. Thurman
45. Earthling
46. Parsley relative
47. French school
49. Freud's "___ and Taboo"
52. Apiece
54. Carpet sample
56. Forest denizen
59. Agent
60. Norse deity
61. Hill VIP
64. Expert
65. Data-collecting org.
66. Strengthen
67. French locale
68. Writer Fleming
71. German eight
72. Venomous snake
73. Forestall
74. Sheriff's gang
75. Say
76. Castle or Dunne
80. Kris Kringle as played by Bryant?
81. Crowbar-user
82. Matzo's lack
84. Beg
86. Staff
87. Flat-bodied ray
89. Zenith
90. Cuban dance
91. Solar body
92. Wow!
96. Trinket
97. Ultimate degree
98. Gear part
102. Gnaws
104. Cordage fiber
105. Be silent, in music
107. Voltaic cell terminal
109. Joplin work
110. Exchange blows
111. Slime
112. Russian range
114. Units of work
115. On
116. Good, to Giorgio
118. Recognized
119. Noted film critic
121. Holds
122. Recipe amt.
124. Numero ___
125. RAM's counterpart

PUZZLE 172

• HER ITINERARY •

PUZZLE 173

• A NEW LEAF •

ACROSS
1. Chop
4. Goat's milk cheese
8. Stride
12. "___ Believer"
13. Holy image
14. Chaste
15. Reject
17. Emerald Isle
18. Morays
19. Fonda and Russell
20. Livestock
23. Diving birds
24. Musical composition
25. Stretchy
28. Atmosphere
29. "Happy Days" actress
31. Rage
32. Camp light
34. Custard dessert
35. Heraldic border
36. Ability
38. Pin
40. Singer Sonny ___
41. Arabian gulf
42. Toll road
46. Dweeb
47. Regarding
48. Zilch
49. Soviet news agency
50. Curds and ___
51. Pig's home

DOWN
1. Strike
2. Ostrich's kin
3. Combat
4. Cuba's Castro
5. French school
6. Hauls
7. Actress Sheridan
8. Talks
9. Subway entrance
10. Toledo's lake
11. Corrals
16. Meshes
19. San ___, Puerto Rico
20. Fossil fuel
21. Western Samoa's capital
22. Flaky pastries
23. Chicken ___ king
25. Aquatic bird
26. Teheran's site
27. Small coin
29. Defrost
30. Mine product
33. Fads
34. Disaster
36. Rich cake
37. Bother
38. Carry on
39. Concept
40. Shrub
42. Playing marble
43. Officeholders
44. Toolbox
45. Tarzan portrayer

PUZZLE 174

• GO BELOW •

ACROSS
1. Blushing shade
4. Actress Gilbert
8. Choir voice
12. British rock gp.
13. Atop
14. Fly aloft
15. Bench
16. Rain gutter element
18. Actress Berger
20. Buyer's delight
21. Plunged
23. "___ of robins . . ."
27. Buckle
29. Aid
32. Judge Lance ___
33. Mist
34. Actor Chaney
35. Sixth Jewish month
36. "We ___ the World"
37. Globule
38. Outlet
39. "M*A*S*H" clerk
41. Rouse
43. Lawsuit
46. Viper
49. Former "20/20" host
53. Eggs
54. French friend
55. Toe holders
56. Method
57. Ground
58. Oak, e.g.
59. Opposite of SSW

DOWN
1. Agents
2. Gen. Robert ___
3. Cut back
4. African region
5. Mil. address
6. Paddles
7. "___ Karenina"
8. Ski resort
9. Card game
10. Greek letter
11. Morsel
17. Lath
19. Cassette
22. Garden green
24. Heavy quilt
25. Baseball's Musial
26. Legal wrong
27. Burn
28. Zhivago's love
30. Feathery wrap
31. Concludes
35. Eager
37. Actor Dourif
40. Longed
42. Flavor
44. Cushy
45. Water pitcher
47. Author Hunter
48. Comic Martha ___
49. Actor Linden
50. June in "Henry & June"
51. Martini liquor
52. By birth

CODEWORD

Instructions for solving Codewords are given on page 11.

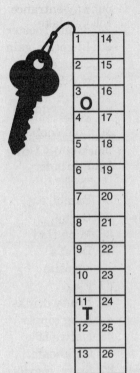

Key/Code table (Puzzle 175):

1	14
2	15
3 O	16
4	17
5	18
6	19
7	20
8	21
9	22
10	23
11 T	24
12	25
13	26

Grid (Puzzle 175):

	14	1	3	13		6		22	15	25	3	20
			1		20	3	12	7	3		3		6
5	1	15	12	7		1		1	15	17	10	14
15		22		15	20	7	26	15		20		7
17	7	15	16	11				20	7	6	9	26
3				2	6	23	6			12		
10	26	19	1	7		3		8	10	7	10	7
		15			4	7	5	10				21
22	3	20	7	16			6	26	9	3	11	
3		6		19	6	18	6	19		10		3 O
11	15	5	3	3		6		24	26	7	7	1
6		3		23	7	26	19	7		16		
23	1	10	23	23		7		26	3	16	7	

Alphabet key (Puzzle 175):

A N
B Ø
C P
D Q
E R
F S
G T̸
H U
I V
J W
K X
L Y
M Z

(Key entries shown: 3 = O, 11 = T)

CODEWORD

Key/Code table (Puzzle 176):

1	14
2	15
3 H	16
4	17
5	18
6 A	19
7	20
8	21
9	22
10	23
11	24
12	25
13	26

Grid (Puzzle 176):

19	21	17	1	9		2	19	20	1	24	1	23
15		16		16 H		13		13		13		8
11	8	19	23	19 A		24	8	22	6	8	4	4
19		17		6		1		17		6		15
21	17	8	4	4		15	6	19	14	1	22	7
		19		18		17		1		19		13
1	10	13	23		18	21	1		4	18	5	5
		13		14		22		22		4		1
13	10	11	8	25	18	1		6	1	15	6	13
12		19		18		12		19		13		6
15	19	23	14	1	11	13		3	1	9	1	11
8		19		1		26		19		1		13
2	16	8	24	23	1	7		16	1	6	13	23

Alphabet key (Puzzle 176):

A̸ N
B O
C P
D Q
E R
F S
G T
H̸ U
I V
J W
K X
L Y
M Z

(Key entries shown: 3 = H, 6 = A)

PUZZLE 177

• SOUP'S ON! •

ACROSS

1. Stag
5. FDR's creation
8. G-man
11. Away from the wind
12. Piece of food
14. Restrain
15. Go-getter
16. Weird
17. City in Algeria
18. Veggie-garnished soup
20. Confounds
22. Female ruff
23. Self-assurance
24. Likely
27. Comparative ending
28. Hammer, e.g.
29. Union
31. Feline
32. Boy
35. Entreaty
36. Swine
37. Butter substitute
39. Shriner's cap
40. Rake
41. Playful exchange
43. Portion
45. Downcast
46. Wrath
47. Charm
49. Single unit
50. Positioned
51. Clear soup
56. Apiece
57. Silly
59. Entrance
60. Sandwich cookie
61. Slender candle
62. Egg-shaped
63. Author Buntline
64. According to
65. Nerve network

DOWN

1. Pilgrimage to Mecca
2. Felipe or Moises
3. Rod's partner
4. Actress Garr
5. Hot dog
6. Whittle
7. Black cuckoo
8. Raises crops
9. Day's march
10. Animal homes
12. Thin layer
13. Tyrant
14. Clear soup-broth
19. A Great Lake
21. Also
24. Sound booster
25. Ill-gotten gain
26. Source of wood
28. Catch-me game
30. Cold soup
31. Atlantic fish
33. Prefix for "high"
34. Bambi, e.g.
36. Derby
38. Mine find
40. Debit's opposite
41. Flag
42. Fruity drinks
44. King topper
45. Native of Oklahoma
47. Stare angrily
48. Sped
50. Unskilled laborer
51. Cloak
52. Smell
53. Relocate
54. Castle ditch
55. ___ Stanley Gardner
58. Fabric pile

PUZZLE 178   Suspended Sentence

The words in each vertical column go into the spaces directly below them, but not necessarily in the order they appear. When you have placed all the words in their correct spaces, you will be able to read a quotation across the diagram from left to right.

ROLLED	ONLY	IT	BED	TO	THAT
THE	AGO	THE	THAT	DIME	AS
FAR	AS	IS	THE	GOES	TEN
YEARS	UNDER	THING	USED		

154

ACROSS

1. Did Smith's job?
5. Newton's heart?
8. Protection
12. Old sailor
16. Aperture
17. Notion
19. Soft drink
20. Musical instrument
21. Short quips
23. Cheating lovers
25. Self
26. Legal thing
27. Adolescent
29. Steamed
30. Spoiled
31. Unmannerly
32. Bustle
33. Surfeits
36. Merit
37. Bridal-registry collection
41. Estonian architect
42. Neptune's orbit?
44. ___ de France
45. Part of ETA
46. TV-remote button
47. Gasp
48. Wheel shaft
49. Was rife
51. Cycle
53. Hungry
54. Congers
55. Sword
56. He directed "Laura"
57. All in
59. Estimate
60. Vacation spot
63. Monad
64. Carreys on?
65. Shelters
67. Bond
68. 32,000 ounces
69. Inept person
72. St. Petersburg's river
73. Awkward
76. Seed cover
77. More achy
78. Legal instrument
79. Provoke
80. Farmyard female
81. Some Asians
83. Suit to ___
84. Grain beard
85. Cote cry
88. 80
90. Restaurant ranking
93. Cager or cagee?
94. River to the Caspian
95. Pass over
96. Mine finds
97. Misfortunes
98. Red-tag event
99. Is in France?
100. Black

DOWN

1. Sabot, e.g.
2. ___ Kong
3. Dieter's option
4. First St.
5. Monetarily penalized
6. March 15, e.g.
7. Eur. land
8. Ms. Lauder
9. Mantua
10. Bachelor's last words
11. Swift, e.g.
12. Organisms' bodies
13. Countenance
14. Erudition
15. French possessive
18. On the ball
22. Ret. plans
24. Fe
28. Paradise
30. "Willard" sequel
31. Great review
32. Scottish lord
33. Card game
34. Swiss river
35. Circus type
36. Soak, as hemp
37. End
38. Disadvantaged hoopster?
39. She, in Soissons
40. Mounted on a peg
42. Lather
43. Part of a 13-piece suit?
46. Intermix
48. Formicary dwellers
50. Converge
51. Luxuriant
52. Crone
53. Western tribesmen
55. Like rappers' jeans
56. Russian city
57. 1984 Nobelist
58. Privy to
59. Culpability
61. Split
62. Lachrymal drop
64. Surface-tension curve
65. Hideaway
66. Wing
70. "Bewitched" boss
71. Perry Mason's underwear?
72. This instant
74. Clio et al.
75. Rainbow goddess
77. Male offspring
79. Inscribed pillar
80. Did a house-keeping chore
81. Work hard
82. Throw
83. Sea east of the Caspian
84. Rara ___
85. Carping remark
86. Mars: pref.
87. Org.
88. Gov. agency
89. ___ pro nobis
91. Presidential nickname
92. Sock end

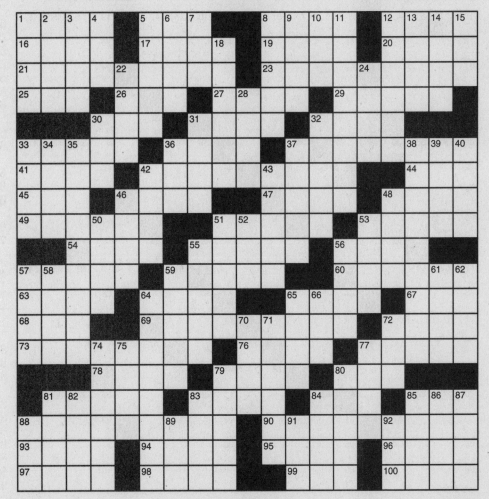

PUZZLE 180

• LEGALESE •

ACROSS
1. Fail
5. Snuggery
9. "Mame" director
13. Casa ____ Orchestra
17. Indolent
18. English horn
19. Ditty
20. Monumental
21. Mrs. Sprat's no-no
22. Horseradish, e.g.
23. Duffer's device
24. Social skill
25. Give orders
28. Bodybuilding pioneer
29. Lil E. Tee's Derby jockey
30. Wright wing
31. "Splendor in the Grass" screenwriter
33. Greenville, South Carolina, neighbor
37. Branch
38. Direction
42. Companion of St. Paul
43. Casual greetings
44. ____ room (network feature)
45. Orbit shape
46. Deceive
47. Trundle ____
48. Stocking stuffers?
49. Greek salad ingredient
50. Footstool
52. Sudden fear
53. Senator Thurmond
54. Highway hazard
55. Feudal baron
56. Scrooge's expletive
57. Rancor
60. MTV watchers, often
61. Political thaw
65. RPM meter
66. Physicist Mach
67. Grimalkin
68. Former Italian currency
69. Tissue additive
70. Indochinese country
71. Carol, to Jan, Marcia, and Cindy
72. Western
73. England's Disraeli
75. Prime ____
76. Irving Berlin song
77. Well-versed
78. Safflower product
79. Freudian term
80. Sandpiper
83. Bernoulli's theorem
90. Lobed organ
91. Meal or bread
92. Unrestricted
93. Arp's art
94. Magwitch of "Great Expectations"
95. Dormer division
96. Compost item
97. Disembarked
98. Look fixedly
99. Redolence
100. Brent Spiner role
101. Portion

DOWN
1. Grinder
2. Mental flash
3. Incapacitate with laughter
4. Enamor
5. Nobel Peace Prize country
6. "____ and Ivory"
7. Lampblack
8. Leashes
9. Inactive
10. Nimbus
11. Walking encyclopedia
12. D.C. figure
13. Literal meaning
14. Fiery gem
15. Biotite
16. Bible book
26. Poems of praise
27. Yale campus tree
28. Identification info
32. Realizes
33. It, to Enrico
34. Slangy negative
35. Position
36. Survival of the fittest
37. Crutch
38. Laminated rock
39. Asseverate
40. Saxophonist Barbieri
41. Susiana
43. Clucker
44. Invents
47. Duffel
48. Liturgical song
51. First name in slapstick
52. "One Night in Bangkok" vehicle
53. Occupied a throne
55. Mortise insertion
56. Play the ponies
57. Try
58. Enclosed area
59. Computer symbol
60. Railroad capacity number
61. Weir
62. Talbot of "Here We Go Again"
63. Deuce topper
64. Rabbit ____
66. "Sesame Street" muppet
67. Cygnet's pop
71. Connecticut harbor city
72. Swan genus
74. Appropriate
75. Duran Duran hit
76. Docket
78. Landlord
79. Occurrence
80. Dross
81. Funnel cloud
82. Don Juan's mother
84. German poet Holz
85. Pacific seaport
86. Economist Smith
87. Gridder Sayers
88. Cut copy
89. Overfill
91. USN noncom

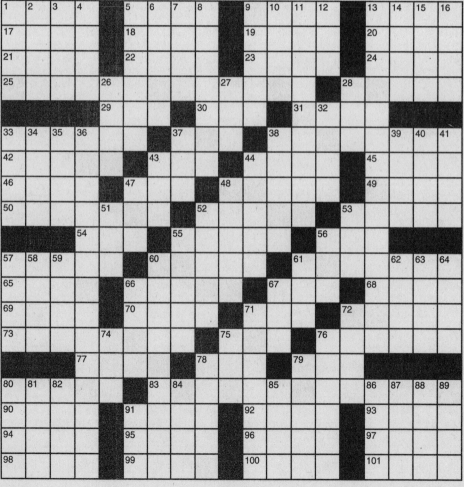

156

ACROSS

1. Affix
6. Remarkable, to Scots
10. Convenient
15. Go ahchoo
16. On land
18. Unattended
19. Loafers
20. Ed's moving truck?
22. Healing drug
23. "Suzie Q" band, shortly
24. Come to know
25. King toppers
26. ___ fizz
28. Pantry tins
31. Mr. Cariou
32. Prizefight
33. Allows
35. There are 24 in a day
38. Groovy!
40. Vane dir.
42. Put turf down
44. Earring
45. Expression of approval
48. Game marble
50. Prevail
52. That guy's
53. Margins
54. Assume as probable
57. Warning wail
59. Unload
61. Removes clothing
63. The Red ___
65. Edition
67. Legislator
69. "___ Hawaii"
70. List-ending abbr.
71. Dad's lady
73. CIA's predecessor
74. Pompous oratory
76. Paper quantity
78. Seize
80. "___-Devil"
82. Foremost
83. Jingle writer
85. Guitar device
87. Quick drinks
89. Society gal
92. Soup veggies
94. Throat occupants
96. Cinema pooch
97. ___ reaction
99. In the past
100. Anklebone
101. Robert's pal?
106. Easter march
107. Spud state
108. New York city
109. Did penance
110. Records
111. Tiptop
112. Cares for

DOWN

1. Bring about
2. John Cougar's summer retreat?
3. Complaints
4. Hebrew prophet
5. ___ Moines
6. Excessive interest, once
7. Gretzky's org.
8. Lassie's breed
9. Acquaints
10. Hard-hearted gal
11. Pacino and Franken
12. Autumn mo.
13. Genetic abbr.
14. Longing
15. Rope-making material
16. Neck scarves
17. Actress Gabor
21. Circle part
23. Mr. Gulager
26. Firm
27. Jackie's boy?
29. SSA IDs
30. Kiefer's property?
32. Physique, briefly
34. Female swine
36. Destructive
37. '60s radical gp.
39. Expels
41. Hi-fi system
43. Belittle, in slang
45. View starter
46. Restricted
47. Sorority letter
49. Ohio River tributary
51. Penpoint
55. Hosp. workers
56. However
58. Jewish cleric
60. Foodie's word
62. Weep
64. Capture
66. Geologic age
68. Frolics
70. Pitcher's stat
72. Singer Davis
75. Pas' mates
77. Ms. West
79. Former Cuban leader
81. Conundrum
84. Cheese-dipped chips
86. Rain gear
88. Workers' gp.
90. Chopin works
91. Founded
93. Egyptian deity
95. Gravy, e.g.
96. Mr. Spelling
98. Pierre's pal
100. "Soap" family name
101. Cambridge univ.
102. Ms. Lupino
103. Faucet
104. ___ Guevara
105. "Star Wars" pilot
106. Caress

PUZZLE 182

CRYPTIC CROSSWORD

British-style or Cryptic Crosswords are a great challenge for crossword fans. Each clue contains either a definition or direct reference to the answer as well as a play on words. The numbers in parentheses indicate the number of letters in the answer word or words.

ACROSS

1. Suppress news of failure in competition (8)
5. Urging, for example, movie rating in German (6)
10. Cake decorator, back before Senator Kennedy, presented a poem (7)
11. First mastiff produced longer dog (7)
12. Every year miss a repeal (5)
13. Sole voter agitated president (9)
14. Composer of verse "Grind" we hear (4)
15. Person from Oz ordered trail sauna (10)
18. Trudeau takes companion to apartment in town (4,1,5)
20. Praise returned twofold (4)
24. Lost son's greed abnormal (9)
26. Stop the French returning plant (5)
27. First contained within it I allow (7)
28. Greek hero uses sly maneuvers (7)
29. Odd code he repeated (6)
30. "Clock Wound" hit mystery novel (8)

DOWN

1. Stop profit agreement (7)
2. Thus small change mounts (7)
3. Character in Betty MacDonald's potboiler? (6)
4. The German follows a French subordinate (5)
6. Lent Guam recycled alloy (8)
7. Tempestuous Ariel is one from the Mideast (7)
8. Unstable substance of story uplifting in spirit (7)
9. I'm Bill the charlatan (8)
16. Forks and knives enlist us in trouble (8)
17. Sail gone—switch to fuel (8)
18. Specific recipes cooked (7)
19. Spin our language (7)
21. Hobart is an imprisoned worker (7)
22. Accumulation is back in storehouse (7)
23. Acted part like a young Eastwood did at first (6)
25. Cash heard first note (5)

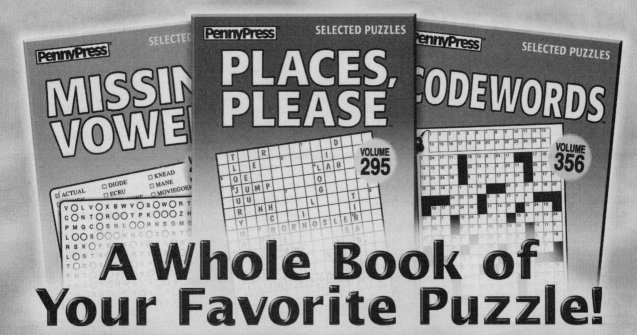

A Whole Book of Your Favorite Puzzle!

Our puzzle collections deliver dozens of your favorite puzzle type, all in one place!

PUZZLE 183

• ECONOMIC FORECAST •

ACROSS

1. Total failure
5. Oat eater
9. Marry secretly
14. Twangy
19. Immaterial
20. Surrounded by
21. Planter
22. Hock
23. Fall in costs
25. Restriction of funds
27. Personal property
28. Lets up
30. Gave a buzz
31. Try
33. Page for views
34. Favor
35. Outdoorsy type
39. Went by wherry
41. Peat places
42. Hit
45. Shun
46. Tom, Dick, and Harry
47. Ancient letter
48. Fly high
49. Flat fee
50. Walked in water
51. Check endorser
52. Handbag
53. "Before" indicator
54. Interlaced
55. Won at chess
56. Fleshy fruits
57. Porking lot?
58. Highways
59. Superior to
60. Entanglement
61. Suppress
63. Low digit
64. Flustered
66. Gushes
68. Kukla's cohort
70. Put on a happy face
71. Hollywood's Joanne ____
74. Neck parts
75. Docks
76. Male deer
77. Trace
78. Horned vipers
79. Praline nut
80. They're tiresome
81. Baseball tap
82. Sets
83. Deposited
84. Grades
85. Dated
86. Sauce ingredient
87. Rhythmic cadence
88. Tack
89. Mumble
90. Tarries
91. Poet Teasdale
92. Shadow
94. Suave
97. Piercing
99. Vapid
104. Business rivals
106. Fiscal conservatism
108. Prospero's sprite
109. Heavenly dish
110. Speck on a map
111. Patella's site
112. Hotsy-____
113. Grand canyon?
114. Feature of some winds
115. Sun. speeches

DOWN

1. Diminish
2. Gladly
3. "Carmina Burana" composer
4. War journalist
5. Affair
6. Wrong
7. Source of agua
8. Writer Ferber
9. Gets away
10. Plundered
11. Had
12. Strokes
13. Stumble
14. Tortilla snacks
15. Dramatist Chekhov
16. Hide
17. Burn soother
18. Advance
24. Behaved
26. Zenith
29. Curved
32. Export imbalance
34. Filleted
35. Nags
36. Prevent
37. The Fed's concern
38. Match
40. Portents
41. Time of low prices
42. Like financial ups and downs
43. Author Joyce Carol ____
44. Compact
46. Nautical
47. Evaluate
48. Stow
50. Barking sounds
51. Surface for traffic
54. Legal documents
55. Months
56. Nudges
60. Fountain treats
62. Head lock?
63. Mountain lake
65. Takes on
66. Obstacles
67. Stroll
69. Interpret
70. Brief
72. Hair coloring
73. Sheer
75. Chimes
79. Predicament
80. Fundamental
81. Blink
84. Boat basins
85. Regular beat
87. Recently
88. Magnates
89. Coined
90. Runs easily
91. Lustrous
93. Lovers' lane?
94. Begone!
95. Muslim Malay
96. Skip
97. Guess
98. Hideout
100. Bugs
101. Long
102. Cato's way
103. Applies henna to
105. "____ Believer"
107. Take advantage of

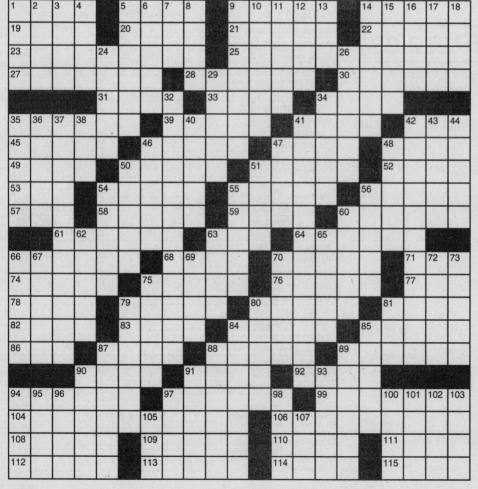

160

ACROSS

1. Jewish cleric
6. Flair
10. Elliott in "JAG"
14. Holler
19. Atlantic or Arctic
20. Current fad
21. Well-known canal
22. Rigatoni, e.g.
23. Stevenson novel, with "The"
25. Shopping plaza
26. Tanker
27. Tokyo fighting sport
28. Fireplace fuel
29. Tyrone Power film
32. Closer
35. Consumer lures
36. Ruddy
37. Blot
40. Aliens' agcy.
41. Green with ___
43. Historic time
45. Wind instrument
49. Loafers
51. Architect Saarinen
52. Clay brick
54. Ms. Tyler
55. Layered rock
56. Semiformal dress
58. Derrick
60. Call's partner
61. Mingo portrayer
63. Indignation
64. Jolts
65. Genesis craft
66. High scorer
67. Composer Orvarsson
69. Terrify
70. Confederate Johnny ___
71. Boyle's detective
74. Cries of surprise
77. Then, to Monique
79. RR depots
80. Hired help
81. Feline
82. Sea between Greece and Turkey
84. ___-fi
85. Gashes
86. Slothful
87. Army rank
88. Power loss
91. Anesthetic choice
92. Nobelist Andric
93. Not as wet
95. Microwave, slangily
96. Irony
97. Society entrants
99. Kookie's real name
100. "Pretty Woman" star
101. ___ Beta Kappa
102. Find a sum
103. Age
105. "My Gal ___"
106. Level
109. Michael Jackson song
115. Rec. vehicle
116. Sorrowful word
120. Happen again
121. Algerian port
122. Showing a profit
125. Mural starter
126. Mentally healthy
127. Comment
128. Russian pancake
129. Exodus figure
130. Mimicked
131. Washstand item
132. Relinquishes

DOWN

1. Plunders
2. Citizens'-rights org.
3. Grin broadly
4. Breakfast meat
5. Pen fluid
6. Mistakes
7. Roomy
8. Way back when
9. Small salamander
10. Treatment
11. Saudis, e.g.
12. Paper money
13. Mr. Lugosi
14. Conversed
15. Coiffure
16. Scandinavian city
17. Colorado Indians
18. Weight allowance
24. Arkin and Hale
30. Mayhem
31. Lobster's cousin
33. Shamrock land
34. Staggers
37. Expel a lawyer
38. Cling
39. Watergate affair, for one
42. Gun-owners' lobby
43. Entertainer Adams
44. Shad ___
46. Tall Australian tree
47. Sty noise
48. December 24 and 31
50. Forest animal
51. Movie critic
52. Courtyards
53. Repeated
57. Muffles
59. Milne character
61. Oak nut
62. Chow hall
64. Twirls
66. On a train
67. Prank
68. TV-viewers' advisory
69. Card game
72. Academy Award
73. Slide
75. Peril
76. Designed
78. Zodiac lion
82. Surrounded by
83. Roof extension
84. Toboggan
85. Pickle veggies
86. Destiny
88. Bridge move
89. Prepared to pray
90. Possessive pronoun
91. Cafe au ___
94. Gambler's town
96. Push
98. Safe
100. Benefited
101. Heated discussion
104. Gumbo pods
105. Ladd role
107. Photo finish
108. Ms. Berry
109. Hat edge
110. Comic Jay
111. Bible book
112. Montgomery's Parks
113. Enfold
114. German article
117. Deposited
118. Skin problem
119. Glides downhill
123. Immediately
124. London media inits.

PUZZLE 185

BATTLESHIPS

The diagram represents the sea, which contains a crossword puzzle; the answer words are Battleships. The letter-number combination to the left of each clue indicates the location in the diagram where a Battleship has been hit (for example, A2 is in the first row, second column). A hit is any one of the letters in the answer word. Using this clue, you must determine the exact location of each answer and whether it is an across or a down word. Fill in black squares to separate words as in a regular crossword. We have filled in the answers to clues A4 and E1.

A2   Comic Kovacs
A4   Conclude
A8   Clock feature
A10 Jazz's Brubeck
A14 Garfield's friend
A15 God of love
B3   Viper
B5   Command
B7   Actor Alda
B13 Make over
C5   Prove human
C6   Realize
C9   Mover's truck
C12 Largest
     continent
D4   Cake layer
D7   Info
D8   Paddle

D11 Grow older
D13 Spring holiday
D15 Fly high
E1   Refinement
E4   Female prophet
E6   Religious dissent
E10 Scant
F6   Tofu source
F7   Puncture
F12 Pencil parts
F14 Norm
G4   Outdated
G7   Sedan, e.g.
G13 Smooth cloth
G15 ____ out (made do)
H1   Await action
H2   Conceit
H5   Hearty meat dish

H8   Colorado Indian
H10 Try
H11 Cowboy film
H14 Named at birth
I2   Author James ____
I4   Tidy
I6   Swerve
I9   Restaurant
I12 Gift
I13 Self-control
I14 Happiness
I15 Chose
J5   Francisco leader
J7   Removes from
     power
J11 Twelve months
K7   Lowest
K8   Begins
K11 Ark's captain
K13 Topics
L3   Talc
L4   Added up
L6   Form of prayer
L9   Falsehoods
L10 Alien's craft
L14 Author Zola
L15 Tractor trailer
M1   Dryer fuzz
M3   Movie star
M7   Great wrath
M10 English school
M11 Owns
M13 Remove from a
     will
N2   ____ fixe
N4   Hawaiian bird
N8   Actress Dey
N9   Mideast native
N14 Aspect
N15 Located
O4   ____ off (angry)
O6   Commonplace
O8   Strong desires
O12 Knight's charger
O13 Come together

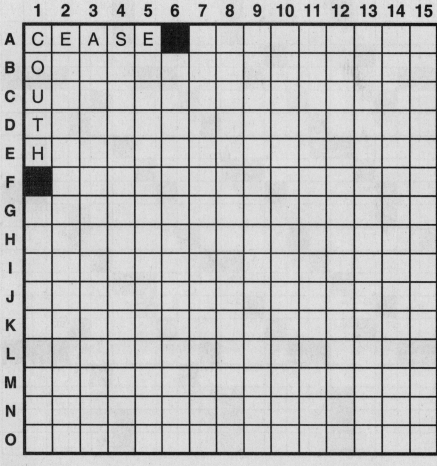

PUZZLE 186

• HEAD HONCHOS •

ACROSS

1. Roe source
5. Fitness clubs
9. Tree anchor
13. Scheme
17. Roman garment
18. Hair divider
19. Not shortened
21. Ham spice
22. "___ the Roof"
23. Earlier
24. Paris subway
25. Tricks
26. VIPs
28. Taro treat
29. Floor bosses
31. Certain dashes
32. Cooking fat
33. Take advantage of
34. Sports events
37. Boggy land
38. Climb
42. Favorable vote
45. Homeric product
46. Haul
47. Fruit pastries
48. Steal from
49. Tattered
50. String of pearls
51. Ointment
52. Kind of maniac
53. Epic tale
54. "What's My ___?"
55. Wooden pin
56. Desist
60. Yank
61. Accumulates
63. Cup handle
64. Ahchoo!
66. Snob
68. Feminine titles
71. Pumpernickel grain
72. Chants
74. Debt marker
75. Meal finale
79. Type of bean
80. Harbor
81. 1492 vessel
83. Be regretful
84. Yemeni city
86. Smells
87. Results
88. Goof
89. Hot chocolate
91. Optimistic
92. Hiatus
93. Sorrow
94. Greek god of light
96. Vital statistic
97. Actress Spacek
98. Farewell, to Caesar
99. Cave dwellers
101. ___ Francisco
102. Military commander
106. Commit perjury
107. Corporate chiefs
112. Gaucho's lasso
113. Floral leaf
115. Lawyer's assignment
116. Provo's state
117. Modify
118. ___ blanche
119. Mournful word
120. Alpha's follower
121. Belgian river
122. Clarinet need
123. Animal skin
124. Urban pollution

DOWN

1. Puny pencil
2. Arizona Indian
3. Highly curious
4. Aykroyd and Rather
5. Soup utensils
6. Trousers
7. Semicircles
8. Holy Fr. female
9. Hearsay
10. Iroquois member
11. Fall mo.
12. Sod
13. Feather
14. Misplace
15. Kiln, e.g.
16. Certainly!
20. Excessively
21. Peaks
27. Listen to
28. Hunger twinges
30. Litter's smallest
32. Pacesetters
34. Rubs it in
35. BB shooter
36. Administrators
37. Swiss money
39. Bachelor party
40. Coolidge, to friends
41. Humorist Bombeck
42. Field of study
43. Berra of baseball
44. Black, to a bard
45. "___ Now or Never"
46. Remove frost from
50. Jacket
51. Stupefy
55. Showy bloom
57. Fiends
58. Glum
59. New-employees' mentors
62. Alliance
65. Storm center
67. Champions
68. Jolly
69. Des ___
70. Roman Catholic Sabbath
73. Knotted loop
75. Detective Nancy ___
76. Continental currency
77. Parched
78. Mexican sandwich
79. Flippered mammal
82. Inquire
85. Buck's abbr.
86. Speak in public
89. Sturgeon delicacy
90. Petroleum-cartel letters
92. Singer Crosby
95. Spheroid-shaped
97. Most rational
98. Later than
100. Felt sick
101. Rope fiber
102. Lubricates
103. Lot
104. Computer key
105. Nurture
107. Cabbagelike veggie
108. British saloons
109. Gossipy bit
110. Defense gp.
111. Thick carpet
112. Beam
114. View starter
115. Billed hat

PUZZLE 187

SPORTING GOODS

ACROSS

1. Flings
6. Seafood delicacy
12. Dorsal ___
15. Conscious
16. Sleep
17. Picnic drink
18. Sparring partners
20. Heavy hammer
24. Eisenhower's nickname
25. Dispensed
26. Rome, e.g.
28. Comparative ending
29. Loch ___
31. USN officer
32. Fights
34. Perpetually
35. Gal
37. Cavities
38. Happiness
39. Plot
42. Emulated a crow
43. Connect
44. African shrubs
45. Dips
46. Taro dish
47. Cumberland ___
50. Bolt
51. Saguaros
52. Disseminates
53. Sib
54. Interrogate
55. Angling rod
57. Granada gold
58. A Tweedle
59. Helm position
60. With joy
61. So-so
62. Porky's home
63. Price ceiling
64. Leans against
65. Daring
66. Slugger Sammy ___
68. "Scent of a Woman" role
69. Merchant
70. Shaping tool
72. Absurdity
73. Former TV host
74. Garden flag
75. Floor covering
76. Alley ___
77. Go to the mall
81. Attack, Fido!
82. History
83. Craftier
85. Pig ___ poke
86. Impounding
88. Serving tool
92. Sigma follower
93. Nook
94. Levels
95. Ajar, in verse
96. Slackened
97. Jaunty

DOWN

1. Log house
2. Got up
3. Jazz instruments
4. Three: pref.
5. "___ in the Clowns"
6. Church instruments
7. Shouts
8. Jane's dog
9. Mazel ___!
10. Compass pt.
11. Saved
12. Goes hungry
13. In a vain effort
14. Born, to Brigitte
19. Ganders
21. Plunging platform
22. Turns right
23. Blunders
27. Possessive pronoun
30. Suave
32. Striking missile
33. Bullfight cheers
34. Yale man
36. Morning hrs.
37. Port-au-Prince's land
38. Idaho river
39. Tossed and tuna
40. Cupboard
41. Goal-making need
42. Hidden reserve
43. Like a bulldog
45. Stationed

46. Combines

48. Come

49. Less wealthy

51. Eyelashes

52. Malice

55. Inaccurate

56. Showy

61. Worries

64. Friendly nation

65. Gun gp.

67. ___ and ahs

68. Musical works

69. Come to a point

70. Memory jogger

71. "La Scala" number

72. Seedy fruit

73. Polished

75. Undefined

76. Green shade

78. Backpacks

79. Humdingers

80. Pushover

82. Break in two

83. Winter forecast

84. Darn!

87. Judge Lance ___

89. Building section

90. Sgt., e.g.

91. Hush-hush org.

PUZZLE 188

ACROSS
1. Broad
5. Get ready
9. Creak
14. Sonnets' kin
15. Harvestable
16. Boom box
17. Remainder
18. Woodwind instrument
19. Not starboard
20. Cosmetics
22. Medical picture
24. Whiskey or bread
25. Competitor
27. Suit to a ___
29. Meekly
31. Circle around
34. Removes
35. Squash
38. Bowler feature
40. Gone by
41. Cast
42. Bedlam
43. Spiders' structures
45. Fall bloomer
47. Pace
48. Force back
50. Wigwams
52. Stubborn animal
53. Bit of land
54. Bizarre
57. Shortly
59. Declare true
63. Fragrance
65. Oversupply
67. Former
68. Morning program
69. Erie or Champlain
70. Parallel
71. Leopard markings
72. Black-___ Susan
73. Hems a skirt

DOWN
1. Bait, sometimes
2. Hunch
3. Cubicle item
4. Honors
5. Drives forward
6. Needle
7. Strong glue
8. Use the keyhole
9. Drearier
10. Quick blow
11. Garlic feature
12. Ethereal
13. Do, re, or mi
21. One: Fr.
23. Surmounting
26. Folk tales
28. Decrease
29. Woods man?
30. Sun-dried brick
32. Enraged
33. Oceans' motions
34. Unfinished
36. Three strikes
37. Competitions
39. Wipe
44. Hot Springs, e.g.
45. As well
46. Kin
47. Decides
49. Reports
51. Canary, e.g.
53. Decorative filling
54. Feeling one's ___
55. Decline
56. Extinct bird
58. Gape
60. Roof feature
61. Dinner course
62. Wallet items
64. Wrestling pad
66. Hilo strings

ACROSS

1. Summer bloom
6. Skidded
10. Tooth ailment
14. Pasture measures
15. Evergreen
16. Rain unit
17. Young drivers
18. Poker opener
19. Broad valley
20. Old Faithful, e.g.
22. Geese formation
23. Not glossy
25. Fish hawks
29. All of two
30. Crater
33. Waikiki wreath
34. Go on stage
35. "Fried Green ___"
39. That's opposite
41. Durable fabric
42. Summer shades
44. Scholastic
46. Outdo
47. Minor falsehood
48. Hired car
50. Moist
51. Agrees to
55. All possible
57. Not he
58. Shopper's card
61. Cash register
63. Entreat
64. Tales
68. At leisure
69. Roof edge
70. Crown
71. Take five
72. Parodied
73. Back street

DOWN

1. Tub
2. Hard water?
3. Unrefined metal
4. Keep at arm's ___
5. Thing of value
6. Reducing camps
7. Boundary
8. Beginning section
9. Cee's follower
10. State further
11. Long for
12. Like Swiss cheese
13. Fencing swords
21. Not nope
23. Frosting flavor
24. Upstairs catchall
26. Shut hard
27. Teacher's ___
28. Civil uprising
29. Fly swatter?
31. Gossip piece
32. Elixir
36. Certain mineral
37. Cafe customer
38. Like some winters
40. Vault
41. Bankruptcy cause
43. CIA agent
45. Brief swim
49. Garden plot
50. Minute point
51. Moving
52. Scold
53. Prison rooms
54. Remnant
56. Sight
59. Great review
60. Viewed
62. Permitted
63. Jacket or soup
65. Lassie
66. "Car 54, Where ___ You?"
67. Announce

PUZZLE 189

167

PUZZLE 190

ACROSS

1. Forbids
5. Indian garments
10. Bench
13. Descended
14. Disguised
15. Row
16. Rude person
17. College
19. Sherpa sighting
20. Awful
21. Was located
22. Browning, e.g.
24. Naked
27. On a voyage
29. Constitution addition
34. Spanish gala
36. Sailor's consent
37. Meat spread
38. Sharp curve
39. "Gremlins" actress
41. Assessment
42. Sad cry
44. Young bug
45. Slims down
48. Renovated
51. Charged particles
52. Broil
53. Makes a mistake
55. Young fox
57. Bruised ___
58. Marched
62. Western
66. Transfer
67. Be indebted to
68. Not as fresh
69. Not windward
70. Pixie
71. Short and sweet
72. Dweeb

DOWN

1. Coddle
2. Plant salve
3. Public disorder
4. Lane boundaries
5. "Moonlight ___"
6. Zealous
7. Race, as a motor
8. Incenses
9. Run aground
10. Luau treat
11. Graze
12. Ironic
14. Sugar square
18. Perplex
23. Meal starter
25. Stun with noise
26. Logs
27. Bridal paths
28. Bun seed
30. Dull finish
31. Private ___
32. Cozy place
33. Casual shirts
34. Have cold feet
35. Skin outbreak
40. Have a cold
43. Marinates
46. Manner
47. Mail carrier
49. Most waterless
50. Extent
54. Pride remark
56. Haul
57. Electric fishes
59. Dramatic part
60. Completed
61. Document
62. Hard row to ___
63. Pussycat's pal
64. Stadium zebra?
65. Links figure

ACROSS

1. Served for a point
5. Purposes
9. X marks it
13. Surfer's wish
14. Person receiving money
16. Docile
17. So be it!
18. Whisk
19. Store sign
20. Gets a flat
22. Tahiti, e.g.
24. Two, in Madrid
25. Stumbling block
30. Overseas
31. Teed off
35. Crop
38. Turmoil
40. Shad ___
41. Weakest, as an excuse
43. Foreign ___
45. Stereo component
46. Heaven's gates
50. Selects
51. Ziti, e.g.
53. Most festive
55. And so forth
57. Valuable stone
60. Hanks movie
63. Sooty dirt
65. Manners
66. Scratchy
71. Toaster ___
72. "God's Little ___"
73. Blender setting
74. Fold up
75. Keg's contents
76. Workout locales
77. Stops

DOWN

1. Grant
2. Small role
3. Not odds
4. Auto mishap mark
5. Times of good fortune
6. Carpenter's blade
7. Look over
8. Glimpse
9. Taken illegally
10. Mama's mate
11. Forewarning
12. Take care of
15. Long tale
21. Tearful moan
23. Clean ___
26. Cruel person
27. Beau, to Lloyd
28. Sailor
29. Grape drink
30. Monkey's kin
32. Grasp
33. Origin
34. Appetites
35. Thunder noise
36. Tibetan holy man
37. Small devils
39. Wilier
42. Quarrels
44. Received
47. Stone or Bronze
48. Squealer
49. Soap ingredient
52. Ridiculer
54. Hang loosely
56. Fragment
57. Donated
58. Edit text
59. Repairs
60. Mop
61. Rate of progress
62. Old stringed instrument
64. Housecoat, e.g.
67. Yank
68. Wail
69. Dress bottom
70. Absolutely!

PUZZLE 191

PUZZLE 192

ACROSS

1. Chew on
5. Trombone's kin
9. Dog-paddle
13. Loll
14. Hackneyed
15. Ocean surge
16. ___ Office
17. Stay
18. Pipe types
19. River deposit
20. Excessively
21. Shovels
23. Date frequently
24. Sandal
26. Brownie
27. Burglar's target
29. Perfect serve
31. Demon
34. "___ It Be Me"
36. Versed in
37. Expensive eggs
38. Soy product
41. Sultan's bevy
43. Sutured
44. Entirety
45. Verb's partner
46. Have dessert
48. ___ culpa
49. Possessive pronoun
50. Harmony
53. In-between
55. Taken ___ (surprised)
59. Prior to, in poetry
61. Stage whispers
64. Time
65. Cha et al.
66. Tarzan's transport
67. Refuge
69. Bookies' concerns
70. Russian saint
71. Broker
72. Expunge
73. Sweater material
74. Shed feathers
75. Sonnets' kin

DOWN

1. Luster
2. Sea forces
3. Blooming shrub
4. Raised bruise
5. Forbidden
6. Labor group
7. Defective
8. Malt beverages
9. Diamond feat
10. Uncontrolled blaze
11. At rest
12. Confusion
14. English city
22. Hammer end
24. Casual shirt
25. Open widely
28. Winter ill
30. Draw near
32. Cut the fescue
33. Coop
35. Commandment start
36. Coffeepot
38. Round cap
39. Toledo shout
40. Pinkish bird
42. Halo
43. Boar's pad
45. Bump
47. Implore
51. Vital
52. Rocking bed
54. Flawless
56. Cut on an angle
57. Kin of ain't
58. "You ___ Hurry Love"
60. Sibilant sounds
61. Openly admit
62. Storage tower
63. Farce
65. Hubbub
68. Back in time

FLOWER POWER

The answers to this petaled puzzle will go in a curve from the number on the outside to the center of the flower. Each number in the flower will have two 5-letter answers. One goes in a clockwise direction and the second in a counterclockwise direction. We have entered two answers to help you begin.

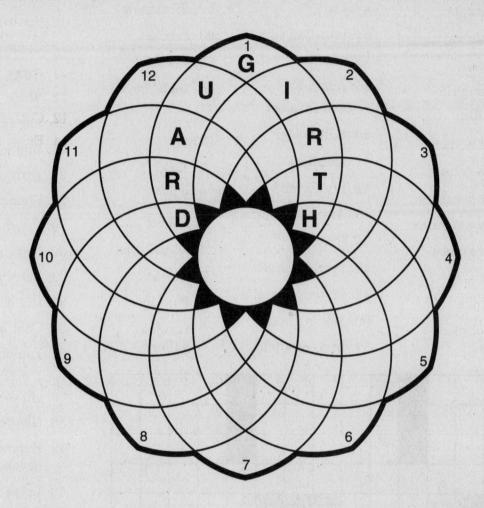

CLOCKWISE

1. Circumference
2. Observe
3. Sects
4. Dim
5. Sail poles
6. Chowhound
7. Gypsy's card
8. Refresh
9. Biblical king
10. ___ Haute
11. Fortify
12. Bee and Em

COUNTERCLOCKWISE

1. Protect
2. Show pain
3. A la ___
4. Mongrels
5. Soil covering
6. Everyone's mother?
7. Assignments
8. Tattered
9. Toast word
10. Caruso's pitch
11. Artist's cap
12. Bow's partner

PUZZLE 194

ON A MISSION

ACROSS

1. Foot digits
5. Certain rays
10. Inspire
14. Knitting rib
15. Gratify
16. "GWTW" home
17. Shrub genus
18. Bottle measure
19. Waste allowance
20. Jason's quest
23. Trick
24. Faux pas
25. Man of many words
28. Valleys
31. Fit
32. First reader
34. Group
37. Ponce de Leon's quest
40. Ball holder
41. Manifest
42. Ivy, for one
43. Arabian ruler
44. Bristles
45. Feather shaft
48. Plated animal
50. Moses's quest
57. Irish republic
58. Billiard shot
59. Province
60. Mr. Kazan
61. Foreign
62. Stratagem
63. Brocket
64. Leases
65. Dads' boys

DOWN

1. Jerk
2. Vow
3. Robert ___
4. Ocean color
5. Chimes
6. Pass by
7. London gallery
8. "___ o'clock scholar"
9. Feudal worker
10. Mentions
11. More scarce
12. Spain's El ___
13. Consumer
21. Away
22. Wary
25. Log float
26. English horn
27. Epoxy
28. Beanery
29. Coach Stagg
30. Not right
32. Liver paste
33. ___ of passage
34. Coat and pants
35. Famous volcano
36. Quaker word
38. Gentler
39. Extends beyond
43. Loom
44. Gloomy
45. Peel's partner
46. Andean country
47. High nest
48. Black-ink item
49. Hammer parts
51. Persian poet
52. Buck or rooster
53. The doctor ___
54. Woody's kid
55. Electric sign
56. Month units

ACROSS

1. Boo's cousin
5. Sign a sublease
10. ___ we forget
14. Lotion ingredient
15. Outcast
16. Exchange premium
17. Boxing brawls
19. Ford's running mate
20. Confucian belief
21. Take out
22. Rendezvous
24. Maintained
25. Table section
26. Red birthstone
29. Sheets, e.g.
33. Kauai cookout
34. Roman bard
36. January, in Juarez
37. Of certain poems
38. Long crest
40. Cultivate
41. Basins
43. ___ there, done that
44. Icelandic saga
45. Conforming to convention
47. A milk cow
49. Gabor and Peron
50. Puts down turf
51. Pekoe pouch
54. 53, to Caesar
55. Kiwi kin, once
58. Greek peak
59. Gardening talent
62. Indigo source
63. Related maternally
64. Catchall abbr.
65. Dispense
66. Chanced
67. Only

DOWN

1. Sword handle
2. Pelvic bones
3. Mediocre
4. Ready
5. Sensory nerve cell
6. Rejoice
7. Cycle or guard
8. Fantasy figure
9. Analyzed
10. Sponge cakes
11. They're inflatable
12. River deposit
13. Piggies
18. ___ fixe
23. Chest sound
24. Slow pitch
25. Cliff shelf
26. Luster
27. Check accounts
28. Savings day?
29. Waited
30. Hackers
31. Lose ground
32. Absolutely not!
35. Xylophones' kin, for short
39. Forbade
42. Hindu deity
46. Turned sharply
48. Crop film
50. Before ocho
51. Warty critter
52. Medieval serf
53. Far East
54. Goneril's father
55. Silent
56. Poet Khayyam
57. Fit
60. Genetic letters
61. Bottom line?

HANDIWORK

PUZZLE 196

OO LA LA

ACROSS

1. Present
5. Photog Adams
10. Tragic king
14. In a lazy way
15. Coconut product
16. 43,560 square feet
17. Enlist again
18. Brittle
19. Slim
20. Puccini opera
22. Overseas
24. October gem
25. Meadow
26. Soldier's lodging
30. Transform
34. Locales
35. Explosion
37. Mr. Sikorsky
38. Loot
39. Andean climber
40. Chills and fever
41. Absolutely, senor
42. Over-50 gp.
43. Cigar
44. Having contact
46. Sawyer and Keaton
47. EMT's action
48. Eastern European
50. Melodic
53. Quixote's birthplace
58. City on the Rhine
59. Slanders
61. Emerald Isle
62. Finch, e.g.
63. Blockade
64. Mailed
65. Mr. Kazan
66. Ford flop
67. French head

DOWN

1. Female
2. Concept
3. Blooper
4. Memo error
5. Take
6. "___ Rae"
7. Hawker's line
8. Hesitant sounds
9. Julio Iglesias song
10. Verdi opera
11. Resound
12. Met show-stopper
13. Separate
21. Readies soil
23. Mr. Franklin
26. Low voices
27. Crocodile Hunter
28. Fewest
29. Another name for the "Mona Lisa"
30. Free ticket
31. Goad
32. Reddener
33. Deuce beaters
35. Bland
36. Rowboat blade
39. Wisconsin city
43. Hindu deity
45. Raises
46. Maiden
48. Swerves
49. Roomy
50. French clergyman
51. Disturb
52. Cross inscription
54. Roost
55. Early Canadian
56. Glimmer
57. Poker wager
60. Top

PUZZLE 197

• Film Wizardry •

ACROSS

1. Twine
5. UV absorber
9. IM's kin
14. Lotion additive
15. Israeli airline
16. Insect stage
17. Path?
20. Reliable
21. Map graphic
22. Half a pair
23. Egyptian skink
25. Fudd, e.g.
27. Proposal
30. Altar slab
32. She's kin
36. Beast
38. "My country, ___ . . ."
40. Brit's pen
41. Quest trio?
44. Lane's love
45. ___ League
46. Ms. Brennan
47. Revoke
49. Road turns
51. "CSI" clue
52. Shortly
54. Church part
56. 6-pt. plays
59. Carries
61. More likely
65. Occupation?
68. Accustom
69. RVs' kin
70. Take out
71. Zsa Zsa ___
72. Craving
73. Signing pioneer

DOWN

1. Low isles
2. Toast topper
3. Tumble
4. "Ryan's Hope" role
5. Chapel seat
6. Cretaceous division
7. Cowshed
8. Mr. Cooke
9. Maryland city
10. Deface
11. Buck chaser?
12. Dr. Pavlov
13. Burden
18. "___ Out"
19. Co. VIP
24. Part of India
26. Basil's "Watson"
27. Rum cake
28. "The Lady ___"
29. Ms. Keaton
31. Remains
33. Having pinnae
34. Spelling bee?
35. Aleera, in "Van Helsing"
37. Wee bugs
39. Soak
42. Momentous
43. Toyota rival
48. Raise
50. Obis
53. Tic-tac-toe win
55. Lyric poem
56. Sprig
57. Ms. Merrill
58. Pencil end
60. ___, Brute?
62. Capture
63. Cigar end?
64. Famed Korean
66. ___-Magnon
67. Is: Fr.

PUZZLE 198

HORSIN' AROUND

ACROSS
1. European range
5. Aid a crook
9. Walk heavily
13. Blooper
17. Pants part
18. Mete (out)
19. Ferris wheel, e.g.
20. Totem ___
21. ___ of Man
22. Roddy McDowell horse film
25. Attacked
27. "The ___ Tattoo"
28. Formal solos
29. Chunk of eternity
30. Outlaws
31. Coastal eagle
33. Crouch
36. Top fighter pilot
37. Pirate's quest
41. Dumbo's wings
42. Venture
44. Mideast native
45. Stephen or Peggy
46. Actress Carol ___

47. Troubles
48. Roman judge
49. Recipe amts.
50. Determine
52. Totally confused
53. Browned bread
54. Mickey Rooney horse film, with "The"
58. ___ lazuli
61. Individuals
62. Takes
66. Release
67. Scruffs
69. Expedition
70. Cry of discovery
71. ___ King Cole
72. Kitchen tool
73. Acorn producers
74. Gloomy
75. Ireland's emblem
77. Misstate
78. Cleanse
79. Hankerings
80. Soft cheese

81. Mas' guys
82. Fragment
85. 100 centavos
86. Scrabble pieces
90. Elizabeth Taylor horse film
94. Red-pencil
95. Forearm bone
96. Writer James ___
97. Roof feature
98. Relay ___
99. Well-behaved
100. Knell
101. Move slightly
102. Diving duck

DOWN
1. Sale condition
2. In order to avoid
3. ___ Alto
4. Sound systems
5. Promo writers
6. Woody ___ of "Cheers"
7. Santa's staffer
8. Apartment balcony
9. Push against
10. Stripe
11. Puzzling

12. ___ Leppard
13. Steeples
14. Geometry points
15. Actress Chase
16. Pod dwellers
23. Actress Skye
24. Kauai porch
26. Floor cleaner
30. Candy units
31. Of a time
32. Mr. Auberjonois
33. Scorch
34. Narrative
35. Food scraps
37. Court event
38. Sky bear
39. Cong. members
40. Bridge position
42. La Scala singer
43. Mr. Guinness
44. Hunches
47. "___ Fair"
48. Actor Rob ___
49. Manner
51. Final bio.
52. "Lou Grant" lead
53. Tick ___
55. Russian penny
56. Sweet singer

57. Sherbets

58. Contact ___

59. Indian nanny

60. Hummus holder

63. Inadequate

64. Criminal

65. Painful

67. Midday

68. Crescents

69. Container weight

72. Philosophy

73. Baltimore team

74. Long overcoats

76. Abundant

77. Gaelic

78. Butter serving

80. Slanting edge

81. "___ Pan"

82. Comfy

83. Angelic headwear

84. ___ time

85. Petition

86. Name on jeans

87. Dutch cheese

88. Food staple

89. Hearty meat dish

91. Short rest

92. Become mature

93. Barrel

PUZZLE 198

PUZZLE 199

MISSING LYRICS

ACROSS

1. Capitol cover
5. CEO, for one
9. Herald
13. Sandwich meat
16. Sermon response
17. Sills or Fleming
18. ___ down (subdued)
19. Athens vowel
20. "There'll be blue ___ the White Cliffs . . ."
22. Assuages
23. Yale nickname
24. Tankard's cousin
25. Is in hock
27. Politician Quayle
28. Holiday drink
30. Leans
32. Old hat
34. Portland's locale
37. Itsy-bitsy
38. Enraged
40. Moon-lander acronym
41. ___ leather
43. Dog's foot
47. British lockup
49. Loop
50. Choir member
52. Relieve
53. Newspaper story
55. Through
56. Sides
59. Mischievous one
60. Leaves
64. Lobbying gp.
65. Bar chairs
68. Tool assortment
69. Down-under sight
73. Relatives
74. Baker's requirement
76. Question starter
78. Tofu source
79. Motivate
82. Stadium sound
84. "Safe" caller
85. Price
86. Room or wear
87. Dominates
89. Twirler's item
92. Forks out
94. Dine in the evening
95. Olympic flame lighter
96. African fox
97. Now
101. Masculine title
102. Dwelling unit
105. "Oh Stewball was a ___"
109. Eisenhower, to friends
110. Pricker
111. He was Terrible
112. Singer Young
113. Brown or Paul
114. Irritated
115. Glory
116. Substitute

DOWN

1. Bits
2. Disregard
3. Scant
4. Conclusion
5. Nigerian native
6. Fourteen, to Nero
7. First lady
8. "Here we come a-___"
9. Crow
10. Switch settings
11. Welsh river
12. Asner and Ames
13. Pays attention
14. Book of maps
15. Orono's state
18. Itty-bitty
21. Busybody
26. Wish for
29. Knot
30. British gun
31. Filter
32. ___ se
33. Sweet drink
34. Russian saint
35. Admiral or guard
36. "You're not the only one with mixed ___"
39. Housetop
42. Tethered
44. "___ and few are the moments . . ."
45. Bit of land
46. Dict. entries
48. It's chauffeured
50. Tune
51. Dead lang.
54. Noncommissioned off.
55. Large container
57. Inclined
58. Train units
61. Augment, of old

178

62. Wrestling move

63. Fly

65. Take to the slopes

66. Canister

67. Kind

70. Pierces

71. Flower cluster

72. Occurs, of old

75. Peace symbols

76. "I ___ I'll ever see you again"

77. Ponderosa guy

80. Expert

81. Actor McKellen

82. Coop denizens

83. Adolescent

86. Atomic particle

88. Soup tools

89. Aromatic herb

90. Identical

91. Grows weary

93. Father

98. Sketched

99. Vietnam's continent

PUZZLE 199

100. Sharp, shrill cry

102. Piggy-bank deps.

103. Eureka!

104. Likewise not

106. A Gardner

107. Machine part

108. Chemical suff.

PUZZLE 200

NAMESAKES

ACROSS
1. Canal boat
6. Boring tool
9. Meat paste
13. He loves, to Cato
17. Embellish
18. Rage
19. Burden
20. ___ Scotia
21. Unbranded-calf namesake
24. Gorilla-expert Fossey
25. Fencer's weapon
26. Declare
27. Responsive movement
29. Fur pieces
31. Oceans
32. Cleverly
33. Affirm
35. Goddess of plenty
36. Norma ___ of "Riptide"
40. Food tidbits
44. Threaded nail
48. Limerick, e.g.
49. Dunks
52. Buckeye State
54. Belgian money
55. Ms. Moorehead
57. Railroad-car namesake
60. Mauna ___
62. Sticky
63. Seventh notes
64. Photo-process namesake
69. Mexican painter Rivera
73. ___ Major
74. Editing term
75. Feudal slave
77. Secondhand
78. Snatches
80. Biblical garden
82. Cartilage
84. "___ Miserables"
86. Resounded
89. British dramatist
93. On vacation
94. Drawer freshener
99. Circus gymnast
100. Individual
102. Top-grade
103. Coal wagon
104. Business-ban namesake
107. Contain
108. Metric measure
109. Sock tip
110. Anesthetic of yore
111. Shadowbox
112. Flip through
113. Eavesdrop
114. Pageant crown

DOWN
1. Diamond features
2. Modify
3. Juliet's guy
4. Porridge
5. Opposite of WSW
6. Goals
7. Tropical fish
8. Flood guards
9. Harbors
10. Black cuckoo
11. Covers snugly
12. Inuit
13. Temperature-scale namesake
14. Slightly wet
15. Applicability
16. Weedy plant
22. Survived
23. Lyric Muse
28. Dozes off
30. Corn portion
34. Math branch
36. Hot spring
37. Pig
38. Hallow follower
39. Women's-costume namesake
41. Ginger or Roy
42. "___ Playing Our Song"
43. Small swallow
45. Jamaican product
46. Memorable period
47. Gained victory
50. Identified
51. Dissolved substance
53. Three strikes
56. Distress letters
58. Mourn
59. Hat

180

61. Classifieds

64. Haul

65. Bruins great

66. "Born in the ___"

67. Devoured

68. Hence

70. Superlative ending

71. Harden

72. Verse form

76. California city

79. Belgrade resident

81. Stair post

83. Ore. neighbor

85. Munchies

87. Insertion marks

88. Mint-family herb

89. Promises

90. Fragment

91. Call to a diva

92. Moral

93. Cook's smock

95. Saguaros

96. Commotion

97. Register

98. Aquarium creature

101. Comply with

105. ___ mode

106. Although

PUZZLE 200

PUZZLE 201

RANDOM RANKS

ACROSS

1. Sheet of cotton
5. Boot liner
8. Globule
12. Tiger's gp.
15. Grades K-12
16. UN agency
17. Leaf part
18. Opener for two Tins?
19. To be, in Toulon
20. Military lullaby?
22. "Whose Life ___ Anyway?"
23. Separate
24. The press
27. Winchester, e.g.
28. Sunbeam
29. Woodworking tool
30. Pinnacle
32. Challenger
35. Sharp projections
37. Chants
41. From ___ Z
42. Sierra ___
44. Guided vacation
46. Storytelling dance
47. Me

49. Spot before home
51. Position
52. Craftsperson
54. This, in Toledo
55. Nursery on high
56. Like a fiddle
57. Diagram
59. Imus or King
60. Banes
63. Scaloppine meat
64. Exasperating
68. Longing
69. On a ___ basis
72. Large ratites
73. Sufficient, to a bard
74. Eternal City
75. Of fatty acid
77. Trig units
78. An archangel
80. Agitated state
81. Give a view
83. Norse poetry
84. Computer nickname

85. Mom of "Rhoda"
86. Queried
89. Automatic habit
95. Mag. font
96. She, in Seville
98. "September ___"
99. Telephone abbr.
100. Go bad
101. Pause
102. Shad's output
103. Virginia willow
104. Vocalize
105. Detect
106. Taxing mo.
107. Plushy

DOWN

1. Complaint
2. Type of clarinet
3. Via, for short
4. ___ del Fuego
5. Brief and forceful
6. Cupid's wings
7. "Bad boys" program
8. Sudden assault
9. Misplace
10. Sapporo sash
11. Stake
12. Collegian's teach

13. "Brown Eyed ___"
14. Opening wager
21. Veteran
23. Cole Sear had it
25. Towering
26. Clio winners
27. Animated Chihuahua
30. Cheer
31. Whittle
32. Tabula ___
33. Road to the Forum
34. Electrical unit
35. Sportscaster Madden
36. Black bird
38. Sorry one
39. Tien Shan mountains
40. Gratify
43. Coup d'___
44. Recipe amt.
45. Inauguration vow
48. Superfluous one
50. Handed out
53. Monica, to Ross
55. Thumbs up!
57. Heart of the wheat

182

58. Demolish, in Soho

59. Three: Ger.

60. Wharf

61. Alcohol burner

62. Old English poet

63. "Twelfth Night" character

64. "___ a man . . ."

65. Everywhere: pref.

66. Atomic particle

67. Latin verb

69. Mr. Rogers

70. Sarge, for one

71. Baba of legend

76. Symphony ending

79. Increase

80. Pouch

82. Regional speech

84. Substantial

85. Secret

86. Pretensions

87. Greek porch

88. Houston suburb

89. Chemise

90. Mrs. Charles

91. Dismiss

92. Doing

93. Underwater barrier

94. Part of QED

96. Meadow mower

97. Song syllables

PUZZLE 201

183

PUZZLE 202

LITERARY GENTS

ACROSS
1. Wheat ___
5. Axioms
11. Appropriate
14. Judge's field
17. Lily species
18. Monkey treat
19. Kingston coll.
20. Shout of surprise
21. Thurber's daydreamer
23. More savage
25. Patella
26. Constantly, to Keats
28. Cracker type
29. Resistance unit
30. Dreadful
33. Shipshape
34. Jetsons' dog
37. Imagine!
38. Realm
41. Moos
42. Soldier's lodging
45. Dismissal
48. Inventor Whitney
49. Cohort
50. Assail abusively
52. Big fuss
53. Regulate
55. Ceramics powder
56. Sparrows, e.g.
58. Sporty sock
60. Hit-or-miss
62. Saturate
65. Mantel
67. Clutched
71. Bambi's mother
72. Highest point
74. Slender nail
75. Ginger ___
76. Jumbled puzzle
78. Vanquish
80. Creek
81. Open, as a jacket
83. Climbing plant
84. Of musical pitch
85. Gymnast Korbut
87. ___ public
90. Illuminated
91. 14th president
94. Energy measure
95. Rewards
99. Subjugate
101. Lewis's preacher
104. Loosen (jute)
105. Brooch
106. Evening party
107. Dizzy or James
108. "Roses ___ Red"
109. Stale
110. Sabers
111. Cathedral section

DOWN
1. Rubberneck
2. Vivacity
3. Audition aim
4. Space rocks
5. Carpenter Norm ___
6. Humid
7. Cuckoo species
8. Gangster's gun
9. Door sign
10. Speaker
11. ___ Wiedersehen
12. Snob
13. Seating section
14. Scott's romancer
15. Leading
16. Groveling
22. Mimic
24. Proportion
27. Disburden
30. Devout
31. Hooter
32. Wilde's age-fearer
34. A Baldwin brother
35. Fly alone
36. Look-alike
37. Miller's salesman
39. Crooner Torme
40. Resembling a protozoan
42. Internet diary
43. Prior to, in verse
44. ___ Haute
46. Find a sum
47. "___ Amigos"
49. Unpaid debts
51. Latin way
54. Sigma's follower
55. Capitulated
57. Scamp
59. Drumstick

61. Phooey's kin

62. Writer Tarbell

63. Calendar abbr.

64. Wren's legionnaire

66. ___ whiz!

68. Pang

69. Jazzy Fitzgerald

70. Wooded valley

73. "Peter ___"

74. Covey

77. Knot

79. Pine tree

80. Circular hall

82. "Annabel Lee" poet

84. Tuneful Turner

85. Puccini work

86. Passenger vessel

88. Ringlet

89. Incandescent

90. Theater boxes

92. Guitar attachment

93. Rotten

95. Reared

96. Footfall

97. Stages

98. "Auld Lang ___"

100. Conclude

102. "O Sole ___"

103. Foul up

1	2	3	4	■	5	6	7	8	9	10	■	11	12	13	■	14	15	16
17				■	18						■	19			■	20		
21				22							■	23			24			
25						■	26		27		■	28						
■	■		29			■	30	31			■	32			33			
34	35	36		■	37			■		38		39	40			■	■	
41				42			■	43	44	■	45					■	46	47
48			■	49			■	50		51			■	52				
53			54			■	55				■	56	57					
■	■	58			■	59		■	60			61		■	■			
62	63	64		■	65			66		■	67			■	68	69	70	
71			■	72	73			■	74				■	75				
76			77			■	78		79			■	80					
■	81				■	82		■	83		■	84						
85	86			■	87		88	89		■	90			■	■	■		
91			92	93	■	94		■		95			■	96	97	98		
99				100	■	101		102	103				■					
104		■	105		■	106					■	107						
108		■	109		■	110				■	111							

PUZZLE 203

FICTIONAL TRAVEL

ACROSS

1. Tots up
5. Survives
10. Turf
15. Etna's output
19. Lothario
20. Anticipate
21. More wan
22. "Rock of ___"
23. Columnist Quindlen
24. "Common Sense" author
25. Cager Houston
26. Central or Hyde
27. Birch is one
28. Actor Josephson
30. Transport in "A Star Is Born"
32. Holy Scripture
34. Of few words
36. Modernize
37. Steam bath
39. Treasure cache
41. "___ By Your Man"
44. Pulled
46. Lofty
48. Office holders
49. Calendar abbr.
52. Joule's kin
53. Gridiron ref
55. Shabby
57. Allot
58. Author Angelou
60. Overturn
62. Fannie or Ginnie
63. Streisand costar
64. Role for Liz
66. Certain poplar
68. Molasses cookie
69. Transport in "Return of the Jedi"
74. Transport on "Bonanza"
76. Persuasive
77. Scrapes
79. Live and pin
80. Harbingers
81. Female GI
82. Packed away
85. Actor Jannings
89. Charter
90. To wit
92. Put forth
94. Caviar, e.g.
95. Superlative ending
96. Sixty secs.
97. Mia Hamm's sport
99. ___ swiss
101. Upset
103. Polish
104. Unbound
105. September bloom
108. Surfaced
110. Temple area
112. Transport in "Meet Me in St. Louis"
115. Spell out
118. Auto-repair place
121. Swiped
122. 1931-32 Best Actress
124. Sault St. ___
125. Convey
126. Boxer's boundary
127. Hockey hall
128. Protection
129. Bahrain bigwig
130. Newspaper page
131. Slogged
132. Connery and Penn
133. Take ten

DOWN

1. Syria native
2. Through
3. Transport on "Baywatch"
4. Very hot
5. Jacket flap
6. Apprised
7. Leave port
8. Ginger portrayer
9. Howling monkey
10. Mineral spring
11. "If These ___ Could Talk"
12. Confederates
13. Twenty quires
14. Bond foe
15. Slipped
16. Anew
17. French novelist
18. Lopsided
29. Doohickeys
31. Footed vases
33. "Diamonds & Rust" singer
35. Aft
37. Arise
38. Emanation
39. Field cover
40. Gather
42. Span
43. Even one
45. Perceive
47. Director Sidney ___
49. Alabama city
50. Garret
51. Fangs
54. Lout
56. Polynesian force
57. Dour
59. Stress
61. Back muscles, for short
63. Guitar part
65. SLR part
67. Ahem's kin
68. Bull or bare
69. Tally

186

70. Apple and pear, e.g.

71. Broker

72. A Saroyan

73. Confronts

75. Exits

78. Prepared emotionally

81. Die down

83. Begin a run

84. Modeled

86. Transport in "Tin Cup"

87. Charles or Burl

88. Fill the hull

90. Zilch

91. Defeat

93. Blockhead

96. Stick in the mud

98. Movie houses

100. Wedding gift

101. Smelled (of)

102. Hauled by cart

105. Dome player

106. Condescend

107. Metaphor, e.g.

109. Actress Worth

110. Charged particle

111. Rude looks

113. Become less hostile

114. "___ Mia"

116. Cab client

117. "My Friend ___"

119. American inventor

120. Cheeky

123. Woeful

PUZZLE 203

PUZZLE 204

SAN FRANCISCO

ACROSS

1. Down source
6. ___ Thomas
11. English composer
15. Med. course
19. ___ suzette
20. Different
21. Urge
22. Singer Amos
23. Portia de ___
24. Lieu
25. Telegraph Hill landmark
27. Frisco shopping district
29. Steep before cooking
30. Entree list
31. Glitches
34. Poppa
35. Of course!
36. Energy unit
39. Invade
41. Chalkboard
43. Cul-de-___
45. Cat talk
47. School gps.
49. Organizes
51. Flock babies
55. Channel
57. Toward the mouth
59. Strips of wood
61. Winnie-the-___
62. Morsel
64. Pupil site
66. Remove slowly
67. Germanic letter
68. This, in Spain
69. Chip with cheese
71. Early show
73. Sunbathe
75. Hippie movement center
79. Chef's meas.
80. Backslide
82. Following
83. Mouth edges
85. Dies ___
86. "___ of Eden"
89. Singer Turner
90. Noses
93. Flat bread
94. Leafy dish
96. Black birds
98. Reach
99. Sows
101. Nat and Natalie
103. Feed the pot
105. Proven
106. ___ Ming
108. Pub servings
110. Saharan
112. Giant slugger
113. Santa's staffer
116. Haul
118. Courtyards
120. Hibernia
122. Thick syrup
125. Waterfront roadway
130. Famous film area
132. Diacritic
133. More certain
134. Profit
135. Actress Adams
136. Uncloudy
137. Fanfare
138. Tolkien talking trees
139. Sample tape
140. Flocks
141. Spools

DOWN

1. Off-white
2. Steel source
3. TV's Arnaz
4. ___ salts
5. Rob or Carl
6. Biting insect
7. Aleutian island
8. Ms. Perlman et al.
9. Finds out
10. Trials
11. Bank abbr.
12. Motel unit
13. Water nymph
14. Spares
15. Like ___ of bricks
16. Not at all
17. Sharp ridge
18. Car parts
26. ___ basin
28. Easy job
32. British lockup
33. Soda sipper
36. Throw off
37. Painter Guido ___
38. Landmark bridge
40. Bold
42. Major ender
44. ___ pants
46. Meshes
48. ___ Jessica Parker
50. Sea World star
52. Hill once known as Parnassus
53. Dog treats
54. Wool giver
56. Tenth
58. Commands
60. Tangles
63. Ridicules
65. Long pole

70. Ancient Roman port
72. Hitching
73. Stumbles
74. Lofty pad
76. Abraham's son
77. Hair tint
78. Intelligence
81. ___-to-wear
84. Verse writer
87. Swine food
88. Actress Shire
91. Tightly drawn
92. Let it stand!
95. Slight hollow
97. Drivers
100. Mambo's kin
102. Limber up
104. Actor Stoltz
107. Evicted
109. Easy as pie, e.g.
111. Pencil topper
113. Roast host
114. "Mean Girls" star
115. Coquette
117. Hollow stone
119. More skilled
121. Draw forth
123. Landers and Jillian
124. Move in water
126. Babylonian storm god
127. Director Kenton
128. Authentic
129. Food scraps
131. New prefix

PUZZLE 204

189

PUZZLE 205

ARNOLD'S FILMS

ACROSS

1. Gentle
5. Not guilty, e.g.
9. Fundamental
14. Floral essence
19. Theater award
20. Rod and ___
21. "A Bell for ___"
22. Mold
23. Arnold's Christmas caper
26. Long-legged bird
27. Emu's kin
28. Writer Levin
29. Sitting above
31. Civil wrong
32. Tiny meas.
33. Grace closer
35. Dome opening
37. Arnold's alien assault
42. Tap lightly
43. Circus worker
44. Pine fruit
45. Estuary
47. Quench
49. South American plain
52. Lawn material
53. "Fiddler on the Roof" role
55. Human trunks

57. Woes
59. Slogan
62. Space or science starter
64. Pottery oven
65. Defense org.
66. Large inn
68. Carnival feature
70. Pet lizards
72. Follower of Dionysus
74. List starter
75. Gentleman
76. Wreaths of leaves
77. Greek god of war
78. Skin prefix
79. Pakistani tongue
80. Harvest crops
82. Showroom model
84. Paddled
87. Benefit
88. Ms. Burstyn
90. Seductress
92. Agnus ___
94. Gin and ___
96. Dutch cheese
98. Relieve (of)
99. Sugar source

100. Vini
102. Father
104. Arnold's soldier story
107. Particle of sand
110. Chip's partner
111. Feel terrible
112. Phoned
113. Name on jeans
115. English brew
117. Achieves
121. Soul
123. Arnold's police picture
126. Heavy ___
127. TV's Linda ___
128. Canal or Lake
129. Apple middle
130. Bean and Penn
131. ___ aves
132. Leading lady
133. Ms. Bennett

DOWN

1. Magic power
2. Wading bird
3. Cloth fuzz
4. Abase
5. Sliced beforehand
6. Actress Remini
7. Wiggly fish
8. "___ Desire"
9. Vacation spot
10. Orange cooler
11. Hindu month

12. Med. course
13. Chicago university
14. Fire remnant
15. Arnold's android actioner
16. Gypsy's card
17. To the left, matey
18. French income
24. Peru's capital
25. Ambush
30. Arnold's weightlifting work
34. Coup d'___
36. Teaching org.
37. Not laptops
38. Space
39. Bike trick
40. Mine deposit
41. Opponent
43. Actress Hatcher
46. Pro vote
48. Keepsake
50. Aircraft
51. Church table
53. Arnold's Martian mission
54. Blunder
56. Ooze
58. Mayday!
60. Arnold's sci-fi shocker
61. Musical sound
63. Greased
67. Former Ford model

69. Portions
71. Army coll.
72. Jacobin leader
73. TV sound
74. ___ Crusader
76. Tote
78. Column type
81. Nautical term
83. Former Russian space station
85. First garden

86. Act
89. Nothing
91. Tokyo, once
93. "Quincy, M.E." actor
95. ER term
97. "The ___ Falcon"
99. Equilibrium
101. More timid
103. Whitetail

105. ___-of-fact
106. Morsel
107. Weight units
108. Indian queen
109. Singer Baker
110. Mideast money
114. "___ Las Vegas"
116. Grows older

117. Concert solo
118. Computer image
119. Edible seaweed
120. Raced
122. Gore and Capone
124. Gene letters
125. Warhol's forte

PUZZLE 206

CHARGE!

ACROSS

1. Cathedral section
5. Doctor's org.
8. Private eye
11. Food items
17. Rejoice
18. Volcanic crater
20. Stick fast
21. Oafish charge
25. Unite, as oxen
26. Baseball's Mel ___
27. Achieve
28. Narrow inlet
29. Afternoon performance
31. Chatty charge
35. Dove and robin, e.g.
37. Truth, once
38. Even if
42. Academy ___
47. Necklace parts
51. Advance charge
55. House of snow
56. African iris
57. Last
58. Burns
59. Gov. branch
60. Guinness's title
61. NYC clock zone
62. Luau dance
64. Soul
66. Inspires anew
71. Toward sunrise
73. Elev.
76. Breakfast food
77. Actress Magnani
78. Scattered
82. Atmosphere
85. Butcher's offering
86. Overthrow
87. Political charge
90. Cultivate again
92. Thwart
93. Examiner
94. Mountain nymph
97. Fall bloom
100. Canine charges
107. Spookiest
111. Ms. Hartmann
112. French painting family
113. Boxer's count
114. Dissolute fellow
116. Leadership charge
122. Hasty glance
123. Game official
124. Conceptions
125. Disco light
126. Storm dir.
127. Lay eyes on
128. Farrago

DOWN

1. Principle
2. Good, in Hindi
3. Frozen rain
4. Timetable info
5. More severe
6. ___ milk
7. Inclusive word
8. Ninth follower
9. Greek muse
10. Chocolate source
11. Delivery truck
12. Actress Lupino
13. Relieved sounds
14. Jacket type
15. Drudge
16. Flower part
17. TV's Tarzan
19. Buenos ___
22. Skipjack
23. Strikes
24. "___ the Woods"
30. Lat. footnote
32. Ad ___
33. Moral
34. Hindu god of love and wealth
36. TV's Thompson
38. Live
39. Units of illumination
40. Glitches
41. Gladden
43. Telegram
44. Money machs.
45. Mob scene
46. ___ and don'ts
48. Unhealthy
49. Bow the head
50. Mayday!
52. Switzerland pass
53. Poetic always
54. Highest
58. Metal refuse
60. Examine
63. Impulses
65. Rhode Island resort
67. Buddhist monks
68. Inactive
69. Maternal relative
70. Sylvan deity
72. Dinner check
73. Competent
74. Merry tune

75. Control

76. System prefix

78. Big ___

79. Mao ___-tung

80. Floor cover

81. Flynn of film

83. Wet dirt

84. Author Ephron

88. Perpetual, poetically

89. Actress Gilpin

91. Microscopic

95. French river

96. Dingy

98. Couch

99. Laughing sound

100. Greek letters

101. Not suitable

102. Los Angeles basketballer

103. Harden

104. Comic DeGeneres

105. Pocahontas's mate

106. ___ it (very well)

108. Rot

109. Bruises

110. Albacores

115. Superman's letter

117. "___ e Leandro"

118. BTO's song?

119. Color

120. Cent. segments

121. That man

PUZZLE 207

Diagramless crosswords are solved by using the clues and their numbers to fill in the answer words and the arrangement of black squares. Insert the number of each clue with the first letter of its answer, across and down. Fill in a black square at the end of each answer. Every black square must have a corresponding black square on the opposite side of the diagram to form a diagonally symmetrical pattern. Puzzles 207 and 208 have been started for you.

ACROSS
1. Poor mark
4. Couple
7. Fired up

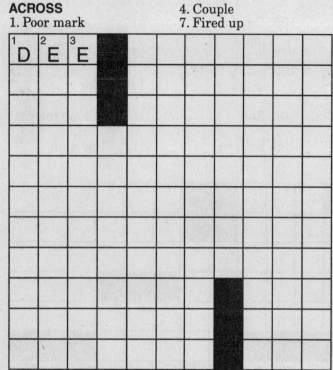

10. Chapter in history, perhaps
11. Green
12. Busy activity
13. Ryan of films
14. Woodcutter's tool
15. Commotion
16. Bounding main
18. Whip
19. Tough
21. Rents
22. Make an exit
24. Head
27. Bug
31. Surrounded by
32. African mammal, shortly
33. Breed of dog
34. Society miss
36. Trip segment
37. Volcanic residue
38. Positive vote
39. Australian bird
40. Determined
41. House shape
42. Canadian whiskey

DOWN
1. Floor models
2. Put up
3. Enthusiastic
4. Daze
5. Floor-shiner
6. Be obliged to pay
7. Punch dipper
8. Fool
9. Forceps
17. Suffered an illness
18. Fruit pulp
20. Knock gently
23. Spoken
24. Fathers
25. Entertain
26. Taut
28. Roofer, sometimes
29. Opponent
30. Scamp
34. Coloring agent
35. Shocking fish

PUZZLE 208

ACROSS
1. A year in Juan's life
4. Tattoo word, perhaps
7. Bounder

8. Right-away acronym
12. Byron's before
13. Individual
14. Constructed
15. Subsequently
17. Round-tripper
18. Sarcastic
21. Flight unit
24. Couch potato's tool
28. Cookie grain
29. ATM code
30. Nourished
31. Rank
33. Seasons on the Seine
34. Different
36. Jargon
40. London transports
44. Skier's tow
45. Debt letters
47. Flock sound
48. Exhaust
49. Doze
50. Tip
51. Gibbon, e.g.

DOWN
1. Future oak
2. Bobbsey twin
3. Shelley offering
4. Voice of Bugs
5. Mouths
6. Encountered
8. I love, in Latin
9. Hammett's Spade
10. Summertime cooler
11. According to
16. Sixth sense
17. Skirt's border
19. Galway natives
20. Family room
21. Mayday!
22. Do knot work
23. Character from Greece
25. O'er and o'er
26. Driving platform
27. Asner and Wynn
29. Place
32. Toddler
33. Go astray
35. Piano exercise
36. ABA dues-payer
37. Baseball stat
38. Needlefish
39. Crude copper
41. Honest fellow
42. Guy
43. Downcast
45. ___ nutshell
46. Alley ___

PUZZLE 209

ACROSS
1. South American rodent
5. Played over
6. Like some ability
7. Clubs and hearts
8. Sweet treat
9. Playwright Shepard
12. Hunger signal
13. Dwindled
15. Plane feature
16. Making clothes
20. Plus
21. Poorest
22. Regard
23. Race timer
26. Tiff
27. Peruses
28. Colleague
29. Reuben bread
30. Pink shade
32. Boston airport
33. Like a clear night
35. Flood protection
36. Calendar's coverage

DOWN
1. Trivial
2. War god
3. Is able to
4. Tiny colonist
5. Foray
6. Breathing organ
7. Warbled
8. Frankness
9. Old sailor
10. Spanish year
11. Cousteau's milieu
12. Pub portion
13. Hope
14. Alleviate
15. Used to be
16. Little ones
17. Curved trajectory
18. Approach
19. Obtain
21. Walk wetly
24. Apiece
25. Method
26. Actor Penn
28. Say grace
30. Apple tool
31. Grimm guy
32. Molten flow
33. Crafty
34. Summer shirt

Starting box on page 562

Throwbacks

PUZZLE 210

You have to throw your mental gears into reverse to play this game. Reading backward there are at least three 4-letter words to be found in each of the longer words. You can skip over letters, but don't change the order of the letters. For example, in the word DECLARE you can find the word RACE reading backward by starting with the next-to-last letter and skipping over the L, but you can't find the word READ without changing the order of the letters.

1. BELUGAS _____ _____ _____

2. BIFEROUS _____ _____ _____

3. OVERFLOW _____ _____ _____

4. MARGINATE _____ _____ _____

5. OPALESCED _____ _____ _____

6. MENDELIAN _____ _____ _____

7. ARBITRAGER _____ _____ _____

8. CONCEPTUAL _____ _____ _____

PUZZLE 211

ACROSS

1. Bits
5. Pate topper
8. Muslim title
11. Begin
12. Marsh bird
13. Of the ear
14. Short letter
15. Dock's site
17. Carried
19. First name in scat
20. Greek porch
21. Intuit
22. Skipped
26. Threaded fastener
27. Away
28. Ano starter
30. Corridor
32. Sock parts
34. Strong alkalis
37. Rely (on)
38. Most eager
41. Wedding attendant
45. Deuce beater
46. Decays
47. Type
48. At any time
49. Charcoal residue
50. Model Carol ____
51. Confiscated property

DOWN

1. Tut's place
2. Mime
3. Floor models
4. Nose
5. Sweltering
6. Have being
7. Viscid substance
8. Bikini, e.g.
9. Ms. Lollo- brigida
10. Statute
12. Perched
13. Escutcheon band
15. Sharp impacts
16. Chicken chow
18. Muck
21. Not a lot
23. Sacred images
24. Levels
25. Aquarium favorite
28. Break bread
29. Stared at
30. Lap pooch
31. Potato bud
32. Religion
33. Discon- tinues
35. Register
36. Tennis stroke
37. Sis's sibs
38. Child
39. Leak slowly
40. Neophyte
41. Two-piece piece
42. Reggae's kin
43. Big bucks, briefly
44. Colony dweller

Starting box on page 562

PUZZLE 212

Categories

For each of the Categories listed, can you think of a word or phrase beginning with each letter on the left? Count one point for each correct answer. A score of 15 is good and 21 is excellent.

	SALAD BAR ITEMS	OCCUPATIONS	POETS	WORLD RIVERS	PHOTOGRAPHY TERMS
C					
L					
O					
N					
E					

ACROSS

1. Diminishes
5. Elevator man
9. County center
10. Actress Lee
11. Scarecrow stuffing
13. Aid in wrongdoing
14. Abraham's wife
16. Texas city
19. Act toward
22. Ambition
25. Having wings
27. Designer Cassini
28. Papal cape
29. Marriage-license info
35. For any reason
36. Physicians, briefly
37. Roman emperor
38. Decay
40. Fixes
43. Closer
47. Corroded
50. Lawn invader
51. Playwright David ____
53. Supplication
54. Tear apart
55. Finch food
56. Arctic slider

DOWN

1. Sibilant sound
2. Wagers
3. Film vamp
4. Kick off
5. Test type
6. Brass bass
7. Ancient road
8. Filled
12. Clash of arms
15. Core
17. Whimsical
18. Some paintings
20. Jai ____
21. Powder base
23. Former soldier
24. Zounds!
26. Legal matter
28. Actor Davis
29. Moving truck
30. List member
31. Weight allowance
32. Isolated
33. Surpass
34. Holy image
39. Lights
41. Beaver's barrier
42. Headliners
44. Player's part
45. Gen. Robert ____
46. Peruse
48. Jannings of films
49. Granular snow
52. Senator Kennedy

Starting box on page 562

Little Puzzler

PUZZLE 214

Place the answers to the clues into the diagram reading across and down, using only the letters given in the LETTERBOX. The answers to each group of clues are in alphabetical order.

LETTERBOX

A A A E E E H I M M O O O P P P R R R S S S T W

ACROSS

Mr. Onassis

Cut down

Swab

Scull

Kitty

Baby carriages

Leaks out

DOWN

Cup handle

Bunny's gait

Larry's crony

Maven

Sample

Iron setting

Cloaks

197

PUZZLE 215

ACROSS

1. Resting place
4. Salary
5. Cargo vessel
6. Viper
9. Rib, e.g.
10. Cognitive
13. Furthermore
14. Win by ____
15. Meander
17. Easy gallop
19. Neighbor of Nevada
22. "Jane ____"
23. Steed breed
24. Reclined
28. Gas-guzzlers
29. Homestead segment
30. Alternative word
31. Warm up
32. Famous loch
36. Athletic event
37. Hypnotic state
39. Chalet feature
43. Lend ____ (listen)
44. Part of rpm
45. Sound system
47. Glazier's item
48. Fine or performance
49. Like some stories
51. Was defeated
52. Be indebted

Starting box on page 562

DOWN

1. Unclad
2. Custard essential
3. Reckon
4. "A Fish Called ____"
5. U2 vocalist
6. Empress Ivanovna
7. Rock
8. Meat pie, to a Brit
9. Candy unit
11. Apiece
12. Sly look
16. Huge painting
18. Tell
20. Sailors
21. Away
23. Tennis term
25. Feel pity
26. Hot under the collar
27. Of recent vintage
33. Periods of time
34. Famous sledder
35. Show contempt
36. No more than
38. Dray
40. To pieces
41. Let off steam
42. Before, in verse
46. Norwegian seaport
47. Model's stance
50. In what way?

PUZZLE 216

End of the Line

For each of the categories listed, can you think of a word or phrase ending with each letter on the right? Count one point for each correct answer. A score of 15 is good, and 21 is excellent.

FAMOUS LOUS OR LOUISES	HOOVED ANIMALS	BROADWAY MUSICALS	LAND FORMATIONS	ASIAN CAPITALS	
					A
					T
					O
					N
					E

198

PUZZLE 217

ACROSS

1. "Fight Club" actor
5. Pointed shafts
8. Gratification
11. Slant
12. Pork piece
14. Grew older
18. Kipling book
19. Lacquered metal
20. Century plant
21. Rodeo rope
25. Delights
27. Gush forth
28. Levee
29. Cobbler's tool
30. Valuable stones
31. Incipient flower
32. Watch winder
34. Steal
37. Nightstand item
38. Vicinity
40. Felicity
45. Second showing
47. Vernacular
48. Abound
50. Michigan's ____ Canals
52. Piggies
53. Put aside
54. Egyptian sun god
55. Gaiety
58. Library habitue
59. Missing

DOWN

1. Evening clothes?
2. Golfer's choice
3. Sit in judgment
4. Huck's pal
6. Mark from a blow
7. Busybody
8. Large deer
9. Broadway's Simon
10. Cash drawer
13. Required
14. Flu symptom
15. Long-jawed fish
16. Eden inhabitant
17. ____ Moines
20. Solicits
22. Resort of sorts
23. Do needle-work
24. Hooter
26. Intend
30. Chewy substance
31. Lourdes lids
32. Take a dip
33. Hamilton bill
34. Train unit
35. Bauxite or galena
36. Apiece
37. Group of poems
39. Spartan
40. Smash
41. Commotion
42. Dessert option
43. Fabric junction
44. Cut off
46. Lunchtime, often
49. Nothing more than
51. Prov. in Canada
54. So be it!
56. Joplin composition
57. Wedding response

Starting box on page 562

Tiles

PUZZLE 218

Imagine that these Tiles are on a table, each tile showing a 2-letter combination. Can you rearrange these Tiles visually to form a 10-letter word?

PUZZLE 219

ACROSS

1. Pi's follower
4. Israeli seaport
6. Optimistic
8. Spanish two
11. Coolidge, to friends
12. Bump hard
14. Quick snooze
17. Bird of prey
18. State further
19. Paul Bunyan's tool
20. Dipstick coating
21. Captivate
24. To wit
27. Checkered vehicle
28. Joust
29. Japanese coin
30. Athenian vowel
31. Potent
34. Motorist's circle
38. Card game of old
39. So-so grade
40. Sings like the Swiss
44. Miserable
47. Bossy's remark
48. Go blond
49. Billboard
50. Savannah
52. Spring-flowering shrub
54. Rhode ___
57. Gained victory
58. Faucet
61. Pouch, in physiology
63. Deface
64. Mouse-sighter's cry?
65. Susan Hayward film
66. Suit accessory
67. Reticent
68. Passed by, as time
72. Lean eater of rhyme
73. Palindromic child

DOWN

1. Hip-hop music
2. Scoot
3. Not working
4. Clutch
5. Ambiance
6. "If I ___ a Hammer"
7. Remiss
8. Forest female
9. Possess
10. Venetian-blind piece
11. Compassionate
13. Fixer
14. Christmas song
15. Become sick
16. Employ busily
22. BLT spread
23. Yoke of ___
25. Model T, e.g.
26. Lion's diet
31. ___ and the Family Stone
32. Excessively
33. Curtain fixture
35. Unreturned tennis serve
36. ___ room (den)
37. But
41. Jannings of "Faust"
42. Balcony section
43. "Moonlight ___"
44. Recommendation
45. Farewells
46. Congeal
49. Went under
51. Obstructs
52. Dazzle
53. Actress Caldwell
55. Nope
56. Dishwasher cycle
59. Lemon quencher
60. Chums
61. Manuscript mark
62. Support
69. Appropriate
70. Specialist
71. Positioned

Starting box on page 562

ACROSS

1. Dandy
4. Astern
7. Rowing items
9. "Days of ___ Lives"
10. Caricature
13. Mends
16. Frank Herbert novel
17. Desperate
20. Sticky stuff
21. Whirling
22. Be next to
23. Hilo wreath
25. Curved bone
27. Deuce
28. Obnoxious plant
31. Splendor
33. Florence's evening
34. Jogged
35. African antelope
36. "What ___ God wrought?"
37. Like the desert
38. Cope
41. Catch
43. "Isn't ___ Lovely?"
44. Convey
45. One-pip card
46. Shoulder ornament
49. Roman avenue
50. Hankering
51. "Gandhi" garb
52. Stare stupidly
54. Hosp. areas
55. Kind
56. Lofty pad
57. Take up, as a skirt
60. Priestly garment
63. Call it quits
64. Ambiance
65. Feathery wrap
66. Among
69. Most brusque
71. Bilge
72. Religious division
76. Black cuckoo
77. Fabulous bird
78. Flail
80. Lira's replacement
81. Do nothing
83. Shaver
85. Lime beverage
86. Birch or pine, e.g.
87. Shifts
89. Teensy particle
91. Finger count
92. Stitch
93. Curse
94. Ogle
97. Made a gull-like sound
99. Game of chance
101. Cattle
102. Lout
103. Grads
105. Massage
108. Got together
109. Ravel
110. Adios!
111. Stomach muscles

DOWN

1. Asta's front limb
2. Granola tidbit
3. Con's counterpart
4. Thumbs up!
5. Mushrooms, e.g.
6. Enlarged duet
8. Fizzy drink
10. Actor's signal
11. Over
12. Bird's beak
14. Matador
15. Fervor
16. He-bee
18. Bewail
19. Carve
21. Rouses from sleep
23. Carpenter's tool
24. Anesthetic gas
26. Ordered
27. Missing-parcel inquiry
29. Boredom
30. ___ citizenship
32. Endure
33. Was in session
38. Irish county
39. TV's Ricky
40. October stone
42. Father
47. 2 x 2 craft
48. Psychic's deck
49. "I Like ___"
53. Windshield cleaner
56. Hardwood
57. Color tone
58. Once, formerly
59. Archimedes's forte
60. Roughened
61. Slacken
62. Tub
64. Tie type
66. Give up, as a right
67. List of names
68. Ceramic slab
70. Roster
72. Collections
73. Discovery cry
74. Embroidery variety
75. Foot digit
79. Assessor
82. Hence
84. Boisterous girls
88. Clinton's instrument
90. Garfield's cry
93. Comfortable
95. Each
96. Slangy sufficiency
98. Prevailed
100. Lacking feeling
104. Sault ___ Marie
106. Lingerie top
107. Smear

Starting box on page 562

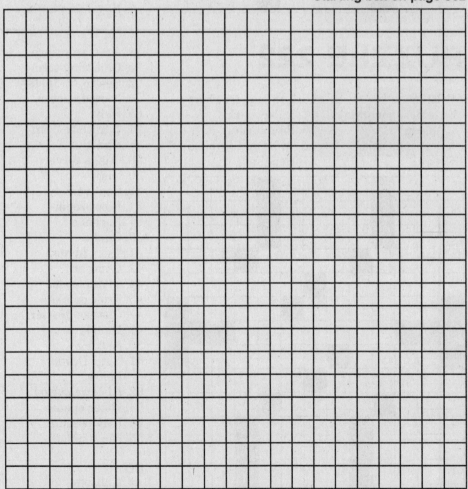

PUZZLE 221

ACROSS
1. Adventure story
5. Association
9. Dove's call
12. Canola and corn
13. Desire
14. Boring device
15. Hubbubs
16. Anticipated
18. Rest
20. Botch it
21. Pave again
23. Highly excited
27. Toy racer
30. Picture
31. Tire input
32. Pricker
34. Sick
35. Covers, as a gift
37. Cowboys' seats
39. Peddle
40. Lamp dweller
41. Wise bird
43. Telegrams
47. Dentist's concern
51. Car for hire
52. Feather stole
53. Clarinet's kin
54. Overlook
55. However
56. Sly glance
57. Fixed charge

DOWN
1. Float aloft
2. Assistant
3. Gooey substance
4. Classify
5. Swift feline
6. Bagel topping
7. Higher of two
8. Brewery output
9. Purring pet
10. Have bills
11. Antique
17. Pack tightly
19. Religious factions
22. Started the day
24. Peggy on "Mannix"
25. Stare rudely at
26. Hardens
27. Cuts lumber
28. Former Italian money
29. ___ hygiene
30. Bombay's nation
33. Cattleman
36. Conspire
38. Creditor's opposite
40. Sphere
42. Lamb's coat
44. Tibetan monk
45. Depart
46. Locale
47. Ease off
48. "___ Send Me"
49. Chow down
50. Tic-tac-___

PUZZLE 222

ACROSS
1. Heidi's mountain
4. Asleep
8. Serpent's noise
12. Rival
13. Lap pup, for short
14. Ruler mark
15. Preschooler
16. "How do I love ___?"
17. Headliner
18. Arabian prince
20. Gambling term
22. Before, to Shelley
23. Narrate again
25. Holy
27. Translate from cipher
29. Coffee servers
30. Gist
32. Coat variety
34. Elbowroom
37. Burdens
39. Quake
41. "___ Abner"
42. Chew on
44. Olympic sled
45. Fruit drinks
47. Clothes presser
49. Dine late
50. Netting
51. "___ Down Below"
52. Historic period
53. Poker opener
54. Play possum
55. Hog's home

DOWN
1. Following
2. Appeared indistinctly
3. Tiny
4. Likely
5. Witnesses
6. ___ out (barely made)
7. Actions
8. That guy's
9. Young doctor
10. Frightens
11. Tear
19. Withdraw
21. Teacup plate
24. Misplacing
26. Kind of embroidery
28. Wiggly fish
31. ABC, NBC, or CBS
32. Lass
33. Most lazy
35. Entertains
36. Custardlike food
37. Andes climber
38. Smell
40. Settle a debt
43. Diva's forte
46. "Ain't ___ Sweet"
48. Once named

202

ACROSS

1. Study hard
5. Thunderous sound
9. Type of race
11. Tour leader
12. Drastic
13. Not present
15. Gloomy
16. Movie backdrop
17. "____ Sharkey"
20. Bit of butter
21. Food fish
23. MacGraw and others
25. Famous frontiersman
27. Peeve
28. Bigfoot's kin
29. Enlightener
33. Friendly nation
34. Rent again
36. Imagine
38. By means of
39. Pipe joint
40. Jackie's second
42. Journey part
45. Crooner Torme
46. First lady
47. Vigoda of "Fish"
48. Thanksgiving vegetable
49. Gab
52. Cooler cubes
54. Commenced
56. Brag
58. Tempo
61. Mascara, for example
65. Stats for Mets
69. Out of the weather
70. Donated
71. Beatty and Sparks
72. Golfer's goal
73. Covered
76. Animal's home
77. Consume a bagel
80. Belfry creature
81. House of Congress
83. Yell
85. Oregon's capital
86. Blouse
87. Tiny particle
88. Bygone days

DOWN

1. Kind of card
2. Vroom the engine
3. Pub orders
4. Female horse
5. Havana's locale
6. "Schindler's ____"
7. Summer drink
8. Writing implement
10. Still
11. Empty space
12. Red-tag event
14. Highway fee
15. Declare
17. Pigeon's purr
18. Mom's man
19. United
22. Actress Susan ____
24. Respectful title
25. Wager
26. Call it quits
27. Male bighorn
29. Yale student
30. Affirmative reply
31. Before, in verse
32. Fam. member
35. Ominous look
37. Very attentive
40. Doctors' gp.
41. Yank's foe
43. Zsa Zsa's sister
44. Sparkler
50. Vital statistic
51. Bandleader Kyser
52. Debtor's note
53. Beanie, e.g.
54. Spelling contest
55. Opposite of pos.
56. Gentle bear
57. Number of toes
58. Seance response
59. Word of lament
60. Mother ____
62. Halfway
63. Mad. or Lex.
64. Barbie's beau
66. Refund
67. Actor West
68. Speedy plane, once
73. Crown of light
74. Bit of news
75. Pol. party member
77. Windy curve
78. "____ Breaky Heart"
79. Small ensemble
82. Singer King Cole
84. Make a faux pas

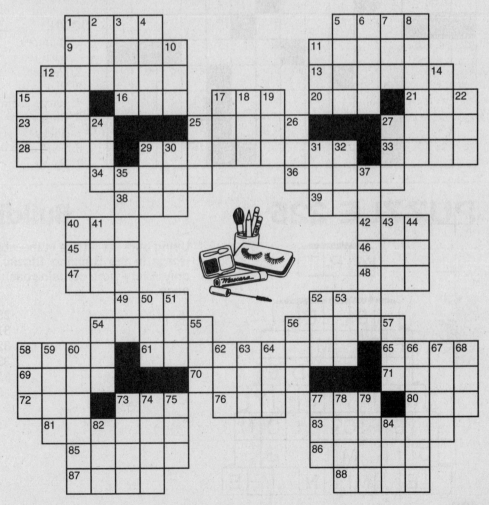

PUZZLE 224

ACROSS

1. Deadly serpents
5. British noblewoman
9. Subways' kin
12. Distort
13. Royal messenger
15. Cut, as branches
16. Wickedness
17. Frozen hanger
18. Hoopla
19. Lily variety
20. Soda-flavoring nut
21. Small drum
23. Canasta card
25. Chubbier
27. Support
30. Mooch
32. Tree-trunk growth
34. Type spaces
35. Allergic reaction
39. Boathouse item
40. More fortunate
43. Cry of disapproval
44. Musical-staff sign
46. Pal of Pooh
47. Term of office
49. Magazine publisher
52. Tiny bits
53. Visionary
56. Poetic twilights
58. 1945 conference site
59. Nomad's abode
61. Holy image
65. Ostrichlike animal
66. Blade holder
68. Roof projection
69. Free (of)
70. Snaky sounds
71. Erupt
72. Get it?
73. Watcher
74. Oodles

DOWN

1. Inspires with fear
2. Collect
3. Prude
4. Large stain
5. Phony ducks
6. Seed coat
7. Pasta
8. Architectural add-on
9. Spiral-horned antelope
10. Cabin
11. Prey's trail
13. Increase
14. Remove errors from
22. Lollapalooza
24. Film spool
26. Beginning
27. Political coalition
28. Irani coin
29. Farm measure
31. Kind of tea
33. Care for
36. Lean against
37. Short-billed rail
38. Tends the garden
41. Respect
42. Harness piece
45. Official decree
48. Most prying
50. Shatter
51. Tenant
53. Colorers
54. Fibrous shrub
55. Escape
57. Old English letters
60. Loosen
62. Guitar device
63. Kiln
64. Breaking story
67. Hurry

PUZZLE 225

Building Blocks

Using only the letters in the word ART, complete the words in the Building Blocks. Words read across only. Every word contains each letter of ART at least once.

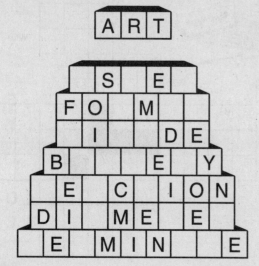

PUZZLE 226

ACROSS

1. Horse gait
5. Mosque priest
9. Form in a mold
13. Bumpkin
14. Pickle marts
16. In ___ of
17. Tons
18. Hogs
19. Oomph
20. Jury member?
21. Country estate
23. Knowl-edgeable
27. Hawaiian porch
30. Pretentious
32. Prod
34. Legal thing
35. Yellowfin, e.g.
37. Flower parts
38. Cookie grain
39. Purple bloomer
41. Crock
42. Most reliable
45. Sky hue
47. Shoe front
48. At hand
49. Convent superior
51. Letter stroke
53. Snatches
54. Escargot
56. Wearing clothes
60. Beijing nanny
63. Golden calves
66. Slick
67. Gray wolf
68. Dissenter
69. Pace
70. Previous
71. Alluring
72. Traipsed

DOWN

1. Web, to a fly
2. Guideline
3. Orchestra instrument
4. Foursome
5. Egos' kin
6. Gull's call
7. Existing
8. Skirt length
9. Make big bucks
10. Be indisposed
11. Ariel's milieu
12. Large cask
15. Market
22. Channel
24. Humor
25. Full-grown
26. Indian princess
28. Modifies
29. Eskimo houses
30. Finds out
31. Insightful
33. East, to Enrique
34. Printing proc.
36. Linen robe
37. ___ diver
40. Wing-shaped
43. Hearing distance
44. Gyrate
46. Decline
50. Accompany
52. Carnival
53. Sphere
55. Fateful date
57. Perjurer
58. Type of saxophone
59. Colored
60. Matterhorn, e.g.
61. Extinct bird
62. Not pres.
64. Villain Luthor
65. Like a fox

Bits and Pieces   PUZZLE 227

Can you identify these hotel terms from the Bits and Pieces shown in the boxes? The first words are always on the top and the second on the bottom.

1.
```
R O O
V I C
```

2.
```
O U B
N C Y
```

3.
```
F R O
E S K
```

4.
```
Y L E
T R Y
```

5.
```
Y M O
U I T
```

6.
```
M P L
K F A
```

7.
```
P O R
T L E
```

8.
```
C K O
I M E
```

PUZZLE 228

ACROSS

1. Drastic
5. Confused
9. Rogers's prop
14. Scent
15. Random try
16. Serving perfectly
17. Inkling
18. On earth
19. Kind of eclipse
20. Boxer Norton
21. Cheek by ___
22. Strong cord
23. Term of affection
25. Wish for
29. Played the leading man
32. Entertainer
35. Oompah horn
36. Scrapes
38. Foot's limb
40. Stopped lying?
42. Unshut, poetically
43. "___ Foolish Things"
45. African antelope
46. Dish wiper
48. Fume
49. Expresses
51. Mysteries
54. Exposes
56. Crazy bird
57. Biblical sibling
60. Impact sound
62. Draw along
65. Storms
67. Nourishing substance
68. Glass unit
69. Insecure feeling
70. Threat's final word
71. Killer whale
72. Irritable
73. Pull dandelions
74. Colorist

DOWN

1. Pier
2. Unemployed
3. Indirect
4. Prior to, in verse
5. Beached
6. Mulligan ___
7. Ahead of schedule
8. Vigoda of "Barney Miller"
9. ___ Vegas, Nevada
10. Future oaks
11. Fodder storage area
12. Break suddenly
13. Fairy-tale meanie
21. Jelly container
24. Significant stages
26. Studio stands
27. Band aid
28. Reddish corrosion
29. Buck
30. Rotates
31. Doze
33. Simple
34. Perch anew
37. Orangutan, e.g.
39. Retrieves
41. James of song
44. Brave sandwich?
47. "___ the ramparts . . ."
50. Best at the job
52. Dodged
53. New England cape
55. Lady's wrap
57. Smell ___ (be suspicious)
58. Destruction
59. Souffle items
61. Flexible tube
63. Previously
64. Wash's partner
66. Messy place
67. Scarcely any
68. Pea abode

PUZZLE 229

Mini-Crosswords

Fill in each of the diagrams with eight different 4-letter words to construct your own crossword puzzles. Only common English words are allowed. You may repeat letters as often as you wish.

1.
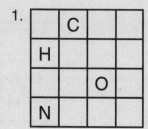

2.
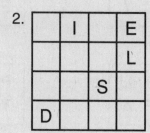

3.
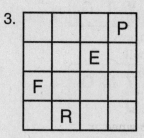

BRICK BY BRICK

PUZZLE 230

Rearrange this stack of bricks to form a crossword puzzle. The clues will help you fit the bricks into their correct places. Row 1 has been filled in for you. Use the bricks to fill in the remaining spaces.

ACROSS

1. Plod heavily
   Amazed
   Clay brick
2. Drifter
   Horseback
      game
   Cycled
3. Poetic black
   Dealer's tip
   Sinned
4. Planting plot
   Never a
5. Belongs to us
   Augmented
6. Lofty
   Warbler, to a
      Brit
7. Condiment
      root
   Grows
      mature
   Soccer's
      Hamm
8. Bother
   Honey
      badger
   Bilk
9. Sock end
   Heap
   Protection
10. Betrayals
    Busy insects
11. Tooth pain
    Inner hand
12. Lip
    Nobility
13. Computer
       missive
    Impersonator
    Fables
14. Shrewd
    Spoiled kid
    Amend text
15. Yonder
    Cola, e.g.
    18-wheeler

DOWN

1. "___ So Cold"
   Cleverness
   Faction
2. Stud site
   Gypsy's deck
   Asian nanny
3. Band
      instrument
   Interrogator
   Cooking herb
4. Venice transport
   Not as difficult
5. Dutch export
   Boot liner
   Caustic stuff
6. More suitable
   From Cork
7. Of forests
   Burn soother
   Toning targets
8. Large deer
   Like a hot
      cereal
   Ace
9. Bambi's mother
   Advantage
   Widen
10. Ships' spines
    Chief artery
11. Lincoln
       nickname
    Golfer
       Ernie ___
    Skillfully
12. Folk-dance skirt
    Women
13. Edible pod
    Roast host
    Metallic vein
14. Pilsner or lager
    Mob scenes
    Clip
15. Crosscurrent
    "___
       Wednesday"
    Bigfoot's cousin

BRICKS

| E A S | ■ ■ R | D ■ ■ | K E D | ■ ■ R |
| A C H | A P E | S ■ E | R E D | ■ P I |

| D I T | L T Y | E R ■ | Y O D | E S ■ |
| E M I | O R E | M I A | ■ A G | ■ ■ ■ |

| S ■ ■ | A T E | S E E | H O B | S A S |
| ■ I L | L E ■ | ■ ■ ■ | E B O | E M A |

| L ■ ■ | B R A | A R Y | C A G | ■ B E |
| S A F | S O D | ■ ■ ■ | T H E | A L M |

| ■ B I | E L L | E Y ■ | O ■ P | D B E |
| ■ E R | E S ■ | R E ■ | N ■ T | O U R |

| ■ T R | O N S | I R K | O L O | O Y A |
| ■ ■ ■ | E ■ P | T O E | O K E | R ■ L |

| T ■ E | L L ■ | C O N | ■ ■ N | ■ T A |
| A ■ S | A B I | E T Y | K E D | W A S |

DIAGRAM

	1	2	3	4	5	6	7	8	9	10	11	12	13	14	15
1	S	L	O	G	■	A	W	E	D	■	A	D	O	B	E
2															
3															
4															
5															
6															
7															
8															
9															
10															
11															
12															
13															
14															
15															

207

PUZZLE 231

ACROSS
1. Redden
6. Biblical book
10. Strong desire
14. Lovers' lane?
15. Hard metal
16. Salon treatment
17. Smudge
18. Law
19. Picket-line crosser
20. A Spelling
21. Egg concoction
23. Jungle swinger
24. Bellow specialty
26. Jeans closer
28. Aardvark's snack
31. Write
32. Agts.
33. Made of oak
35. Free (of)
36. Egyptian snakes
40. Embellish
41. Fruit spread
42. Kilt fold
43. Sasquatch's cousin
44. Old witch
45. Tourist's must
46. Bungle
48. Damp and cold
49. Intersected
50. Tiny
53. Hair colorant
55. Amaze
56. Think over
58. Exploding star
62. Old sayings
64. Ms. Evans
65. Shun
66. Excursion
67. Sign
68. Calibrated
69. Wriggly
70. Get a flat
71. Pungs

DOWN
1. Pronto
2. Prom auto
3. Client
4. Destroyed
5. Not him
6. Flyboys
7. Mean
8. Peal
9. Went ahchoo
10. FedEx competitor
11. Sum up
12. Raisin's ancestry
13. Smoldering coal
21. Pepin's prop
22. Nib
25. Doing business
27. Sunday song
28. Absent
29. Bump
30. Beep
32. Cup edge
34. Deviate
35. Dustcloth
37. Look like
38. Peel
39. At once, to an MD
41. Boxing punch
42. Future queen, maybe
44. Cigar box
45. List
47. Youngster
48. Begrudge
50. Sew loosely
51. Mindful
52. Handrail support
53. Ms. Hunt
54. Blacksmith's tool
57. Sport
59. Seep
60. Competed
61. Attaches
63. Heaven
65. Horse's kin

PUZZLE 232

ACROSS

1. Brake part
5. Downs' partners
8. Likewise
12. Armed conflicts
13. Towels off
15. Shipment
16. Circle segments
17. Beginning part
18. Corrosive
19. Mind one's manners
21. Certain cans
23. Observe
24. Fresh
25. Kind of hound
28. Sock menders
32. Play unit
33. Frosted
35. Dozed off
37. Istanbul native
39. Turns white
41. Foal's mother
42. Solemn
44. Clenched hand
45. Ink holder
46. Country manors
48. Jabbered
51. Tyke
52. Shad ___
53. Flamenco dancer's need
58. Threaten
61. Slender woodwind
62. Vine fruit
64. Irritable person
65. Healing plant
66. Warning whistle
67. Basil or parsley, e.g.
68. Extend credit
69. Egyptian snake
70. Keats poems

DOWN

1. Large mop
2. Bunny's kin
3. Musical groups
4. School papers
5. Container
6. Middle Eastern bread
7. Songs from admirers
8. Woeful expression
9. Crazy
10. Glide
11. Bettor's numbers
13. Casino cube
14. More aching
20. Neckline shape
22. Possesses
25. Sluggers' sticks
26. Extremely serious
27. Pointed end
28. Cold-cut shops
29. Shady tree
30. Showed up again
31. Buying frenzy
34. Lunch hall
36. Cultivate
38. Toolbox
40. Hog's pad
43. Computer input
47. Pincers
49. "You ___ My Sunshine"
50. Rain gear
53. Furnace fuel
54. Efficient
55. Presently
56. Mounted on a peg
57. ___ and feathers
58. Knights, e.g.
59. Worry
60. Flows back
63. Zip

PUZZLE 233

ACROSS

1. Hot tubs
5. Blue
8. In the distance
12. Floor square
13. Beat
15. Hoop place
16. Troop group
17. Repeat
18. Finished together
19. Title
20. Stylish
21. Witnesses
23. Liveliness
25. Couple
26. Additional
29. Relieve
34. Blemish
37. Atlantic coast
39. Bend in prayer
40. Metered car
41. Levees
43. Monk's room
44. Met performance
46. Skinny
47. Dangerous snakes
48. Juries
50. Power tool
52. Matterhorn, e.g.
54. Heaping
58. Kind of spray can
62. Clever
63. Hair-care goo
64. Precipitate
65. Inasmuch as
67. To boot
68. Small landmass
69. Got word
70. Campers' beds
71. Naval responses
72. Apply henna to
73. Throw lightly

DOWN

1. Cuff fasteners
2. GI's poster
3. Excuse
4. Backdrop
5. Molt
6. Circle part
7. Be skeptical
8. Female singer
9. Thwart
10. Still snoozing
11. Blushing colors
13. Jogged
14. Makes tea
20. Combine
22. Fasten
24. Turn in
27. Banister
28. Questioned
30. Available for duty
31. Golfing gadgets
32. Improve
33. Room additions
34. Street sign
35. Mama's mate
36. Steers
38. Salty drop
42. Clipped
45. Oh, woe!
49. Wade
51. Aglow
53. Carried on
55. Arctic structure
56. Bird abodes
57. Luster
58. "Tosca" solo, e.g.
59. Simple
60. Madden
61. Singles
62. Building lot
66. Negative answer
67. Feat

ACROSS

1. Goes astray
5. Endorse
9. Set in
14. Seepage
15. Peer
16. Hose hue
17. Bethlehem trio
18. Electric sign
19. Emblem
20. Heavy hammer
22. Like an igloo
24. Forest creature
26. Hacienda brick
29. Made believe
34. "If I ___ a Rich Man"
36. Site
37. Visualized
38. Hem's partner
39. Deal
40. Bar fare
42. Relieve
43. Spud bud
44. Dollar division
45. Preholiday nights
46. Decorator's advice
48. Put together
50. Take a break
52. Set down
53. Passes up seconds
56. Most recent
61. Race
64. Fridge foray
66. Despise
67. Ascended
68. Earlier
69. Fair
70. Dos and ___
71. Prepared a golf ball
72. Evergreen plants

DOWN

1. "Desire" trees
2. Actual
3. Explode
4. Slip
5. Filleted
6. Become mature
7. Lump of soil
8. Gambling game
9. Receded
10. A Soprano
11. Make an offer
12. Hen grenade?
13. Barely passing grade
21. Capture
23. Ticked off
25. Works, as dough
27. Act
28. Obliterated
29. Solemn request
30. Diminish
31. Dog ___ dog
32. Sandwich sellers
33. Nail polish
35. Lea grazers
36. Imitator
41. Insisted
42. Adult elver
47. Senior
48. Hatchet
49. So long!
51. Staffers
54. Harness-racing gait
55. All there
57. Curds and ___
58. Roof feature
59. Irish or beef
60. Decades
61. Feeling low
62. Not amateur
63. Long period
65. Polar sight

PUZZLE 235

ACROSS

1. Potato
5. Mouth margin
8. ___ go bragh
12. Tasting of port
13. Paddy grains
15. Not taped
16. Matching
17. Gush
18. Nights before
19. Phi ___ Kappa
20. Clamor
21. Buy stocks
23. Encounters
25. Last letter
26. Take off
29. Sogginess
33. Wood cutter
34. Alex Trebek, e.g.
37. Tourist or booby
38. "The ___ Bug"
40. Vaselike vessel
41. Moby Dick, e.g.
42. Appealed
43. Wash
45. "Sanford and ___"
46. Flashing lights
49. Far East
51. Daiquiri liquor
52. "Green ___"
54. Blazing
57. Piece of soap
58. Set down
62. Unkempt one
63. Synagogue official
65. Can. province
66. Ring
67. Produce
68. Christmastime
69. Of sound mind
70. Tavern drink
71. Moore of "Ghost"

DOWN

1. Mop
2. Spear point
3. Department
4. Energetic person
5. Boundary
6. Computer graphics
7. Fido or Fluffy
8. ___ hour
9. Split
10. Currier and ___
11. Egg holder
13. Cash in
14. Snatch
22. After taxes
24. Smooth
26. Coarse files
27. Praise
28. Poem's rhythm
29. Journeyed
30. Delete
31. Boutique
32. Paid out
35. Baby bears
36. Timespan
39. Charming
41. "The Way We ___"
44. Dreadful
47. Tramp
48. Abrasive material
50. Tahiti or Crete
52. Certain convent
53. Telegram
54. Slithery biters
55. Dog's parasite
56. Borrowed sum
59. Lotion ingredient
60. It's on the agenda
61. Spanish artist
64. "The ___ Up There"

ACROSS

1. Ripped
5. Grape drinks
9. Mops
14. Territory
15. Unaccompanied
16. Poisonous snake
17. Lad's girl
18. Wall component
19. Go over again
20. Fabric
22. Boise's locale
24. Compass pt.
25. Tops
27. Consent to
31. Certain deer
32. Against the law
34. Hinder
36. Explosive letters
37. Likewise
38. Bus
39. Medic
40. Prowled
41. Ham
42. Derby, e.g.
43. Rock groups
44. Made even
46. Cauldrons
47. Library stamp
48. Seeger or Rose
49. Copy
52. Staid
54. Immerse again
56. Caravan stop
60. Be enough
62. Give (out)
63. Snow crystal
64. Scored on serve
65. Having talent
66. Not as many
67. Flower sites
68. "A Fine ___"

DOWN

1. Powders
2. Some exams
3. Plant again
4. Side of Manhattan
5. Horse's kin
6. Loving to excess
7. Avoid capture
8. Bubbly beverage
9. Roll of parchment
10. Anguish
11. Major network
12. Swimsuit part
13. Chump
21. Deck opening
23. Sentry's word
26. Acorn source
28. Masters
29. Leered
30. Hornets, e.g.
31. Bulb's holder
32. Business abbr.
33. City parcel
34. Jeered
35. Immature insect
36. Youngster
38. Noncommissioned off.
39. Mom's man
40. Furnish food
42. Deli sandwich
43. Cave denizen
45. Lower
46. Skilled
48. Freedom from war
49. Kind of brick
50. Tablets
51. Fencing swords
53. Talk too much
55. Type of cheese
56. Switch word
57. Pub offering
58. Cut wood
59. "I Like ___"
61. NFL scores

PUZZLE 236

213

PUZZLE 237

ACROSS
1. Swindle
5. Acted like
9. Puts into service
13. Color quality
14. Night vision
16. Blacktop
17. Skin woe
18. "___ Dawn"
19. Cabbage salad
20. Molar, e.g.
22. Nourishes
24. Poem type
25. Declare
26. Cake decorator
28. Angle
30. Mink or sable
31. Right-minded
32. Bunny
36. Doze off
37. Butts into
41. Statues of gods
42. Canine beast
43. Eskimo canoe
44. Foretell
45. Stein
46. Ripe old age
47. ___ out (barely made)
49. Warm
50. "On ___ Pond"
53. Certain amphibian
54. Know the ___ and outs
57. Sunbeam
58. Jacksonville bowl
60. Alpine song
62. Spring flower
64. Scold
66. Metal thread
67. Entree list
68. Studio stand
69. Adore
70. Rim
71. Unites
72. Pace

DOWN
1. ERAs, e.g.
2. Wintertime drink
3. Bother
4. Tournament
5. Do sums
6. Like better
7. Moray fisherman
8. Social appointment
9. Raises, in poker
10. Beauty parlor
11. Steer clear of
12. Norton's domain
15. Zany
21. Stereos
23. Male delivery?
27. Sever
29. Showed again
31. Hang down
32. Torso bone
33. Big fuss
34. Physique, for short
35. Extort money from
36. Egg drink
38. Pro vote
39. Cushion
40. Height limit?
42. Faulty firework
43. Money pool
45. Danger
46. Presently
48. Small cask
49. Gathered, as cattle
50. Filthy matter
51. Rowed
52. Fibbing
53. Library no-no
54. Blockhead
55. Daring
56. Doze
59. Liquefy
61. Night birds
63. Prosecute
65. Tracks up?

ACROSS

1. Apex
5. ___ roe
9. Defrosts
14. Cajole
15. Dial sound
16. Be ready for
17. Author Hoag
18. Grand-scale tale
19. Basil sauce
20. "Broken Arrow" costar
22. Feeling low
24. Drain
25. Fund-raiser
28. ___ and outs
29. Carpenter's blade
32. Feathery scarf
33. Flower holders
35. Small branches
37. Ocean journey
40. Sasquatch's cousin
41. Fowl for food
42. Housekeeper
46. Dangled
48. Show pain
49. Tint again
51. Storm center
53. Evergreen shrub
54. Corral
55. Designated
58. Aardvark's snack
59. Border
60. Proclaim
65. Cheerfully
68. Brokaw's forte
70. Not aweather
71. TV host
72. Annoying fly
73. Merriment
74. Oliver and Lou
75. Not evens
76. Begs

DOWN

1. Performs
2. Furnace fuel
3. "I Remember ___"
4. Freeway sign
5. Two-channel player
6. Short flight
7. Licorice-tasting seed
8. Kind of coffee
9. Road guide
10. Ram's mate
11. Movie collie
12. Giants
13. Halts
21. Diminishes
23. Couch
26. Of ships
27. Earmark
29. Swine's home
30. Dumbfound
31. Comedian
34. Large truck
36. Coat with gold
38. Ajar, in poetry
39. Alpine call
41. Obvious
43. "___ Day Now"
44. Cream or pick
45. Morning mist
47. Comics' Olive ___
48. Takes a spouse
49. Suggest another title
50. Tempt
52. Leavening agents
54. Beeper
56. Church game
57. Fix, as text
61. Legend
62. Angled additions
63. Smell strongly
64. Pullover shirts
66. Supervised
67. No problem!
69. Crumple

PUZZLE 238

215

PUZZLE 239

ACROSS

1. Get a whiff of
6. Betting numbers
10. Twinge
14. Newspapers and radio
15. Enfold
16. Small recess
17. Agreement
18. Certain bean
19. Snout
20. Belly
21. Ponders
23. Charges
24. Mustang food?
25. Attempt again
27. Lunch meat
31. Floral necklace
32. Taxi
35. Perfume
36. Vroom the engine
38. Attack
40. ___ down (moderated)
42. Baked pastry
44. Bag
45. Plastic card
47. Circle part
49. Broad valley
50. That girl
51. Fanatic
53. Cooked in an oven
55. Unveiling
57. Tissue layer
58. Tear
61. Tint again
63. Lyric poem
66. Juvenile
67. Celebrity
68. Settle a debt
70. Metal-bearing rocks
71. Alternative word
72. Strong thread
73. Barber's sign
74. Unwanted plant
75. Hunts

DOWN

1. Conceited
2. Predinner reading
3. Change for publication
4. Ignited
5. One of the flock
6. Night people
7. Less moist
8. Maiden
9. Fitness center
10. Pester
11. Dove's comments
12. Party thrower
13. Supplements
22. Employer
23. Crunchy
24. Pierced
26. Boston ___ Party
27. Bungle
28. Worship
29. Recluse
30. Not nope
32. Diamond weight
33. Supermarket lane
34. Run together, as colors
37. Through
39. Soapy
41. Banqueted
43. Make a misstep
46. Vat
48. Ape
52. Mobile-home owner?
54. Warns
55. Dimwitted
56. Torment
58. Halt!
59. Guy in white
60. Sway
62. Famous Scott
63. Mayberry lad
64. Unpleasantly damp
65. "Bright ___"
67. Attach buttons
69. Lamb's mom

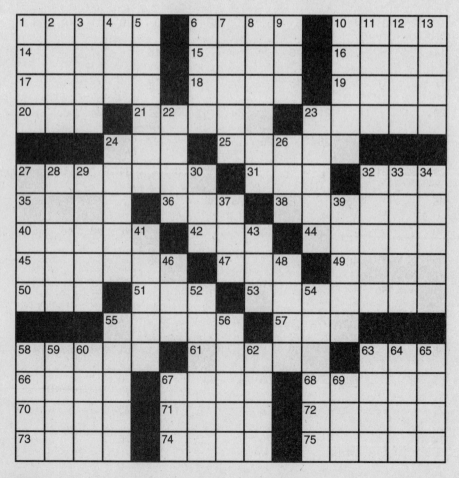

FULL CIRCLE

To complete this circular puzzle fill in the answers to the AROUND clues in a clockwise direction. For the RADIAL clues move from the outside to the inside.

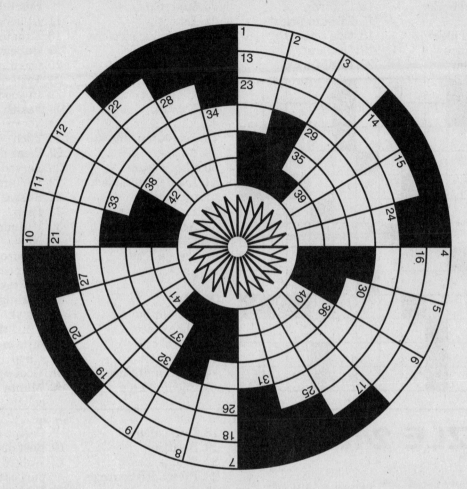

AROUND (Clockwise)

1. Novel
4. Donkey
7. Neptune's realm
10. Time period
13. Assumed name
16. Facial features
18. Bridge support
21. Armed conflicts
23. Spicy cake
26. Final settlement
29. Walking stick
30. More weird
32. Culture medium
33. Searches slyly
35. Express
   disapproval

36. Unlit
37. Large pond
38. Jason's ship
39. Butterfly snare
40. Snick's mate
41. Stitch
42. Chair

RADIAL (Out to in)

1. Old horses
2. Actor Wallach
3. Windlass
4. Priest's robe
5. Father
6. Goes quickly
7. Asterisk
8. Make a mistake

9. Of the ears
10. Female sheep
11. Battering devices
12. Sports buildings
14. Once more
15. Detect
17. Wrapping material
19. Adventure tales
20. Reptile
22. Sleep sound
24. Relax
25. Dreadful
27. Matured
28. Ancient Roman
   garb
31. Supplement
34. Cooking vessel

PUZZLE 241

ACROSS
1. Stags and bucks
4. Likewise
8. Mummy's place
12. Acorn source
13. Past curfew
14. At any time
15. Captive
17. Tibetan priest
18. One's equal
19. Deal out
20. Road turns
23. Shade trees
25. Give temporarily
26. ___ in (get a closeup)
27. Young boy
30. Ice-cream dish
32. Detect
34. Browning's before
35. Medicine
37. Little songbird
38. 12 inches
39. Unkempt
40. Excites
43. Lawn pest
45. Secret writing
46. As one
50. Many years
51. Land surrounded by water
52. Baseball stat
53. Ark builder
54. Degree
55. Twisted, as a grin

DOWN
1. Sock or bunny
2. Lobe place
3. Patrol or instructor
4. Medicinal lilies
5. Bowling area
6. Audio system
7. Above, to a poet
8. Reveals
9. Egg-shaped
10. Written reminder
11. Ill-behaved child
16. Exhaust
19. Bullets, to a GI
20. Or ___! (threat)
21. Tart
22. In good mental health
24. Yearn
26. Zilch
27. Wear out
28. Served perfectly
29. Declare untrue
31. Fusses
33. Peep
36. Ultimate
38. New
39. Snooze
40. Glance at
41. For takeout
42. Inkling
44. Gawk
46. "___ the season . . ."
47. Chop
48. Goof up
49. Manta ___

PUZZLE 242

ACROSS
1. Collect
6. Corn coverings
11. Spotted ponies
13. Small village
14. Boundary
15. Mountainous
16. Agate
18. Draw along
19. Befitting
22. Bridge fees
23. Pretended courage
25. Sample
30. Certain parasites
31. Wool producer
33. Sty fare
34. Express feeling
36. At the beach
38. Lad
40. Miniature
41. ___-been
44. Regard highly
46. Available for duty
48. Library user
52. Artist's pad
53. Pitcher's goal
54. Scheduled
55. Sheer

DOWN
1. Monkey
2. Combine
3. Aardvark's snack
4. Restrain
5. "Moonlight ___"
6. Most healthy
7. Ref's cousin
8. Narrow slash
9. Casino game
10. Beef dish
12. Walked purposefully
13. Lobby
17. Tire mishap
19. Competent
20. ___ and proper
21. Tortilla treat
24. Dobbin's doc
26. Powdery residue
27. Ponderous
28. Sped
29. Weapon for a duel
32. Enrolls
35. Facial feature
37. Bed linen
39. Capital of Norway
41. Trebek, e.g.
42. Not pro
43. Swamp covering
45. Shopping place
47. Citrus quencher
49. Metal mold
50. ___ out (barely make)
51. Sales agent, for short

DOUBLE TROUBLE

PUZZLE 243

Not really double trouble, but double fun! Solve this puzzle as you would a regular crossword, except place one, two, or three letters in each box. The number of letters in each answer is shown in parentheses after its clue.

ACROSS

1. Spotted horse (5)
3. Clutch (5)
5. Nearby (5)
7. Iced (7)
9. Bottle-nosed ___ (7)
10. Reasons (7)
11. Pet rodents (7)
13. General Bonaparte (8)
15. Leading lady (7)
17. Glacial ridges (6)
18. Athlete trainer (5)
19. Humid (8)
21. Spain's continent (6)
24. Portable heat source (6)
26. Summit (4)
28. Trap (7)
30. Swift character (5)
32. Pedicurist's concern (7)
34. College official (4)
35. Colorists (5)
37. Chants (7)
39. Unabashed (9)
41. Perfumed (7)
42. Wild dogs (7)
43. Refuge (7)
45. Studio (7)
48. Remove from print (4)
49. Flow-control device (5)
50. Thinking organ (5)

DOWN

1. Squeeze (5)
2. Labor (4)
3. Diagram (5)
4. Triangular sail (9)
5. Moisturizer (6)
6. Baby cows (6)
8. Record books (7)
9. Kewpies (5)
10. Lawn pest (4)
12. Cafe (6)
14. Faker (6)
15. Confront boldly (6)
16. Betrayal of trust (9)
17. Moving staircases (10)
20. Plumbing tube (4)
22. Unwraps (5)
23. Make beloved (6)
25. Ark builder (4)
27. Barbie's friend (3)
29. Stadiums (6)
31. Heaps (6)
33. Sickness (7)
36. Jewish school (7)
38. Precede (8)
39. Manacle (7)
40. Lunch and dinner (5)
41. Cub or girl (5)
42. Green gem (4)
44. Dig (5)
46. Zodiacal scales (5)
47. Ireland, poetically (4)

[Crossword grid with numbered cells: 1, 2, 3, 4, 5, 6, 7, 8, 9, 10, 11, 12, 13, 14, 15, 16, 17, 18, 19, 20, 21, 22, 23, 24, 25, 26, 27, 28, 29, 30, 31, 32, 33, 34, 35, 36, 37, 38, 39, 40, 41, 42, 43, 44, 45, 46, 47, 48, 49, 50]

Exploraword

PUZZLE 244

How many common words of four or more letters can you form from the letters of the given word? A letter may be used only as many times as it appears in the given word. Proper names, abbreviations, contractions, and foreign words are not allowed.

REALTOR

PUZZLE 245

ACROSS

1. Pouches
5. Shed tears
9. Use a swearword
13. Morally bad
14. Makes cookies
15. Knowledgeable about
16. Peace symbol
17. Impartial
19. Pleasantly
21. Nada
22. Period
23. Colorful carp
24. Risk
25. Thing, in law
26. Shoot the breeze
29. Nerve network
31. 1 + 9, 5 + 5, etc.
33. Regretful person
35. Card game
37. News paragraph
40. Length x width
41. Bootleg, as tickets
43. Guitar adjunct
44. Cow's house
45. Unique person
46. Recognized
47. Band bookings
50. Mistake
52. Comfortable room
53. Religious brother
55. Staff member
57. Amigo
59. Opposite of neath
60. Island garland
61. Habitual
65. Clearance event
68. Musical conclusion
69. School club
70. Elaborate display
71. Rich Little, e.g.
72. Medieval slave
73. Traded for cash
74. Grasslands

DOWN

1. Garden plots
2. Admit
3. Shell out
4. Chic
5. Curvy
6. Increase
7. Contour feather
8. Rock concert souvenir
9. Bamboozle
10. Comprehend
11. Cordwood measure
12. Bubbly beverages
14. Values
18. Out of the weather
20. Rocky hill
24. Disturb
26. Seize
27. Radiance
28. Outdoor tavern
30. Tex-Mex treat
32. Tiny notch
34. Rajah's wife
36. Butterlike spread
38. Fencing equipment
39. Cut, as a lawn
42. Soothsayer
48. Spectacular party
49. Blockades
51. Remote
53. Valley ___
54. Film spools
56. Dancing spot
58. Not express
61. Garbed
62. Negative response
63. Think-tank product
64. Sedans, e.g.
66. Golfer's peg
67. Fully

PUZZLE 246   Add One

Add one letter to each of the words on the right to form the answer to one of the clues on the left. The added letter may be at the beginning, at the end, or in the middle of the word. Place that letter in the box next to its clue. The added letters, read from top to bottom, will spell a 6-letter word.

1. Necklace bead   ☐   a. FINALE

2. Planting   ☐   b. TRY

3. Wheedle   ☐   c. AUNT

4. Excursion   ☐   d. SWING

5. Busboy's platter   ☐   e. DUPED

6. Threw away   ☐   f. PEAR

ACROSS

1. Fibrous material
5. Ocean plant
9. Deadly reptiles
13. Top-grade recipient
14. Clock faces
16. Barre bend
17. Three musicians
18. Pastoral poem
19. Horse's gait
20. Soda-fountain dessert
22. Fled to wed
24. Seize forcibly
27. River barrier
28. Significant period
31. Suitable
35. Stringy
36. Weaker, as an excuse
37. Limb
39. Emulate Tomba
40. Sharp bark
41. Actress Pamela ___ Martin
42. Bowling frames
43. Duplication
45. Slumbered
47. Delayed
49. Flourless cake
50. Annapolis initials
51. Darn again
53. Blessed
56. Appear
60. Property measure
61. Pixieish
65. Pink, as a burger
66. Footwear item
67. Middays
68. Lively spirit
69. Rough-cut
70. Lap pup, shortly
71. Young society women

DOWN

1. Sunbonnets
2. Pale beige
3. Chicken chow ___
4. Generate
5. Fifi's farewell
6. Pan cover
7. Frolicsome
8. Every bit
9. Self-assurance
10. Swine food
11. Old King Cole's request
12. Future flower
15. Kind of hammer
21. Wan
23. Bear necessity?
25. Put trust in
26. More apparent
28. Formerly, formerly
29. Jabbed
30. Express an idea
32. Obstruct
33. Surgical beam
34. Burst
38. Dispense
43. Satchel
44. Hal ___ of "Barney Miller"
45. Bloom support
46. Reduced
48. Mulligatawny vessel
52. Hearing or taste
53. Cloth belt
54. Muscle strain
55. Brag
57. Breath sound
58. Snatch
59. Bards' twilights
62. Prune
63. Enemy
64. Squid's squirt

PUZZLE 247

1	2	3	4		5	6	7	8		9	10	11	12
13					14				15	16			
17					18					19			
20				21					22	23			
			24			25	26		27				
28	29	30				31		32			33	34	
35						36					37		38
39						40					41		
42				43	44				45	46			
		47		48					49				
			50				51		52				
53	54	55							56		57	58	59
60					61	62	63	64		65			
66					67					68			
69					70					71			

End of the Line

PUZZLE 248

For each of the categories listed, can you think of a word or phrase ending with each letter on the right? Count one point for each correct answer. A score of 15 is good, and 21 is excellent.

BOYS' NAMES	THINGS THAT FLY	POETS	DOG BREEDS	BODIES OF WATER	
					T
					R
					E
					N
					D

PUZZLE 249   THREE-D CROSSWORD

Here's a crossword with a third dimension! Each of the three faces (A, B, and C) is a crossword with words reading across and down. As you solve this puzzle, you'll see that some of the answers from one face continue on another face of the cube. Watch your ABCs, and you'll find that this is a real blockbuster.

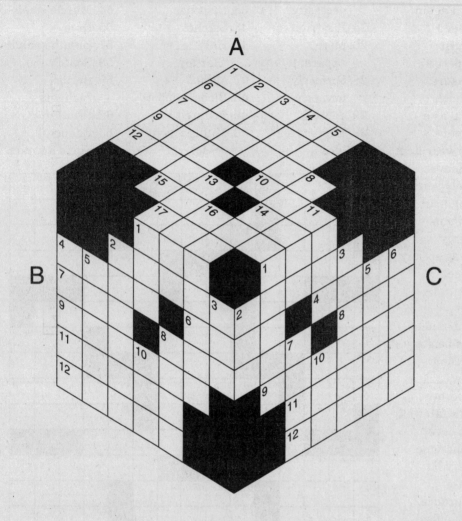

B CLUES

ACROSS

1. Cheerleader's yell
2. Had a party
4. Withered
6. Graceful horse
7. Microscopic
8. Creeps
9. Ark's resting place
11. Giant
12. "____ Like Old Times"

DOWN

2. Make
3. Lingerie item
4. Smacks, as a fly
5. Ghostly
8. Preserves food
10. Bump hard

C CLUES

ACROSS

1. Mom's guy
4. Palm variety
8. Actor Kilmer
9. Firstborn
11. Chief artery
12. Newsman Jennings

DOWN

2. Uncooked
3. Turn aside
5. Thick glue
6. Sacred table
7. Insult
10. Female deer

A CLUES

ACROSS

1. Price tag
6. Attentive
7. Fondle
9. Be mistaken
10. Stockholm's country
12. Property title
14. Part of Q.E.D.
15. Trustworthy
17. Obtain

DOWN

1. Spiked (the punch)
2. Knowledgeable
3. Like a jail cell
4. ____ out a living
5. Minus
8. Term of endearment
11. Seabird
13. Unit of heat
16. Chime

222

Instructions for solving Codeword puzzles are given on page 11.

Puzzle 250 key:

1	14		
2	15		
3	16		
4	17		
5	18		
6	19		
7	20		
8	21		
9	22		
10 A	23		
11	24		
12	25		
13	26 M		

Puzzle 250 grid:

17	3	24	8	3	■	1	■	■	22	25	21	10
22	■	10	■	19	21	10	22	20	■	10 A	■	21
3	9	8	20	21	■	17	■	10	22	26 M	3	22
■	■	14	■	1	14	10	1	■	25	■	26	■	8
22	25	4	26	21	■	22	■	24	3	3	1	21
21	■	■	■	■	18	8	2	8	■	7	■	■
5	10	15	8	20	■	■	■	10	1	18	21	2
■	■	22	■	21	1	12	21	■	■	■	■	10
13	11	3	14	21	■	8	■	16	10	6	21	22
11	■	14	■	23	11	26	19	3	■	3	■	■
10	26	21	19	10	■	19	■	11	24	12	10	22
7	■	7	■	4	3	11	12	16	■	10	■	11
18	8	14	21	■	■	1	■	21	7	24	10	14

Letter grid (A–Z): A (crossed out), B, C, D, E, F, G, H, I, J, K, L, M (crossed out), N, O, P, Q, R, S, T, U, V, W, X, Y, Z

Puzzle 251 key:

1	14		
2	15		
3	16		
4 N	17		
5	18		
6	19 A		
7	20		
8	21		
9	22		
10	23		
11	24		
12	25		
13	26		

Puzzle 251 grid:

13	18	19	15	19	■	19	■	4	19	22	10	7
21	■	5	■	3	2	6	3	10	■	23	■	2
19	7	5	23	3	■	19	■	25	19	5	24	16
11	■	2	■	10	12	1	2	■	■	5	■	10
11	10	24	24	14	■	■	■	6	19	17	2	21
5	■	■	■	■	9	2	20	19	■	2	■	■
10	26	18	21	3	■	19	■	11	9	14	12	1
■	■	11	■	19	4	22	1	■	■	■	■	2
15	10	13	19 A	4 N	■	■	■	11	23	8	18	10
23	■	21	■	■	5	19	15	19	■	18	■	7
15	23	19	4	7	■	5	■	12	21	10	7	2
23	■	7	■	23	4	19	4	10	■	10	■	25
7	25	10	5	24	■	21	■	21	19	4	23	4

Letter grid (A–Z): A (crossed out), N (crossed out), B, C, D, E, F, G, H, I, J, K, L, M, O, P, Q, R, S, T, U, V, W, X, Y, Z

PUZZLE 252

ACROSS

1. "___ I'm With You"
5. Get older
8. Uninteresting
12. Place for a gutter
13. Morsel
15. Military clerk
16. Two-masted vessel
17. Jeweled headband
18. Component
19. Offer for cash
20. Build on
21. Battery terminal
23. Large wading bird
25. Use an axe
26. Sharp knock
29. Candy ingredient
31. Fairway cry
32. Chaos
33. Having blemishes
34. Squirreled away
35. Skier's line
36. Prospector's find
37. Slipperier
38. Sheer
39. Portland's st.
40. Knot
41. More painful
42. "And I Love ___"
43. Homely
44. Chartered
45. Tentacle
46. Cook in fat
47. "___ That a Shame"
48. Data
50. Printing liquid
51. Part of a.k.a.
55. Fillet
57. Composed
59. Novel, e.g.
60. Zenith
61. Famous
62. Ms. Turner
63. Student's bane
64. Lived
65. Nervous

DOWN

1. Fly traps
2. Aesop racer
3. Vicious
4. Nightie
5. Boric and citric
6. Alumnus, for short
7. Corn unit
8. Release money
9. Poetry and prose
10. Picnic refreshment
11. Dress bottom
13. One of a flight
14. Wall-covering hanger
22. Had creditors
24. "The ___ Seed"
25. Shanty
27. Doted on
28. Strength
29. Record keeper
30. Weakens
31. Tinker Bell, e.g.
33. Luau greeting
34. ___ anteater
37. Like some toenails
38. Easily carried
40. Nonsense
41. Wrongdoing
44. Walked
47. Pays up
49. ___ of kin
50. Tad
52. Shipment
53. Ditty
54. Agree
55. Casey's club
56. Unlatch, in an ode
58. Paddle

224

ACROSS

1. Expansive
5. Certain vipers
9. Untidy type
13. Hooked on
14. Jumping insects
16. Roadway marker
17. December forecast
18. Valley ___
19. Acted like
20. "___ Miss Brooks"
21. Piece of advice
22. Scratch
24. Bump hard
25. Hatchet
26. Use a shovel
27. Dread
30. Wildcat
32. Backbone
34. Fink
35. Tire filler
37. Scholastic
39. Title of respect
42. Closer
44. Legend
45. Forefather
47. Mask or lift
49. Boxing count
50. Paddled
52. Small particle
55. Ma that baas
56. Not bright
57. Wise bird
59. Dense mist
61. Knows how
62. Gloom
63. On behalf of
64. Mama's guy
67. Glowing coal
70. Italian money, once
71. Watcher
72. Staggers
73. Served well
74. Await judgment
75. Blue jay's home
76. Joins together

DOWN

1. Helmet part
2. Yearly
3. "___ Weather"
4. Pull
5. Attach
6. Inclines
7. According to
8. Sink or bend
9. Leave a mark
10. Prune
11. Quarter of four
12. ___-and-breakfast
15. Educational meetings
21. Cab
23. Elderly
26. Chop
27. Service branch
28. Postpone
29. Clearly outline
31. Moniker
33. Clergyman
36. Legal fee
38. Project
39. Husband or wife
40. Afresh
41. Pimples
43. Standard
46. Fountain beverage
48. Leafy vegetable
51. Wooden rods
53. Place of business
54. Gave berth to?
58. Most vile
60. Diploma receivers
61. Credit ___
64. Pizazz
65. Shipboard yes
66. "The ___ is mightier . . ."
68. Grown boys
69. Honey producer
70. Statute

PUZZLE 253

225

PUZZLE 254

ACROSS

1. Agents
5. Soft drink
9. Cougar, e.g.
12. Land measurement
13. Badge
15. Reverent dread
16. Front of a ship
17. Wield
18. Frying need
19. Dine
20. Plunged
21. Clog
23. Regarding
25. British rank
27. More capable
29. Blackboard need
31. Swigged
33. Familiarized
37. Before, poetically
38. Three minutes, to Ali
40. Horse feed
41. Wandering
44. Salad-bar item
47. Sugar trees
49. Goofed
50. Fourscore minus ten
53. Potters' media
55. Metallic sound
56. Plummet
57. Incline
60. Floor covering
61. Alpine comebacks
64. Man Friday
65. Excitement
66. Extinguishes
67. Poetic contraction
68. For each
69. Young voter
70. Pharmacy measure

DOWN

1. Chats
2. Eggshell
3. Airplane device
4. Alter slacks
5. Pocket money
6. Pigsty sound
7. Directed
8. Completely
9. Roasting bird
10. Attentive
11. Belief
13. Avoid
14. Judge's decision
20. Royal title
22. Brass instrument
24. Nope's opposite
25. Square-dance locale
26. Comment to the audience
27. Many years
28. Loni's ex
30. Cheek cosmetic
32. Dribbled
34. More parched
35. Chalet feature
36. Went auburn
39. Single
42. Pulpit word
43. Jerked
45. Tide type
46. Remove moisture
48. Protect
50. Small piece
51. Duck
52. Vim
54. Negative profit
56. Pharmacist's amount
58. Proposal
59. Make curly
62. Camp bed
63. Tinge
64. "Stand ___ Deliver"

226

ACROSS

1. Carry
5. Favorite
8. Cement chunk
12. Press pleats
13. Record
15. Daft
16. Bistro
17. Jewish teacher
18. Repeat
19. Defame
20. Individual
21. Nails
23. Pasted
25. Sty dweller
26. Playmate
28. Sire
31. Burned brightly
32. Tourist's aid
33. Moisture
35. Kitchen gizmo
36. June honoree
37. Flavoring
39. "Bells ___ Ringing"
40. Loud call
41. Moral excellence
42. Victor's prize
45. Most stable
46. Constrictor
47. Gabs
48. Brews
51. Gym wing
52. Hen grenades?
56. Breezy
57. Develop
59. Grandma
60. Ms. Russo
61. Shabby
62. Scratch
63. Angered
64. Short farewell
65. Has a meal

DOWN

1. Muscle twitches
2. ___ hygiene
3. Bean curd
4. Activate
5. Smoothed
6. Subsided
7. Vat
8. Toboggan
9. Canal feature
10. Feel bad
11. Hisses
13. In the area
14. Accident
22. Kettle
24. Look at slyly
26. Tease
27. Sports car
28. Passing fashion
29. Corrects copy
30. Sever again
31. Woman's purchase
32. Merry month
34. Miniature
36. Like a desert
37. Basin
38. Attendance
40. Follower
41. Dell
43. Heeded
44. Explode
45. Greet
47. Irritable
48. Bombay garb
49. Level
50. Coastal flier
53. Grand party
54. Pesky insect
55. Cutting tools
58. Grab hold of

PUZZLE 256

ACROSS
1. Cougar
5. In need of kneading
9. Dieter's milk
13. Dollars
14. Nap
16. Pull strings?
17. Shade
18. White bear
19. Beak
20. Part of a flight
22. Parsley portion
24. Nourished
25. Evaluates
27. Seinfeld's field
29. That girl
31. Nasty mutt
32. Greek cheese
33. Labeled
35. Take the high road?
36. Poker token
40. La Scala solos
41. Uncle Sam's target
42. Album entry
43. Has-___
44. Go out with
45. Treated pleats
46. Slangy refusals
48. A Whitney
49. Middle of summer
50. Damage
53. Pastry shop
55. Zilch
56. Whoppers
58. Unloads
61. Afresh
63. Foundation
65. Lawn pest
66. At hand
67. Gregg expert
68. Cannon report
69. Crosscurrent
70. Anxious
71. Opposed

DOWN
1. Cauldrons
2. Complete entity
3. Zoo
4. Moving
5. Viper
6. More proximate
7. Supports
8. Decade division
9. Wolf pack component
10. Dagger
11. Lounged
12. Like old cheese
15. Expensive
21. Ethnic groups
23. Obtained
26. Bomb
28. Manly
29. Spear
30. Now's partner
32. Winter ill
34. Heavenly dish
35. Hardly a friend
37. Wedding trip
38. Scoop
39. Shells
41. Toady's reply
42. Jimmied
44. Bushes
45. Kind
47. Be indisposed
48. Soothing
50. Absurd
51. Dug
52. Request urgently
53. Cleared tables
54. Cuban dance
57. Running behind
59. Flower bed
60. 18-wheeler
62. Crooked
64. Asian sauce

ACROSS

1. Help in crime
5. Camera's need
9. Toward the center of
13. Color changer
14. Craze
15. Stingy
16. Cold-cuts store
17. Ell
18. Squares of butter
19. Pieces
21. Burrow
23. Shirt style
24. Jacket part
27. Observant
29. Luau strings
30. Fall behind
33. Mork et al.
35. Storage box
36. Argument
38. Comes to a stop
40. Districts
41. Ship's stabilizer
45. Disregard
47. Cherry-tree chopper
48. Yearns for
50. Gaze at
52. Apparatus
53. Feel about
54. Cousins' mothers
56. Charter
57. Dull routine
60. Northern seal
62. Calms the appetite
64. Uses the microwave
66. Mama's fellow
70. On a voyage
71. Details
72. Heroic poem
73. Fix
74. Pulls
75. Get a flat

DOWN

1. Find a sum
2. Adios!
3. Grown grig
4. Clan
5. Admirers
6. Hostelry
7. Was untruthful
8. Skirt type
9. Little demon
10. Straighten up
11. Spuds
12. First symptoms
14. Wrestling surface
20. Under the weather
22. Stride
24. Grease job
25. Alike
26. Hang fire
28. Onionlike veggie
31. Old saying
32. Daughters
33. With speed
34. Hearty
37. Envision
39. Crisp cookie
42. Merit
43. Withdraw
44. Voyage parts
46. Incessantly
48. Fold
49. Spoiled
51. Bend an ___
53. Shine
55. Case or crust
58. Text division
59. Ballet skirt
60. Clothing edges
61. Pack animal
63. Sorry
65. Nail holder
67. Mimic
68. Bobby or cotter
69. Play section

PUZZLE 258

HEADHUNTING

Don't lose your head as you fill in the diagram. The first letter of each answer word will go somewhere within the word itself; all the other letters appear in order. For example, CART might be aCrt, arCt, or artC. (NOTE: The second letter of the answer word is always first.) Look for the letters which are shared by across and down words.

ACROSS

1. Escapade
6. Not injected
10. Of a time
14. Malign
15. Caesar's city
16. Mr. Lacoste
17. Fine mist
18. Tent holders
19. Lends a hand
20. Motionless
22. Fierce feline
24. Attack a sub?
25. Drive the getaway car
27. Pivot
29. Hideaway
33. Curb
34. Saw logs
35. Ferry
40. Church part
41. Succinct
42. An inning has six
43. Bridesmaid, e.g.
45. Blender button
46. Erelong
47. Bluff
49. Meal
52. Comic Martha ___
53. Snitch
54. Graph starter
56. Not quite
61. Tiff
63. Persian sprite
65. Racket
66. Cupcake finisher
67. Dagger of yore
68. Lovers' lane?
69. ___ majeste
70. Truck follower
71. DeGeneres series

DOWN

1. Pat down
2. Mimic
3. Oceans
4. Platter
5. Iona artisans
6. Mine find
7. Range
8. Bang shut
9. Playful mammal
10. Wrath
11. Plane spotter
12. Past or present
13. Thrill
21. Crackerjack
23. Diamond cover
26. Wickerwork
28. Essence
29. Hide
30. Manuscript mark
31. Field
32. Primps
33. Watchman
36. Operated
37. Reminder
38. Urge on
39. Flight part
41. Fragrant
44. Feed the kitty
45. Uproar
48. Grant foe
49. Serenity
50. The cruellest month?
51. Quenches
52. Velocities
55. Colombian coin
57. Cruise
58. Meet defeat
59. Medieval slave
60. Solar disk
62. 66, e.g.
64. Bakery item

230

ACROSS

1. Zest
6. Fusses
10. Impair
13. Aim
15. Bee Gees, e.g.
16. Self-conceit
17. Two-channel player
18. Cashier's drawer
19. Morsel
20. Paint this red
21. Prance
23. Please
25. Command to Fido
26. Grinned
27. Covered with spots
32. Damp
33. Metal mixtures
34. Bark at the moon
35. Woolly bleaters
39. Fur scarf
40. Gave a meal to
41. Ratify
42. Famous diamond
43. First ___
44. Simmer
45. Grain storage bin
47. Car style
48. Beset
51. Up-to-date
52. The same
53. Orange's peel
54. Group of wolves
58. Natural mineral
59. Nerd's kin
61. Fit for food
63. Pollinating insect
64. White House room
65. Instant ___
66. Put a stop to
67. Makes a hue turn
68. Garden invaders

DOWN

1. Essence
2. Golden-rule word
3. Worry
4. Coastal bird
5. United
6. Storage area
7. Spigot problem
8. Tin Man's need
9. Serious
10. Athlete's goal
11. Marble
12. Dressed
14. Prepares, as a salad
22. Glove material
24. Compared
26. Announce
27. Move quickly
28. Voice part
29. Plunk
30. European weasel
31. Corrosive material
32. Father
34. Gardener's plot
36. Electric unit
37. Resounding sound
38. Stair
40. Tall tale
41. Always, in poetry
43. Feel poorly
44. More melancholy
46. Ran wild
47. Deary
48. Sun-dried brick
49. Temptress
50. Mount
51. Kitchen gloves
53. Go upward
54. Corncob or meerschaum
55. Willing's partner
56. Dressed
57. Door openers
60. Manner
62. Mountain ___

PUZZLE 260

ACROSS
1. Not pro
5. Don't go
9. Breathes relief
14. Toe woe
15. Temptation
16. Parcel out
17. Cattle calls
18. Flexible armor
19. Pack animal
20. Halted
22. Enter data
24. Rookie socialite
25. Mourning
27. Bro's sib
29. Boat power
31. Overlay
34. Attack, Fido!
35. Fuzzy fruit
38. Like a chalet roof
40. It's of miner concern
41. Honors
43. Excitement
44. Hanker
46. Transfer, as property
47. Excavate
48. Informer
50. Bounded
53. Vegas cube
54. Name
56. Island drink
59. Cover the roof again
61. Medicated
65. Swiftly
67. Woe is me!
69. QB's call
70. Outspoken
71. It's passed in class
72. Be an also-ran
73. Foe
74. Was aware of
75. Decorative pitcher

DOWN
1. Pinnacle
2. "High ___"
3. Tramped
4. Implant
5. Addition result
6. Instruct
7. Getting grayer
8. Cry
9. Soup go-withs
10. Abed
11. Pollyanna's word
12. Where the heart is
13. Guess
21. Penn and Teller, e.g.
23. Put to good ___
26. Irritates
28. Mako's milieu
29. Bogs down
30. Where the buoys are
31. Contended
32. Escape
33. Decorated again
34. Type of bean
36. Hankering
37. Dainty
39. Lassie, e.g.
41. Completely
42. Liquefy
45. Cast off
49. Can opener?
51. No spring chicken
52. Streisand hit
54. Hawk's weapon
55. Upset
56. Babble wildly
57. Once's follower
58. Defensive spray
60. Gas container
62. Sluggish
63. Comfort
64. Lock changer?
66. Type of shaft
68. Darn

ACROSS

1. Grates
6. Highbrow
10. Trots
14. Oak fruit
15. Island dance
16. Touched ground
17. The press
18. Gambler's concern
19. Opera star
20. Lark
22. Football team
24. Boggy
27. "Ain't ___ Sweet"
28. Finish
29. Electrified atom
30. As of now
32. Skirt type
34. Apparel
36. Be next to
38. Spasm
41. Peddle
42. Pokes
43. Corn holder
45. Door opener?
46. Very eager
47. Contain
48. Tragic
50. Antlered beast
53. Secure
54. Actor Erwin
57. Tiger, e.g.
58. Sings a Swiss tune
60. Made like a pig
62. Pickle portion
64. Judge
65. Admired one
67. Resided
71. Stumble
72. Like
73. In flames
74. Lot's wife, ultimately
75. Watched
76. Firm

DOWN

1. Male sheep
2. High or low card
3. Clump of turf
4. Refracting crystal
5. Quick
6. Clog, e.g.
7. Unclothed
8. Ancient
9. Singles, e.g.
10. Green gem
11. Ms. Oyl
12. Specified
13. Put up with
21. Seedy bread
23. Guided
24. Poses
25. Courted
26. Aspect
27. Smear
31. Archer's aim
33. Restless desire
35. Husky's burden
37. Ghost's cry
39. Peeved
40. Courteous
42. Perfect place
44. All the queen's men
49. Freezer cube
51. Drain-opener chemical
52. Australian marsupials
54. Kinds
55. Sparkly headgear
56. Up to the time that
59. Float aimlessly
61. Held onto
62. A few
63. Appealed
66. Time division
68. Contend
69. Botch
70. Informal room

PUZZLE 262

ACROSS

1. Hopeful
5. Roadies' plug-ins
9. Thin board
13. Skilled
14. Lingers
16. Soothing plant
17. Christmas plant
19. Not busy
20. Fix definitely
21. Untruth
22. Seeded breads
24. Hidden microphone
25. Feathered scarves
28. Horror
31. Center
33. Cry
35. Marble markings
36. Circle
38. Bring legal action
39. Unruly kids
40. Browns quickly
41. Scorch
42. Bottle lid
43. Pesters
44. Removed the pit
45. House addition
46. Go ___ over
47. Resounded
49. Grown grigs
51. Easter bonnet
52. Nautical cry
55. Sense of humor
56. Deluge refuge
59. ERA or RBI
62. Barbecue spit
65. Right-hand person
66. Bolt together?
67. Big game hunter?
68. Look
69. ___ over (faint)
70. Table doilies

DOWN

1. Yaks
2. A woodwind
3. Thin opening
4. Tokyo currency
5. "Anchors ___"
6. One of a pair
7. Deep hole
8. Mix with a spoon
9. Rodeo rope
10. Fully
11. Furthermore
12. Chop
15. Verbalize
18. Hits hard
23. Kind of tide
24. Storage boxes
26. Guarantee
27. Went bad, as milk
28. Feminine
29. Wavelet
30. Not here
31. Neigh sayer
32. ___ and downs
34. Fold up
35. Wrongdoing
37. Mighty tree
40. Drink daintily
41. Navy recruit
44. Talks idly
46. Lenten Wednesday
48. Carve
50. After
53. Mine rock
54. Sunnyside-up part
55. Rub off
56. Opera highlight
57. Revolt
58. Actor Howard et al.
59. Tree liquid
60. Hog-___
61. Summer beverage
63. Water tester
64. Stately tree

PUZZLE 263

ACROSS

1. Browned bread
6. Hit
10. At once, to an MD
14. Icy abode
15. Bishop of Rome
16. Wrong
17. With sarcasm
18. Spoils
19. Punter's action
20. Bigfoot's kin
21. Forbid
22. Certain fly
24. "That ___ Cat"
26. Chinese frypan
27. ___ Maria
30. Stogie
32. Proposal
36. Flushed
38. Society newcomer
40. Pond organism
42. Informed of
43. Stadium
45. Cry out
46. Shortage
47. Sass
48. Team pet
50. Lackluster
52. Random tries
54. Pair
55. Puffin's kin
57. Throw
59. Side streets
63. Dove's murmur
64. Recuperate
68. Attitude
69. Ferrous metal
71. Greetings!
72. Source for repro
73. Microwave, slangily
74. Water holes
75. Climb
76. The Bee ___
77. Lawn material

DOWN

1. In order
2. Fiend
3. Dismounted
4. Like a rock
5. Yo-yo, e.g.
6. Pounced
7. Ducklike diver
8. Liable
9. Pasta topping
10. Well-being
11. Tease
12. Semicircles
13. Tot
21. Suite or veil
23. Slalom
25. Jet hotshot
26. Little bird
27. "East of Eden" role
28. Ivy-covered
29. Enroll
31. Proficient
33. "Happy ___"
34. Vote into office
35. Luminous
37. Fizzy drink
39. Hollow reed
41. Chorus voice
44. Danger
49. Mule's father
51. Cooking leaf
53. Makes up (for)
56. Working
58. Trim, as wool
59. Love, Italian style
60. Singer Morgan
61. Actress Nettleton
62. Outskirts
63. Coal by-product
65. "Born Free" star
66. Bar brews
67. At a ___ for words
70. Be regretful
71. Greedy person

235

The answers to this petaled puzzle will go in a curve from the number on the outside to the center of the flower. Each number in the flower will have two 5-letter answers. One goes in a clockwise direction and the second in a counterclockwise direction. We have entered two answers to help you begin.

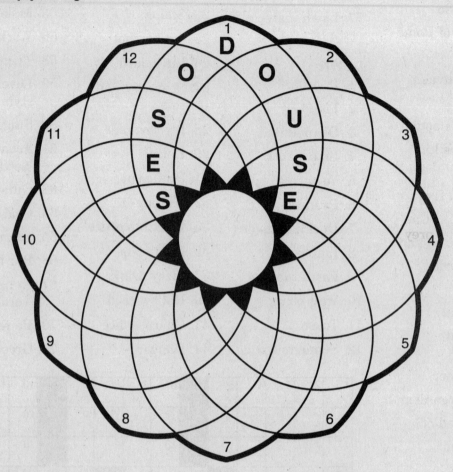

CLOCKWISE

1. Put out
2. Do a body search
3. Pretty, in Glasgow
4. Under, to a poet
5. Hint
6. Tractor name
7. Newspapers and TV
8. Uncovers
9. Flat hills
10. Major followers
11. Theater feature
12. Roadway

COUNTERCLOCKWISE

1. Medicates
2. Pollutes
3. Cruel person
4. Clamor
5. On edge
6. Guzzled
7. Substantial
8. Nut-bearing tree
9. Mexican mom
10. Chilling
11. Baffled
12. Moreno and Rudner

FLOWER POWER FANS! *Fun is always in full bloom with every volume of Selected Flower Power. To order, see page 159.*

ACROSS

1. Horse feed
5. Mustang fuel
8. Seed
12. Kennel pest
13. Beginning
15. Not windward
16. Sense
17. Host's speech
18. Tibetan priest
19. Recede
21. ___-evident
23. Frying utensil
24. Imitate
27. Viper
29. Sniggler's prey
30. Perch
31. "The ___ Bunch"
33. Ingest
35. Balanced
37. Bestowed
39. Be in debt
40. Ogler
41. Wipe out
43. Bossa ___
47. Cargo weight
49. Forgave
51. BLT topping
53. "___ a Living"
54. Host
55. Valise
56. Sharp turn
58. Tilling tool
60. Winding curve
61. Great fury
62. Australian birds
64. Large coffeepot
66. Croon
68. Walkways
70. Bible book
74. Conscious of
75. Nose
76. Castle's defense
77. Snug retreat
78. Dumbfound
79. Anxious

DOWN

1. Not at work
2. Brewery order
3. Casual top
4. Boutique event
5. Sloe ___ fizz
6. Abilities
7. Easy or Wall
8. Miss
9. Pass
10. Stay
11. Intended
13. Babies' napkins
14. Doughnut feature
20. Coves
22. Went by airplane
24. Sound
25. Use rosary beads
26. Roof part
28. Coworker
32. Filthy
34. Modify
36. Scorpion's poison
38. Female fowl
39. Above, in poems
42. Scarf
44. ___ in a lifetime
45. Victory symbols
46. Orange drinks
48. Slime
50. Moose or elk
51. Nautical
52. Brokers
53. "The Night of the ___"
55. Plains animal
57. Mischievous kids
59. Banish
63. Store
65. John Doe, e.g.
67. Acquired
69. Color tone
71. Atlantic fish
72. Running game
73. Barnyard enclosure

PUZZLE 266

ACROSS

1. Sidewalk border
5. Knock
8. Move, as wings
12. Follow instructions
13. Liquid measure
15. Lion's den
16. A la ___
17. Cherish
18. Askew
19. Cooking leaf
20. Pace
21. Favorite
23. More expensive
25. Foamy brew
26. Moose's cousin
29. Veto
30. Green onion
32. Warmth
34. Fashionable
35. Fairy-tale beast
36. Clothes
37. Wear away
38. "Of ___ I Sing"
39. Uttered
40. Louse eggs
41. Fragments
42. Perfumes
44. To's mate
45. Not he
46. On in years
47. Chopin, e.g.
51. Pair
52. Noblemen
53. Attach buttons
54. Memo error
57. Clearances
59. Florida Key, e.g.
60. Listen to
61. Precise
62. Stubborn sort
63. Narrative
64. Flock mother
65. Pain in the neck

DOWN

1. Hair detanglers
2. WWII craft
3. Change the color of again
4. See you later!
5. Commuter
6. On
7. ___ your request
8. Level
9. Decree
10. Balloon input
11. Nose around
13. Kind of paint
14. Substitute for
20. Roast holder
22. Snakelike fish
24. Make possible
25. Sour compounds
26. "___ Is Enough"
27. Folk tales
28. Reflex site
30. Photographs
31. Moisturizer
32. Severe
33. Delete
34. Yelled
36. Departs
37. Confine
41. Swimsuit tops
43. Currently
44. Earliest
47. Cake unit
48. Put forth
49. Vends
50. Chirp
51. Shredded
52. Cabbage salad
54. "___ kingdom come . . ."
55. Supporting vote
56. Bogey beater
58. Wood chopper
59. Brat

ACROSS

1. Applaud
5. Maiden
9. Chicks' sounds
14. Air
15. Sore
16. Bayou
17. Cloudburst
18. Hammer end
19. Quartz variety
20. Fellow
21. Preserve
23. Unfamiliar
24. Flock babies
29. Polka ___
31. Uncertainties
34. Easter flowers
36. Regularly, in poems
39. Toddler
40. Bumbling
41. Work dough
43. Hatchet
44. Family
45. Female fowl
47. Honest ___
48. Depart
50. Dummy
52. Junior
53. Jump or pole
54. Strive
55. Go for it
56. Canine comment
58. Racing rowboat
60. Fitting
63. ___ a girl!
65. Taverns
69. Played over
71. Unexciting
75. Flunk
76. Posts
77. Diva's delight
78. Sicilian volcano
79. Fur wrap
80. Nomad's abode
81. Paper amount

DOWN

1. Deuce, e.g.
2. Hawaiian party
3. Desertlike
4. Wall section
5. Lick, as a cat
6. Topnotch
7. "Ain't ___ Sweet"
8. Harmony
9. Softly, to Bach
10. Neighbor of Scot.
11. Vivacity
12. Tennis's Sampras
13. Hearty meat dish
22. Product pitches
25. Similar
26. Kind of skirt
27. Mixes
28. Taste
30. Heavy weight
31. Lang. of Rome
32. Sly critters
33. T-bone, e.g.
35. Cultural
37. Lavish meal
38. Small drum
41. Bow down
42. Refuse
46. Neutral color
49. By way of
51. Raises, in poker
54. Behind
57. Washer cycle
59. Permanent inmate
60. Weapons
61. ___ moss
62. Larry, Curly, and Moe
64. Datum, for short
66. "___ and Hayes"
67. Foch or Simone
68. Bridge feat
70. The works
72. "Roses ___ Red"
73. 60 secs.
74. Chow down

PUZZLE 268

WHEN IN ROME

ACROSS

1. Tip, as a hat
5. Light brown
9. Health facilities
13. Ames locale
17. Fitzgerald of scat
18. Has-___
19. Beatles' movie
20. Object of worship
21. Asian nation
22. Blind part
23. Sector
24. Salon request
25. All-terrain chariot feature?
28. Roars
30. Quaint lodging
31. Summer month
32. Beget
33. Actor Edward James ___
36. Mixed breed
37. Rat-a-tat sound
41. Singer Celine ___
42. Roman weapon?
44. Flush
45. Eggs
46. Typeface

47. Voiceless sound
48. Average
49. Renaissance
51. Lane or Keaton
53. Cousins' moms
54. Combatant
55. Taxis
56. Greek letter
57. Computer component
60. Cafe order
61. Hoffman film
65. Beneficiary
66. Curse
67. Crooked
68. California fort
69. Send out
70. Caesar's senate proposal?
73. Attitude
74. Type of feed
76. Suffers
77. Au pair
78. Bobbles
79. Reflex site

80. Tenn. neighbor
81. Portugal's peninsula
84. Roman rhyme?
89. Actor O'Shea
90. Rhythm
92. Car make
93. Eurasian sea
94. Inter ___
95. Puzzled
96. Reclines
97. Hollow
98. Honey beverage
99. Chop ___
100. Sprint
101. Fin finish

DOWN

1. Hero shop
2. Scandinavian saint
3. Cascade
4. Style
5. "Barnaby Jones" star
6. Chamber
7. Cope with change
8. Fib
9. Shear
10. French father
11. Bistro brew

12. Madrid resident
13. Toga with a jacket?
14. Poetic tributes
15. Donned
16. Charity
26. Nav. rank
27. Division word
29. Tolkien creature
32. Cordwood measure
33. Garlic feature
34. Not taped
35. Utah city
36. Ho Chi ___ City
37. Astonishes
38. English river
39. Ordeal
40. Yoko et al.
42. Make a choice
43. Japanese port
46. ___ bad to worse
50. Cato's nightcap?
51. Russian villa
52. German self
53. Sailor's hail
55. The Ritz, e.g.
56. Toe woe

PUZZLE 268

57. Head cook
58. Actress Moore
59. Social reformer Jacob ___
60. Ancient Mexicans
61. "___ the night . . ."
62. Promptly
63. Hard metal
64. Mini whirlpool
66. Farmers' garb
67. Shout of jubilation
71. Rajah's wife
72. Spotted
73. Artificial
75. Diagnostic procedure, briefly
77. Composer Rorem
79. Feline
80. Stuffed dough dish
81. Islamic leader
82. Ill temper
83. ___ Kazan
84. Woman's first name
85. March time
86. Ticks off
87. Coolidge and Ripken
88. She, to Gigi
91. Lender's receipt

PUZZLE 269

NOT UP AND IN . . .

ACROSS

1. Flog
5. Crosswise
10. Canine
13. Toward shelter
14. ___ firma
15. ___ pop
16. Not a step up, but . . .
18. Taunt
19. Desire
20. That girl's
21. Daze
23. Male heirs
24. Phobias
25. Slanted
28. Roxie ___
29. Yank
32. Rains
33. Pretense
34. Radio company
35. ABA member
36. Coffeepot
37. Darling
38. Mongrel
39. Learned
41. Desist
42. Compass dir.
43. British party
44. Ran into
45. Make right
47. Drill
48. Sides
50. Leisure
51. Card game
54. Netman Arthur ___
55. Not giving in first, but . . .
58. Food plan
59. River mammal
60. Consumer
61. Dejected
62. Indigent
63. Foundation

DOWN

1. Lord's wife
2. Burn salve
3. Patched
4. Cackler
5. Show up
6. Grizzlies
7. Discord deity
8. Airport abbr.
9. Experts
10. Not up with salmon, but . . .
11. Lyrical
12. Fence door
15. Celebrity
17. Footwear
22. Estimate
23. Limber
24. Dim
25. ___ shuttle
26. ___ position
27. Not held in, but . . .
28. Rush
30. Edict
31. Pierced
33. Protect
37. Greek township
39. Let it stand
40. Rainy season
41. Troubles
44. Prayer's beads
46. Encounter
47. Bundled
48. Crazes
49. ___ Minor
50. Kitchen or major ender
51. Actress Kudrow
52. Singles
53. Grimm giant
56. Utah Indian
57. Vat

242

PUZZLE 270

1998 CINEMA HIT

ACROSS

1. Zhivago's beloved
5. Irrigate
10. Fraud
14. Military sch.
15. Garnish
16. Tempo
17. Half of title film
19. Charity gifts
20. Comprehend
21. Country's Haggard
22. Angers
23. Stable mate
24. Stripe
25. Detach
28. Ignited
29. Comic Hope
32. Pivot point
33. Frankie in title film
36. Gay Nineties, e.g.
37. Aria singer
38. Speechify
39. Desertlike
40. Ring legend
41. Lela ___ of title film
42. Croaker
43. Gumshoe
44. Good times
45. "McQ" actor
46. Suffers
48. Roseanne's surname
50. Derrick
52. Rent contract
54. Lobster trap
57. Existence
58. Half of title film

60. Spin like ___
61. Cruising
62. Milky stone
63. Subsequent
64. Hanker
65. Vend

DOWN

1. Statutes
2. Muscle strain
3. Funny lady Martha ___
4. Calculate
5. Thin biscuit
6. Cherish
7. Implement
8. ___ Stanley Gardner
9. Hosp. workers
10. Madrid's site
11. Star of title film
12. Pinnacle
13. Army chow
18. General Bradley
22. "Puttin' on the ___"
23. Flat hill
24. Tablecloth fabric
25. Egypt's Anwar ___
26. Deport
27. Star of title film
28. Jared ___ of "Panic Room"
30. Heavenly hunter
31. Cop's shield
33. Circles
34. Rainbows
35. Stadium cheer
39. A ways off
41. Govern
45. Small bird
47. Clumsy
48. Cotton bundler
49. Japanese, e.g.
50. Family
51. Observance
52. Not early
53. Movie feline
54. Pontiff
55. Elliptical
56. Blab
58. Ms. Wray
59. ___ Angeles

PUZZLE 271

• CHEAT •

ACROSS
1. Fast horse
5. Title of respect
8. "Murder, ___ Wrote"
11. Locations
13. Individual
14. Candle ingredient
15. Cheats
17. Caesar's three
18. I-toppers
19. Pennies
21. Changes
24. Learned person
25. Throng
26. Steering device
27. Black cuckoo
28. Contained
29. Flightless bird
32. Diced
35. Diamond weight
37. Request
39. Bother
40. Twig broom
41. Yours and mine
42. Picnic pest
43. Cheat
48. Foot part
49. Lamb's mom
50. Small stream
51. Sin
52. Lair
53. Type of bag

DOWN
1. Shade of blond
2. River, in Madrid
3. From ___ Z
4. Planted, as in a garden
5. Male children
6. Pen fluid
7. Save
8. Cheats
9. Port-au-Prince's land
10. Live
12. Cussed
16. "___ Not Unusual"
20. Opposite of WSW
21. Cry of discovery
22. Chaney of film
23. Cheat
24. Doctoral deg.
26. Roll of bills
28. That girl
30. Function starter
31. Colorado Indian
33. E.T.'s transport
34. Failed
35. Chocolate substitute
36. Classify
37. Diminish
38. Mexican mister
39. Center of activity
41. Sign of the future
44. Astound
45. Animal park
46. City parcel
47. ___ out a living

PUZZLE 272

• FICTIONAL PLACES •

ACROSS
1. Put (away)
5. Airport abbr.
8. Stage drama
12. Fasten securely
13. Actor Mineo
14. Ceremony
15. Legendary sunken island
17. Barbara or Anthony
18. New Zealand native
19. Pretentious display
21. Run away
23. Malt-drying ovens
27. Meadow
30. Swift's island of tiny folk
32. Montezuma's people
35. Unusual thing
36. "The Thorn Birds" ranch
38. Part of a wk.
39. Pacific island group
40. Give off
43. Persia, today
45. Tropical fruit
49. Health farms
52. Town of robotic wives
54. Highland skirt
55. Cup handle
56. Liberate
57. Affirmative votes
58. Beer's kin
59. Tilts, as a plane

DOWN
1. Close noisily
2. Good-bye, in London
3. Scandinavian city
4. Pier
5. NYC clock zone
6. Capital of Taiwan
7. In addition
8. Not C.O.D.
9. Cover
10. Devoured
11. Craving
16. Zilch
20. Shape
22. Otherwise
24. Expectorate
25. Ballet skirt
26. Eye woe
27. Youths
28. Poet Pound
29. Molecule part
31. Rich soil
33. Conceited people
34. Blacken
37. ___ floss
41. Mischievous child
42. Chewy candy
44. Voyaging
46. Mrs. Charles
47. Expanded
48. Emotional poems
49. Heavens
50. Dessert choice
51. In the manner of
53. Before, in verse

Fill in each row and column of the Wordsworth diagram with at least two words. The number of words in a row or column is indicated by the number of clues. Words are not separated by extra squares, so all the squares will be filled in when the diagram is completed.

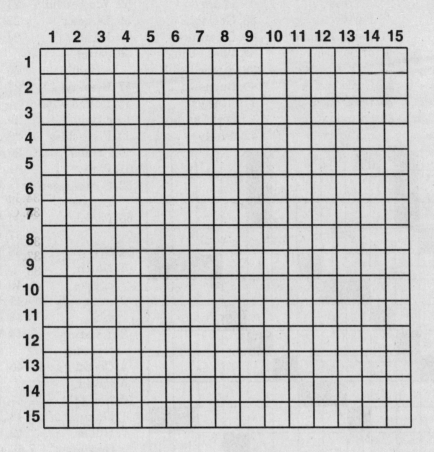

ACROSS

1. Cautious • Bistro • Lantern

2. Go back (on) • Hindu queen • Unclear

3. Strange • Marsh bird • Evokes

4. Swerve • Mechanic's garb • ____-tzu

5. Beige • Barren land • Revise

6. Railed • Kindle • Ingested

7. Manners • Native of Naples

8. Say • Nab • Appropriate • Parched

9. Favorite • Key, e.g. • Required

10. Different • Moisture • Lubricate •

    Ms. Moreno

11. Stable bit • Covert • Whittled

12. Faults • Angered • Time periods

13. High peak • Egyptian deity • Fib • Tear

14. Ganders • Track event • Prairie • Conger

15. Gaelic • Lair • Postpone • Sprite

DOWN

1. Adage • Parody • Mellow

2. Scarlet • Card game • Higher

3. Below • Records

4. Elk • Shoshonean • Digits • Sage

5. Poultry product • Emotional poem • Sad

6. Courage • Supped • Felony

7. Forest sights • Silly • Up

8. Feline • Baseball's Jackson • Poured forth

9. Close, in verse • Nothing • Routine •

    Follower's suffix

10. Stuff • Ill-fated ship • Valley

11. Wicked • Day's march • Statute • Abundance

12. Natural resin • Ore refinery • Return a favor

13. Nimble • Succor • Plummet • Female ruff

14. TV's "____ X" • Glacial ridge • Centerboard

15. Chilean coin • Gainsay • Pop • Ego

PUZZLE 274

• ZESTY •

ACROSS

1. Constantly
5. Small drum
10. Dory
14. Refute
15. Ms. Astaire
16. Soda flavor
17. Kitty builder
18. Descartes and Lacoste
19. Norse war god
20. Actress Farrow
21. Large primate of Borneo
23. To wit
25. Cycle prefix
26. Beseeched
28. Of unknown maturity
32. Comic DeGeneres
33. "Where's ____?"
35. Year, to Pedro
36. Garlands
37. Clearances
38. Wise about
39. Rustic hotel
40. Buenos ____
41. "Ragged Dick" author
42. Avidly
44. Lances
45. Once called
46. Hire
48. Having four right angles
52. You betcha!
55. Director Kazan
56. Jewel weight
57. Bean type
58. Italian wine city
59. First-class
60. Related
61. Pare
62. Copenhagen natives
63. Portal

DOWN

1. Dutch cheese
2. ____, vidi, vici
3. Twisting together
4. Cereal grain
5. Paved
6. "Let's Make ____"
7. Hill or Goodman
8. Cassini of fashion
9. Echoes
10. Nova ____, Canada
11. Finale
12. Actor Ken ____
13. Designer Vera ____
21. Boding
22. Loosen
24. "Battle of the ____"
26. Misrepresent
27. Verdugo of films
28. Rubber trees
29. African lake
30. Go in
31. The ____ (rock group)
33. Unsure
34. Hops beverage
37. Quieted
38. Dairy-case buy
40. Field of study
41. Copycat
43. Necessitate
44. Uses an ice rink
46. Shroud of ____
47. Winged
48. Harvest
49. Otherwise
50. Quote
51. Ball
53. Emanate
54. Mentally sound
57. Dawdle

PUZZLE 275   Drop-Ins

Using only the letters given in the box, fill in all the dashes to form 8-letter words. Each letter is used only once.

> AAA CC DD EEEEEEE F G HHH III
> KK LLLLLL M NNN R T UU V W

1. E __ K __ O __ N __

2. A __ J __ C __ N __

3. S __ I __ L __ U __

4. C __ E __ I __ A __

5. S __ A __ E __ G __

6. A __ Y __ H __ R __

7. B __ C __ F __ R __

8. J __ V __ N __ L __

9. B __ C __ E __ O __

10. D __ A __ O __ A __

DOUBLE TROUBLE

Not really double trouble, but double fun! Solve this puzzle as you would a regular crossword, EXCEPT place one, two, or three letters in each box. The number of letters in each answer is shown in parentheses after its clue.

ACROSS

1. Dexterous (4)
3. Decease (6)
7. Becomes serious (6)
9. Salve (9)
11. Plant pests (6)
12. Daily fare (4)
13. Bring up (4)
15. Carol (4)
16. Impetuous (5)
18. Strange (5)
19. Demolish, to some (8)
21. Became sluggish (9)
22. Remedy (8)
24. Inconsiderate (7)
27. Evensong (7)
30. Recover (5)
31. Forces (on) (6)
32. Spicy Mexican sauce (4)
34. Pelt (3)
35. Lean, as a boat (4)
36. Seat (5)
37. Chagrined (7)
40. Stir up (6)
41. Extract (6)
42. Shut in (4)

DOWN

1. Condenses (8)
2. Fewer (4)
3. Judge (4)
4. In vogue (6)
5. Small land mass (5)
6. Yalie (3)
7. Daytime dramas (5)
8. In arrears (6)
10. Implore (7)
14. Merited (6)
16. Main impact, as of a blow (5)
17. Worker for a cause (8)
18. Straighten (5)
20. Litter (5)
21. Asserts (6)
23. Performs (4)
24. Feudal peasant (4)
25. Designer Ashley (5)
26. Young mare (5)
28. Press or wave (9)
29. Petition (7)
31. Promote the growth of (6)
33. Before, to a bard (3)
35. Citrus fruit (4)
36. Computer component (4)
38. Roe source (4)
39. Rapid descent (4)

(Crossword grid with numbered cells 1–42)

Domino Theory

Arrange the four dominoes on the left into the pattern on the right so that a correct multiplication problem is formed. The number of dots on each half-domino is considered a one-digit number; for example, a half with six dots represents the number 6.

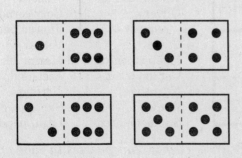

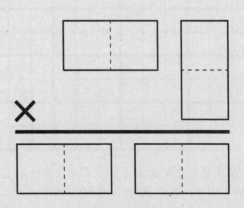

PUZZLE 278

BRICK BY BRICK

Rearrange this stack of bricks to form a crossword puzzle. The clues will help you fit the bricks into their correct places. Row 1 has been filled in for you. Use the bricks to fill in the remaining spaces.

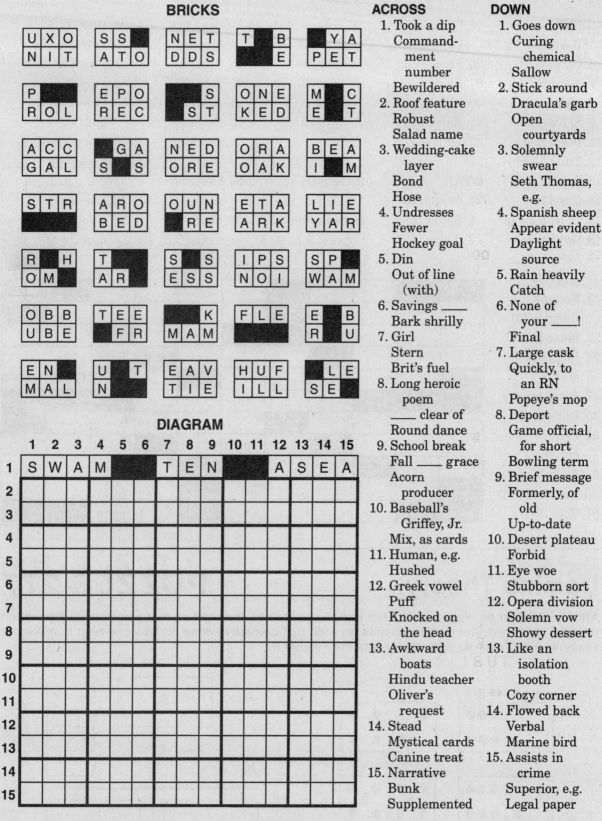

BRICKS

ACROSS

1. Took a dip
   Commandment number
   Bewildered
2. Roof feature
   Robust
   Salad name
3. Wedding-cake layer
   Bond
   Hose
4. Undresses
   Fewer
   Hockey goal
5. Din
   Out of line (with)
6. Savings ___
   Bark shrilly
7. Girl
   Stern
   Brit's fuel
8. Long heroic poem
   ___ clear of
   Round dance
9. School break
   Fall ___ grace
   Acorn producer
10. Baseball's Griffey, Jr.
    Mix, as cards
11. Human, e.g.
    Hushed
12. Greek vowel
    Puff
    Knocked on the head
13. Awkward boats
    Hindu teacher
    Oliver's request
14. Stead
    Mystical cards
    Canine treat
15. Narrative
    Bunk
    Supplemented

DOWN

1. Goes down
   Curing chemical
   Sallow
2. Stick around
   Dracula's garb
   Open courtyards
3. Solemnly swear
   Seth Thomas, e.g.
4. Spanish sheep
   Appear evident
   Daylight source
5. Rain heavily
   Catch
6. None of your ___!
   Final
7. Large cask
   Quickly, to an RN
   Popeye's mop
8. Deport
   Game official, for short
   Bowling term
9. Brief message
   Formerly, of old
   Up-to-date
10. Desert plateau
    Forbid
11. Eye woe
    Stubborn sort
12. Opera division
    Solemn vow
    Showy dessert
13. Like an isolation booth
    Cozy corner
14. Flowed back
    Verbal
    Marine bird
15. Assists in crime
    Superior, e.g.
    Legal paper

DIAGRAM

	1	2	3	4	5	6	7	8	9	10	11	12	13	14	15
1	S	W	A	M				T	E	N			A	S	E	A
2															
3															
4															
5															
6															
7															
8															
9															
10															
11															
12															
13															
14															
15															

BRICK BY BRICK FANS! *Get a ton of Brick by Bricks—over 50 fun puzzles in each of our special collections! To order, see page 159.*

PUZZLE 279

• CENTRAL •

ACROSS

1. Matterhorn's range
5. Japanese beverage
9. Part in a play
13. ____-bargain
14. Met musical
16. "The Good Earth" heroine
17. Mountain lake
18. Cybercafe patrons
19. Darn
20. Route from West Africa to the Americas
23. Cape fox
24. Discolor
25. Trail behind
28. Sailor's yes
29. Poisonous snake
32. Sub in a tub
36. Sweater neckline
38. Country home
40. Avoiding extremes
44. Ta ta, in Tours
45. Chorus syllable
46. Code breakers
47. Tease, as hair
48. Tear
51. Summer, in Paris
53. Helpers
55. Archibald of basketball
59. Period of Egyptian history
63. Cover with gold
64. Put on cloud nine
65. Region
67. Threatening word
68. Discourage
69. Wilbur's talking horse
70. Anthropologist in Samoa
71. Dealer's car, for short
72. "Buona ____, Mrs. Campbell"

DOWN

1. Fitting
2. Andes animal
3. Persian pixies
4. Smooths, as wood
5. "Heart and ____"
6. Church recess
7. Holds on to
8. Printing mistakes
9. Ancient Italian
10. Designer Cassini
11. Bowling alley
12. Finish
15. Ore test
21. Actress Dolores ____ Rio
22. Strainer
26. Caesar's greeting
27. Prefix for earth
29. Lotion ingredient
30. Do in, as a dragon
31. Steno tablets
32. Epps or Sharif
33. "____ Rose" (song title)
34. Correct text
35. "____ to Joy"
37. Young newt
39. Rankle
41. Sensational
42. Three, in Turin
43. Head topper
49. Dawdled
50. Prepared spuds
52. School subj.
53. Did sums
54. Compete on ice
56. Second president
57. Yankee manager
58. Moslem ruler
59. Runner's distance
60. "Casablanca" lady
61. List component
62. Fictional sleuth Wolfe
63. Jewel
66. Dentists' gp.

Riddle Me This

PUZZLE 280

Here are five riddles and their mixed-up answers! Unscramble each group of letters to form a word. Use those words to fill in the answer blanks.

IDETR   ELTMNA   TEH   EEARDR   SI   LSOGS   IHRGT
SUSIEBSN   DGO   EPDSE   AOHNC   ECLIS

1. What name is given a police officer with a radar gun? ___ ___ ___ ___ ___ ___

2. What is a Mexican restaurant called? ___ ___ ___ ___ ___ ___   ___ ___ ___ ___ ___ ___ ___ ___

3. What is superficial learning called? ___ ___ ___ ___ ___   ___ ___ ___ ___ ___

4. How was Fido after chasing a car? ___ ___ ___ - ___ ___ ___ ___ ___

5. What is a good name for a deli? ___ ___ ___   ___ ___ ___ ___ ___ ___ ___
___ ___ ___ ___ ___

249

PUZZLE 281

Instructions for solving Codewords are given on page 11.

Letter key grid (left):

1	14
2	15
3	16
4	17
5	18
6	19
7 A	20 N
8	21
9	22
10	23
11	24
12	25
13	26

Main grid:

26	12	20	14	■	19	7	20	7	■	16	25	7
15	2	15	4	■	7	21	15	26	■	2	15	10
7	20	3	11	■	14	11	16	3	■	7 A	2	26
■	■	16	25	11	26	3	■	1	20 N	15	15
19	24	22	3	11	■	■	18	11	1	15	4
15	1	15	■	23	24	12	3	15	13	■	■
2	15	13	■	24	16	18	15	4	■	12	7	22
■	■	13	15	15	19	15	13	■	22	4	12
8	5	7	4	16	■	15	16	3	15	4
26	11	26	17	■	8	12	20	13	12	■	■
15	26	26	■	22	24	19	15	■	7	9	7	4
7	8	15	■	11	10	15	21	■	6	12	26	15
3	18	17	■	3	15	20	3	■	15	3	7	16

Alphabet key (right): A̶ N̶ / B O / C P / D Q / E R / F S / G T / H U / I V / J W / K X / L Y / M Z

PUZZLE 282

Letter key grid (left):

1	14
2	15
3 I	16
4	17
5 D	18
6	19
7	20
8	21
9	22
10	23
11	24
12	25
13	26

Main grid:

22	8	21	■	8	17	12	14	■	22	16	17	8	7
8	13	6	■	17	6	8	19	■	25	8	19	8	15	6
14	8	11	■	22	16	17	6	■	16	11	6	25	8	19
2	16	23	■	■	14	6	6	18	6	21	■	■
8	23	9	25	■	6	8	21	19	14	■	23	8	23	8
■	■	9	7	7	■	16	23	14	■	20	16	22
■	26	8	19	16	23	9	21	14	■	22	17	10	25	6
3	10	16	23	6	■	22	8	17	■	9	8	21	6	18
10	18	18 D	6	21	■	6	1	6	14	9	21	6	14
8	15	6	■	1	6	19	■	6	17	24	■	■
18	6	14	24	■	5	6	19	9	19	■	14	8	13	19
■	■	21	8	16	18	6	18	■	■	22	16	6
8	4	8	16	17	14	■	8	18	18	14	■	8	22	23
7	16	17	17	6	23	■	22	17	16	6	■	21	6	23
23	6	17	17	14	■	■	14	1	19	11	■	23	21	1

Alphabet key (right): A N / B O / C̶ P / D̶ Q / E R / F S / G T / H U / I̶ V / J W / K X / L Y / M Z

ACROSS

1. Wooden box
6. Tentacles
10. Cave sound
14. Employs
15. Frog or year
16. Wallop
17. Bread bakers
18. Cassette
19. Tress
20. Guy
21. Good buddy
22. Obligated
24. Dais
27. Clip
28. Pipe joints
29. Subscribed again
33. Breakfast fare
36. Cow's chew
37. Baled commodity
38. Chopping
39. Blot
40. Strainer
42. Small bit
43. Skillet
44. More soggy
45. Sniffed
48. Recreation
49. Belonging to us
50. Last
54. Small branches
57. Commandment word
58. Floor-shiner
59. Came to ground
60. Tiny amount
62. Rattler
64. Rubberneck
65. Fit of temper
66. Peeler
67. Spectator
68. Golf-ball props
69. Intermediary

DOWN

1. Bite down
2. Challenger
3. Spot for sports
4. Twice five
5. Winding curve
6. Sacred tables
7. Kingdom
8. Traveler's need
9. Participated in a bee
10. Get free
11. Association
12. Throw
13. Stare at
21. Survey
23. Electrified atom
25. Promgoer
26. Pennant
29. Polish
30. Hone
31. Overhang
32. Colorer
33. Broadway hit
34. Huge quiz
35. Fair feature
36. Tuna container
39. June honoree
40. Highway vehicle
41. List member
43. Stick with it
44. Light-bulb word
46. Hang around
47. Pull with effort
48. Brags
50. Loosen
51. Mindful
52. Seized
53. Put forth
54. Cooking herb
55. Romp
56. Ready to eat
61. Individual
62. Health spring
63. Hassle

PUZZLE 283

PUZZLE 284

IT'S ALL FOR . . .

ACROSS

1. Epochs
5. Some cheese
10. Bewildered
15. Early TV host
19. Gold cloth
20. Diva Callas
21. Group of notes
22. Regarding
23. Setting for exhibits
25. Something difficult to deal with
27. Agave
28. Relieves
29. News flashes
30. Orig. texts
33. Curbs
35. Author Brown
36. Second name?
37. Hawke et al.
39. Forum wear
41. Kingdoms
44. Lozenges
45. Classroom activity
49. Wetlands agcy.
51. Moistens, poetically
52. Rude person
53. Patton command
54. Mine entrance

55. MIT workplace
56. Possess
57. Butter substitute
58. Garment cut
59. Australian bird
60. French film
61. Room, to Rene
63. Golfers' woes
64. Abase
66. Grouchy
67. Fine fiddle
68. UFO riders
70. Hair coloring
71. Ripens
72. Crooner Cole
75. Street markers
76. Skater Brinker
77. Arm bone
78. Compass pt.
79. Carol
80. Roman Ares
81. ___ Antilles
83. Workers'-aid gp.
84. Shapely curve
85. Revue
87. Silver salmon
88. Fortune
90. Learning method
91. Pakistan city
92. In the manner of

93. Midmorning
94. Speedy
97. Joined
98. Gather up
101. Irate
103. Point
104. Dressage events
106. Amateur's revue
112. Actress Archer
113. Home of the brave?
114. Quickly!
115. Billion ending
116. False god
117. Water jugs
118. Harass
119. Douses

DOWN

1. Loop trains
2. Cheer
3. Latin I verb
4. Baste
5. Beams
6. Capital of Vietnam
7. Cosmetics name
8. ___ Grande
9. Pappy
10. Relating to Greece
11. Plural of that
12. Vexed
13. Slips
14. Flurry
15. Soft-hued

16. Tennis ace
17. Proton's place
18. Aisles
24. Alerts
26. Enemy
28. Ventriloquist Bergen
30. Interfere
31. Rivulet
32. Its capital is Hollywood
34. Potbellied ___
36. Elusive
38. Camera type, briefly
40. Chalk up
41. San ___, Italy
42. Elixirs are sold here
43. Quill, e.g.
45. Ladd movie
46. Flung
47. Dawdle
48. It grew in Brooklyn
50. Actor Roscoe ___
52. Fills in gaps
54. Disembarked
57. Earthenware jar
58. Sad word
60. Containers
61. Phoenix five
62. Prince Valiant's son
63. Bedaub
65. Bounder
66. Feel

252

67. Nixon's veep
68. Dermal disorder
69. Unfettered
70. Famous spy
71. Moreover
73. On the beach
74. Heckled
76. Bunny's kin
77. Guide
80. Conductor Eduardo ___
81. Former Australian leader Joseph ___
82. Approx.
83. Aah's mate
85. Waltz, to Jacques
86. Locks
87. Plebe
89. Dangling ornament
91. Finch
93. Fortress
95. World carrier
96. Segment
98. "Pequod" captain
99. "___ Lisa"
100. Wild buffalo of India
101. Masticate
102. Twine
105. Canonized fem.
106. Label
107. Primate
108. Adage
109. Hasten
110. Table scrap
111. Director Craven

PUZZLE 285

WHAT A THRILL!

ACROSS

1. Hits
5. Sloping walk
9. Set ablaze
12. Benefit
14. Nimble
16. Rage
17. Tremendous!
19. Curly's pal
20. Wind dir.
21. Antonym's ant.
22. "The ___ Cometh"
24. Nightly need
26. Actress Alicia
27. Awesome!
34. Bacon chunk
37. ". . . who lived in ___"
38. Perfume
39. Jul. follower
40. Take a load off
41. Egg cells
42. Split
44. Celts
46. Woeful expression
47. Exciting!
50. Darjeeling, e.g.
51. Satisfies
54. Mournful sounds
57. Scoundrel
58. Milne character
60. Cinnabar, e.g.
61. Invigorating!
64. Fleur-de-___
65. Strange
66. Regional
67. N.Y. time
68. Cub houses
69. Mrs. Ed?

DOWN

1. Diamond corner
2. Bread bakers
3. Jurors
4. Sibling, for short
5. Precipitate
6. Bygone days
7. Maxi's cousin
8. Appease
9. Capital of Peru
10. ___ horse
11. PGA prop
13. Surgical beam
15. TV's Verdugo
18. Outgoing personality
23. Kind of shark
25. Peter (out)
28. Very, in music
29. Pickpocket
30. Fiercely
31. Icon
32. PBS series
33. Foie ___
34. Free from risk
35. Storm break
36. Novelist James ___
43. Prefix with plasm
44. Bestowed
45. Rope-making material
46. Rep.
48. Josh
49. Of birth
52. Author Jong
53. Underwater radar
54. Grate
55. Take five
56. Patriarch
57. Laments
59. Leer at
60. Fiesta cheer
62. 60 secs.
63. Singer Petty

ACROSS

1. Disagreement
5. IRS employees
9. Skill
14. Sacred
15. A Guthrie
16. Vietnam's capital
17. Purposes
18. Soybean paste
19. Caper
20. Parkman classic
23. Neither's follower
24. Jewel
25. Chitchat
28. Chute starter
31. Biblical songs
36. Concur
38. A woodwind
40. Diving bird
41. Longfellow verse
44. Sinful
45. Pierre's pate
46. Doctrine
47. Western New York tribe
49. Few
51. Snaky sound
52. Liable
54. Compass pt.
56. Lazarus poem
64. Coliseum
65. Roof extension
66. Yugoslavian president
67. Danger
68. Dueling sword
69. Margarine
70. Marsh grasses
71. Grizzlies' caves
72. Fence support

DOWN

1. Slam
2. Swanky
3. Helm position
4. Boxer Mike ___
5. Tourist's must
6. Puritan
7. Too
8. Chinese family
9. Amulets
10. Frog genus
11. Against
12. Thwart
13. Twitch
21. Rodeo competitor
22. Sioux dwelling
25. Gawks
26. Century plant
27. Boston skater
29. Gallivant
30. Aids a felon
32. "God's Little ___"
33. Back areas
34. Styles
35. Lets it stand
37. Ms. Macpherson
39. Snack cookie
42. Day's march
43. Office clerk
48. Erie and Suez
50. Free-for-alls
53. Wool material
55. Halt legally
56. Birch, e.g.
57. Present!
58. Oklahoma city
59. ___ Canaveral
60. Kiln
61. Farm tower
62. Shoshoneans
63. Chimney dust
64. Rainy mo.

PUZZLE 287

TURNAROUNDS

ACROSS

1. Bogus butter
5. Smack
9. Rims
14. Red-pencil
15. Drifter
16. Nary a soul
17. Moves by
19. Jay feature
20. Army gp.
21. Common couple
22. Corset parts
24. "Lolita" star
26. Geologic stratum
27. Ms. Thurman
30. Begins operating
33. Negative link
34. Turquoise
37. Fourth letter
38. ___ Hawkins Day
40. Rock type
41. Track shapes
44. Plateau's kin
45. Foot lever
47. Hilo gift
48. Music and dance
49. Ang or Spike
50. Parvenus
54. Goof
55. Piglet's pal
56. Latin verb
59. Sorrow
61. D.C. figure
63. Notable span
65. Faint
67. Assumes command of
70. Vexation
71. Malevolent
72. Place for a tie
73. Affirmatives
74. Corded fabrics
75. Food scraps

DOWN

1. Smell this
2. On one plane
3. Lament
4. Above, to a bard
5. Fake
6. Stir-fry pans
7. Mr. Burrows
8. Flings
9. Bivouac
10. Small boat
11. Fails in business
12. Type measures
13. Collection
18. Canvas cover
23. Greek letter
25. Honshu port
26. Furtiveness
28. Damp
29. Neighborhoods
31. Big deal
32. Give the gas to
34. Cider source
35. Peculiar
36. Experiences
39. Accumulate
42. Grassy spot
43. Gentleman
46. Tall blooms
51. Mystery writer
52. Quieter
53. Decades
57. Cut off
58. Upright
60. Stray
61. Bypass
62. Slender fish
64. Torah cabinets
65. Eavesdrop
66. Minute
68. St. crosser
69. Yoko ___

ACROSS

1. Isinglasses
6. Omit
10. Long-range weapon inits.
14. Helm direction
15. Architect Saarinen
16. Fishing boat
17. Start of quip
19. Major work
20. Big combos
21. Article topper
23. Bro's sibling
25. ___ gratias
26. Tibetan gazelle
27. Snaky swimmer
28. Boyer of baseball
30. Part 2 of quip
33. Dozing
35. Baby hooter
36. Abrade
37. Frankie or Cleo
39. "The Producers" role
43. Completely
45. Telephone button
47. Part 3 of quip
51. Store lights
52. Klee contemporary
53. Asian fete
54. Snack
56. Classic prefix
57. Prevented
59. Israel natives
61. Ink smudge
62. End of quip
66. Differently
67. Lather
68. Mocking look
69. Bread grains
70. Coxcombs
71. Is inclined

DOWN

1. Flower time
2. Wall St. occurrence
3. Legal advisers
4. With the bow, musically
5. Straphanger
6. Melees
7. Beer buys
8. High dudgeon
9. Low-quality book
10. False god
11. Imitated
12. Sultanate of Borneo
13. Yours truly
18. Formerly named
22. Eastern school
23. Old wound
24. Rick's love
26. Belle's dress
29. Somewhat warm
31. French soldier
32. Piano exercise
34. Used as a foil
38. Much
40. Springsteen song
41. Swimmer's path
42. Plus
44. Designate
46. Commit
47. Talk fast
48. Out loud
49. Revolted
50. Kingdoms
55. Attorneys' gp.
58. Rds.
59. Cookie type
60. Ms. Meara
63. Court
64. Crimson
65. Cal. confines

PUZZLE 288

DOWN TO EARTH

PUZZLE 289

FLOWER POWER

The answers to the petaled puzzle will go in a curve from the number on the outside to the center of the flower. Each number in the flower will have two 5-letter answers. One goes in a clockwise direction and the second in a counterclockwise direction. We have entered two answers to help you begin.

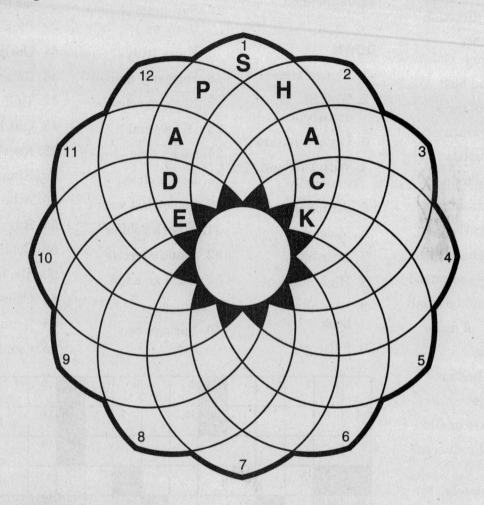

CLOCKWISE

1. Rough cabin
2. "___ of Fortune"
3. Stream
4. Vote in
5. Get tangled
6. Part of AKA
7. Bobbin
8. Display
9. Style
10. Multitude
11. Breakfast item
12. Recreation

COUNTERCLOCKWISE

1. Gardener's tool
2. "___ Line Is It Anyway?"
3. Layout
4. Assemble
5. Finely contoured
6. Bend in prayer
7. Nibble
8. On a ship's left side
9. Angry dog's comment
10. Egret, e.g.
11. Of sound
12. Remorseful

PUZZLE 290
• SIXTH SENSE •

ACROSS
1. Lets stand
6. Formerly, formerly
10. It may be bright
14. Annoying Internet ad
15. ___ beer
16. Ponder, with "over"
17. City in upstate New York
18. Yesteryear
20. Pier
21. Marine bird
22. Soundtrack
23. Finish the lawn
25. Puts a spell on
26. Apartment dweller's lack
31. Broods
32. Like pie?
33. They deliver the goods
36. Like the Sahara
37. Severe
39. Fencer's tool
40. Fishing gear
41. ___-service
42. Hindu chant
44. Speed measure
46. Violin top
49. Geometry concern
50. A place to remember
51. Real mad
53. Average
57. High point of the Rocky Mountains
59. Sneeze sound
60. Writing on the wall
61. Major or Minor
62. Rhythm
63. Take ten
64. Heaters
65. German steel city

DOWN
1. Cager Webb
2. Oz visitor
3. It's a long story
4. ___ out (tired)
5. Bather's facility
6. Antipasto follower
7. Bridle strap
8. Inter- changeable
9. Uno e due
10. Tainted
11. Pairs
12. Commercial bovine
13. Choir members
19. Cheeky
21. Wedding dress shade
24. Calendar box
25. Fine wool
26. Leave a mark
27. Pamplona runner
28. "Metamorphoses" poet
29. They do the lord's work
30. ___ de deux
33. Until
34. Inca country
35. Broil
38. Ginger ___
39. Improves
41. Grain towers
43. Modern art?
44. Blink of an eye
45. Winter coats
46. Flavor
47. Weather region, poetically
48. Gathers leaves
51. Blood parts
52. Hops kiln
54. Resistance units
55. Hitchcock classic
56. Cow's hurdle
58. Wrinkly dog
59. Got fed up?

Progressions

PUZZLE 291

Can you follow the mathematical progression to find the fifth number in each series?

A.	9	10	13	18	___	34	45	58	73
B.	3	10	20	27	___	61	122	129	258
C.	49	53	48	54	___	51	46	52	45
D.	27	24	33	30	___	36	45	42	51
E.	51	53	57	63	___	73	77	83	91
F.	35	30	26	29	___	26	22	25	27
G.	26	35	27	34	___	33	29	32	30

PUZZLE 292

• DWELL ON IT •

ACROSS
1. Lion's share
5. Skillful
9. ___ Bunny
13. Hautboy
17. Singer James
18. Darn it!
19. "Hair" hairstyle
20. Opera box
21. Editor's mark
22. Rail prefix
23. Lunchtime, for some
24. Pickle seasoning
25. Hardly haute cuisine
28. Breakfast treats
30. Last word, often
31. Roller-coaster bonus
33. Kanga's baby
34. Hoi ___
38. Categories
40. Macaroni shape
44. Battle song?
45. Madrid Mrs.
47. Young boy
49. Lotto adaptation
50. Herbal drinks
51. Diamond section?
55. Give the boot
56. Smarty Jones, e.g.
58. Scientist Marie ___
59. Manors
61. Ghoul follower?
63. Zesty flavors
65. Pioneer Carson
66. Skunk
70. Trite
72. Oft-counted animal
76. Film's Guinness
77. Macaulay Culkin film
80. Atop
81. Change decor
82. Previously
83. Actress Grier
84. Mr. ___ (Lorre role)
85. Wanders
87. Each
91. Milwaukee player
93. Browning's before
95. "___, Brute?"
96. Furthermore
97. Devious reasoner
101. European festival
107. Melville work
108. Evening, in Florence
110. Without, to Henri
111. Cain's brother
112. MacDonald had one
113. Julia's brother
114. Gaelic
115. Actor Neeson
116. Forest filler
117. Lengthy tale
118. Tinted
119. Allows

DOWN
1. Fit together
2. Sarge's dog
3. Goblet part
4. London museum
5. Reprimand
6. Offspring
7. Long and lean
8. French star
9. Maine city
10. Alien ship
11. Get bigger
12. Detection device
13. Swanee River song
14. Seethe
15. Rude look
16. Slithery fish
26. Corporate exec
27. Nice refusal?
29. Rival
32. Anti-fur org.
34. Walkway
35. Sandwich cookie
36. Fibber
37. Canine film
38. Entire range
39. Glut
41. Musical rhythm
42. Story starter
43. Stir-fry pans
46. Mythical bird
48. School furniture
52. Wipe off
53. Nina's sister ship
54. Allowed by law
57. Computer key
60. "___ the season . . ."
62. Laughter
64. Incline
66. Young cod
67. Bread spread
68. Castor's mother
69. Party attire, perhaps
71. Bambi's aunt
73. Enough, to a bard
74. Luncheon finisher
75. Penniless
78. Pout
79. Like some wedding invitations
86. ___ Lanka
88. New York college town
89. Letter from Greece?
90. Used a bad word
92. Drivel
94. Sibilant sounds
96. Stressed out
97. Tender
98. Baseball's Moreno
99. Study carefully
100. Trillion prefix
102. Diversify
103. Place for a concert
104. Tony's relative
105. Vegetarian's no-no
106. Shade providers
109. Equip

PUZZLE 293

• ALSO KNOWN AS •

ACROSS
1. Mr. Kristofferson
5. Wound remnant
9. Boring
13. Live in the woods
17. Bump
18. Walking aid
19. Genesis twin
20. English-horn's kin
21. "____ the Rainbow"
22. Fast horse
23. Feathery plant
24. Holiday log
25. Oregon
28. Kid's vehicle
30. Infuriation
31. Canvas shelter
33. Bonnet
34. ____ shuttle
37. Benedict Arnold's crime
40. Uptight
44. Ocean motion
45. Spy org.
46. Sword type
48. Find a buyer
49. Call ____ day
50. "Seinfeld" character
53. "Blueberries for ____"
54. Dog's wagger
55. Saunter
57. Lullaby, e.g.
59. Boat race
61. Doctors' gp.
62. Senator Kefauver
64. Encountered
65. Curious box opener, of myth
69. Man of the hour
70. Gusto
74. Abbr. for a copy's source
75. Sixth sense, briefly
77. Become more forgiving
79. Certain boot width
80. Bridal-gown trim
81. Civil disorder
83. Opposite of ext.
84. Comedian Carvey
85. Vigilant
87. Pie option
90. Jewish feast
91. ____ Lanka
93. "Dukes of Hazzard" role
94. Bamboozle
95. "Soul Sacrifice" group
99. Minnesota

105. Vicinity
106. Liberate
108. Tear apart
109. "____ What You Did"
110. Gold coating
111. Flair
112. Ms. Brickell
113. High heel, e.g.
114. Macpherson of "Sirens"
115. Easy victory
116. Kennel comment
117. "Guarding ____"

DOWN
1. Door handle
2. Roam
3. Mental flash
4. Ceremony
5. Spook
6. Pullman and diner
7. Surgeon-to-be's subj.
8. Money-back offer
9. Protection
10. Put to good ____
11. Phyllis's husband
12. Noontime repast
13. South Dakota
14. Be next to

15. Lawn pest
16. Gaze
26. Poet's before
27. Herbal drink
29. Kind of bran
32. First-rate
34. Blend
35. Bread with a pocket
36. Cain's father
37. Carrere of "True Lies"
38. Pay hike
39. At hand
41. Spiffy
42. Slash
43. Jazzy Fitzgerald
45. More obvious
47. Component
50. A Muppet
51. Snack
52. Keyboard key
56. Wisconsin
58. "Breathless" star
60. Polite chap
63. Like a rock
65. Silents' Negri

66. Caspian's neighbor
67. Friendly
68. China's site
71. Enjoy a novel
72. Hackman or Wilder
73. 52 weeks
76. Flag holder
78. Compass pt.
82. Trig function
84. Cavity filler
86. ____-la-la
88. Bossy's remark
89. Fish hawk
90. Mayday!
92. Deduce
94. Crawl
95. Wise seasoning?
96. Seed covering
97. Actress Carter
98. A Guthrie
100. Animal skin
101. Sermon topic
102. Tennis's Arthur ____
103. New Mexico resort
104. Meadow mamas
107. ____ de Cologne

PUZZLE 294

• WEATHER FORECAST •

ACROSS
1. Flows back
5. Asterisk
9. Hole punch
12. Froth
17. Harvest
18. Musical conclusion
19. Ms. Salonga
20. H_2O
21. ___ spumante
22. Is beholden to
23. Big Blue's acronym
24. Glacial ridge
25. 1972 Neil Simon play
29. Kindled
30. At any time
31. Full of spunk
35. Supply food for
38. Urgent
40. "Mayberry ___"
41. Pedal digit
42. Chinese gelatin
43. Knockout count
44. Mope
46. Thrice said, it's a movie
47. Gratuity
48. 1952 Gene Kelly film
52. Priest
54. Greek marketplace
55. TV's Tarzan
56. Leggy bird
57. New Deal acronym
58. Item of value
62. According to
64. Actress Zasu ___
66. Chant
67. 1936 Margaret Mitchell classic
72. Indian flatbread
73. Mr. Redding
74. Assistant
75. Prince Valiant's son
76. Diplomacy
77. High-arced toss
78. Corrida cry
79. Sup
81. Sumter and Knox
82. Barren place
84. Wilson of "Zoolander"
86. Islet
87. 1972 Dean Jones film
93. "El Capitan" composer
96. One, to Helmut
97. Author Bombeck
98. Gravy vessel
100. Go back to zero
101. Female ruff
102. Stratum
103. Companion of Artemis
104. Ryan or Castle
105. Sibilant letter
106. Dispatched
107. Broad smile

DOWN
1. Paleozoic, for one
2. Outdo
3. Lavage
4. Extravagant talker
5. Reconnoiterer
6. Small city
7. Citrus drinks
8. Slice of bacon
9. Garment cut
10. Unit of magnetic flux
11. Essayist Charles ___
12. Influenced
13. Zoroastrian
14. Colorado native
15. Convened
16. Sooner than, poetically
26. Boot-camp address?
27. "___ Got a Secret"
28. ___ record (confidential)
32. Greek portico
33. A Spelling
34. Bear young, as goats
35. Drawback
36. Nimble
37. Grow narrow
38. Bear cave
39. Swenson of "Benson"
40. Furrow
43. Muscle twitch
44. Lafitte, e.g.
45. Ms. Munson
46. Lover's rendezvous
48. Tendon
49. Cause to burn
50. Civil War side
51. Oxlike antelope
53. Lassos
59. Sub finder
60. Legislate
61. They're pitched
63. Theater district
64. Advanced deg.
65. Cygnus
66. Tavern
67. Midas's metal
68. Oklahoma tribe
69. Penpoints
70. Even score
71. Fury
76. Carryall
78. Elaborate
79. ___ Rio, Texas
80. Rias, e.g.
81. Balsam, for one
83. Ruhr Valley city
84. Theater awards
85. Diminishes
86. Separated
88. "___ No Angels"
89. Pennsylvania port
90. Marvel characters
91. Acidulous
92. Rani's dress
93. Indian mister
94. Bardic above
95. Employ
99. Beachgoer's shade

262

ACROSS

1. Stead
5. Actress Moore
9. Hot spot
10. Uttered
11. Standard of excellence
13. Waikiki wreath
14. Schemed
18. Pas' mates
21. Tiny sphere
22. Portent
24. Hogwash!
27. ___ nutshell
28. Laser ray
29. Etats-___
31. Japanese sash
32. Groovy!
33. Farm critter?
34. RR depot
35. Officer
36. Dimple
38. Boas and asps
40. Showed the way
41. Ike's monogram
42. Cracker topper
45. "___ a Girl in My Soup"
48. Focal point
49. Stereo equipment
51. Michigan canals
52. Mature
53. Menu phrase
54. Untamed
56. Crooned
57. Rarer than rare
58. Kind of sale
59. Restraint
61. Kiss
62. Docs
63. "Night Fever" group
65. Get hitched
66. Meeting leader
72. Corn servings
73. On the briny
74. Engrave
75. Timid

DOWN

1. Tennis shot
2. "___ Got a Secret"
3. Dusk, in verse
4. Without clothes
5. Game tile
6. RBI's kin
7. Blemish
8. Sort
12. Biddy
14. Soil enricher
15. Felon's flight
16. Outback bird
17. Bear caves
18. Actress Rogers
19. Prolific auth.
20. Motorcycle pouch
21. Warped
23. Louse eggs
24. Rotating lever
25. Hautboy
26. Detective hints
28. Cutting tool
30. Tunnel digger
37. Big foot?
39. Summer cooler
42. Fireside event
43. Maui dance
44. Turkish bigwig
45. Lots and lots
46. Mild oath
47. Bastes
50. Commoner
51. Smart answer
55. Casino cube
56. Boy of song
60. Rather recent
61. Uproar
64. Berlin's pl.
66. Pecan middle?
67. Bowler, e.g.
68. Rainbow shape
69. Chemical suffix
70. Billy ___ Williams
71. Prattle

• TAKE A LOAD OFF •

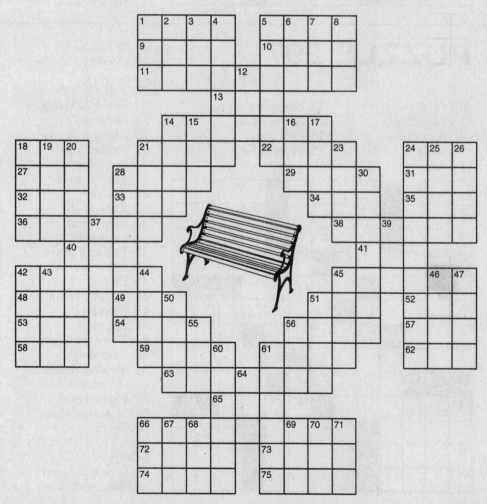

PUZZLE 296

ACROSS
1. Guy's date
4. Sore
8. Thailand, once
12. Mellow
13. Sky hue
14. Release
15. Feathery scarf
16. "Crash and ___"
17. Flower stalk
18. Entrance hall
20. Cartwright son
21. Gulp
23. Against
26. Layer
27. Clog, e.g.
28. Fib
31. Concealed
33. Progressing
35. Stake
36. Stare stupidly
38. Footnote abbr.
39. Dress for Caesar
40. Blushing
41. Scorch
44. More timid
47. Dash
48. Storage building
49. Tee preceder
52. General feeling
53. Ring
54. Groove
55. Ran, as dye
56. Affectedly bohemian
57. Eavesdrop

DOWN
1. Chitchat
2. Give it ___
3. Greenest
4. Popular columnist
5. Helpful hint
6. Cheer
7. Craving
8. Fish delicacy
9. Division term
10. Citrus drinks
11. Dads' wives
19. Grimm villain
21. Ticket receipt
22. Sherry, e.g.
24. Breakfast niche
25. Knockout number
27. Glitch
28. Workers
29. Bearded bloom
30. Crosscurrent
32. Self-esteem
34. Telegram
37. Clothes cleaner
39. Stair part
41. Alaskan king ___
42. Lug
43. Realty unit
45. Miami team
46. Leisurely
48. Health farm
50. Dine late
51. Eye ailment

PUZZLE 297

ACROSS
1. Classifieds
4. Hero's tale
8. Cease
12. Lulu
13. Shopping plaza
14. Angel's hat
15. Golf peg
16. Florida Key, e.g.
17. Tomahawks
18. Grocery vehicle
20. Counsel
22. Make a web
24. Come to terms
26. Minor role
28. Abstain (from)
32. Tarzan's pal
33. Doctrine
35. Seek to marry
36. Sea cow
38. Exhilarate
40. Sleeveless garments
42. Historic times
43. Ask
46. Placed
48. Requirement
49. Plunder
51. Slippery
54. Newborn horse
55. Contended
56. Maiden-name indicator
57. Exclusively
58. Miscalculates
59. Fetch

DOWN
1. Quick to learn
2. Casino cube
3. Laboratory sample
4. Turkish official
5. Macaroni, e.g.
6. Bedridden
7. Proved innocent
8. Electric razor
9. Hired hack
10. Bullring cries
11. Sit for a photo
19. Actress Sue ___ Langdon
21. "Robinson Crusoe" author
22. Con game
23. Daddy
25. Shake hands with
27. Group of eight
29. Giving
30. Minute amount
31. Refusals
34. Stockpile
37. Eagerly
39. Flower garland
41. Foxier
43. Facts, briefly
44. Lighting gas
45. Schnitzel meat
47. Tallies up
50. ___ conditioner
52. Average grade
53. Thus far

ACROSS

1. Terminate
5. Manufacture
9. Glided
13. Fork part
14. Mounds of sand
15. Roll call response
16. Coarse file
17. Group of eight
18. Psychology topics
19. Bitter resentment
20. Compared
22. Squid emission
23. Customer
25. Geologic divisions
27. Yolky
29. Sniffed
32. Martini garnish
35. Home with the flu
37. Zigzag
38. Relatives
39. Sight organ
40. ____ the knot
41. Relays, e.g.
44. Guided
45. Handle skillfully
47. Displayed
49. Type of dive
51. Coastal bird
52. Elaborate
56. Mauna ____
58. Moon valleys
62. Feather stole
63. Besides
65. Bakery workers
66. Anthem
67. Ooze
68. Eliminate completely
69. Almost round
70. Give a party
71. Remainder
72. Printer's term

DOWN

1. Peel
2. Regal headpiece
3. Beginning
4. Vivacity
5. Mire
6. Contribute to the pot
7. Finely sharpened
8. Regard highly
9. "Murder, ____ Wrote"
10. Pass bills
11. Steel source
12. Classroom item
14. Nothing ____!
20. Theater box
21. Detective Nancy ____
24. Gun, as a motor
26. Brewery order
28. Produce
29. Snow coasters
30. Wicked
31. Achievement
32. Southern vegetable
33. False witness
34. Grows larger
36. Drain-opener chemical
42. Corn portion
43. Harmony
45. "Star ____" (Lucas film)
46. Roadside lodging
48. More uncanny
50. Not as good
53. Overhead
54. Of sound
55. National symbol
56. Place for mascara
57. Margarine
59. "God's Little ____"
60. Breakfast beverages
61. Formerly, formerly
64. Select
66. Clump of turf

Across and Down

Place the answers to the clues into their correct places in the diagrams so that the same words read both Across and Down.

A.

1. Backslide
2. False name
3. Tablets
4. Latin music
5. Composition

B.

1. Light wood
2. Coral island
3. Certain train
4. Work hard
5. Narrow lane

PUZZLE 300

ACROSS
1. Ointment
5. History
9. General Powell
14. Operatic melody
15. Resonate
16. Clay brick
17. Spool
18. Coral barrier
19. Deserve
20. Small chicken
22. Employ
24. Double curve
25. Photo
27. Haul
29. Garment ticket
34. Fire remains
37. Rich deposit
38. Unflappable
40. Felled
42. Baking need
43. Twig
44. Alley
45. Two ___ in a pod
46. Soft wood
47. Actress Lanchester
48. Skiing surface
50. Criminal
53. Director Howard
54. A Bobbsey twin
55. Sort
58. Strange
60. Gather
65. Insignificant
67. Capri, e.g.
70. Salad veggie
71. Inclined
72. Paw roughly
73. In the sack
74. Cavalry sword
75. Tense
76. Danson and Koppel

DOWN
1. Sharp point
2. Turf
3. Hold on property
4. Fountain treat
5. License
6. Highest card
7. That girl
8. Bean curd
9. Carved brooches
10. Poetic form
11. Folk wisdom
12. Large wading bird
13. Tennis court dividers
21. Gorilla, e.g.
23. Pursue, as prey
26. Desert plants
28. Sea mammals
29. Make a splash
30. Rambles
31. Best
32. Suppress
33. Leaving
35. Praise
36. Feeling
39. Saltwater body
41. "___ Abby"
43. Squander
49. Not as good
51. Specifically
52. Type of antelope
55. Scamps
56. Milan money, once
57. Door handle
59. Ten-cent piece
61. Shoo!
62. Cylinder
63. ___ out (barely managed)
64. Ruby and crimson
66. Half a pair
68. Glum
69. Pull with effort

PUZZLE 301   Fan Words

Place the 5-letter answers to the clues into the fan to discover an 8-letter word reading across the outlined area. As an added help, pairs of answers are anagrams (1 is an anagram of 2, 3 is an anagram of 4, etc.).

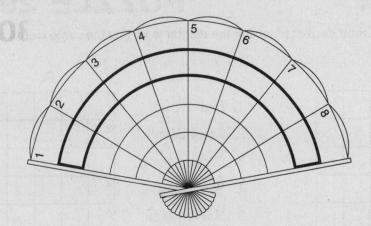

1. Capture
2. Gains income
3. Incorrect
4. Matured
5. Language units
6. Excalibur, e.g.
7. Fragrant wood
8. Curved

ACROSS

1. Gift paper
5. Cured pork
8. Word to the wides
12. Judge
13. Crossed a creek
15. Atop
16. Bloodhound's clue
17. Passageway
18. Snarl
19. Nothing
20. Class
21. Least messy
23. Iron or driver
26. Attendee
27. Mariner's yes
28. Eternities
30. Frigate hand
33. Sombreros
36. Small nail
38. Reign
39. Radiate
40. Mass of bees
42. Dark, to a bard
43. Borders
44. Hawaiian feast
45. Monopoly card
46. Sonnet's kin
47. Girl
49. Mata Hari, e.g.
51. Tennyson piece
53. Honored
58. Transport system
61. Dance noisily
62. Ostrich kin
63. Dumbstruck
64. Gown fabric
66. Summer drinks
67. Ascot event
68. Sway to and fro
69. Dryer residue
70. Observer
71. ___ off steam
72. Mats

DOWN

1. Not right
2. "Talk ___" (film)
3. Ring-shaped reef
4. Each
5. Japanese verse
6. Classifieds
7. Liquefy
8. Motherless calf
9. Tire filler, perhaps
10. Athenian vowels
11. Illegal act
13. Billfolds
14. Condescend
20. Frosty
22. Positive guidelines
24. Abstains from food
25. For the reason that
29. Southern vegetable
31. Sunburn remedy
32. Rip up
33. Big sandwich
34. Inside
35. Watch, e.g.
37. Hole punchers
38. Tint again
41. Hardy horse
47. Actor Ayres
48. Gather up
50. Liveliness
52. More mature
54. Be miserly
55. Newspapers and TV
56. Revise
57. Cleans
58. Unusual
59. "Far and ___"
60. Two-masted vessel
65. Make a knot
66. European mountain

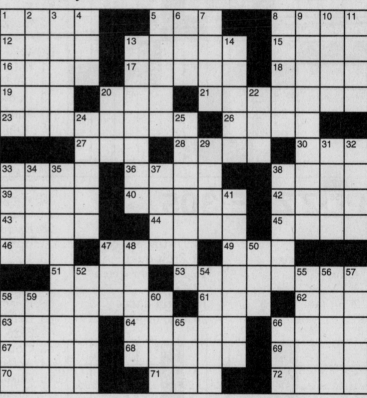

Blockbuilders

PUZZLE 303

Fit the letter blocks into the diagram to spell out the name of a famous person.

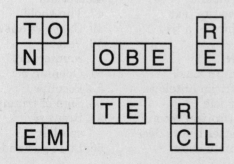

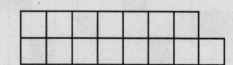

PUZZLE 304

ACROSS
1. Raccoon's kin
6. Swarm
11. Church instruments
13. Soaper, e.g.
14. Dodgers' Reese
15. Shady bowers
16. Dried plum
18. Pekoe, e.g.
19. Shaping tool
22. Doctrines
24. Kitchen wrap
26. Obscured
30. Opponent
31. Fabric layer
32. Not taped
33. Distribute again
35. Reflex-test joint
36. Hairdressing
39. Finale
40. Sit-ups targets
43. Sleep disorder
44. Second shooting
46. Good for farming
51. Scratched
52. Run off the tracks
53. Foxier
54. Fender-mishap marks

DOWN
1. Patrolman
2. Gold source
3. Iron or Bronze
4. Marble
5. Bungling
6. Regarding this point
7. Sphere
8. Mob scene
9. Risk
10. Actress Lanchester
12. Parched
13. Rationally
17. Not sterile
19. Remotely
20. Completed
21. Tubular pasta
23. Pout
25. Speech defect
27. Eat supper
28. Fifty-fifty
29. Feat
31. Raised, as oil
34. One who drenches
37. The Grateful ____
38. Having handles
40. Curves
41. "The ____ Jar"
42. Stick around
45. Amaze
47. "You ____ Sixteen"
48. Declare taboo
49. Kindled
50. Chicago transports

PUZZLE 305

ACROSS
1. Pole or lodge
4. Top
8. Swabs
12. Situate
13. ____ tide
14. Distinctive quality
15. Fruit quaff
16. Hawaiian goose
17. Liquor
18. Latin dance
20. Jets or Mets
22. Winged
24. Gem weight
28. Exclusively
31. Burrow
33. "____ Blue" (song)
34. Creatures
36. Clergyman
38. Poison ____
39. Dribble
41. Skin sac
42. Cranky
44. Apiece
46. Customer
48. Serengeti scavenger
52. ____ Office
55. Dispense
57. Prison inmate
58. Sandwich mart
59. Bee ____ ('70s group)
60. Crude shelter
61. Profound
62. Rewrite text
63. Third of a trio

DOWN
1. Ship's mast
2. African antelope
3. Article
4. Historical record
5. Letter before dee
6. Hindu chant
7. Duel weapon
8. Molten rock
9. "____ Gang"
10. Supportive of
11. Droop
19. Howls
21. Land parcel
23. As well
25. Risque
26. Singer Tori ____
27. Hue
28. Solemn notice
29. Actress Campbell
30. Deposits
32. Thought
35. Playthings
37. "____ Breaky Heart"
40. ____ in (aimed)
43. Dutch flower
45. Bureau
47. Threshold
49. Canyon's answer
50. Verb's counterpart
51. Opening bet
52. Peculiar
53. Sign of triumph
54. Brewery specialty
56. Luau garland

CODEWORD

Codeword is a special crossword puzzle in which conventional clues are omitted. Instead, answer words in the diagram are represented by numbers. Each number represents a different letter of the alphabet, and all of the letters of the alphabet are used. When you are sure of a letter, put it in the code key chart and cross it off in the alphabet box. A group of letters has been inserted to start you off.

Code key chart:

1	14
2	15
3	16
4	17
5	18
6	19
7	20
8	21
9 N	22
10 O	23
11 C	24
12	25
13	26

Alphabet box:

A ~~N~~
B ~~O~~
~~C~~ P
D Q
E R
F S
G T
H U
I V
J W
K X
L Y
M Z

Codeword grid:

12	8	3		1	8	13		6	13	6		10	3	6
8	2	6		8	25	19		20	26	4		23	6	6
23	8	2	3	26	3	6		12	7	26	21	26	8	5
			8	5	6	7	12		6	12	8			
5	8	26	11		9	6	13	6	7		14	15	8	22
8	9	12				12	26	5		20	15	7	7	24
22	26	25	11		11	10	9	20	6	7	6	9	11	6
				16	10	10			9	10	7			
9	10	17	8	9	25	5	8	9	22		10	7	16	10
8	13	8	7	6		10	21	8			24	6	3	
24	6	12	26		8	3	10	7	12		23	6	6	12
			9	8	2		13	7	10	12	6			
10	11	6	8	9	26	11		8	9	8	2	7	8	17
7	19	10		10	5	8		12	8	9		6	7	8
23	26	9		9	6	23		6	5	18		25	18	24

(grid contains the inserted letters C O N at squares 11 10 9)

Letter Tiles

Form four words reading across and five words reading down by placing the eight Letter Tiles into the diagram. Horizontal tiles go into horizontal spaces, vertical tiles into vertical spaces. In the example, three tiles fit together to form the words SAW, ONE, SO, AN, and WE.

Example:

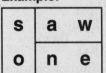

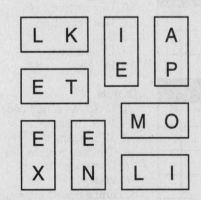

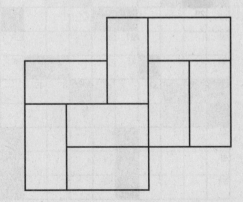

PUZZLE 308

• TEE TIME •

ACROSS
1. Ripens, as cheese
5. Tiny
8. Tennis great
12. Farm structure
13. "2001" computer
14. ____-do-well
15. Bobby Jones wore them
17. Terrible tsar
18. Baby fox
19. Cordwood measure
20. Yearned
23. Pie nut
25. Evil plan
26. Corporate symbol
27. Annoy
30. Song gal
31. Jeweler's weight
32. Regret
33. Sheepish she
34. Unpaid
35. Mine find
36. Computer symbols
38. Flax product
39. Discussion group
41. Take a chair
42. Black, poetically
43. Links hazard
48. Shipped
49. The self
50. Roof overhang
51. Sonnets' kin
52. Bar bill
53. Gather

DOWN
1. Inquire
2. Cotton machine
3. Wallach of film
4. Electrical outlet
5. Sharpen
6. Lobe's site
7. City trains
8. Singer Bryant
9. Chip-shot club
10. Get wind of
11. Marine bird
16. Small goat
19. Glasgow native
20. Basilica part
21. Talon
22. Golfer's aim
23. Ponders intently
24. Mild oath
26. Grassy area
28. Ill-mannered
29. Perceptive
31. Not warm
35. Scattered debris
37. Small change
38. Can top
39. Mexican coin
40. Sleeping
41. Snooty person
43. Gel
44. Turkish title
45. Actress Charlotte ____
46. Frank's ex
47. Vim

PUZZLE 309

• BAA·BAA •

ACROSS
1. Bashful
4. Zhivago's love
8. Revealer's cry
12. So-so grade
13. Syrian, e.g.
14. Chilled
15. Sky Altar
16. Fail to hit
17. Son of Zeus
18. 1930 Oscar winner
21. Function
22. Gun-lobby gp.
23. Pointy tools
26. Winning serve
27. Curved line
30. Brooklyn neighborhood
34. Cooking vessel
35. Type spaces
36. Split
37. Meyers or Fleischer
38. Division of the HHS
40. Consequence
46. Angel's crown
47. Victuals
48. Cal.'s neighbor
49. Egg-shaped
50. Decorative case
51. Bee secretion
52. Sup
53. Uncommon
54. PC key

DOWN
1. Read, as a bar code
2. Sub, to some
3. 12 months
4. Tibetan monks
5. Come up
6. Hasty
7. Opposite of presence
8. Coronet
9. Land parcel
10. Venison source
11. Promos
19. Artist's inspiration
20. Bailiwick
23. Horned viper
24. "Tommy" group, with "The"
25. Authorize
26. Checkup sounds
27. Burrows or Vigoda
28. Operated
29. Dancer Charisse
31. Persian genie
32. Nose
33. Mild expletive
37. Certain agave root
38. Scrub hard
39. ____ Hawkins Day
40. Sitarist Shankar
41. Alda or Thicke
42. Smidgen
43. Hawkeye State
44. Spoken
45. Immediately following
46. Brick carrier

BRICK BY BRICK

Rearrange this stack of bricks to form a crossword puzzle. The clues will help you fit the bricks into their correct places. Row 1 has been filled in for you. Use the bricks to fill in the remaining spaces.

ACROSS

1. Con
   Kelp
   Rub
2. Heavy reading
   Equine
   coloring
   Integrity
3. Demolish
   Dissolve
   Boredom
4. Misbehave
   Ooze
   Bullring cheer
5. How come?
   Toning targets
   Fine
6. Halter
   New England
   cape
   Wild party
7. Champion
   Thailand, once
   Atop
8. Skating leap
   Threaded nail
   Served
   perfectly
9. Sly trick
   Coastline
   eagle
   Radiation
   quantities
10. Headliner
    Saute
    Supervised
11. Jellystone
    bear
    Pursue busily
    Marvy!
12. Mal de ___
    Diminish
    Strong glue
13. Egg shapes
    Admire
    Touched
    ground
14. Bad habits
    Burn soother
    Diamond team
15. Sad poem
    Hide-and-___
    Clothing

DOWN

1. Hay
   Hems
   and ___
   Relocate
2. Sofa
   Door sign
   Sinful
3. Friendship
   Track event
4. Bill of fare
   Short jacket
   Voyage
   segment
5. Norm
   Vaporous
6. Provide
   guns
   Game fish
   Little lie
7. Loamy
   deposit
   Bakery
   worker
   Mournful
   word
8. Nerve
   Tote
   Mosaic piece
9. Dissenter
   Premonition
   Tea type
10. Fashionable
    Healthy
    Cartoon cry
11. Facial
    feature
    Lens opening
12. Sweetie
    On ship
    Breathe
    hard
13. Complication
    Book page
14. Disgusting
    Plant stalk
    Chopping
15. A Great
    Lake
    Masons'
    troughs
    Memory
    units

BRICKS

Row 1: NOR / NUI | ATE / LIK | OXY / LIT | UP■ / ■AB | STA / ■■Y

Row 2: W■A / E■R | CRE / ERN | OAN / ELT | LED / LY■ | ■CO / IAM

Row 3: AXE / WIL | ASH / NTO | ■■■ / FAB | ■D■ / ■■O / B | ■E■R / ■N■M

Row 4: ■■■ / HER | ALO / SEE | ■EP / E■A | ME■ / OKA | BRA / O■S

Row 5: ES■ / GY■ | OLE / Y■■ | ■AB / LS■ | SLI / S■■ | CED / EMS

Row 6: INE / OGS | TOM / RUI | RY■ / ■■P | ACT / WHY | E■N / K■T

Row 7: MER / OVA | VIC / ELE | L■S / E■■ | ■HO / ■EN | R■F / OGI

DIAGRAM

	1	2	3	4	5	6	7	8	9	10	11	12	13	14	15
1	S	C	A	M	■	A	L	G	A	■	C	H	A	F	E
2															
3															
4															
5															
6															
7															
8															
9															
10															
11															
12															
13															
14															
15															

PUZZLE 311

ACROSS

1. Subways' kin
4. The two together
8. Question starter
12. Flaky dessert
13. Zone
14. Courageous one
15. Intense fury
16. 52-week period
17. Very black
18. Small role
20. Fido or Felix
22. Electric light
25. Cold-cuts stores
29. Sage or thyme
32. Legendary creature
34. Had brunch
35. Bunyan's tool
36. Characteristic
37. Type of neckline
38. Health club
39. Cattle group
40. Flirt
41. Mr. Ed, e.g.
43. Trailer truck
45. Relay section
47. America's Cup vessel
51. Sailor's hail
54. Border on
57. Yo!
58. Mine deposit
59. Place for mascara
60. Tick off
61. Look narrowly
62. Grows older
63. OK grade

DOWN

1. Grand
2. Italian money, once
3. Appear
4. Louisiana marsh
5. Mining product
6. Hot drink
7. "The Grass ___"
8. Snowy
9. Female fowl
10. Genesis ship
11. Yo-yo, e.g.
19. Ease off
21. Ready for print
23. Old instrument
24. Grizzlies
26. Volcano flow
27. List component
28. Trickle
29. Mince
30. World's fair, e.g.
31. Raise upright
33. Ocean surge
36. Biblical pronoun
40. By way of
42. Slicker
44. Folk tales
46. Colorful
48. Fashionable
49. Present!
50. Tot
51. Matterhorn, e.g.
52. Garden tool
53. Poem
55. Sack
56. Advantage

ACROSS

1. Bridge offer
4. Cooking utensils
8. Tug
12. Had pizza
13. Send off
14. Pressing tool
15. Freezer abundance
16. Competently
17. Mr. Ruth
18. King's chair
20. Baste again
21. Government agency
24. Skedaddle!
27. Tall tree
28. Sweet tuber
31. Vatican leader
32. Before, poetically
33. Fashion length
34. Liable
35. Honolulu handout
36. Pedaled
37. Football team
39. Twisted
43. Eye parts
47. Crosby crony
48. Intertwined
50. Fedora or bowler
51. Bloodhound's trail
52. Prepare to publish
53. Eden dweller
54. Fix
55. Flower plots
56. Dawn's moisture

DOWN

1. Fish enticement
2. Poison-ivy result
3. Doe or stag
4. Goober
5. Fossil resin
6. Naught
7. Porker's home
8. Agree
9. Historic times
10. Kimono, e.g.
11. Recognized
19. Wind instrument
20. Daiquiri liquor
22. Strange
23. Bubbly beverage
24. Health farm
25. Law officer
26. Choose
28. Shaggy ox
29. Wood chopper
30. The center of
32. Slippery as an ___
33. Short skirt
35. Journey stage
36. French caps
38. Colorful
39. "For ___ the Bell Tolls"
40. Went by cab
41. Informed of
42. Geek
44. Discard
45. Roof overhang
46. Hearty dish
48. Spider's structure
49. Verse of praise

PUZZLE 312

PUZZLE 313

ACROSS
1. Patriarch
4. Rim
8. Overseer
12. Frozen
13. Medical photo
14. Be next to
15. Not he
16. Kind
17. Matador's foe
18. Aromatic wood
20. Nest noise
21. Eastern temple
25. Majority
28. Copier
29. Public vehicle
32. Ram's mate
33. Past its prime
34. Elect
35. Tennis barrier
36. Skin
37. A snap
38. Attack
40. Tub
44. Brainpan
48. Bereft of moisture
49. Tributes in verse
52. Take legal action
53. Cash register
54. Dilly
55. Diamond stat
56. Benefit
57. St. Paul's Cathedral feature
58. Burrow

DOWN
1. Record
2. Pang
3. Applied henna
4. Spare
5. Withered
6. Crack
7. Storm's center
8. English town
9. A woodwind
10. Certainly
11. Hit the brakes
19. Likely
20. Concern
22. Microsoft bigwig
23. October gems
24. Greek letter
25. Gents
26. Have unpaid bills
27. Complete collection
29. Feather scarf
30. Increases
31. Porky's home
33. Bridge
37. Moose's relative
39. Distribute
40. Nocturnal fliers
41. Operatic highlight
42. Fine cloth
43. Immobile
45. Exploited
46. Tempt
47. Not fatty
49. Archaic
50. Pair
51. Freddy's street

ACROSS

1. So long
5. Fashionable
9. Smidgen
12. Froster
13. Champion
14. Mine extract
15. Within sight
16. So be it!
17. Shark's limb
18. Viper
20. Showy
22. Plastic
25. Horrible
26. Lime drink
27. As well
30. Little bits
34. Encountered
35. Sugar tree
37. Lobster eggs
38. Former time
40. Baby's pop
41. Pipe shape
42. Manner
44. Pint-size
46. Utensil
49. Oahu garland
50. Crow call
51. Checkers, e.g.
54. Taunt
58. Mature
59. Timespans
60. Dorothy's dog
61. Planted plot
62. Rents
63. All right

DOWN

1. Cookie box
2. Maven
3. Hot beverage
4. Draw up
5. Guy
6. Tailor's concern
7. Fury
8. Cuban dance
9. Bean curd
10. Like the Gobi
11. Hold back
19. Grand ___
21. Calculate
22. Flirt
23. Notion
24. Seines
25. Gutsy
28. Woman
29. Fancy resort
31. Zone
32. ___ weevil
33. Merchandise
36. Life of Riley
39. Couple
43. Halo wearer
45. Gloves
46. Wound cover
47. Attendant
48. Was in the red
49. Fewer
52. Exist
53. Scatter rug
55. Court
56. Contraction
57. Moreover

PUZZLE 314

275

PUZZLE 315

ACROSS
1. Tentacle
4. Sandwich source
8. Toy for windy days
12. Unpaid
13. Like
14. Carol
15. Road bend
16. Coral ridge
17. Bed-and-breakfasts
18. Portion
20. Fool
22. Infomercials
24. Denominations
28. Highway vehicle
31. Building curve
34. Gardener's aid
35. Doing business
36. Pine
37. Muck's partner
38. Hopper
39. Reminder
40. Froze
41. ___ diver
43. Lion or cougar
45. Breakfast item
47. Hay
51. Ship pole
54. Berserk
57. Time period
58. Duet
59. Folk wisdom
60. Be unwell
61. Cockeyed
62. Copycat
63. Mouse's kin

DOWN
1. Grape drinks
2. Hustle
3. Small plateau
4. Risked
5. Barely make
6. Speak falsely
7. Data
8. Cutting tool
9. Charged atom
10. ___-gallon hat
11. Subways' cousins
19. Heavy drizzle
21. Volcano's output
23. Vault
25. Fashionable
26. Ripped apart
27. Plant starter
28. Blubbers
29. Long poem
30. Diner list
32. Hoop edge
33. Gator's kin
37. Oven glove
39. Periodical, for short
42. Juicy fruit
44. Inquisitive one
46. Party
48. Stern
49. Concert solo
50. Whitman or Disney
51. Mountain resort
52. Handle roughly
53. Hot-___ balloon
55. Swab
56. Mine deposit

PUZZLE 316

ACROSS

1. Chops
5. Hole punches
9. Hen's product
12. Sunburn soother
13. Castle's trench
14. Cote call
15. Husky's burden
16. Jumping stick
17. Sweetie
18. Horse's kin
20. Atmosphere layer
22. Horned mammal, briefly
25. Hot spring
26. Charged atom
27. Hasty
30. Petition
34. Cook's item
35. Pay the tab
37. Coffee server
38. Put on cargo
40. Concocted
41. Gallery exhibit
42. Cold
44. Cheer
46. 747, e.g.
49. Glide over snow
50. Natural
51. Dealer's car
54. Wind toy
58. Cain's mother
59. Like
60. Cruel
61. Stuff
62. Scarlet hues
63. Look like

DOWN

1. Possesses
2. Building wing
3. Gloom
4. Family auto
5. Hi-fi parts
6. Romance
7. Dally
8. Lower oneself
9. Repeated sound
10. Hired thug
11. Missing
19. Separate
21. Microwave
22. Rends
23. Owl's sound
24. Fascinated by
25. Roe source
28. Land force
29. Baltic or North
31. Hawaiian party
32. Misjudges
33. Poker offering
36. Tropical wood
39. Triumph
43. Fragrant tree
45. Tyson and Wallace
46. Make ready
47. Volcano's liquid
48. Dazzled
49. Male offspring
52. Squeak by
53. Central
55. "___ Got Sixpence"
56. Even score
57. Popular street

PUZZLE 317

ACROSS
1. ___-and-cheese sandwich
4. Boxers do it
8. Borrowed sum
12. Pub order
13. Albacore
14. "Do ___ others . . ."
15. Baltic or Bering
16. Chooses
17. Track competition
18. Howdy!
20. Jump
22. Fairy
24. Colorers
28. Male deer
31. Annoy
34. Judge's field
35. Burst open
36. Period of note
37. Go down the slopes
38. ___ of Aquarius
39. Flower support
40. Look
41. Miles or Vaughn
43. Deadly snake
45. Glimpse
47. Hitching
51. Stylish
54. Fabricated
57. Gentle animal
58. Sedan or coupe
59. Froster
60. Fortune
61. Brood's home
62. Juvenile
63. Nanny has two

DOWN
1. Jumble
2. Out of the weather
3. Breakfast, e.g.
4. Seat
5. Baby dog
6. Picnic insect
7. Skin irritation
8. Hardly smooth
9. Undivided
10. Had pasta
11. Commandment word
19. Chair support
21. "___ to Joy"
23. Be distressed
25. Other than
26. Leaf gatherer
27. Enjoy a pool
28. Some resorts
29. Nero's garment
30. Rich Little, e.g.
32. Animosity
33. Buddhist monk
39. That woman
40. Secret watcher
42. Broad tie
44. Harsh
46. Shoot forth
48. At rest
49. Lunch hour
50. Understands
51. Food tin
52. Shade
53. ___ a living!
55. Top fighter pilot
56. Low grade

ACROSS

1. Cold-cut shop
5. Bit of smoke
9. Occupation
12. Dry
13. Kind of code
14. Ostrich kin
15. Facts
16. Raise
17. Sibling, for short
18. Barnyard female
20. Pool of money
22. Porch
25. Swindle
27. Burst
28. Tad
30. Favorites
34. Become mature
35. Hex
37. "Bells ___ Ringing"
38. Grandma
40. Fat
41. Take legal action
42. Mongrel dog
44. Stream
46. Inched along
49. "___ Belongs to Me"
50. Youth
51. Legend
54. ___ one's time
58. Coop product
59. Departure
60. Sinful
61. Service cost
62. Agts.
63. Corrosive liquids

DOWN

1. Mom's guy
2. Important time
3. Ignited
4. Spud state
5. Caution
6. Bad humor
7. Bering, e.g.
8. Hooded jacket
9. Quip
10. Skip over
11. Full of activity
19. Hero's story
21. Brat
22. Bridge length
23. Nero's garment
24. "___ sesame!"
25. Walk proudly
26. Valise
29. Unseat
31. Ill at ___
32. Faithful
33. Search
36. Engrave with acid
39. Electrical unit
43. Say
45. Troublemaker
46. Musical symbol
47. Extreme anger
48. Outskirts
49. Collections
52. Chopper
53. Sass
55. Trailing plant
56. Casino cube
57. Subways' kin

PUZZLE 319

ACROSS
1. Big bash
5. Invites
9. Glimmers
14. Sulfuric ___
15. Dryer fuzz
16. Opening
17. School dance
18. On a cruise
19. Pitfall
20. Junior's dad
22. Engrave on glass
24. Strive
25. Farm butter
26. Ms. Claiborne
27. Shout
28. Hastier
32. Feel concern
34. Mare's morsel
35. Bomb
37. Responds
41. Arctic, e.g.
44. Young louse
46. Errand
47. Rates of speed
49. Strong java
51. Pod occupant
52. Self-images
54. Refined
57. Jack, e.g.
60. Spoil
62. Knight
63. Have debts
64. Store
65. Pass
69. Cowboy's tool
71. Slice
73. Soda choice
74. Traffic jam
75. Stop!
76. Major periods
77. Stairs
78. Stretches
79. Like morning grass

DOWN
1. Intervals
2. Plat portion
3. Father of the pride
4. Idolize
5. Frightened
6. Brother's sib
7. Bow
8. Radio noise
9. List type
10. Stopover spot
11. Work hard
12. Risk
13. Girder metal
21. Clumsy person
23. Russian ruler
27. Slangy yes
28. Kick
29. Marathon
30. List member
31. Dash
33. Kind of room
36. Gloomy
38. Manage
39. Family chart
40. Zoo favorite
42. Imitated
43. Eggy drink
45. Yank
48. Classify
50. Arid places
53. Calm
55. Naught
56. Copied
57. Foals
58. Remain
59. Witness again
61. Pinch
64. Drenches
66. Ponder
67. Side dish
68. Effortless
70. Dine
72. Hops brew

ACROSS

1. Etui
5. Lard
8. Boring
12. Hideous
13. Clothing
15. Opie, to Ron
16. Factual
17. Pause mark
18. Imitator
19. At any time, in poetry
20. Bantam
21. Snivel
23. Color again
25. Bureaus
28. Beer barrel
29. Tad
30. Flabbergast
32. Incite
34. Despaired
35. Hushed
36. Holier-___-thou
37. Tuck, e.g.
38. In addition
39. Irritate
40. Loaded
41. Transport
42. Signal
43. Skunk feature
44. Bar bottle
45. Storekeeper
47. Dance or exercise
51. Thick stuff
52. Choice word
53. Self-esteem
54. Wishing hole
57. I give!
59. Store news
60. Toward shelter
61. Gypsy's card
62. Prick
63. Slip
64. Belly
65. Flurries

DOWN

1. Prettier
2. Approve
3. Drink loudly
4. Look over
5. Forward end
6. Troops
7. Beret's kin
8. Donkeys' cries
9. Chop off
10. Dark brew
11. Not him
13. Serving well
14. Boater
20. Cake part
22. Devour Rice?
24. Equivalent
25. Cagney part
26. Eagle's claw
27. Saber
29. Less cordial
31. Fleecy mama
32. Shoulder motion
33. Thief
34. Enthusiasm
36. ___-tac-toe
37. Movie ending
38. Note
40. Insane
41. Confident
44. Change the clock
46. Flirted
47. Parcel out
48. Vandyke, e.g.
49. Snow abode
50. Campus gals
52. Beige
54. Used to be
55. Lodge member
56. Floral wreath
58. Bug
59. Workout site

PUZZLE 320

PUZZLE 321

ACROSS

1. ___ and tucker
4. Cry
8. Steep
12. Juicy drink
13. Roster
15. Aggravate
16. Kirk's diary
17. Make beloved
18. Capri, e.g.
19. Hindered
21. Twosome
22. Writing table
23. Active
24. Flaky dessert
26. Adriatic, e.g.
28. Tarot reader
30. Weep
33. Runs
36. Stroll
37. Past
38. Secular
39. Pirouette
41. Adverse
42. Crackerjack
43. Lunch option
44. Worn down
47. Rose plot
48. Nylons
49. Give the gas
50. Deary
51. Saline drops
55. Lagoon
58. Night person
61. Wasp
62. Fraud
63. Working-class cat?
65. Freezer cube
66. Besides
67. Dieter's food
68. Seed
69. Colored
70. Safeguard
71. Type spaces

DOWN

1. Model wood
2. Sacred cows
3. Sired
4. Fasten
5. Plus
6. Lot growth
7. Oahu feast
8. Gowned lady
9. Get up
10. Annexes
11. Seven days
13. Smirked
14. Plane device
20. Smart
25. Bother
27. Study of stars
28. Steal
29. Maize spike
30. Spoken
31. Peer
32. Daring
33. Inform
34. Add liquor to
35. Watched
40. Lived
43. "___ Will Buy?"
45. Reply
46. Through
50. Biblical king
52. Biscotto flavor
53. Spy mission, for short
54. Worries
55. Garbed
56. Slick
57. Glass jar
59. Dog's bark
60. Sled
61. Flock
64. Burn cause

ACROSS

1. Fight
5. Furry foot
8. Musical work
12. Book leaf
13. Infants
15. Force
16. News piece
17. Dark
18. Oklahoma Indian
19. Part of a bowler's split
21. Blooper
23. Leftover
24. Paint base
26. Dull
27. Chum
30. Skin designs
33. Fiesta figure
35. Hacienda
36. Office workers
37. Restaurant list
40. Fool
42. Sobbed
43. Get even for
46. Tale
49. Small coin
50. Camper
53. Deer's relative
54. Frantic
56. Silent
57. Bear's lair
59. Savory jelly
61. Dress part
63. Indian outfit
66. Dog's warning
68. Reed instrument
69. Steers
70. Ghostly
71. Slipped
72. Adept
73. Society entrant
74. Wiggly ones

DOWN

1. Malice
2. Obvious
3. Program
4. Office sub
5. Cooking utensil
6. Skilled
7. Bizarre
8. Bloodhound's clue
9. Match
10. One, to Juan
11. Fr. holy woman
13. Toe ailment
14. Removes
20. Tiny amount
22. Exclude
25. Cuckoo
27. Glass unit
28. On the apex of
29. Most recent
31. Torso
32. Mine tunnel
34. Banister support
37. Lion's pride
38. Wicked
39. ___ of the woods
41. Till the soil
44. Jewels
45. Go by, as time
47. Trinket
48. Chauffeured car
51. Fit to be food
52. Jump back
55. Ate in style
58. Calls for
59. Grammatical no-no
60. Concern
62. Patient's portion
63. Clump of turf
64. Hewing tool
65. Ump's cousin
67. Needle

PUZZLE 323

ACROSS
1. Lined up
5. Cinder
8. Enthusiasm
13. Van or skirt
14. Slick
15. Excellent
16. Opinion sampling
17. Race unit
18. Hazardous
19. Mode
21. Ribs, e.g.
23. Musket, e.g.
24. Desk wood
26. Taverns
29. Lookout's platform
34. Desqueaks
37. Leap
38. Village
39. Luminous
41. Purchaser
43. Consider
46. Granny
47. Earn
49. Rations
51. Scar
52. Herb
53. Later
55. 18-wheeler
57. Librarian's date
58. Chop down
61. Military
64. Large parrot
68. More wicked
71. Above, to a bard
73. Auction
74. Consequence
75. Cove
76. Shoot forth
77. Residue
78. Personal pronoun
79. Allows

DOWN
1. Electrical units
2. Street brawl
3. Solely
4. Weepy tree?
5. Feel terrible
6. Ripoff
7. Promotion
8. Bar staple
9. Downs' partners
10. Exclusively male
11. Soy product
12. Public
15. Pavlova's skirt
20. A side of New York
22. Prone
25. Realize
27. Anaconda
28. Autograph
29. Pal
30. Valentine gift
31. Theater glasses
32. Ma that baas
33. Take a whiff
35. Alpaca kin
36. Submarine locater
40. Mr. Cleaver
42. Big trucks
44. Understood
45. Tended the garden
48. Ball holder
50. Snare or bongo
53. Ventilate
54. Sneaky person
56. Store
58. Grazing group
59. By any chance
60. Smart
62. Crowds
63. Slangy assent
65. Appeared
66. Deplaned
67. Saturates
69. Haul
70. Raised trains
72. Whiskey type

PUZZLE 324

ACROSS

1. Deck opening
6. Sink
9. Noah's scout
13. Type of type
15. Chart shape
16. Stove part
17. Starchy food
18. Guiltless
20. Bad e-mail
21. Talked wildly
23. Regret
24. Prize money
26. Name list
28. Tearful moan
31. Pas' mates
32. Fabled loser
33. In support of
34. Multiple
36. Organs of sight
40. Sour compounds
42. Big bucks
43. Have a cigar
44. Fictional work
45. Recollection
47. Hankering
48. Majors et al.
50. Card game
51. Curious
52. Plan
55. Yard barrier
57. Tick off
58. Yawning
60. Movie
64. Tyke's bike
66. Make certain
68. Hubbub
69. At any time, to Keats
70. Wandered
71. Approximately
72. Time period
73. Printed mistakes

DOWN

1. Haunches
2. On the pinnacle
3. Cheerio
4. Vise
5. Popular song
6. Cactus's defense
7. "___ No Sunshine"
8. Army rank
9. Medic
10. Candid
11. Scene of action
12. Come in
14. Horse pen
19. Fragrance
22. Guesses
25. Refs' kin
27. Appear
28. Lovers' tiff
29. Whale
30. Cook in water
32. Type of lamp
35. Wheel part
37. Toy on a string
38. Added to
39. Convey
41. Grocery section
43. Harmony
45. Endangered
46. Feat in horseshoes
49. Like an omelet
52. Duplicate
53. Faux pas
54. Slides
55. Impassioned
56. Short paper
59. Court response
61. Mound
62. Lunchbox dessert
63. Unites
65. Bird cry
67. Nary

285

PUZZLE 325

ACROSS

1. Prig
5. ___ cutlet
9. Pimples
13. Lhasa leader
14. Account
15. Fawns' mothers
16. Not odd
17. Metal suit
18. Fastener
19. Royal family
21. Towel word
23. Pig's pad
24. Fanatic
25. Empty
27. Pasta
31. Music system
34. Earlier than, in poems
35. Stable babies
37. Highway exit
38. Mails
40. Kind
41. Judgment
42. Wager
43. Caves
45. First named
46. Fence steps
49. Mimicked
51. Park pest
53. Nourished
54. Stamping tool
56. Lapse
57. Lift up
61. Attaches
63. Tint again
65. Glazed
66. Depart
67. Weeps
68. Rugged rock
69. Examination
70. Laborer
71. Wriggly

DOWN

1. Winter toy
2. Blue or bean
3. Sign
4. Yellow fruit
5. Diversify
6. Shade giver
7. Hilo hello
8. Song's words
9. TV breaks
10. Restriction
11. Orderly
12. Notice
14. Skin decal
20. Rides the waves
22. Took a pew
25. Film heavy
26. Dweeb
27. Plateaus
28. Don't exist
29. Many-legged creatures
30. Fastener
32. Roast host
33. Chose
36. Dieter's milk
39. Sub store
41. A Lauder
44. Firearms
47. ___ foo yung
48. Hunt
50. Counsel
52. Soap ___
54. Senseless
55. Doing nothing
57. Viewed
58. Ranch unit
59. Duck
60. Overwrought
62. Adjust
64. Ruckus

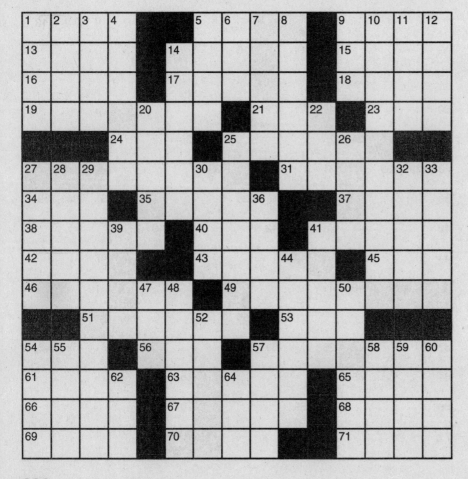

ACROSS

1. Bar brews
5. Wooden shoe
9. Slapping noise
14. Count (on)
15. Fence
16. Came up
17. Opponent
18. Sluggish
19. Home on the range?
20. Fragrances
22. Appetite
24. Cloth junction
25. Not him
26. Raises
28. Diamond call
30. Playground game
32. Recipe measures
38. Way off
40. Wound up
41. Milk producer
42. Scale
44. Etna ejection
45. Puccini product
47. At least two eras
48. Unwarranted
50. Incline
51. Fast warship
53. Offspring
54. Before now
55. Down-under bird
57. Legal decree
60. Rogues
63. Seize
66. Foolish
68. Very overweight
70. Garlands
72. Contribute a chip
73. Radio receiver
74. Desire
75. Retain
76. Manner
77. Those persons
78. Drops the ball

DOWN

1. Embarrass
2. Jouster's weapon
3. Amuses
4. Pelt
5. Crunchy
6. Boy
7. Slick
8. Cheerfulness
9. Made a lap
10. Right away!
11. Easy stride
12. Bewildered
13. Abound
21. Jerk
23. Muzzle part
27. Stable
29. French twist, e.g.
31. Extension
33. Follow
34. Stick
35. "QE2," e.g.
36. Average
37. Exchange
38. Hit a perfect serve
39. Polar floater
43. Small town
46. Tennis teacher
49. Midday
52. Loafer ornament
53. Solar body
56. Pulpy
58. Fall bloom
59. Bawls
60. Bunks
61. Share a boundary
62. Turn down
64. Touched ground
65. "Little Women" role
67. Stir
69. Poetic before
71. Frozen dessert

PUZZLE 327

ACROSS

1. Absorbed
5. Against
8. Campus group
12. "Star Wars" knights
13. Gypsy's card
15. Parasites
16. Ifs, ___, or buts
17. Verdi work
18. Concerning
19. Took a nap
21. Was without
23. Bark
26. BPOE member
27. Ease up
31. Scorched
33. Atlas entry
36. ___ of thumb
37. Party's candidates
38. Before, to Keats
39. Dairy product
41. Sprite
42. Assessor
44. Drop the ball
45. Desirable thing
47. Jerk
48. Polka partner
49. Dated
50. Hold up
51. "___ Yeller"
52. Flat receptacle
54. Fell behind
57. Garden tool
62. Egg shape
63. Nobility
67. BLT topping
68. Inlet
69. Went on wildly
70. Gossip bit
71. Was in debt
72. Misters
73. Canvas sheet

DOWN

1. Slightly closed
2. Hereditary factor
3. Chances
4. Main point
5. Lid
6. Mine find
7. Neither's mate
8. Movie, slangily
9. Hockey site
10. Property measure
11. ___ off
13. Commotion
14. Natural ability
20. Meadow mama
22. Tailor
24. Fixate (on)
25. Most complete
27. Moved in a curve
28. Pack animal
29. With it
30. British drink
32. Roof beam
33. Tin, e.g.
34. Stadium
35. Enthusiastic
40. Sugar tree
43. Yes, at sea
46. More melancholy
50. Hair tint
51. Leered
53. Frightened
54. Daft
55. Declare firmly
56. Delivered
58. Send off
59. Facts
60. Observer
61. Play
64. Robber's run
65. "___ Got a Secret"
66. Half a score

CRISS-CROSSWORD

The answer words for Criss-Crossword are entered diagonally, reading downward, from upper left to lower right or from upper right to lower left. We have entered the words CAGE and WAR as examples.

TO THE RIGHT

1. Pen

2. Used to be

3. Car types

4. Carpet

5. Torment

6. Of the nose

7. Cut the grass

9. Lease

11. Agitate

12. Sports group

16. Mansard features

18. Supplemented

19. Soak through

22. Exam

24. Merit

25. Revived

28. Detective

30. Dunce

31. Weaving machines

34. Bog product

35. Noisy dance

37. Tire groove

39. Ancient

TO THE LEFT

2. Battle

3. Wise guys

4. Takes offense

5. New flower

6. Cancel

7. Insane

8. Stockings

10. Ocean breaker

13. Orderly

14. Admire

15. Layer

17. Rescues

20. Tree filler

21. Not imagined

23. Screen

26. School truant

27. Scheme

29. Gazes

32. Christmas songs

33. Burden

36. Spoiled child

38. Mire

40. Boy

PUZZLE 329

ACROSS
1. Washington bill
4. Days gone by
8. Have a little talk
12. Pear-shaped fruit
13. Bouncing sound
14. Went by rail
15. Blossomed
17. Informed about
18. Great rage
19. Most arid
21. Shout
24. Tavern treats
25. Extremely serious
27. Part of FBI
31. Through
32. Make another attempt at
34. Flock female
35. Instruct
37. Dueling swords
39. Operator
40. Gambling term
41. More precious
44. Building addition
46. Eager
47. Hemingway, e.g.
52. Plow
53. Location
54. Sign of triumph
55. Otherwise
56. Extend credit
57. Affirmative vote

DOWN
1. ____-limits (forbidden)
2. Nothing
3. ____ trip
4. Look closely
5. Land tract
6. This girl
7. Tyke
8. Sea voyage
9. Comedian Bob ____
10. Hubbubs
11. Collapsible shelter
16. Basketball's Chamberlain
20. Tint again
21. Underground cavern
22. Battery fluid
23. Hawaiian gala
24. In pursuit of
26. Wipe clean
28. Hollow grass
29. Dazzled
30. Minus
33. Everlasting
36. Turn sour
38. Survey
41. Calendar entry
42. Hateful
43. Needs aspirin
44. ____-steven
45. Precede
48. Crude metal
49. Climbing plant
50. Observe
51. "____ and Sympathy"

PUZZLE 330

ACROSS
1. Capp and Capone
4. Opera highlight
8. Touched
12. Intersected
13. Mama ____ Elliot
14. Adrift
15. Feasted
16. Pinball boo-boo
17. Flower stalk
18. Catch the waves
20. Dweeb
22. "You ____ So Beautiful"
23. Javelin
25. More angry
27. Fly alone
28. Modified copy
29. Present
31. Baby's shoe
33. Gambling game
36. Dried plums
37. Horse's sound
39. Decay
40. Pass over
43. Extinct bird
44. Gawk
46. Concept
48. Bear's burrow
49. Membership fees
50. Antlered animals
51. Dillydally
52. Fixes the table
53. Stench
54. Some city trains

DOWN
1. Stockpile
2. Pauses
3. Music system
4. Play section
5. Downpour
6. Wight, e.g.
7. Straddling
8. Fourth notes
9. Country manor
10. Gazed slyly
11. Meeker
19. Hawk's cousin
21. Has a sip
24. Paths
26. Show up for
28. Shakespeare's before
30. More hazardous
31. Irish accent
32. Plug's location
34. Noggin
35. Trying experience
36. Pushes
38. Serving utensil
41. At rest
42. Lap pup
45. Curvy letter
47. Request

DOUBLE TROUBLE

PUZZLE 331

Not really double trouble, but double fun! Solve this puzzle as you would a regular crossword, except place one, two, or three letters in each box. The number of letters in each answer is shown in parentheses after its clue.

ACROSS

1. Hobby (7)
4. Constable, perhaps (6)
7. Band (5)
10. Skiing type (6)
11. Isaac or Otto (5)
12. Reply (7)
13. Hard to get (4)
14. Walleye (5)
15. Sales talk (5)
16. Sailor (7)
18. Heirloom (7)
20. Bill of ___ (4)
22. Cleave (5)
23. Lopez film, with "The" (4)
24. Playground meanie (5)
25. Respectful gesture (7)
27. Off the beam (9)
30. Clear up (5)
31. Assuage (4)
33. Insult (4)
34. Garment feature (4)
35. Tussle (7)
36. On the far side (6)
39. Mired down (5)
40. Lug (5)
42. Shoemaker/Levy discovery (5)
43. Rosary section (6)
45. Call it a day (6)
46. Salad green, sometimes (7)
47. Impassioned (7)
48. Buy stocks (6)
49. Incited (5)

DOWN

1. Broad view (8)
2. Spoon, sometimes (7)
3. Doc (5)
4. Furniture roller (6)
5. Possibly, poetically (9)
6. Tattered (4)
7. Distend (7)
8. Grate (4)
9. Duck's domain (4)
14. Contradictory (8)
15. Cotton fabric (5)
17. Newspaper supplement (6)
19. Rudder handle (6)
20. Incredible (8)
21. Depend (on) (4)
25. Sewer (7)
26. Leaven (5)
28. Armed or highway (7)
29. Close at hand (6)
30. Pop (4)
32. ___ service (9)
35. Smash-up (5)
37. Approaching (8)
38. Uninvolved (8)
39. Alumnus, once (7)
41. Stop (6)
43. Shelve (5)
44. Spelunker's spot (4)
45. Constraint (4)
46. Encourage (4)

Double Up

PUZZLE 332

Each puzzle consists of four 5-letter words that use ten different letters exactly twice apiece. Thus, since there are already two A's in the first puzzle, you cannot use another A. There is only one S in that puzzle; think of a word using the second S.

1.
S O L _
_ E A _
A R N _
_ I G

2.
U E D _
_ H R _
T A E _
_ U C

3.
C U T _
_ O C _
R N E _
_ H R

4.
E T A _
_ S L _
S L T _
_ I E

291

PUZZLE 333

ACROSS
1. Sitting above
5. Burn slightly
9. Good-bye, in London
13. Wait
14. Brink
15. Bill collector?
16. Tokyo waistbands
17. Appointment
19. Cast out
21. Touch lightly
22. Dirty place
23. Enjoy a buffet
24. By what method?
26. Assemble
28. Shoot forth
30. Scarcity
33. Groovy!
37. Jolt suddenly
39. Full-strength
40. Eskimo canoe
41. Baseball stat
42. Show up repeatedly
43. Incensed
44. Drowse
45. Bothered
46. Impassive
49. Stomped
51. Pepper-picker Piper
53. "All About ____"
54. Turkish hat
57. Slangy coffee
59. Airport abbr.
60. Pique
62. For adorn-ment
66. Butterfly snares
67. Bakery employee
68. Oodles
69. Lump
70. DEA agent
71. Impact noise
72. Catch sight of

DOWN
1. Dwelling
2. Shinbone
3. Shelley, e.g.
4. Mexican dollar
5. Capitol Hill VIP
6. Energy measure-ment
7. Playing marble
8. Esteem
9. Singer/ guitarist Petty
10. Dumbfounded
11. Campground home
12. Affectedly bohemian
14. Scorpion's poison
18. Blunted rapier
20. Edible gastropod
25. Shrivel
27. Antic
29. Mystical deck
31. Factual
32. Bovine gathering
33. Glides downhill
34. Skin woe
35. Big surprise
36. Gravy server
38. Priest
42. TV's "Knight ____"
47. List unit
48. Despise
50. Racetrack shapes
52. Ponderosa, e.g.
54. Gasoline and kerosene
55. Halt legally
56. Tangy
57. Unite
58. "Jaws" boat
61. Fairy-tale start
63. ____ de Triomphe
64. Sorority letter
65. Say more

PUZZLE 334

Slide-O-Gram

Place the seven words into the diagram, one word for each row, so that one of the columns reading down will spell out a 7-letter word that is related to the others. Each given letter is part of one word.

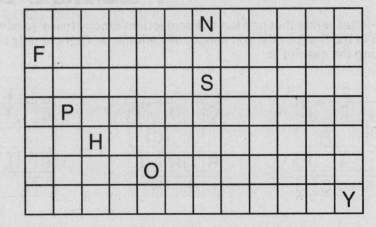

Custom

Fashion

Habit

Pattern

Practice

Tendency

Wont

292

ACROSS

1. One opposed
5. Clerical garment
8. Mosque official
12. Weaving frame
13. Part of the head
15. Part of TV
16. Minestrone, e.g.
17. Metal suit
18. Glided
19. Gumbo vegetable
20. Pekoe portion
22. Sash for a kimono
23. Watch secretly
25. Mocking
27. Deletions
32. Shoot the breeze
33. Japanese noodles
34. Mournful
39. Curved edge
40. Scrubbed
42. Raven's call
43. Most snobbish
45. Swiped
47. Massage
48. Leading ladies
50. Expel a lawyer
53. Country hotel
54. Printing liquid
55. Scoops
59. Carry along
63. Increase
65. Cheek makeup
66. Wild goat
67. "___ the Night"
68. Safe-crackers
69. Naught
70. Sample
71. Legal thing
72. Understands

DOWN

1. Additionally
2. Corner
3. Take in the sights
4. Deadlock
5. Pasture measure
6. Tibetan monk
7. Small lump
8. "___ My Party"
9. Large fruit
10. Excuse
11. Doc
13. Woodland deity
14. Grassland
21. Male descendant
24. On time
26. Make a choice
27. Goofs up
28. Cloud juice
29. Caisson's contents
30. Duel tool
31. Cut
35. Kitty builder
36. Revered image
37. Hollow
38. Woolly females
41. Book collection
44. Sphere
46. Shading
49. Ascends
50. Finger, e.g.
51. Absurd
52. Short comedies
56. Activist
57. Sled
58. Omelet needs
60. Wind instrument
61. Camper's cover
62. Former spouses
64. Commandment word

Rapid Reader

Ten 5-letter words appear backward in these lines of letters. Can you find them all in four minutes or less? Underline each word as you find it, as we have done with the first word, JUMBO.

```
Q C S R E V I R V A H L A O B M U J O S
K T C E R E S Y C M T E R A H S T O C K
E S I A R T M O G X D D N U O H R L U P
A R I Z T S Y R T N O L E M W L Y U H H
T N L E T O M F W R U Q T I M T R A H C
```

PUZZLE 337

BRICK BY BRICK

Rearrange this stack of bricks to form a crossword puzzle. The clues will help you fit the bricks into their correct places. Row 1 has been filled in for you. Use the bricks to fill in the remaining spaces.

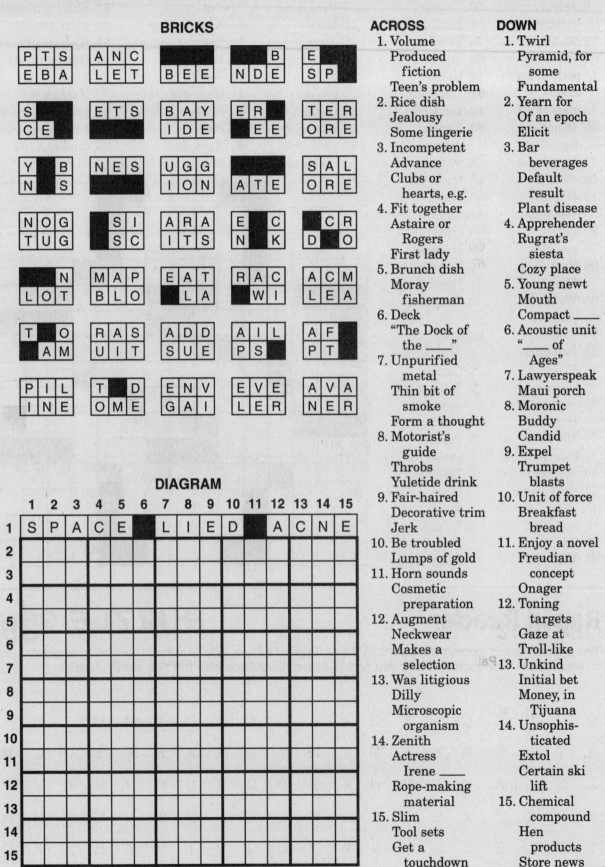

BRICKS

ACROSS

1. Volume
   Produced fiction
   Teen's problem
2. Rice dish
   Jealousy
   Some lingerie
3. Incompetent
   Advance
   Clubs or hearts, e.g.
4. Fit together
   Astaire or Rogers
   First lady
5. Brunch dish
   Moray fisherman
6. Deck
   "The Dock of the ___"
7. Unpurified metal
   Thin bit of smoke
   Form a thought
8. Motorist's guide
   Throbs
   Yuletide drink
9. Fair-haired
   Decorative trim
   Jerk
10. Be troubled
    Lumps of gold
11. Horn sounds
    Cosmetic preparation
12. Augment
    Neckwear
    Makes a selection
13. Was litigious
    Dilly
    Microscopic organism
14. Zenith
    Actress Irene ___
    Rope-making material
15. Slim
    Tool sets
    Get a touchdown

DOWN

1. Twirl
   Pyramid, for some
   Fundamental
2. Yearn for
   Of an epoch
   Elicit
3. Bar beverages
   Default result
   Plant disease
4. Apprehender
   Rugrat's siesta
   Cozy place
5. Young newt
   Mouth
   Compact ___
6. Acoustic unit
   "___ of Ages"
7. Lawyerspeak
   Maui porch
8. Moronic
   Buddy
   Candid
9. Expel
   Trumpet blasts
10. Unit of force
    Breakfast bread
11. Enjoy a novel
    Freudian concept
    Onager
12. Toning targets
    Gaze at
    Troll-like
13. Unkind
    Initial bet
    Money, in Tijuana
14. Unsophis-ticated
    Extol
    Certain ski lift
15. Chemical compound
    Hen products
    Store news

ACROSS

1. Throw
5. Hen's product
8. Farm tower
12. Neighborhood
13. Extensive
15. Lacking rain
16. Commits perjury
17. Plato's market
18. Vittles
19. Chinese game
21. Cook in hot oil
22. Landers and Jillian
23. ___ cube
24. Shankar's instrument
26. Adolescent
28. Sand
31. Puckered
33. Complete failure
34. Ignited
36. Fox's dance?
37. Ridiculous
39. Word before angle or open
40. "Stand ___ Deliver"
41. Skirmish
42. Disgraced
44. Vendor
46. Spheres
47. Dough
49. Clump of turf
50. Settee
53. Income ___
54. Clamor
58. Astringent substance
59. Practice piece
61. Folklore giant
62. Italian currency, once
63. Silly people
64. Radar-screen spot
65. Playthings
66. Stimpy's pal
67. Slithery swimmers

DOWN

1. Dogie
2. Battle song?
3. Witnessed
4. Most flavorful
5. Energy unit
6. Botches
7. Military post
8. Kenyan tour
9. Heavy metal
10. Maned male
11. Bookie's concern
13. Ruin
14. Dawn-to-dusk periods
20. Skin problem
25. Priest's garment
26. Rotates
27. Wear away
29. Ascend
30. Clerks
31. "Harper Valley ___"
32. Conducted
33. Bark at the moon
35. Newsman Koppel
38. Storyteller
39. Clothes collection
41. Winter ailment
43. Basketball target
45. Andes animals
48. Ooze
49. Brings to court
50. Snow melter
51. Hodgepodge
52. Rage
55. Flirty look
56. Nutmeg cover
57. D.C. figures
60. Ameche or Rickles

Halftime

Pair off the groups of letters to form ten 6-letter baseball terms.

BAT	EUP	KIE	SEC	_____	_____
BLE	IKE	LIN	SLI	_____	_____
DER	IRE	OND	STR	_____	_____
DOU	ING	OUT	TER	_____	_____
DUG	INN	ROO	UMP	_____	_____

PUZZLE 340

AT 6'S AND 7'S

Clues to all the 6- and 7-letter entries in this crossword are listed first, and they are in scrambled order. Use the numbered clues as solving hints to help you determine where each one belongs in the diagram.

6-LETTER ENTRIES

Beginning
Guide
Mournful
Reveled
Table linens
Card suit
Grown-ups
Talks back
Drink
Dry gulch
Magician's word
Meager
Daze
Disposition
Ecclesiastical councils
Piano compositions
Golf scores
Mexican dish
Treats for Fido
Takes a nap

7-LETTER ENTRIES

Returned
Became visible
Concurs
Prince Charles, e.g.
Feels regret
Greed
Clergymen
Rustles, as silk
Downpours
Bargain shopper's action
Restrains
Certain heroes?
Furry pet
Rests

ACROSS

8. Ego
12. Bar bill
16. Stair part
18. Bustle
20. Come together
21. Coffee cup
22. Burning
23. Nile vipers
25. Willy or Moby Dick
27. Taverns
28. Biblical word
33. Goofed
35. Army dining hall
36. Paper amount
38. Unseals
44. Card game of old
45. Perfume oil
49. Medleys
50. Searches
52. Serenity
53. Fabric fold
54. Notable time
57. Thugs
59. Ivan or Peter
60. Indian garb
63. Express
72. Pie's kin
74. Verdi offering
75. Got up
76. Wild cat
77. Mixes the batter
78. Freckle
79. Romanced
84. Sight organ
85. Binge
87. Instant lawn
88. Hamilton bills

DOWN

5. Despise
6. Previously, in verse
7. Family car
9. Marine birds
10. Luau garland
11. Mrs. Sprat's diet
17. Wet, as grass
24. Wine glass part
28. Employer
30. Narrative poem
34. Chess castle
40. Spinning toy
41. Building wing
42. Cravat
44. Actress Thompson
46. Outdoor game
47. Expert
48. Carpet color
51. Formerly
56. Tall spar
58. Umpire's call
59. Streetcar
71. Bastes
73. Speed detector
76. Striking end of a hammer
77. Smack
80. Choose
81. Miner's quest
83. "All About ____"

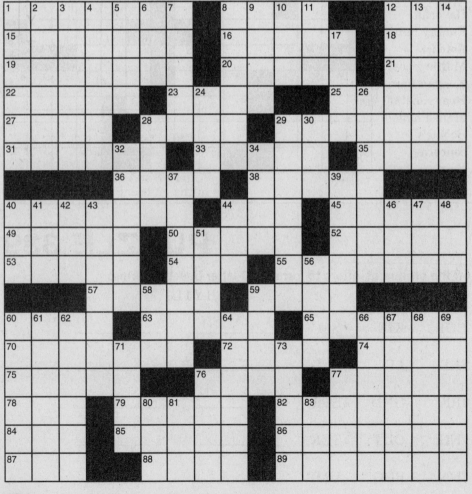

CODEWORD

Codeword is a special crossword puzzle in which conventional clues are omitted. Instead, answer words in the diagram are represented by numbers. Each number represents a different letter of the alphabet, and all of the letters of the alphabet are used. When you are sure of a letter, put it in the code key chart and cross it off in the alphabet box. A group of letters has been inserted to start you off.

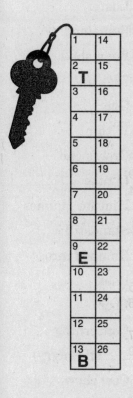

Code key chart:

| 1 | 14 | | 2 (T) | 15 | | 3 | 16 | | 4 | 17 | | 5 | 18 | | 6 | 19 | | 7 | 20 | | 8 | 21 | | 9 (E) | 22 | | 10 | 23 | | 11 | 24 | | 12 | 25 | | 13 (B) | 26 |

Alphabet box:

A N
B̷ O
C P
D Q
E̷ R
F S
G T̷
H U
I V
J W
K X
L Y
M Z

Codeword grid:

21	10	26	3			26	16	1		10	12	11	15
10	22	16	9		2	14	23	16	13		22	16	24	9
13	9	24	2		23	10	13	13	11		11	10	12	13
		26	14	11	22	11			24	16	13		
10	22	19	14	10	13 (B)	9 (E)	2 (T)		8	4	11	26	14	9
24	9	9		23	10	2		21	4	2		16	10	7
3	9	23	1	9	22		7	16	9		1	9	25	2
	21	10	12		7	11	2		18	9	17		
26	14	4	6		13	10	1		19	9	2	11	2	9
16	4	23		22	16	17		6	10	23		24	10	5
6	9	5	24	9	23		26	10	24	24	9	2	2	9
		25	11	20		10	22	2	9	23			
24	10	3	9		16	25	1	9	23		6	10	6	10
11	15	9	10		11	23	16	1	5		16	15	16	23
26	20	10	23			5	9	10		2	16	16	3	

Mix and Mingle

Unscramble the letters to the right of each row and place them in the correct squares to spell out nine compound words or phrases. In addition, the initial letters of the answers can be rearranged to form a bonus compound word or phrase.

#	1	2	3	4	5	6	7	8	Letters
1.	O		F	S		R		N	GFIP
2.		A		T			O	R	RHWEM
3.	P		A		T		N	G	HYIL
4.		A			T	A		R	ERKCE
5.	N	E		S			U	N	ODWH
6.		A	C			O		S	E	HERR
7.	A	R			E		E		MNCYH
8.		E	R			E		N	GEREV
9.	N			N		O		T	ANYAG

BONUS: _____

PUZZLE 343

ACROSS
1. Hoard
6. Crown of light
10. Harass
13. Chops
15. Wickedness
16. Wise bird
17. Adjust to surroundings
18. Temperate
19. In addition
20. Dunce
21. Imitated
23. Corn coverings
25. Silky fabric
27. Light boats
28. Conspired
31. Comrade
32. Tranquil
33. Emulate a tailor
34. Came to rest
38. Reigned
39. Boo-boo
40. Likely
41. Sasquatch's kin
42. Roll
43. Adult
44. Competed
46. Sailed
47. Peaceful
50. Fogs
51. Bumpkins
52. Forbidden thing
53. "Billy Budd" direction
56. Massage
57. Deuces
59. Take tiny bites
62. Huge fuss
63. Icicle's spot
64. Wraps
65. Stroke
66. Talk to God
67. Lovely

DOWN
1. Drive away
2. Famous plantation
3. Like
4. "___ Loves You"
5. Barnyard fowl
6. Strong males
7. Greedy
8. Adjective for Abner
9. Dated
10. Untrue
11. Got out of bed
12. Luster
14. Remained
22. Bean shell
24. Digs up
25. Got
26. Within
27. Crow's call
28. Limber
29. Hint for Holmes
30. Standstill
31. Bumped into
33. Bask
35. Boor
36. Concerning
37. ___ off (angry)
39. Cow chew
40. Treaty
42. Honey source
43. Bricklayers
45. Foot arch
46. Yang's partner
47. Leftover piece
48. Duck
49. Automaton
50. Saunter
52. PBS series
53. Skilled
54. Split
55. "___ Pilot"
58. Conflict
60. "___ Alive!"
61. Archer's weapon

ACROSS

1. Sofa part
4. Promote
8. Reprimand
13. Icy center
14. Sports spot
15. Knight wear
16. Cackler
17. Cargoes
18. Give up
19. Escape
21. Highway
23. Hearty soup
24. Bungle
26. Intensity
28. Saguaro, e.g.
31. Make a bow
32. Ox's kin
35. Santa's laugh
36. Old pronoun
38. Lake boats
40. Submits to
42. Moray ___
44. Dish up
45. Blotted out
47. Joined
49. Matured
50. Pop
51. Feel unwell
53. More beloved
55. Solemn
57. ___ and flow
58. Charge
61. Hog fat
63. Verse
67. Maui dances
69. Alcohol
71. Hymn of praise
72. Keen
73. Hermit
74. Guys
75. Flung
76. Differently
77. Light tap

DOWN

1. Hurt
2. Rod's mate
3. Food list
4. Expert
5. Hurdle
6. Opened
7. Rubber ring
8. Viewed
9. Collide
10. Drop
11. Sweetheart
12. Depicted
14. On guard
20. Phony ducks
22. Legendary
25. Road groove
27. Hyson and cha
28. Hooded snake
29. In front
30. Not he
32. Ravine
33. When pigs fly!
34. Applied
35. Weeded
37. Evergreen
39. Within reach
41. Pew
43. Governed
46. Watch face
48. Aberdeen's river
52. Obligated
54. More fit
55. Utter
56. Slobber
58. Converse
59. Ow!
60. Garble
62. Puts on
64. Play
65. Concept
66. Red ___
68. Mend
70. Last letter

PUZZLE 345

ACROSS
1. Nuisance
5. Fluster
9. Bits of land
14. Solemn statement
15. Gone
16. Whisk
17. Concluded
18. Dracula's garb
19. Unfortunately
20. More secluded
22. Smear
24. Water walker
26. Harass
29. Help (in crime)
31. Give ___ (listen)
33. Tuck's partner
35. Horsy noises
37. Strong drink
39. Bedlam
40. Feelings
41. Moral
43. Coal receptacle
44. Intersected
45. Ramble
46. Called up
48. Bad humor
49. Soap ingredient
50. Lodge fees
51. Grab
54. Meddled
57. Penny
59. Extreme
63. Legal suits
66. Pearly gem
68. Tortilla dish
69. Aside
70. Small amount
71. Gumbo item
72. Full of gossip
73. Hive habitues
74. Ocean ridge

DOWN
1. Needy
2. Roof edge
3. Stop
4. Hurler
5. Confronted
6. Conscious
7. Microwave
8. Black-___ pea
9. Magazine unit
10. Mops
11. Supervised
12. Electric ___
13. Snoop
21. Become ragged
23. Outside
25. Exercise program
27. Empower
28. Straightens
29. Tees off
30. Infant's shoe
32. Curved line
34. Frog's hangout
35. Trucker's rig
36. Purloined
38. Skated
42. Baled commodity
47. Account examiner
52. Bakery workers
53. Tangy
55. Speak in public
56. Clearances
58. Mausoleum
60. Torte, e.g.
61. Pasture measure
62. Bread unit
63. Film container
64. Monkey's uncle?
65. Viewed
67. Filled dessert

ACROSS

1. Weapons
5. Infant
9. High point
13. Wild cat
14. Sniggler
16. Itinerary
17. Wise about
18. Grind
19. Hiker's house
20. ___-friendly
21. Emerge
23. Bronze, e.g.
24. Empower
27. Winery worker
29. Shelley poem
30. Hindu leader
31. Trust
35. Trendy
36. Cleanser
40. Surrounded by
41. Succeeded
42. Milky
43. Newsman Roger ___
44. Get it?
45. Carpenter, often
46. Sport blade
48. Apparatus
49. Wet
52. Cable
57. Ante up
58. Cockloft
60. Enrage
61. "Aida" solo
63. Bind again
65. Ids' kin
66. Split
67. Sharp cries
68. Eternities
69. Fringe
70. Poor grades
71. Deuce beater

DOWN

1. Audibly
2. Wash off
3. Bates, e.g.
4. Sleep noise
5. Implore
6. Charge with gas
7. Shriek
8. Bigfoot's kin
9. Prone
10. Soccer shoe
11. Dog's bane
12. Go in
15. Relax
22. Corn unit
25. Flat bell
26. Insert
28. Fish roll
30. Rummy game
31. Aswan, e.g.
32. Queensland bird
33. Seal herd
34. Wound up
35. Weeding tool
37. Vinegar's mate
38. Breakfasted
39. According to
41. Little
42. Minimum ___
44. Guard
45. None
47. Coat or soup
48. Chef's secret
49. Fifth wheel
50. Rowed
51. Losing oomph
52. Name
53. Encounter
54. Strictness
55. Isolated
56. Slipshod
59. ___ off (annoyed)
62. Juicy drink
64. Sharp curve

PUZZLE 347

ACROSS

1. At the peak of
5. Con
9. Waters down
14. Ride the wind
15. Friend
16. Check the books of
17. Bruised
18. Repents of
19. Divinity
20. Most cunning
22. Barn bird
23. Spaghetti
26. That thing's
29. Neckwear item
30. Proverb
31. Most irritated
34. Favorite
35. Ms. Magnani
37. Mock
38. Lime drinks
40. Confederation
42. Guns
46. Corn serving
48. Water body
50. Music of Hammer
51. Least refined
54. Aspect
56. Golf norm
57. Lock's partner
58. Comforted
59. Coffeepot
60. Runaway groom
64. Brings up
67. Stud's place
68. Carpet feature
72. Arrangement
73. Press
74. Sinister
75. Foe
76. Act
77. Tints

DOWN

1. Wild donkey
2. Overly
3. Wooden propeller
4. Immediately
5. Garment of India
6. Hint
7. Stout brews
8. "___ Pizza"
9. Small boy
10. Shade of color
11. Fools
12. Simpleton
13. Elegance
21. Dalai ___
23. Dad
24. Removed summarily
25. Particular place
27. Show appreciation to
28. Short drink
31. Motel
32. Dogs' waggers
33. Poetic always
36. Barton, e.g.
39. "The ___ Wolf"
41. Grain
43. Periods
44. Bouquet holder
45. Accelerated
47. Deluge refuge
49. Duel tool
51. Sway
52. Flowery
53. Facial feature
55. Kept on about
56. Bag
61. Knowledge
62. Woodwind
63. Await action
65. Daiquiri liquor
66. Snoop
69. Trailing plant
70. Tell tales
71. City railroads

PUZZLE 348

ACROSS

1. Whopper
4. Part of a glove
8. Rowing blades
12. Lyric poem
13. Duplicates
15. Scheme
16. Cheer
17. Bear witness to
18. Roman wear
19. Yield
21. Persian ruler
23. Convent member
24. Made like
27. Uneven
29. Behaves
32. Robin Hood's skill
35. Linen offering
37. Stockpile
41. Chap
42. Says again
44. Which person
45. Longhorn
47. Listen secretly
49. Morning crower
51. Yeas
52. African tour
55. Fit of anger
57. Breeze
58. Spill
61. Moth repellent
65. Radar light
67. Make angry
70. Mete out
71. Ogle
72. Transferred land
73. Hinged top
74. Whirlpool
75. Glimpse
76. Winners

DOWN

1. Grub
2. Unoccupied
3. Hamburger meat
4. Lobster ___
5. Befitting
6. Reclines
7. Network
8. Choose
9. Beside
10. Scoundrel
11. "___ by Me"
13. Complain
14. Wide-eyed look
20. Middle or Far
22. Annoy
25. Comfort
26. Window coverings
28. Phys ed room
29. Hole-punching tools
30. Yak
31. Current
33. Spiked sneaker
34. Hoists
36. Mistakes
38. Cockeyed
39. Wingtip, e.g.
40. Drenches
43. Gull's kin
46. Geologic span
48. Dried fruit
50. Lubricated
52. Fur
53. Suffered an illness
54. Sauteed
56. Chilled
59. Small bills
60. Type of school
62. Hero's home?
63. Similar
64. Rose and ruby
66. Interfere
68. Big fuss
69. Fetch

PUZZLE 349

ACROSS
1. Part of TGIF
6. Irritate
9. Glass section
13. Using oars
15. Signal
16. Acknowledge
17. Fugitive groom
18. Omelet item
19. Metal tube
20. Large deer
21. Sentence piece
23. Citrus coolers
24. Change the color of
25. Humorous one
26. Week unit
28. Therefore
30. Not qualified
34. Narrow roads
37. Glad
39. Manage
40. Disciple
42. Spotted cat
44. Gun, as an engine
45. Cinema path
47. Protuberances
48. Sketches
50. Relaxed
52. Permit
53. Egyptian cobra
54. Trot
57. Legitimate
60. Take in, as a crop
62. Hooter
63. Charged particles
64. Sweetie
66. Dotted game tile
68. Thin board
69. Wonderment
70. Pencil tip
71. Actor Donahue
72. Married
73. Door

DOWN
1. Cornered
2. Christmas greenery
3. Emerged from sleep
4. Small bite
5. Recognized
6. Summer quencher
7. Carpet
8. Beer holder
9. Tropical fruit
10. Enthusiastic
11. Slangy negative
12. Wool producers
14. Matured
22. Wealth
26. Hoodwink
27. Tennis, ___?
28. "___ So Fine"
29. Country manor
31. Actor Pitt
32. Entice
33. Pass catchers
34. Cooking grease
35. Impersonator
36. Bossa ___
38. Gladden
41. Shopper's aid
43. Pea shell
46. Figured out
49. Meaty
51. Digging tool
54. Beam
55. Possessor
56. Splendor
57. Pinball mishap
58. Crowd's sound
59. "Do ___ others . . ."
61. Ponder
64. Hem's partner
65. Have debts
67. Adult boy

304

ACROSS

1. Hornets, e.g.
6. Liquid rock
10. Finish
14. Aflame
15. Betwixt
16. Wild cat
17. Rough
18. Emeralds, e.g.
20. Cask
21. Deadlocked
23. Songbirds
24. Naturally!
25. Mariner
26. Vegas machine
28. Competent
29. Blue above
30. Tug
34. Duplicates
37. Stadium part
39. Fawn's mother
40. Smell
41. Getaway
42. Hard wood
44. Sidekick
45. Urban pall
47. Shuts
48. Extensions
50. Who ___ you?
51. Put
52. Outskirts
54. Dino, to Fred
55. Curve
58. Narration
61. Stereo system
62. Scand. land
63. Not spoken
66. Obscure
68. Gape
69. Up-and-down toy
70. Nobility
71. Customs
72. Not west
73. Slumber

DOWN

1. Nutty
2. Come to terms
3. Hits hard
4. Seed holder
5. Climbing plants
6. Light beer
7. Prayer ender
8. Vigor's pal
9. Radio spots
10. Flashy
11. Lullaby
12. Warning sign
13. Lapse
19. Couple
22. Cauldrons
26. Browse
27. Sodium solution
28. Get a bead on
29. Phase
31. Fusses
32. Nary a thing
33. Clues
34. Cod, for one
35. Voiced
36. Survey
38. Kinfolk
41. Folk tales
43. Young man
46. ___ wheels
47. Musical sign
49. Waits on
53. Hue
54. Aviator
55. Stones song
56. Turnpike
57. Jerk
58. Frosty's material
59. Cato's wear
60. Nothing but
61. Feeds, as horses
64. Deli loaf
65. Feather scarf
67. 100%

PUZZLE 351

ACROSS

1. Noodles
6. Feat
9. Society newcomers
13. Harmony
15. Quiet!
16. Turf
17. Dazed state
18. Foot digit
19. Mr. Griffin
20. Sewn borders
21. Sound system
24. OK mark
25. Extra tire
26. Thick gloves
28. Talk idly
31. Always, in poems
32. ___ se
33. Formerly
34. Jog
36. Short sock
40. Received
41. Battling
43. Head flanker
44. Shocked
47. Egg-shaped
49. Exist
50. Teensy
51. Mature
52. Go by air
53. Computer part
56. Kilt, e.g.
58. Single
59. Antelope
61. Hot rocks
65. Tiger ___
67. Grease
68. Beginner's book
70. Lug
71. Victory symbol
72. Recluse
73. Break
74. High railways
75. Showy flower

DOWN

1. Country walk
2. Land unit
3. Hoax
4. Weights
5. Circle part
6. Starflower
7. Errand
8. You, once
9. River blockade
10. Create
11. Chapeau
12. Rescues
14. Frantic
22. Gypsy's card
23. Warning
25. Harden
27. Bug
28. Bonkers
29. Excited
30. "___ Sides Now"
32. Essay division
35. Pair number
37. Four-___ clover
38. ___ Grey
39. It beats a deuce
42. Advantage
45. Wonder
46. Big rig
48. Say yes
53. Sheds
54. Burger garnish
55. "___ Dawn"
56. Sales talk
57. Green veggies
60. Transfer
61. Italian bread, once
62. S.W.A.T. need
63. Blood carrier
64. Bohemian
66. Uh-huh
69. Agent

306

ACROSS

1. Castle ditches
6. Stomach muscles
9. Cooks
14. Fool
15. Snapshot
16. Pathway
17. Object
18. Lobe place
19. Plains abode
20. Diamond, e.g.
22. Chopped
24. Tibetan beast
25. Angora fabric
28. Form of address
30. Drain
31. Door feature
33. Eyeglasses
36. Fury
37. Located
39. Tender spots
41. Peel
43. Not drunk
45. Desire
46. Smirk
48. Cowboy, at times
50. Dotted cube
51. Own up to
53. Vatican resident
54. Sad
55. Track shape
57. Disposition
59. Prone
62. Ids' mates
64. A Costello
65. Barnyard sound
67. Winter woe
69. Ringlet
73. Thrust
74. Mr. Arnold
75. Chilling
76. Lab compound
77. Sure!
78. Respond

DOWN

1. Central
2. Shelley poem
3. Point
4. "___ Enough"
5. Spells
6. Act like
7. Inclination
8. Shoo!
9. Dozes
10. Rush
11. View
12. Dog's pest
13. Search for
21. Skirts
23. Lived
25. Berth place
26. Unbolted
27. Helicopter part
29. Kitty's cry
30. Titles of respect
32. Jazz style
34. Nursery item
35. Elder
38. Terminal
40. Worry
42. Prototype
44. Fend off
47. "Rosie the ___"
49. More secluded
52. Label
56. Towering
58. Thick soup
59. Qualified
60. Not minus
61. Pup ___
63. Type of gin
66. Mature
68. Strike caller
70. Timespan
71. Attack, Fido!
72. Collection

PUZZLE 353

MOVIES & TELEVISION

ACROSS

1. Hayworth and Gam
6. Cable-TV channel
9. Actor Handler
13. Ryan and Cara
15. Marine mammal
17. Caron film
18. Basinger film
19. Lew ___
20. Stage org.
21. Refute
23. Unger's virtue
25. Disney fish
29. Actor Clark
31. Ms. Lindstrom
32. Actor Brooks
34. Indian dwelling
36. "What's Eating Gilbert ___"
41. Marcel ___
43. Trim down
45. Actress Markey
46. Ursula ___
48. "The Great ___"
50. Narc's org.
53. "___ Wolf"
54. Costner role
56. Cong. member
57. "Sports Night" name
59. Actress Anderson
62. Greek war god
63. Frank Gorshin, e.g.
65. The F in FBI
69. "Beau ___"
71. ___ Fudd
73. Actress Neal
74. TV partner, often
76. Hemsley series
78. ___ shark
79. ___ Bilko
84. "American ___"
86. "The Sopranos" actor
87. Oyster find
89. Daytime drama
94. 1492 vessel
95. J.R.'s mom
96. "___ Man"
97. Ena Hartmann role
98. Drumstick
99. Ganders

DOWN

1. ___ Tin Tin
2. Gershwin brother
3. Actor Danson
4. Singer DiFranco
5. Forward
6. Biblical pronoun
7. Cowshed
8. Surprise hit
9. Richard or Aeryk
10. Ivy, e.g.
11. Reps.
12. Peeples and Vardalos
14. Kernel
15. Garth's buddy
16. Actor Morales
22. PBS science show
24. ___ sale
25. "China Beach" locale
26. Ms. Marie Saint
27. Bardot's sea
28. Willy, e.g.
30. Actor Omar ___
33. Role for Barbra
35. Art stand
37. VCR button
38. Gasteyer and Alicia
39. Peace ___
40. "Exit to ___"
42. Miss Quested
44. "___, Indiana"
47. Georgia ___
49. Sleuth Sam ___
50. Pull behind

51. "Jane ___"

52. Summer coolers

55. Batman's butler

58. NYC clock zone

60. "___ la Douce"

61. Foster film

64. Actor Roberts

66. "___ Lobo"

67. ___ Buchanan

68. Football's Dawson

70. Actress Plumb

72. Author Zola

75. "___ Fear"

77. Cyrano's feature

79. Drop

80. Director Kazan

81. Lease

82. Actress Erin ___

83. "Tall ___"

85. TV's Shelley ___

88. Big truck

90. Mr. Ventura

91. Bakery treat

92. USN officer

93. Shad ___

PUZZLE 354

ACROSS

1. Noblewoman
5. Willowy
9. Swipe
14. Spoil
15. Corn cake
16. Knowing
17. Jars
18. Fruit waste
19. Famed
20. Skirt length
21. Amid
23. Musician's job
25. Supply with oxygen
29. Stick together
31. Loud noise
33. Guard
35. Belly
36. ___ Grey
38. Turn
40. Painter's work
41. Helped
43. Baby wear
44. Frail
46. Stared at
47. Deed
48. Subway fee
49. Nary a thing
51. Brim
53. Handy
55. Blubber
56. Accounts book
59. Every
63. Porcelain
67. Chalet part
68. ___ of Wight
69. Pointer
70. Did in (the dragon)
71. Adjacent
72. Home on the range
73. Wallet items
74. Rubberneck

DOWN

1. Bongo, e.g.
2. Distinctive air
3. Impudent female
4. "___ Pulver"
5. Twig
6. Cut of meat
7. Hostels
8. In the middle
9. More sensible
10. 1 + 1
11. Wolf down
12. Have being
13. Headed
22. Celsius unit
24. Perfect model
26. Toward the stern
27. Makings of a cuppa
28. Lure
29. Part of FBI
30. Playful swimmers
31. Bikini piece
32. Outer-space man
34. Arrears
35. Fishing hook
37. Madison or Park
39. Weirder
42. Concentrated solution
45. Spelling ___
50. Firstborn
52. Coloring
54. Signaling light
55. Ships' hands
57. Blow
58. Commensurate
60. Puzzled
61. Applaud
62. This place
63. Siamese, e.g.
64. Rush
65. Unruly child
66. Born

PUZZLE 355

ACROSS

1. Second Greek letter
5. Harvest
9. Peak
13. Prayer word
14. Dodge
16. At what time?
17. Ladder part
18. Recently
19. Yogurt word
20. Sibilant sounds
22. Weeds
24. Flee
25. Deviation
28. Coldly
30. Yardstick
33. Puffy do
34. Downs' opposites
35. Sewing spike
37. Trim
41. Expense
42. Snake
43. Help
45. Blue bird
46. Suspect
48. Certain fly
50. Maven
51. Conceit
53. Inscribed
55. Lift
58. Laundry machine
59. Naval off.
60. Long stride
63. Grating
67. Wine region
69. Pack animal
72. Bargain event
73. Wreck
74. Related by marriage
75. Tied
76. Gull's kin
77. Category
78. Ruby and cerise

DOWN

1. Unclad
2. Australian birds
3. Wallet bills
4. Cherubs
5. Skillet
6. "___ Got No Strings"
7. Pasture worker
8. Metric weight
9. Hole-making tool
10. Texas dish
11. Lead or zinc
12. Foe
15. Tint
21. Spa feature
23. Man's title
26. Immediately
27. Leaks out
29. Patrolman
30. Hand warmer
31. Duel blade
32. On the briny
33. Scrappy
36. At another time
38. Partly open
39. Speed
40. Looked at
44. Discourage
47. Gun the engine
49. Old
52. Congeal
54. Blackboard item
55. Vital organ
56. Follow directly
57. Awake
61. Tokyo sash
62. Kick
64. Safeguard
65. Begged
66. Appetites
68. Motel
70. Knock
71. Be in debt

PUZZLE 356

ACROSS
1. Lazes
6. Tyke
9. Desire
13. Snare
15. Hubbub
16. It's often read
17. Chump
18. Milk maker
19. Wound cover
20. Saturate
21. Enhance
23. Present!
24. Low voice
26. Watered
27. Uniform color
30. Red gem
34. More uncanny
36. Bazaar
37. Dress bottom
40. Smirk
41. Due
43. Boyfriend
44. Lay turf
45. Watcher
46. Pester
48. Billboard
50. Goods
51. Agitate
54. Unsightly
56. Sole
57. Investigate
60. Pursue
63. Bends
64. Slack
65. Decreasing
68. Empty
69. Develop
70. Sharper
71. Join
72. Itch
73. Honkers

DOWN
1. Not so much
2. Informed of
3. Above
4. Bushy do
5. Slump
6. Shell food
7. Fragrance
8. Suburb
9. Outcome
10. Contests
11. Glower
12. Implant
14. Bog product
22. Poodle, e.g.
24. Like
25. Tell a fib
26. Not him
27. Barrels
28. Long lunch
29. Parched
31. In flames
32. Sought office
33. Near
35. Acuff et al.
37. Listen to
38. Soften
39. Rumple
42. Dampen
43. Donkey call
45. Eternity
47. Pointed tool
48. Format in advance
49. Chef's spicy coating
51. Assert
52. Crowd
53. ___ Fester
55. Nerd
57. Romp
58. Current fad
59. Steers
60. Sherry, e.g.
61. Wallet items
62. Grimm villain
66. Entreat
67. Drone

PUZZLE 357

ACROSS

1. Guess
5. Talk idly
9. UN HQ site
12. Wee
13. Rated
15. Pro vote
16. Intense fury
17. Pinker
18. Operated
19. Have life
20. Sound reverb
21. Scrub, as a mission
23. Cautiously
26. Small combo
28. Of the nose
31. Critter
35. Dim
38. Fuzzy fruit
40. Ear piece
41. Bronze or Iron
42. Shaggy bovine
43. Race, as a motor
44. Rebuke
46. Division preposition
47. Shabby
49. Office worker
51. Skier's locale
53. Turndowns
55. Gasped
59. Linguine, e.g.
62. Publicize
65. Route
66. Infirm
67. Tickle pink
69. Get up
70. Sock end
71. Jerked
72. Bakery employee
73. Evergreen plant
74. Lichen's kin
75. Sets

DOWN

1. Sipping tube
2. Elegant headgear
3. Ire
4. Toodle-oo!
5. Gator's relative
6. Meat medley
7. Simpleton
8. Originally named
9. Singer Laura ___
10. Calendar total
11. Tilt
13. Joel and Zane
14. Water outlet
22. Churn
24. Scribe's fluid
25. Nonprofessional
27. April shower
29. Comparable
30. Itemizes
32. Additional
33. Still not up
34. Impose, as a tax
35. Sloop's pole
36. Unattractive
37. Harvest
39. Lamb product
42. Take the bait
45. Pub order
47. Luxury resort
48. Yet, poetically
50. Foamy
52. Chose
54. Shorthand, for short
56. A couple of times
57. Art supporter
58. Colorists
59. Compassion
60. Burn balm
61. Heap
63. Mighty trees
64. Functions
68. Getaway
69. Big truck

313

PUZZLE 358

ACROSS

1. Caribbean dance
6. Mule's kin
9. Tree growth
13. Highly curious
17. Outcast
18. Dine
19. Concept
20. Mama's man
21. Mr. Fudd
22. "Tell ___ About It"
23. Car straps
25. Young person
26. Sham
28. Perjure oneself
29. Tow behind
33. Bass bait
35. Sister's son
40. Yankees, et al.
44. Deputy
45. Jogged
46. Type of saxophone
47. Epic
48. Not suitable
49. Omelet ingredient
50. Colorists
52. "The Prince of ___"
54. "___ a Living"
55. Matured
57. Title
59. Felt concern
61. Egyptian structure
65. Crowd
67. Boat basins
71. Curved roofs
73. Doll's date
75. Wow!
76. Tavern
79. Milky stones
81. Confiscated
85. Freezer cube
86. Verbal exams
88. Preschoolers
90. Provoke
91. Grassy layer
92. Folklore giant
93. Pleasantly brief
96. Soup legume
98. Duo
99. Establishes
100. Signal yes
102. Fierce rage
103. Excursion
107. Objective
112. Brief snooze
115. Hoist
116. ___-do-well
117. Hound's prey
118. Tavern drink
119. Chilling
120. "___ Wars"
121. Husky's load
122. Mineral spring
123. Aroma

DOWN

1. Encounter
2. Car part
3. Imitate
4. Mixes
5. Above, in poems
6. Volcanic dust
7. Bring to court
8. Spread out awkwardly
9. Abuse
10. Solemn lyric poem
11. Close firmly
12. Shiny fabrics
13. Simian
14. Young woman
15. Choose
16. Motor fuel
24. Spelling ___
27. Camp beds
30. Scan a book
31. Competently
32. Turnstile
34. Houdini's specialty
36. "Peter ___"
37. Phonograph
38. Modify text
39. Soaks
40. Loose-fitting
41. Wrath
42. "___ Jim"
43. Lady's title
45. Gather crops
48. Consumer
51. Total
53. Historic timespan
56. June honoree
58. Marsh
60. Remove sand
62. Cows' sounds
63. Unruly child
64. "___ of a Salesman"
66. However
68. Ruckus

314

PUZZLE 358

69. Neckwear
70. Tool hut
72. Sailing craft
74. Narrative
76. Billiards game
77. Yearning
78. Stable
80. Tense
82. Baby goats
83. At another place
84. Small salamander
87. Authorize
89. Agitate
93. Two-toed animals
94. Coliseums
95. Honor
97. Rural hotel
101. Knob
104. Occasional
105. Bad
106. Ship bottom
107. Officeholders
108. Tennis need
109. English brew
110. Blunder
111. Mineral source
113. Swiss peak
114. Split ___ soup
115. "___ So Fine"

PUZZLE 359

ACROSS

1. Rural unit
5. Halters
9. Hoarder
14. Beat this
15. Calm
16. Witch
17. Out of ___
18. Certain woodwind
19. Cheer
20. Fade away
22. Cut
24. Cow's chew
25. Pedigree diagram
27. Promise
28. Muffet's fare
29. Stipend
30. Bill, eventually
32. Couch
34. Electrical measure
35. Strong alkalis
37. ___ of Man
40. Resort
41. Surround and attack
44. Northern toymaker
46. Memo error
48. Chisel, e.g.
49. EPA's concern
50. Viewed
53. Beckon
54. Porker's place
55. Wound's leftover
58. Important times
60. Duel blade
62. Woolen cap
63. Obstacle
64. Expert
65. Period
67. Muck's partner
69. Previous
73. Place
74. Lily species
75. Petition
76. Moved gradually
77. Foreteller
78. 52 weeks

DOWN

1. Magazine fillers
2. Call out
3. Race
4. TV host
5. Small lump
6. Summon the genie
7. Honolulu howdy
8. Rains ice
9. Look through
10. Body part
11. Affirm
12. Result
13. Thin
21. Hotel employee
23. Gossiper's query
25. Attract
26. Settle a debt
27. Has a mortgage
28. Lived
29. Sols preceders
31. Affirmative vote
33. Baseball player
36. Use a chair
38. Tenant's document
39. Superior
42. Ages
43. Sticky material
45. Use a wok
47. Part of rpm
51. Twilight, in verse
52. Serious plays
55. Comic Martin
56. Dressed like Dracula
57. In the midst of
59. Spry
61. Red flower
63. Lean-to
64. Look intently
66. Stick for billiards
68. Caviar
70. Bubbly brew
71. Where whales wallow
72. La Brea goo

ACROSS

1. Yeas
5. Bolted
9. Gooey stuff
12. Diva's aria
13. Play
15. Right you ___!
16. Fit of anger
17. Lower
18. Bathing-suit part
19. Intense
21. Followed
23. Upper body
26. Frock
27. Past
28. Workout spots
32. Dynamite
33. Major-leaguer
34. Fine powder
35. Rent
36. Puts
38. Dish
40. Lodge members
44. Humble ___
46. Starring role
48. Third of a trio
49. Previous
51. Baseball's Rose
52. Toll
53. Yelled
54. Consumed
56. Dundee boy
58. Cabin and deck
61. Moreover
62. Second ___
64. Labels
68. Hot diamonds
69. More wicked
70. Concept
71. Blokes
72. Reel shockers?
73. Caper

DOWN

1. Pale gray
2. Not me
3. Brownie
4. Couches
5. Worry
6. Be defeated
7. Overhead trains
8. Routine food
9. Postpones
10. Imprison
11. Enjoys Koontz
13. Winter ill
14. Baby's bed
20. Price
22. Peeved
23. Faucets
24. Beast
25. Base
29. Kind of doll
30. Completely
31. Head part
32. Meadow cry
37. Snooped
39. Golf accessory
41. Attic
42. Leg hinge
43. Spotted
45. Antiseptic
47. Bottomless
49. Strut
50. Harassed
53. Assertion
55. In motion
57. Roof edge
58. Yank
59. Mine rocks
60. "___ the ramparts . . ."
63. Hitch
65. Hoopla
66. Trinket
67. Tree juice

317

PUZZLE 361

ACROSS

1. Twitches
5. Mesh
8. Thin tuft
12. Pine
13. Managed
15. Ditto, of a sort
16. Shark type
17. Talk
18. Telephone part
19. Being
21. Caroled
23. Forest animal
24. Furthermore
25. Vital vessel
27. Angelic child
30. Tiny
33. Paddle
34. Had a bit of
36. Sand hill
40. Foamy brew
41. Weary
42. Far down
43. Fuss: hyph.
45. Thrilled
47. Part of a foot
48. Dark
50. Amber and mastic
52. Lactic and pectic
55. Strive
56. Container
57. Atlantic coast
61. Standards
64. Lime peel
66. Fire starter
68. ERA, e.g.
69. Confused
70. Subdues
71. "Swan Lake" costume
72. Active
73. Not dry
74. Prayer word

DOWN

1. Yarn
2. Saintly picture
3. Babbled
4. Elder
5. Struggle
6. Generations
7. Alpha's follower
8. Elope
9. More slippery
10. "Thou ___ not kill"
11. Lively dance
13. Modest
14. Lair
20. Publicize
22. Lass
26. Antique
27. Cloak
28. Light ring
29. Perkins role
30. Wander off
31. Converge
32. Serpent
35. Soft material
37. Final demand
38. Lunch hour
39. Woolly ones
44. Weird
46. End or heat
49. Operate
51. Snooze
52. Emanations
53. Crunchy
54. ___ sanctum
58. Rearward
59. Cabbage salad
60. Duration
61. Part of TGIF
62. Delayed
63. Shock
65. 24 hours
67. Mesh

ACROSS

1. Blemish
5. Practice boxing
9. Barbecue skewers
14. Ballerina's skirt
15. Advise
16. Spring flower
17. Like the Gobi
18. Gutsy
19. Foot joint
20. Angered
22. Encouragement
24. Make a seam
25. Kid
26. Over
28. Clever humor
30. Roll tightly
31. Cannoli filler
35. Fringe
39. Wine holder
40. ___ deck
41. Groans
42. Beach color
43. Imprecise
44. Capri or Man
45. Because
46. Magician
47. Use again
49. Hustle
50. As well
51. Sailor's hail
52. Glum
55. ___ it up (overact)
58. Took an oath
60. Gambling game
62. Choose
64. Intention
66. Gooey stuff
67. Turmoil
68. Lark's lair
69. Part
70. Jewish feast
71. Patella's place
72. Building add-ons

DOWN

1. Commence
2. Novelty item
3. Slanting
4. Discourteous
5. Stand-in
6. Explored
7. All lit up
8. Renovate
9. Radio noise
10. Wordplay
11. Kinds
12. Domino piece
13. Pour out
21. Daybreaks
23. Gulp
27. Nitpick
29. November's gem
31. Hightail it
32. Roman garment
33. Guided vacation
34. Imitated
35. Asian ruler
36. Medicinal measure
37. Showy
38. Incompetent
39. Pickle container
42. Santa's gift
43. Imitation leather
45. Circulate
46. Pay suit to
48. Placard
49. Dairy food
51. Actress Eve ___
52. Counter seat
53. Bikini, e.g.
54. Dummies
55. Hesitation sounds
56. Opposed to aweather
57. Blend
59. Hog's remark
61. Grimm heavy
63. Fair grade
65. Devoured

319

PUZZLE 363

ACROSS

1. Storage area
6. Batman's wear
10. Prohibit
14. Immature insect
15. Yoked animals
16. Surrounded by
17. Envy color
18. Dweeb
19. Decoy
20. Solicit
21. Unusual
23. Spring flowers
25. Sub sandwich
26. Zealous
27. System of belief
29. Was sorry for
30. Big do
33. Scam
34. Honest
36. Browning's work
37. In the past
38. Type of bean
40. Wheel rod
41. Elderly
42. Suit part
43. College head
44. Cool, man!
45. Frankly declare
47. Sound
49. Dirt
50. Only
51. Mottled cat
54. Unsmelted metal
55. Starchy root
58. Felt obligated
59. Lollapalooza
62. Female kin
64. Kaput
65. Church word
66. Nonsupporters
67. Glimpse
68. Skewer
69. Loses traction

DOWN

1. Seaweed
2. Coal products
3. Voyage
4. "___ Got to Be Me"
5. Paddled
6. Co-op's kin
7. Cutting tool
8. ___ se
9. Salad veggie
10. Legitimate
11. Flightless birds
12. Exhaust
13. Sonnets' kin
22. Sag
24. Clear (of)
25. Jinxed
26. Uncles' wives
27. Cuban dance
28. Competed
29. Modernize
30. Tricked
31. Transmit
32. Portent
33. Frost
35. Swivel
36. Priest
39. Alternate
45. Spark
46. Instruments
48. Sports complexes
49. Slaphappy
50. Cowboy's ride
51. Area ___
52. Astounds
53. Vault
55. Himalayan creature
56. Lab fluid
57. ___ hall
60. Strike caller
61. "Hawaii" prop
63. Sign

All of the 4-letter entries in this crossword puzzle are listed separately and are in alphabetical order. Use the numbered clues as solving aids to help you determine where each 4-letter entry goes in the diagram.

4 LETTERS

ALOE
AMIE
AREA
BEEP
COPY
DELI
EAST
EMIT
EPEE
HAIR
HARE
ISLE
KEEL
LAUD
MADE
MENU
MINI
OBOE
OLDE
PORK
ROLE
SCAB
SILK
SLOT
TALE
TEAL
TEEN
TOMS
TRAM
WIPE
YELL
YOKE

ACROSS

5. Corn unit
13. Yes, to Henri
16. Stick out
18. Pigpen
20. Extend
21. Nearly transparent
24. Cover
25. Baseball hat
33. "We ___ the World"
34. Large parrot
36. Spanish river
40. Popular street name
41. Partook of
43. Summits
45. Composure
48. Yearning
49. Stumbling block
57. Olive or safflower
60. Hairstyling goo

DOWN

1. ___-and-cheese sandwich
2. Pub drink
3. Charged particle
4. Utilize again
6. "___ House" (song)
7. Life story, for short
8. Narrow band
17. Duo
28. Frozen cube
38. Soft, light color
42. London brew
44. Opponent
50. Gear part
51. Whopper
53. "O Sole ___"
54. Scribe's fluid
55. Connection

PUZZLE 365

ACROSS

1. Highway vehicle
5. "Less ___ Zero"
9. Soak (up)
12. What bit Cleopatra
15. Unfold
16. Legendary Himalayan creature
17. Anchors
19. Ghostly word
20. Soil
21. Get ready
22. Unfasten
23. Small boy
24. Amass
26. Sketch ___
28. Dodgers
30. Bunny's step
31. Prison
33. Info
34. Bathing-suit top
36. Cooking pot
40. Fall
44. Geologic division
45. Factions
46. Sticker
48. Above, in poems
49. Competent
50. One or more
51. Biblical your
53. Caution light
55. Effect
57. Almost round
58. Probes
59. Snooze
61. Secure
62. Singer Bennett
65. Sharp pain
68. Keats works
70. Cheered (for)
74. Zodiac sign
76. Nannies
78. Subside
79. Trailing vine
80. Hog
81. Sunday song
83. Jeopardy
85. Bachelor
86. Cling
88. Climb
90. Compass dir.
91. Punt
93. Branches
94. Dine
96. Olive stuffer
99. Sign
100. Runways
103. Picnic cooler
104. Enormous
106. Past curfew
109. Wooer
110. Caribbean, e.g.
111. Flies alone
112. Leave
113. Farm measure
114. Fri. follower
115. Criticize
116. Home rooms
117. Requirement

DOWN

1. Baking ___
2. Heroic poem
3. Traders
4. Prelim
5. Use a keyboard
6. The lady's
7. Munched
8. Coldest
9. Opie, to Andy
10. Flowed out slowly
11. Personal
12. Fit
13. Fly aloft
14. Seed holders
17. Kiddie's pie
18. Pancake flipper
25. Rich
27. Swiss mountain
29. Water blockade
31. Fourth of ___
32. False show
34. Yogi, e.g.
35. Lasso cord
37. Cousins' mothers
38. Vibrant
39. Grandma
41. Short cuts?
42. Onion's relative
43. Goofs
47. Conveyor ___
52. Elevate
54. Deli spread
56. Force along
60. Roman wear
61. Crews

63. Circle around

64. Most regal

65. Mama's fellow

66. Desertlike

67. Near

69. Give (out)

71. Watch, e.g.

72. Writer Hunter

73. Force unit

75. Coils

77. Glittered

78. Pitching stats

82. Part

84. Large tree

87. ___ out a living

89. Knows how to

92. Australian animal

95. Metropolitan

96. Overtake

97. Inkling

98. Veal, e.g.

99. ___ a living!

100. Arranges

101. Trim down

102. Took to court

105. Yuletide drink

107. Lumberjack's tool

108. Shallow pan

PUZZLE 365

PUZZLE 366

DOUBLE CROSSER

When you fill in the correct missing letters in the crossword diagram, those letters, transferred to the correspondingly numbered dashes below the diagram, will reveal a quotation. Make sure no word is repeated in the diagram. Proper names, abbreviations, contractions, and foreign words are not allowed. There are different possibilities to fill the diagram, but only one way will give you the correct quotation.

S	P	A	12	■	31	C	T	S	■	46	R	B	A	6
H	5	I	R	■	C	11	A	36	■	L	E	A	S	E
A	R	8	Y	■	M	4	C	A	■	N	37	G	H	27
P	I	E	■	P	14	L	T	■	R	A	G	■		
E	15	D	25	19	16	I	V	18	■	N	A	M	E	
		R	O	T	■	21	O	L	A	■	C	23	N	
S	A	22	E	3	A	S	39	A	L	■	O	R	E	
T	E	A	■	L	O	45	■	A	33	E	■	35	A	M
34	R	R	■	E	7	I	17	L	E	■	O	24	L	Y
R	I	30	■	9	D	L	E	■	D	I	43			
N	E	1	R	■	40	T	C	28	■	C	E	A	S	20
■		O	13	N	■	L	O	P	48	■	L	29	A	
A	D	44	G	E	2	■	O	A	L	■	E	10	I	32
47	E	V	U	E	■	E	U	R	41	■	L	A	Z	E
T	W	38	E	D	■	26	D	Y	■	42	E	E	L	

```
 1    2  3  4  5  6  7      8  9  10 11 12     13 14 15 16
____  __ __ __ __ __ __     __ __ __ __ __     __ __ __ __

17 18     19 20 21 22 23 24 25 26     27 28 29
__ __     __ __ __ __ __ __ __ __     __ __ __

30 31 32 33 34 35 36 37 38 39 40     41 42     43 44 45 46 47 48
__ __ __ __ __ __ __ __ __ __ __     __ __     __ __ __ __ __ __.
```

PUZZLE 367

Step by Step

In five steps change each word one letter at a time into a new 5-letter word so that by the fifth step each letter has been changed. Do not rearrange the order of the letters. You do not have to change the letters in order.

Example: Rouge, Rough, Cough, Couch, Conch, Cinch

1. CLASH

___
___
___
___
___

2. PEONY

___
___
___
___
___

3. CHIMP

___
___
___
___
___

4. BRING

___
___
___
___
___

PUZZLE 368

ACROSS
1. Whitish gemstones
6. Barges
11. Western shows
13. Ideal place
14. Reddish-brown pigment
15. Raga instruments
16. Make dim
18. "For ___ a jolly . . ."
19. Blot
22. Nicely warm
24. Refined
26. Partially open
30. Gaucho's tool
31. Sports facility
33. Cabbagelike veggie
34. Dateless
35. Field flowers
37. Curving
40. Court call
41. Ph.D holders
44. Certain antiseptic
46. On the contrary
48. Car safety device
52. Baltimore player
53. Geological layers
54. Nice fathers?
55. Chemical compound

DOWN
1. Conjunctions
2. Luau dish
3. Citrus refreshment
4. Advance, as cash
5. Brahms piece
6. Work shift
7. Bivouac bed
8. Colorful fish
9. Telegram
10. Brashness
12. Polynesian garment
13. Puts into service
17. Loud insect
19. Society gals
20. Tons
21. Mr. Lugosi
23. Tibetan oxen
25. Overly enthusiastic
27. Confine
28. Out of the wind
29. ___ and relaxation
32. Obsessions
36. Kindle
38. Cambodian dollars
39. Essence
41. Plummet
42. Barely cooked
43. Rustle
45. Fouls up
47. Ready the soil
49. Baseball implement
50. Munched
51. Long-jawed swimmer

PUZZLE 369

ACROSS
1. Part of a.k.a.
5. Kind of room, shortly
8. Tropical American rodent
12. Adore to excess
13. Have debts
14. Gather
15. In any way
16. Carries out
18. In accordance with
19. Untamed
20. Monkey's relative
21. Small quake
23. Coats with a dull finish
25. Float aloft
26. Shrivel
27. Fiasco
29. Finished
31. Bullets, to a GI
34. Complain
35. Slinks
37. Sooner than
38. Having a roof overhang
40. Pied Piper's follower
41. Apprehended
43. BLT spread
44. Forum wear
45. Timetable info
46. Bakery worker
47. Let it stand
48. Male offspring
49. Fill abundantly

DOWN
1. Skilled
2. Romeo and Juliet, e.g.
3. Music system
4. Above, in poems
5. Cowboy, at times
6. Water server
7. Potter's clay
8. Paid athlete
9. Charge with gas
10. Recreational vehicle
11. Cathedral recesses
17. Mesa
19. Predicts
22. Term of address
24. Topic
26. Bundle
28. Scolds
29. Root vegetable
30. Develop
32. Gourd-shaped instrument
33. Approved
34. Irish poet
35. Passenger car
36. Save
39. Prohibit
42. Take food
43. Wire measurement

PUZZLE 370

Codeword is a special crossword puzzle in which conventional clues are omitted. Instead, answer words in the diagram are represented by numbers. Each number represents a different letter of the alphabet, and all of the letters of the alphabet are used. When you are sure of a letter, put it in the code key chart and cross it off in the alphabet box. A group of letters has been inserted to start you off.

Code key chart:

#		#	
1		14	
2		15	
3		16	N
4		17	E
5		18	
6		19	
7		20	
8		21	
9		22	
10		23	
11	M	24	
12		25	
13		26	

Alphabet box:

A	N (✗)
B	O
C	P
D	Q
E (✗)	R
F	S
G	T
H	U
I	V
J	W
K	X
L	Y
M (✗)	Z

Grid (numbers):

Row 1: 26 21 3 21 5 · · 23 16 21 15 · 22 17 6
Row 2: 21 25 7 26 17 · 10 2 1 6 6 · 21 15 7
Row 3: 11 7 19 7 26 · 2 16 22 6 17 · 11 7 25
Row 4: · · 23 7 25 21 · 5 17 16 · 14 1 15
Row 5: 19 7 26 17 · 21 6 19 17 26 · 2 23 17
Row 6: 1 26 17 · 23 19 1 26 · 15 5 7 23 19
Row 7: 20 21 25 · 14 21 19 17 · 12 21 14
Row 8: 20 6 7 2 26 · 12 21 8 · 26 17 20 17 26
Row 9: · 26 1 11 · 25 7 11 17 · 21 14 17
Row 10: · 19 21 16 15 7 · 6 7 21 11 · 19 1 17
Row 11: 24 17 17 · 16 17 17 25 12 · 14 17 22 9
Row 12: 17 26 26 · 21 23 14 · 11(M) 7 13 17
Row 13: 18 26 21 · 6 7 7 23 17(E) · 1 16 21 16 17
Row 14: 26 7 19 · 19 7 4 1 16(N) · 17 16 25 7 8
Row 15: 21 26 17 · 7 16 12 4 · 8 17 25 15 17

LOVE CODEWORDS? *Enjoy hours of fun with our special collections of Selected Codewords!* *See page 159 for details.*

PUZZLE 371

Quotefinds

In each diagram, start at the circled letter and draw one continuous path moving from letter to adjacent letter, horizontally, vertically, and diagonally, to discover a quotation. Each letter will be used once. The path does not cross itself.

1.

E	I	P	F	I	N	F	O
N	T	A	O	A	S	B	L
C	(A)	H	L	U	R	H	E
S	E	A	D	F	T	S	B
W	I	T	N	E	H	U	A
O	R	H	M	O	R	A	N

2.

L	P	O	E	P	E	L	I
E	I	S	H	T	N	K	E
L	K	A	L	A	H	I	A
N	I	E	L	F	(S)	I	L
G	N	I	O	N	T	H	G
T	H	G	D	T	U	B	T

BRICK BY BRICK

Rearrange this stack of bricks to form a crossword puzzle. The clues will help you fit the bricks into their correct places. Row 1 has been filled in for you. Use the bricks to fill in the remaining spaces.

ACROSS

1. Epochal
   Submarine
   Sad cry
2. Lasso's kin
   Coral ring
   Supportive
   beam
3. Occupied
   Anytime
4. Fat
   Boat basin
5. Strong
   Small crow
6. Raised RRs
   Like a
   shooting
   star
7. Milk source
   President's
   "no"
   Nook
8. Policeman
   Pedicure
   concern
9. Hard metal
   Flat bread
   Energy
   units
10. Insane
    That lady
11. Cot
    Purified
12. Conforms
    Wood
    turner
13. Italian
    evening
    Percussion
    instru-
    ment
14. Diving duck
    Boor
    Lunch stop
15. Sculls
    Beginner
    52 weeks

DOWN

1. Lessens
   Selves
   Low singer
2. Defeat
   Attic
   Plant disease
3. And
   Secure
   Defier
4. Basketball shot
   Fastened
   Bears' feet
5. Wee particle
   Chin hollow
6. Contains
   "____ Only Just
   Begun"
   Dangerous
7. Airport abbr.
   Perpetual
   Consume
8. Filch
   Soak to soften
   Farm insect
   Quaker pronoun
9. Bravo!
   Film scenes
   Craggy peak
10. Madagascar
    primate
    Unique chap
    Old card game
11. Coat cut
    Edit out
12. Golden ____
    Motion picture
    ____-longlegs
13. Furious
    Autos
    Cedar, e.g.
14. Coliseum
    Elevated
    Island dance
15. Fodder
    Extra
    Arab ruler

BRICKS

E L S / G O A	R I C / ■ N I	T H E / R U M	O E N / N ■ E	A ■ A / Y A S
U T ■ / P O W	T E O / E T O	A D A / S E R	W ■ Y / S ■ ■	D E R / ■ F I
M A R / U L ■	A I L / R G S	A N G / L T E	■ ■ ■ / E R F	I C E / E L ■
T O L / A B E	■ M E / T ■ V	■ ■ ■ / C H E	E L I / E A R	A H O / T Y R
■ L A / L E D	■ ■ ■ / B E D	O F F / S T E	E D ■ / R E D	S T O / ■ ■ ■
■ ■ ■ / E T T	S H E / ■ ■ ■	B O L / B U S	I R T / V E R	S M E / O A R
L ■ G / E ■ E	I N A / D A W	P T S / A ■ K	O ■ D / O ■ Y	R ■ T / N A A

DIAGRAM

	1	2	3	4	5	6	7	8	9	10	11	12	13	14	15
1	E	R	A	L	■	H	E	R	O	■	A	L	A	S	
2															
3															
4															
5															
6															
7															
8															
9															
10															
11															
12															
13															
14															
15															

PUZZLE 373

ACROSS
1. Opposite of pro
5. Ms. West et al.
9. Shoot the breeze
13. Shredded
14. Himalayan nation
15. Residence
16. Taken by mouth
17. Accustom
18. Summit
19. Horsemanship school
21. Incline
22. Boldly forward
23. Goblet feature
24. Flower part
26. Circle segment
28. Came across
30. Summarizes
33. Neither rhyme ____ reason
34. Defective bomb
36. Protect
38. Passes over
41. Bubble ____
43. Relish
44. Emerge
46. Jazz type
48. Unlock, poetically
49. Gazer
51. Prohibit
53. Thing, to a lawyer
54. Italian city
56. Little bit
58. "The ____ Must Be Crazy"
61. Chimp
62. Tidily
65. Solemn notice
66. Swing about
68. Stead
69. Strong affection
70. Fortune-tellers
71. Face shape
72. Anxiety
73. Goes astray
74. Hawaii state bird

DOWN
1. Potent particle
2. Author Ephron
3. Written copy
4. Narrow channel
5. Sixty secs.
6. Borders on
7. Creepier
8. Vast plains
9. Padre
10. Crosby's pal
11. Neighbor of Can.
12. Printed words
14. Swarmed
20. Precious stone
25. Head woe
26. Dwarf buffalo
27. Frolics
29. Jerk
31. Derogatory
32. Slant
35. Title
37. Hides the gray
39. Truckdriver
40. Hindu dress
42. Crowd
45. Setback
47. Artists' pigments
50. Small sword
52. Fish eggs
55. "____ Cry Wolf"
57. Eagle's claw
58. Links game
59. A woodwind
60. Prima donna
63. Lacking fat
64. Santa's time
67. Hospital surg. areas

(crossword grid with numbered squares 1–74)

PUZZLE 374   Squares

Each of the Squares contains an 8-letter word. It can be found by starting at one of the letters and reading either clockwise or counterclockwise. In the example the word STANDARD is found by starting at the letter S and reading counterclockwise.

Example:

D	R	A
S		D
T	A	N

1.

P	N	O
Y		T
H	C	I

2.

I	L	O
D		S
I	F	Y

3.

S	W	O
U		N
O	R	D

4.

I	N	I
T		F
E	I	N

5.

I	N	A
D		L
R	A	C

6.

H	G	U
T		O
H	O	R

7.

C	D	R
U		A
P	B	O

8.

I	M	D
A		I
L	C	S

9.

A	N	U
R		L
G	R	A

328

ACROSS

1. Hospital section
5. Podium
9. Bridge fee
13. Wings
14. Multitude
15. Pennsylvania port
16. Maidenhair
17. Licorice-flavored seasoning
18. Sports competition
19. Wavered
21. Drain, as energy
23. Verse type
24. Tavern
27. Biblical pronoun
30. Curtsies
31. Green soup
33. Comparative word
34. Vend
36. Western movie
38. Meringue's lack
39. Adjusted accurately
41. Viewpoint
42. Quarries
44. Catholic calendar
45. Weeds
46. Printing measures
47. Scoundrels
49. Capsize
51. Walked purposefully
53. Ginza belt
54. Fearful wonder
55. Like some sailors
60. "Desire Under the ___"
63. Writings
65. Merchandise
66. Kind of opera?
67. Golfer Woods
68. Medieval slave
69. Polo mount
70. Luxury hotels
71. Flower stalk

DOWN

1. Float
2. Away from the wind
3. Lightly cooked
4. Small hollow
5. Receiver
6. Saharan
7. Freud's concerns
8. Playground feature
9. Pace
10. Metallic rock
11. Recline
12. ___ off steam
14. Toughest
20. Chunk of eternity
22. As well
24. Fixed a boot
25. Choice
26. Required
27. Rosebush prickers
28. Healthiest
29. Dark in color
30. Smears
32. Mars's Greek counterpart
33. Category
35. Corrode
37. Tennis's Arthur ___
40. Skeptic
43. Freight barge
48. Experts
50. Olive center
52. Hoarse
53. Watering holes
55. "Spartacus" attire
56. Has obligations
57. Malt kiln
58. Marine bird
59. Reckon
60. Sixth sense
61. Old card game
62. Fellow
64. ___ Van Winkle

PUZZLE 375

(crossword grid)

Bubbles

PUZZLE 376

In each of the circles is the name of a fabric minus one letter! Find that missing letter to complete the fabric's name. Then arrange the missing letters to spell the bonus name.

1.

2.

3.

4.

5.

6.

1. _____

2. _____

3. _____

4. _____

5. _____

6. _____

BONUS: _____

329

PUZZLE 377

DOUBLE TROUBLE

Not really double trouble, but double fun! Solve this puzzle as you would a regular crossword, except place one, two, or three letters in each box. The number of letters in each answer is shown in parentheses after its clue.

ACROSS

1. Use a phone (4)
3. Ten-year periods (7)
7. "Mamma Mia" group (4)
10. ___ you kidding? (3)
11. Potentially existing (8)
12. Gushes (6)
13. Sty dwellers (4)
15. Spicy spice (6)
17. Not offs (3)
18. Picketer, perhaps (9)
20. Chemical compound (7)
22. Diva's solo (4)
24. Spiral pasta (6)
26. Team's symbol (6)
29. ___ de corps (6)
31. Calm (6)
32. Kind of pie? (5)
34. Tibetan monk (4)
36. Steel, e.g. (5)
38. Poetry and prose (10)
42. Mardi ___ (4)
43. False argument (7)
45. Demolish (6)
46. Exterior (5)
48. Mis-prints (6)
50. Long scarves (4)
51. Food fish (5)
52. Transmit (4)
53. Snacked (3)

DOWN

1. Drive-in waiter (6)
2. Fast, in music (7)
3. Oscar ___ Renta (4)
4. Divisions (10)
5. Gouging (7)
6. Sneakiest (6)
7. Deadly reptile (3)
8. Lapel decor (11)
9. Deep tone (4)
14. Fr. holy woman (3)
16. Back end (4)
19. Celeb (4)
21. Melees (5)
23. Taxing time (5)
25. Diamond team (4)
26. Singer Davis (3)
27. Troop leader (11)
28. Make a knot (3)
30. Lucky charm (8)
33. JFK postings (4)
35. Chess term (4)
37. Horses, at times (6)
39. Indian physicist (5)
40. Harbor sight (7)
41. Let go (7)
42. Tile filling (5)
44. Charter (4)
47. Trounce (4)
49. Small amount (3)

PUZZLE 378

Crypto-Riddle

To read this riddle, you must first solve this simple substitution code. The same code is used throughout.

QUESTION:

ZUIQ WBCCBX FXTHSNU KFOL LFWBCFN SQN

BZX GINQ QFXNF NSCGHP LP OFIOOIXTSXT SQN

HFQQFON?

ANSWER:

FIQ LFWBCFN IQF.

PUZZLE 379

ACROSS
1. October's gem
5. Sallow
9. Chew the fat
12. Etna efflux
13. Road to Rome
14. "Xanadu" band
15. Exterminate
17. Child's play?
18. Land parcel
19. Sale caveat
20. Time and again
23. Vocal ensemble
26. Stadium cries
27. Large party
29. Bruin great
30. Elk's kin
31. Dance move
33. Angora garments
35. Aquatic indentation
36. Brandish
37. Thin biscuit
38. Multitude
40. Station purchase
41. Commotion
42. Finish
48. Singer Rawls
49. Asia's ____ Sea
50. Actress Falco
51. Scrap of food
52. Colorful salamander
53. Go along

DOWN
1. Spanish bravo
2. Links standard
3. Ms. Gardner
4. Soup scoops
5. Early Briton
6. ____ glance
7. Say yes to
8. Afore
9. Eliminates
10. Jai ____
11. Marshes
16. Charged bit
19. Assistance
20. Conquistador's quest
21. Grower's tract
22. Discards
23. Tonal combination
24. Serpentine sound
25. Single
27. Dirty
28. Donate
30. West of films
32. According to
34. Strike
35. Edible nut
37. Used to be
38. Circle of light
39. Nose wrinkler
40. Covered with gold
42. Poor review
43. Mining yield
44. Regulation
45. Poet's offering
46. Five-spot
47. Sustained

PUZZLE 380

• WHERE'S THE FIRE? •

ACROSS
1. North Carolina campus
5. Eden figure
9. Man ____ mouse
12. Innocent one
13. Mrs. Dithers
14. First gear
15. Speak idly
17. Expected
18. More briny
19. Floats
21. Saturn's wife
22. Cad
23. Enter
26. Text portion
29. Grass bristle
30. Belt's location
32. .001 of an inch
33. Straighten again
35. Be inclined
36. Delicate
37. Gaze at
39. Stacked
41. Stamp
45. Harem chamber
46. Dynamic person
48. Guitarist Paul
49. Mass booklet
50. Zest
51. Light gray
52. Bring up
53. Don't go!

DOWN
1. Diminishes
2. Refrain syllables
3. Ancient Greek coin
4. Unit of force
5. Pinnacles
6. Way out
7. Biblical craft
8. Life jacket
9. Former sweetie
10. Decisive defeat
11. Stuns
16. Drink a little
20. DDE rival
22. Owns
23. Slender fish
24. Be indebted to
25. Very quickly
26. Needle's kin
27. Bar staple
28. Antiquity
30. British house
31. Mature
34. Prevaricate
35. Entices
37. Miscue
38. Jabber
39. Actress Negri
40. March time
41. Spoken fanfare
42. Land map
43. Moon goddess
44. Like an omelet
47. "Before" indicator

PUZZLE 381

Diagramless crosswords are solved by using the clues and their numbers to fill in the answer words and the arrangement of black squares. Insert the number of each clue with the first letter of its answer, across and down. Fill in a black square at the end of each answer. Every black square must have a corresponding black square on the opposite side of the diagram to form a diagonally symmetrical pattern. Puzzles 381 and 382 have been started for you.

ACROSS
1. "We ____ the World"
4. Bucks, e.g.
7. Star's resort
10. Spar
11. Birthday number
12. Haul behind
13. Kind of butterfly
16. Receive
17. Yule drink
18. Creche figures
20. Himalayan creature
23. Be obliged to pay
24. Wire thickness
25. Brash
27. Gridiron stat
28. Help
30. Best
31. Waste away
36. Unrefined metal
37. Ewer
38. Sal, for example
39. Blazer fuel
40. Ran across
41. Printers' concerns

DOWN
1. Sit-up target
2. Quarrel
3. Overstates
4. Arrest
5. Bruised ____
6. Machine-stitched
7. Supervise a show
8. Hawaiian dish
9. Boring tool
14. Flower wreath
15. Fiddle
18. Unruly hair
19. Dread
21. Involuntary spasm
22. Sort
26. Bond
27. Mister
29. Percussion instrument
30. Refusal word
31. Beagle or collie
32. Gay Nineties, e.g.
33. Annoy
34. Stocking color
35. High tracks

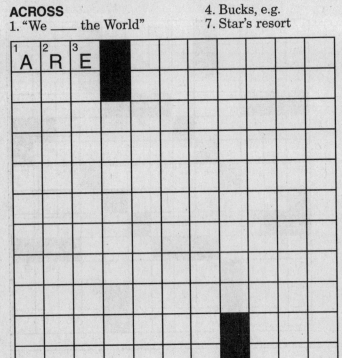

PUZZLE 382

ACROSS
1. Cohort
4. Bro or sis
7. Escape
9. Bill's partner
10. Revised
11. Palm's location
12. Ballet move
13. Tavern
14. Sturgeon delicacy
15. Hibernation spot
16. Plunge
17. Squirmed
21. Honored fighter pilot
22. Cackler
23. "____ Always Loved You"
24. Daryl Hannah role
27. Zorro's mark
28. Igloo block
29. Rooter
30. Small insect
31. Ernie's roommate
32. Small wildcat
34. Resounded
37. Thus far
38. Ponder
39. Fleecy female
40. Parting word

DOWN
1. Dab
2. Orange drink
3. Escorted
4. Wound covering
5. Charged particle
6. Physique, for short
7. Singer Adams
8. Contest
10. Runaway groom
11. Suspended
12. Cost
13. Wooden pin
15. Ruckus
16. Grand Coulee, e.g.
17. Performed nuptials
18. Lounge ____
19. Noteworthy happening
20. Letter after cee
22. Speed
25. Impudent female
26. Play a role
29. Provide food for
30. Card game stake
31. Opposite of cheer
32. Soap ingredient
33. Certain evergreen
34. ____ tide
35. Bawl
36. Digger

PUZZLE 383

ACROSS

1. Pub order
4. Loud sound
6. Football circle
8. Hopeful
9. Mighty tree
11. Arrived
12. English architect
14. Saw the light
16. Deficiency
18. Caftan
19. Close by
21. Cut the grass
22. Cow's comment
24. Mysterious
27. Bridge
28. Slug
30. In that place
31. Hurdle
33. Wharf
34. Chopping tool
35. Bread growth
36. Air passage-way
38. Observe
39. Certainly!

DOWN

1. Mistreat
2. Refined woman
3. Outcome
5. Radiance
6. Abode
7. Merit
8. Garden tool
10. Avid
11. Spider's net
13. First named
14. Upper limb
15. Timber
17. Draft regulator
20. Bellow
23. Individual
25. Finless fish
26. Appeal
27. Lean-to
29. Hired car
30. Ceramic piece
32. Keystone State's founder
33. Jabs
35. Companion
37. Plaything

Starting box on page 562

In and Around

PUZZLE 384

Place the 4-letter answers to the clues into the diagram, from the outside to the inside. When you have finished, two 12-letter words will be revealed, reading from 1 to 12 on both the outermost ring and the third ring from the outside.

1. Plumbing tube
2. In this place
3. Clarinet's kin
4. Finesse
5. Candid
6. Sudden wind
7. Hazard
8. Desertlike
9. Puddle
10. Sharpen
11. Verve
12. Depend (on)

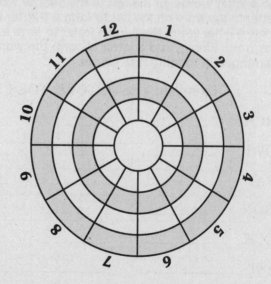

333

PUZZLE 385

ACROSS

1. Oodles
5. Clod
8. Charlatan
9. Run in neutral
10. Division term
11. Demeanor
12. Flog
14. Copied, as a drawing
16. Pound sounds
17. Gumshoe
18. Crude dwelling
19. Cool, formerly
20. Notable time period
23. Mechanical man
26. Term of respect
27. Atlas inclusion
28. Competently
29. Flop
30. Nose-down descent
31. Unknown's name
32. Grey or Woods
33. More positive
34. Do needle-work
35. Whimsical
36. Fashionable
37. Near the bottom
38. Ascended
39. Sprawl site
42. Guitar device
43. Rocky hill
44. Not injected
46. African fox
47. Frolic
48. Hollywood's West
49. Raid the fridge

DOWN

1. Pseudonym
2. Cloth fuzz
3. Cereal grain
4. Certain horse
5. Like Pindar's poems
6. Helm direction
7. Ward (off)
9. Apple product
12. Wine word
13. Small newt
15. Ribbed fabric
16. Sailor's greeting
19. Safe-guarded
20. Qatari leader
21. Go on wildly
22. Rich Little, e.g.
23. X-ray dosage units
24. Wind instrument
25. Huffed and puffed
26. Bask
29. Calendar bit
30. Ranch novice
32. Infant
33. Adequate
35. Dedicated to
36. Broom's relative
37. Olympic event
38. Alice's husband
39. Hustle
40. ___ Major
41. Corrupt
42. Machine parts
45. Kanga's kid

Starting box on page 562

PUZZLE 386   Give and Take

Change the 4-letter words on the left to the 5-letter words on the right by giving and taking letters. Add one letter to the word on the left to form a 5-letter word. Then subtract one letter from that word to form a new 4-letter word. Next add a letter to form a new 5-letter word; subtract a letter to form a new 4-letter word. Finally, add a letter to form the word given on the right. The order of the letters may be rearranged in forming new words.

Example: VEST, STOVE, TOES, THOSE, SHOT, SHORT

1. ARCH _____ _____ _____ _____ MAJOR

2. BOWL _____ _____ _____ _____ NOVEL

3. TRAY _____ _____ _____ _____ SHARP

4. NEON _____ _____ _____ _____ STEIN

5. ROCK _____ _____ _____ _____ CARVE

6. FAST _____ _____ _____ _____ GREAT

334

PUZZLE 387

ACROSS
1. Morally low
5. Sermon response
6. High-chair wear
9. Bestows
11. Botch
12. Malevolent being
14. Condemn
16. Synthetic textile
18. Biblical skipper
20. Think-tank product
22. Crochet
24. Fear greatly
28. Sales prop?
30. Waffle topper
32. January 1 to December 31
33. Do sum math?
34. Actress Olin
35. Relaxes
37. Gam
38. West Pointer
39. Disallow
40. Cold-cuts store
42. Circuits
44. "Contact" author
47. Boutique
49. Wand
51. Valuable rock
52. Parts
54. Court divider
55. Colt's mom
56. Crab or pea

DOWN
1. Capture
2. In the thick of
3. Pitt film
4. Rival
6. Bunk
7. Fairway club
8. Streams
10. Dense
13. Wordless yes
15. Luzon Island city
17. Katmandu's land
19. Brought on board
21. Provided relief
23. Adjust the pitch
24. Hide the gray
25. Peruse
26. Artist's prop?
27. Sports venues
29. Boundaries
31. Butter square
36. U-shaped pipe
38. Havana export
41. Research site
43. Physically tender
45. Particles
46. Pitcher Ryan
48. Dino, to Fred
50. Notorious emperor
53. Use needle and thread

Starting box on page 562

Spinwheel   PUZZLE 388

This puzzle works two ways, outward and inward. Place the answers to the clues in the diagram beginning at the corresponding numbers.

OUTWARD
1. Cleared
3. Thespian
5. Sprinter
7. Repeat
9. Dividing membranes
11. Monster
13. Supplied

INWARD
14. Shelve
12. Bearded animal
10. Old Spanish coin
8. Go to bed
6. Bugs's snack
4. Academy student
2. Finger count

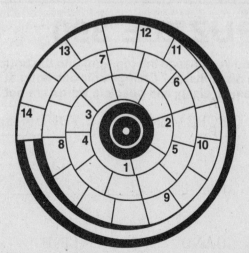

PUZZLE 389

ACROSS

1. Glum
4. Ticked off
7. Bawl
8. Current craze
11. Pub drink
12. House
13. Sound of relief
15. Bedding item
17. Sub shop
18. Flying mammals
19. Chow down
20. Eyelash enhancer
22. "___ and Peace"
23. Scream
24. Kirk Douglas, e.g.
27. Health resort
30. Rock and ___
32. Cigar residue
33. Sack
35. Full amount
36. Ordinary
38. Adam's lady
39. Frog's resting spot
40. Sylvester or Garfield
42. Fish lung
44. Still
45. Pertaining to the nose
47. Ill fortune
49. Ref's kin
50. Grunt's hairdo
53. Progress through time
54. Pod dwellers
55. Middle Easterner
57. Thinning on top
59. Placid or Tahoe
60. Cowboy's prod
62. Hill insect
63. Drumstick
64. ___-been
65. Not no
66. Fleecy one

DOWN

1. Film-star George C. ___
2. Limb
3. Colorant
4. Mediterranean island
5. Woe!
6. Cozy room
8. Ahead: abbr.
9. Excuse me!
10. Put off
12. Vital organ
14. Smarter
15. Watering hole
16. Hollywood's Stacy ___
18. Orbs
21. Influence
22. "I ___ a Teenage Zombie"
25. Follow orders
26. Rant and ___
27. Maple fluid
28. Blueprint
29. Robert or Alan
31. Haul
32. Permit
34. Retrieve
37. Helpers
40. Humped animal
41. Swiss peak
43. Native
46. Sweetener
48. Wall painting
50. Pennies
51. Tatter
52. Seize
53. Exploit, as a privilege
54. Yearn
56. Beseech
58. Week part
60. That female
61. Handle roughly

Starting box on page 562

PUZZLE 390   Changaword

Can you change the top word into the bottom word in each column in the number of steps indicated in parentheses? Change only one letter at a time and do not change the order of the letters. Proper names, slang, and obsolete words are not allowed.

1. FORE (4 steps)   2. FOUL (6 steps)   3. SAND (7 steps)   4. SLAM (7 steps)

HAND   LINE   TRAP   DUNK

ACROSS

1. Verge
5. Earthenware pot
6. Trapping device
8. Dispatch boat
10. Shiny cloth
12. Madras mister
15. More healthy
17. Zoomed
18. East Indian pepper
20. Trio
21. Coat with gold
23. Interrogate
25. Mites
27. Supporting structure
28. Time-honored
30. Hang around
31. Turkish decree
32. River horse
34. Royal address
35. Collection
37. Possesses
38. Mountain nymph
40. Botched
42. Foxier
44. Teen woe
45. Annoyance

DOWN

1. Romaine
2. Arm bone
3. Zagreb natives
4. Outcast
7. Institute
9. Lubricated
11. After expenses
12. Binge
13. Coral formation
14. Chemical ending
16. Carmine, e.g.
17. Wedge
19. Remains
20. Server
21. Strong wind
22. Rage
24. Swimsuit top
25. Culture media
26. Grant
28. Solo for Sills
29. Command to Fido
30. Mushroom-to-be
31. "Sort of" suffix
33. Golf instructor
36. Lobe
39. Work on a windshield, in winter
41. Family rooms
43. Soak, as flax

Starting box on page 562

Fitting Description

Fill in the blanks to complete a Fitting Description of a famous pair of television characters. Place the letters you have added into their corresponding boxes to form the name of those characters.

$$\underline{}_1 \ \underline{}_2 \ S \ T \quad F \ \underline{}_3 \ \underline{}_{11} \ E \ \underline{}_{10} \ \underline{}_7 \ S \quad O \ \underline{}_6$$

$$S \ \underline{}_8 \ S \ \underline{}_5 \ M \ \underline{}_{12} \quad S \ T \ \underline{}_9 \ E \ E \ \underline{}_4$$

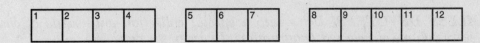

PUZZLE 393

ACROSS

1. Nasal cavity
6. Isolated
7. Pantry pest
11. Bar
12. Hem's partner
14. Sent a telegram
16. Carved brooch
18. Astronaut's thumbs-up
19. It follows Fri.
21. Luau dish
22. Boring tool
24. Full-strength
25. High spirits
27. Large parrots
29. Chigger, e.g.
30. Gush
31. Convent residents
33. "Long ___ Tomorrow"
34. Rail-splitter Lincoln
35. "Ask ___ what your country . . ."
36. Voyage segment
37. Lacking moisture
38. Craggy peak
39. Toward the back, matey
42. Increase, archaically
43. Cinch
45. Tonto's horse
47. Chief exec.
48. Limber
50. Witticism
52. Fight for honor
53. Spade's kin
54. Loony
55. '60s do
56. Ampersand
57. Aviation show feature
59. Knitting stitches
61. Businessman Iacocca
62. Beam of light
63. Squirming
69. Mortise filler
70. Hits hard

DOWN

1. Baglike pouch
2. Category
3. Neighbor of Swed.
4. One, to Juan
5. Briny expanse
7. Mean mutt
8. Corpulent
9. Succession
10. Stage hog
11. Spear point
13. Frail
14. Became frayed
15. Cartoon chipmunk
16. Codger
17. Wilson, of "I Spy"
18. Signature
20. Scarlett's plantation
21. Smoking device
23. Washed
24. Park birds
26. Bath basin
28. Diver's tube
29. Fountain drinks
32. Peeper problems
39. Hydrochloric ___
40. Haze
41. Sod
44. College figure, for short
45. Neuter
46. Canvas covering
47. Humorous wordplays
49. Bellow
50. Glowing coal
51. Grieve
52. Tim or Tyne ___
58. Flat-needled shrub
60. Cloth scrap
64. "___ a Small World"
65. Hairstylist's aid
66. Wildebeest
67. Diary
68. Election winners

Starting box on page 562

DIAGRAMLESS DEVOTEES! Delve into a special collection with loads of challenging puzzles in every volume of Selected Diagramless. To order, see page 159.

PUZZLE 394

ACROSS

1. Tiny vegetables
5. O'Hara home
9. Skulk
10. Taken wrongfully
12. Nonsense
14. Maintains
15. Greek war god
16. Golden ____
17. Gather
18. Embarrassed
23. Appointment calendar
27. Sweetie
28. Whirlpool bath
31. Fastener
32. Corsage spot
34. Tropical nut
36. Shredded
37. James Bond, e.g.
40. Wading birds
42. Deep-dish dessert
43. Coffee shop
45. In the know
46. For each
49. End
51. Petite
53. Stop talking
55. Circle's width
57. Heaven
58. Church instrument
60. Cool!
61. Slip
63. Cover with wood
64. Cured pork
65. Kimono wearer
67. Eye
68. Zhivago's love
72. Portal
73. Sample food
78. Humdingers
80. Caustic stuff
81. Loom operator
84. Living
87. Midnight movie
89. Intention
90. Wither
91. Finance
92. Flowering bushes
96. Comforts
99. School break
100. ____ Cooper
101. New York nine
102. Amount owed

DOWN

1. Possibility
2. Long, long time
3. Astonish
4. Cunning
5. Overly
6. 100%
7. Blushing
8. Ques.'s reply
9. Kilt features
10. Race
11. Crowd number
12. Troubadour
13. District
14. Yuck!
16. Inquire
19. Chum
20. Mr. Gershwin
21. Drink slowly
22. "____ Haw"
24. Sis's sib
25. Above, in verse
26. "To Each His ____"
28. Hit the slopes
29. More opulent
30. Ship's position
33. Hoisting device
35. Cleo's serpent
37. Erupt
38. Spinet
39. Certainly
41. Fighting fish
43. Family unit
44. Intend
46. Fruit stone
47. Pleistocene, e.g.
48. Echo
49. Barbecue item
50. ____ Allan Poe
52. Ruled
53. Innocence
54. 502, to Caesar
56. Metric foot
59. It comes after pi
61. Deviled item
62. Authentic
66. Espy
68. Bagel topper
69. Black cuckoo
70. Legal thing
71. Prehistoric object
74. Boring tool
75. Caspian or Dead
76. Do knot work
77. Christmas ____
79. Beguile
82. Dangerous curves
83. Ostrichlike birds
84. Woolly mom
85. Pacific goose
86. Youngsters
88. Conjunctions
92. Coat sleeve
93. Last letter
94. False front
95. "____ Miserables"
96. Cheerless
97. Bullring cry
98. Ad-____

Starting box on page 562

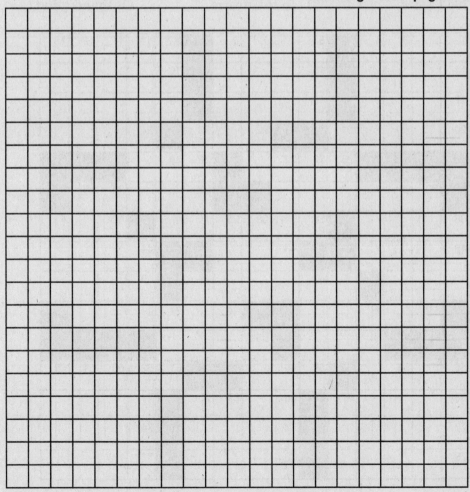

339

PUZZLE 395

ACROSS
1. Hits the slopes
5. Wails
9. Hockey, e.g.
14. Parasites
15. Notion
16. Sound
17. Detail
18. Lived
19. Not right
20. The press
22. Ink stick
24. Pesters
25. Truck sections
28. ___-white
30. Tourist's must
33. Trifled
36. ___ tie
37. Four-leaf plant
40. Victory sign
42. In the center of
43. ___ anemone
44. Knocks
45. Longing
46. Craves
49. Bustles
50. Wigwam's kin
52. Lump of gold
54. Shoemaking tool
55. Matching
56. Latch
59. Sweet potato
61. In the future
66. Deposes
68. Filter
71. Surface a road
72. Group of ships
73. Appeal
74. Former spouses
75. Overdue
76. Ooze
77. Filth

DOWN
1. Slender
2. Wind plaything
3. Like some tea
4. 18-wheeler
5. Bro or sis
6. "___ to Joy"
7. Pager noises
8. Of sound mind
9. Wood cutter
10. Cleanse
11. Skunk's defense
12. Skating site
13. Clothing
21. Expert
23. Brief message
26. Circle section
27. Light wood
29. Pro
30. Halley's discovery
31. Dress cut
32. Fashionable
34. Dodge
35. Terminal
36. Inlet
38. Above, to a poet
39. Letter-turner White
41. Superman's logo
44. Scrap
46. Evergreen
47. Slippery
48. Quantity
51. Caressed
53. Harden
55. Grin
56. Tender
57. Type of hoop
58. Consumer
60. Serpents
62. Parodied
63. Urban ride
64. Always
65. Remainder
67. Messy place
69. Charge
70. Faucet

ACROSS

1. Includes
5. Hack
9. Marched
13. Feel pain
14. Tuck, for one
15. Get hold of
16. Agree
17. Corroded
18. Freshly
19. Evergreen plant
20. Change color
21. Diary item
22. Scary word
24. Tied
28. Waste metal
30. Tow behind
31. Mas' mates
34. Coupled
36. Plus
37. Punch
38. Quits
39. Proclamation
41. Commotion
42. Christmas drink
43. Cut reminder
44. Owl
46. Actress
    Ruby ___
47. Dislike
48. Stood
49. Vigilant
51. Beer quantity
52. Leg part
56. Magazine fillers
58. Closet bar
61. Take the bus
62. Extremely small
65. Slugger Ruth
66. Household
    appliance
67. Sharp
68. Informed of
69. Animal skin
70. Some grains
71. Those people

DOWN

1. Nautical hello
2. British
   nobleman
3. Moat span
4. Pig's home
5. Unkind
6. Possessive
   pronoun
7. Cereal grass
8. Jimmy
9. Lighter ___ air
10. Rave
11. Finished
12. Moist
14. Cook in fat
20. Dummy
21. Border
23. Rowing blades
25. Fancier
26. Gator's cousin
27. Dry land
28. Exhaust
29. River craft
31. Picture
32. Staffers
33. Accumulate
35. Sticker
40. Palm fruit
41. Zoomed
43. Iranian ruler,
    once
45. Acorn bearers
50. Little pies
52. Expedition
53. Employ
54. Movie hero
55. Well-mannered
    guy
57. Bambi's mom
59. Clarinet's cousin
60. Reject
62. Disfigure
63. Arctic
64. Signal
65. Except

PUZZLE 397

ACROSS
1. Deteriorates
5. Talon
9. Lived
12. Newspaper item
13. Wakes up
15. Work on the garden
16. Sample
17. Abate
18. Hotel
19. Observer
20. Pool circuit
21. Leaked
23. Tangles
25. Not against
26. Baking vessel
29. Be in hock
30. Evening meal
33. Green and black fruits
35. Tire filler
36. Pile
38. Hard metal
39. Naughty being
40. Whittle
41. Social grace
42. Spinning toy
43. Smaller
44. Unlock again
46. Gerbil, e.g.
47. Type of wood
48. Geologic age
49. Waiters' items
51. Store up
54. Buzz
55. Bit of smoke
59. Dispute
60. Motor
63. Concept
64. Hearing organ
65. Dressed in
66. Frolic
67. At least one
68. Carpets
69. Electric swimmers

DOWN
1. Came by horse
2. Conform
3. Hour
4. Baby deliverer
5. Make
6. Speech problems
7. Pack animal
8. Dainty
9. Smart kid
10. First-class
11. Forward
13. Tolerates
14. Nose around
22. Waif
24. Christmas word
25. Natural coat
26. Mail
27. Priest's table
28. Sibling's child
30. Short drink
31. Scary
32. Untangle
34. Kills a bill
35. Stereo component
37. Salon treatment
39. Charged particle
40. Metropolis
42. Bowler's frames
43. Joined up
45. Modeled
46. Dried plums
49. Object
50. Steal
51. Field of study
52. Complain
53. Askew
56. Futile
57. Close up
58. Reimburses
61. Neither
62. Large antelope

342

PUZZLE 398

ACROSS

1. Yankees' foes
5. Corned beef dish
9. Coal wagon
13. Bluish green
14. Cafe order
15. Peeve
16. Mongrel dog
17. Held title to
18. Takes advantage of
19. Cavity
20. Key
21. Smaller
22. Races
24. Hold up
28. Canadian whiskey
29. Rug cleaner, shortly
30. Bummed out
33. Put down
36. Cried
37. Bashful
38. Raring to go
39. Water jugs
41. Shade
42. Diamond gal
43. Stunt
44. Repeated
46. Wapiti
47. Uneven
48. GOP member
49. Laundry machine
51. Entrance halls
54. Fountain order
57. Recently
59. Freckle
60. Support in crime
61. Flush
63. Serve tea
64. Mound
65. Construct
66. Detroit product
67. Bustle
68. Army vehicle
69. Dance move

DOWN

1. Highway exits
2. Outfit
3. Trigger's pal
4. Took a chair
5. Wolf cry
6. Having blemishes
7. That female
8. Once possessed
9. Sincerely
10. Increase
11. Milwaukee brews
12. Chow hall
14. Lichen's kin
20. Inventor's start
23. Watched
25. Always
26. Error
27. Behave
30. Hollowed, as a melon
31. Tiptop
32. Changed colors
33. Ms. Evans
34. Sinful
35. Strapped
36. Soaking
40. Walk in the surf
41. People in general
43. Supporting
45. Brag
49. Postal machine
50. Black bird
51. Soft material
52. Path
53. Razor sharpener
54. Weakens
55. Last writes
56. Hoagie shop
58. Guitar part
61. Rent out
62. Time period
63. Mas' guys

343

PUZZLE 399

ACROSS
1. Fashionable
5. Electric units
10. Shells
14. Ness, e.g.
15. Hi from Ho
16. Quartet
17. Downwind
18. Floor exercise
19. Pay dirt
20. Only
21. Opal or sapphire
22. Frogs' homes
23. Peruse
26. Gaucho's tool
28. Raw toast?
30. Tales
33. A tight squeeze?
34. Sweepstakes
38. Clumsy one
40. Eye
41. Coils
43. Blended whiskey
44. Entanglement
45. Mason's tool
46. Suture
47. Long gun
50. Meeker
52. Martial art
54. Peek at
55. Confuse
58. Mellow
60. Bottleneck
64. At any point
65. Blizzard
67. Alleviate
68. Hitched
69. Cliff hanger?
70. Property claim
71. "___ Well . . ."
72. Hail
73. Bland

DOWN
1. Chowder mollusk
2. Greens feature
3. Baker's aide
4. Cheddar, e.g.
5. Existed
6. Adjust
7. Convey
8. First finger
9. Drain, as energy
10. At sea
11. Nursery rhyme hurdle
12. Newsman Roger ___
13. Mined products
22. Layer
24. Balloon baskets
25. Conformed
27. Egg creations
28. Termite, for one
29. Jewish scholar
31. Pony
32. Speaker
33. Hair ornament
35. Christmas tree
36. To's companion
37. Bill, eventually
39. Scarcely any
42. Wallop
48. Norwegian bays
49. Carry
51. Personally
53. "Shane," e.g.
54. Unearthly
55. Second Greek letter
56. Bad
57. Touch
59. Skirt panel
61. Carpenter's need
62. Offshore
63. Polite chap
65. Slump
66. Ran across

ACROSS

1. Pinnacle
5. Of the nose
10. Remove
14. Hisses
15. Quick
16. Oratorio solo
17. Shanties
18. Officials
20. Unlock, to a bard
21. Bumped into
22. Mister
23. Have a good eye
24. Free
26. Fool
28. Undies item
29. Baloney
34. Meadow baby
37. Recognized
39. Ideal spots
40. Island instrument
41. Marine plant
43. Hit
44. Dog of song
46. Make curly
47. Tense
48. Imperil
50. Dessert in a shell
52. Piece of soap
53. Rented space
57. Acknowledge
60. Comic Arnold
62. Sardine can
63. Flintlock, e.g.
64. Detective
67. Settled
68. Filled tortilla
69. Turnpike fees
70. Movie tattoo
71. Gush
72. Young bird
73. Washstand item

DOWN

1. Scorn
2. Passenger car
3. Motor court
4. Curlicue
5. Junior
6. Marble
7. Go wrong
8. Word of lament
9. Foreign ____
10. River blockade
11. Mine yields
12. Good
13. Fortune
19. Obliterated
21. Deface
25. Subside
27. Nourished
29. Later
30. Debtor
31. Dweeb
32. Crimp
33. Catch a glimpse of
34. Grease job
35. Equivalent
36. Patch
38. Neck area
41. "Moonlight ____"
42. Most vacant
45. Prattle
47. Always, in poetry
49. Cavern
51. Charged bit
53. Manner
54. Radiant
55. Pretense
56. Go in
57. Decides
58. Enclose
59. French city
61. Cat's call
65. Swear
66. Angled piece
67. "You ____ Sixteen"

Codeword is a special crossword puzzle in which conventional clues are omitted. Instead, answer words in the diagram are represented by numbers. Each number represents a different letter of the alphabet, and all of the letters of the alphabet are used. When you are sure of a letter, put it in the code key chart and cross it off in the Alphabet Box. A group of letters has been inserted to start you off.

Code Key Chart

1	2	3 S	4	5	6 D	7	8	9	10 O	11	12	13
14	15	16	17	18	19	20	21	22	23	24	25	26

Grid (Across rows):

22	21	16	■	22	3	3	■	15	10	2	■	1	10	5
1	22	22	■	25	5	13	■	25	2	23	■	22	12	22
1	23	4	25	19	19	22	■	9	22	2	■	13	22	25
■	■	1	21	22	22	5	■	■	17	25	12	■	■	■
17	25	14	1	■	25	21	22	■	3 S	25	21	23	8	25
25	20	22	10	21	6	■	19	18	10 O	■	25	7	23	21
14	10	13	13	10	■	3	23	6 D	22	3	13	22	5
■	■	■	6	22	5	10	3	25	21	■	■	■	■	■
3	5	25	26	22	14	25	2	■	3	21	22	5	13
25	19	26	18	■	23	2	2	■	13	22	22	13	18	22
26	10	24	11	22	13	■	22	20	10	■	8	25	23	2
■	■	11	14	5	■	■	21	25	19	20	22	■	■	■
9	10	23	■	10	16	16	■	4	22	25	21	10	11	3
22	25	19	■	26	10	10	■	22	19	19	■	25	3	9
25	19	22	■	18	22	7	■	19	10	1	■	16	22	15

Alphabet Box

A B C Ð E F G H I J K L M N Ø P Q R Ŝ T U V W X Y Z

346

ACROSS

1. Walk loudly
6. Wheat ___
10. Toss
14. Backpacker
15. Greenish blue
16. Comrade
17. Outraged
18. Certain football kick
19. Chowder
20. Remit money to
21. "___ Don't Preach"
23. Cling
25. Corsage spot
26. Fitting
27. Dyed
30. Spider's lacework
33. Remains
34. Remote
35. Signal assent
37. Characters
38. Stick out
39. Marconi's invention
41. Shark's domain
42. Bar
43. Slightest
44. Yell
47. Wants
48. Easel display
49. Shy
50. Rock concert souvenir
53. Excited
54. Bloom-to-be
57. Similar
58. Erie or Champlain
60. Din
62. Bestow
63. Former spouses
64. Dined
65. Drove over the limit
66. Bucky ___ of baseball
67. Sheath

DOWN

1. Poker penny
2. Italian money, once
3. Approval
4. Faced
5. Fixes
6. Split
7. Tied
8. Hightail it
9. Bullfighter
10. Curved nut
11. Burn-soothing plant
12. Insult
13. Category
22. Gorillas
24. Name
25. Metal deposit
27. Convertibles
28. Woodwinds
29. Fragrant shrub
30. Cougar, e.g.
31. One who finishes
32. Idaho's capital
34. Entertainment
36. Polka followers
38. Toast topping
39. Stepped down
40. Desertlike
42. Fought
43. Office note
45. Poured
46. Get it wrong
47. Absorb
49. Caught
50. Stickers
51. Pass over
52. Bee home
54. Sink your teeth into
55. Avails
56. Cub Scout units
59. Chopper
61. Long paddle

PUZZLE 403

ACROSS

1. Tramp
5. Mama's spouse
9. Plaster splint
13. Once again
14. Of the nose
15. Greasy
16. Pitcher Nolan ___
17. Prior to
18. Cover
19. Boundary
21. Press, as clothes
23. Cain's mother
24. Raised border
25. Paid off
27. Clutched
31. Dealer's vehicle
32. Be sickly
33. Sticky stuff
35. Want
39. Twirls
42. Clump
44. Erode
45. Tiny
47. Society girl
49. Poet's before
50. Wheelbarrow's kin
52. Passed, as time
55. Foot-shaped device
59. Bird of prey
60. Small child
61. British noble
62. Grips
66. Liberal ___
68. Dupe
70. Jacket
71. Brainchild
72. Fragments
73. Threshold
74. Geek
75. Ship's company
76. Regard

DOWN

1. Rabbit's cousin
2. Black stone
3. Rhythm
4. Proprietors
5. Frying ___
6. Out of bed
7. Coupled
8. Permitted
9. Elsie, for one
10. Ventilated
11. Unpaid worker
12. Put into print
14. Eggnog spice
20. Quick bite
22. Appointed
26. Wine choice
27. Shocked response
28. Fully grown
29. Touched ground
30. Spaded
34. Fashionable
36. Chills
37. Infrequent
38. Leered
40. Well-mannered
41. Declare
43. Second letter
46. Variable
48. Obstructs
51. Great fear
53. Cobbler's tool
54. Located
55. Dye for wood
56. Large crowd
57. Sea mammal
58. Creme de la creme
63. Manner
64. Book leaf
65. From ___ to stern
67. Heavy-hearted
69. Crow's call

PUZZLE 404

ACROSS

1. Property measure
5. Weakens
9. Cherry seeds
13. Any moment
14. Wheel shafts
16. Repeat
17. Ahem's kin
18. Jeweled headdress
19. Young female
20. Stainless ___
22. Smell
24. Third letter
25. Equipment
27. Long fish
28. Junior
29. Bizarre
32. Complains
35. Employed
37. Thorns
39. Make a seam
40. Memo error
41. Adjust
43. Burn healer
47. Had been
49. 366-day period
51. Extensive
53. Dress size
54. Bitter anger
55. Toolbox
56. Have
58. Batch
60. Fiery
61. Keats et al.
64. Float aimlessly
68. Sad cry
70. Telecast again
72. On a boat
73. Punt
74. Took a car
75. Chunk
76. Very black
77. Beef dish
78. Towel marking

DOWN

1. Certain vipers
2. Charge
3. Ascended
4. Infiltrate
5. Positioned
6. Pivot point
7. Intend
8. String
9. Wooden nail
10. Frozen formation
11. String
12. Fixed a shoe
15. Vault
21. Trounce
23. Chimney part
26. Celebrations
29. Select
30. Moistureless
31. Submerse
33. Lip color
34. Sunday song
36. Persuade
38. Heifers
39. Delay
42. Black-eyed ___
44. Hawaiian keepsake
45. Rowing device
46. Previous to, in verse
48. Above
50. Walk heavily
51. Stringed instrument
52. Invade
53. Scoffs
55. Uniform color
57. Term
59. Refuse
62. Jogging gait
63. Collect
65. Bit of land
66. Be scared
67. Flaps
69. Cloud's site
71. Mint

PUZZLE 405

ACROSS

1. Not this
5. Fair
9. Coffee, slangily
13. Opulent
14. Cornhusk
15. Circle's kin
16. Coastal bird
17. Male voice
18. Jewelry metal
19. Sharper
21. Family
23. "___ Got a Secret"
24. Ready to strike
26. More bizarre
28. Basic nature
31. Facet
33. Kin of hiss
34. Quickly, to Welby
36. Fruit juice
40. Electric light
42. Pass a bill
44. Curly greens
45. Makes fun of
47. Concoct
49. Parent
50. Almonds, e.g.
52. Checks
54. Chapel responses
57. More wary
59. Deposit, as eggs
60. Profit
62. Street sign
66. Branch
68. Stake
70. Soda flavor
71. Ore source
72. Sporting blades
73. Expedition
74. Cooking herb
75. Valley
76. Places

DOWN

1. Travel
2. Lease
3. Skin blemishes
4. From there
5. This woman
6. Prevention measure
7. Reprimands
8. Gumbo veggie
9. Dogtrot
10. Evade
11. Flow-control device
12. Birch
14. Most stern
20. Geologic ages
22. Bump
25. Not fatty
27. Group of cards
28. Lessens
29. Broth, e.g.
30. Diva's aria
32. Insides
35. Bar bill
37. Scottish caps
38. Very many
39. Radiation measures
41. German city
43. Rock mass
46. Meld
48. Songbird
51. Grate against
53. Constructs
54. Former students
55. Chaos
56. Regarding
58. Treetop ornament
61. Startled
63. Was attired in
64. Dismounted
65. Dog cries
67. To a ___
69. Wriggler

ACROSS

1. Ski lift
5. Legal tender
9. Emmy, e.g.
14. Desire
15. Pivot
16. Party prize
17. Mine finds
18. Bring up
19. Profession
20. Remove clothing
22. Long scarf
24. Bering —
25. Game official
26. Bro, to sis
27. Cartoon ant
28. Novice
32. Staff symbol
34. Wiggle
35. Allow
37. Go by, as time
41. Gnaw away
44. Title
46. Leaf
47. Unit of heat
49. Hair goo
51. Carry
52. Additionally
54. Earth science
57. Squeeze
60. — bono
62. Guy's date
63. Embrace
64. Babble
65. Lead remover
69. Motto
72. Bright sign
74. Skirt length
75. Copper, e.g.
76. Alumnus
77. Bone-dry
78. Quarries
79. Has wings
80. Movie sites

DOWN

1. Quaker pronoun
2. Hatched
3. Mimicker
4. Vacation spot
5. Painstaking
6. Hewing tool
7. Hunks
8. Courageous
9. Stern
10. Clash of arms
11. Stop, matey!
12. Wild West show
13. Imagine
21. Buzzer
23. Qualified
27. A ways off
28. Flabbergasted
29. Equine mother
30. Absorbed
31. Comic Buttons
33. Gremlin
36. Yank
38. Water sport
39. Cozy
40. Jumpy
42. Liquid measure
43. Flexible fish
45. Panhandle
48. View
50. Myths
53. Grove product
55. Rowboat item
56. Andean pack animals
57. Victor
58. Sassier
59. Semiprecious stone
61. La Scala offering
66. Beget
67. Rewrite copy
68. Frees of
70. Joyous
71. Overhead transports
73. Cereal grain

PUZZLE 407

FLOWER POWER

The answers to this petaled puzzle will go in a curve from the number on the outside to the center of the flower. Each number in the flower will have two 5-letter answers. One goes in a clockwise direction and the second in a counterclockwise direction. We have entered two answers to help you begin.

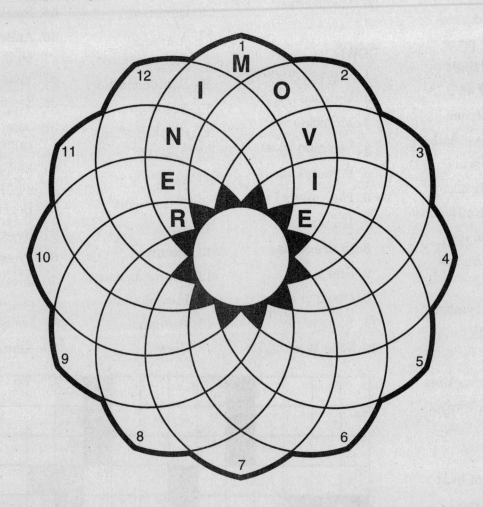

CLOCKWISE

1. Film
2. Toronto ___ Leafs
3. Din
4. The things there
5. Poorer
6. Pretense
7. Slice a turkey
8. Measuring device
9. Stationery
10. Drain
11. Of sound
12. Pale purple

COUNTERCLOCKWISE

1. Gold digger
2. Back tooth
3. Of warships
4. Subject
5. Although
6. Silly creature
7. Evil spell
8. Elevate
9. Pocketbook
10. Balm
11. Wigwam's kin
12. Bring down

ACROSS

1. Particular
5. Poe, e.g.
9. Emulate Oprah
13. "Fame" actress
14. Flow-control device
15. Grain
16. Pearly gem
17. Finisher
18. Beast
19. Cuddle
21. Improved
23. Hearing apparatus
24. Horse's leash
25. Thingamabob
28. Reimbursed
32. Swindled
33. "Wag the ___"
35. Spoiled
37. Show feeling
40. Do the lawn
42. Glimmer
43. Dangers
45. Pekoe
47. Forefoot
48. Say from memory
50. Ill-behaved
53. Spiciness
55. Rainless
56. Parasol
60. Domain
64. Rod
65. Swallowed
67. Matinee ___
68. Yan's prop
69. Scamper
70. Joint
71. Small amphibian
72. Coastal flier
73. Youngsters

DOWN

1. Church picture
2. Cassette
3. Ages
4. ___ milk
5. Criticize
6. ___ and wiser
7. Equalizer
8. Scottie, e.g.
9. Large reptile, briefly
10. Towering
11. Farm fraction
12. ___ off (mad)
14. Swerved
20. Dally
22. Enter data
25. More willing
26. Treasure
27. Huck's pal
29. Ditty
30. Not fitting
31. Erode
32. Cool, once
34. Earned
36. Dawn dampness
38. Involuntary spasm
39. Superior
41. Spider's net
44. Least fresh
46. Passionate
49. Intertwine
51. Militarize
52. Office worker
54. Jacksonville bowl
56. "Wish ___ a Star"
57. Shift
58. Was windy
59. Sublease
61. Theory
62. Street
63. Tall trees
66. Epoch

PUZZLE 409

ACROSS
1. Grimm baddie
5. Totes
9. Itinerary
13. Soared
14. Related by marriage
16. First-class
17. Kisser
18. Neutral color
19. Fence opening
20. Important span
21. Slender nail
22. Deteriorated
24. Word another way
26. Completed
27. Breezy
28. Argued
32. Hollow
35. "___ Town"
36. Building vine
37. Slipperier
38. Tango number
39. Bizarre
41. Glimpse
42. Grease
43. Bellybuttons
44. Teach
47. Nude
48. Hill insect
49. Hated
53. Fair-haired woman
56. Assault
57. Battle
58. Lend
59. African mammal
61. Pocket bread
62. Informed of
63. Lucky number
64. Over
65. Of top quality
66. Rosy hues
67. Hideouts

DOWN
1. Bid
2. Glower
3. Sum up
4. Lamb's mom
5. Book-lending site
6. Worried
7. Coast
8. Sink or bend
9. Chinese temple
10. Burden
11. Poker opener
12. Shortcoming
15. Garden tool
21. Thorny plant
23. Make fun of
25. Hearty
28. Twins
29. Weary
30. Cruel
31. Tints
32. Clamping tool
33. Mastered
34. In ___ of
35. Hooting bird
38. Bind
39. Having handles
40. Special nights
42. Water animals
43. Countries
45. Is unable
46. Plus
47. Hit on the head
49. Go by auto
50. Cord
51. Gobbled up
52. Stalemates
53. Lump
54. Unaccompanied
55. Cereal grains
60. Pronoun
61. Cushion

354

ACROSS

1. Flex
5. Took a dip
9. Enfold
13. Stallion's mate
14. Which person's
15. Now's partner
16. Fiber source
17. Beeps
18. Grace ending
19. Was ahead
20. Seed
21. Overseas
23. House annex
24. Unnerve
27. Rearward, nautically
28. Abominable Snowman
30. Not any
32. Easter basket item
35. Army insect
37. Health clubs
38. Comprehend
39. Stopper
42. Assesses
44. Goblet feature
45. Sprinted
46. Legend
47. Spade's kin
49. Have bills
50. Frank
51. Amazed
54. Hole punch
56. Exploit
59. Trawl
61. Tears up
64. Motor coach
65. Merry
66. Ice-cream holder
67. Claw
70. Distort
71. Retired
72. Vocal solos
73. Stare
74. Trunk
75. Red root
76. Unlockers

DOWN

1. Stroll
2. Seldom
3. Nursery item
4. Fox's prey
5. Displayed
6. Triumphed
7. Question
8. Tableland
9. Dock
10. Furthest
11. Region
12. Await judgment
14. Stop horse!
20. Twirl
22. Howls
25. Moment
26. Cloak
29. Label
31. Skin woe
33. Golly's partner
34. Ruby, e.g.
36. Corner
39. ___ and con
40. Statute
41. Not deserved
43. Eons
44. Darn
46. Peddled
48. Filly's food
52. Involve
53. Fondly
55. Overgrown
57. WWII craft
58. Convent residents
60. Varieties
61. Wound protector
62. Drifter
63. Random try
68. Exist
69. Recline
70. Chinese pan

PUZZLE 410

PUZZLE 411

ACROSS

1. Surface a road
5. Efficient
9. Dance move
13. Subside
16. Fiery jewel
17. Smile
18. Extent
20. Timid
21. Bears' shelters
22. Just before deadline
24. ___-armed bandit
25. Kind of maniac
27. Spur
28. Improves
30. Mas' mates
33. Hold title to
35. Perfect example
38. Master
39. Exceed
41. "___ to a Nightingale"
43. Obtain
45. Surrounded by
48. Film celebrity
49. Loud
51. Sticky substance
53. Nero's garment
54. Barely manage to earn
55. Beginning
57. Deceive
58. Sunday seat
60. Cleanliness
62. Gallery exhibit
63. Cake layer
65. City athletic dept.
66. Hideous
68. Bowling target
69. Bombarded
74. "Leave ___ to Heaven"
75. Feed-bag tidbit
76. Scanty
77. "___ Got Sixpence"
79. Unit of farmland
83. Protect
85. Sink feature
87. Hunted animal
88. James ___ Jones
89. Yearning
90. Subways' cousins
91. Biblical your
92. Shocking fish
94. Risked
97. Maris of "Nurses"
99. Flower plot
100. Insight
103. Pub pints
105. Tourist's stop
107. Scalding
108. Large, seedy fruit
112. Craving
116. Had a taco
117. Kitchen cooker
118. "The Old Grey ___"
119. Bank transaction
120. Young boy
121. Weeder
122. Went lickety-split
123. Subtraction term

DOWN

1. School of whales
2. Orangutan, e.g.
3. Family vehicle
4. Word in a threat
5. Aflame
6. Bathing-suit section
7. Speak imperfectly
8. Contestants
9. Dive home
10. Foil metal
11. Down-under bird
12. Middle Eastern bread
13. Thrifty
14. Goldfinger's foe
15. Farewells
19. Office sub
23. "The ___ Squad"
26. Muck
29. Significant timespans
30. Etiquette's Emily ___
31. Sedan, e.g.
32. Men-only party
34. Cranny
36. Encore!
37. Shelflike projection
40. Fall in folds
42. Reducing regimen
44. "___ Magic Moment"
46. Scrimshaw stuff
47. Accident leftover
49. Recently made
50. Sang Swiss-style
52. Result
56. Wedding missiles
59. Delete
61. Pupil site
63. Royal headdress
64. Curious
67. Chart
68. Bishop of Rome

356

70. Peppy

71. "___ by the Bell"

72. Stadium

73. "___ M for Murder"

74. Coop denizen

78. Travel endorsement

80. Bassinet

81. Lacoste of tennis

82. Viewed

84. Snowy-weather toy

86. Reclaims

91. Dark beige

93. Depressions

95. More unusual

96. Popular street name

98. Banqueted

100. "___ a Wonderful World"

101. Speck

102. Arithmetic

104. Insult

106. Empty

109. Also

110. Christmas ___

111. Natural resource

113. Costly cracker-spread

114. Freon, e.g.

115. Naval off.

PUZZLE 411

PUZZLE 412

ACROSS
1. World holder
6. Mouthpieces
10. Small boat
14. Doctrine
15. Spoken exam
16. Diva's song
17. Within reach
18. Urban region
19. Coin
20. Nest items
21. Scarf
22. Quiver
23. Use a throne
24. Hole-making tool
25. Probable
26. Pungent pod
28. Rough
33. Wandering
35. Fourth notes
36. Dress style
39. Comrade
40. Mails
42. Meshwork
43. Hate
45. Lack of faith
48. Hospital divisions
51. Itty-bitty
52. Cay
53. Pilfer
55. Remove
58. Inadequate
60. Shoe bottom
61. "High ___"
62. Heavenly instrument
63. Of sound
64. Meaningless
65. Before
66. Pick
67. Narrated
68. Deck wood
69. Knots

DOWN
1. Longs
2. Disastrous
3. Duration
4. Finds a sum
5. Tofu bean
6. Homegrown
7. Springtime bloom
8. Garden walk
9. Clever
10. Pleasure craft
11. Field
12. Blink
13. Unpunctual
21. Move in water
22. Mountain resort
24. Balm
25. Curvature
27. Tourist lodging
28. Change to fit
29. Beak
30. Conditions
31. Large container
32. Snake shape
34. Makes like
36. "Harold ___ Maude"
37. Hawaiian gift
38. Common contraction
40. Say a rosary
41. Above, to bards
43. Expected
44. Person in debt
46. Enlaced
47. Sales agent, for short
49. Buzzed
50. Comfort
52. Russian penny
54. Punches
55. Irritated state
56. Bustle
57. Rock's partner
58. Section of glass
59. Humpback's kin
60. Han ___
62. Warm
63. Decade

PUZZLE 413

ACROSS

1. Fiddler's cake?
5. Support
9. Quiets
14. Lion's pad
15. Actor's quest
16. Indian, e.g.
17. Soup vegetable
18. Final notice
19. Peachy keen!
20. Cease
22. Arrogant
24. Flock's perch?
25. Go to "People's Court"
26. Church official
28. Foul odor
31. Formally withdrew
35. Pledge
36. Doll, e.g.
38. Fast
39. An out
42. Pen part
44. Destroyed
45. Most stable
47. Photo
49. Swatter's target
50. Arbor
52. Brags
55. Florida seaport
57. Liable
58. In what way
61. Poetic contraction
62. Brought up
66. Oscar or Emmy
68. Historical ages
70. Marco ___
71. Variety show
72. Attention
73. Successfully dieted
74. Laundry machine
75. Psalm
76. Scrapes by

DOWN

1. Clumsy one
2. Lawn tool
3. Haughtiness
4. Cook slowly
5. Defend
6. Steal with force
7. Green shade
8. Potpourri components
9. Links
10. Big heart?
11. Perform a jete
12. Pal, in Perth
13. Blizzard stuff
21. "Empire of the ___"
23. March 15th, e.g.
27. True
28. Kind of eclipse
29. String
30. Deary
32. Outline
33. Wicked things
34. Withhold
35. Immense
37. Kennel comment
40. Tract
41. Hawaiian, e.g.
43. Baby's garb
46. Clock (a race)
48. Make rougher
51. Address
53. Act like
54. Basic food item
56. Assortment
58. Tough
59. Bill collector?
60. Uneven
63. Chess piece
64. If not
65. Small spots
67. Be repentant
69. Branch

359

PUZZLE 414

ACROSS
1. Food fish
5. Party thrower
9. Fixed vision
14. Mountain cat
15. Gambling stake
16. Fruit pulp
17. Got down
18. Appear
19. Flourish
20. Wireless sets
22. Long poem
24. Foxy
25. Zilch
26. Stallone film
28. Aerie chick
31. Pick
34. Muzzle
35. Used a shovel
37. Fill again
39. Big deal
42. Lump
44. Bread serving
45. Choir members
47. Crude metal
49. At once
50. Small river
52. Entry
55. Parents
57. "___ Gang"
58. Skirt's bottom
61. Camp dwelling
62. Badger
66. Excuse
68. Commotion
70. Fiddler ___
71. Edition
72. Cloth-making device
73. Mummy's bed
74. Musical pauses
75. Fidgety
76. Hot tubs

DOWN
1. Boxers do it
2. Kind of hoop
3. During
4. Courting
5. Bothered
6. Attuned
7. Guide
8. Rates of speed
9. Spots
10. Prom wear
11. Circle portions
12. Movie spool
13. Slippery
21. Type of paint
23. Bakery employee
27. Cheer
28. Chalet features
29. 007, e.g.
30. Pull
32. Nickels, e.g.
33. Meals in shells
34. ___-up-and-go
36. Icky stuff
38. Morning mist
40. Standard
41. Peace agreements
43. Swimsuit piece
46. Ditto
48. Low-priced fare
51. Sleeveless cloak
53. Actor's hint
54. Puts up
56. Arose
58. Head growth
59. If not
60. ___ by a mile
63. Fall sharply
64. Tibetan monk
65. ___ and flows
67. However
69. Spaniel, e.g.

ACROSS

1. Storage spot
6. Gasoline
10. Like some cheese
14. Dinner plates
15. Bullets, for short
16. Bear's home
17. Large pieces
18. Rotated
19. Musical notation
20. It came first?
21. Head toppers
23. Oily
25. Cathedral benches
26. Ocean liner
27. Speak slowly
29. Apparition
32. Kind of tradition
33. Tossed
34. Not high
36. Conquered
37. Short trips
39. Owing
40. Flight record
41. Broadway lights
42. "___ Misbehavin' "
43. Insist
45. Telecast
47. Mom's sister
48. Conceal
49. Pampered
52. Hill's opposite
53. Authority
56. Lacking moisture
57. Voyeur
59. Bypass
61. Electricity carrier
62. Vast timespans
63. Cowboy's tool
64. Actress Cheryl ___
65. Hustle
66. Curl the lip

DOWN

1. Pang
2. Hoodlum
3. Metallic sound
4. Squid's camouflage
5. Type of nut
6. Goes without food
7. Refs' kin
8. Swift-running bird
9. Script
10. Receive
11. Party
12. Nights preceding
13. Dare
22. Cobbler's tool
24. Chimes
25. Best friend
26. Ignores
27. Sag
28. Cookstove
29. Factory
30. Classic song
31. Heap
32. "Harry Potter" pet
33. Apply icing
35. Sopping
37. Develop
38. Rudolph, e.g.
42. "Diamonds ___ Forever"
44. Ambushed
45. Feel poorly
46. Ethics
48. Severe
49. Sob
50. Opera tune
51. Cardinal, e.g.
52. Shelters
53. Be a model
54. Grow
55. Aroma
58. "___ Send Me"
60. Mover's vehicle

PUZZLE 416

ACROSS

1. Droops
5. Marvy!
8. Sundown direction
12. Three voices
13. Blame
15. Wheel shaft
16. Appends
17. Succession
18. Hustle
19. Fall asleep
21. Tint
23. Face feature
24. Dehydrate
25. Gather
28. Hog's sound
30. Major artery
31. Grows older
32. Mocked
35. Curves
37. Friendly
40. Farm cylinder
41. Singing voices
42. Chef's need
43. Will beneficiary
44. Smug
45. Garden foe
46. Jotted reminder
48. Criminal fire
51. Playground chute
53. Monk
54. Young chap
57. Against
58. Harbor vessel
61. Burning
63. Avenue
65. Pay the ___
68. Not shut
69. Till
70. Scoff
71. Affleck and Blue
72. Quick farewells
73. Title
74. Besides

DOWN

1. "___ by Me"
2. Enthusiasm
3. Lightheaded
4. Ho-hum
5. Canine's coat
6. Help out
7. Ran, as colors
8. Lived
9. Like some clubs
10. Destroyed
11. Entice
13. Errand runner
14. Undertake
20. '60s do
22. Souffle item
26. For any reason
27. Incomplete
29. Fame
30. Idolized
31. Mule's kin
32. Blond shade
33. ___ a la mode
34. Remove
36. Deadly snake
38. Third letter
39. Leftover
41. Formerly
47. Intersected
49. Sting
50. Fool
51. Rub vigorously
52. Crazy
54. Coat fold
55. Prayer words
56. Thick
59. Good times
60. Clear liquors
62. Earring's place
64. Rules to follow
66. Luau dish
67. Botch things

ACROSS

1. Offshore
5. Giant moth
10. Baby powder
14. Long skirt
15. Gaucho's tool
16. Where to worship from
17. Hyde Park stroller
18. Extend "Life"
19. Folk tales
20. Likewise
21. Floating zoo
22. Mitt
23. Press clothes
25. Gape
28. Knock
29. Deceive
31. Self-importance
33. Chowder, e.g.
35. Preholiday night
36. Distant
38. Rim
42. Gloomy
44. Cauliflower ___
45. Bright sign
46. In a different way
47. Communion tables
50. Little bit
51. Powerful wind
53. Not nope
54. Overhead rails
55. Cobra's kin
58. Greek cheese
60. Harmony
62. Printer's mark
64. Get tangled
66. On the pinnacle
69. Regretted
70. Lagoon's boundary
72. Marceau, for one
73. Cooled
74. Provoke
75. Roulette bet
76. Negate
77. Glitch
78. Drive

DOWN

1. Electrical measures
2. Actress Mia ___
3. Inspectors
4. Pointer
5. Organize
6. Cake level
7. Scrawny
8. Consumed food
9. Cutting tool
10. Not short
11. In progress
12. Immature insect
13. Crawl
22. Type of antelope
24. Across, to Keats
26. Off course
27. Anguish
29. Relinquish
30. Almost round
32. Frittata
34. Calligraphy tool
37. Cookie grain
39. Wolfe, e.g.
40. Ambition
41. Football positions
43. Cask
47. Bistro brew
48. Cattle thief
49. Snoop
52. Stern
55. Pungent
56. Gravy, e.g.
57. Trim with a beak
59. Romance
61. Entitles
63. Duane or Nelson
65. Moreover
67. Prophetic sign
68. Hang fire
70. Hotshot
71. Roofing stuff

PUZZLE 418

ACROSS

1. Hustle
5. Big trucks
9. Summits
14. Fuss
15. Neutral color
16. Cay
17. Kind of roast
18. Without dread
20. Individually
22. ___ horse
23. Unclose, poetically
24. But
25. Branches
27. Dangle
30. Lock's companion
31. Dad
35. Dime's worth
40. Pilfered
41. Circle's kin
42. Peep
44. Camp abode
45. Created again
47. Buy
49. Foe
50. Letter after cee
51. Vigor
53. Honey drink
54. Held
57. Many times, in poems
60. Fleecy mama
62. Contrive
64. Castle entrance
68. Vexes
69. Putrefy
70. Phony
71. Soup vegetable
72. Cache
73. D and Labor
74. Goofs up

DOWN

1. Pound prisoner
2. Car type
3. Let in
4. Pine
5. Quotation
6. Hard water?
7. Grazing matter
8. Convinced
9. It's in the sky?
10. Hazardous curve
11. Likewise
12. Iodine source
13. Eye problem
19. Room for experiments
21. Soap block
26. Legend
28. ___ for (pick)
29. Cubicle
32. Excuse
33. Corrals
34. Casino action
35. Wrenched
36. Equal
37. Identify
38. Holding tool
39. Little drink
40. Jam knives
43. Unmannerly
46. Change color
48. Transfer
52. ___ annum
53. Press
54. Employer
55. Inquirer
56. Editors' stations
57. Likelihood
58. Worry
59. Burrito's kin
61. Frenzied
63. Horrid
65. Strife
66. Toodle-oo!
67. Jolly

ACROSS

1. Work
6. Model
9. Papas' mates
14. Mindful
15. Tissue layer
16. Roused
17. Seized
18. French peak
19. The press
20. Spud bud
21. ___-tac-toe
23. Kind of tide
25. USNA grad
26. Salary
28. Charged atom
30. Bore
32. Chef's need
34. On
38. College VIP
39. October's stone
41. Part of TV
42. Anxious
43. Exterior
45. Component
46. Calf-length skirt
47. Ponder
48. Guns a motor
49. Otherwise
50. Miss
51. Cross
53. Beam of light
55. Guardian ___
57. Befitting
60. Ref's cousin
62. Connecting word
63. Gorilla
66. Grieve
68. Pacino et al.
70. Challenger
72. Flight path
73. Fink
74. Spare
75. Stashes
76. Snoop
77. Aerie homes

DOWN

1. After hours
2. Gone
3. Cook
4. Metal source
5. Apartment, e.g.
6. Opening
7. Unwell
8. Category
9. Caribbean dance
10. Dazzle
11. Fashion
12. Like
13. There are seven of them
22. Ice house
24. Hopper
26. Breezier
27. Kitchen tool
29. Organic
30. The ___ made me do it!
31. Forays
33. Bar brews
35. Belief
36. ___ Oyl
37. Cats, e.g.
38. Notre ___
40. Cougar
44. Govern
50. Exercise room
52. Blush
54. Cousins' mothers
56. Foul
57. Berserk
58. Study hard
59. Pipe
61. Golf norms
63. Handicrafts
64. Sassy
65. Periods
67. Tear
69. Lick up
71. Hatchet

PUZZLE 420

ACROSS
1. Ship's personnel
5. Cloth belt
9. "Alice" role
12. Folk legends
13. Thought
14. Cup edge
15. Highest point
16. Dinner hour
18. Snow runner
19. Closed hand
20. Bridle strap
21. Writing implement
23. Leans
25. Fix, as leftovers
27. Ifs, ____, or buts
28. Checks
30. Harmony
32. Principles
35. Mars, e.g.
37. Narrated again
39. Long, easy stride
40. Designer Saint-Laurent
42. Armed conflict
43. Fruit pastry
45. Primitive dwelling
46. Last letter
47. Polite chap
48. Native minerals
49. Remark further
50. Keats poems
51. ____ and ends

DOWN
1. Grasp
2. Granny's chair
3. White weasel
4. Petite
5. Like
6. Lemon coolers
7. Benches
8. "Shallow ____"
9. Pal
10. Draws the line
11. Premonitions
17. Rapid ____
19. Hostile
22. Strait
24. Woodworking tools
26. Golf gadget
29. Roads
30. Inclined
31. Jabbered
33. Chicken
34. Drudged
35. "____ Suite"
36. Used a keyboard
38. ____ rehearsal
41. Grape plant
44. Psyche part
45. Bill and ____

PUZZLE 421

ACROSS
1. Deep cut
5. Hired help
9. Bunny's step
12. Initial wager
13. Cake froster
14. ____ carte
15. Work hard
16. Got out quickly
18. "Duke of ____"
19. Slight advantage
20. Night fliers
23. RBIs, e.g.
27. ____ Francisco
30. Banish
32. Mimic
33. Investigator
35. Came to terms
37. Sunburn remedy
38. Ireland
40. Adriatic, e.g.
41. Gin's partner
43. "Cheers" regular
45. Nanny or billy
47. Scent
51. Predicaments
55. California wine region
56. "Bells ____ Ringing"
57. Myers or Todd
58. Deadlocked
59. Resting place
60. Yemeni port
61. Camper's home

DOWN
1. Airport exit
2. Small buffalo
3. Commotion
4. Howdy!
5. Towel monogram
6. Entry
7. Geek
8. Hauls
9. Cured pork
10. Bullfight shout
11. Cushion
17. Parking-lot timer
21. Sorrow
22. Entice
24. Hotshots
25. "Of ____ I Sing"
26. Fizzy drink
27. Minor quarrel
28. Woody's boy
29. Midday
31. Poi source
34. Light brown
36. Berlin's lang.
39. Amount consumed
42. Punctuation mark
44. French painter
46. Surrounded by
48. Mr. Letterman
49. Exposed
50. Talk wildly
51. Dry gently
52. Ill temper
53. Conducted
54. Member of Cong.

ACROSS

1. "Now It ____ Be Told"
4. Dana ____ of "Diff'rent Strokes"
9. "White ____"
12. "Murder for ____"
13. Light-show beam
14. "Never Give a Sucker an ____ Break"
16. "____ County"
17. Smarted
18. Lew ____ of "Lime Street"
20. "Coming of ____"
21. Moses Pray's nickname on "Paper Moon"
23. Booger Dawson, for one
25. "____ Got a Secret"
26. "The ____ Patrol"
27. Diahann's role on "Lonesome Dove: The Series"
28. "The ____ Bears Movie"
29. Rain heavily
30. Had a meal
31. "It's in the ____"
32. Dolenz of "Ferris Bueller"
34. "____-22"
37. Neck hair on Simba
38. George Peppard series, with "The"
42. Moon ____ Zappa of "Heartstopper"
43. Cutter of "Perfect Strangers"
44. Hargitay of "Ghoulies"
46. Dreyfuss of "Empty Nest," e.g.
47. "Hawkeye" cast-member Jed ____
48. Frank ____ of "Leave It to Beaver"
49. "The ____ Soldier"
50. "Divorce ____ Style"
52. Black Beauty's father
53. "____ Me No Flowers"
54. Claire ____ of "My So-Called Life"
55. "Maisie ____ Her Man"
56. Honor's part in "Goldfinger"
57. "Desk ____"
59. Cassidy ____ of "Models, Inc."
60. "____ Air"
61. Coach Parseghian and others
64. "Evening Shade" character
66. Robin Hood's weapon
67. "____ Busters"
70. Cariou of "Louisiana"
71. "Who Has ____ the Wind?"
72. "Hey ____"
73. Ill-humor
74. Julie's portrayal on "Extreme"
76. "Championship Bridge with Charles ____"
78. Nolan of "Julia"
80. "Jane ____"
81. "____ Nation"
82. "What's My ____?"
83. "The Ballad of the ____ Cafe"
84. Duncan of "The Hogan Family"
85. Fr. holy woman

DOWN

1. "Tom Corbett, Space ____"
2. "Cheers" serving
3. Mike ____ of "The Monkees"
4. "Dark Justice" star Begona ____
5. "Arsenic and Old ____"
6. "____ Wednesday"
7. "Sabrina the ____ Witch"
8. "Law & ____"
9. "Hot ____ & Cold Feet"
10. Peggy's persona on "Step by Step"
11. "____, Indiana"
12. "____ of the Vagabound"
15. Campbell of "Catwalk"
16. "My Mother the ____"
19. Sch. term
22. Verse of praise
24. Stephen ____ of "The Crying Game"
28. Prop for Charlie Chaplin
29. Small monkey
30. "____ of Aggression"
31. "Calamity Jane and Sam ____"
33. McCain of "The Rifleman"
34. "Henry Aldrich Plays ____"
35. Corsaut of "House Calls"
36. "____: The Story of Michelangelo"
37. Appearance
39. Rob ____ of "Silk Stalkings"
40. "Movin' On" star
41. Patinkin of "Chicago Hope"
43. Nicholas ____ of "The Commish"
44. "Presenting Lily ____"
45. Sue ____ Langdon
47. "The ____ of Louis XIV"
48. "Love at First ____"
51. "____ Than Zero"
52. Connery or Penn
53. "A Walk in the ____"
55. Cereal mix
56. Eleanor and Jane
58. Ess follower
60. "The Bride Came ____"
61. Menu phrase
62. Russo of "Sable"
63. "____ Gang"
65. Robert Urich series
66. "The Bugs ____ Show"
67. "The ____ Lucas Show"
68. Gross of "The Couch Trip"
69. Shirt size abbr.
71. "The Bad ____"
72. Title of ownership
75. Acronym for Wonder Woman's computer
77. "____ Tin Tin K-9 Cop"
79. Eng. course

PUZZLE 423

ACROSS

1. Certain apartment
6. Athenian vowels
10. "Centennial," e.g.
14. Noncitizen
15. Hawaiian goose
16. Plenty, formerly
17. Deposits river sediments
18. Fence door
19. Teheran money
20. Firefighter's need
21. Not 'neath
22. Resides
24. Astute
26. Yang's mate
27. Made lace
29. Chest muscles, for short
32. Cookie sheet
33. Washstand pitcher
35. Convey
37. Icicle hanger
39. Came up
41. Chinese coin
42. Crunchy
44. Selects
46. Bro's sib
47. Voice range
48. Disturber of the peace
50. Before, poetically
52. Beholds
53. White herons
56. ___ and outs
57. Engrave chemically
61. "___ Here to Eternity"
62. Clock sound
64. Long scarf
65. Floor square
66. Racetrack shape
67. Moving
68. Zoomed
69. Heap of wood
70. Chirps

DOWN

1. Handy money
2. Miscellany
3. Zeros
4. Perceive
5. Switch positions
6. Beget
7. Weepy
8. Picnic insect
9. Dingy
10. Calmly
11. Dye source
12. Soccer score
13. Cobblers' tools
21. Type of street
23. Rub dry
25. Had food
27. Royal headwear
28. Heavy iron block
30. Make happen
31. Step
32. Slangy sleuth
34. Pal of Pooh
35. Binds again
36. Printer's measures
38. Respected
40. Drizzle
43. Harbor town
45. Miss Piggy, e.g.
49. African fly
51. Halt legally
52. Acting priest
53. Newts
54. Clench
55. Star's quest
58. Shopping bag
59. Paper holder
60. Not his
63. Trailing plant
64. Syrup source

PUZZLE 424

Blips

Place one of the given letters in each circle to form nine 3-letter words reading from top to bottom. Use each letter only as many times as it is listed. Do not repeat a word in your solution.

Y E B W N E G T E W K A O

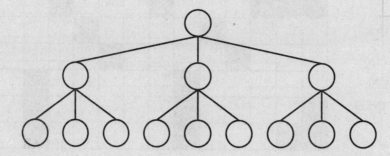

368

DOUBLE TROUBLE · PUZZLE 425

Not really double trouble, but double fun! Solve this puzzle as you would a regular crossword, except place one, two, or three letters in each box. The number of letters in each answer is shown in parentheses after its clue.

ACROSS
1. Stratagem (6)
4. Rapscallion (5)
6. Eton's rival (6)
8. Black-ink items (6)
9. Chocolate candy (7)
10. Worked hard (7)
11. Valuable stone (3)
12. Fear greatly (5)
13. Walking sticks (6)
15. Very desirable (8)
17. To such an extent (7)
20. Like a judge (5)
21. Benevolence (7)
23. Christmas sticker (4)
24. Roller coaster units (4)
25. Stoppers (5)
26. Locust tree (6)
27. Beseeches (4)
28. Widgets (7)
29. Uncultured (5)
30. Aerial (7)
32. Fine-wool garments (9)
34. Look up to (6)
36. Uncovers (5)
37. Luxurious (5)
39. Sawhorse (7)
41. English nobleman (7)
43. Willowy (7)
44. Esprit de corps (6)
45. Departs (4)
46. Stays away (7)

DOWN
1. Stuffing herb (4)
2. Rooks and pawns (8)
3. Competitions (5)
4. Flat-heeled slipper (5)
5. Most adequate (7)
6. Place of refuge (6)
7. Wrangled (5)
9. Foot pedal (7)
10. Lariat (5)
12. Less bright (7)
14. Similarity (8)
16. Eye shades (6)
18. Connective tissue sheath (6)
19. Not imagined (4)
21. Harmonious sounds (6)
22. Awkward boats (4)
24. Social division (5)
25. Musical close (4)
26. Scholarly community (7)
27. Commenced (5)
28. Bestow (6)
29. Squeezes (7)
31. Snuggle (6)
32. Minnelli vehicle (7)
33. Dazzling (11)
35. Commerce restriction (7)
38. Wedding attendants (6)
39. Shaking (6)
40. Shopper's magnet (4)
42. Individuals (4)
43. Certain foundations (5)

Make the Connection · PUZZLE 426

Place the words into the diagram reading across only so that the same letter appears in boxes that touch above or below.

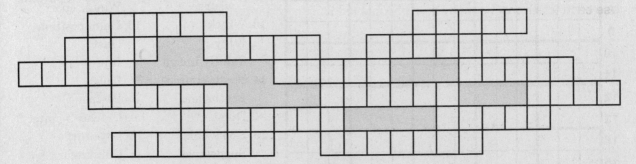

ACROBAT ARMADA CHARM LARGE RAMP
AMOEBA ATOLL EPOCH LEAF RIFLE
AMPULE BANDANA HUSBAND MOLAR SCRAM

PUZZLE 427

BRICK BY BRICK

Rearrange this stack of bricks to form a crossword puzzle. The clues will help you fit the bricks into their correct places. Row 1 has been filled in for you. Use the bricks to fill in the remaining spaces.

BRICKS

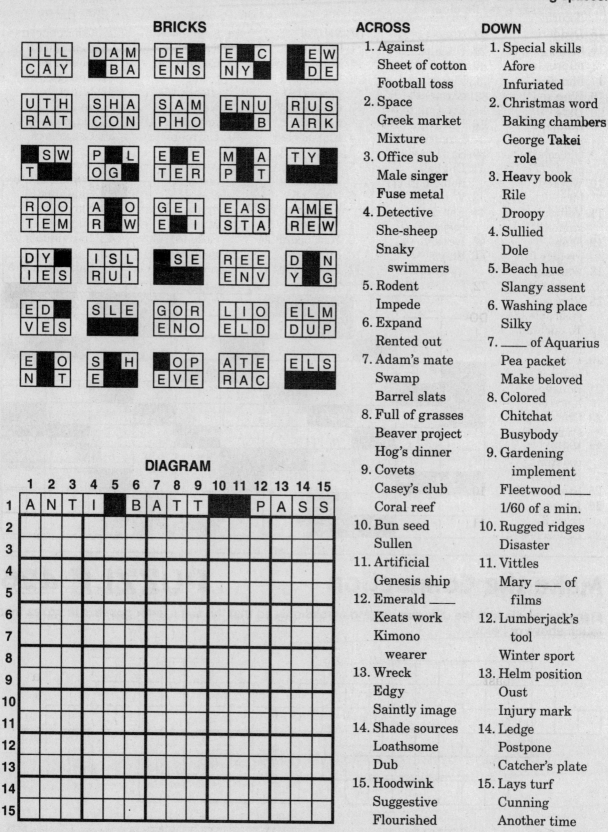

ACROSS

1. Against
   Sheet of cotton
   Football toss
2. Space
   Greek market
   Mixture
3. Office sub
   Male singer
   Fuse metal
4. Detective
   She-sheep
   Snaky
      swimmers
5. Rodent
   Impede
6. Expand
   Rented out
7. Adam's mate
   Swamp
   Barrel slats
8. Full of grasses
   Beaver project
   Hog's dinner
9. Covets
   Casey's club
   Coral reef
10. Bun seed
    Sullen
11. Artificial
    Genesis ship
12. Emerald _____
    Keats work
    Kimono
       wearer
13. Wreck
    Edgy
    Saintly image
14. Shade sources
    Loathsome
    Dub
15. Hoodwink
    Suggestive
    Flourished

DOWN

1. Special skills
   Afore
   Infuriated
2. Christmas word
   Baking chambers
   George Takei
      role
3. Heavy book
   Rile
   Droopy
4. Sullied
   Dole
5. Beach hue
   Slangy assent
6. Washing place
   Silky
7. _____ of Aquarius
   Pea packet
   Make beloved
8. Colored
   Chitchat
   Busybody
9. Gardening
      implement
   Fleetwood _____
   1/60 of a min.
10. Rugged ridges
    Disaster
11. Vittles
    Mary _____ of
       films
12. Lumberjack's
       tool
    Winter sport
13. Helm position
    Oust
    Injury mark
14. Ledge
    Postpone
    Catcher's plate
15. Lays turf
    Cunning
    Another time

DIAGRAM

	1	2	3	4	5	6	7	8	9	10	11	12	13	14	15
1	A	N	T	I		B	A	T	T			P	A	S	S
2															
3															
4															
5															
6															
7															
8															
9															
10															
11															
12															
13															
14															
15															

PUZZLE 428

ACROSS

1. Lowly
5. Colas, e.g.
10. Mournful cry
14. Cake decorator
15. Doddering
16. Salon offering
17. Menaced
19. Wise man
20. Date frequently
21. Capri currency, once
22. Advantageous
24. Mas' guys
25. Perform
26. So far
27. Verify
31. Puccini work
33. Charge
34. Project
36. Greek marketplace
40. To the left, matey
42. Nothing's alternative
43. Auto polisher
44. Diameter parts
45. Florida islands
47. Shut in
48. ___ on (urged)
50. Chic
52. Corroded
55. Personal pronoun
56. Twosome
57. Spanish gala
59. Nimble
60. Female relative, for short
63. Wide-mouthed jar
64. Certain jungle
67. Roger ___ of "Frida"
68. Expunge
69. ___ von Bismarck
70. Goofs
71. Removed from print
72. Puff of smoke

DOWN

1. Morsels
2. Pang
3. Desiccated
4. Poet's before
5. Gratify fully
6. Lulus
7. Merrill of "The Meal"
8. Beer's cousin
9. Win over
10. Cathedral part
11. Covered in foliage
12. Dispute
13. Small food fish
18. European mountains
23. Fodder
25. Suitably
27. Remotely
28. Appetizer
29. Stepped
30. Spooky
31. Lubricated
32. Wide open
35. Creator
37. Farm team
38. Split apart
39. Pretentious
41. With no slack
46. Overfed
49. Equipped
51. Printing method
52. Previously, previously
53. Roofer, e.g.
54. Moray fisherman
56. Solid
58. Talk rudely
59. Clock feature
60. U.S. program to find aliens
61. Novel endings?
62. Cease
65. "We ___ Not Alone"
66. Fracas

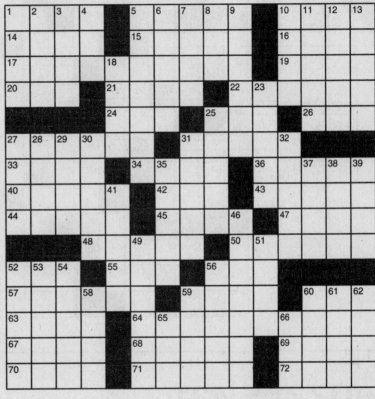

Pulling Strings

PUZZLE 429

Place the answers to the clues into the squares. Squares that are connected with lines contain the same letter. Don't get tangled!

1. Roast
2. Keepsakes
3. Bog
4. Maned mama
5. Kingdom

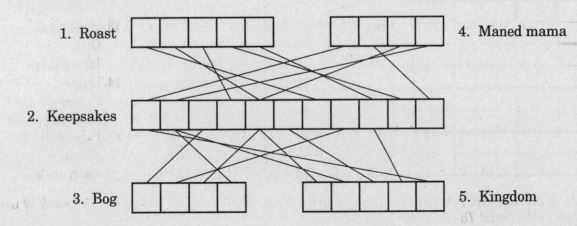

Codeword is a special crossword puzzle in which conventional clues are omitted. Instead, answer words in the diagram are represented by numbers. Each number represents a different letter of the alphabet, and all of the letters of the alphabet are used. When you are sure of a letter, put it in the code key chart and cross it off in the alphabet box. A group of letters has been inserted to start you off.

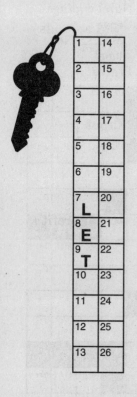

Code key chart:

No.	Letter	No.	Letter
1		14	
2		15	
3		16	
4		17	
5		18	
6		19	
7	L	20	
8	E	21	
9	T	22	
10		23	
11		24	
12		25	
13		26	

Alphabet box:

A N
B O
C P
D Q
E̷ R
F S
G T̷
H U
I V
J W
K X
L̷ Y
M Z

Grid:

16	14	9	■	9	20	16	13	■	■	2	23	20	14	18
14	7	8	■	20	14	3	8	■	8	4	1	14	9	8
10	7	14	9	11	20	16	5	■	12	1	9	9	8	20
■	■	14	17	8	5	■	21	16	14	■	■			
19	14	7	7	■	8	19	8	■	21	14	5	24	16	
14	2	6	7	1	17	■	16	13	13	■	18	16	16	20
2	22	8	■	15	11	23	15	8	20	■	2	9	6	8
■			15	8	5	16	■	23	16	18	8			
2	14	20	11	■	23	1	23	15	16	16	■	10	20	16
8	25	11	9	■	8	20	14	■	7	11	4	1	11	13
9	8	18	8	8	■	2	18	14	■	1	20	12	8	
■			26	11	8	■	17	14	12	11	■			
18	16	8	9	11	23	■	6	1	7	8	9	11	13	8
8	5	7	14	23	8	■	14	2	8	14	■	5	16	12
9	8	17	18	9	■	18	8	8	20	■	15	8	12	

(Starter letters shown in grid: **L E T**)

PUZZLE 431 — Letterdrop

Discover the sayings concealed in these lines. Drop one letter in each pair and decide where words begin and end.

1. CE HV EO RU LY KB NO DE IY LV TA WU NG HI

   LS DI NC DT OH EL SK NA MO UE GL AE DN IG

   UN TA GH EY

2. CT HR AE SI WL LE VE TA IE SN DT OY FE XA

   OL LM SU OJ EU NR GD AS MI SU TP LR EA IV

   SO EL

ACROSS

1. Fur
5. Street fight
9. Tower top
14. Gawk at
15. Greed
16. Turned white
17. Rawhide
18. Metal fastener
19. Ticked off
20. Etna's output
22. Cut of meat
24. Shrewd
25. Pathways from hearts
28. Periodical, briefly
30. Merge
31. Suitable
32. Broken-bone brace
35. Mr. Carney
36. Televised again
38. Put down
40. Demean
42. Have a mortgage
43. Avoid
44. Postman's load
45. Apprehensive
47. Bar staple
48. Worldwide
51. Last letter
52. Stags
53. Combine
54. Herons
56. Pen pal?
59. Lemon coolers
62. Donkey
63. Dale or Linda
65. Burn
67. Like
71. Lease again
72. Embrace
73. Big quiz
74. Unruly kids
75. Certain poems
76. Positions

DOWN

1. Jump
2. Birthday number
3. Needing Dr. Welby
4. Patch the roof
5. Change in form
6. Newhart TV home
7. Roundish
8. Misprint
9. ___ column
10. Golf goal
11. Sorts
12. Fishing gear
13. Whirlpool
21. Gape
23. Scamp
25. Auto safety device
26. Certain soup
27. Walk leisurely
29. Bass feature
30. Title of respect
32. Cause for a blessing
33. Zero
34. Straightens up
37. Reverence
39. Sanctums
41. Gradual
43. Observers
46. Best wishes
49. Wild animals
50. Total
55. Curved letters
56. Catnip, e.g.
57. Kaput
58. Festivity
60. Parrot
61. Not barefoot
64. Actual profit
66. Stein filler
68. Bunyan's tool
69. Bathroom rug
70. Type measures

PUZZLE 433

ACROSS
1. Dog's greeting
4. Obligation
8. Belfry denizens
12. Guns
16. Byron's always
17. Affirms
19. Charley horse
20. Opera offering
21. Historical period
22. TV and newspapers
23. Become larger
24. Kind of tide
25. Bread for hummus
27. Upper limb
29. Deposes
31. Observed
32. Values
35. Vitality
39. Loses energy
41. Allergic reaction
43. Happy face
44. Enchanting
47. Blunder
48. Snaky curve
50. Faint
51. Stood up
52. Teasingly shy
53. Major roads
55. Mermaid's milieu
56. Delirious
59. Western prop
60. After-shower sprinkle
62. Office staff
64. Tune for two
68. Garret
70. Lifts
72. Fabric layer
73. Burrito wrapper
76. Unlock, in a sonnet
77. Aromatic wood
79. Birthday count
80. Caustic stuff
81. Payable
82. Mother-of-pearl source
84. Move slowly
86. Campus bigwig
88. Group of lions
89. Plains tent
90. Lasted
92. Deal (with)
96. Enthusiasm
99. Hit the slopes
100. Deuce beater
101. Ballerina's jump
104. Equivalent
106. Show feeling
110. Lime beverage
111. Choir member
112. Turn loose
113. Blood fluid
114. Roofing substance
115. Secluded valley
116. Fruit pastry
117. Lee's men, briefly
118. City trains

DOWN
1. Cries
2. Cliff hanger?
3. Grind, as cheese
4. Beaver's barrier
5. Genesis name
6. Flower's spot
7. Court cases
8. Caddie's tote
9. Crossword direction
10. Quaker pronoun
11. Mends with thread
12. Kidnapper's demand
13. Previous to, to a poet
14. Passing through
15. Tree liquid
18. Rani's gown
26. Nonsupporters
28. Carousels
30. Fixes, as a salad
32. Women's undergarment
33. Conger, e.g.
34. Distant
36. Skirt length
37. Ballet bend
38. Clothing borders
40. Cake topper
42. Valiant types
44. Spar
45. Place
46. Aim
47. Huge timespans
49. Fur piece
52. Around
53. Sharpshooter Oakley
54. Cardinal's color
57. Skillfully
58. Concealed
61. Feline

PUZZLE 433

63. Neck part

65. Lofty hairstyle

66. Brilliance

67. It's stored in a boot

69. Rudder handle

71. Large amount

73. Social grace

74. Horrible monster

75. Gather in a crop

78. Opt

81. Mr. Aykroyd

82. "You ___ My Love"

83. Auction action

85. Sword or rifle

87. Spookier

88. Early reader

91. Hawaiian instruments

93. Speak formally

94. Bike's accelerator

95. Gazers

97. Silly

98. Gumbo pod

101. Loiter

102. Addition shape

103. Had a snack

105. Snare

107. Native mineral

108. Place to bathe

109. Type measures

PUZZLE 434

ACROSS

1. "Casino" quote
5. Sculpture
9. Musical range
14. Cry
15. Till
16. Like a sprite
17. Gold fabric
18. Claim
19. Ceremonies
20. Winter vehicle
22. Hosiery mishap
23. Yet, poetically
24. Cigar container
28. Graph
31. School wing
32. Have feelings
33. Type of rug
34. Wight or Man
36. Sloe ___
37. Approximately
38. Electric signs
40. Mellowed
41. Command- ment word
42. Milk-giving animal
43. Wishes
44. Prayer finale
46. Thrust
47. Ward off
49. Restoration
51. To and ___
52. Dunk
53. Trouble
58. Green sauce
61. British noble
62. Rich supply
63. Nimble
64. Take the bait
65. Hold
66. Rodeo competitor
67. Raised
68. Social insects

DOWN

1. Night hooters
2. College official
3. Sample recording
4. Discharge
5. Report
6. Joining
7. Meat dish
8. Freight measure
9. Truth ___
10. Outpatient center
11. "Billy Budd" direction
12. Deceive
13. Certain dashes
21. Part of mpg
22. Jamaican product
24. Zoo giggler?
25. Sharp weapon
26. Acquaint
27. Divides
28. Auto trim
29. Rush
30. Previously
31. Dimness
33. Sub finder
35. Actor George ___
39. Frightened
40. OK, to McHale
45. Cuddle
46. Tap
48. Swear
50. Beau
51. Strength
53. Fur
54. Seaweed
55. Ripped
56. Censor
57. Agents
58. Average
59. Freudian topic
60. Little drink
61. Flow back

ACROSS

1. Pan handler?
5. Flying stinger
9. Garble
13. Ship's bottom
14. "___ and Dangerous"
16. Tiptop
17. Clarify
19. Get an "F"
20. Dads
21. Third letters
22. Deceitful
24. Stern
25. Paddle's cousin
26. Swiss cottage
28. Key employees?
32. Defrosted
33. Transit coach
34. Explode
35. Hockey spots
36. Bill
37. Home, on a diamond
39. Not young
40. Judgment ___
41. Charred
42. Throw out
45. Court clown
46. Recline
47. Year part
48. Gear for Ansel Adams
51. Attache
52. Damage
55. "___ the Hill"
56. 6:00, to many
59. Bond
60. Slalom competitor
61. Sonnets' kin
62. Says further
63. Lobe locales
64. Money factory

DOWN

1. Dip's companion
2. Hippy dance
3. Annexes
4. Common ailment
5. Sprinkled
6. Catch
7. Break violently
8. Favored one
9. Belted jacket
10. Goof off
11. Module
12. Put faith (in)
15. Phony ducks
18. Weighing devices
23. Emulate Ice-T
24. "Hudson ___"
26. Cook-off dish
27. Gives
28. Open container
29. Certain tire
30. Carrier
31. Floored it
32. Stomped
33. Chesapeake ___
36. Little bit
37. Bug
38. Thin strip
40. Fears
41. Exporters
43. Store workers
44. Ventilate
45. Connector
47. Craze
48. Soda flavor
49. Eager
50. Fix
52. Calf-length skirt
53. Grace period?
54. Take a load off
57. Likable guy?
58. Male turkey

PUZZLE 436

ACROSS

1. Unwinds
7. Handiworks
11. Solicit
14. Kind of type
15. Buy and sell
16. Bar
17. Roof window
18. Skirt type
19. "___ Waited So Long"
20. Snoop
21. Shadow site
23. Buck's love
24. Groom
26. Ones who yield
28. Clinic visitor
31. Uncovered
32. Straightens
33. Open container
34. Many
38. Least good
39. Young boy
40. Old saying
41. Explore
42. Appetite
43. Hope loftily
44. Notion
46. Feared
47. Threads
50. "Oh, Pretty ___"
51. Hurried
52. Cathedral
54. Notable time
57. Frequently, to poets
58. Puff up, as bread
59. Choice
62. Neath's mate
63. Level
64. Weighted, as dice
65. ___ and con
66. Head flankers
67. Border trimmers

DOWN

1. Disposes of
2. At the summit
3. Differ
4. Lawn tree
5. Recline
6. Partitions
7. Jingle writers
8. True
9. Urban car
10. Patio door, perhaps
11. Live
12. Relish
13. Leg joints
22. Up to this point
24. Football
25. Sublease
27. Expressionless
28. Doggy feet
29. Lotion ingredient
30. Drain
31. Nip in the ___
33. Shade of brown
35. Deposited
36. Folklore giant
37. ___ off (mad)
39. Steeped drink
40. On a cruise
42. Jewish school
43. Garment opening
45. Judge's decision
46. Physician
47. Company
48. Crisp cookie
49. Emcee's speech
50. Songbirds
53. Operator
54. Staff officer
55. Active one
56. Closes
60. Pea holder
61. Touch game

ACROSS

1. Scram!
5. Celebrity
9. Bassinet
13. Mast
14. Cheerless
15. Went by cab
16. Church image
17. Ghostly
18. Reed instrument
19. Extremely
20. Ordinary
21. Blow mark
22. Jungle trip
24. Mischievous
27. Ode, e.g.
29. Japanese coin
30. Select
33. Gumbo must
36. Often-dried fruit
38. Meal course
40. Off-white
42. Boy
44. Clans
45. Combined
47. Maiden
49. Hold out
50. Pa's boy
51. Had been
53. Dish
55. Included
57. Hot spring
61. Restrain
64. Burn
66. Great anger
67. Voiced
68. Dugout
69. Gush
70. Monster
71. Alter
72. Metallic vein
73. Stare impolitely
74. Acapulco money
75. Like some cars

DOWN

1. Roasting rods
2. Winter drink
3. Remote
4. Toe count
5. Bowser's bane
6. Lofty abode
7. Mostly
8. Barely earn
9. English coin
10. Judge's garb
11. Sacred statue
12. Sugar root
14. Faith
20. Supportive
23. Detached
25. Stipend
26. Rustic hotels
28. Wire measure
30. Seal hunter
31. Hamsters, e.g.
32. Trial
33. Major work
34. Bingo's kin
35. April shower
37. Squelch
39. Mr. Savalas
41. Bawdy
43. Particle
46. Pater
48. Recorded
52. Bun seed
54. Tiny
55. More competent
56. Sups
58. Farm buildings
59. Wear away
60. Marry again
61. Awesome!
62. Compulsion
63. Not common
65. Forbidden thing
68. Mushroom top
69. Common malady

PUZZLE 438

FLOWER POWER

The answers to this petaled puzzle will go in a curve from the number on the outside to the center of the flower. Each number in the flower will have two 5-letter answers. One goes in a clockwise direction and the second in a counterclockwise direction. We have entered two answers to help you begin.

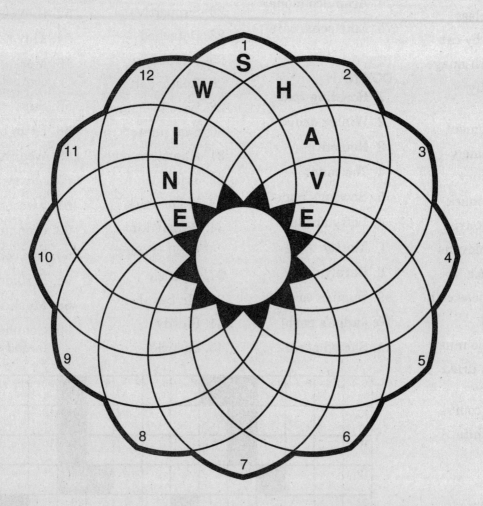

CLOCKWISE

1. Shear
2. Lariat
3. Pulverize
4. Rabbit
5. Impertinent
6. Card game
7. Guard
8. Small songbird
9. Thick
10. Elton's instrument
11. Patterned fabric
12. Heavy string

COUNTERCLOCKWISE

1. Sty dwellers
2. African mammal, shortly
3. Jack's foe
4. Courageous
5. Hotel option
6. Heavenly food
7. Injury
8. Not plain
9. Jingle
10. English coins
11. Tweak
12. Rubbish

ACROSS

1. Beat it!
6. Town, briefly
10. Bullets, to a GI
14. Motto
15. Confused
16. Urge
17. Peelings
18. Branch
19. Slime
20. Qty.
21. Hoopla
23. Gel
25. Mexican money unit
27. Not outs
28. ___ ear
29. Sawbucks
31. Throb
35. Lasso
38. Mock
39. Powder ___
40. Live
41. Biddy
42. Twist
44. Swiss peak
45. Downcast
46. Noises
47. Fate
50. Litigated
51. Half a pair
52. Harm
53. Casual
57. Different
60. Not ons
62. Shad ___
63. Banister
64. Price
66. Verdi work
68. Friendly
69. Withdraw
70. Sand hills
71. ___ dog
72. Disobey
73. Divided

DOWN

1. Discard
2. Offense
3. Leases
4. Build on
5. Peat ___
6. Sinks
7. Consumers
8. VCR button
9. Shower spot
10. Oak seeds
11. Attitude
12. Labyrinth
13. Yoke beasts
22. Color
24. Be unwell
26. Milo's pal
30. Devour
31. Dowel
32. Similar
33. Cultivate
34. Bacon's pals
35. Guide
36. Wheel shaft
37. Slits
38. Apple color
41. Fodder
42. Trouble
43. Fresh
45. Scoffed (at)
46. Waves
48. Labored
49. Squid fluid
50. Protection
52. Theme
54. Coliseum
55. More achy
56. Baking need
57. Coffeepots
58. Spike
59. Adult nits
61. Soft drink
65. Chopper
67. Baby dog

PUZZLE 440

ACROSS
1. Ho-hum
5. Shindig
10. Reiner or Sagan
14. Promise
15. Proportion
16. Mind
17. Jungle
19. Harken
20. Home sick
21. Equip
22. Gravy scoop
23. Star, briefly
25. Seles stroke
26. Adhesive
28. Think
32. Throbs
33. Animal facilities
34. Shredded
36. Colonist
37. Overly
39. Reporter's query
41. Wrath
42. Deadlocks
44. Shabby
46. Plant again
48. Drastic
50. Antelope's playmate
51. Clear
52. Cotton bundler
55. Allege
58. Restrict
59. Couple
62. Play
63. Desolate place
67. Summit
68. With speed
69. Between
70. "___ Times"
71. Fringe benefits
72. Vets' patients

DOWN
1. Indian garb
2. Face shape
3. Stain
4. Part of BYOB
5. Grill
6. Big
7. Nibbled
8. Female sib
9. Bambino
10. Live together
11. Asleep
12. True-to-life
13. Ancient instrument
18. Most liberated
22. Fire fuel
23. Incision
24. Life sci.
25. Cowboy La Rue
26. Bottled spirit
27. Paint type
29. Trimmed
30. Racket
31. Miscue
32. Baseball club
33. Speed
35. ___ Delhi
38. Due
40. Commands
43. Like a zebra
45. Southern soldier, to a Yank
47. Byron's always
49. Curb
53. To the rear
54. Rural roads
55. Rocky cliff
56. Loony tunes
57. Bullets, briefly
59. Knight's lady
60. Troop group
61. Betting numbers
63. Afternoon sleep
64. Ajar, to Keats
65. Damage
66. Baby's seat

382

PUZZLE 441

ACROSS
1. Play a guitar
6. Roe source
10. Branches
14. Tantalize
15. Oceanic surge
16. Wooer
17. Roof parts
18. Public
19. Still
20. Who ___ you?
21. Factory
23. Connect the ___
24. Talking bird
26. St. Peter, e.g.
30. Your, of yore
32. Pencil ends
36. Lark
39. Family fight
40. Dove's cry
41. English drink
42. Ornamented
45. Pork product
46. Dinghy paddle
47. Impose, as a tax
48. Eat away at
50. Struggle
52. Arid
53. Parched
56. Effortless
60. Bullets
63. Keats or Frost
65. Island necklace
66. Sunny
67. Send out
69. Put ___
   (reserve)
71. Farmland unit
72. Not prompt
73. Competitor
74. Cane
75. Give a meal to
76. Popular fad

DOWN
1. Vapor
2. Weepy
3. Crowlike bird
4. Employ
5. Chow hall
6. Slouch
7. African animal
8. Fruit drink
9. Family room
10. Remains
11. Renovate
12. Ice-cream treat
13. Brings to court
22. Alfalfa
25. Had wings
27. Viewed
28. Bona fide
29. Fireman's aid
31. Vitality
33. Repeating sound
34. Route
35. A few
36. Stash away
37. Bosc, e.g.
38. Barely cooked
39. Cook in fat
43. Pickle seller
44. Blown lead-in
49. Saloon drink
51. Packed away
52. Color
54. Ill will
55. Hauled
57. Existing
58. Enclosed car
59. Produce
60. A long way off
61. Spice
62. Mud
64. Vinegary
67. Sprite
68. Actress Murray
70. Man's title

383

PUZZLE 442

ACROSS

1. Jewish scholar
6. Fish start
9. Float
13. Individually
15. Timespan
16. Efficiently
17. Cash in
18. Above, in verse
19. Bath bar
20. Extinguished flames?
21. Crunchy
24. Molokai strings
25. Marine mammal
26. Survived
28. Road curve
31. Identify
32. Japanese wrestler
33. Advanced
35. Oversize
36. Light fixture
40. Sensational
41. Pine
42. Ocean vessel
43. Turn
44. Brooch
45. Interfere
46. Enlist in
48. Ms. Leoni
49. Piggish place
50. Evade
53. Not hearing
54. Bemoan
55. Burdensome
57. Strike out
61. Homely
63. Felon
64. Worn away
66. Bloodless
67. Hen grenade
68. Delirious
69. Easy gait
70. 24-hour period
71. Trivial

DOWN

1. Not common
2. Highest point
3. Wait
4. Bloom buzzers
5. Igloo block
6. Grease again
7. Metals
8. Noise muffler
9. Used to be
10. Circa
11. Snow unit
12. Keyed
14. Hosted
22. Cloth doll
23. Holiday spud
25. Raced
27. Hard
28. House wings
29. Bouillon
30. Indian dress
32. Mister
34. Edo warrior
35. Coal box
37. Conjunctions
38. Thaw
39. Victim
41. Shark part
42. Fall faller
44. Pricked
45. Scanty
47. Make a selection
48. X
50. Gush lava
51. Creme brulee topping
52. Ma's strings
53. Drab
56. Calming exercise
57. Bird that coos
58. Reword
59. Church season
60. Jumpy
62. Thus far
65. Hip-hop music

PUZZLE 443

ACROSS

1. Statutes
5. Kind of skirt
9. Sis's sibs
13. Converse
14. Faulty car
15. Banish
16. Maui dance
17. Enter data
18. Wight, e.g.
19. Green gem
21. Hotel worker
23. By way of
24. Authentic
25. Hostile
28. Bungled
31. Concealed
32. Ascended
35. Legal code
37. ___-advised
38. Movie texts
40. Mine product
41. Spot
42. Chinese mammal
43. Caress
44. Less moist
46. Smirked
50. Plans
52. Victory sign
53. Attire
56. Most bare
60. Wooden shoe
61. Used a keyboard
63. Glen
64. Snout
65. Upper class
66. Dusks
67. Rams' mates
68. Stains
69. Mr. Gingrich

DOWN

1. Pain
2. Buddy
3. Fable
4. Famish
5. Darn
6. Sprite
7. Uncertainty
8. Bank rate
9. Kettle
10. Hurry
11. Norway city
12. Stair
14. Purple bloom
20. Ventilate
22. Entices
25. Rasped
26. Lazy person
27. Merit
29. Go off to wed
30. Ventured
31. ___-and-hers
33. Weed out
34. Whitish gem
36. Soaked
38. Lance
39. Covered in rugs
45. Pictures
47. Dodge
48. Wiggly fish
49. Blush
51. Sneakily
53. Skin woe
54. Till
55. Model
56. Gambles
57. Roof part
58. Heap
59. Big quiz
62. Bakery item

PUZZLE 444

ACROSS

1. Dunk
4. For takeout
8. Histories
13. Shade
14. Helm direction
16. Lifeless
17. Stray
18. Pore over
19. Strange
20. ___ Albert
22. Agts.
24. Spouse
25. Shut
27. Slobber
29. The works
30. Broadcasts
31. Bridal path
33. Chart again
35. Commotion
38. Result
39. Fruit cooler
40. Yellow resin
44. Attorney
46. Bend
47. Look at
49. Foray
50. Toupee
51. Float
55. Dips
56. Coral ___
58. Skirt length
59. Cover
60. Interior
62. Saying
64. Climbing vine
67. ___ bear
68. Yoga position
69. Born as
70. Cancel
71. Customs
72. Capture

DOWN

1. That lady
2. "___ Town"
3. Acts
4. Flavor
5. Select
6. Squash
7. Command
8. Pizza ___
9. Afresh
10. Weekly show
11. Minor thing
12. Hard metal
15. Memo mistake
21. Attack
23. ___ opera
25. Concern
26. Legal claim
28. Pale purple
32. Japanese warrior
34. Fuzzy fruit
35. Alfalfa
36. Keats poem
37. Poet's above
41. Entwining
42. Wicked
43. Beatty film
45. Not who
47. Hot dog
48. Meeting plan
50. Compose
52. Test tube
53. Furnish
54. Gaucho's tool
55. Grace word
57. G-men
61. Dark bread
63. Man
65. Low neckline
66. Up to now

ACROSS

1. Large mop
5. Relay portion
8. Parade entry
13. Exploding star
14. Exist
15. Dog breed
16. Similar
17. ___ peeve
18. Reveal
19. Organ levers
21. "___-Devil"
23. Closet bar
24. Carol
26. Atop
29. Distantly
31. Fitting
33. Ewe's young
36. Bedridden
37. Ms. Delaney
39. Lawn trimmers
41. Reminder
42. Men
44. Immerse
45. Develop
48. Amount
50. "___ Day Now"
51. Dumbfound
52. Wilt
53. Competently
55. Boar's tooth
57. Dreaded person
59. "___ So Shy"
62. Nervous twitch
64. Fished
68. Individually
71. Filch
73. Provide
74. Weeping tree?
75. Hooting bird
76. Prayer ender
77. Chastise
78. Tiny
79. Promising

DOWN

1. Crisp cookie
2. Roused
3. Eager
4. Yellow fruit
5. Slight error
6. Sooner than
7. Fetches
8. Cunning animal
9. Chop
10. Perfume
11. As well
12. ___ off (irate)
15. Chick's remark
20. British noble
22. Shack
25. Rural road
27. Ancient
28. Nitpick
29. Grads
30. Speedy
32. Chinese mammal
34. Award
35. Salty
36. Igloo block
38. 21, e.g.
39. Curvy turn
40. 007, e.g.
43. Jonathan ___ of "CSI: Miami"
46. Wagon track
47. Wildebeest
49. Draw wages
52. Slope slider
54. Tramp
56. Hearty soup
58. Clark ___
59. Coach commands
60. Spectacular
61. Barn's neighbor
63. Brag
65. Luxury auto
66. Dusks
67. Refute
69. Plumbing joint
70. Cape ___
72. Be in debt

387

PUZZLE 446

ACROSS

1. Domicile
5. Load
9. Life stories, shortly
13. Pound
17. Bodily radiance
18. Proposal
19. Cornfield measure
20. Killer whale
21. ___ of lamb
22. Caper
23. Avid
24. False witness
25. Ponder
26. Splashed
28. Block or Long
30. Cashew or pecan
32. Born
33. Beep
35. Part of RPM
38. Chipper
40. Dismal
42. City vehicle
45. Maui guitar
47. Outfit
48. Elude
50. Phi ___ Kappa

51. Missing links
54. Crest
55. Ten-year time
57. Printers' measures
60. Eight musicians
61. Complete circuit
64. Paris's river
65. Stared in wonder
67. Officeholders
68. Fragrances
70. Squealer
71. Banished
73. Allot
74. Antiseptic
76. Clarinet's kin
80. Turkey accompaniment
82. "___ It Romantic?"
84. Overacting
86. Poetic adverb
87. No more!
89. Degree
90. Ask earnestly
91. Sharp taste
92. Lamb Chop's mama?

94. Fishing boat item
96. Oahu's site
100. Informed
103. Tramp
107. Forewarning
108. Pisa dough, once
110. Geometry term
111. At the top
112. Animal fur
113. Break ___
114. Shift course
115. Shopping site
116. Finales
117. Roulette bets
118. Guitarist Duane ___
119. Dramatic production

DOWN

1. Cultivate
2. Polynesian feast
3. Curves
4. Occupied
5. Gold medal position
6. Admired actor
7. Sour
8. Mistake
9. Make a cake

10. Summer drink
11. Crude metal
12. 12th-grader
13. ___ weevil
14. What a diva sings
15. Browse
16. Solid
27. Shrub border
29. Eye woe
31. Consume
34. Galley blade
35. Bar
36. Gain with effort
37. Ditch
39. Mend
41. Went back on
42. Desert growths
43. Jingle writers
44. Borscht ingredients
46. Boy
49. Cleaner, shortly
52. Actress Skinner
53. Conference
56. Twisting turn
58. Skirt style
59. Piano type
60. Sonnet's cousin
61. Mountain resort

388

62. Worship

63. Arctic

66. Simple

69. Race (an engine)

72. Freckle

75. Additional

77. Child's neckwear

78. Till bill

79. Humpty Dumpty, e.g.

81. Abominable snowman

82. Charged atom

83. Sweetened

85. Ajar, in verse

88. Carpenter, at times

89. Burnt

93. Move to and fro

95. Dull sound

96. "___ and Glory"

97. Blessing close

98. Join metals

99. Picnic crashers

101. Forbids

102. Future flower

104. October stone

105. South American lasso

106. Just

109. "___ Got a Secret"

PUZZLE 447

ACROSS

1. Blackthorn
5. Stand
10. Ranch
14. Father
15. Info gathering
16. Island event
17. Maui strings
18. Sudden downpour
20. Begin again
22. Cancel
23. Copy
24. Even one
26. Phooey!
28. Chore
31. Fruit pie
33. Black
36. Queensland bird
37. Maps
39. Song for two
41. Moat
43. Crow's cry
44. Poorer
45. Longing
46. Withdraw
48. Briny deep
49. Change
51. Leg middle
52. Snake shape
53. "Cheers" cry
55. Boxing count
56. Amiss
59. Thin
61. Brewing need
66. Southern spread
69. Helpful hint
70. Desmond ___
71. Heavenly dish
72. Unusual
73. Beheld
74. Doze
75. Utilizes

DOWN

1. Encourage
2. Huron, e.g.
3. Unlock
4. Lighten
5. Lob's path
6. Meet event
7. Holy image
8. Fit
9. Bears
10. Winter illness
11. Emanation
12. File
13. Silent
19. Tell all
21. Timepiece
25. Slangy no
27. Commotion
28. "Star Wars" knights
29. Passes over
30. ___ Cassidy
32. Follow
34. Caregiver
35. Pro votes
38. Blackjack goal
40. Herbal drinks
42. Jaw part
44. Tiny
46. Flows
47. 4th letter
50. Army post
54. Iron, e.g.
56. Decides
57. Chimney duct
58. Lot
60. Sup
62. Hosiery hue
63. Woeful cry
64. Doubtless
65. Golf pegs
67. Habit wearer
68. Siesta

PUZZLE 448

ACROSS
1. Smug
5. Boat propeller
8. Soft food
12. 1492 vessel
13. Poison ___
15. Pot donation
16. Uninvited picnickers
17. Cease-fire
18. Radiate
19. Grow choppers
21. Ledge
23. Bad humor
24. Nurture
25. Enrolled
27. Clod
29. Ms. Leoni
31. Glitzy party
32. "Cheers" quaff
33. Not at work
35. Violent
39. Weary
42. Cruise or Hanks
44. Indian craft
45. Maneuvers
47. Mass
49. Prosecute
50. False witness
52. Hardwood
54. Ballpoint contents
55. Clearly shaped
59. Oven
61. Pronoun
62. Knight's lady
63. Passes (laws)
66. Wapitis
68. Kitchen gadget
70. Insignificant
71. Escape
72. White
73. Facial ridge
74. Seltzer
75. Hair tint
76. Gels

DOWN
1. Biting bug
2. Queue
3. Meddle
4. Stitch loosely
5. "___ Gang"
6. Delight
7. Speeding
8. "Time," for short
9. Dark
10. Shop
11. Cleft
13. Hi-fi
14. Basement
20. Derby, e.g.
22. Blooming bush
26. Legend
27. Fillies' fodder
28. Dismounted
30. Fore-and-___
34. Dense mist
36. Dishonest
37. Part of speech
38. Nerd
40. Squiggly creatures
41. Withered
43. Bossy's comment
46. Greens dishes
48. Muffin mart
51. Jog the memory
53. Kith and ___
55. Gourmet cooks
56. Howdy!
57. Irritated
58. Fake duck
60. Meadow babies
64. Fox's dance?
65. Embroiders
67. Caribbean ___
69. Woolly female

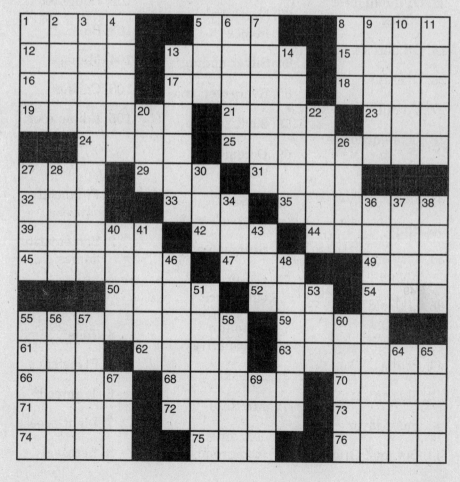

PUZZLE 449

GLOBE TROT

ACROSS

1. Alcatraz features
5. Sch. groups
9. Cookie guy
13. Like Willie
16. "___ Around" (Beach Boys song)
17. Soprano Mills
18. ___-car
20. Even's counterpart
21. Come closer
22. Of the highest caliber
24. Oil derrick
25. Overdue
27. Untruth
28. Like anchovies
30. Ample
31. Forest
33. Ship
34. City on the Rhone
36. Like old milk
37. Gate
41. Sculls
42. Magna ___
43. Paint layer
44. Botanist Gray
45. Sick
46. Knitting stitch
47. Dreamy
49. Author Stoker
50. "Waking ___ Devine"
51. Incensed
52. Beard on grain
53. Stingers
54. Except
56. Bergen et al.
59. Hocks
62. North Pole helper
64. Silver ending
65. Evergreen tree
68. 2006 Yankee
69. December song
71. Stove compartment
72. Sturgeon eggs
73. Gooey substance
74. Acapulco affirmative
75. ___-ski
77. Mr. Rose
78. ___ difference (compromise)
80. Convey orally
81. Spatial
82. "___ Mable"
83. Filled
85. Pour
86. Cavalry sword
88. Gov. agcy.
89. Walked silently
92. Formerly
93. Influential country
98. Hence
99. Turkish title
100. Composer Erik ___
101. Tiger's roar?
102. Delighted
103. Bon ___
104. Manage
105. Caring
106. Edible root

DOWN

1. Financial squeeze
2. Screenwriter James ___
3. Opposite of imaginary
4. Toils
5. Flycatcher
6. Tramped
7. Light breeze
8. Betrayal
9. Curved
10. Blanc or Ferrer
11. Put ___ pedestal
12. Ave. crossers
13. Global conflicts
14. Censor
15. Tense
19. Aver
23. Scenic exhibit
26. Gridiron meas.
29. Whatever
31. Cardinals' 2006 victory
32. Communist nations, once
33. Suspension
34. Cut of pork
35. Noted locksmith
36. Hindu dress
38. French negative
39. Hurry-up abbr.
40. Candied tubers
42. Tress
46. Brooches
48. Have a mortgage
49. Coll. degrees
53. Small songbird
54. German conjunction

55. ___-mo

57. Courtroom rapper

58. Greek deity

59. Servings of butter

60. ___ on the knuckles (sharp rebuke)

61. Ethnic music

63. Crew cut

65. "Rockin' in the ___"

66. Pinch

67. Spool

69. Point out

70. Ex-ember

74. Casts about

76. Like some labels

77. Pupil

79. Superlative suffix

81. High peak

84. Summed

85. Canned

86. Union

87. Jason's ship

89. Shore bird

90. Yikes!

91. Dummy

94. Galoot

95. Hwy.

96. McCarthy of "The Blue Knight"

97. Romance

PUZZLE 450

ACROSS

1. Cunning
4. Large mop
8. Glimmer
13. Sorrow
14. Aristocrat
15. Right now!
16. Behave
17. Small combo
18. Pearl maker
19. Soggy
21. Feel sore
23. Sea eagle
24. Flower necklace
26. Eartha ___ of song
28. Blouses
31. Dead heat
32. Feathery scarf
35. Heroic
36. Mister
38. Grid shoes
40. Portrayals
42. Incision
44. Wood strips
45. Shaped
47. Life story
49. Quaker pronoun
50. Prince ___ Khan
51. Pecan, e.g.
53. Occupation
55. Oil barrel
57. Cat's coat
58. Not at work
61. Door sign
63. Talking birds
67. Scribbles
70. Clutch
72. Afflicted
73. Tiers
74. Corridor
75. Thick stuff
76. Apple pips
77. Category
78. With it, once

DOWN

1. Did the crawl
2. Loony
3. Hairy Himalayan
4. Hunting dog
5. Hostilities
6. Met solo
7. Hinder
8. Cook in fat
9. ___ Alamos
10. Opening wager
11. Gang ending
12. Antler
15. Lyrical
20. Slashed
22. Popular song
25. "___ My Party"
27. Snitch
28. Bobbin
29. Not flat
30. Attack!
32. Scrub
33. Alternate
34. African fox
35. Humorist Bombeck
37. Polish
39. Restaurant
41. Export
43. Muscle twitch
46. Pressure
48. Clod
52. Prom wear
54. Deep sound
56. Strength
58. Night fliers
59. Liberate
60. Finger count
62. Dish carrier
64. Near
65. Burn reliever
66. Splash
68. Mr. Turner
69. City trains
71. Swiss peak

ACROSS

1. Sever
6. Fight
10. Excited
14. Jeweled headdress
15. Cherish
16. Recreation
17. Agitated
18. Proofread
19. Deplaned
20. Gamble
21. Burdened
23. Food plans
24. Pilfer
25. Of yore
27. Observe
30. Bark
31. Former GI
34. Land force
35. "___ Are There"
37. Dotted tile
39. Appears
41. Weep
43. Carrier
44. Mom, e.g.
46. Pronto!
48. Gentle
49. Heaven
50. Mission
52. Curiously
54. Curved
56. Clod
57. Slant
60. Prepared
62. Hole puncher
65. Tibetan priest
66. Edges
67. Snow house
69. Cake froster
70. Health herb
71. Eminent
72. Fender nick
73. Talking bird
74. Silly bird

DOWN

1. Short end
2. Peace ___
3. Final
4. Great rage
5. Skin design
6. Bend
7. Western show
8. Eagerly
9. Besides
10. Once more
11. High wind
12. Leave out
13. Acquires
22. Competently
23. Station
24. Verse
26. Pa
27. Hiatus
28. ___ board
29. Medic
31. Essential
32. Nemesis
33. Shredded
34. Egypt's snakes
36. Coffee server
38. Theme
40. Capture
42. There
45. ___-tac-toe
47. Lumber
51. Only
53. Adage
54. Divided
55. Speed ___
57. Glided
58. Doily fabric
59. Warning sign
61. At a loss
62. Female singer
63. Sorrows
64. Mother ___
66. Cut of pork
68. Thick stuff

PUZZLE 452

ACROSS

1. Fasten
6. Wall support
10. Fruit discards
14. Wit
15. Car part
16. Feel sore
17. Sports ring
18. Skin woe
19. Number suffix
20. Toe count
21. However
23. Went by
25. Comic's one-___
27. Saharan
28. Tolerate
30. Rewrite
32. The limit?
35. Mistletoe unit
36. Joy
37. Garden tool
38. Rigid
39. Simmer in liquid
40. Faculty bigwig
41. Rainbow, e.g.
42. Drafted
43. Cries
44. Swarming insect
45. Fireman's item
46. Heavy jacket
47. Tier
48. Resided
50. For real
53. Exasperate
54. ___-duty
57. Snub
58. Divisible by two
61. Bald ___
63. Monarch
64. Scanned
65. Made angry
66. Reducing spots
67. Pairs
68. Scads

DOWN

1. Gab
2. Fishing decoy
3. Pew word
4. Enos, to Seth
5. Beseeching
6. One of fifty
7. ___-tac-toe
8. Vase
9. ___ apple pie
10. Sucker
11. Freezes
12. Quaker pronoun
13. Transmit
22. Conclusion
24. Humanities
25. Cafe au ___
26. Kin
28. Extra
29. Peace agreement
31. Chop finely
32. Arab chief
33. Australian animal
34. Longings
35. Attempt
36. Jeers
39. Thieves, e.g.
40. Scamper
42. Stop!
43. Those who stroll
46. Part of rpm
47. Ladder steps
49. Curves
50. Questions
51. China flaw
52. Albacore
54. Peer
55. Soared
56. G-men
59. Sign of triumph
60. Corrode
62. Be unwell

ACROSS

1. Head bone
6. Luxury resort
9. Youngsters
13. Tropical fruit
15. High peak
16. Beige
17. Fled to marry
18. Screen
19. Grin
20. Burrow
21. Tinted
23. Toad bumps
24. Plus
26. Chatter
27. Farm tower
29. Consumers
32. King beater
35. Small branch
36. Plunk
37. Harbor
38. Whistle
39. Crone
41. Green stone
42. Vast timespan
43. Toward shelter
44. Exterior
45. Handle
46. ___ printer
48. Brood
49. Cut wood
50. Doubtful
52. Phony
55. Canter
57. Wide st.
60. Greek war god
61. Fracas
62. Heavy
65. Granny
66. "Chances ___"
67. Folk tale
68. Dell
69. Joined
70. Survives

DOWN

1. Hurried
2. Garden green
3. Aware of
4. Child's seat
5. Soap ingredient
6. Rational
7. Appealed
8. Befitting
9. Shish ___
10. Cake topper
11. Dang!
12. Amounts
14. Attaches
22. Second person
23. Bee's kin
24. Aglow
25. Diary
26. Flourish
27. Bobbin
28. Twist of fate
30. Buying event
31. Ms. Keats
32. Decrease
33. West Pointer
34. Witness
35. Pace
39. Side order
40. Stags
41. Panel
43. Woe is me!
44. ___-key
47. Slit
49. Ms. Lucci
51. Tripped
52. Blast
53. Spoken exam
54. Actor Kelly
55. Wisdom
56. Had debts
57. Fruit drinks
58. Air shaft
59. Finales
61. Uncooked
63. Conger, e.g.
64. ___ Khan

PUZZLE 454

ACROSS

1. Openings
5. Paves
9. ___ Cruces
12. Civil melee
13. Close by
15. "I Like ___"
16. Loafing
17. Dresser
18. Bikini half
19. Transmit
21. Great fear
23. Macaroni, e.g.
24. Scrubs
25. Pure
28. Mets' former home
29. Bagel topping
30. Eye problem
33. Trickles
37. Mimics
39. Long period
40. Birthmark
41. Piano part
43. Opponent
45. Kidman, to pals
46. Chatters
48. Old-time girdle
51. Deli buy
54. Gleam
56. Dilemmas
57. Authorized
61. Horse's kin
62. Walk
64. Crest
65. Sever
66. Threefold
67. Central
68. Type spaces
69. Mind
70. Bobbles

DOWN

1. "True ___"
2. Staffer
3. Voter survey
4. Brews
5. Faith
6. Chief artery
7. Weep over
8. Grab
9. October sign
10. Ohio city
11. Broils
13. Humiliates
14. Fenced
20. Kitty
22. Equip again
25. Thunder sound
26. ___ chest
27. Felled
28. Posted
31. British brews
32. Poet's there
34. Charged atoms
35. Ballet move
36. Denomination
38. Legends
42. Least convincing
44. Frozen hanger
47. Cafe
49. Undivided
50. Title again
51. Climb
52. Fiery crime
53. Speech problems
54. Incline
55. Not flat
58. Burn mark
59. Asian ruler
60. Burrows
63. Josh

ACROSS

1. Dull
5. Mister
8. "___ the Roof"
12. Lawn broom
13. Simple
15. Dalai ___
16. Spirited
17. Arctic house
18. Stumble
19. Mob
20. Become mature
21. Bracelet sites
23. Sassy has three
25. Vagrant
26. Poke
29. Tie the knot
30. Sums
33. Disburden
35. Beam
36. Watch sound
38. Strict
39. Floor cover
40. Lazy ___
41. Promgoer
42. "Adam's ___"
43. Shrine
44. Shoveled
46. Shallow pot
47. Spy
48. June, to Beaver
49. Hurls
51. Eliminate
54. Kindled
55. Clips
59. Broiler
60. Buzz
62. Be adjacent
63. Converge
64. Affirmatives
65. By oneself
66. Miscalculates
67. G-man
68. Aid

DOWN

1. Boast
2. Molten rock
3. Related
4. Row of bushes
5. Slumped
6. The British ___
7. Pedro's river
8. Final demand
9. Norms
10. Exclude
11. Siestas
13. Prejudiced
14. Dallas player
22. Groove
24. "___ Lake"
26. Fair
27. Chips in chips
28. Remove, TV-style
30. Running game
31. Speaks imperfectly
32. Weighing device
34. Decorations
35. Massage
37. ___-slapper
39. Relieve
40. Shipped
42. Medicine
43. Samples
45. Freckle
46. Hurt
49. Shut
50. Long cut
51. Arched ceiling
52. Always
53. Sly gaze
56. Clarinet's kin
57. Tug
58. Cease
61. KO counter

PUZZLE 456

ACROSS
1. Sill
6. Halt!
10. Lofty
14. TV sound
15. Couple
16. Soprano's solo
17. Takes a plane
18. Bit of land
19. Fasting time
20. Have a meal
21. Submerged
23. Leave
25. Humor
26. Read hastily
28. Suitmaker
31. Concealing
35. Daybreak, poetically
36. Tin, e.g.
38. Extra
40. Door sign
41. Beanie
42. Bewildered
43. Intelligent
44. Doomed
46. Paraphernalia
47. Breakfast food
49. Weakest, as an excuse
51. ___ monster
53. Retort to "t'ain't!"
54. Quit
58. Cargo
60. 747, e.g.
63. Microwave ___
64. Duplicate
66. Steered
68. Soft cloth
69. Gutter spot
70. Compare
71. Comrade
72. Saloon orders
73. Rectify

DOWN
1. Strongbox
2. Polynesian dance
3. Revise text
4. Falsify
5. Dinosaur bone, e.g.
6. Whirl
7. Jobs
8. Canola ___
9. Predominate
10. Fine powder
11. Realm
12. Dryer fuzz
13. Past due
22. Source of energy
24. Plus
25. Cold season
27. Small church
28. Poisonous
29. Ascend
30. Remember
32. Visions
33. Beaks
34. Terrific
35. Kitten noise
37. Create lace
39. Cauliflower ___
44. Dimmer
45. Information
48. Easter edible
50. Central
52. Vibrant
54. Activist Parks
55. Morally bad
56. Market
57. Dark in color
59. Dollar bills
60. Gag
61. Constant
62. Baby-sit
65. Custom
67. Margin

CODEWORD

Codeword is a special crossword puzzle in which conventional clues are omitted. Instead, answer words in the diagram are represented by numbers. Each number represents a different letter of the alphabet, and all of the letters of the alphabet are used. When you are sure of a letter, put it in the code key chart and cross it off in the Alphabet Box. A group of letters has been inserted to start you off.

1	2	3	4 T	5	6	7 A	8	9	10	11	12	13
14	15	16	17 R	18	19	20	21	22	23	24	25	26

Alphabet Box

A B C D E F G H I J K L M N O P Q R S T U V W X Y Z

401

PUZZLE 458

ACROSS

1. Short breath
5. ___ Stanley Gardner
9. Doe's beau
13. On the peak
17. Limo, e.g.
18. At no time, in verse
19. Corridor
20. Wander
21. "Klute" role
22. Pasta variety
24. Tiny pest
25. Police officer
27. Taro dish
28. Spiced drink
30. Overhead trains
31. Cul-de-___
33. Gunk
35. Moray catcher
38. La-la lead-in
39. Beat
41. Criminal
43. Crackpot
47. Shock
48. Time period
50. "Surfin' ___"
51. Jack's tote
52. Spanish houses
54. Green parrot
55. Society miss
56. Keyboardist's boo-boo
57. Cumbersome
58. Flavoring herb
59. Dangerous curve
60. "Twilight" heroine
62. Aromatic herb
64. Caribbean, e.g.
67. Advance
68. Blacksmith's workshop
70. Mama's guy
74. "Ben-___"
75. Fast plane
76. Sensations
77. Mosque priest
78. Gp.
79. Shelley work
80. French cay
81. Lack of transparentness
84. "Cheers" bartender
86. Powdery
88. Indian dish
89. Spirited horse
91. Once named
92. Chimpanzee, e.g.
93. Sheep's cry
96. Turn of phrase
98. Fish eggs
101. Widen
103. "Titanic" obstacle
106. Financial officer
109. ___ Domini
110. Matching
111. Smooch
112. Quote
113. Flag feature
114. Jewels
115. Turkish general
116. Get the news
117. Bargain event

DOWN

1. "The Misfits" lead
2. Acoustic
3. Frets
4. Sonnet, e.g.
5. Entangle
6. D.C. figure
7. Vault
8. Hence
9. This lady
10. Skin decoration
11. Choir member
12. Skate across
13. Sock pattern
14. Coal weight
15. Eggs, to Caesar
16. ___ peeve
23. Interstate
26. Nora's dog
29. Conquers
32. Figured out
34. Mineral deposits
36. Sneak away
37. Thorny blooms
39. Assignment
40. Fridge freshener
42. Catches
43. Take one side
44. Doris ___
45. Submerse
46. Small lump
49. Bottle dweller
53. Winged
57. Extort money from
58. Colt's mom
61. Relished
63. Legendary
64. Exhibit
65. Continental coins
66. Jargon
68. Sieves
69. Submit to
71. Pierre's friend
72. Butter square
73. March girl
76. Clamping tool
82. Wall-covering hanger
83. Mr. Trebek
85. Stoops (to)
87. Separate
90. Chicago Bears name
93. ___ ray
94. Record of an event
95. Idolize
97. Auth.
99. Sound of pain
100. Great Lake
102. Overtake
103. Pouch
104. ___ out (make do)
105. Boundary
107. Sly ___ fox
108. Timetable info

PUZZLE 459

ACROSS
1. Garner
6. Heavy club
10. Penniless
14. Postman's path
15. Eager
16. Ramble
17. Wading bird
18. Extra large
20. Court
21. Not right
23. Forerunners
24. Moreover
25. Social miscue
27. Claims
31. Insect stage
34. Desolate
35. Toll roads
38. Branch
40. Salon offering
41. Loathed
42. Reason
43. Hang low
44. Like some stones
45. Parallel to
46. Shish ___
48. Japanese warrior
50. Wear down
53. Monthly pub.
54. Knights' mates
57. Unsuitable
59. Freudian concept
62. Pachyderms
64. Like many roofs
66. Ascended
67. Scallion's kin
68. Overturn
69. Within reach
70. Transgresses
71. Naps

DOWN
1. Expanded
2. Company symbol
3. Lira replacement
4. Lunched
5. CBS, e.g.
6. Shark variety
7. Getting grayer
8. Cuban dance
9. Hen's output
10. Early reader
11. Slime
12. Cookie cooker
13. Cincinnati team
19. Divans
22. Disintegrate
24. Word
26. Deserted
27. Venomous snakes
28. Cut of beef
29. Army noncom
30. Hot springs
32. Heroism
33. Concert site
36. "___ My Party"
37. Florida islands
39. Creche figures
41. Drifter
42. Drain stopper
44. Swamp
45. Novice
47. Pager
49. Hi-fi item
51. Luncheonette
52. Record
54. Laura or Bruce
55. African succulent
56. Flat formation
58. Inquires
59. Nights before
60. Lady's guy
61. Bookie's quote
63. Bar order
65. Jungle beast

Rounders

PUZZLE 460

The names of three minerals are hidden in these Rounders. For each one, start at one of the letters and read either clockwise or counterclockwise.

1.
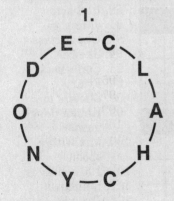

2.
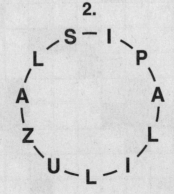

3.
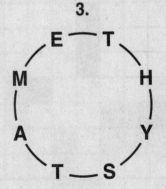

PUZZLE 461

ACROSS
1. Absent
5. Door clasp
9. Food fish
13. Apr. guru
16. Cherish
17. Bellowing
19. Hors d'oeuvre spread
20. Dinghy paddle
21. Sharpening wheel
23. Set of clothing
25. Ques.'s reply
26. Final bio.
27. Shudder
29. Burrows and Lincoln
30. Named at birth
31. Synthetic
33. Picnic drink
36. Geek
38. Pig product
39. Congers, e.g.
42. Islamic sovereign
44. Old freezer tools
48. Great respect
50. Fly alone
51. Harm
52. No rocks, please
53. Sale agt.
54. Hula accompaniment
58. Story
59. Type of neckline
60. Filled tortilla
63. Not long.
65. Notched
67. Compass dir.
68. Riviera resort
70. Elegance
72. Computer key
73. Alluring
74. English brew
75. Musical sound
79. Six, to Sophia
80. Brings
82. Bridle
84. Sample tape
86. Slender fish
87. Aquatic bird
89. Ryan or Tilly
90. Smoldering ashes
93. Nutty
94. Totals
97. Overjoy
99. NBC's peacock, e.g.
100. Luxury resort
103. Forbid
105. Rafting rapids
108. Stopover spot
109. Habitual course
110. Auriculate
111. Catch-all abbr.
112. Tut tut!
113. Zipped
114. Mindful
115. ___ and cons

DOWN
1. Pond-scum ingredient
2. Eroded
3. Rara ___
4. Yearning
5. Falling star?
6. More pretentious
7. Chimney dirt
8. Omelet maker
9. Gum flavor
10. "Big" star
11. Lost
12. "Gidget" actress
13. Baseball's Ty ___
14. Lose color
15. Greek war deity
18. Legal matter
22. Actress Dixon
24. Rat trap?
28. Pile
32. Examiners
33. Mule's father
34. Twosome
35. Remodeling result
37. A ___ a dozen
38. From now on
40. Baby bug
41. Sugary
43. Guided vacation
45. Contact
46. Cancel
47. Cabbagelike plants
49. Duel tool
55. Monarch's realm
56. Being of service
57. Nearby
60. Pons and Arthur
61. Without a shepherd
62. Fasten again
64. Layer
66. Housing fee
69. Moved to another country
71. Political cartoonist
76. Unit of resistance
77. Links peg
78. Work measure
81. Far-reaching
82. Sad play
83. Fund generously
85. Engage, as gears
88. Bad actor
91. Jazz style
92. Upper class
94. Skewer
95. Coffeepots
96. Friar
98. Sheep's ma
99. Italian dough, formerly
100. Mix with a spoon
101. 100 centavos
102. Rainbows
104. Tax org.
106. "Hee ___"
107. Hi-fi component

DOUBLE TROUBLE

Not really double trouble, but double fun! Solve this puzzle as you would a regular crossword, except place one, two, or three letters in each box. The number of letters in each answer is shown in parentheses after its clue.

ACROSS

1. Doctor's gp. (3)
3. Make taboo (3)
5. Daze (4)
7. Use a colander (6)
10. Absorb (10)
12. Roller coaster, e.g. (4)
13. Missive (7)
15. Sure thing (5)
16. Travel across (8)
18. Parisian river (5)
19. Mom's brother (5)
20. Jeopardy (5)
21. Hotel patron (5)
23. Weep (3)
24. Glide over snow (3)
25. Fashionable (4)
26. Tortilla snack (4)
28. Assist a crime (4)
30. At any time (4)
31. Hold on property (4)
32. Endure (9)
34. Pant joint (6)
36. Twice five (3)
38. Come closer (4)
39. Essay topic (5)
42. Over the top (10)
45. Pout (4)
47. Farm structure (4)
48. Fireplace shelf (6)
49. Evil demon (5)
50. Chilly (5)
51. Summer hue (3)
52. Relax (4)
53. Roster (4)
55. Fad (5)
56. Diminish (5)
57. Colleagues (5)
59. Grating (8)
62. Enamored (4)
63. Oblong nut (6)
65. Received (3)
66. Charming (10)
69. Point out (8)
70. Speak (5)
71. Pointed stick (5)
72. Kilns (5)

DOWN

1. Compile (5)
2. Goal (3)
3. Whiten (6)
4. Starting wager (4)
5. Compete (6)
6. Below (5)
7. Dance move (4)
8. Salary boost (5)
9. Natural impulse (8)
11. Frozen hanger (6)
14. Apprehensive (5)
16. Beaten path (5)
17. Smooth transition (5)
19. Cosmos (8)
20. Rate of interest (10)
22. Barrel strip (5)
24. Yarn bundle (5)
25. ____ con carne (5)
26. Cassette, e.g. (4)
27. Eye part (6)
29. French cap (5)
33. Preach (9)
35. Quantity (6)
37. No more! (6)
40. Pause (8)
41. Honeydew, e.g. (5)
43. Vine support (7)
44. Eternal spirit (4)
46. Energized (5)
48. Orchestrate (10)
52. Cancel (6)
54. Small flap (3)
55. Desire strongly (5)
56. Desert (7)
58. ____ boom (5)
60. Spicy stew (6)
61. Child minder (6)
62. Relinquish (7)
64. See socially (4)
66. Nuisance (4)
67. Higher than (5)
68. Camera feature (4)

LOOKING FOR DOUBLE TROUBLE? *You've found it! Treat yourself to special collections of your favorite puzzles—over 50 in each! To order, see page 159.*

PUZZLE 463

BRICK BY BRICK

Rearrange this stack of bricks to form a crossword puzzle. The clues will help you fit the bricks into their correct places. Row 1 has been filled in for you. Use the bricks to fill in the remaining spaces.

BRICKS

ACROSS

1. Clipped
   Freebie
   Glided
2. Lavalava
   Arab
   garments
   Road's
   scholar?
3. Room at
   the top?
   Mild
   antiseptic
4. Legal matter
   Forfeits
   Dispatch craft
5. Plot
   Did really
   well
6. Continuing
   story
   Something
   extra
7. Metamorphic
   stage
   Prized marble
   Reggae's kin
8. With
   Bird no more
   Discoloration
9. Varnish
   ingredient
   Violinist's
   direction
   Homely
10. Preside over
    Grain
11. Political
    groups
    Verily
12. Expunge
    Reveille
    obeyer
    Big bucks,
    briefly
13. Vacation spot,
    maybe
    Tropical palm
14. Not fer
    Debtor
    Pronged
15. Fast time
    Ferber or Best
    Lyric verse

DOWN

1. Lock horns
   Confidant
   Mideast carrier
2. Abhorrence
   Poisonous
   plant
   Craze
3. Food scraps
   Period
   Related
4. Portuguese
   king
   Fiber source
   Missing
5. Atomic centers
   Duplicities
6. Ladies' room?
   For
   Gardening
   device
7. Some reds,
   informally
   Meek sort
   Gang
8. High winds
   Sticky glop
   Dangerous
   damsel
9. Swamp
   Stare stupidly
   Watery fluids
10. 23rd of 24
    Eastern tie
    Cyclops's
    singleton
11. Light boats
    Judge again
12. Newly hairless
    Cat fish
    Pants mishap
13. Geometric
    points
    Practice
    Less, musically
14. Egyptian
    wader
    Dexterity
    Glazed
15. Bird no more
    Indefinite
    number
    Put cargo
    aboard

DIAGRAM

406

PUZZLE 464

• GREENGROCER'S STOCK •

ACROSS
1. Part of LST
5. Avec's opposite
9. Likelihood
13. Expenditure
17. Chisel, e.g.
18. Nile queen, for short
19. Bog fuel
20. Aware of
21. "____ Karenina"
22. Walk, with "it"
23. Pollster Roper
24. Demeanor
25. Accountant
28. Cheerleader's props
30. As well
31. Slangy affirmative
33. Slant
34. '60s do
37. Slugger Slaughter
40. Bond's school
42. "Angela's ____"
45. Forever and a day
46. Dings
48. North Carolina college
50. Usher's find
51. Every
53. Domain
55. Dutch treat
57. King of Judah
58. Corners
60. Cool
62. Sower's device
64. Sycophant
68. Affair
71. Wipe away
72. Princeton athlete
76. "Xanadu" gp.
77. Cabbage Patch Kid, e.g.
80. Form of trapshooting
82. Otherwise
83. Swimmer's circuits
85. Debatable
87. Blunder
89. Shoshonean language
90. Skeletal bone
92. Bend
94. Laborer of yore
95. Angry
96. Pay to play
98. Unwavering
100. Chicago-to-Detroit dir.
102. Touching
105. He's a watcher
111. Egg-shaped
112. Chore
114. Lt. Kojak
115. Cast
116. Not any
117. Jannings of film
118. Republic of Ireland
119. Nutmeg coat
120. Punkie
121. Lacoste of tennis
122. Defraud
123. City in California

DOWN
1. Wild guess
2. Sharpen
3. Hebrides island
4. Sow
5. Tall beer glass
6. Felipe, Jesus, or Matty
7. Sign gas
8. Pushover
9. Run
10. Md.'s neighbor
11. Moist
12. 3-legged chair
13. Hiker's aid
14. Andy Griffith film
15. Stalk
16. "Sixteen ____"
26. College gal
27. Wide-shoe width
29. ____ culpa
32. Cavity
34. Yard units
35. Bellow
36. Fairy-tale starter
38. Former NBA star Shaquille ____
39. Trite
41. Silent assent
43. Slacken
44. Sun, e.g.
47. Slant
49. Part of a folk-rock trio
52. Warmth
54. Heaths
56. Convene
59. Hurried
61. Snow unit
63. New York Indian
65. Formal dance
66. Rhone feeder
67. Tarot users
68. Liquefy
69. Kirghizia's ____ Mountains
70. Head honcho
73. Dejected
74. This, in Tijuana
75. Oboist's need
78. Base
79. Goof off
81. Symphonic story
84. Sleeveless jersey
86. Drip
88. Gambler's city
91. Noshed
93. Expert, for short
97. Stage direction
99. Muffles
101. Frome of fiction
102. Chinese mafia
103. English river
104. Unexciting
106. Trendy
107. Wife of Zeus
108. Mystique
109. Excursion
110. Spanish pot
113. Break a Commandment

PUZZLE 465   DILEMMA

Except for 1 Across, there are two clues for each number and two identical sides in the diagram. Your Dilemma is to discover which answer goes on the right side and which answer goes on the left. Note: The heavy lines indicate the ends of words as black squares do in regular crosswords.

ACROSS

1. Dickens novel
9. Entrance
   Old wound
10. Oracle
    Bellow
11. Voice range
    Italian capital
12. Golden-rule word
    Destroy
13. Loiter
    Loop trains
15. Deceit
    Less
18. Demeanor
    Horse goad
20. Scandinavian
    Turkish title
21. Metal suit
    Bicycle part
23. Gremlin
    Social insect
25. Stand-in
    Night before
28. Shanty
    Striped cat
29. Parsley unit
    Sofa
30. It's after zeta
    Bard's before
31. Gunk
    Hubbub
32. Chicken
    Winter forecast
36. Gab
    Lodge member
37. Swarm
    Revise
38. Wharf
    Originate
40. Set of three
    Near or Far
42. Not once
    Map graphic
44. Switch position
    Feasted
45. Aid in crime
    Small stick
47. Spew out
    Persia, today
48. Pop flavor
    Pink wine
49. Zoo pen
    Paddy crop
50. Surplus
    Christmas greenery
51. Hamilton bill
    Wager

DOWN

1. Hymn
   Challenges
2. Mr. Menjou
   Filled pastry
3. Mouse's kin
   Vigor
4. List member
   Croaker
5. Ancient Celt
   Single printing
6. Swindle
   Lamprey
7. Actress
   Thompson
   Meal starter
8. Not poetry
   Laundry machine
14. Jewel
    Take to court
16. Inexperienced
    Mental picture
17. Ocean vessel
    Not yet
    acquainted
19. Observe
    Discuss again
21. Pack tightly
    Analyze
22. Oil derrick
    Chaney of films
24. Fad
    Dish
26. Fiddle
    Keep current
27. Draw forth
    Penniless
33. "Made in ___"
    Raffle
34. Botch things
    Tiny vegetable
35. Performing
    Building
38. Sales attempt
    Type of drum
39. Gauge
    Stately
41. Doctrine
    Frequently
43. Waistcoat
    Window ledge
44. Exclude
    Steed breed
46. Crate
    Flirt with

PUZZLE 466

• GLUED TO THE TUBE •

ACROSS

1. TV E.T.
4. Pro-am, e.g.
8. Canadian Indian
12. Blissful state
18. Aloha gift
19. "___ Zapata!"
20. Cultivated
21. Persist
22. Notice spot
25. Wears down
26. Aesop offering
27. Bruin legend
28. But
30. About
31. Fragrant bushes
33. Circular
35. Rough house
37. ___ acid
38. Artificial audio
40. Masterpiece
43. Not much
44. Place near
46. Style of dress
47. Token amount?
48. Grimm girl
50. Oxford fellows
51. Comprehensive work
52. Sanction
53. Rudolph of racing
57. Sycophant's reply
58. Quite a feast
59. Memo header
60. Chili addition
62. Call
63. "Mrs. Miniver" player
64. Military instructions
69. News newbie
72. Scorch
73. Drip
74. Yikes!
75. It makes the sun burn
78. Jaw
81. China's Chou ___
83. Vichy waters
84. Common contraction
85. Stud location
86. Reversals
88. Nice noggin
89. Jumble
90. Clerical helper
93. Edible kernel
95. Baglike structure
96. Knitting pattern
98. Gloomy, in literature
100. Concerning this point
102. Port-___
103. Indeed
104. Large family
106. Saturn's wife
108. Went first
109. Hedge component
110. Promising
112. Ad graphics
117. Turned away
118. Calla
119. Attach with hinges
120. Murmur softly
121. Thawed
122. Nil, in Seville
123. Orchestral tuner
124. Crucial

DOWN

1. Mass robe
2. Bucharest bread
3. DVD collection
4. Cold-weather wear
5. Hummus dippers
6. Terribly bad
7. Bobbsey twin
8. Rockette, e.g.
9. Thundered
10. Auction end
11. Vortex
12. Fan center
13. Straying
14. ___-garde
15. Arcade staple
16. Square
17. Catbird seat?
21. Silk substitutes
23. Bank deal
24. Horse pill
29. Fairies
31. Boyo
32. Think of
33. ___ Fighters
34. Prepared
36. Great service
38. Traditional editing device
39. Polar floater
41. Humorist Bombeck
42. Honey drink
45. Flock's perch?
47. Roll up
49. Paris summer
51. Chic hotels
52. Five-spot
54. Natural resin
55. Med. procedure
56. Miscellany
58. Walter Scott, e.g.
61. Past times
62. Bacchanal
64. Worn out
65. Balance part
66. See red?
67. Stimpy's pal
68. Md. neighbor
69. Upholstered chair
70. Remarkable
71. Batter's space
72. Theater
74. Atop, in verse
75. Greasy substances
76. Chemical fertilizer
77. Bolt cutter
78. Rapid rate
79. Main course?
80. Sanctify
82. Skater Midori ___
85. Like a duck
87. Deficiency
89. Wild, wild West
90. Tough situation
91. Practice exercise
92. Show piece?
94. Taste
96. Make up
97. Jewish law text
99. Hollywood's Julia
101. Former critic Roger ___
103. Horned mammal, briefly
104. Mine conveyance
105. Gad about
107. Skim
109. Striker's bane
111. Spread, as hay
113. Mouths
114. Pi's follower
115. Fish, at first
116. Trifle

PUZZLE 467

• HERO WORSHIP •

ACROSS
1. Bath powder
5. Hat material
9. Emulate Dr. Dre
12. General Bradley
13. Author James ___
14. United
15. Forest sight
16. Margot Kidder role
18. Nick and Nora's pet
20. Cook's aid
21. Erroneous
23. Slugger Willie ___
25. Invest. plan
26. Early man
28. PDQ's kin
32. Buddhism form
33. Heavy fabric
35. E.T. vessel
36. Goes the other way
38. Hamlet, e.g.
39. Omelet implement
40. Tiny bit
42. Reporter's question
44. Not these
47. Flag feature
48. George Reeves role
51. Wading bird
54. Pub quaff
55. Science series
56. Convergence points
57. Bled, as a color
58. Dance movement
59. Senate votes

DOWN
1. Better
2. Pierre's pal
3. Kristin Kreuk role
4. Salad ingredient
5. White House pet
6. ___ trip
7. Waikiki wear
8. On edge
9. Wander
10. Green Gables girl
11. Look closely
17. Homer's daughter
19. Blue-green
21. Bubbly water
22. Kind of code
23. Woman's title
24. Grace ending
27. Extinct bird
29. Gerard Christopher role
30. At a distance
31. Cornbread
34. Sort of salamander
37. Type of encl.
41. Coastal birds
43. Israeli port
44. Rasputin's ruler
45. Grass-skirt dance
46. Ready for business
47. Quick retort
49. Witty remark
50. Hail, Caesar
52. Cooler cooler
53. Bro's sib

PUZZLE 468

• INSTANT REPLAY •

ACROSS
1. Guy's date
4. Brahma worshiper
9. Hot under the collar
12. Hole in one
13. Dunkable treats
14. Tokyo, formerly
15. Racing implement
17. Golfer's gadget
18. Holm or McKellen
19. Always, in verse
21. Yellow pigment
24. Traveler's spot
28. Greek letter
29. Lassie and Benji
31. Wild ox
32. Nice water?
33. Lowland
35. Japanese accessory
36. Curly do
38. Balanced
39. Diameter measure
40. Debase
42. Prom goers
44. Tennis call
45. Step on it!
46. Oklahoma city
48. It may be punched
54. Ballet step
55. Cherish
56. Louis XIV, e.g.
57. QB's goals
58. Judicial togs
59. Hold title to

DOWN
1. Freon or neon
2. Behave
3. Sign of summer?
4. "___ End"
5. Persian Gulf land
6. Court divider
7. Bashful's pal
8. Seat finder
9. Rhythm marker
10. Picnic drink
11. Bambi's mom
16. Flaky dessert
20. Govt. agency
21. Mountain nymph
22. Irritate
23. Type of figure
24. Desert plant
25. Small landmass
26. Batman's sidekick
27. Coin side
30. Had creditors
34. Lures
37. Raw metal
41. Rose oil
43. Slithery fish
45. Roll-call reply
46. Suitable
47. Andy, to Opie
49. Chapel vow
50. Unruly bunch
51. Gold, in Spain
52. Milk source
53. Kith's companion

Instructions for solving Codeword puzzles are given on page 11.

1	14 H
2	15
3	16
4	17
5	18
6	19
7 I	20
8	21
9	22
10	23
11	24
12	25
13	26

Grid (Puzzle 469):

2	17	6	13	10		11		1	17	26	7	6
17		22		6	14 H	7 I	21	15		7		17
23	17	21	24	17		1		4	20	8	17	21
		7		25	14	7	10	16		20		
3	15	6	16					10	7	21	20	25
15				9	13	15	10	14		1		7
23	15	22	17	13		7		17	19	17	7	18
17		15		7	21	4	15	25				20
1	17	16	20	21				10	14	13	21	
	16		20	26	17	12	22		15			
2	5	7	4	4		26		20	21	19	17	22
15		21		4	7	15	21	15		17		20
18	17	24	8	15		4		5	20	6	13	1

A	N
B	O
C	P
D	Q
E	R
F	S
G	T
H̸	U
I̸	V
J	W
K	X
L	Y
M	Z

1	14
2	15
3	16
4	17
5	18
6	19
7	20
8	21
9 R	22
10	23
11 O	24
12	25
13	26

Grid (Puzzle 470):

2	13	18	8	22		12		11	9	21	13	18
11 O		13		15	19	18	23	17		23		3
9 R	8	6	21	19		19		23	20	20	8	13
20		23		16	19	20	1	7		23		20
22	19	9	14	19		4		23	15	24		
13				18	9	19	22			13		12
22	13	25	8	23				26	23	18	18	7
23		8			11	9	16	19				6
		13	9	14		11		5	23	20	11	6
12		16		20	8	1	10	23		13		23
22	23	14	11	23		23		15	13	16	13	18
19		23		15	19	20	19	13		2		9
20	11	20	23	18		18		20	23	23	1	7

A	N
B	O̸
C	P
D	Q
E	R̸
F	S
G	T
H	U
I	V
J	W
K	X
L	Y
M	Z

PUZZLE 471

ACROSS
1. Water jug
5. Impudent
9. Store transaction
13. Crucifix
14. Basic tenet
16. Mountain goat
17. Streetcar
18. Frighten
19. Word in a threat
20. Highway vehicle
21. Anglo-Saxon peon
22. Catches
23. Inclined walk
26. Equivalent
28. Originated
31. Malt kiln
34. Impassive
35. Village's kin
37. Not him
39. Frat letters
40. Recycle
42. Alluring
43. Ditty
44. Export
45. Form a thought
47. Dollar component
49. Cairn and kin
51. Ogler
53. Lyrical verses
54. Patsies
57. Blow gently
59. Moreover
63. Egress
64. Elaborate display
66. Feral
67. Nerve network
68. Express
69. ____ out a living
70. Winged
71. Fleche weapon
72. Moistens, poetically

DOWN
1. Food scraps
2. Folk knowledge
3. Garden soil
4. Navy officers
5. Dads
6. Excluding
7. Inlets
8. Wind-storms
9. Reddish-brown pigment
10. Partner of ready and willing
11. For fear that
12. 24th letters
15. Humbly docile
24. Black bird
25. Mexican mother
27. Electrically-charged particle
28. Rule of conduct
29. Silk fabric
30. Musical composition
32. Clip sheep
33. Writings
34. Bath, e.g.
36. Strange
38. Ham on ____
41. Post-intermission overture
42. Vacillated
44. Dirty place
46. Game cube
48. Many a bird
50. Turn
52. Certain sheep
54. Antitoxins
55. Figure-skating jump
56. Flat bread
58. Flutter
60. Enjoy
61. Destroyed
62. Tout's numbers
65. To a ____

PUZZLE 472   Carry-Overs

Add and subtract letters from the ROOT WORDS to form answers to the CLUES. Start with the first ROOT WORD, subtract one letter, and rearrange the remaining letters to form the answer to the first CLUE. Carry over the letter you subtracted to the next line, add it to the second ROOT WORD, subtract the number of letters indicated, and rearrange the remaining letters to form the second answer. Continue solving in this way.

	ROOT WORDS		CLUES
1.	ABSENT	- 1 = _____	Sew loosely
2.	□ + STRIPE	- 2 = _____	Publish
3.	□ □ + PLAIN	- 2 = _____	Walkway
4.	□ □ + CASTLE	- 3 = _____	Asian land
5.	□ □ □ + TONE	- 0 = _____	Challenge

PUZZLE 473

•TEAM COLORS•

ACROSS

1. Rickey ingredient
5. Musician Artie ___
9. Humid
13. "___ in Calico"
17. March 15, e.g.
18. Film plantation
19. Daredevil Knievel
20. Marie Wilson role
21. Helena's st.
22. Actress Moran
23. Bristle
24. Hollow plant
25. Depressed marauders
28. Allowance
30. Actor Mineo
31. Lively dance
33. Type of collar
34. The Greatest
37. Famous loch
40. Oil container
42. General Rommel
45. Mesh fabric
46. Pitfalls
48. Short cut?
50. Darnel
51. Hull feature
53. List of candidates
55. Recognize
57. Through
58. Galahad's garb
60. Coral reef
62. Hate
64. Gilded ground squirrels
68. Select
71. Two under par
72. Studio stand
76. Paddle
77. Birthright peddler
80. Drizzles
82. Italian city
83. Woeful word
85. Tangy
87. Franco and Peter
89. Kildare's org.
90. Conviction
92. Taj Mahal site
94. Gossip
95. Launch or lily ___
96. Smooth-talking
98. Hibernia
100. Subway alternative
102. Outstanding
105. Scarlet current
111. Shiny cloth
112. Chore
114. Elevator direction
115. At a loss
116. Cake finisher
117. Arena shape
118. Author Hunter
119. Camera's eye
120. Loads
121. Diamond number
122. Lacoste of tennis
123. Etta ___ of comics

DOWN

1. Arm or leg
2. Admired person
3. Waiter's handout
4. Mr. Kefauver
5. Robbers
6. Mata ___
7. Like the Gobi
8. Baseballer Paul ___
9. Final course
10. St. or rd.
11. Queens nine
12. Shallow dish
13. Heathrow, e.g.
14. Emerald greeting
15. Pulpit word
16. Diane or Cheryl
26. Bellow
27. Kind of wine
29. Native suffix
32. Skulk
34. Singer Paul ___
35. Smirk
36. Dating couple
38. Light lunch
39. Outburst
41. 60 secs.
43. Garden bloom
44. Like a pin
47. Slingshot ammo
49. Fashion
52. Company emblem
54. English composer
56. "The Way We ___"
59. Thorny flower
61. Michael York role
63. Russian monarch
65. For fear that
66. Worked at
67. Painter Matisse
68. Layer
69. Hearty's partner
70. Citrus fellows
73. Hotel freebie
74. Austen novel
75. Clue
78. Driver's org.
79. Egg on
81. Paris school
84. Retailers
86. Drip slowly
88. Confound
91. Sesame plant
93. Schedule abbr.
97. Wand
99. Pillow filler
101. Celery serving
102. Skirt feature
103. Tortilla snack
104. Sitarist Shankar
106. Shake a leg
107. Water bird
108. Got it!
109. Bumper blemish
110. Dawn's direction
113. Jose or Juan

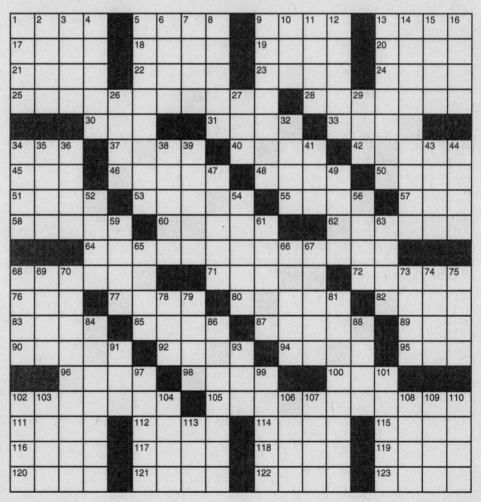

PUZZLE 474

• MEETING PLACE •

ACROSS

1. Alcohol-awareness gp.
5. Netman Smith
9. Illegal scheme
13. Christiania, today
17. Peerless person
18. Type of cotton
19. Fast-food entree
20. Compost item
21. Carolina rail
22. Tarbell and Wells
23. Cote females
24. Bibliography abbr.
25. Boss Tweed's organization
28. "My ___" (hit by The Knack)
30. Certain magazine pages
31. Dancer Montez
33. Panache
34. Punch
37. Surmounting
40. Willing
42. Dumas hero
45. ___ of Tranquility
46. German misters
48. Jim ___ of the Red Sox
50. Icicle hanger
51. Religious journey
53. Uproarious events
55. Pharmacist's concern
57. Canon
58. Bestow
60. Cyberspace service
62. Crosby, ___ & Nash
64. Palace of Versailles room
68. Bearing
71. Offensive move
72. Cartoon character Fudd
76. Osprey's kin
77. Redolence
80. Brazilian port
82. German article
83. Ginger portrayer
85. Burnoose wearer
87. Biblical mountain
89. "A Spy in the House of Love" writer
90. Wrong
92. Presentiment
94. Thessalian peak
95. Banned insecticide
96. British school
98. ___-eyed
100. Snorkel, e.g.
102. Savant
105. Talk-show host
111. Rime
112. Deice
114. Bed support
115. Lover of Rose
116. "___ Need Is the Girl"
117. Newswoman Magnus
118. Military clerk
119. Scope or graph starter
120. Black-tie affair
121. Molly ___ (Blair Brown role)
122. Vintage
123. Polaris, e.g.

DOWN

1. "Happy Days" actor
2. Sulawesi ox
3. Prefix meaning skin
4. Inge forte
5. Like Emily Dickinson
6. Antimacassar
7. Far East nanny
8. Twangy
9. Outstanding
10. Crow's comment
11. "Easy ___" (radio program)
12. Arens or Dayan
13. Perform surgery
14. New Jersey university
15. Director David ___
16. Louisiana town
26. Esau's wife
27. Fireplace fuel
29. Wing
32. In the thick of
34. Connors's nemesis
35. Stop gradually
36. "Charlie's Angels" actress
38. Cantilevered winder
39. Introductory hoopla
41. "Foucault's Pendulum" author
43. Cameo shape, often
44. Makes clothes
47. ". . . and thy ___ they comfort me."
49. It, to Enrico
52. ___ Dory (marine fish)
54. "Barefoot in the Park" playwright
56. French I verb
59. Steve Martin's birthplace
61. Former Maltese money
63. Bali Ha'i, for example
65. Clytemnestra's mother
66. Percentage
67. "___ Daughter"
68. Bristle
69. Barbershop request
70. 1977 Oscar-winning film
73. Intellect
74. Tennyson heroine
75. "La Boheme" update
78. ___ y plata
79. Pro-football team
81. Tom Selleck movie
84. Queens section
86. Overdue
88. Emilia's husband
91. Fa follower
93. Scan. nation
97. Appointed
99. Emerson output
101. "___ Life"
102. Certain hairstyle
103. Tropical nut
104. Renovate
106. Composer Siegmeister
107. Nil, in Seville
108. Help on a heist
109. Ms. Kedrova
110. Sidelong glance
113. Removable cover

PUZZLE 475

• NAME DROPPING •

ACROSS

1. Arctic
6. Manor lands
12. Madras mister
15. Friend, in Barcelona
16. Petty officer
17. Boy without a shadow
18. Soupy's gathering?
20. Sagittarius, e.g.
24. ___ Na Na
25. Hollandaise ingredients
26. Like the White Rabbit
28. "___ Maria"
29. Per
31. French preposition
32. Thumbs through
34. Faux pas
35. Yeah, right!
37. Risky feat
38. Currency
39. Chum
40. Lowed
41. Casino town
42. Delicate
45. Chessmen
46. Excavated
47. Sizzle
50. That's a laugh
51. Free-for-all
52. Pueblo Indian
53. Adversary
54. From ___ Z
55. Anita's twelve?
57. Simile center
58. Sea dog
59. Stirs
60. Cone home
61. Throw off
62. Swift jet, once
63. Wrath
64. Diaphanous
65. Handwriting on the wall
66. Position
68. Companies
69. Baby beagle
70. Chips in?
72. Recital pieces
73. Hurry
74. A way out
75. Pointer
76. O'Hare est.
77. Thanksgiving side
81. Patriotic org.
82. Botanical balm
83. Seen better days
85. Mr. Gehrig
86. Least gregarious
88. Forecast from Gale?
92. Roman road
93. Cleans up
94. Seasonal visitor
95. Musical aptitude
96. Quick as a wink
97. Moslem prince

DOWN

1. Old hat
2. D-Day beach
3. Fragrant flower
4. Epoch
5. Optimistic
6. Embroidery trim
7. Tries to find
8. Wee ones
9. Parisian buddy
10. Prepare hides
11. United Kingdom division
12. Outdated footwear
13. Steak order
14. Letterhead abbr.
19. Poser
21. Arsenio?
22. Wickedness
23. D.C. figures
27. Hill insect
30. St. Augustine's home
32. Sharon's pitch?
33. Stage signals
34. Trespass
36. ___ of Pigs
37. Johnny Appleseed, e.g.
38. Start
40. Men
41. Indian coin
42. "___ My Line?"
43. Tiniest bits
44. Novel by Martin?
45. Black tea
46. Earthmover, for short
48. Violin treatment
49. "The Second Coming" poet
51. Juan's mom
52. They may be high
55. Entices
56. Regards
61. Void
64. Farm building
65. "___ Town"
67. Noun suffix
68. Timberlands
69. Winter jacket
70. Tacks on
71. Ham's father
72. B'way sign
73. Ready for bed
75. Rite field?
76. Outfitted
78. Set straight
79. Cassino or Carlo
80. Glucose
82. Tibet locale
83. Party spread
84. Irish
87. Night before
89. Hint
90. Shelley offering
91. Viet ___

415

PUZZLE 476

CRYPTIC CROSSWORD

British-style or Cryptic Crosswords are a great challenge for crossword fans. Each clue contains either a definition or direct reference to the answer as well as a play on words. The numbers in parentheses indicate the number of letters in the answer words.

ACROSS

1. Croatian intially seems like a very interesting character (6)
4. Totaled auto—mend on the move (8)
9. Guide at Everest hides dream (6)
10. Given to studying city Lana flips over (8)
12. Rashly, I banned key ingredient of chili (6,4)
13. Drop from eye laceration (4)
15. Quarrel made steering clumsy (12)
19. An angel's duly playing New Year's tune (4,4,4)
22. Single large A (4)
23. Crafters' Haven carries mens' accessory (10)
26. Note in oboe upset Dancer, e.g. (8)
27. Island language of Southeast Asia packs a wallop (6)
28. No way French marshal takes Florida athlete (8)
29. Business log annually features motto (6)

DOWN

1. Like glue or like a twig? (6)
2. Silver butt and a slate (6)
3. Stupidly, I'd ply niter without fear (10)
5. Essence of Romanians' frenzy (5)
6. Sad-looking fruit, by the sound of it (4)
7. Theodore has that place all tied up (8)
8. Tack a medal on knockout to speak audibly (8)
11. Get boat in another way (6)
14. Bill's net, an odd bit of court equipment (6,4)
16. Phosphorus settles, showing an autumnal hue (6)
17. An old cur upset kettle (8)
18. Tribe ruler making noises with chains (8)
20. Wide-open joke about wrestler's goal (6)
21. Lousy singer quit (6)
24. Refer to Eddy with more liberty (5)
25. Revise new diet (4)

To receive a free copy of our guide, "How to Solve Cryptic Crosswords," send a self-addressed, business-sized, stamped envelope to Cryptic Clues, Penny Press, 6 Prowitt Street, Norwalk, CT 06855-1220 or visit the Puzzler's Corner section of our website at PennyDellPuzzles.com.

PUZZLE 477

• DUDS •

ACROSS
1. Bindle stiff
5. Freud colleague
10. Avoided a tag
14. Virgule
19. Made one's point?
20. Three-wheeler
21. Ponderosa, e.g.
22. Forbidden
23. Off-the-rack apparel
25. Ballet-class wear
27. Greek consonant
28. Uh-oh!
29. Yours, once
31. Roof ends
32. Excite
34. Academic
35. Influences
37. Pismire
38. Waterproof cover
39. Condition
40. Andy Capp's wife
43. Wounded
46. Unfamiliar
48. Of national government
50. Promise
51. Cuts with a scalloped edge
52. Beginnings
54. Market
55. Biblical Syria
56. 'Tis a pity!
57. Exaltation members
58. Serenity
59. Mountain-to-be?
61. Cloaks
62. Long
63. Say it ain't so
64. Predicated
65. Doughnuts
66. Protective group
69. Germinated grains
70. Maturity
74. Eats
75. Tumbles
76. Man from Gdansk
77. Rubberneck
78. Something to spin
79. Move furtively
80. Went on and on
81. Enlarged
82. Take for granted
84. Clung
86. Duck milieus
87. Spread for drying
88. Potato concoction
90. Makes a scene?
91. Adage

92. Whey accompaniment
93. Vichy very
94. Italian desserts
98. British royal name
101. Gashes
103. Suffers
104. Forbid
105. Informal semiformal attire
107. Go-to-meeting threads
110. Total
111. Spoken
112. Record
113. Manipulator
114. Merchandise
115. Parisian pop
116. Butter factory
117. Stout's Wolfe

DOWN
1. Western writer
2. Raft
3. Humdinger
4. Queer
5. As a maximum
6. Hang loosely
7. Caps and tams
8. Scratch (out)
9. Rejuvenates
10. Hit the road
11. Creditor's claim
12. Consume

13. Early condensation
14. Deviated
15. Sheepish types
16. Explorer Tasman
17. Put out
18. "Bonanza" offspring
24. Juvenile
26. Shooting marbles
30. Arizona Indian
33. Sibling's inheritance
34. Signature substitutes
36. Floats
38. Having a musical key
39. Slept noisily
40. Have a cow
41. Knight stick?
42. More venerable
43. Took a dip
44. Corrida performer
45. River to the Caspian
46. Paddock youngster
47. Sour fruit?
49. Fancy dress
51. Put on a coat?
53. Authorizes
57. Endures
58. Whittle
60. For the lady
61. Gave a ring
62. Kept the faith
64. Love song
65. Like a mosaic
66. Copt's domain
67. Entrap
68. Had feelings
69. Deranged
70. Wanders about
71. Deserve
72. Exceeded the limit
73. Sutures
75. Area of expertise
76. Components
79. Know-it-all
80. Set back
83. Loan sharks
85. Stag
86. Violet variety
89. Guarantee
91. Emolument
92. Encrusted
93. Pugilist's pursuit
94. Sweet or hard drink
95. Corpulent
96. Beam acronym
97. Preface
98. Self-satisfied
99. Oz pooch
100. Till
102. Makeup artist?
103. Oppositionist
106. Soak (up)
108. Movies' Merkel
109. Roll

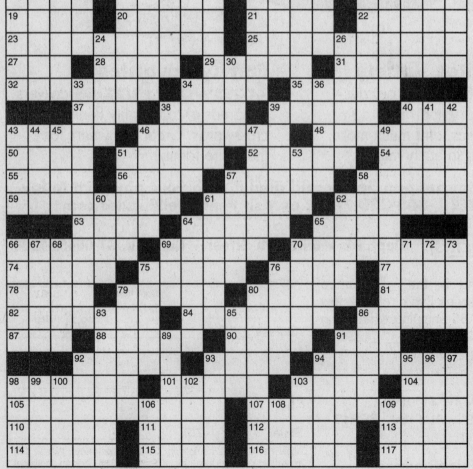

ACROSS

1. Truman's birthplace
6. Lull, mostly
10. Indonesian isle
14. Food fish
19. Fleet of foot
20. Tide phase
21. Muscat's land
22. Court story
23. Not in order
25. Expel
26. Bye!
27. Spotted
28. That guy's
29. Attract attention
32. They're not there
35. Albanian cash
36. Little rascal
37. Louse
40. Small colonist
41. Curved molding
43. Dean's partner
45. Commuter's egress
49. Sharply
51. Jolt
52. Cashew tree
54. Tokyo closer
55. Barely enough
56. Retire
58. Poet Charles ____
60. Speaker's platform
61. Frosh, finally
62. Bolted
63. Already adjusted
64. Big deal
65. Mr. Preminger
66. Family group
68. Designer Karan
69. Cooped-up female?
70. Labor action
73. ATM maker
76. Camera conveyance
78. Roughly wrought
79. Place
80. Casino cube
81. Even if
83. More for Maria
84. Fixes
85. Sicily sight
86. First and third, e.g.
87. Agent's refuge
90. Aligns
91. Ad ____
92. Spirit
94. Holiday season
95. Dynamic start
96. Does something appealing?
98. Caustic stuff
99. Father
100. Is for two?
101. Indian bread
102. Ballet step
104. Mover's ride
105. Overhaul
108. Friction easers
114. Denials
115. MacGraw et al.
119. It's spam a lot
120. Cross
121. Quite dark
124. Neck vestment
125. Festive
126. Thought of France
127. Metal mix
128. Copier solution
129. Grad exam
130. Pucker-producing
131. Together

DOWN

1. Vientiane's locale
2. Flu symptom
3. Bit
4. Beside
5. KO counter
6. Volunteer
7. Minimum
8. Resinous substance
9. Line of wk.
10. Tiny shoe
11. Frenzied
12. Tie
13. Division word
14. Oregon city
15. Grips
16. Customary practice
17. Do as you're told
18. Terrible
24. Artificial
30. Hebrew letter
31. Spanish girl
33. Cease
34. Bridge position
37. Algerian district
38. Submit
39. Large rattler
42. Clock-setting std.
43. San ____
44. Ms. Tan
46. Sleep poorly
47. AKA hautboy
48. Ale selection
50. "CSI" evidence
51. Two-legged support
52. Will not
53. Eye piece?
56. Angrily
57. Rub off
59. Writer Deighton
61. Height enhancer
63. Nudges
65. Studious-looking
66. Movement
67. Inc., abroad
68. Sad song
71. Ship
72. Rear
74. Movies
75. Conclude
77. Done, to Donne
81. Turkish title
82. Tolstoy et el.
83. Mature filly
84. Sovereign
85. Afore
87. Announce
88. Rushing
89. Your and my
90. Those people
93. Further
95. Criticize
97. Unite
99. Summer wear
100. Wading bird
103. Fitter
104. Stringed instrument
106. Record
107. Becomes tiresome
108. Drummer's concern
109. S.W.A.T. need
110. Reclined
111. Legendary vessel
112. Din
113. Sputter
116. Film composer Schifrin
117. Desktop picture
118. Part of the Hebrides
122. Director Lupino
123. Sheepish greeting

PUZZLE 479

CLAPBOARD

In this crossword puzzle all words in the same row or column overlap by one or two letters.

ACROSS

1. Gypsy dance
8. Egg entree
14. Peru's capital
15. Imitators
16. Prom goer
17. Love, for Luigi
18. Writer Jong
19. Make right
21. Sulked
24. Good buy
25. Communist hero
27. Evergreen shrub
28. Blooper
31. Author Ayn ___
33. Space explorer
35. Present time
37. Italian farewell
38. Smells
41. Locale
43. Cain's mother
44. Snag
45. French heads
46. Prophet
47. Of an age
50. Bird's abode
53. ___ kwon do
54. Oklahoma city
55. Amusing
56. Foreigners
58. Step
60. Chest rattle
61. Rival
62. Oarsman
63. Sudden assault
64. Flop
66. Borders
67. French philosopher
68. The Emerald Isle
69. Kernel
70. Obtuse
71. "Jane ___"
72. Film holder

DOWN

1. Pancake
2. Luxury ride
3. Sum
4. Bazaar
5. Fencing sword
6. Dweeb
7. Town ___
8. Academy Award
9. Feast
10. Go in
11. Wild cat
12. Timespan
13. Hip
20. Columbus ship
22. Novice
23. Lyric verse
24. Indicates
25. City parcel
26. Advocate Ralph ___
29. Unique
30. Tsar's realm
31. Way to learn
32. Of ships
34. New Mexico city
35. Equal
36. Shouted
38. Frisky swimmer
39. College bigwig
40. Tenants
42. Scottie, e.g.
44. Scalawags
48. Band crew member
49. Enchantment
51. Pass over
52. Blockade
55. Journal
57. Scents organ
58. "___ Lake"
59. Comic Johnson
62. Crimson
65. Singer Shannon

1	2	3	4	5	6	7	8	9	10	11	12	13
14			15				16					
17			18			19			20			
21		22	23	24		25		26				
27			28	29	30		31		32			
33	34				35					36		
37		38	39		40	41		42	43			
44		45			46		47	48	49			
50	51	52	53		54		55					
56			57	58		59	60					
61		62			63			64		65		
66		67			68							
69		70		71		72						

ACROSS

1. "___ and the Swan"
5. TV's Lansbury
11. Islet
14. Turkish title
18. A Baldwin
19. Painted
20. Touched ground
22. Ms. Horne
23. Wharf
24. Like a mosaic
25. Pocket-size book
27. Child's plaything
29. Sci-fi transports
31. Pacify
32. Feels sick
33. Stretch
34. Stash
35. Polluted
38. Boors
40. Lure
41. Embrace
44. Whets
45. Home movie
46. Delivers by post
47. Kimono closer
48. Feat
49. Hunter's wear
50. Stale
51. Oaf
52. Greek letter
53. Picnic dish
56. Beseech
57. Daily deliverer
59. Intense beam
60. Warm and cozy
61. ___-et-Cher
62. Clubs and spades
63. Indian garment
64. Fall
67. English Channel feeder
68. Disposable tumbler
72. Tacks
73. Ineffectual person
75. One, in Glasgow
76. French priest
77. Daggers
79. Singer Burl ___
80. Recipe qty.
81. Mr. Mineo
82. Feathered talkers
83. Fervor
85. Doze
87. Compass pt.
88. Garcia or Gibb
89. Peaceful
90. Covered with calcite
91. Approve
92. Oompah horn
93. Ignore
94. Startles
97. Sweetheart
98. Office item
103. Flimsy
105. More genuine
107. Ireland
108. ___ Major
109. Vocalist Ono
110. Badgerer
111. Italian capital
112. Stained
113. Berlin's lang.
114. Constant
115. Brittle cookie

DOWN

1. Certain Scandinavian
2. Director Kazan
3. Profound
4. Land
5. Tartly
6. Taboos
7. Impudence
8. List ender: abbr.
9. Luau welcome
10. Signify
11. Tender chicken
12. Oh, woe!
13. Kennel sound
14. Jostle
15. Pork or lamb
16. Yardstick unit
17. Gather leaves
21. Irritably
26. Haley novel
28. Equips
30. Musical notes
33. Author Grafton
34. Declared
35. Keen
36. Coffee flavor
37. "___ of Old Smoky"
38. British sailor
39. Aroma
40. Farm machine
41. Pits
42. WWII craft
43. Silly
45. Mist
46. Specks
49. Bungalow
50. Learn well
51. Debussy's "___ de Lune"
53. High-school balls
54. Fattens
55. Likes, in Paris
56. Attentive reader
58. Avoid capture
60. Records
62. Marinates
63. Wiser
64. Demean
65. Citified
66. Dining surface
67. Spatter
68. Swivel
69. Supply food for
70. NASCAR's Al ___
71. Energetic
74. Ocean movement
77. Long-ruling family
78. ___ 500
82. Inventor
83. Hair colors
84. Estuary
85. Provoke
86. Cavalry soldiers
89. As being
90. Fortified wine
91. Mountain deity
92. Male voice
93. Zoom
94. Tater
95. Grant of films
96. Cathedral part
97. Cycle
98. Hotel employee
99. Plankton
100. Detroit athlete
101. "My Friend ___"
102. Chirp
104. Sty dweller
106. Graze

PUZZLE 481

SINGLE SYLLABLE

ACROSS

1. Small newt
4. ___ Lanka
7. Furthermore
11. Barrier
15. Harvest crops
17. Glance at
18. Similar
19. Actress Shawkat
20. Extended, single syllable
22. Foraged, single syllable
24. Bar
25. "___ the One"
27. ___, set, go!
28. Over
30. Welcomes
32. Stockpile
36. Chicago airport
38. Glided
43. Defraud
44. Region
45. Reporter's query
46. Cougar
47. Not rich
48. Dispatch
49. Easy as ___
50. Mischievous
51. Prowled
53. Warp
54. Terra ___
55. Comfy shirt
56. Honks
58. Picasso work
59. Compassion
62. Angry
63. Removed cornhusks
67. Asian nannies
68. Sine ___ non
69. Makes a choice
71. Lease
72. Minstrel's item
73. However
74. ___-di (Beatles' lyric)
75. Aladdin's pal
76. Louis Kahn's middle name
78. Foreign farewell
79. Milk giver
80. King's home
82. Not for
84. Apart
88. Crunchy
90. Tapioca's source
95. Crumpled, single syllable
97. Carried, single syllable
99. Apple, e.g.
100. Repair
101. Track down
102. Sasquatch's cousin
103. Smack
104. Leisurely
105. TV's Koppel
106. Period

DOWN

1. Formerly, formerly
2. Greek cheese
3. Canvas cover
4. Chatted, single syllable
5. "Norma ___"
6. ___ 500
7. Promise
8. Dough
9. Screamed, single syllable
10. Surprised cry
11. Diminish
12. Pond growth
13. Fibbed
14. ___ Godiva
16. Part of mpg
17. He gets away free?
21. Brown bread
23. ___ Major
26. Fairy-tale beast
29. Sound unit
31. Moreover
32. Current measures
33. Atomic particle
34. Burn reliever
35. Itched, single syllable
37. Plus
39. Stained, single syllable
40. Cluster
41. Release
42. Comic Carvey
45. Breaks the tape
48. View
49. Verve
50. Neutral hue
52. Clock winders
53. Good grade
56. Prizefight

57. Historic epoch

58. Relieved sounds

59. African nation

60. Flightless birds

61. Pro ___

62. Silenced, single syllable

63. Stopped, single syllable

64. Humane

65. Great lake

66. Doe

69. Kimono closer

70. Not guilty, e.g.

73. Swimsuit part

74. Shelley works

75. Appearance

77. Store sign

78. With sourness

81. Spatial

83. Chatter

84. Deadly snakes

85. Freight barge

86. Marie Wilson role

87. Opera song

89. Attention getter

91. Eavesdrop

92. Copied

93. Turn down

94. Mine entrance

96. Greek letter

98. High note

PUZZLE 481

PUZZLE 482

ACROSS

1. Large ponds
6. Wash out
10. Pack
14. "Aida," e.g.
15. Eons
16. Genuine
17. Played over
18. Jars
19. West's opposite
20. Goof
21. At a standstill
23. Incidents
25. Declare
26. Bites
27. Lotions
29. Polar sight
30. Round vegetable
33. Scissors
34. Sorrow
35. Getaway
36. Excellent
37. Cage
38. Captivate
40. Unwell
41. Baptize
42. Quickly
43. Dessert choice
44. Healthy
45. Affluence
46. Tribe
48. Track
49. Harmonize
51. Toil
52. Vat
55. Burrow
56. Jacob, to Esau
58. Intermission
60. Herbal healer
61. Zest
62. Possessed
63. "You ___ Me"
64. Former spouses
65. Crocodile ___

DOWN

1. Fables
2. Imitator
3. "Quo Vadis?" actress
4. Pitching stat
5. Clean
6. Imperfections
7. Come to terms
8. Rumpus room
9. Fragrance
10. Sheer
11. Repot
12. Banish
13. Drenches
22. Beaver barriers
24. Contend
25. Couch
27. Texas dish
28. Thought
29. Electrified atom
31. Home planet
32. Munitions, for short
33. Prune
34. Spider's parlor
37. Situate
38. Eccentric
39. Breach
41. House's alcove
42. Prickly ___
44. Enthusiast
45. Injustices
47. Attracted
48. Cord
49. Mournful sigh
50. Parable
52. Albacore
53. ___-friendly
54. River bottoms
57. Floor-shiner
59. Astound

ACROSS

1. Poise
5. Complain
9. Inner man
13. Empty
14. Condor's habitat
16. Roundish
17. Right to property
18. Winter rain
19. Office note
20. Oolong
21. Shoat's pad
22. Protection
24. Frozen asset?
26. Wordy birdie
27. Compromise
29. Arts' partner
34. Mumble
37. Edible root
38. Noble
39. Instances
41. Family room
43. "Hamlet," e.g.
44. Wards off
46. Pecan, e.g.
48. Hymn ending
49. Hound variety
50. Robe material
52. Banco deposit
54. Evicted
58. Cutting tool
62. Entirety
63. Fashion
64. Space
65. Shish ___
67. Come about
68. Revolt
69. Decay
70. "Happy Birthday" writer
71. Sound
72. Fable
73. Hardens

DOWN

1. Leans
2. Good-bye
3. Neat
4. X
5. Command
6. Nothing more than
7. Citrus quencher
8. In want
9. Not all
10. Constant
11. Felonious flights
12. Berg
15. Foul odor
21. Sink or bend
23. Managed
25. Riskers
26. Souvenir
28. Lobe's place
30. Places in order
31. Bubbles
32. 4:02, e.g.
33. Flip through
34. Picket-line crosser
35. Hot stuff
36. Applies
40. Paces
42. Stage prompt
45. Sirloins
47. Misfortune
51. Daiquiri liquor
53. Brushed
55. More than once
56. Art stand
57. Tinters
58. Prison-cell decor
59. Diva's highlight
60. Bright sign
61. Court
62. Jib, e.g.
66. Feather stole
67. Apparatus

PUZZLE 484

ACROSS

1. Chin hair
6. Copycats
10. Boutique
14. Repeat
15. Scat!
16. Inlet
17. Smell
18. Abrasive tool
20. ___ Lancelot
21. Joy
23. Observant
24. Egg producer
25. "Ice ___"
26. Elderly
27. Leg bone
29. Incredible
33. Packed down
36. Clip
37. Stir-fry vessel
38. Says yes
39. Request
40. Crack
42. Mend
43. Consume
44. Prejudiced
45. Unvarying
48. Pillage
49. Rowing blade
50. Quaker pronoun
51. Buzzer
54. Tennis, e.g.
57. Phantom
59. Manta ___
60. More mischievous
62. Wipe clean
64. Initial bet
65. Other than
66. Reduce
67. Nuisance
68. Lime drinks
69. ___ a hand

DOWN

1. Cheeky
2. Spooky
3. Tree nut
4. Island drink
5. Dreary
6. Appoint
7. Aspect
8. Vast times
9. Turf unit
10. Burns with water
11. Ms. Lange
12. Above
13. Perky
19. Whiten
22. Placed down
26. Have title to
27. Agent
28. "___ So Fine"
29. Help
30. Night birds
31. Budge
32. Barely earned
33. Bean curd
34. Related
35. Long skirt
36. Deep hole
39. Dull thud
40. Attack!
41. Mighty tree
43. Misstep
44. Inlets
46. Misplace
47. Vow
48. Coasts
50. The ones here
51. Muscle
52. Soothed
53. Watchers
54. Cinch
55. Glass unit
56. Not ins
57. Coat with gold
58. Inform
61. Pekoe, e.g.
63. Shad ___

ACROSS

1. Insulting
6. Buck
10. Reach
14. Telegrams
15. Ear part
16. To boot
17. Healing herbs
18. Atop
19. Favorites
20. Twist
21. Small stones
23. Who —— you?
24. Bashful
26. None
27. Blue
28. Hole punch
31. Electric unit
33. Narrow lane
35. Frothy
37. Tiny
40. Fast-food order
41. Dugout
42. Flat
46. Thin
48. Ambition
49. Call on
51. Snoop
53. Greeted
54. —— and tonic
55. Caustic liquids
58. Table part
60. Curve
61. Hypothesis
63. Batters
67. Store
69. Formal solo
70. Coat fold
71. Mountain cat
72. Tiger ——
73. Soap ——
74. Grain
75. Fewer
76. French hat

DOWN

1. Mop
2. Egypt's river
3. Wrought ——
4. Actions
5. Double curve
6. Garble
7. November gem
8. Higher than
9. Produce
10. Fool
11. Gladden
12. Off course
13. Nuzzled
21. Health club
22. Laze around
25. Fodder
28. Astern
29. Romance
30. Linger
32. Agenda
34. Rude look
36. Peat ——
38. Rural hotel
39. Playthings
41. Mayor's office
43. Vigor
44. Adam's wife
45. Profit
47. Scot's skirt
48. Hue
49. Moral excellence
50. Earnings
52. Fabric layer
54. Pants
56. Uncanny
57. Dirties
59. Vine fruit
62. Light beams
64. Mimicker
65. Simple
66. Blind part
68. Gob
70. Soft toss

PUZZLE 485

PUZZLE 486

ACROSS
1. Fodder
6. Adds to
10. Faux ___
13. Australian marsupials
15. Dalai ___
16. Earlier than, to Keats
17. Eat
18. Snail's cousin
19. Promptly
20. Actress Sandra ___
21. Tent
23. Flavoring seed
25. Bigfoot's kin
26. Cold tea
27. Place
30. Beanie, e.g.
33. Ring legend
34. Certain fly
37. Arm, e.g.
39. Drain-clearer chemical
42. Everything
43. Raised flatland
45. Far down
46. Seventh letter
47. Pond plant
48. Pitcher's goal
50. Entirety
52. Goof
54. Dollars
55. Bag
57. Recently
60. Burn balms
62. Fiend
64. Tarzan's chum
67. Chop
68. Utilized
70. Filched
72. Go to court
73. Honey drink
74. Manhattan square
75. Clio winners
76. Grand Ole ___
77. Reposes

DOWN
1. Slip
2. Mood
3. Have a fit
4. Capp's order
5. Refuse
6. Other than
7. Cabbage's kin
8. Ostrich's cousin
9. Long story
10. Antibiotic
11. Came up
12. Stitched
14. Editor's mark
22. Snapshot
24. Zip
25. Nevertheless
27. Buck
28. Small landmass
29. Stargazers' tools
31. Church table
32. Apple dessert
33. Touch against
35. Junk e-mail
36. Gym wing
38. More, to Pedro
40. Ox's harness
41. Woolly moms
44. Ripen
49. Oar
51. Hilo strings
53. Run into
55. Spicy dip
56. Audible
58. Snack
59. Sign up
61. Japanese wrestling
62. Darling
63. Duane ___
64. Woeful cry
65. Hide
66. Stops
69. Fall month
71. Mine load

FLOWER POWER

The answers to this petaled puzzle will go in a curve from the number on the outside to the center of the flower. Each number in the flower will have two 5-letter answers. One goes in a clockwise direction and the second in a counterclockwise direction. We have entered two answers to help you begin.

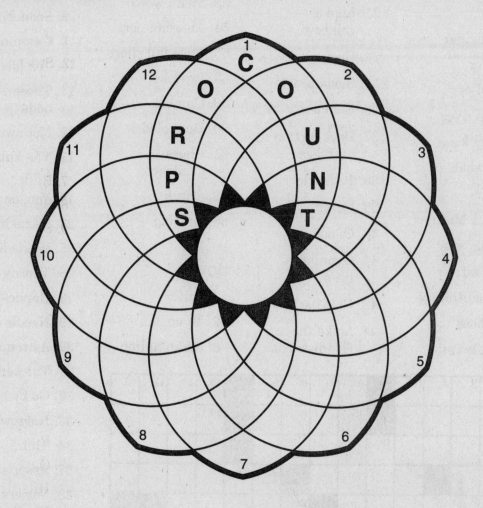

CLOCKWISE	COUNTERCLOCKWISE
1. Dracula, e.g.	1. Unit of soldiers
2. Like fresh lettuce	2. Cuban line dance
3. Moon period	3. Overly modest one
4. Arrive at	4. Thick-skinned animal, briefly
5. Explosion	5. "Beauty and the ___"
6. Cohort	6. Necklace part
7. Body organ	7. Prayer before meals
8. Clipped, as sheep	8. Walk through water
9. Utter confusion	9. Repeat rhythmically
10. Dad	10. Bogus
11. Flat-bottomed vessel	11. Room and ___
12. Certain apartment	12. Roasting fowl

PUZZLE 488

DISTANCE DENOTED

ACROSS

1. Tag
6. Commoner
10. Louver
14. Small egg
15. Swiss river
16. Merry king
17. Improbable
19. Lulu
20. Singer McGraw
21. "Mask" star
22. Park officer
24. Spread thickly
26. Boo-boos
27. Female ruff
28. Spattered
31. Like a rainbow
34. Casino's decoy
35. Sioux brave
36. Gold leaf
37. Does certain exercises
38. Bedazzle
39. Furor
40. Of soil
41. Gymnast's need
42. Gets back to
44. Make the ___ fly (disturb)
45. Tickle pink
46. Party giver
50. Half a score
52. Section
53. Menu word
54. Algerian port
55. They fall short
58. Provoke
59. Gamble
60. Duel blades
61. Cheesy sandwich
62. Check
63. Grating

DOWN

1. Attics
2. To no ___
3. Asian nation
4. Ferrell film
5. Sponged
6. Harness-racing horse
7. Lion portrayer
8. Sooner
9. Camping gear
10. Tea biscuits
11. Those with low odds
12. Not aweather
13. The Yukon, in Can.
18. You, once
23. Kazakh sea
25. Waste allowance
26. Thorny
28. Crevice fillers
29. Needle case
30. Astronaut Eisele
31. Thickener
32. Go by bus
33. Narrow escape
34. Tint
37. Asserts
38. Variety
40. Burden
41. Less practiced
43. Sun revolver
44. Mold
46. ___ pants
47. Relaxes
48. Hibernation
49. Cheeky
50. Frosh abode
51. Ohio lake
52. Whittle
56. Feast
57. Dieter's resort

ACROSS

1. Not hers
4. Water growth
8. Tossed
14. Ref's kin
15. ___ estate
16. Bad luck
17. Hot spring
18. Wheat ___
19. Dodged
20. Skipper clipper
23. Musician John
24. Shocking fish
25. Chinese skillet
28. Emblem
29. Train sounds
32. Cook bread
33. Large lizard
35. Display
36. One pun
39. African nation
40. Dished out
41. Arab prince
42. Body part
43. Computer sci. rule
47. Likely
48. HRH's fliers
49. Mortise's mate
50. Royal loyal
54. Instructor
57. Folk hero
58. Inventor Whitney
59. Highest point
60. Gawk at
61. ___ can

62. Witnesses
63. Snares
64. Glimpse

DOWN

1. Soothes
2. Pierce
3. Ancient Greek city
4. Inert gas
5. Nasty look
6. Attire
7. ___ mater
8. Ancient Nile city
9. Shack
10. Bellow
11. Bizarre
12. Deep sorrow
13. Head motion
21. Venezuela coin
22. Best wishes
25. Skin bump
26. Authorize
27. Lock need
29. Slice
30. Barn area
31. Open
32. Spans
34. Card game
35. St.
36. Sugar cube
37. Modify text
38. Brit. rock group
39. Bering, e.g.
42. Samples
44. Map features
45. Hockey player
46. Connected
48. Speedster
49. Stories
50. Pen
51. Large cat
52. Rim
53. Electrical unit
54. Comic Rowan
55. Wall St. event
56. Freckle

RHYME TIME

PUZZLE 490

AT STEAK

ACROSS

1. Visual's mate
6. In order
10. Sweet potatoes
14. Like a chip
15. Zone
16. Jai ——
17. Formation side
19. Lug
20. Snaky letter
21. Bother
22. Groovy
23. "The Name of the Rose" author
24. Franklin's bill
27. Snakes
30. Clock part
35. Florida city
37. Terra follower
38. Mai ——
39. Rabbit ears
41. Pompous speech
43. Put
44. Destiny
46. Gilbert et al.
47. Vatican sentry
50. Mrs. Munster
51. Elliott of rap
52. Wrath
54. Covered vehicle
57. Greek letter
58. "Surfin' ——"
61. Ferrigno role
62. Funny pages feature
66. Suit to ——
67. Cooker
68. American bird
69. Having foot digits
70. Sudden pain
71. Stinks

DOWN

1. Yard unit
2. Geller et al.
3. Slangy home
4. Sheep follower
5. Of the eye
6. Gab
7. Writer Levin
8. Hideout
9. Shaggy ox
10. Jehovah
11. Wings
12. Rough up
13. Window part
18. Gift tag word
22. Vapors
23. "Babe" role
24. Admiral on the seas: abbr.
25. Protein-rich snack
26. Mr. Preminger
27. Gather
28. Tendon
29. Ms. LaBelle
31. Son of Daedalus
32. Early video-game maker
33. Of the snout
34. Silly
36. Signs, permanently
40. Pesters
42. Hay unit
45. Might
48. Had a cigar
49. Compact ——
53. Platform
54. Huh?
55. Car
56. Merriment
57. Pong's mate
58. Prompt
59. Luxurious fabric
60. Mimics
62. Patrolman
63. Eggs
64. Guys
65. Inventor's monogram

MEADOW LAMENT

ACROSS

1. Acknowledge
6. Gallivant
10. Aid a felon
14. Habituate
15. Grandma Moses
16. Succotash part
17. Outboard, e.g.
18. Long tooth
19. Cave
20. Filming technique
22. Norwegian port
23. Luncheonette
24. A Murrow: abbr.
26. Draft group: abbr.
29. Mr. Koppel
30. Thief
34. Cuts wood
36. Ridiculous
37. Fleming solo
38. Hoisin-sauce base
39. Roman orator
40. Luxuriated
43. Hammered
45. Varnish
46. Panel truck
47. King of Judah
48. Boat mover
49. Line dance
51. From the top
54. Wedding attendant
59. Run easily
60. English river
61. Stan's buddy

62. Coatrack
63. Folk dance
64. Loam and mire
65. So be it!
66. Quits
67. Honeyed

DOWN

1. Sleep stages: abbr.
2. Organic compound
3. Limo, e.g.
4. Gang
5. White ant
6. Traveled like Huck
7. Studio sign
8. ___ Domini
9. X-Men foe
10. Ration
11. Prejudice
12. Actor Jannings
13. Poi root
21. People
25. Early drops
26. Deli orders
27. Singer Vaughan
28. Farm gate
30. Tricky
31. Woody vine
32. ___ Park, Colorado
33. Harper sitcom
35. Fright night
36. Atlantic catch
38. Dry, as wine
41. Spanish wave
42. Armed conflict
43. Dormer unit
44. Fascinate
46. Sajak sells them
49. Removed the pit
50. Blazing
51. Utah resort
52. Average
53. Duel tool
55. Legal claim
56. Netman Nastase
57. Bug
58. For fear that

PUZZLE 492

BLOOMING WONDERS

ACROSS

1. Fellow
5. Switch
9. Confidence game
13. Curdle
17. Patriot Nathan ___
18. King of the road
19. Capital of Italia
20. Gallivant
21. Buck character
22. Unpleasant task
23. Momentarily
24. Beame and Burrows
25. Its bracts may be brilliant
28. Ocean officers
30. Be out of the pink
31. Sink feature
33. Middling grade
34. Discouraged
39. Math class
41. Sufficient
45. Hair base
46. Close-mouthed person
48. Idle of Monty Python
50. Solar cycle
51. Printer's need
52. Pressed the horn
54. Building shape
55. Tabula ___
56. Outmoded
58. Fend off
60. Squeals
62. Tractor part
64. Miles or Bette
66. Zip
67. Island commonwealth
71. Resided
73. Stars
77. Ripening agent
78. Animal pouch
80. Most recent
82. Educators' org.
83. Colleen
84. Letter drop
86. Gravy no-no
87. Lee of comics
88. Call to Babe
90. Fed. revenuer
92. Reproducing illegally
94. ___ billing
96. Inferior
98. Man/mouse link
99. Talk out of
103. Its petals may be fringed
109. On the Caspian
110. Turnstile
112. Hurry like a bee
113. Beseech
114. Vitality
115. Broad expanse
116. Make gentle
117. Jelly ___ Morton
118. Feminine suffix
119. Snake's home
120. Went like the wind
121. Sir Geraint's love

DOWN

1. Pork ___
2. Ethereal light
3. ___ Mountains (Asian range)
4. Stadium flapper
5. Boot string
6. Habit
7. Touch on
8. Hypothesize
9. Madrid Mrs.
10. Plot
11. Out of control
12. Agitated
13. It has crinkled clusters
14. Place for a stud
15. ___ easy
16. Miss Trueheart
26. Error-marking word
27. Craftsmanship
29. Mendel subject
32. "___ We There Yet?"
34. Spigot problem
35. An O'Neill
36. Yan's pans
37. Luge
38. Sealed a box
40. Coated with gold
42. Clang
43. Emit coherent light
44. Historic divisions
47. ___ detector
49. Reunion group
52. Girder
53. ___-may-care
57. It has bell-shaped flowers
59. Adversary
61. Pinball word
63. Male voice
65. Frame

434

67. Luggage

68. Money-changer's fee

69. Knight in shining armor

70. Pretzel coating

72. Prefix for half

74. Against

75. James or Dizzy

76. Harmonized

79. Strives

81. Germinated

85. Lao-tzu's doctrine

87. Height

89. Second-person pronoun

91. French negative

93. Mus. adaptation

95. Heathen

97. Log vessels

99. Fog

100. "___ True?" (Brenda Lee song)

101. Propelled

102. Take the plunge

104. Wallop

105. Interval

106. Curling ___

107. Jamaican tangelo

108. Fuse

111. Grab some vittles

PUZZLE 493

HANNA-BARBERA

ACROSS
1. Party thrower
5. Root or Yale
10. "Lord ___"
13. Short leaps
17. Actress Shawkat
18. Fooled
19. In history
20. ___ Hershiser
21. Darling
22. Harbingers
23. Crate
24. Roman fiddler
25. The boy adventurer
27. Emphasize
29. Italy's cont.
30. Dwelling
32. Cartoon sound
33. ___ l'oeil
37. Excellent
39. Allotted
43. Hindu deity
44. Right away
46. Not closed
48. Nick's wife
49. Auth.
50. Nasal tone
53. Volcano's dust
54. Broad smile
55. Hairy creatures
57. Caesar's cry
58. Having a litter
60. Research room, for short
62. Cool, once
64. Delighted cry
65. Genuineness
70. Insignia
73. March composer
77. Thomas ___ Edison
78. List-closing abbr.
79. Heroic tales
81. Ms. Munson et al.
82. Unhealthy air
83. Chimney black
85. Make a choice
86. Write with acid
87. Integrity
89. Courting
92. Release oxen
94. Dispute
96. Fossil
97. Dentist's gp.
98. Improbable
102. The suited superhero
108. Combine
109. Beckon
110. Claw
111. "Thirteen" role
112. Snitch
113. Murmur fondly
114. Quick-witted
115. Stable mate
116. ___ podrida
117. Med. provider
118. Legal holdings
119. Winter toy

DOWN
1. Muslim pilgrimage
2. Bread spread
3. Actress Phillips
4. Mountain lake
5. Silver-tongued
6. Small primate
7. ___ fixe
8. Island of Japan
9. Free from obstruction
10. The talking shark
11. Mad scientist's aide
12. Chutzpah
13. The kung fu canine
14. Sandwich cookie
15. Inca territory
16. ___ machine
26. Not nope
28. Actor Beatty
31. ___ culpa
33. Helen of ___
34. Seldom seen
35. Overlook
36. The store window ape
37. Slap
38. Wild party
40. Actress Petty
41. Ireland, to poets
42. Drat!
45. Have creditors
47. Carla on "Cheers"
51. Ultimate
52. Estimate
56. ___ Francisco
59. Song syllables
61. Busy insects

63. Edible size

65. Hotheaded

66. Red Muppet

67. Bard of ___

68. Load cargo

69. The mystery-solving dog

71. Highly excited

72. Drink like a cat

74. Golden-rule word

75. Bag

76. Netman Arthur ___

80. Pupils

84. Likewise

88. Seoul soldier

90. Put in place

91. Bhutan language

93. Complain

95. Country lass

97. Oak fruit

98. ___ no good

99. Dramatist Coward

100. Lounge around

101. Tower

103. Helm direction

104. Skirt edges

105. Racetrack shape

106. Regal title

107. ___ off (irate)

PUZZLE 494

MAGIC FOLKS

ACROSS

1. Finance
5. Drama
9. Volcanic landform
13. Gossip
17. Bread spread
18. Olympic sled
19. ___-de-camp
20. Carson's successor
21. Deep blue
22. Dash
23. Foie ___
24. Mr. Preminger
25. Magic man
28. Rests
30. Shoe width
31. Taro's kin
33. Spigot
34. Gel
37. Stead
40. Crazy
42. Repeat
46. Magic man
49. Rant
51. Prayer closer
52. Author Roberts
53. Stop
54. Singer Ritter
55. Boom box
57. Analogy phrase
60. Refreshment table
63. Magic woman
67. Anybody
70. Shadowbox
71. Fall flower
75. Work by Keats
76. Car fuel
78. Allie's roommate
81. Fork prong
82. Declare again
85. Magic man
87. Consumed
88. Takei role
90. Greek portico
91. Moore film
92. Fam. member
94. Disallow
96. Spanish aunt
98. "___ and Isolde"
102. Magic man
108. Sari wearer
109. Hanker
111. Bellow
112. Mideast nation
113. Kind of sax
114. Away from the wind
115. Amos or Spelling
116. Oscar ___ Hoya
117. Farm worker
118. Entrance
119. Line of wk.
120. French state

DOWN

1. Stable youngster
2. Forearm bone
3. Nuremberg no
4. "La ___ Vita"
5. Common
6. Doozie
7. Chinese isinglass
8. Busybody
9. Big bottle
10. Ventilate
11. Hebrew month
12. Adjust
13. Mistake
14. Permits
15. Starting bet
16. Hisses
26. Morays, e.g.
27. Exam type
29. Segment
32. Manner
34. Cicatrix
35. Ms. Bombeck
36. Even
38. Roxy Music name
39. Language group
41. Kunta ___
43. Ms. Moreno
44. Over, in Berlin
45. Subsequent
47. Game bird
48. Soothes
50. Yemen port
56. Galleon gold
58. Cookbook amt.
59. Honshu bay
61. Rap sheet info
62. ___ Rica
64. "Picnic" writer

438

PUZZLE 494

65. Gets close

66. Streetcars

67. Hurt

68. Halls

69. Ham, e.g.

72. Shade

73. Children's author

74. Leash

77. Earring

79. Asian holiday

80. Recondite

83. Term

84. Bad mood

85. Jupiter's wife

86. Shower

89. Register

93. Greens

95. Mongol tents

97. Battery terminal

98. Capture

99. Chest noise

100. Toward

101. ___ contendere

103. Glop

104. Jack rabbit

105. "___ a man with seven wives . . ."

106. Simba's friend

107. Pesky one

110. New prefix

439

PUZZLE 495

ALL DRIED UP

ACROSS

1. Flock father
4. Illegal scheme
8. "Deputy ___"
12. Scrub in the tub
17. "Diamonds ___ Forever"
18. French bread?
19. Gen. Robert ___
20. Disney mermaid
21. Arid role for Johnny Depp?
24. Sherpa's home
25. Hesitant sounds
26. Concert extra
27. Inhales sharply
28. "The Zoo Story" author
31. Aperitif of white wine
32. Actor Mineo
34. Fox's spurned target, eventually?
39. At sixes and ___
44. Vb. type
45. British gun
46. Grind, as teeth
48. Writer James ___
49. Feels poorly
51. Division term
53. Originally named
54. Without ice
55. Tic-___-toe
57. Regional dlr.
60. Some statues
61. Arid Steinbeck novel?
66. Cloaks
67. Biblical verb
68. Stool pigeon
69. Skater Brinker
70. Poetic dusk
71. Secure
74. Mil. branch
78. Melville work
79. Lebanese port
82. Abrade
84. Battery size
85. Small piano
87. Oklahoma winery in a drought?
90. Staff
92. Somme summer
93. Kent's colleague
94. Certain inn
98. Canopy
101. Clean-air gp.
102. Romance
103. Desiccated jelly source?
108. Coward
109. Concrete
110. Mideast nation
111. Nabokov book
112. Look after
113. Latin being
114. Distribute
115. Chasing game

DOWN

1. Joplin piece
2. "Exodus" hero
3. Crooner Torme
4. Female fortuneteller
5. Mongrels
6. Gallery piece
7. Extra
8. Freeing of frost
9. Loser
10. Water barrier
11. Heredity factors
12. Slip-on bracelet
13. Territory
14. Gratuities
15. Stack
16. Plumbing joints
22. Ale's cousin
23. "Diana" performer
28. Atlas section
29. Actress Petty
30. Singer Ives
33. Tennis champ
35. New York city
36. Writer Deighton
37. Blasting letters
38. ___ Domingo
40. Pacific republic
41. Throw out
42. Not o'er
43. Deposits
47. Vassal
50. Child by marriage
52. Garfield's pal
56. ___ Antiqua
58. Leaders
59. JFK sights, once
60. Bandeau

440

61. Step heavily

62. Vietnam's capital

63. Concept

64. Sound-related

65. Wrench

66. Grinch's targets

70. This, senora

72. Celestial Altar

73. Devotee

75. ___ souci

76. Heavy club

77. Lyricist Sammy ___

80. Spanish escorts

81. Item

83. Grill fuel

86. Bud

88. Gambling town

89. Jai ___

91. Mother-of-pearl

94. Big fiddle

95. Dijon date

96. Sniffer

97. Fine powder

99. Miseries

100. Bleak

101. Part of QED

104. Rap's Dr. ___

105. GRE's kin

106. Ms. Lupino

107. Harass

PUZZLE 496

OLD MAXIMS

ACROSS

1. Polite address
6. Church nook
10. Clump of dirt
14. Small amount
17. Marble type
18. Legume
19. Nurse's ___
20. Actress Alicia
21. Lord Byron's maxim, "Truth is ___"
25. Bank feature
26. Unfamiliar
27. ___ Stanley Gardner
28. Portray
31. Dollar bills
32. Place
33. Delete
34. Flinch
36. Tennis's Arthur ___
38. Mold
39. Formal name
40. Flat serving dish
41. "On My ___"
44. Mao ___-tung
45. Brooklyn's ___ Island
46. Parcel
47. Tooth pain
48. River crossing
49. Tire input
50. John or Sean
51. St. Paul's maxim
58. Competitor
59. Ore.'s neighbor
60. Curds and ___
61. ___-steven
62. Colony dwellers
64. Antigone's uncle
66. Swimsuit component
69. Director Craven
70. Garfield's pal
71. ___ Sales
72. School official
73. Laundry appliance
74. Tour of duty
75. Seashore
76. Fabric design
79. Gorilla-expert Fossey
80. Dress
81. Plant anchor
82. Straighten
84. More confident
86. Thomas a Kempis's maxim
92. Actress Hagen
93. Wine city
94. Theater award
95. Gentler
96. ___ Moines
97. Dill seed
98. Louse spawn
99. Glitches

DOWN

1. Barker and Kettle
2. FBI official
3. The Beastmaster
4. Resurgence
5. Peril
6. Cain's brother
7. Perky
8. Positioned
9. Intensify
10. Cato's dog
11. ___ preserver
12. Norse deity
13. Winter mo.
14. Laissez-___
15. "___ Gay"
16. Receded
22. Belly
23. Nautical position
24. French noggin
28. Adroit
29. Greek love god
30. Whittle down
31. Merely
32. Meek
34. Breezy
35. Devoted suffix
36. Actress Meyers
37. Song gal
39. Civil wrong
40. Alpine pool
41. Eight prefix
42. Sudden notion
43. Maui goose
45. Spiral
46. Caesar's 1002
47. Pale gray
48. TV's Drescher
49. Turkish bigwig
50. Egyptian deity
51. Work group
52. Bee's home
53. Blvds.

54. Quick meal
55. McMahon and Ames
56. Used a broom
57. Nautical hello
62. Commotion
63. Anais ___
64. Invent
65. Operate
66. Defeat

67. Impulsive
68. Initial stake
70. Table scrap
71. Elizabeth Cady ___
72. Hotel employee
73. Division word
74. ___ of relief
75. Fissures
76. "___ Mary"

77. Turnpike
78. Tiny bits
79. Finger, e.g.
80. ___-Magnon
82. Gp.
83. Lo-cal
84. Court action

85. Colorado tribe
87. Flight-safety org.
88. Kimono sash
89. "___ Believer"
90. Not pos.
91. AMA members

PUZZLE 497

SEA TO C

ACROSS

1. Soupcon
5. Sour
10. Combat group
14. Tub
19. One, to Fritz
20. ___ system
21. Darling dog
22. Serrated
23. Last part of a patriotic song, briefly
26. Greenland community
27. Bow material
28. Mr. Kenton
29. Lynx
30. Agua
31. Cain's nephew
32. Wallace ___
33. Actor Green
34. Seedlings
37. Approximately
38. Celebration
40. Lee's org.
43. Doily stuff
44. Hunky-___
46. Made of cashmere
48. Male cat
49. Be human
50. Eyes
52. Wander
53. Donated
54. Orange or lime drink
55. Qumran find, briefly
59. TV's Ken ___
60. Hoods' gals
61. Young adults
62. Avarice
63. Chaperons
66. Tortilla chip
67. Checks
69. African grasses
70. Eyelashes
71. Chinese, e.g.
72. Promptly
73. Where Eastwood was mayor, briefly
76. Thurs. follower
79. New Mexico town
80. Stead
81. Anoint
82. Lass's pal
83. Finale
84. More embarrassed
86. Coach Stagg
87. Liver delicacy
88. "Stand" band
89. Dunking cookie
90. Behold!
92. Glance at
94. Frenzied
96. Disdain
97. Pair
98. Insertion sign
100. Weapons storehouse
102. Jug handles
103. Match a bet
106. Leg joint
107. Tongue twister opening, briefly
110. Scoff
111. Scope prefix
112. Ancient Greek region
113. Gridlock sound
114. Lugs
115. Cereal grasses
116. Cloudless
117. Samoa's capital

DOWN

1. Flout
2. Rich one's suffix
3. Neve material
4. Dress edge
5. Houston players
6. Chills
7. Different
8. Stadium cry
9. Graft
10. One bushy eye topper
11. Mrs. Reagan
12. ___ Swenson
13. Poise
14. Amidst
15. Buddhist saint
16. Jack London collection, briefly
17. Wight, e.g.
18. ___-do-well
24. Penny
25. Nay votes
31. Wind dir.
32. Kind of acid
33. Flower parts
34. Guilty, e.g.
35. Grease
36. Farm fraction
38. Nitwits
39. Mideast airline
41. Part of USSR
42. Revises
44. Doubles
45. Auto pioneer
47. Maine college town
50. Perfumes
51. Stone ax
53. Bridge expert
56. Worn out
57. Director DeMille
58. Restored building
60. Groans
62. She's amazing!
63. Spring holiday
64. "Alias" role

65. Place to buy shrimp, briefly
66. Lady of the Lake
67. Cinders
68. Cambodian coin
70. Belief
71. ___ time
73. Office worker
74. Caddie, e.g.
75. Mandarin's residence
76. Blemish
77. Large rodents
78. ___ fixe
84. Cheerleaders
85. Lounges
86. Artist's medium
87. Pea home
91. Treatment
92. College official
93. Hasty
95. Brawl
96. Small silver fish
97. Ancient Romania
98. List of actors
99. Part of A.D.
100. Concerning
101. Ratite bird
102. Medieval menial
103. Sty fare
104. "The Time Machine" people
105. This, in Tijuana
108. Chat room giggle
109. Airport info

PUZZLE 498

EXISTENCE

ACROSS
1. Not rigid
5. Acts
10. Gets going
15. Let it stand
19. Scent
20. Pond plants
21. Bay of Naples isle
22. Whaler's direction
23. Observe one's equines?
26. Level, in London
27. More pert
28. Lab burner's name
29. Hotel offering
30. Outcast
33. Spelling ___
34. Study in a hurry
36. Husband of Ephrath
39. Love
41. Pale
43. OK
46. Too
48. Disparage a nursery-rhyme shepherdess?
51. Scottish negative
52. Dawn deity
54. Hurry
55. Author Levin
56. Uncommon
57. Boy's date
59. Increases
61. Waste cloths
63. Ms. Osmond
64. As well
65. Neck area
67. Pour forth
68. Drizzled
69. Scrimp on fireplace materials?
73. Poses
76. Tick off
77. Stratagem
78. If not
82. Actress Noriega
83. Subarctic native
84. Tasty!
85. Cherished
86. DCCLI times II
87. ___ Baba
88. Como follower
92. Stroke gently
94. ___ carte
95. Happening only to celebs?
99. Is generous
101. Early trombone great
102. Last letter
103. Script direction
105. Conditioner
106. Fiber source
107. Patriotic group: abbr.
109. One who makes declarations
111. Place
114. Sounded annoyed
117. Hockey players
121. Timespans
122. Scold one's family members?
125. Heal
126. Ms. Verdugo
127. Forward
128. Dart
129. Decimal numbers
130. Like a nerd
131. Dundee adjective
132. Lincoln son et al.

DOWN
1. Throws
2. Concept
3. Hardness scale
4. Flourish
5. DJ's device
6. Ohio city
7. Past
8. Greek letter
9. Certain Slav
10. Teatime treat
11. Baby's auto chair
12. Church part
13. Medieval tableware items
14. Bro's sib
15. Play a guitar
16. Ethnic cuisine
17. Compass point
18. Trap, in a way
24. Accountable
25. Arrogance
29. Alabama's Monte ___
31. Envoy: abbr.
32. Field worker
35. Ms. McEntire
36. Line dance
37. Profit
38. Ogles
40. Arctic native's tool
42. A little
43. Hanker
44. Spooky
45. Zoom
47. Cy and Neil
49. Whirring sound
50. Spoke well of
53. Shadowbox
58. Indian tobacco
60. Driving
62. Right now: abbr.
63. Ms. West
66. Actress Sedgwick
67. Gosh
68. Word repetitions
70. British sports group: abbr.

71. Some English songs
72. Sudden overthrow
73. Latin dance
74. More weird
75. Put on a pedestal
79. Gain knowledge
80. Boutique bargains
81. Rub out
83. Patrons
87. ___ mater
89. Not mono
90. Make leather
91. Handiworks
93. Indication of trouble
96. House member
97. Place for petrol
98. Collection
100. Transport by plane
104. Sleeve style
106. Foundations
108. In check
110. Flatterer
111. Faction
112. Real
113. Merit
115. Peter Fonda role
116. Blah
118. Wisconsin town
119. Ms. Markey
120. Former JFK sights
122. Implore
123. Greek letter
124. Netherlands village

PUZZLE 498

447

PUZZLE 499

THEY GET IT DONE

ACROSS

1. Small songbird
5. Barber's need
10. Osaka's locale
15. Gutsy
19. Ring of light
20. Covet
21. Bowie's last post
22. Opportunist
23. Indiana's Bayh
24. Torn apart
25. Step part
26. So long!
27. Julio Gallo, e.g.
29. Chanel and Versace, briefly
31. Accessible
32. Certain minor
33. Nut-weevil treats
34. Liberty figure
38. Political alliance
39. Departed
41. Gold measure
42. Hardhearted
44. Lily leaf
45. Wedges
50. Like Liam Neeson
51. Settles up
52. "Daniel Boone" role
54. Clarinet kin
55. Shed
56. Most, for short
57. Easy gallop
58. Felix's remark
59. Squeezes (out)
61. Interlace
63. Entreaty word
65. Doyle's creation
68. Ladled
69. Bordered
70. Diminishes
71. Crib wheel
72. "Hulk" star
73. Divulge
74. Washes away
76. Singer Janis ___
77. Seaweed bed
81. Like some excuses
82. Achier
83. Part for Shalhoub
85. Rose part
86. Entangle
88. ___ Moines
89. Producer Michaels
90. Stadium
91. Defeated soundly
93. Once a filly
94. Autumn apple
95. Kind of daisy
99. Bud holder
100. Yule
102. Dolly Levi et al.
105. McCain and Pelosi, e.g.
110. Self: pref.
111. Expend
112. Drive-time medium
113. First: abbr.
114. Comic Laurel
115. Kent portrayer
116. Happening
117. Tinware art
118. Present!
119. Ski spot
120. Move clumsily
121. Whole bunch

DOWN

1. Sound of relief
2. Musician Shankar
3. Oomph
4. Zip
5. Scour
6. Toddler vehicle
7. Lustrous black
8. Wrapped up
9. Paddock
10. Jolted
11. Noncitizen
12. Wile away
13. "Life With Father" star
14. Role in "Psycho"
15. London swaggerer
16. Willow tree
17. Memorize
18. Waste
28. Oral cavity
29. Not accept
30. Statutes
32. Casks
34. Conceal profits
35. Edible tuber
36. Nutmeg coat
37. Martha Stewart, e.g.
38. Baby in blue
39. ___ poster
40. Inch along
42. Hot tubs
43. Tab add-on
44. Kind of claw
46. June Cleaver and Debra Barone, e.g.
47. Girder type
48. Certain bull
49. Stitched
52. Site of Casco Bay
53. Oliver Twist, e.g.
56. Mishmashes
57. Thickens
60. Legend
61. Black suit
62. Conundrum

PUZZLE 499

64. Football's Dawson
65. Montezuma features?
66. It's south of Buffalo
67. Alpaca's kin
68. Made points
72. Harden clay
75. Took a limo
76. Rural lodge
78. Summers abroad
79. Narrow way
80. Braid
83. Encore!
84. Mesabi find
85. Simon, Randy, and ___
87. Strip of wood
89. Gal
92. Tripod topper
93. Weasel
94. Faraway
95. Shatter
96. ___ cuisine
97. Perfume oil
98. Oatmeal cake
99. Liveliness
100. 2000 candidate
101. In debt
103. Tomahawks
104. Reserve
105. Fluid rock
106. Baby foxes
107. Carbon compound
108. Vex
109. Brood
112. Man in gray

PUZZLE 500

COMMUNICATE

ACROSS

1. Obey
5. Bind
10. Lean
14. Gooey stuff
18. Sandwich cookie
19. Michelangelo piece
20. Harden
22. Move upward
23. Moos
24. Translator
26. Convenience
27. USNA grad
28. Dowel
29. Author Jong
30. Part of FAA
32. Analyzes critically
35. Finito
36. Fired up
37. Escape from
39. Baum barker
41. Amusing
45. Railroad station
46. Glide
47. Mute bird
49. Wheel hub
50. Command for Mr. Ed
51. Make law
53. Hornet's bite
54. Chutzpah
55. Go wrong
56. Gamble
57. Duty
58. Rocky cliff
59. Vision
60. Coughed
61. Of flight
62. Maggie or Kate
64. Exists permanently
66. Irritable
68. '70s do
69. Slipperiest
70. Rectify
72. Poet's dawn
73. Form of trapshooting
74. Prance
75. 60 secs.
78. Dreadful
79. Smart ___ (wise guy)
80. Advantage
81. Lennon's wife
82. Ashwell or Olin
83. Stable femme
84. Tear in half
86. Harshly pungent
88. Window above a door
90. Soapstone
91. Social group
92. Bathtub ___
93. Wray et al.
95. Wimpy
98. Amplify
102. Alpine ridge
104. Trunk cover
105. Artfully shy
108. ___-tat
109. Indirect message
112. Game on horseback
113. Bobby and Peter's brother
114. Italian city
115. Garry or Demi
116. Swirling current
117. East, to Enrique
118. Evening, in Rome
119. Lab compound
120. Mexican coin

DOWN

1. Lawn pest
2. Smooth out
3. Journal
4. Spanish two
5. Informers
6. Whisper
7. Steep flax
8. Leg or man ending
9. Paulie and Polly
10. Mythical enchantress
11. Close by
12. Cashew
13. Nonkosher
14. Hallmark purchase
15. Deceitful one
16. Thessaly peak
17. Compost item
21. Soon
25. Swivel
28. Grammatical tense
31. Faint
33. Confusion
34. Wall Street data printer
37. Sharpness
38. Deviate suddenly
40. Bit of granola
41. Flogged with a stick
42. Cubicle
43. Zoo's bird house
44. Dismiss
46. Spending money
47. Kindle
48. Mass media agency
52. Approaching
53. Sawed-off
57. Thorax
59. Finger spelling
60. Facial feature

450

62. Nudger

63. Boat basin

65. Dorothy, to Em

66. Teamster's rig

67. Unsuccessful, at Belmont

68. Small silver fish

69. Major religion

71. Water-filled trench

75. Series of dots and dashes

76. Name abbr.

77. Central point

79. Between

80. Inclusive word

84. Peeper problems

85. Diversion

87. Calico or Persian

89. Guinness's title

93. Hindu ascetic

94. NBA site

96. Flame

97. Certain clerk

98. Impel

99. Standards

100. Editor's word

101. Flightless birds

103. Personalities

106. Ransom Eli ___

107. Kind of dieting

110. Lode yield

111. Commandment word

112. Verve

PUZZLE 501

Diagramless crosswords are solved by using the clues and their numbers to fill in the answer words and the arrangement of black squares. Insert the number of each clue with the first letter of its answer, across and down. Fill in a black square at the end of each answer. Every black square must have a corresponding black square on the opposite side of the diagram to form a diagonally symmetrical pattern. Puzzles 501 and 502 have been started for you.

ACROSS

1. Limit
4. What person?
7. Bogey beater
10. Pub offering
11. Biddy
12. Prior to, poetically
13. Tyke
14. Needle opening
15. Feel terrible
16. Intone
18. More inferior
20. Healthy
21. Young American bird
22. Tough plastic
24. Expands
27. Advantage
31. Garden tillers
32. Garnish
33. Gulped down
34. Building wing
36. Lobster eggs
37. Lass's pal
38. Seeded bread
39. Large flower, for short
40. Sibilant letter
41. Casual shirt
42. Snoop

DOWN

1. Lay hold of
2. Oahu greeting
3. Daisy ray
4. Hone
5. Yoo-hoo!
6. Type of street
7. Oyster gem
8. Come up
9. Rent again
17. When pigs fly!
19. Flirted with
21. Printers' concerns
23. Order form, sometimes
24. Marine mammal
25. Small quantities
26. House papers
28. Campus dwellings
29. Gathering
30. Foe
32. Nautical direction
35. Drain-opener chemical

PUZZLE 502

ACROSS

1. Hair line
5. Parcel (out)
9. Turkish title
10. Canvas prop
11. Rice dish
13. Uncertain
14. Protect
17. Large shrimp
19. Dog's bane
20. Archaic pronoun
21. Auctioned off
24. Object
25. Having no brand name
27. Observe
30. Modify text
31. Steal
34. Pretension
35. Chinese temple
37. Snag
40. TV's Lorenzo ____
41. Blender output
43. Appearance
44. Paved course
45. Hand over
46. Neutral hue

DOWN

1. Pizazz
2. During
3. Aggravate
4. Gridlock cause
5. Equal
6. Themed paper
7. Abound
8. Go by, as time
10. "____ of Eden"
12. Experienced
15. Maiden-name word
16. Beaver creation
18. Hollywood's Skye
22. Blazed the trail
23. Faucet woe
25. Hand signal
26. Slanted type
27. Shrew
28. Lubricate
29. Journey
31. Wanderer
32. Saying
33. Army post
36. Willing
38. Gator's cousin
39. Find out
42. School's URL ender

PUZZLE 503

Starting box on page 562

ACROSS
1. Bovine baby
5. Gas-guzzler
8. Detecting system
9. Dude
10. Aromatic spice
12. Extra
13. Heir, sometimes
14. Salon offering
16. Elemental bit
17. Plan
18. Calendar square
19. "___ There Was You"
20. Turn over
21. The largest part
22. Incidental effect
25. Vitality
26. Pro votes
27. Extol
29. Bluish purple
32. Deteriorate
35. Cinema pooch
36. Poetic piece
37. Printer's need
39. Fraternity letter
40. Coffee holders
41. Meat spread
42. "Save me!"
44. Contrary term
45. Inane
46. Vitamin B component
48. Humdinger
49. Polish coin
50. Eternally, in verse
51. Catch sight of

DOWN
1. Enumerate
2. Picnic spoiler
3. Lantern
4. Liberty
5. Oil source
6. Astringent substance
7. Legal thing
8. Nose around
9. Design
11. Clutch
12. Fly swatter?
13. Skirt feature
15. Legendary story
17. Addition word
20. Burr, to Hamilton
21. Mr. ___ (Lorre role)
23. Liquid rock
24. Caustic stuff
25. Your and my
27. Alley yowlers
28. Eye
29. Speed ratio
30. Colorless
31. Employ
32. Tilt
33. Infant's attire
34. Enroll
36. Dramatic device
38. Florida island
40. Agreement
41. Southern bread
43. Playmates
45. Gentle animal
47. Beat walker

Deduction Problem

PUZZLE 504

Ten Cards

Ten cards, numbered 1 through 10, are shuffled and placed face down in a row on the table. The number on the second card from the left is equal to the average of the numbers on the first and third cards. Similarly the number on each of the third through seventh cards from the left is the average of the numbers of its two neighbors. The cards numbered 1 and 10 are not at either end. The first card on the left is larger than its neighbor. Can you figure out the numbers on each card in the row, going from left to right?

PUZZLE 505

ACROSS

1. Previously
4. Locations
6. Clerical garment
9. Large seabird
13. Mr. Mineo et al.
15. Tranquil
16. Back talk
17. Intense
19. Low digit
20. Lingerie item
22. Work measure
23. Bullfight bellow
24. Spree
25. County exhibitions
27. Vault
29. Dads
30. Soak up, as gravy
32. At least one
33. Dispatched
34. Keaton of film
36. Barley beard
37. Sp. lady
38. Tent stake
39. Quotes
41. In what way?
44. Mock
47. Hubbub
48. Hockey legend
49. Fork prong
50. American symbol
53. After taxes
54. Appears
55. Officeholders

DOWN

1. Composer Khachaturian
2. Receive
3. Crew blade
4. Up to the task
5. Fuses, as metal
6. Sharp ___ tack
7. Varnish ingredient
8. Toronto player
9. Play division
10. Asian language
11. Mr. Caesar
12. Eavesdrop
14. Subway loop
18. Breakfast favorite
20. Raise a glass
21. Inventor Whitney
25. Devotee
26. Piece of turf
27. Turner and Wood
28. Hydro-carbon suffix
29. Tux-wearing creature?
31. Handguns
33. Perspire
35. Have being
36. Talented
39. Semi section
40. Neighbor of Ore.
41. Swine
42. Nocturnal predator
43. Minute
45. Compass pt.
46. Hanoi holiday
48. Radio buffs
51. ___ gratia
52. Nighttime, in verse

Starting box on page 562

PUZZLE 506

Substitutions

In these addition problems letters are substituted for numbers. When the letters are placed in order from 0 to 9, they will spell a 10-letter phrase. The same code is used in all three problems.

```
  C A T T L E        M E A T         H A M
+   C A M E L      + R I C E       + E G G
  ─────────────    ──────────      ────────
  6 4 3 3 7 7        1 5 9 4 1       1 1 1 1
```

10-LETTER PHRASE: ___ ___ ___ ___ ___ ___ ___ ___ ___ ___
          0 1 2 3 4 5 6 7 8 9

PUZZLE 507

ACROSS

1. Cheerio
5. Disfigure
8. Seed covering
9. Came to ground
11. "Ally McBeal" role
12. Horse feed
13. Two-hulled boat
19. Out of kilter
21. Ralph Kramden's wife
22. Greek letter
24. Brilliant
25. Chemical compound
27. Lacquered tin
28. Occasionally
31. Overlook
33. Thwart
34. Edit again
35. Jabber
36. Bouquet
37. Beast of burden
41. Pass through
46. Hamill's jump
47. Kuwaiti leader
48. Niblick number
49. Blessing concluder
50. Petition
51. Body of knowledge

DOWN

1. Fine powder
2. Opera tune
3. Coloration
4. Pond growth
5. "I Remember ____"
6. Alack's partner
7. Endanger
10. Heat control
14. Comprehensive design
15. Not quite
16. Iranian monetary unit
17. Cornfield measure
18. Web
20. Sudden notion
23. Small number
25. Suppose
26. Athenian vowel
29. Clinging vine
30. Emeril's creation
31. Nothing but
32. Image
34. Strike sharply
38. Rotational center
39. Food list
40. Nautical direction
42. Down-to-earth
43. Bullets
44. Seating section
45. Marine eagle

Starting box on page 562

Hexagrams

PUZZLE 508

One of the letters in the hexagons has been circled because it and the letters in the six surrounding hexagons can be unscrambled to form a 7-letter word (in this case TOURISM). We were able to form 13 other words in this manner.

TOURISM _____   _____

_____   _____

_____   _____

_____   _____

_____   _____

_____   _____

_____

PUZZLE 509

ACROSS

1. Motorist's buy
4. Charter
5. "___ the night before . . ."
9. Hodgepodge
10. Blood vessel
12. Smidgen
14. Boot liner
17. Numeral type
18. Ocean surge
19. Storybook monster
21. Eye problem
23. Ricelike pasta
24. Competes
25. Give out
27. Comes to a close
28. Position
29. Thus
30. Brit's baby buggy
31. Climax
34. Adrift
37. Business arrangement
38. Distinctive times
39. Devout
40. Door lock
41. Lobster's cousin
43. Exclusively
47. Actor Christian ___
48. Ploy
49. French condiment
52. Certain bread
53. Home ruler?
54. Initiated
55. Mother, to Brigitte
58. Early light
59. Send off
60. Floor covering

DOWN

1. Beautician's aid
2. Black bird
3. Short visit
4. Cowboy event
5. Mariner
6. Seek to marry
7. Tentacles
8. EMT's word
11. Whatever
12. Wheel cushion
13. Shaping tool
15. Ripening
16. Summary of beliefs
18. Indian pole
20. Superman's letter
22. Muslim official
26. Athens vowel
28. Sauna's locale
29. Conger or moray
31. Hacienda brick
32. Cartoon frame
33. BLT spread
34. Bellowing
35. Actress Field
36. Admirer
38. Fade away
39. Door clasp
41. Vinegar bottle
42. Island drink
44. Seize
45. Produced fiction
46. Hindu discipline
50. Rule
51. Overnight accommodation
56. Australian bird
57. Big truck

Starting box on page 562

PUZZLE 510   Exploraword

How many common words of 4 or more letters can you form from the letters of the given word? A letter may be used only as many times as it appears in the given word. Proper names, abbreviations, contractions, and foreign words are not allowed.

ANGELIC

PUZZLE 511

ACROSS

1. African fox
5. Cato's greeting
8. Pare
9. Diamond gal
10. Red dyes
12. Complainer
16. Be situated
17. Nothing more than
18. Sesame plant
19. Assuage
20. ___ tai
22. Common contraction
24. Pay ending
25. Blue-pencil
26. Adriatic wind
28. Skunk
31. Dry watercourse
33. Sac
34. Sheet
37. School subject
39. Skillfully
41. Seasons in France
42. Bridal-page word
43. Capitalizes on
44. Nighttime, to a bard
45. Hit on the noggin
47. Masculine address
49. Lamb's pseudonym
50. Dove's call
51. Missive
54. Tossed
57. Compass pt.
58. Derisive cry
59. Farm pen
60. Is obliged to

DOWN

1. Cathedral part
2. Rorqual
3. Washington VIP
4. Overhead railways
5. Clerical vestment
6. Contend (for)
7. Uncompounded
10. Inventor Whitney
11. Dipstick coating
13. Deed
14. Sounds of hesitation
15. Female ruff
18. Jeweled headdress
20. Wild bunch
21. Beneath decks
22. Bright thought
23. Command to Fido
25. Differently
27. Paid notices
28. Groaners
29. Grampus
30. Afternoon brew
32. Winter gliders
33. Hive inhabitants
35. Dogpatch name
36. Skedaddle
38. Adherent's suffix
40. Japanese currency
43. Military division
45. Animation frame
46. Madrid cheer
47. Scatter, as seed
48. Charged atom
50. Army beds
52. Approx.
53. Spanish king
54. Yet, briefly
55. Reporter's question
56. Caviar source

Starting box on page 562

Finish the Fours   PUZZLE 512

Place letters into the empty squares in the diagram to form a string of overlapping 4-letter words. A 4-letter word begins in each numbered square. If you choose the correct letters, they will reveal the name of a singer, reading in order from left to right.

1		R		2	Y	A		3	D	E		4	T		I	P		5	S		I		6		E	V	E		7	E	V	E
8		O	M	P		9	P		10	S	T	A		11	L	U		12	H	U		13	L		W		14	E	E			

457

PUZZLE 513

ACROSS

1. Smooth-talking
5. Jelly fruit
6. Notice the absence of
10. Endeavored
12. Earthenware pot
13. Speak from a soapbox
14. Belief
19. "The Bell Jar" author
21. Insect stage
22. Jacket fastener
23. Caught sight of
25. Fortune-teller
26. Well-being
27. Duplicate
28. Angered
29. Scottish headwear
30. Long way off
34. Grippe
35. Casino game
36. Doubled
38. Voila!
43. Call forth
44. Internet search engine
45. Principles
47. Reheat
48. Takes a spouse
51. 1 + 1
53. Devout
54. All in favor say it
55. Injure
56. Sheer force
58. Overhead
59. Crowd
63. Know instinctively
66. Minstrel's item
67. Medicinal shrub
68. Comedienne Radner
69. Distrustful
71. Electron tube
72. Huge quantity
73. Roads
75. British beverages
76. Handle skillfully
77. None

DOWN

1. Stringed instrument
2. Wash
3. "____ Got Sixpence"
4. Musical combo
5. Wine source
6. Sulk
7. Woes
8. Whacks
9. Fill full
10. Saturates
11. Bona fide
15. Harden like bone
16. Distort
17. Cosmetics
18. Parodied
20. Strong guy
24. Dealer's car
30. Assists a thief
31. Basketball side
32. Promptly, in a sonnet
33. Gather leaves
35. Eccentric
37. Steep (jute)
39. Pumpernickel grain
40. Respectively
41. Scat!
42. Pliers, e.g.
46. Sculpture
47. Tot's garment
48. Dry watercourse
49. Regarding
50. Drillmaster?
52. Composed
55. Foyer
57. Bridal veil material
59. Graceful
60. Verbally
61. Protuberance
62. Turns to the right
64. Inventor's start
65. Choice marbles
70. Exhibit boredom
71. Venison animal
74. Passing through

Starting box on page 562

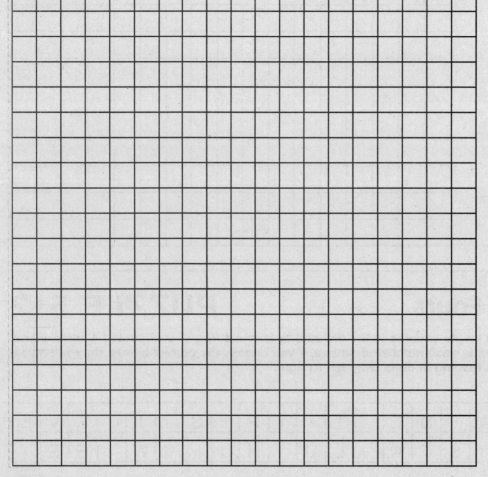

458

PUZZLE 514

ACROSS

1. Bushy do
4. Reef
7. Head front
8. Hasten
9. Rich supply
10. Mischievous being
11. Dillydally
12. Process leather again
16. Triumph
19. Waterlogged
20. Appendage
21. Batter's goal
23. Bring to court
24. Dozing
25. Longings
27. Memory unit
28. Sports official
30. Double
33. Mild expletive
35. Athenian vowel
37. Burnt wood
40. "Alice" spinoff
41. The entirety
42. Not deep
46. Common ailment
47. ___ culpa
48. Fictional character
49. "___ Lobo"
50. Slangy sleuth
51. Almost hailed
52. Halloween mo.
53. Actress Carol ___
54. Comrade
55. "Rhoda" mom
58. Director Craven
59. Colored
61. Edible tuber
64. Epic poetry
66. Moist
69. Tweeter's mate
71. Congou, e.g.
72. Climbing devices
73. Be mistaken
74. Come what ___
75. Boring
76. Mountain crest
78. Bewitch
79. Natural resin
81. Boxer's bane
83. Become mature
84. Web-footed bird
85. Bankroll
86. Bro, e.g.

DOWN

1. Croaker
2. Closet bar
3. Bill collector?
4. Lower jaw
5. Objective
6. Nope's opposite
7. Utter loudly
11. Permit
13. Elementary
14. Correct
15. Adjust
16. Debris
17. Key
18. Named at birth
19. Cleanse
21. Bark at the moon
22. That lady
26. Be adequate
27. Mr. Lugosi
29. Mistakenly
31. Rations out
32. Gehrig or Costello
33. With spirit
34. Put into office
36. Pit vipers
38. Opening
39. Sharpen
43. Save me!
44. Designated space
45. Watercourse
49. Paddles
50. Small amount
56. Put off
57. Monkey business?
60. Library stamp
62. Gone
63. "The ___ Squad"
65. Conjunctions
67. Simple
68. Comb's creation
70. Curious
72. Negligent
74. Cruel
76. Performed well on
77. Salamanders
78. Rosemary or thyme
79. "L.A. ___"
80. Muslim leader
82. Maui handout

Starting box on page 562

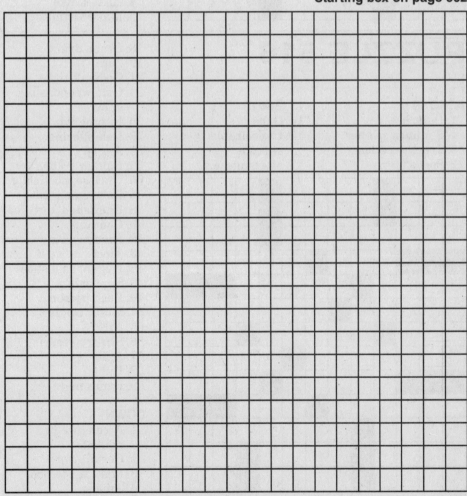

459

PUZZLE 515

ACROSS
1. Retired for the night
5. Shoo!
9. With it
12. Dramatic part
13. Per
14. 100%
15. Shopper's mecca
16. Initial wager
17. Apply
18. Powder mineral
20. Ran in neutral
22. Polite address
25. Land parcel
27. Previous to, poetically
28. List of options
30. Fades
34. Add spice
36. Chest of drawers
38. Angel's headpiece
39. Reckon
41. Had pasta
42. Male singer
44. Trails
46. Seashore
49. Swear at
51. Poke fun at
52. Aroma
54. Data
58. Ailing
59. Dawn, in verse
60. Gateway
61. Short farewell
62. TV and jet
63. Sidle

DOWN
1. Coat sleeve
2. Feathery wrap
3. House addition
4. "___ Dawn"
5. Make airtight
6. French dance
7. Ham it up
8. Not our
9. Lug
10. Choice word
11. Appealed
19. Bullets, for short
21. Forest creature
22. Screen
23. ___ code
24. Business arrangement
26. Six-sided solid
29. Terminates
31. Tempo
32. Basin
33. Brings to court
35. Blubbers
37. Strike callers
40. Accompany
43. Potent particles
45. In reserve
46. Baby's bed
47. Greasy
48. Having talent
50. Coffee containers
53. Bambi's mom, e.g.
55. Give silent consent
56. London forecast
57. Miner's find

PUZZLE 516

ACROSS
1. Dark bread
4. Sunburn soother
8. Truck sections
12. Poet's always
13. Bewail
14. Gape
15. Undesirable animals
17. Mortgage, e.g.
18. Grape drink
19. Zero
21. Godiva's title
24. Give weapons to anew
26. In progress
28. Deli offering
32. Angry
33. Bald or golden
35. Unclose, poetically
36. Bake-sale treat
38. Cherished
40. Contains
42. Hive insects
43. Alert
46. Fasten, as a shoe
48. Supper, e.g.
49. Each person
54. Water carrier
55. Nil
56. Stir-fry vessel
57. Agile
58. Duos
59. Ram's mate

DOWN
1. Accelerate in neutral
2. Certain vote
3. Make a boo-boo
4. Among
5. Recluse
6. Cereal type
7. Entangle
8. Pillar
9. Very eager
10. Dull
11. Mailed
16. BLT spread
20. Disney's mermaid
21. Meadow baby
22. Remotely
23. Fuddy-duddy
25. Urged (on)
27. Choir member
29. Bird that coos
30. Three-sided blade
31. Beatty film
34. Malady
37. Completely
39. Comply with
41. Shorthand pro
43. Little devils
44. Tide type
45. Bazaar
47. Enrages
50. Solemn promise
51. Have bills
52. Pronto!
53. ___ out (make do)

ACROSS

1. Auction action
4. Bridle part
7. Pop
11. Buck
12. Lemon drink
13. ___ paper
14. Exclusive residential area
17. Omani, e.g.
18. Doing nothing
22. United States, e.g.
23. Judah Ben ___
25. More joyful
27. Major or Minor
28. With the most marbles?
31. ___ Inn (hotel chain)
32. Whittle (down)
33. Cracker type
35. Commandment number
38. Sewer line?
39. Canola ___
40. Not at work
43. Ham it up
45. Piggies
47. Diddly
48. Crowbar, e.g.
49. Baking qty.
50. Like some humor
51. Participated in a race
52. Shade provider
54. Simple syllable
56. Music players
59. Made eggs
61. Have something
62. Declared
64. Procrastinate
65. Pea's place
66. Double-helix stuff
67. Cocktail lounge
69. Lyric poem
70. Pert
73. Historical novel
75. ___ Kai-shek
77. Nastier
79. Eastern European
83. North American heron
85. City trains
86. Make a cryptogram
88. Optic problem
89. Lighten up
91. Dog family member
94. Radiate
95. Grounded bird
96. Made a lap
97. Pen points
98. Jazz composition
99. Secret agent man

DOWN

1. Nuts and ___
2. Where Hindi is spoken
3. Art style
4. How do ewe do?
5. Some have pictures on them
6. Tie up
7. Microwave button
8. Above, to a bard
9. Apothecary measure
10. Pub purchases
14. Stocky antelope
15. Dinghy thingy
16. Switch positions
18. Cookbook author Rombauer
19. Oahu attraction
20. Directed
21. Notable time
24. Operate
26. Go, team!
29. Simian
30. '60s war zone
33. "___ Milk?"
34. Laugh and a half
35. Address book no.
36. Capital in the land of Oz
37. PBS program
38. Feminine pronoun
41. Douglas ___
42. Take wing
44. Is inclined
46. 300 spoiler
53. Farm outbuilding
54. Touch
55. Brazilian resort
57. Bright color
58. Dirty dishes collector
59. HST's predecessor
60. Pigment
63. Calendar unit
67. Coal-storage place
68. Good service?
71. Despise
72. Vane letters
73. Sniggler's pursuit
74. Joe Montana, e.g.
75. "JAG" network
76. Success
77. Bumps into
78. Vroom
79. Discard
80. Towering
81. Flurry
82. Madden
84. Calling-card info
87. Famous loch
90. Sis, e.g.
92. "___ Believer"
93. Carry with effort

PUZZLE 517

• VERY VALUABLE •

461

PUZZLE 518

ACROSS
1. Kermit's comment
6. Drink heartily
10. Scottish family
14. Mantel
15. Grandma
16. Golfer's target
17. Common viper
18. Pesters
19. Frosting user
20. Two, in Madrid
21. Affirmative gesture
23. Punted
25. Guarded
28. Place for books
30. Model T, e.g.
31. Nib
34. Title of respect
35. When all ___ fails . . .
37. Andes climber
39. Deep female voice
40. Run-down
42. Historic times
43. Itty-bitty
45. Come up
46. Clothes
47. Snaky curve
48. Chalet feature
50. Intense, as pain
52. Pendant shape
54. Damage
58. Whichever
59. Misbehaving
62. The Grateful ___
63. Copycat
66. Speechify
68. Leisure
69. Conquer
70. Eagle's weapon
71. Picnic annoyances
72. Watcher
73. Opponent

DOWN
1. Garbed
2. Make over
3. Track numbers
4. Stage of life
5. Corn piece
6. Insulting
7. Strife
8. Squid fluid
9. Joint seal
10. Fashionable
11. Canal feature
12. Not aweather
13. Dull person
22. Bid
24. Matinee headliner
25. Speed ___ (fast driver)
26. Less pleasant
27. Tunes for two
28. Bargain events
29. Loathes
31. Fortune-teller's card
32. Appearance
33. Quarterback's throw
34. Partner
36. Immature insect
38. Diminish
41. Long
44. Tibetan creature
49. Supply with oxygen
51. Wolflike animal
53. Challenger
54. Thought
55. Stingy
56. Previous
57. Fruity drinks
59. Unit of cotton
60. Nature's building block
61. Say no to
64. Income
65. ___ out a living
67. Managed

PUZZLE 519

Piece by Piece

We have eliminated the spaces between the words in a message and divided all the letters into 3-letter pieces. Rearrange the pieces to reconstruct the message. The dashes indicate the number of letters in each word.

AKI ART ATH EEL EIN ERE EVE EYW GAG HOS HTH NGG NIF
NSI OFB OFM OME OOD STS TCO THE TSF UES WIS YOU

___ ___ ___ ___ ___ ___   ___ ___ ___ ___ ___ ___ ___ ___ ___   ___ ___ ___ ___ ___ ___ ___ ___   ___ ___ ___ ___ ___ ___ ___

___ ___ ___ ___ ___   ___ ___ ___ ___ ___ ___ ___   ___ ___ ___   ___ ___ ___ ___   ___ ___ ___

___ ___ ___ ___ ___ ___   ___ ___ ___   ___ ___ ___ ___ ___

___ ___ ___ ___ ___ ___ ___ ___ ___   ___ ___ ___ ___ ___ ___ ___

PUZZLE 520

ACROSS

1. Honolulu hello
6. Feather scarf
9. Bursts
13. Champagne cocktail
15. Large coffeepot
16. Nautical position
17. Publishes
18. Gender
19. Compass point
20. Used a chair
21. Glimpse
23. Nitwits
25. On the loose
26. Complain
27. Aerial
30. Got too big for
34. Deceitful person
35. African fly
37. Bitter anger
38. Aquatic bird
39. Fireplace residue
40. Farm unit
41. Work onstage
42. Detected
45. Humble
46. Aretha hit
48. Archives
50. Not so much
51. Plumber's problem
52. Tilted
55. Chapel song
56. Lass
59. ___-a-lug
60. Mimic
62. Power
64. Diner's card
65. Female pig
66. Having more morning moisture
67. Rim
68. ___ and yang
69. Solid

DOWN

1. Current measures
2. Former Milan money
3. Skip over
4. Deary
5. To the rear
6. Bustling
7. Native metal
8. Upset
9. Handling roughly
10. Bread spread
11. Annoying one
12. Collections
14. Comply
22. Serfs
24. Calendar entry
25. Common plant
26. Maternal
27. Church area
28. Dorothy, to Em
29. Little pies
31. Kitchen tool
32. Did wrong
33. Time periods
36. Superman's letter
40. Frenzied
42. Recognized
43. Rapture
44. Considered
47. Calamity
49. Put in a tin
52. Apex
53. Cast off
54. Breathing organ
55. Chopped
56. Smirk
57. Matures
58. Harplike instrument
61. Luau dish
63. Wool producer

In the Middle

PUZZLE 521

Fill in the squares to form a word that is the missing link to connect the two given words. For example, if the two given words were CRAB and SAUCE, the missing link would be APPLE (Crab apple, Applesauce).

1.

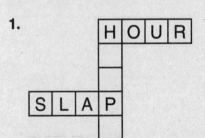

2.

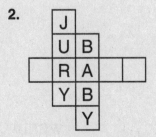

3.

PUZZLE 522

ACROSS

1. Layered mineral
5. Cathedral area
9. Race type
13. Skunk's weapon
14. Overindulge
15. Tantrum
16. Arched ceiling
17. Ranch eatery
19. Santa's helper
20. Determination
21. Mental picture
22. Leered at
24. Conclusion
26. Take for a time
28. Dracula's garb
29. That lady
32. Misbehave
33. Customers
35. Check
36. Plank
37. Booty
38. Protective sheet
40. Ms. Hopper
41. Building extensions
42. Bowler feature
43. Football shirt
44. Coordination
45. French hat
46. Desert relief
49. Holland export
50. Awesome!
53. Sounds familiar
56. Pulled violently
57. Scottish group
58. Mr. Savalas
59. Indigo dye
60. Poisonous serpents
61. Wriggly
62. Jamaican fruit

DOWN

1. Way
2. Groupie's obsession
3. Quilts
4. "We ___ the Champions"
5. Garden pest
6. Sulk
7. Thus, to Cato
8. Lodge member
9. Stage offering
10. Sitar music
11. Highly curious
12. Chromosome part
14. Metal fastener
18. Make broader
20. Unappetizing food
23. Sourpuss
24. Rock pile
25. Unbarred, to a bard
26. Sew loosely
27. Base eight
28. Assert
29. Impulsive
30. Sidestep
31. Pass along
33. Baby's woe
34. "Being ___"
36. Catch fire
39. Chasm
40. Sage or thyme
43. Toast topper
44. Roadway markers
45. Threaten
46. Whale of a movie
47. Feels unwell
48. Break sharply
49. Sunday toller
51. Seed coat
52. Sub shop
54. Gulped down
55. Andy's aunt
56. Greek letter

PUZZLE 523 — Changaword

Can you change the top word into the bottom word in each column in the number of steps indicated in parentheses? Change only one letter at a time and do not change the order of the letters. Proper names, slang, and obsolete words are not allowed.

1. POST (4 steps)   2. MISS (4 steps)   3. POKE (5 steps)   4. SHOP (5 steps)

CARD   IONS   WEED   WORN

464

BRICK BY BRICK

Rearrange this stack of bricks to form a crossword puzzle. The clues will help you fit the bricks into their correct places. Row 1 has been filled in for you. Use the bricks to fill in the remaining spaces.

ACROSS

1. Tater
   Display box
   Hence
2. Tasting of port
   Incan climber
   Dirt
3. Prewar
   Stack
4. Maui meal
   Laser units
   Baklava
   dough
5. Intervene
   Befuddled
6. Commercials
   Work bit
   Greek letter
7. Additional
   Economic
   decline
8. Cassette
   Aches
   Presage
9. Conquers
   Blemishes
10. Got hitched
    Fling
    Diving bird
11. Vocal
    Jewelry buy
12. White whale
    Atlas spot
    NFL player
13. Blue bloom
    Time past
14. Desqueaks
    Shoe bottoms
    Coffeepots
15. Char
    Salamander
    Big pond

DOWN

1. Exchanges
   Store
   Life stories
2. Grape type
   Blacktop
   Song canal
3. Loosen
   Acted like
   Actress Lee
4. Color
   Kitchen gizmo
   WWII nation
5. Groom's mate
   Heavy shoe
6. Scrubs
   Cheers
7. Comrade
   Cuban dance
   Eternity
8. Chip dip
   Bard's before
   Fine thread
9. Large bird
   Factions
   Hearty soup
10. Electrical units
    Most skilled
11. Witches
    More certain
12. Glimpse
    Boffo!
    Mr. Brynner
13. Make muddy
    Strong cotton
    Verdi work
14. Fish organ
    Weeder
    Wind up
15. Toast spread
    Hostelries
    Stallion

BRICKS

(brick grid)

DIAGRAM

(15x15 grid, row 1: S P U D _ _ C A S E _ _ E R G O)

PUZZLE 525

ACROSS

1. Not ons
5. Concept
9. Coarse files
14. Beaut
15. Invalid
16. Pull strings?
17. Snare, e.g.
18. Trucker's rig
19. Express
20. Feat
22. Former soldier
24. Save
27. Powder ___
28. Noteworthy period
29. Baby's word
31. Hand warmer
36. Gaucho's tool
38. Polka ___
39. Copying
41. Judgment
43. Workout area
45. Hoard
46. Flood wall
47. Sawbones
49. ___ gin
50. Mends
52. Role model
54. High railways
55. Tease
57. Snuggle
59. Spear
64. Moral crime
65. Miss Oyl
66. Bestowed
69. Eye
73. Water tubes
74. Cattle
75. Street
76. Advances
77. Writing
78. Hauls

DOWN

1. Ancient
2. Mink's coat
3. Winter ill
4. Poison ___
5. In lieu
6. Proper
7. Shade giver
8. Vital
9. Corrosion
10. Stake
11. Excel
12. Pocket bread
13. Witnessed
21. Cow's chew
23. Hen output
24. Mutiny
25. Wore away
26. Lip wetter
27. Grasshopper
30. Hound
32. ___ Palmas
33. Elects
34. Purple
35. Register
37. Sampras, e.g.
40. Honkers
42. Derek's number
44. Up-to-date
48. Approval
51. ___ slope
53. Luau welcome
56. Metal mold
58. Grunt
59. Mr. Lennon
60. Burn herb
61. Travel permit
62. Anytime
63. Minus
67. Wood chopper
68. Irritate
70. Gunk
71. Decree
72. Koch and Ames

ACROSS

1. Pile up
6. Chemin de ___
9. Toupee spot
13. Saskatchewan city
15. Age of note
16. Estate unit
17. Encircled
18. Large weight
19. Harness part
20. Openings
21. Most recent
23. Horned vipers
24. Some hardwoods
25. Turf piece
27. Loose
29. "___ Alibi"
32. Retain
35. Skirt type
36. Stopwatches
38. Breed of dog
40. Project
41. Satire's kin
42. Road marker
43. Sprechen ___ Deutsch?
44. Love seat
45. Teen's woe
46. Dance outfit
48. Suture
49. Retiring
50. Scribe's need
52. Landed
55. Cognizant of
58. Grander
61. Drag
64. Resounded
65. Gorilla, e.g.
66. Digestion aid
68. Kind
69. Mr. Heflin
70. More trite
71. Snow coaster
72. High railways
73. Correct

DOWN

1. Jason's ship
2. Israel's Golda ___
3. Taj Mahal's site
4. Mr. Caesar
5. Fishing gadget
6. Celebration
7. Amor
8. Throws a fit
9. Cavalcade
10. Mavens
11. Excursion
12. Poetic nights
14. Early man?
22. Casual wear
24. Way out
26. Approves
27. Boundary
28. Good-bye
30. Gush
31. Revival
33. Period
34. Involving wordplay
35. French pronoun
36. Deadlock
37. Bread grain
39. Holy cow!
42. Play players
44. Solar body
47. Tinted
51. Rascal
53. Minus
54. Upset
55. Footed vases
56. Bucket
57. Earlier
59. Fiery gem
60. Affleck et al.
61. Clay square
62. Cooker
63. Beaver's dad
67. Flee

PUZZLE 527

ACROSS
1. Cunning
4. TV's Griffin
8. Trite
13. Seek the love of
14. Edible bulb
16. Lineup
17. Wintry
18. Rubbish
19. Express
20. Positive
22. Third letters
23. More unusual
24. Snitch
26. Night sight
28. Sporty socks
32. Entered data
36. Mink's coat
37. Cling
40. Choppers
42. Soothing herbs
44. ___ League
45. Piece
46. Back end
47. Address
49. Many
50. Quick bite
52. High fliers
54. Snake sound
57. This lady
58. Large nail
62. ___ moss
64. Sell
68. Recluse
69. Pungent
71. Bird call
72. Fall flower
73. Memo pro
74. Spicy
75. Fake
76. Scholar
77. Not offs

DOWN
1. Guzzle
2. Daft
3. Child's toy
4. Trim
5. Passed laws
6. Get up
7. Ballots
8. Tasty
9. Plodded
10. Parched
11. Shoestring
12. Ogler
15. Coop seat
21. Evaporate
25. Too bad!
27. Wolfed down
28. Yonder
29. Guidelines
30. Creak
31. Boat
33. Friend
34. Deport
35. Room style
38. Night before
39. Bar orders
41. Pairs
43. Baseball stat
45. Persian king
47. Snow slat
48. With a price of
51. Red fruit
53. Gun a motor
55. Health spots
56. Factions
58. Spank
59. Elegant
60. Involved with
61. Alert
63. Site
65. Canyon sound
66. Lunch hour
67. Dabs
70. Bambi's mom

ACROSS

1. Attired
5. Gold fabric
9. Sanctify
14. Lodge
15. Utah city
16. Variety show
17. High point
18. Brewed drinks
19. Spy
20. Small plateau
21. Summer shade
22. Irritates
23. "O Sole ___"
25. Seer's card
29. Playful animal
32. Tease
33. Cee's follower
36. Matched
38. Fair feature
39. Lawn tree
40. House annex
41. Certain gasket
43. Corn core
44. Lobster eggs
45. Random try
46. Flee
49. Furthermore
50. Coop dweller
51. Tanker
52. Toy bear
54. Rural hotel
55. Hearty meal
58. Ancient
60. Actor Jannings
64. Reviled
66. Pagan god
67. Skirt style
68. Church fixture
69. Marie's mom
70. Greek deity
71. Bothersome
72. Appealed
73. Chair, e.g.

DOWN

1. Silent type
2. Boot tie
3. Goals
4. Visionary
5. Gambling game
6. Scope
7. Signified
8. Dash lengths
9. Bikini half
10. Lawful
11. Eternally
12. Plunged
13. Puts
24. Ill temper
26. Related
27. Line of hills
28. Lyric poem
29. Verdi's forte
30. Bird's claw
31. Like a mosaic
33. Transferred art
34. Run off to wed
35. Live coal
37. Was overfond
38. Make fun of
42. Writer Ayn ___
45. This lady
47. Male child
48. Theaters
52. Pinch
53. Alpine call
54. Lounged
55. Bloke
56. Healthy
57. Baseball's Mel and family
59. Knowledge
61. Deep mud
62. Conception
63. Directory
65. Not damp
66. Small demon

PUZZLE 529

ACROSS

1. Weapons
5. ___ stick
9. Little bird
13. Orderly
14. Rates
16. Healthy
17. Hired car
18. Bother
19. Keats works
20. Throw
22. Morse ___
24. Drama part
25. Waterfowl
28. Signals
30. Fold over
33. Snack
34. At once
35. Flightless bird
36. Phooey!
39. Oyster find
43. Diamond, e.g.
44. Oval shape
46. Mushy stuff
47. Slowpoke
49. Reflex site
50. Loop rails
51. Lubricate
53. Fairy
55. Lousy grade
56. Quickly
59. Lazy person
61. Wiggly fish
62. Smooth
64. Compact ___
68. Crimson hues
70. Spare
73. Adhesive
74. Thought
75. Defies
76. Spanish hello
77. Wildcat
78. Mimic
79. Reveal

DOWN

1. Tiny insects
2. Genuine
3. Skirt type
4. Bee bite
5. Tent spike
6. Rowing blade
7. Elegance
8. Atop
9. Rock's The ___
10. Plane spotter
11. Choose
12. Bird homes
15. Car type
21. Golly!
23. Flee to wed
26. ___ Grey tea
27. Stem
29. Meadow mama
30. Table parts
31. Hymn ender
32. Cougar
37. Can metal
38. Haste
40. Matured
41. Stage part
42. Misplace
44. Nobility
45. Persuade
48. Charged atom
52. Adored
54. Supplied food
56. Hazard
57. Marshy
58. Of yore
59. Prelim
60. Not left
63. Quiz
65. Gin fruit
66. Select
67. Emblem
69. Clinton's horn
71. ___ room
72. Solicit

PUZZLE 530

ACROSS

1. Current measures
5. Tramp
9. Converse
13. Tot's toy
14. In a pen
15. Brave man
16. Absent
17. Took on
18. Relay, e.g.
19. Canary or cat
20. Clearance
21. Consommes
23. Bridge supports
25. Focus
26. Hitched
27. Branch of math
31. Broken-bone brace
34. Nothing
35. Shred
36. Warn
37. Louse
38. Serpent
40. Price to pay
41. Shirt
42. Praised
43. Hearing range
46. Owl or eagle
47. Spider's trap
48. Carefully
52. Movie house
55. Carry on
56. Shade
57. On a cruise
58. Pursue
60. "___ Breckin-ridge"
61. Vegas machine
62. Protect
63. Iowa city
64. Wallet items
65. Bard's poems
66. Termite, e.g.

DOWN

1. Change to fit
2. Lawn cutter
3. Shallow dish
4. Shrewd
5. Cheered
6. Tyrants
7. Honey producer
8. Weird one
9. Auto trim
10. Warm
11. Curved structure
12. Piggies
14. Swiss cottage
20. Tour of duty
22. Gear
24. Fuss
27. Rescue
28. Small nail
29. Leaf gatherer
30. Ancient
31. Burglar's target
32. Request
33. Amorous look
34. Siesta
37. Bunk
38. Army noncom
39. Unclothed
41. Snuff stuff
42. Loiter
44. Perspires
45. Sewn edge
46. Prejudices
48. Serious
49. Verse
50. Entices
51. Baker's need
52. Angler's throw
53. Bit of land
54. Bright light
59. Coal bucket
60. Street guide

PUZZLE 531

ACROSS
1. Rice dish
6. Glory
10. Did the butterfly
14. Dodge
15. Fund advance
16. Mild
17. Less dated
18. Goofs up
19. American composer
20. Gaucho's aid
22. Boxing venue
23. MTV offering
26. Got an A+ on
28. Kitchen alcove
30. Shirt part
31. Knock
34. Caper
35. Handiwork
37. Tranquil
39. Indifferent
41. Lobe's site
43. Head supports
44. Drizzled
46. Groaner
48. Current unit
49. Picnic crasher
50. Pull
52. Grows
54. Center
56. Necessities
57. Quantity
61. Wall hanging
63. "Aida" air
64. Feminine suffix
65. Chewy candy
70. Inner man
71. Venerable
72. Cast out
73. Loathe
74. Hardy girl
75. Premiere

DOWN
1. Animal's cage
2. Detect ending
3. Order's mate
4. Lime drink
5. Polecat
6. Tiny jumper
7. Vital vessel
8. Spanish rattle
9. Half ems
10. Hubbub
11. Breaker
12. So be it!
13. Arizona city
21. Bit
22. Jingle writers
23. Fiddle
24. Least open
25. Train stop
27. Hosp. rooms
28. Ibsen output
29. Prior to, in poems
31. Tape
32. Leg joints
33. Irritants
36. Draw off
38. Follies
40. Go and get
42. Bar bottle
45. Dyad
47. Granny
51. Farmers' group
53. Quizzed
55. Marine birds
57. Hit hard
58. Location
59. Lean
60. Coffeehouse
62. Beatty film
64. Sup
66. Chopper
67. Falsehood
68. Common virus
69. Until now

CLUES IN TWOS

Some of the Clues in this crossword are In Twos. Fill in two different answers to the same clue in the squares indicated.

ACROSS

1. ⎤
4. ⎦ Fling
8. Roma robe
12. Bullring cheer
13. Sector
14. Affirm
15. ⎤
17. ⎦ Salve
18. Carry
19. Pact
21. ⎤
24. ⎦ Snatch
28. Flee
31. Foundation
34. Conducted
35. Single
36. Piece
37. Boy
38. Put in curlers
39. Cow's milk gland
40. Cunning
41. Promise
43. Pen
45. March date
48. Other
52. ⎤
55. ⎦ Buffs
58. Wicked
59. Increase
60. Doze
61. Printer's term
62. Sailboat
63. Endeavor

DOWN

1. Bounty
2. Medley
3. Crooked
4. Beret on the brae
5. Mineral
6. Transmit
7. Gratify
8. Postpone
9. Eggs
10. Hair tamer
11. Limb
16. Decimal unit
20. Declare
22. Ridiculous
23. Uncovered
25. Troubles
26. Ardor
27. Whirlpool
28. Defeat
29. Afresh
30. Dole
32. Puppeteer Krofft
33. Frosts
42. Lane
44. However
46. Uneasy
47. Antitoxins
49. Fasting period
50. Singe
51. View
52. Nourished
53. Hail
54. Nothing
56. Pledge
57. Night bird

PUZZLE 533

ACROSS
1. Clod
4. Slacken
8. Rogues
12. Long, long ____
13. Encourage
14. Site
15. Lantern fuel
17. Grain grinder
18. Birthday greeting
19. Amend copy
20. Monastery
23. Furthermore
26. ____ monster (lizard)
27. Summit
28. Mexican year
31. Ex-sinner, at times
33. Chipped
35. Confederate Johnny ____
36. Humble
38. Chauffeured car
39. Has dinner
40. Glory
41. Short reminder
44. "____ the night . . ."
46. Constantly
47. Hair clasp
51. Chardonnay, e.g.
52. News flash
53. Manner
54. Garble
55. Hideouts
56. Ajar, to a bard

DOWN
1. Acorn bearer
2. Get older
3. "____ the Boys"
4. Thesis
5. Impersonator
6. Ice-cream treat
7. Prior to, in verse
8. Carved gem
9. Parched
10. Salami seller
11. Pepper's mate
16. Atlantic, e.g.
20. Food thickener
21. Nibble
22. Soft lump
24. Tall and thin
25. Use snow runners
27. Make ready
28. Comparable
29. Verne captain
30. Stink
32. Outback avian
34. ____ shave
37. Country manor
39. More achy
40. Injures
41. Kittens' sounds
42. Wicked
43. Entree list
45. Little songbird
47. Bridge move
48. Duo
49. Faucet
50. Needle hole

PUZZLE 534

ACROSS
1. Nearly all
5. Pot donation
9. "Harper Valley ____"
12. Move slowly
13. Dolt
14. Meal starter
15. Wound mark
16. Dental problem
18. Trailer truck
19. Lariat
20. Hawaiian gift
22. Istanbul native
26. Embrace
30. Midafternoon
31. Mauna ____
32. Spicy dish
34. Cavity
35. Judge's seat
37. Musical event
39. Voice range
40. Sailor's yes
41. Regularly
45. Reckless
49. Maintain
52. World's fair, e.g.
53. Shad delicacy
54. Sly gaze
55. Healing plant
56. Bird of prey
57. Camera part
58. "____ Make a Deal"

DOWN
1. Fail to hit
2. Formerly
3. Hoax
4. Wave of excitement
5. Do away with
6. Bossa ____
7. Piggies
8. Slips up
9. Luau fare
10. Create lace
11. Feasted
17. "____ Sides Now"
21. Every
23. Hankering
24. Back end
25. Held onto
26. Exile isle
27. Yuletide
28. "____ Hardly Wait"
29. Photo
30. Very small
33. Repair-shop rentals
36. Pigeons' purrs
38. Breakfast food
42. Tripped
43. Hickory, e.g.
44. Level
46. Wheel shaft
47. Dirt stain
48. Weeding tools
49. Con's foe
50. Propel a boat
51. Skinny fish

474

DOUBLE TROUBLE

PUZZLE 535

Not really double trouble, but double fun! Solve this puzzle as you would a regular crossword, except place one, two, or three letters in each box. The number of letters in each answer is shown in parentheses after its clue.

ACROSS
1. Fuzzy fruit (5)
4. Stake (5)
7. Part of REM (5)
10. Poi party (4)
11. Hire (6)
12. Kind of scout (6)
13. Finger woe (8)
15. Certain shop (9)
16. Notebook binding (6)
17. Birthmark (4)
18. Soft wool (8)
21. Grilled cheese, e.g. (8)
24. City in North Italy (5)
25. Noisy brawl (6)
26. Texas town (6)
28. Defense building (8)
30. Very best (6)
31. Spot (5)

32. Grimm guy (5)
33. Risky undertaking (7)
36. Camaraderie (10)
39. Fragrant rootstock (5)
40. Prickly plants (5)
41. Brink (5)
43. 39.37 inches (5)
44. Stew staples (6)
45. Wander (4)

DOWN
1. Ring (4)
2. Beginning point (4)
3. Lug (4)
4. Kind of heating (7)
5. Light beer (5)
6. Mirror product (5)
7. Proportion (5)
8. Chums (4)
9. Card or crisis (8)
14. Motivate (7)

15. Large shorebird (6)
17. Worker's bane? (6)
18. Tube top? (3)
19. Form (5)
20. Singer Ethel ___ (6)
21. Yellow-orange (7)
22. Cut cleaner (6)
23. Game of kings? (5)
25. Once more (5)
27. GRE's kin (3)
29. Sample (5)

30. Tail (6)
32. Vine ladder (7)
33. Poison (5)
34. Castle tower (6)
35. Part of a flight (5)
36. Clique (7)
37. Catch a chill (6)
38. Malayan boat (4)
40. Hoodwink (3)
42. Treasured one (3)

Build-A-Quote

PUZZLE 536

Fill in the diagrams by putting the lines of letters VERTICALLY into their squares. The letters in each line must remain in the same order. The lines are given in jumbled order. When finished, you will be able to read a saying ACROSS the rows in each diagram.

1.

A C T L T S
N D W I Y S
O E E R A I
M R E W H T
L I R S S B
Y O I A A E

2.

T B E S Y E
S S S D U U
U O M Y Y L
S L E O O F
T Y A A B R
A M R L U S

PUZZLE 537

ACROSS

1. The Red ____ (Snoopy's foe)
6. Mark permanently
10. Moist
14. "Home ____"
15. Opera solo
16. Lamb's pen name
17. Mississippi, e.g.
18. Waist accessory
19. Tuna containers
20. ____ whiz!
21. Eye
23. Makes like Chubby Checker
25. Make ____ meet (get by)
27. Slithery swimmer
28. Box top
29. Scottish cap
31. Fundraiser
35. "M*A*S*H" character
38. Corn and canola
40. "Car 54, Where ____ You?"
41. Aware
42. Expert
43. Toga wearer
45. Body of water
46. Warmth
47. Modify
48. Retirement money
51. Health resort
52. Actor Chaney
53. "Murder, ____ Wrote"
55. Actor's part
59. Explain clearly
62. Musical sound
64. Rocky pinnacle
65. Dry
66. Narrow cut
68. Helicopter part
70. Provoke
71. Floor square
72. Over-weight
73. Golf gadgets
74. Holler
75. Fathered

DOWN

1. Flat-bottomed vessel
2. E.T., e.g.
3. Wandered
4. "____ Day at a Time"
5. Fiddling emperor
6. Expensive fur
7. Fisher-man's basket
8. Feel sick
9. Babies' noise-makers
10. Choose
11. Woe is me!
12. Julep flavor
13. Football throw
22. Jewel
24. Gain victory
26. "A ____ Is Born"
30. Comic Carney
31. Ink spot
32. Widespread reputation
33. Iraq's neighbor
34. Watch over
35. Grate
36. Away from the wind
37. Actor Martin
38. Not closed
39. Gershwin brother
43. Musical style
44. Actor Sharif
46. Truthfulness
49. Playground features
50. Charged particle
51. Congressman: abbr.
53. Not moving
54. "Grand ____"
56. Playful aquatic mammal
57. Not tight
58. Blundered
59. Pub missile
60. Great Lake
61. Manicurist's tool
63. Greek god of love
67. Fib
69. Kimono sash

PUZZLE 538   Linkwords

Add a Linkword to the end of the word on the left and the beginning of the word on the right to form two compound words or phrases. The dashes indicate the number of letters in the Linkword. For example, if the words were PEANUT _ _ _ _ _ _ FLY, the Linkword would be BUTTER (Peanut butter, Butterfly).

1. PAN __ __ __ __ WALK

2. DRY __ __ __ __ FLOWER

3. SCHOOL __ __ __ __ HORSE

4. SAIL __ __ __ __ SWAIN

5. TOLL __ __ __ __ PLANT

6. CART __ __ __ __ __ BARROW

7. WHIRL __ __ __ __ __ FALL

8. WILD __ __ __ NIP

9. MOUSE __ __ __ __ DOOR

10. STAR __ __ __ __ PAN

476

PUZZLE 539

ACROSS

1. Computer device
6. Tell all
10. Agony
14. Not sleeping
15. Olden days
16. Before
17. Surrendered
18. Highland hats
19. Fume
20. Dangerous curve
21. Thing
23. Casual top
25. Gooey substance
26. Mama's boy
27. Treatment center
30. Couple
31. Man
34. Very dry champagne
35. Father
37. Buoyant wood
39. Pledge
40. Confined area
41. Active person
42. Geek
44. Affect
46. Fat
47. Chicago railways
48. Ostrichlike bird
50. Confesses
52. Firm up
53. Chatter
54. Brunch beverage
58. Cake layer
60. Keats poem
63. Aroma
64. Attendee
66. Judge's mallet
68. Soothing plant
69. Tapered sword
70. Paragon
71. Butterfly snares
72. Crimson hues
73. Techies

DOWN

1. Defensive spray
2. Is indebted to
3. Patriarchs
4. Make do
5. Highway divider
6. Computer term
7. Fertile soil
8. Give guns to
9. Present, as a gift
10. Stylishly elegant
11. Opposer
12. Froster
13. Certain amphibian
22. Stumble
24. Haughty person
25. Church's portion
26. Poem division
27. Go very slow
28. Stringed instruments
29. Detergent measure
31. Crow
32. Clients
33. Scotland ___
34. Foretell
36. Podded vegetable
38. Improvise
43. Entreats
45. Sidle
49. Inadequate
51. Page border
54. Wail
55. Sit around
56. Hypothetical
57. Lode loads
58. Mounted on a peg
59. Incenses
60. Atop
61. ___ Sea Scrolls
62. Wings
65. Unclose, poetically
67. Summer refresher

Hubcaps

PUZZLE 540

Insert two letters into the center of each circle below to form three 6-letter words reading across and diagonally (top to bottom). When you are finished, the letters you have entered, reading across, will spell a bonus word.

1.
2.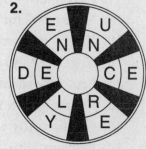
3.
4.

BONUS WORD: ___

477

PUZZLE 541

CAMOUFLAGE

The answers to the clues can be found in the diagram, but they have been camouflaged. Their letters are in correct order, but sometimes are separated by extra letters that have been inserted throughout the diagram. You must black out all the extra letters. Each of the remaining letters will be used in a word reading across and a word reading down. Solve ACROSS and DOWN together to determine the correct letters where there is a choice. The number of answer words in a row or column is indicated by the number of clues.

	1	2	3	4	5	6	7	8	9	10	11	12	13	14	15
1	W	H	I	I	T	H	E	N	P	R	S	T	A	W	N
2	O	V	L	P	E	U	R	I	A	V	A	R	R	E	A
3	N	U	D	Z	H	G	E	A	L	W	M	O	S	H	T
4	N	L	E	A	A	R	N	R	A	E	C	B	E	L	Y
5	D	M	A	I	S	H	U	Y	A	B	U	L	T	Z	T
6	E	A	V	V	E	C	O	S	C	U	L	F	A	T	E
7	A	G	L	O	O	A	K	T	M	T	E	E	S	M	T
8	R	E	S	T	I	V	I	V	E	S	T	A	W	I	R
9	D	R	S	S	N	E	W	I	T	D	E	E	N	N	H
10	I	M	M	A	N	S	I	O	C	N	M	B	F	U	M
11	E	L	Q	L	A	P	S	T	E	A	C	R	E	S	E
12	B	A	L	A	N	Z	S	C	E	R	E	I	L	S	E
13	U	N	U	T	G	I	L	K	N	E	E	U	A	E	L
14	W	V	Y	B	E	N	V	Y	Y	O	E	A	S	T	H
15	T	E	R	E	C	F	E	A	Y	E	M	L	E	O	T

ACROSS

1. Bleach • Shrimp
2. "Aida," e.g. • Zone
3. Prod • Just about
4. Discover • Revolt
5. Meadow flower • Border
6. Icicle's spot • Kiss
7. Crow over • Abound
8. Balky • One of a flight
9. Doodled • Adolescent
10. Stately house • Silent
11. Pass • Unit of property
12. Remainder • Annoy
13. "Wait ____ Dark" • Bow down
14. Urge • Brewing need
15. Ball holder • Shoelace hole

DOWN

1. Amazement • First appearance
2. Luau entertainment • Relevant
3. Flawless • Foxy
4. Vitally important • Broke bread
5. Razz • Silly
6. Solemn • Twirl
7. Heretofore • Ocean oasis
8. Not any • Thickset
9. King's residence • Quite small
10. Negate • Capture
11. Protective charm • Pageant host
12. Lounging wear • Atmospheric
13. On the briny • Or ____! (threat)
14. Bruise • 18th-century dance
15. Talk incessantly • Dissolve

CODEWORD

PUZZLE 542

Instructions for solving Codewords are given on page 11.

Letter key (542):

A = (crossed out)
B
C
D
E
F
G = (crossed out)
H
I = (crossed out)
J
K
L
M
N
O
P
Q
R
S
T
U
V
W
X
Y
Z

Code reference column (542):
1 / 14
2 / 15
3 / 16 — T
4 / 17
5 / 18 — N
6 / 19
7 / 20
8 / 21
9 / 22 — I
10 / 23
11 / 24
12 / 25
13 / 26

Grid (542):

24	23	21		26	15	11	18		9	26	22	25
18	17	23		11	25	22	16		14	17	25	7
19	18	13		15	14	25	15		25	26	2	18
11	18	18	15		16	23	23	11	18			
			26	15	18		24	18	15	26	11	3
1	4	22	25	22		19	22	10		9	26	6
24	14	3		11	12	14	26	3		26	17	23
26	25	18		3	14	5		23	2	24	26	11
8	26	16	8	23	23		26	5	22			
			14	5	3	22	25		5	26	20	18
26	14	3	23		22	21	23	25		17	18	25
10	24	26	7		5	18	5	18		18	3	26
18	5	21	11		17	26	17	26		21	23	5

CODEWORD

PUZZLE 543

Letter key (543):

A
B = (crossed out)
C
D
E
F
G = (crossed out)
H
I
J
K
L
M
N
O
P
Q
R
S
T
U
V
W
X
Y
Z

Code reference column (543):
1 / 14
2 / 15
3 / 16 — T
4 / 17
5 / 18
6 / 19
7 / 20
8 / 21
9 / 22
10 / 23
11 / 24
12 / 25 — O
13 / 26

Grid (543):

25	17	17		16	21	20		2	21	16		5	2	10
11	7	7		9	25	1		10	2	15		2	19	19
10	16	11		16	8	16		7	11	4		14	10	2
3	11	15	2			10	14	16	7	7		14	2	14
			12	16	7	3	11			11	6	2	12	16
11	22	11	7	16	11		21	16	3	2	21	16	16	
10	25	21	16	7	9		11	21	25	23	11			
5	25	16			23	11	24	16	21		17	2	21
			10	24	11	3	16		26	1	11	21	3	25
	23	11	3	2	19	16	16		1	14	21	25	10	16
18	2	19	9	7		3	5	16	10	16				
16	23	10		7	11	10	10	25		11	7	20	11
19	25	8		13	1	3		18	16	3		25	2	7
1	10	16		25	21	16		16	21	21		25	6	2
16	11	21		9	11	8		21	11	9		19	16	3

Given letters in grid (543): T O (row with 26 1 11 21 3 = T O)

479

PUZZLE 544

ACROSS
1. Clash of arms
4. Lobe insert
8. Steered
13. Color
14. Instance
15. Came closer
16. ___ a girl!
17. Skating feat
18. Truly
19. Abyss
21. Records
23. Operative
24. Cavity
25. Stretches
27. Earn
29. Extend
31. It measures rpm
35. Bind again
37. Broad street
39. Go wrong
42. Highest
44. Desire
45. Toxin
47. Bureau
49. Person opposed
50. Slangy refusals
52. Pipe
55. Drip
57. Religious women
59. Band aid
62. Change
65. Ship bunk
66. In abundance
68. Creeper
70. Fabrication
71. Eaten away
72. Prepare (copy)
73. Have being
74. Tailored
75. Salesmen
76. Vigor

DOWN
1. What one?
2. Novelist
3. Secondhand
4. Con
5. Government levy
6. Spent
7. Sub seller
8. Compact
9. Fab!
10. Mined metals
11. Gore, once
12. Nelson or Duane
15. Sobriquet
20. Singe
22. Large amount
26. Holy fem.
28. Mexican money
29. Quick drink
30. Roost
32. A few
33. Signal
34. Coop bird
36. Burrowed
38. Suit item
39. Fitness farm
40. Charged particle
41. Baby bug
43. Doubters' words
46. Ann, to Abby
48. Melody
51. Suitable
53. Gunny
54. Complete
56. Having handles
58. Cote denizen
59. Eternity
60. Maned mama
61. Cultivate
63. Perpetually
64. Take a cab
65. Risks cash
67. Byron product
69. Nibble

PUZZLE 545

ACROSS
1. Darns
5. Phonograph
9. Satchels
13. Three voices
14. Part of BLT
15. Ranch unit
16. Bright
17. Sins
18. Skinny
19. Picnic cooler
20. Hard metal
21. Pup ___
22. Allow
24. Unruly
27. Smooth
29. Petite
30. Prevail
33. Record
36. Stick up
38. Withdraw
40. Love
42. Excessively
44. Colorless gas
45. Levels
47. Radio promos
49. Emerald ___
50. KO count
51. Torso bone
53. Entry
55. Road turns
57. Baseball unit
61. Chess piece
64. TV wire
66. Maiden
67. Utilizes
68. Check word
69. ___ mater
70. Boyfriend
71. Adjust
72. Attendee
73. Welfare
74. Twerp
75. Hurried

DOWN
1. Purse band
2. Eat away
3. Smarter
4. ___ sauce
5. Own
6. More frigid
7. Tail
8. Those elected
9. Crazy
10. Feel pain
11. Beam
12. Shipped
14. Gambler
20. Man's title
23. Tiny
25. Mr. Craven
26. Buck
28. Negative word
30. Unites
31. False god
32. Maui goose
33. Dizzy
34. Dormant
35. Before long
37. Big snake
39. Rocky monument
41. Fouls up
43. Curious
46. Bro's sibling
48. Stained
52. Suited
54. Unit
55. Develop
56. Speaker
58. Snow house
59. Title giver
60. Shine
61. Saloons
62. Confused
63. Frail
65. Turn
68. Skillet
69. Rep.

PUZZLE 546

ACROSS

1. Smudge
6. Fades
10. Mexican fare
14. Bass's kin
15. Metal bar
16. Above
17. Attached
18. With skill
19. Pitched item
20. Tell a fib
21. Prime
23. Bible story
27. Ran wild
31. Noisily
34. Trunk
35. Large fruit
37. Lord's wife
39. Cleopatra's snake
40. Sweetie
41. Wine source
43. Have in view
44. Not in
45. Look like
46. Some tubs
49. Shorthand, shortly
51. Cotton fabric
53. Menace
55. Tool
59. Hockey player
62. Tennis expert
63. Narrow board
66. Seepage
67. Leafy dish
69. Pontiff
70. Event
71. Merge
72. Felled
73. Toboggan, e.g.
74. Groups of computer bits

DOWN

1. Head part
2. TV and radio
3. Senior
4. Bubbly brew
5. Fishing gear
6. Rubbed away
7. Slugger Ruth
8. Paper money
9. Wilier
10. Skin decor
11. Took food
12. Bamboozle
13. Elect
22. Urban place
24. Completely
25. Scary sound
26. Fencer's move
28. Litter
29. Certain curves
30. Dummy
32. Andean animal
33. Bark sharply
35. Tooth locale
36. Keyboard key
38. Ledger column
40. Emcee
42. ___ room (den)
45. Saturate
47. Hole in one
48. Heavy weight
50. Roosted
52. Skulked
54. Powders
56. Tear in half
57. Vexed
58. Ore deposits
60. Wild duck
61. Slacken
63. Health spring
64. Bagel topping
65. Clumsy oaf
67. Pinch hitter
68. Random choice

482

ACROSS

1. Deadly snakes
5. Fibbed
9. Sprinted
13. Honk
14. Pointer
16. Ali, once
17. Aroma
18. Happiness
19. Garden tube
20. Berth places
22. Heeded
24. Dads
25. Sunday song
27. Victim
29. Lard
30. Sushi fish
33. Noisy
34. Buccaneer
36. Swiss peak
38. Shade source
39. Fasten
40. Dowel
41. Busy insect
42. Society miss
43. Implant
45. Doe
46. Epic tale
48. Plaything
49. Dog's cry
50. Metropolitan
52. Egg ___
53. Dresser
56. Epicure
60. Imitates
61. Devotee
64. Roof overhang
65. Ferry, e.g.
66. Made
67. Peepers
68. Finales
69. Reckless
70. Kind

DOWN

1. Tiny particle
2. Fizzy water
3. Needy
4. Like a zebra
5. Buddhist monks
6. Blue bloom
7. Bungle
8. Period
9. Design
10. Stratagem
11. Soothe
12. Colored
15. Stop!
21. Denial
23. Run, as colors
25. Golf score
26. Sparkling
27. Warsaw natives
28. Latin dance
29. Spanish party
31. Price tag
32. Doze off
33. Governed
34. Clip
35. Child
37. Apiece
39. Jeweled headpiece
44. Vast timespan
45. Ranks
47. Visitors
49. "___ Are There"
51. Onion, e.g.
52. Compass point
53. Film pig
54. Aware of
55. Scan
56. Hair goops
57. BLT topper
58. Continually
59. Sample
62. "___ Town"
63. Through

PUZZLE 548   OVERLAPS

Place the answer to each clue into the diagram beginning at the corresponding number. Words will overlap with other words.

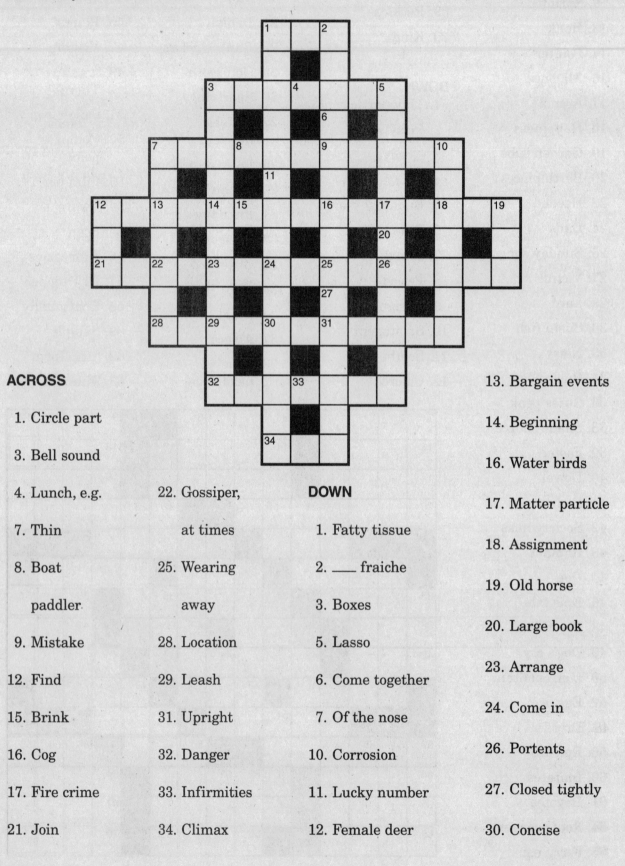

ACROSS

1. Circle part

3. Bell sound

4. Lunch, e.g.

7. Thin

8. Boat

   paddler

9. Mistake

12. Find

15. Brink

16. Cog

17. Fire crime

21. Join

22. Gossiper,

   at times

25. Wearing

   away

28. Location

29. Leash

31. Upright

32. Danger

33. Infirmities

34. Climax

DOWN

1. Fatty tissue

2. ___ fraiche

3. Boxes

5. Lasso

6. Come together

7. Of the nose

10. Corrosion

11. Lucky number

12. Female deer

13. Bargain events

14. Beginning

16. Water birds

17. Matter particle

18. Assignment

19. Old horse

20. Large book

23. Arrange

24. Come in

26. Portents

27. Closed tightly

30. Concise

ACROSS

1. Wise one
5. Ship operators
9. Parsley unit
14. Factual
15. Opening
16. Popeye's girl
17. Bun
18. Measure
19. West Pointer
20. Current measure
21. Betsy or Diana
22. Coal receptacle
23. Hobby
25. Glimpsed
28. Sorbet
29. Blue Oyster ___
30. Carpenter's tool
32. Gleamed
35. Joylessly
36. Caribbean, e.g.
37. Publicize
38. Splurge
39. Embraced
40. Picnic intruder
41. Put in order
42. Ineptly
43. Busy insect
44. Dramatist Coward
45. Winter ill
46. Mythical reptile
48. Earth science
52. Nourished
53. Boxing match
54. Stage signal
55. Not in bed
58. Walk heavily
59. Wild duck
60. Certain tire
61. Went up
62. Noble
63. Summoned
64. Had a debt
65. Ifs, ___, or buts

DOWN

1. Purse band
2. Odor
3. Swallows quickly
4. Shocking fish
5. Metal finish
6. Wake
7. Additions
8. Itty-bitty
9. Group
10. Board
11. Disburden
12. "___ Got a Secret"
13. Receive
21. Paddy harvest
22. Southern beauty
24. Color
25. Chubby
26. Slackened
27. Reside
29. Suez ___
31. Woman
32. Attempt
33. Put an edge on
34. External
35. Seductress
38. Ponder
39. Lug
41. Enraged
42. Pat dry
45. Quarreled
47. In flames
48. Swimming bird
49. Atlantic, e.g.
50. Security officer
51. Screams
53. Punch
55. Viper
56. Resort
57. Running game
58. In support of
59. Hot brew

PUZZLE 550

ACROSS
1. Plant stalk
5. Not 'tain't
8. Dwell (on)
12. Military body
13. Heavenly food
15. Cake finisher
16. Discomfort
17. Cancel
18. Water sport
19. Ankle injury
21. Baby's wear
23. Tease
24. Dozes
27. Rebound
29. Policeman
32. Huge number
34. Speechify
36. Keanu role
37. Flying toys
41. Leading man
42. Fresh
43. Delay
44. Sample
45. Preholiday night
46. Pithy
47. Strong coffee
50. Bench
51. Fireside
54. Evening sight
55. Jeanne d'____
56. Dipping food
58. Felt hat
63. Failure
65. Majestic
68. Eager
69. Bright thought
70. Blunder
71. Flower vessel
72. Experiment
73. Nosh
74. BPOE members

DOWN
1. Tires
2. Golf hazard
3. Arab bigwig
4. Avian gabber
5. Basker's reward
6. Wayside stop
7. Ignore
8. Stylish
9. Tree nut
10. Artifact
11. Investigation
13. Estate
14. Legal excuse
20. Hobbies
22. Novel shop
25. Main meal
26. Shirt parts
28. Join forces
29. Layer
30. Killer whale
31. Strokes
33. Minimum
35. Carrier
38. Canvas cover
39. Otherwise
40. Scads
48. Dial
49. More secure
51. Wont
52. Wear down
53. Zeniths
57. Tiny opening
59. Kline flick
60. Racetrack
61. Jeopardize
62. Citrus drinks
64. Baseball club
66. Lingerie buy
67. Land tract

486

ACROSS

1. Tater
5. Ship's pole
9. Dancer Falana
13. Prong
14. Left, at sea
16. Approval
17. Skating leap
18. Flight part
19. Yearning
20. Copious flow
22. Luau fare
23. Fresh talk
24. Date
25. Squiggly fish
28. Fruit pastry
30. Deceitful
32. Dad's boy
33. Actor Torn
36. Green gems
38. Pay dirt
39. Burn
42. Pierre's key
43. Once more
44. Nasser's gp.
45. Preached
49. Tinting agent
50. Horse's cousin
51. Arctic plain
54. Pick
55. Tool hut
56. Dined
58. Links game
61. Hurt
63. Sputters
65. Be adjacent to
66. Feel
69. Puts to work
70. Had on
71. Follow
72. Coal source
73. Quick-witted
74. Does, e.g.
75. Ifs, ____, or buts

DOWN

1. Headliners
2. Sprites
3. Bumpy
4. Edit out
5. Pas' mates
6. Likely
7. TV dramas
8. Small group
9. Scoundrel
10. Soup pod
11. Hangs back
12. Pro votes
15. Camera holder
21. Paper amount
26. Supplement
27. Song's words
29. Winners
31. Continually, in a poem
32. Detective
33. Mr. Silver
34. Incense
35. Sunday seat
37. Elev.
39. Cow's mouthful
40. Hit the ____
41. "You ____ Sixteen"
43. Include
45. Baby's perch
46. Plantation
47. Ms. McClanahan
48. Outcomes
52. Dried grape
53. Go to
54. Regularly
55. Melting snow
57. Sibilant sounds
58. Stare stupidly
59. Band member
60. Tempt
62. Electrified atoms
64. Cougar
67. Prompt
68. Tom and drake

487

PUZZLE 552

FLOWER POWER

The answers to this petaled puzzle will go in a curve from the number on the outside to the center of the flower. Each number in the flower will have two 5-letter answers. One goes in a clockwise direction and the second in a counterclockwise direction. We have entered two answers to help you begin.

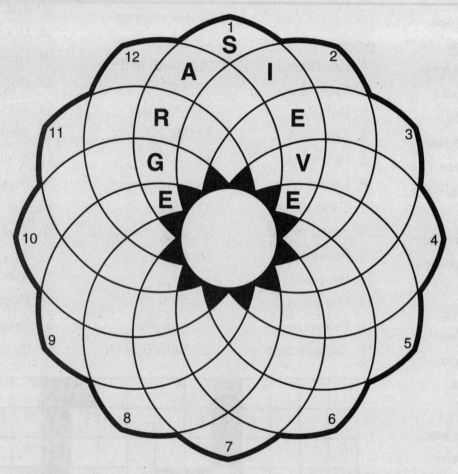

CLOCKWISE

1. Strainer
2. Bird's resting place
3. Brute
4. Smack
5. Fishing net
6. Inferior
7. Fake
8. Co-op's kin
9. Rough shelter
10. Church-hall game
11. Circumference
12. Do the lambada

COUNTERCLOCKWISE

1. Bilko, for short
2. Spotted horse
3. Nut-bearing tree
4. Tennis stroke
5. —— shuttle
6. Dog-walking cord
7. Pencil tip
8. Thick lump
9. Untied
10. Pretty, to a Glasgow lad
11. Lightheaded
12. Australian dog

ACROSS

1. Popular soda
5. Unite
8. Hot tubs
12. Spirited
13. Soft hat
15. Ship feature
16. Nevada city
17. Prepared
18. Bygone time
19. Immediately
21. Dine late
22. Apple pastry
23. Butt
25. Wheel tooth
27. Wind around
28. Blockhead
31. Vote to accept
33. Carol
35. Feel awful
36. Legendary beast
37. Hair knot
38. Sincere
40. Serape
42. Apiece
46. Destiny
48. Well-kept
50. Enemy
51. Polish
53. Veranda
54. Draw along
55. Getaway
56. To's mate
58. ___ out (barely earn)
59. Heidi's peak
60. Part of TGIF
62. Shrine
67. Slide
69. Stringed instrument
71. Spoken
72. Dashed
73. Condescend
74. Camera's eye
75. Worry
76. Be in hock
77. Small child

DOWN

1. Criticize
2. Done
3. Sales pitch
4. Fusses
5. Miniature
6. Historic ages
7. Subtract
8. Heavens
9. Folks
10. Antenna
11. Nap
13. Widest
14. Printed mistake
20. Waiter's aid
24. Wool eater
26. Wildebeest
28. Stable morsel
29. Make public
30. Winter ill
32. Baby grand
34. Single
37. Asphalt
39. Fairy
41. "The Way We ___"
43. Near the stern
44. Dove's cry
45. Use an axe
47. Out of tune
49. Biblical pronoun
51. Voting round
52. Ballpark judge
53. Spud
55. Survives
57. Barbecue order
61. Falling flakes
63. Shed feathers
64. Quarry
65. Thin
66. Threat word
68. Chapel bench
70. Mr. Pesci

PUZZLE 554

ACROSS
1. Minded
6. Smooth wood
10. Lids
14. Attentive
15. Say grace
16. White gem
17. Big ponds
18. Like
19. Himalayan legend
20. Caustic material
21. Old salt
23. Worked hard
25. Ventilate
26. Gym pad
27. Restrained
30. Sagest
33. Pyramid resident
34. Long tales
36. Decree
38. Miner's rock
39. Still life, e.g.
40. Chop
41. Ruin
42. Aviator
44. Satisfied
46. Song's text
48. Barked
50. Pub order
51. Decay
52. Come before
56. Corral
57. Patrolman
60. Cherish
61. Mexican meal
63. Solemn
65. Customer
66. Notable times
67. Canvas prop
68. Chow hall
69. Poker term
70. Tired

DOWN
1. Phone
2. Gone
3. Lawn tool
4. Stretch
5. Fate
6. Ship pole
7. Noah's craft
8. Tack
9. Energetic
10. Prairie wolf
11. Imitator
12. Head
13. Coasted
22. Who ___ you?
24. Game fish
25. Aspire
27. Rustic
28. ___ board
29. Bargains
30. Clever
31. Bluish gray
32. Burdened
33. Mother
35. Not amateur
37. Unite
42. Heap
43. Summer drink
44. Mooches
45. Befitting
47. Speeders
49. Strong rage
52. Purple fruit
53. Stood up
54. Nightfalls
55. Derive
56. Stance
57. Box
58. Hot spot
59. Rawhide
62. Feline
64. Knock

490

PUZZLE 555

ACROSS

1. Astound
4. Attack terms
8. Restrict
13. Ms. Tyler
14. Blood passage
16. Cleanse
17. Poetic work
18. Bow
19. Rhyme
20. Therefore
22. Drooping
24. Flee
25. Against
26. Interviewer
27. Deli breads
28. Apprehend
30. Naked
32. Mixes
35. Satellites
39. Grand
40. Mexican Mrs.
41. Suez ____
42. Aerosol bomb
44. Scrappy
45. Double reed
46. Footed vase
47. Shock
50. Liver, e.g.
53. Choice word
57. Overcame
58. Correct
59. Tanned
60. Lopsided
62. Brazil's dance
64. Horse doc
65. Deck
66. Step
67. Lobe locale
68. Forty winks
69. Stuffed shirt
70. Withered

DOWN

1. Hilo hi
2. Extend
3. Incident
4. Well-being
5. Charged bit
6. Salad item
7. T-bone, e.g.
8. Tariff
9. Great fury
10. Wed
11. Edition
12. Young adults
15. Math subject
21. Baking spice
23. Clutch
26. Torso muscles
27. Legal fee
29. Make up
31. Kitchen gadget
32. Bikini top
33. Charter
34. Psyche part
35. Hockey great
36. Print concerns
37. Fink
38. Shady
40. Female medium
43. Swoop
44. Enjoyment
47. Barters
48. Add up
49. Join
51. Tiny pests
52. Jingle writer
54. Cherished
55. Pledge
56. Door
58. On the apex
59. Prong
61. Lounge
63. Med subject

491

PUZZLE 556

"ATION" BREAKS

ACROSS

1. Avoid
6. Fire sign
11. Guitar's kin
14. Long sandwich
17. Noble gas
18. Bagel toppers
19. Mr. Luthor
20. Lennon's mate
21. Anvil in the ear
22. Met solos
23. The Big Apple: abbr.
24. Toss
25. Country obsessed with deer?
27. Elk
29. Monopoly token
30. Actor Will ___
32. Depth charge, in slang
35. Viper's sound
36. Steal from
38. Lab fluids
39. Work out
40. Chart again
42. Aliens: abbr.
44. Followers: suff.
45. Rabbi's book
48. Audible dashes
51. Spittle
54. Heeded
57. Future junior: abbr.
59. Decorative bloom
62. Ms. Carangi
63. Speech during a break?
66. Apollo's son
67. Liquidize
69. Carnival
70. Oregon volcano: abbr.
72. Radiance
74. Hardly happy
76. Signs
77. Gas light
79. Soft shoe, for short
81. Music hall
84. Video-game site
87. Troubles
90. Barley beard
91. Nationwide group: abbr.
94. Outlined
95. Dos' mate
97. Unending, to bards
99. Embody
101. Tatting allotment?
103. Hit the slopes
105. Western Indian
106. Scales sign
107. Author H.H. ___
108. ___ Bravo
109. Foot digit
110. Tiny landmass
111. Painter Degas
112. Motel
113. Decade parts: abbr.
114. Frets
115. Students' tables

DOWN

1. Lives
2. Slow passages
3. Takes the lid off
4. Baker's need
5. Trap
6. Level
7. Singer et al.
8. Self-evident truths
9. Villain
10. Curved letter
11. Radius' mate
12. Calculator feature
13. Tax on tobacco
14. Honorable mention in the arias?
15. One, to Pedro
16. Mr. Saget
26. Bit of matter
27. "___ My Line?"
28. Succeed
31. Three, to Mario
33. "___ Maria"
34. Sega competitor: abbr.
37. Faulty
40. Sunbeam
41. Former
43. Garment of India
45. Clothes
46. Off-Broadway award
47. The right place?
49. Horse's foot
50. Freewheel clutch
52. Weaver's tool
53. "___ It Romantic?"

55. Cupid

56. Fifth book: abbr.

58. Tresses

60. Snatched

61. Finales

64. Originate

65. Small combo

68. Craziness

71. That guy

73. Boisterous

75. Jerry's group: abbr.

77. ___ King Cole

78. Mess up

80. Dove's sound

82. Jug

83. Wild

85. Appointed helper

86. Lou Grant, e.g.

88. Join up

89. Secure

91. Washers

92. Warm jacket

93. Mexican sirs

96. Fastener

98. Musical work

100. Charges

102. Chows down

103. ___ Lanka

104. Family

106. Fleur-de-___

PUZZLE 557

• ROYAL FAMILY •

ACROSS
1. Evergreen shrub
4. Vipers
8. External covering
12. French friend
13. Had on
14. Vetch
15. Groaner
16. Miner's entry
17. Gifts of charity
18. Israel's Moshe ___
20. Excellent!
21. Attention-getter
23. Teatime treat
25. Hotel unit
26. RBI's kin
27. Humbug's partner
30. Botch
31. Tennis, e.g.
33. Tavern drink
34. Okay
35. Canine comment
36. Sluggish
37. Black birds
39. Sermon response
40. Fancy headwear
43. Texas landmark
45. Scandinavian city
46. Wing-shaped
47. Jamaican export
50. Gymnast Korbut
51. Distribute
52. Happy ___ clam
53. Pipe problem
54. On a cruise
55. Allow

DOWN
1. Jabber
2. Outback bird
3. Edward VIII, George VI, etc.
4. Not here
5. Soft drinks
6. Charles, e.g.
7. Part of a match
8. Gawk
9. Wrinkly vegetable
10. "___ la Douce"
11. Cozy spot
19. Money mach.
20. Tiny fly
21. Target
22. Sensitive
24. Bruin Bobby ___
27. Scottish castle
28. Burn soother
29. Shaped with an ax
31. Poet Teasdale
32. Con's foe
36. "Cheers" role
37. Frog's call
38. Bluish gray
40. Hammer, e.g.
41. Bit of land
42. Pond growth
44. Neighborhood
46. Doctor's org.
48. Consume
49. Wrestling pad

PUZZLE 558

• ANIMAL EXPRESSIONS •

ACROSS
1. Intertwine
5. Bro's sib
8. Like the desert
12. Soprano's solo
13. Cycle starter
14. Entryway
15. Early bird's opposite
17. Statistics
18. Yearning
19. Martini garnish
21. Dawn to dusk
22. Ancient Assyrian city
24. Seasoned
28. Distinction
31. Seaweed gel
32. Curved molding
33. Thin layer
36. Short-legged hound
38. Feeling
40. Instant lawn
42. Swagger
43. Health resort
46. Asset
48. Independent operator
50. Paddy crop
51. Wrap up
52. Actor Sharif
53. Oxen's harness
54. Winding curve
55. Game of chance

DOWN
1. Quite a few
2. Famous canal
3. Indication
4. Triumphant sound
5. Impassive
6. Golfer Hale ___
7. Cloud lining?
8. State further
9. Obstructive drivers
10. Tiny amount
11. Low cart
16. Sound pitch
20. First lady
23. Baseball's Slaughter
24. Actor Mineo
25. Turkish title
26. Unsuccessful incumbent, for a while
27. Slender
29. Like Willie Winkie
30. Actual profit
34. Negatives
35. Former prime minister
36. Leaps
37. Feed the kitty
39. Presses clothes
40. Agile
41. Melange
43. "___ Like It Hot"
44. Scheme
45. Curly coif
47. Date
49. Stir-fry skillet

BATTLESHIPS

The diagram represents a sea that contains a crossword puzzle; the answer words are Battleships. The letter-number combination to the left of each clue indicates the location in the diagram where a Battleship has been hit (for example, A2 is in the first row, second column). A hit is any one of the letters in the answer word. Using this clue, you must determine the exact location of each answer and whether it is an across or a down word. Fill in black squares to separate words as in a regular crossword. We have filled in the answers to clues A2 and D1.

A2 Soaked
A4 Pair
A8 Plus
A10 Endeavor
A14 Dalai ____
A15 Chip in chips
B3 Bird's crop
B6 Helper
B7 More frosty
B9 Sushi delicacy
B12 Uniform
B13 Assert
C1 Corporate symbol
C2 Inscribed
C6 Wheeled platform
C12 Relief
C15 Experiment
D1 Garbed
D3 Supped
D8 Shriveled
D11 Evil spell
D14 Clutter
E3 Zealous
E5 Bowler hat
E7 Point total
E10 Snare
E11 Beanie
F5 Church council
F6 Outcome
F8 Sudden takeover
F10 Contrite
F15 Mexican "Rah!"
G1 Early dwelling
G4 Crib
G5 Frankness
G8 Muzzle
G9 Preceding, poetically
G13 Niven of "Magnum Force"
G15 Sword
H1 Exist
H3 Approach
H6 Pinch
H9 Sped
H11 Salamander
H13 Edible pod
H14 Mass of eggs
I1 Routing term
I7 Microscopic

I12 Suave
I14 Maned male
J2 Puccini piece
J3 Corn portion
J5 Confined
J6 Desk slider
J7 Warp
J10 Soap ingredient
K7 Steel beam
K12 Wager
K15 Tolerate
L2 Dipper
L3 Antelope's pal
L4 Magnificence
L5 Large tart
L9 Pause
L11 Rendezvous
L14 20th letter
M1 Shrill

M4 Margarine
M7 Masculine
M8 Perpetual
M9 Artifact
M12 Soup dish
M15 Remove from print
N1 Patron
N2 Furthermore
N6 Angry
N10 Encore!
N12 Lamb's lament
N14 Stair post
N15 Downwind
O2 Small boat
O7 Before now
O9 "La ____ Vita"
O10 Since, to a Scot
O12 Whole
O13 Coral island

	1	2	3	4	5	6	7	8	9	10	11	12	13	14	15
A	■	W	E	T	■										
B	C														
C	L														
D	A														
E	D														
F	■														
G															
H															
I															
J															
K															
L															
M															
N															
O															

PUZZLE 560

• CLIMATOLOGY •

ACROSS
1. Terra _____
6. Swedish band
10. Further
14. Places
15. Back part
16. December air
17. Survive
20. Kind
21. _____ Moines
22. Occasions
23. Mr. Redding
25. Equitable
27. Rap
33. Ranch resident
34. Drinks at the bar
35. Witticism
36. Out of control
37. Practice session
39. Sugar source
40. Everybody
41. Canine comment
42. Sign of spring
43. Vacillate
47. Borders
48. Checks out
49. Fussy couple?
52. Shepherd's charge
53. Bring to light
57. Be feverish
61. Skip
62. Clark's friend
63. Withers
64. Former frosh
65. Faction
66. Slightest

DOWN
1. Crow calls
2. Snack in a stack
3. Pull to pieces
4. Like some sailors
5. Wood for bats
6. Seize
7. Puts up the farm
8. Humbug!
9. Live
10. Whole
11. Come into view
12. Really dry
13. Tall trees
18. Put in a good word?
19. Mixes
24. Craggy peak
25. Cut down
26. Second son
27. Quiet
28. Howdy!
29. Israeli seaport
30. It's spam a lot
31. Regulated for use
32. Somme summers
33. Clear the decks?
37. Not a happy fate
38. Goes bad
39. Track support
41. Bridge's forerunner
42. Point of no return?
44. Circle of greens
45. Most recent
46. Colorist
49. Amor
50. Weighty wrestling
51. Crop
52. Bigger than big
54. Luau entertainment
55. Table scraps
56. Occident
58. High rollers?
59. Larry's crony
60. Cobbler's punch

PUZZLE 561

Connections

Place the 7-letter answers to the clues into the diagram, each answer starting at the top with the letter C and ending at the bottom with the letter E. When the diagram is filled, a 9-letter word will read across the outlined row of the diagram.

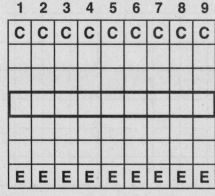

1. Atmosphere
2. Bathe
3. Associates
4. Wind system
5. Overturn
6. Bungalow
7. Singing group
8. Perfumed liquid
9. Red shade

DOUBLE TROUBLE

PUZZLE 562

Not really double trouble, but double fun! Solve this puzzle as you would a regular crossword, except place one, two, or three letters in each box. The number of letters in each answer is shown in parentheses after its clue.

ACROSS
1. Utter (8)
4. Bombard- ment (7)
7. "Pygmalion" playwright (4)
9. Stickum (5)
10. Light brown (5)
11. Common duck (7)
12. Verve (4)
13. Box lightly (4)
14. Pieplant (7)
16. Fantastic (10)
18. Minister (6)
20. ____ the hill (4)
21. Garfield's snooze (6)
23. Two-masted vessel (5)
25. Wastrel (8)
27. Make an afghan (7)
28. Most nimble (7)
29. French fathers (5)
30. Urgent (8)
31. Clog, e.g. (4)
32. Have faith in (5)

34. Hire, as a bus (7)
36. Park nuisance (6)
38. Extreme anger (4)
39. Cut with an axe (3)
41. Theater feature (7)
43. Saucer-shaped bell (4)
45. Like some dissertations (8)
46. Hut (5)
47. Took in, as food (8)
48. One who boots the ball (6)

DOWN
1. Force (6)
2. Nice (8)
3. Beret's place (4)
4. Cruel (9)
5. "Norma ____" (3)
6. Radioactivity detector inventor (6)
7. "The meek ____ inherit . . ." (5)
8. Prize (5)
11. Sculpting stone (6)

13. Cash user (7)
15. Shiny wheel accessory (6)
17. Dismissal (7)
19. Shaky (7)
21. Outfielder's skill (8)
22. Fisherman's tool (3)
24. Trunk (5)
25. Prim and ____ (6)
26. "Reader's ____" (6)
27. Irritable (5)
28. Binge (5)

30. Fame (8)
31. Deficiency (8)
33. Indian money (5)
34. Used a credit card (7)
35. Oratory (8)
37. Continuing (7)
40. "____, Texas Ranger" (6)
41. Wetland (5)
42. Charlatan (5)
44. Robin's roost (4)
45. Landing pier (4)

Circle Sums

PUZZLE 563

Each circle, lettered A through I, has its own number value from 1 to 9. No two circles have the same value. The numbers shown in the diagram are the sums of the circles that overlap at those points. For example, 12 is the sum of circles A and D. Can you find the value of each circle?

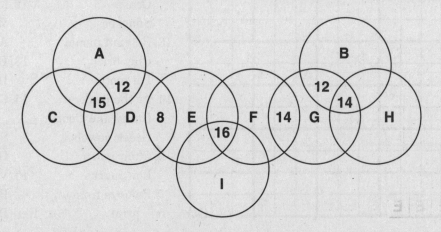

497

PUZZLE 564

BRICK BY BRICK

Rearrange this stack of bricks to form a crossword puzzle. The clues will help you fit the bricks into their correct places. Row 1 has been filled in for you. Use the bricks to fill in the remaining spaces.

BRICKS

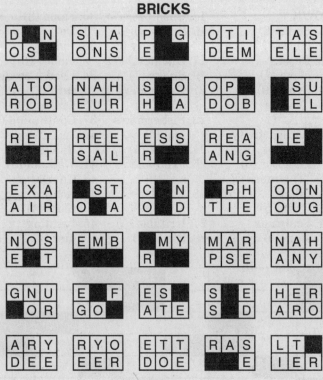

ACROSS

1. Zeros
   Choice term
   Star's transport
2. Hearing-related
   Middays
   General Bradley
3. Floor model
   Moola
   Church recess
4. Rudimentary
   stage
   Prosecutes
   Snaky letter
5. Bard's eternity
   Happiness
   spreader
6. Word group
   Fragrant flower
7. Dead heat
   Conceit
   Beauty parlors
8. Elevate in rank
   Stocky antelope
   Chatty bird
9. More breezy
   Bruins great
   "Ask ___ Girl"
10. Used tire
    Annoy
11. Romantic dances
    Bambi's mother
12. Slangy negative
    Cease
    Snacker
13. Belgian money
    Clay brick
    Poi root
14. At the peak
    Busey and Cooper
    Greek vowels
15. Choir gown
    Low marks
    Remove from
    print

DOWN

1. Bump
   Salty drop
   Adjacent
2. Detail
   Sprite
   Car
3. Branch
   Object of love
4. Goal maker
   Former Capri
   cabbage
   Unlock, in a
   sonnet
5. Indeed!
   Pre-adult
   years
6. Sign a check
   Bedraggled
7. Pool forfeit
   Coop product
   Gadget
8. Immerse
   Yoko ___
   Fern seed
9. Swallow up
   Large vase
   Brief farewell
10. Scissors
    Blushing
    quality
11. Hot vapor
    Also
12. Mauna ___
    Wriggly
    Analyzed
13. Detached
    Despise
14. Catholic
    service
    Silly
    Of an epoch
15. Valuable lodes
    Pale
    Pink wine

DIAGRAM

	1	2	3	4	5	6	7	8	9	10	11	12	13	14	15
1	N	I	L	S		E	L	S	E			L	I	M	O
2															
3															
4															
5															
6															
7															
8															
9															
10															
11															
12															
13															
14															
15															

PUZZLE 565

ACROSS
1. Blacken
5. Diminish
9. Polish
13. Volcano flow
14. Fiery crime
15. Raison d'____
16. Similar
17. Continues
18. Mounted on a peg
19. Ordinary
21. Encloses
23. Mail date
26. Accomplice
29. Staggers
32. Head cook
33. Seasonings
35. Holds
37. Race divisions
39. "____ Town" (Wilder play)
40. Weepy
42. Vintage-film sta.
43. Pregame period
46. Autocrat
47. Reef
49. Pouched fish-hunting bird
51. Sunnier
53. Rower
56. With hands on hips
61. Danube's shade
62. Flies high
65. Came out even
66. Elevator name
67. Roast host
68. Bedecked
69. Geologic divisions
70. Plants firmly
71. Towel marking

DOWN
1. Edible mollusk
2. Cod's kin
3. Raring
4. Delhi princess
5. Half of a bikini
6. Wild donkey
7. Clan symbol
8. Trap
9. Cause (oneself) to go
10. Shoshoneans
11. Liberate
12. G-men
14. Apportions
20. Well-suited
22. Summit
24. Lethargy
25. Victory
26. Throat sounds
27. Daytona or Miami
28. Young newt
30. Capital of Tibet
31. It's a wrap!
32. Half a dance
34. Vinegar bottle
36. Damascus' site, shortly
38. Throng
41. List-closing abbr.
44. Pen names
45. Polite word
48. Fixate on
50. Taunt
52. Troll
53. Clarinet's cousin
54. Higher than tenor
55. Spoil
57. Scratch
58. Marathon segment
59. Grizzly ____
60. Chances
63. False front
64. Second notes

Satellites

PUZZLE 566

Form ten words by placing one syllable in each circle. The center circle will contain the first syllable for each of the ten words. Each syllable will be used once. Words read outward from the center. If you need help getting started, you will find the first syllable on page 561.

A   AL   BE   BIL   COME

DAZ   DLE   EN   FORE

FUD   GIN   HAV   HE

HOLD   I   IOR   LENT

LIEV   MOTH   NEV

NING   O   TY   ZLE

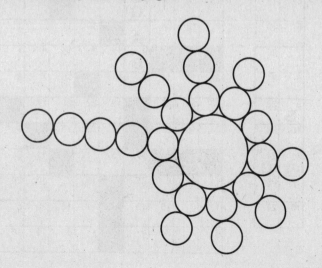

PUZZLE 567 CODEWORD

Instructions for solving Codewords are given on page 11.

Key:

1	14		
2	15		
3	16		
4	17	**O**	
5	18		
6	19		
7	20		
8	21	**T**	
9	22		
10	23		
11	24	**L**	
12	25		
13	26		

Main grid:

23	4	8	8		24	13	7	14		26	7	15
25	10	6	11		13	16	14	4		7	11	25
21	7	17	6		7	6	14	25		16	4	8
		14	7	6	8				1	25	21	
4	7	5		26	11	4	21		26	4	8	8
					L	**O**	**T**					
18	12	25	16	7		16	13	11	11			
23	25	16	7	9	25		26	7	6	21	25	14
		15	6	21	20		8	3	6	15	25	
26	25	10	12		7	6	23	8		8	25	2
11	25	6				22	4	4	5			
7	11	11		4	15	20	4		7	2	11	8
20	25	25		15	4	7	16		19	25	25	3
25	15	15		25	14	22	12		25	14	14	12

A	N
B	Ø
C	P
D	Q
E	R
F	S
G	T̸
H	U
I	V
J	W
K	X
L̸	Y
M	Z

PUZZLE 568 CODEWORD

Key:

1	14		
2	15		
3	16		
4	17		
5	18		
6	19		
7	20		
8	21		
9	22	**B**	
10	23		
11	24	**A**	**G**
12	25		
13	26		

Main grid:

17	7	17	18	11		26	8	11	16		26	11	15	13
20	15	8	20	1		20	17	16	20		7	5	20	15
9	15	8	1	1		20	14	8	25		13	20	3	10
			26	12	1	6	10		22	26	7			
7	2	22		25	11	10		2	20	11		9	11	10
13	20	25	24	8	16		1	11	25	7		20	4	8
			G											
1	16	20	11		10	11	6	1		6	25	20	17	11
			A											
			9	12	25	15	8	1	23	12	8			
			B											
21	15	11	1	1		15	7	8	12		8	22	8	8
20	11	25		12	22	20	17		8	1	6	8	25	1
24	10	2		11	15	16		9	8	16		4	11	1
			11	15	11		11	8	25	7	8			
11	21	8	25		19	7	17	24		16	12	17	8	25
1	8	25	13		11	15	20	8		21	25	11	14	8
6	8	24	1		1	6	11	16		26	20	17	8	5

A̸	N
B̸	O
C	P
D	Q
E	R
F	S
G̸	T
H	U
I	V
J	W
K	X
L	Y
M	Z

500

PUZZLE 569

• ANIMAL MAGNETISM •

ACROSS

1. Feats
5. Defeat
9. Gala
13. Snapshot
15. Sector
16. Indy entrant
17. Mr. Woods
18. Locomotive part
20. Type of sofa
25. Presidential "no"
26. Bend
27. Car
30. Vowed
31. Deliver
33. Ms. Stapleton
36. Dripping
37. Printing measures
38. Feed-bag contents
42. Solo for Sills
43. Columbus's state
44. Pedestrian
47. Bivalve mollusk
49. Ms. Bartok
50. "I Like ____"
51. Slumbering
54. Lower in pitch
58. Ali, once
59. Writer Zane ____
60. Bronte heroine
61. Doctors' gp.
64. Heidi's peak
67. "____ With the Wind"
68. Use a hose
70. Island feasts
72. Ireland, to the Irish
73. Prune
74. Munch
77. Poison mushroom
82. Diplomas
87. Hood's missile
89. Prevention measure?
90. Notion
91. Large: pref.
92. Glimpse
93. Way in
94. Country road

DOWN

1. Befitting
2. Stylish
3. Garment for Nero
4. Stalk
5. Shortage
6. Spanish gold
7. Darn
8. Animal pouch
9. Statistic
10. Parrot
11. Casual pullover
12. Drop the ball
14. Mine find
16. 66, for ex.
19. Stratford's river
21. Ordinance
22. Thing to furrow
23. Property unit
24. Jazz's Baker
27. Mr. Vigoda
28. Coffee server
29. "____ the season . . ."
30. Cast of two, in craps
32. Zeroes
33. Mandible
34. Mesozoic, e.g.
35. Feel poorly
39. Exclamations of joy
40. Dead heat
41. Sun, in Seville
45. First lady
46. Yak
47. Central
48. Hawaiian guitar
51. Air hero
52. Sneaky
53. Household god
55. Specialist
56. Smooth, to Keats
57. Ham on ____
61. Businessman Onassis
62. Blemish
63. Yes, Captain!
64. Besides
65. Moon goddess
66. Remitted
69. Church benches
71. Increases
74. Heredity unit
75. Collar locale
76. Repeat
77. Russian ruler of old
78. Flat hat
79. Spoken
80. Seal hunter
81. Forsaken
82. Soak up
83. Color tone
84. Jest
85. Altar answer
86. Keanu, in "The Matrix"
88. Grief

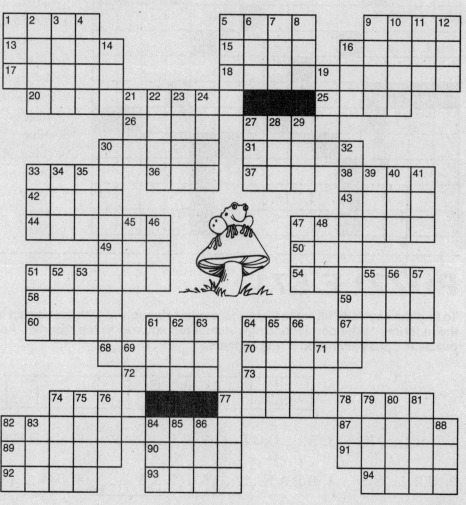

PUZZLE 570

ACROSS

1. Knocks lightly
5. Daisylike plant
10. Abandoned
14. Continental currency
15. Stage
16. Greenish blue
17. Seed coat
18. Legal wrongs
19. Tousle
20. Put aside
21. Shad delicacy
22. Creature
23. Adjust
26. Seeing organ
28. Soap-making substance
29. Young newt
31. Shut hard
33. Damage
35. Poplars
40. Existed
41. One who yields
43. Lotion ingredient
44. Skunk's identification
46. Jury option
48. Roughened
50. Kiwi's extinct kin
51. Globe
54. Card game of old
55. Confuse
57. Risk
59. Commandment count
61. Egyptian symbol
64. Yale students
65. Mooch
67. Greek porch
68. Iranian coin
69. Whims
70. Lofty
71. Land unit
72. Colorists
73. Thin board

DOWN

1. Afternoon socials
2. Atmosphere
3. Jean Lafitte, e.g.
4. Repaired, as shoes
5. Fitting
6. Deficit
7. Polynesian tuber
8. Value
9. Thing, in law
10. Fancy fabric
11. Even
12. Picky
13. Savor
22. Snoozing sites
24. Solicit
25. Imitation medication
27. Pined
29. Loses intensity
30. Stew
32. Press
34. Tropical cuckoo
36. Inner shoe
37. Basic
38. Forbidden thing
39. Bristle
42. Put in jeopardy
45. Become a bore
47. Unusual
49. Traffic circle
51. "Madama Butterfly," e.g.
52. Memento
53. Tobacco pipe
56. Perseveres
58. Bit of land
60. Rim
62. Soda-flavoring nut
63. Pause
65. Cow's chew
66. Double curve

PUZZLE 571

Keyword

To find the Keyword, fill in the blanks in words 1 through 10 with the correct missing letters. Transfer those letters to the correspondingly numbered squares in the diagram. Approach with care—this puzzle is not as simple as it first appears.

1	2	3	4	5	6	7	8	9	10

1. T R I __ E
2. G R __ S S
3. S __ O O P
4. G R A N __
5. C L __ M P
6. D R A W __
7. __ H E R E
8. S H __ N E
9. P __ R C H
10. E R O __ E

ACROSS

1. Bookie's concern
5. Nick and Nora's pet
9. Pumpkin's beginning
13. Spoiled kid
14. San Antonio mission
16. Church nook
17. Little bit
18. Long-legged bird
19. Joke's punch ___
20. Extra tire
22. Soothe
23. Frosted
24. Gun, as an engine
26. Daughter's brother
28. Possibility
33. Parasite
37. ___ Rico
38. Filled with wonder
40. Maui necklace
41. Colored eye-part
42. Heavy inert gas
44. General's assistant
45. Rating for Bo
46. Bonfire
47. Like some car windows
49. Words of consent
51. Took into custody
53. ___ Newton
55. Provide weapons to
56. Fisherman's hook
59. Ewe's young
62. Startle
67. Bogus butter
68. Sun-dried brick
70. Baking chamber
71. Food thickener
72. Anchor-lifter
73. Ukrainian city
74. Small arrow
75. Dole (out)
76. Rafter's peril

DOWN

1. Japanese sashes
2. Let fall
3. Computer fodder
4. Constellation member
5. Exclamation of delight
6. Shirt section
7. Scarlett's plantation
8. Singer Tori ___
9. Salty solution
10. Monumental story
11. Medieval slave
12. Property title
15. Wallet stuffers
21. Formerly, of yore
25. Strong glue
27. Timeworn
28. Blender setting
29. Bridle controls
30. Hospital surg. areas
31. Chair mender
32. Tango requirement
34. Nobility
35. Surrendered
36. Hurried
37. "Town Without ___"
39. Door sign
43. Notable period
44. Aardvark's morsel
46. Omega's preceder
48. Theories
50. Exertion
52. Bunny
54. Pleased
56. Prod
57. Pond organism
58. Terror
60. Genesis gent
61. Chess action
63. Coal by-product
64. Enthusiastic
65. Bamboo shoot
66. Green with ___
69. French summer

PUZZLE 572

Top to Bottom

PUZZLE 573

Place the letters given below each diagram into the squares to form eight 4-letter words reading from top to bottom from square to connected square. The top letter is the first letter of all eight words, each letter in the second row is the second letter of four words, and so on.

Example:

Bare, Bark, Balk, Ball, Bulk, Bull, Burl, Burn.

1.

E L M O R T T

2.

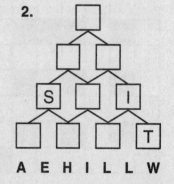

A E H I L L W

British-style or Cryptic Crosswords are a great challenge for crossword fans. Each clue contains either a definition or direct reference to the answer as well as a play on words. The numbers in parentheses indicate the number of letters in the answer words.

ACROSS

1. Promote advantage baby bear had (8)
5. Magazine worker to ride with changes (6)
10. Speak ill of Barnum and unravel (7)
11. Sanguinary inmate holds lips (7)
12. A male spy (5)
13. Act of beau not exactly turnaround (5-4)
14. Suits fitting in commercials (6)
16. Shaking fist, Cree most aggressive (8)
18. Add time for political treatise (8)
20. California lets ruined princely mansion (6)
23. Storm rang—violent force! (6-3)
25. Hand out Kleenex after commencement (5)
27. Charge complex pen's electric core (7)
28. Roster features the most nimble (7)
29. Warm to a pigpen (6)
30. Jockey outraced teacher (8)

DOWN

1. Gary's home in Vreeland (7)
2. Hide money in report (5)
3. Person from Massachusetts howls, "Spud!" (3,6)
4. Giant ensnaring fifth martial artist (6)
6. Flow opening dam fissure (5)
7. Will's final, final word at prayer time (9)
8. Most putrid dilapidated tankers (7)
9. Partially concoct opinion for army figures? (6)
15. Pay carhop after transcribing religious writings (9)
17. It's a relic unusually practical (9)
18. Cushiest job occupied by this woman (7)
19. Revolutionary patriot in Connecticut cottage (6)
21. Voter role, etc., manipulated (7)
22. Walked in the morning, then ran (6)
24. Nine people a risky situation for trapeze artists? (5)
26. Scented fish (5)

PUZZLE 575

• COUNT ME IN! •

ACROSS
1. Ann and May
6. Et ___ (and others)
10. Horned vipers
14. Got up
15. Protracted
16. Actress Ward
17. Winner's position
19. Peruse
20. Corrode
21. Canine, e.g.
22. Mob scenes
23. Sluggish creature
24. Omen
25. Earthenware maker
28. Turntable shaft
31. Pined
32. Part of the crew
34. Mooch
35. China flaw
36. Took on (cargo)
37. Plucked instrument
38. Get it wrong
39. Captain of industry
40. Invade
41. Most embarrassed
43. Full of avarice
44. Shot on the green
45. Father of psycho-analysis
47. Chars
49. Narrow valleys
50. Set price
53. Remedy
54. Final chance, on the gridiron
56. Music and dance
57. Film terrier
58. Having handles
59. Items for play
60. Subsequently
61. Color changers

DOWN
1. Bistro
2. "Tosca" tune
3. Sailor's layover
4. Double curve
5. Colonized
6. Apportion
7. Reluctant
8. Creep
9. Birthday concern
10. Designate
11. Diamond bag
12. Land map
13. Without
18. Inferior
22. Journalist Jacob ___
23. One of a flight
24. Exceeded the limit
25. Indiana athlete
26. Earth tone
27. Incidental participant
28. British gun
29. Enticed
30. Vacant
32. Trading center
33. Hubbub
36. Not least?
37. Take note of
39. Lays odds
40. Passed over lightly
42. Coercion
43. Classy fella
45. Champagne glass
46. Broadcast again
47. Shoo!
48. Continental currency
49. Golly!
50. Links warning
51. Water jug
52. Outcomes
54. Portly
55. Calendar square

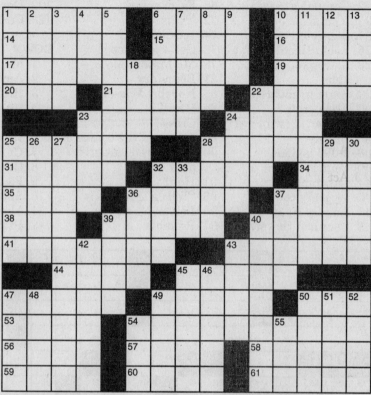

Number Sleuth

PUZZLE 576

One of the numbers in the hexagons has been circled because it and the numbers in the six surrounding hexagons are all different. There are 14 others like this. Are you a sharp-eyed sleuth who can find them all?

PUZZLE 577

• WAY TO GROW! •

ACROSS

1. Tease
5. Emulates Olivier
9. Ointment
13. Humid
17. Ireland, to the Irish
18. Midday
19. Ancient Greek city
20. Unwritten
21. Top-billed
22. Campus group: abbr.
23. "Giant" actor
24. Sensible
25. Robin Hood's haunt
28. Astronauts' group: abbr.
29. Bit of granola
30. Alien craft
31. Buster Brown's dog
33. Cloudy
38. 2,000 pounds
40. Pounce
44. Lawn moisture
45. Weasel's cousin
47. Actress Ryan
49. Common flower
50. Low in pitch
52. Nosher
54. Lived
56. Crawford's ex
57. Binge
59. ___ Pyle
61. Small songbird
63. Unit of electricity
65. Actor Bruce
67. In past days
68. Farm vehicle
72. Yarns
74. Incident
78. Get a move on
79. Mr. Matheson
81. Boundary
83. Nobelist Wiesel
84. Poet T.S. ___
86. Cross
88. Removed the center of
90. Registered caregiver: abbr.
91. Hunt
93. "Tell ___ About It"
95. Lebanon's region
97. Prompts
99. Aunt, to Juan
101. Forbid
102. Turkish ___
105. Minnesota county
112. Voyaging
113. Sally ___ (bun)
114. Layer
115. Cognizant of
116. Scorch
117. Blue-pencil
118. German waterway
119. Type of monster?
120. Cattle group
121. Religious procedure
122. Depend
123. Care for

DOWN

1. Ms. Harper
2. Among
3. "Dies ___"
4. Intense fear
5. Critique
6. Designer Chanel
7. Croaker
8. Confused situation
9. Fourposter site
10. Sailor's direction
11. Minimum
12. Praying ___
13. Chicago suburb
14. Elaborate solo
15. Bulk
16. Appeal
26. Texas town
27. Frequently, to bards
32. Frosh's concern: abbr.
33. Betting factor
34. Al Gore, e.g.
35. Widemouthed jug
36. Dateless
37. Rocky Mountain range
39. Unprecedented
41. Roman road
42. Franco or Peter
43. Enlarged
46. Send payment
48. Sedan fuel
51. Fuzzy-fruit source
53. Majestic
55. Restful resort
58. Paramedic: abbr.
60. Artifact
62. ___ of Aquarius
64. Kettle
66. Defective auto
68. Three, in Tijuana
69. ___ of thumb
70. Far East
71. Glass part
73. Parent
75. She, to Miguel
76. Pinches
77. Nylon shelter
80. ___-jongg
82. Gum flavoring
85. Fort Worth college: abbr.
87. Easing of political tension
89. Sketch
92. "Catch-22" author
94. River, in Tijuana
96. Plenty
98. ___ Arabia
100. Following
102. Johann Sebastian ___
103. Wimbledon winner
104. Salty droplet
106. Woven
107. Neap or ebb
108. Command to Rover
109. Mayberry lad
110. Toy figure
111. Cinch

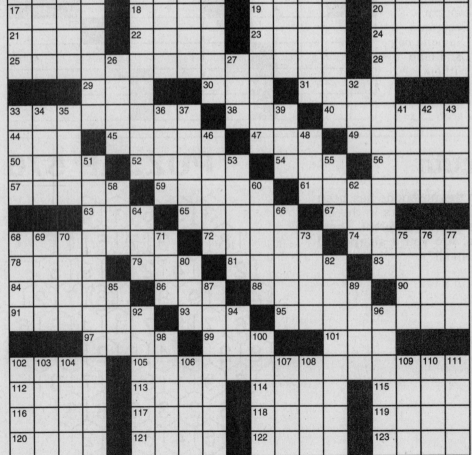

506

ACROSS

1. Glass unit
5. ____ Nui (Easter Island)
9. Links cry
13. Up to the job
17. Voyaging
18. Verve
19. Designer Cassini
20. Eurasian river
21. Catherine ____ (Henry's sixth)
22. Set down
23. At hand
24. Luggage holder
25. Rocky's opponent
28. Ousts
30. Tibetan native
31. Wheel part
33. Mariner
34. Set up
38. Engrossed
40. Conspiracy
44. Olympic sled
45. New Haven tree
47. St. Anthony's cross
49. Ali ____
50. Czech river
51. "I'm Coming Out" singer
55. Burden of proof
56. "Casino" star
58. Simulacrum
59. Squirrel away
61. "God Bless the ____"
63. Biblical verb
65. Fourth grade?
66. Maple sugar sugar
70. Articulate
72. "Blonde" novelist
76. Stick around
77. Oscar-winning choreographer
80. Molten flow
81. Sharp
82. High note
83. ____ Jima
84. Persia, now
85. Rulers of 84 Across, once
87. Fictional sailor
91. Aromatic tea
93. Take in
95. The good earth
96. Young bug
97. Venezuela city
101. "The Story of Vernon and ____"
107. Aid
108. Tatters
110. Radar's drink
111. Sham
112. Letter opener
113. Arch type
114. Mend
115. Diarist Frank
116. Dormant
117. Pullovers
118. Belt
119. Joins

DOWN

1. Daddy
2. Pronto, initially
3. Famous fiddler
4. Nobleman
5. Changed clips
6. Alas!
7. Two of a kind
8. ____ condor
9. Nuzzle
10. Fiesta cheer
11. Librarian's advice
12. Graceful wader
13. Northern lights
14. Some lingerie
15. Frilly trim
16. Big deer
26. Caustic stuff
27. Business card abbr.
29. Special interest gp.
32. Within: pref.
34. Complete failure
35. Fresh
36. Eons
37. "War of the Worlds" show
38. Holy men
39. Itar-____ (Russian news agency)
41. Spoiler
42. Touch
43. Emit a beam
46. Number in a Roman deck?
48. Secondhand
52. Minor prophet
53. Playing marble
54. Has a lease
57. Late start?
60. Office VIP
62. Tennis great
64. Not so hot
66. Fast fliers
67. Beehive State
68. "____ Mia"
69. Slippery ones
71. Like sashimi
73. Twelve Oaks neighbor
74. Novelist Hunter
75. On one's rocker?
78. Track
79. Taking in
86. Cul-de-____
88. Sounds
89. Taproom
90. Recompense
92. "Give ____ rest!"
94. Seer's deck
96. Jacket style
97. Muslim judge
98. Tucked in
99. Bona fide
100. Wise one
102. "Hud" star
103. "Arms and the Man" playwright
104. Pitch
105. Touch down
106. Demi and Bruce, e.g.
109. Gosh!

PUZZLE 578

• OH, HEAVENS! •

507

PUZZLE 579

• ET-TOO? •

ACROSS

1. Operatic voice
6. Complain
10. Those folks
14. Not so hot
19. Above a whisper
20. Jai ____
21. Charge
22. Solitary
23. Bee-shaped flute?
25. Pay to play
26. Poker Flat creator
27. African nobelist
28. "Tarzan" extra
29. Lowest point on a spacecraft?
32. Rear
35. Mr. Paul
36. Sandpiper
37. Conifer
40. Mr. Silver
41. Equips
43. Reggae rock
45. "The Man" Musial
49. Ratifies
51. Helm position
52. Cast
54. Carnival city
55. Rude look
56. Square printer's mark?
58. Give the slip
60. Road measure
61. Bavarian river
63. Cover
64. Faberge egg glaze
65. Highlands one
66. Dispatch
67. Greek earth goddess
69. Snick and ____
70. The puck stops here
71. Impressionist sculpture?
74. Both Begleys
77. "Common Sense" author
79. Height prefix
80. Low marks
81. Madre's brother
82. Glittering
84. Tut, tut!
85. Hollywood segment
86. Duel memento
87. "R.U.R." playwright
88. Great French Renaissance music?
91. Rubberneck
92. Barcelona bravo
93. Like Georgia Brown
95. Troubles
96. Seabird
98. Pastry piece
100. Oft-misused contraction
101. Army sch.
102. A Kennedy
103. Like Rhine wine
104. Medium power
106. Tropical cuckoo
107. Peter of Peter, Paul & Mary
110. Bedtime poetry?
116. Philosophical ideal
117. Swiss river
121. "____ Doone"
122. Destroy, in York
123. Carpenter's apprentice?
126. Vocal group
127. Slugger Slaughter
128. Tribe
129. Southern miss
130. "____ the Sidewalk Ends"
131. Stored
132. Corrodes
133. Stock

DOWN

1. Thai coin
2. Baseball family
3. Do a mailroom chore
4. First light
5. Tribute in verse
6. Come about
7. Visa carrier
8. Hit
9. Dock
10. Vestiges
11. Aaron and Williams
12. Major follower
13. Athletic occasion
14. Western lake
15. Delights
16. Left on a ship
17. Math term
18. Consider
24. Polynesian tubers
30. Ancient Mexican
31. Dietary fiber
33. Comic Carney
34. Claw
37. Petty officer
38. Locomotive
39. Greenbacks?
42. Writer Stout
43. Yukon transport
44. Marlowe's nickname
46. Musician's ID?
47. Assistant
48. Yuletide
50. Fair mark
51. Tolerate
52. Tuck's title
53. Science fiction and romance
57. Cover story
59. Northern Thai
61. Bully
62. Last of the Stuart monarchs
64. Kriemhild's husband
66. Sneers
67. Folklore robot
68. Sternward
69. Old dagger
72. Spoil
73. "Awake and Sing!" playwright
75. Bum wrap?
76. Very
78. "Chances ____"
82. Argyll native
83. Indian rhythm
84. Adversaries
85. Forward
86. A noncom
88. Lay odds
89. Caravan stop
90. Actor Roth
94. Rub
96. Argentine leader
97. Tokyo, once
99. Sawbuck
101. Turmoil
102. Gets in shape
105. Ray
106. Man with morals
108. No longer on deck
109. Race refresher
110. Squander
111. Lomond, e.g.
112. "Vissi d'____"
113. "Enterprise" journey
114. Wind instrument
115. ____ homo
118. Up to it
119. Audition goal
120. Viewed
124. Menu phrase
125. Tide type

ACROSS

1. Common commodity?
6. Trudge
10. Silent type
14. Carries on
19. They clear snow
20. After the bell
21. Topnotch
22. Quarters
23. Buenos ____
24. Leaf angle
25. Gaga
26. June celebrant
27. NFL team
29. Breakfast side
32. Actor Morales
33. Colorado brave
35. Jabber
36. Adjutant
37. Tough
40. Florentine surname
44. Sommer of films
47. Manly
50. Insuperable barrier
53. Noun suffix
54. Some poplars
56. It's of miner concern
57. Pharmacist's heart
58. Lost
60. Landlord's charges
62. Just plain creepy
65. Disqualifies (oneself)
67. Group of verses
68. Outfit
70. Samovars
72. Saul's grandfather
73. "____ a Lady"
74. Mahogany pooch
78. Actor Edmund ____
82. Hunky-dory
84. ____-chef
85. Bob Hope's gp.
86. ____ de Pascua
87. Firing mechanism
91. Yorkshire city
94. Wall covering
96. Crude vessel
97. Co. without bias
99. Had wings
101. Realm
102. Angled add-on
103. Oboe's kin
108. American dramatist
109. Expensive
111. Antarctic penguin
112. Kudos
114. Hardy girl
116. Refrain opener
118. Draft org.
119. Race units
123. Terrace portals
129. Current
131. Lasso
132. Bogus butter
133. Asia's ____ Mountains
135. Widemouthed
136. Good quality
137. Opinion
138. Ms. Skye
139. Mouselike mammal
140. You have to have them
141. Merit
142. Eye drop
143. Budges

DOWN

1. Alley pickup
2. Inventor Howe
3. Waterwheel
4. Muscular manipulation
5. Latin verb
6. Credit card
7. Careless
8. Auditory
9. Put off
10. Appetizers
11. Garish
12. Against
13. Flat formation
14. Synagogue sight
15. Chafe
16. Mute
17. Poi ingredient
18. Beheld
28. Capek play
30. Handle
31. Accomplish perfectly
34. Back talk?
38. Roger Rabbit, e.g.
39. Flag
41. Passable
42. ____ Jima
43. Singer Vicki ____
45. Genuflection joint
46. Athenian characters
47. Partners
48. Hebrew letter
49. Lake craft
51. Originally called
52. Give the punch punch
55. Labor action
59. Fruity candy
61. Polite address
63. Charlotte ____
64. Vexation
66. Signs up
69. Soldiers, for short
71. Erwin of television
75. Cirque du ____
76. Tint
77. Medium's medium
79. Lauder of cosmetics
80. Vigilant
81. Nostrils
83. Fairy-tale heavy
87. Like some stockings
88. Get to
89. Uncomfortable
90. Way to send a ltr.
92. Morse syllable
93. Call it a day
95. Mil. addresses
98. Spanish root word?
100. Does wrong
104. Humorous poet
105. Take a load off
106. Deli delicacy
107. More unpleasant
110. Let
113. Equal prefix
115. Emulates Ella
117. Look for
120. Certain mites
121. Daily delivery
122. Multitudes
123. Ollie's pal
124. Court order?
125. Intertwined
126. Pelvis pieces
127. Not e'en once
128. Flavoring for gin
130. Throw
134. Literary olio

PUZZLE 581

FULL CIRCLE

To complete this circular puzzle fill in the answers to the AROUND clues in a clockwise direction. For the RADIAL clues move from the outside to the inside.

AROUND (Clockwise)

1. Molten rock
6. ___ soup (dense fog)
9. Oft-visited site
14. Young amphibian
17. Bitterly pungent
18. RBIs, e.g.
20. Mindful
21. Clever
23. Rein
24. Savor
25. In no case
26. Private teacher
27. See-through
29. Too soon
31. Spud state
33. Rotate rapidly
35. Winter jacket
36. Abide
37. Volume unit
38. Sasquatch's cousin
39. Chirp
40. After taxes
41. Semester
42. Went first

RADIAL (Out to in)

1. Shopping plaza
2. Expert
3. Hold tightly
4. Small disaster
5. Stick fast
6. School org.
7. Tripod
8. Acquire
9. Numerous
10. Fleecy mom
11. Frivolous objection
12. Attribute
13. Vent
14. Ostrichlike bird
15. Arbuckle's nickname
16. Gardening tool
18. Leather band
19. Suffice
21. Blizzard
22. Stale
28. Gain with effort
30. Allow
32. That girl
34. Get free (of)

ACROSS
1. Dot
5. Smear
9. Son of Seth
13. Buck, e.g.
17. Honey factory
18. Seine feeder
19. Stride
20. Sicilian spouter
21. Cry for Yorick
22. Dark brews
23. Precinct
24. Rustle
25. Barbara Hale role
28. The first was in 1095
30. Craft
31. Scut
33. Walk
34. Hack
37. Seepage
40. Limerick, e.g.
42. "Stormy Weather" composer
45. Gray of botany
46. Synthetic fiber
48. ___ tide
50. Fable
51. Loan
53. Cankers, e.g.
55. Retain
57. Spy gp.
58. Lady
60. Cool!
62. Close up again
64. Australian tennis great
68. Humans, e.g.
71. Sic
72. Canine woe
76. Tribute in verse
77. Sinister
80. Pay up
82. Prod
83. Sublet
85. Machinate
87. Summary
89. Archaic
90. Italian port
92. Shipment
94. Vend
95. No
96. Yin and ___
98. Colt's gait
100. Spanish article
102. Pistol sheath
105. American explorer
111. He was, to Brutus
112. Ibsen woman
114. North Carolina college
115. Asian lake
116. Green Gables girl
117. Horse color
118. Pay to play
119. Dinner bun
120. Jury member
121. Literary Lazarus
122. Blob
123. Patch place, maybe

DOWN
1. Roe source
2. Stack
3. Egg-shaped
4. Magnetic density unit
5. Crowers
6. Rhythmic cadence
7. Customer
8. Adjust
9. Blissfulness
10. Likewise not
11. Vienna-based gp.
12. Scorches
13. Napoleon, perhaps
14. Sundance's girlfriend
15. Camelot woman
16. Infrequent
26. A Guthrie
27. "The Raven" monogram
29. Kind of lizard
32. Onion's kin
34. Collected
35. Very confused
36. Ensemble
38. With
39. '50s conflict site
41. Capp's Daisy ___
43. Director Kazan
44. Dahl's wife
47. Approaches
49. Andes nation
52. Gal
54. Drive
56. Salon job
59. Concocted
61. Aquatic mammal
63. Sans date
65. Invitation abbr.
66. Attends
67. In reserve
68. Netman Bjorn ___
69. ___ fixe
70. 1967 Beatles hit
73. Midday
74. Fete
75. Whirlpool
78. Sick
79. Plunder
81. Taproom requests
84. Kitchen appliance
86. California town
88. Blueprint
91. "B.C." insect
93. Forest female
97. Film noir, e.g.
99. Metal bar
101. Set off
102. Mound
103. French river
104. Space
106. Arm bone
107. Oodles
108. Press
109. Garden green
110. Fashion magazine
113. Aries

PUZZLE 583

• STATESIDE REALTY •

ACROSS

1. Hoosegow
5. Grain tower
9. Appoint
13. Vale
17. Current
18. Cattle stall
19. Fe
20. Falco of "The Sopranos"
21. African lily
22. Bluff
23. Eft
24. Mellows
25. National Park in Wyoming
28. Tidies up
30. Memorable timespan
31. Scruff
33. Game cry
34. Finish second
37. Highland instrument
40. Prevent
44. Went
45. Raven's remark
46. Near
48. Sector
49. D.C.'s country
50. Upper House
53. Murmur fondly
54. Hollywood's Neeson
55. Berlin native
57. Famous citizen
59. Tanning light
61. Fore's partner
62. Rub out
64. Behold
65. Xylophone tools
69. Con game
70. Honda competitor
74. Huge quiz
75. From ___ Z
77. Sidewinders home
79. Plat
80. Saxophone type
81. Grease
83. Geologic period
84. Harden clay
85. Integument
87. Neophytes
90. Canned
91. Sweltering
93. Milan money, once
94. Devour
95. Secured with wedges
99. Island group of Florida
105. Mrs. Chaplin
106. Soft wood
108. Shakespearean fiend
109. Furry rodents
110. Tel ___
111. Islamic nation
112. Waterless
113. Not odd
114. French noggin
115. Liability
116. Endangered goose
117. Brood's home

DOWN

1. Remain
2. Mosaic piece
3. Adored one
4. Choose again
5. Vowel sound
6. Author Murdoch
7. Merry tune
8. Rectangular
9. Bowler's target
10. Exist
11. Cut down
12. Key in
13. Desert basin in California
14. Brink
15. Mortgage, e.g.
16. Minus
26. Gold source
27. Carpet pile
29. Driver's org.
32. Heroic tale
34. Tout
35. ___ majesty
36. At a distance
37. Outlaw
38. Wide-eyed
39. Inner selves
41. Assam silkworm
42. Enlarge a hole
43. Pack down
45. Midmost
47. Astros' home
50. Vault
51. Sailors
52. Ratify
56. Cavern site in Kentucky
58. Jacob's twin
60. Very bright
63. Host
65. Warmth
66. Spindle
67. Tatamis
68. Shock
71. Actor Epps
72. Profits
73. Made like
76. Ancient Greek coin
78. Mayday!
82. Obvious
84. Hydrocarbon substance
86. Perfect, per NASA
88. Seconds abbr.
89. ___ Islands, West Indies
90. Lard
92. Wishy-washy
94. Ravage
95. Winter garment
96. Lifted with force
97. Step ___!
98. Dreadful
100. Zoomed
101. Norse god
102. Donate
103. High cards
104. Mailed
107. Capture

512

ACROSS

1. Thin cut
5. Downey or Maffia
9. Tool housing
13. No, in Moscow
17. Fuss
18. Grace ending
19. Part of TV
20. Tiny amount
21. State firmly
22. Clenched hand
23. Train track
24. Pirate's drink
25. Al Stewart hit
28. Greek city
30. Building annex
31. Doze off
32. Smack, as a fly
33. Pie ingredient?
36. Trust
39. Dish rag
43. "Green ____"
45. Drivers' org.
46. Shakespearean king
47. Common dog's name
48. "Now ____ me down . . ."
49. Healthy
50. Style
51. Baseball's Speaker
52. Football pass
54. Crude
55. Scarlett's suitor
56. Mare's morsel
57. Jaded
58. Suit accessory
59. Soaring
62. Fabric
63. Bull session
67. Julep flavor
68. Rise's partner
69. Repair
70. Finished
71. Ruler mark
72. Garden tube
73. Nada
74. Cast out
75. Pittsburgh team
77. Kind of hat
79. Ancient lang.
80. Sticky substance
81. Part of FYI
82. Perform
84. Abundant
87. Hangover cure
93. Astonished
94. Dutch cheese
96. Brief bio
97. Heavy cord
98. Ration
99. Cleave
100. Had on
101. Garble
102. Equal
103. Proof of ownership
104. Prophet
105. Differently

DOWN

1. Don't go
2. Cherish
3. Hunch
4. Yankee manager
5. Lottery
6. Leave out
7. Network
8. Rabbit ears
9. Leather band
10. Miami cagers
11. Ivy Leaguer
12. Small state
13. Jack Higgins novel
14. Yesteryear
15. Bond's school
16. Labels
26. Auto pioneer
27. Scoundrel
29. Make a doily
32. Chars
33. Send by post
34. USC rival
35. Phooey's kin
37. Bucket
38. Nosh
39. On edge
40. Metal thread
41. Red-pencil
42. Missing
44. Theme of "Rocky III"
46. Dog restraint
49. Chubby
50. Prepare cheese
53. Mouse's kin
54. Exact copy
55. Poke fun at
57. Utter contentment
58. Tariff
59. French friends
60. Dryer leftover
61. Story starter
62. Ironing, e.g.
63. Desert monster
64. Villain's forte
65. Ward of "Sisters"
66. Waste allowance
68. Flock tender
69. Fish limb
73. Decreases in width
74. Per capita
76. ____ Vegas
77. Luau fare
78. Be important
81. Well-known
83. To the point
84. Genie's home
85. Author James ____
86. Campaign quest
87. Contain
88. Reed instrument
89. Dismiss
90. Child's toy
91. Musical work
92. "Pretty Woman" star
95. "____ Hard"

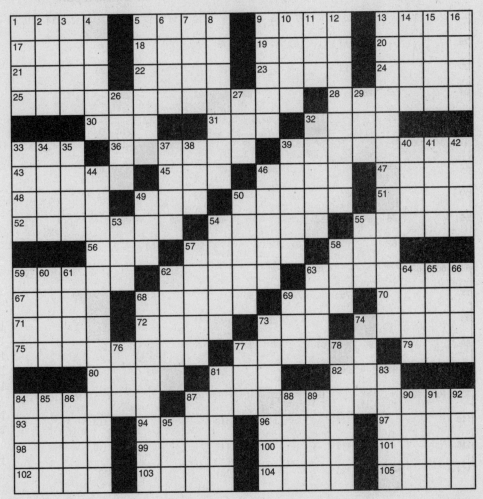

PUZZLE 585

• DOMICILE •

ACROSS

1. Pro ____
5. Facts
9. Stench
13. River bottom
16. Persia, now
17. Sprightliness
18. Closing passage
19. Maui dance
20. Fringe benefit
21. Escapade
22. Served a winner
23. Exclusively
24. Bargain hunter's delight
27. Testimonials
29. Dustcloth
30. Washstand item
32. Tax org.
33. Type of turnip
38. Send forth
40. Lofty nest
44. According to
45. Vapid
47. Entity
49. Costa ____
50. Ltd.'s kin
51. Evade
53. Prior to, in verse
54. Patron
55. Cabinetmaker's tool
58. Ameliorate
60. Interminable
62. Egg cells
64. Springe
66. "Curly ____"
67. Component
71. Dandruff site
73. Attempt
77. Relocate
78. Ditto's sister
80. ____ basin
82. Gay Nineties, e.g.
83. Roman date
84. Beget
86. No way!
88. Goal
89. Leases
91. Falls behind
93. Springs back
95. Greek goddess of dawn
97. Complain
99. High mountain
100. Bake in sauce
104. Winter boredom
110. African nation
111. Misfortunes
113. Further
114. Pleasant
115. Swine
116. Quick look
117. Baseball's Slaughter
118. Mrs. Copperfield
119. Work by Keats
120. Marsh bird
121. Completed
122. Elide

DOWN

1. Mature
2. God of war
3. Pie
4. Capital of Turkey
5. Representative
6. Cry of pity
7. Scarlett's place
8. Tarsus site
9. Wood sorrel
10. School of thought
11. European river
12. Wheel spokes
13. Batter's ploy
14. Fashion magazine
15. Calendar squares
19. Casino's regulations
25. File-folder features
26. Female sheep
28. Bikini top
31. Australian bird
33. Balustrade
34. Forearm bone
35. Diplomacy
36. Big party
37. Grads
39. Recap, for one
41. Go up
42. Frosts
43. Pinnae
46. Perfect places
48. Sawbucks
52. Pass into law
56. Settles land, like some pioneers
57. Poetic nightfall
59. Sap
61. Fitting
63. Added stipulations
65. Church officer
67. Arab chieftain
68. Rich vein
69. Level
70. Labor
72. Cover with asphalt
74. Mr. Connery
75. Dry
76. Sweet potatoes
79. Treader
81. Native of Beirut
85. It's often inflated
87. Massage, in a way
90. Musical syllable
92. Component of the USAF
94. Makes topsy-turvy
96. Berths
98. Identified
100. Imitate
101. Wearing boots
102. Pen
103. Ersatz butter
105. Former Palm Springs mayor
106. Fe
107. Stringed instrument
108. Beige
109. Nurture
112. Resort

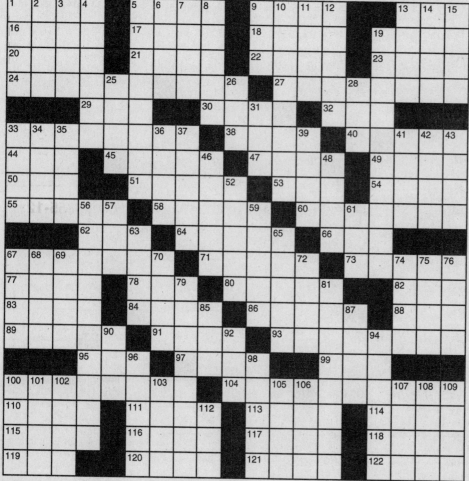

PUZZLE 1

```
ICY        GAS          BASK
OLAV      DELTA        ADEN  CONE
TALE    DILBERT       ATOP   OBOE
ANTE     DELI    ATOP  LILABNER
   GARFIELD       LILABNER
      AERY         ELSE
      BYTE         STEPS
AWL                      EEL
NOOSE               ELATE
GONER               SANTA
ELDER               SOULS
LEI                   TEE
   NEIGH        ODDS
     LOOP       BRER
SUPERMAN      ALLEYOOP
SOME  YETI  DOOM      PLOD
TUBE    SHELDON      ALLY
USER     SCALD       LAKE
BARS      EWE         SAD
```

PUZZLE 2

```
STEM   PAW   DEWS
NOVA   ERE   RAIL
ODIC   RED   ISLE
BOLA   INDEBTED
     ROOTED
ABROAD   DISPEL
BRENT     BLOKE
EASIER   SLATED
     RUSHES
LOOKSFOR    HODS
AXLE  FLU   IDOL
DELL  LOB   NOSE
SNAP  ESS   GREW
```

PUZZLE 3

```
HAM  OHMS  ALBS
OLE  NEAP  LIRA
TIN  CANE  LEAN
   AWED  ABOUND
ITCH   SURLY
ORIOLES   USAGE
NUN  OTHER  LOW
AEGIS    ENTWINE
    BEARD   EGGS
ASSERT   OATH
MINX  LAWN  TAT
PLIE  AGED  EYE
SOPS  SODS  DEN
```

PUZZLE 4

```
ARIA  REIN  ABHOR
LEND  UPDO  CRAVE
OPTS  LIEN  TALES
OER  DECAF  WONT
FLORA      AMEN
   IMPOSTOR  HAS
DAWN  RAT  URGENT
ALAS  ORALS  LATE
STREWN  TIS  EDIT
HOT  ETCETERA
   IDOL    ONSET
SPAR  ABBOT  CAR
CUBIC  WEAN  PURE
AMUSE  EASE  ABLE
BATHE  DUES  LAYS
```

PUZZLE 5

1. Mild child, 2. Fleet feet, 3. Truth sleuth, 4. Cheap creep, 5. Peak shriek.

PUZZLE 6

```
DADS   IRIS   RESIN
EXIT   NOON   ERODE
ELSE   FETA   NEWER
DECADE   AIDE   SAD
   ODOR   LOGO
BAN   GNAW   LEVEE
RUT   MOBILE   AXED
ARENA   LEI   FLARE
SANE   DELETE   GIN
   STAKE   DUET  GET
      RIFT   ACHE
SAP   STUB   CHARGE
ALOES   NOSH   GALL
STOKE   ALEE   ATOM
HOLED   SOAR   REPS
```

PUZZLE 7

1. Silverfish, 2. Birthright, 3. Straightforward.

PUZZLE 8

```
TORE   ACED   IRS
LOPER   FLOE   DEAR
ARETE   RANT   OKRA
WAR   LOW   RELIEF
SHASTA   SHAW   NET
   ARCH   YIELD
ITALY   OMEN   ELAN
NOVA   LOONS   AERO
ATOM   IRMA   UNDER
   CIRCA   SAKE
BRA   YOYO   DERIVE
LETTER   VIA   RIG
AMIE   IRED   STENO
BIOS   CURE   PINES
TNT   ETTA   APED
```

PUZZLE 9

1.   2.   3.

1. Rogue, Raven, Risky, Relic, Rhyme.
2. Drawl, Divot, Dogma, Daily, Decor.
3. Often, Oasis, Occur, Orbit, Owing.

PUZZLE 10

```
SACS   MALA   EFT
OGEE   AGER   ROO
LORE   LEACHING
   ERRING   ONTO
FAB   ACTUAL
ABRADE   ELICIT
CLARA   LEASH
EELERS   DARTLE
   OSPREY   EEN
HOWL   LESSER
ADHESIVE   PETS
FOE   ONER   ERAL
TRY   WELT   ESPY
```

PUZZLE 11

```
PIANO      SPICE
ANGORA   SPIRAL
STATIC   TATERS
TOR   GARISH
   NICER   YARD
LACONIC      NAY
AXED   AIL   FIRE
ILL      TOTALED
DELI   REWAX
   GRADER   ISM
ITALIC   STUDIO
MOROSE   TAKERS
PEKOE      RESET
```

PUZZLE 12

```
KIN   CEL   SPA   ROB
IRE   AXE   ERN   ERA
WOE   RUG   TOO   EAR
INDEED      SNIFFLE
   BLEST   GNU
BABE   PIP   TENTH
ALL   SCREAM   LIRA
RAT   SUE   SIS   NIL
CZAR   BATTLE   JET
HERON   DEE   QUAD
   VOW   ALBUM
WIRETAP   REPAIR
ODE   ADE   FIN   COO
LEI   TEE   REC   ITS
FAN   ERR   ORE   DAY
```

1-G, 2-Q, 3-N, 4-U, 5-Z, 6-K, 7-P, 8-C, 9-S, 10-F, 11-R, 12-V, 13-L, 14-Y, 15-E, 16-B, 17-J, 18-H, 19-T, 20-W, 21-O, 22-X, 23-D, 24-A, 25-I, 26-M.

PUZZLE 13

1. Fin and feather, 2. Happy and healthy, 3. Light and airy, 4. Far and away, 5. Snow and rain, 6. Point and shoot, 7. Stand and fight, 8. Sit and think.

PUZZLE 14

```
GSA   DIRT   BASE
ULT   ODOR   ANIL
MOO   TIMECLOCK
PENCE   PEAS
   EADS   SAWED
POTS   EMMA   ALI
EMIT   MIA   ASIN
TIM   MILK   STAG
STENO      ETTE
   ITAL   HATED
LUNCHTIME   ITO
AMOK   OMAR   MOM
BARS   PARE   ENE
```

PUZZLE 15

```
ALP   RAP  SECT
CAR  TERR  ACHE
TWO  RENO  THIN
   PROFESSIONS
SHEET    PAN
CARD  PREY  PLY
ALT   ROC   RAE
TOY  POET  ROLL
    EAT  DECAL
PROGRESSIVE
LAIR  SHIN  ELI
OGLE  TOTE  DON
WEST  SEE   SUN
```

PUZZLE 19

```
MAAM  DISC  NOW
ALSO  ECHO  ADE
RAPT  LEER  NOR
   OWL    AWARE
THERE    ISLE
HAY  DODO  BEDS
ERE   AIL   PIE
MERE  ROOF  IVE
    BEST  RECAP
DOUBT    FOX
INS  HIDE  TWOS
ACE  ARIA  RARE
LED  NEER  AREA
```

PUZZLE 23

```
SWAM  MESA  PAT
PAPA  ORAL  ALE
AGED  TAXI  CON
   ASH   BAKED
CLAMP    KID
RAM  ANTE  STIR
AIM  NOUNS  EOE
BROW  OBOE  STA
   HEN   METAL
TACOS    TIE
ERR  SAGE  RODS
LIE  AREA  IDOL
LAW  YELL  EDGY
```

PUZZLE 16

```
HASP  DORY  HONOR
IDEA  OLEO  EVOKE
DIRT  MEND  METRE
ETERNE  TEN  READ
   OAST   LAST
JANITOR   POUCH
BUS  LITER  BROAD
SITE  CAMEL  NAVE
ACIDS  LILAC  TOR
ERGOT   TITANIC
   ELAN   CINE
PROW  BOA  TEETHE
LAPIS  BLEU  DOOR
UKASE  LARD  LOAN
MELEE  ESSE  ETRE
```

PUZZLE 20

```
ELMS  TWAS  ACT
BEAU  HAIL  RAY
BITS  AXLE  IRK
   HAW   EVADE
ANTIC    SKI
PEA  ECHO  ACID
EEL  SHARK  ADE
DREW  AMEN  PEW
   OPT   ESSAY
DARER    FEW
ALE  URGE  IDOL
SOL  DEER  NANA
HEY  EVEN  EYED
```

PUZZLE 24

```
LOT  STEW  WAGE
AGO  WOKE  OMEN
PRO  EYER  OPTS
SETUP    ELL
   STEP   ISSUE
SAFE  AIDE  AND
ERA   SPA   GIG
AIR  FEET  MATE
MAMBO    DEMO
   ARC   ABOVE
SPOT  LEAK  NIL
HALE  URGE  ELS
ENDS  BEER  SEE
```

PUZZLE 17

```
CAP  ZONE  WAND
OIL  ERAS  ALOE
ONE  BEGS  RISE
STAIR    OPTED
   CARPED
WAGE  HIDE  VEE
RYE  SINGS  INK
YET  ANTE  WADE
   VOODOO
SHAKE    TOKYO
PORE  WATT  NOG
OBOE  ALEE  ERR
TOWN  GEAR  WEE
```

PUZZLE 21

```
ARC  SUDS  SAGA
PAR  TRIO  ITEM
EGO  ONES  TEMP
RECUR    TOGO
   SKI    UNDUE
GATE  SLIM  IRK
ASH   LID   AGE
SEE  PEEL  ALES
PANDA    END
   AWED   OOZED
SPOT  TACT  ORE
AIDE  CLUE  NAB
PEER  HEED  ESS
```

PUZZLE 25

```
USURP  COWS  TAB
REPEAT  LUAU  ALA
GROTTO  ARRANGED
EEN  SPEW  IVE
   HYMN   LENTO
OLLA  ODDLY  EARN
PEAS  SORA  VIA
TARP  TREND  BEER
EGG  SAKI  ERNE
DUEL  SEMIS  ANTS
ERUPT    ERST
   CUR  CROC  EWE
FOLKLORE  BUDDHA
ADO  SLED  ELUDES
NAG  ELSE  LOONY
```

PUZZLE 18

```
ADE  ROAM  REIN
HAY  AUTO  EAVE
ODE  ITEM  DREW
YARDS    SPY
   REVS   RECUR
SPRY  ECHO  ALE
TOO   IRE   RAP
ASP  GLUE  PENS
THESE    BLUE
   YET   PASTA
SCAR  ALOE  URN
LULU  PAWN  RUN
YELP  SPED  FEE
```

PUZZLE 22

```
OWED  BARB  ALP
POLO  AREA  NIL
TOFU  LEFT  TEE
   BUD   HYENA
SLOTS    VISE
HIP  EDIT  SOSO
ERE  RESEW  BOX
SAND  LIMO  ODE
   OMIT   OCEAN
SINCE    PLY
ADE  WINE  CHEF
SEE  ERAS  LULL
HAD  DEBT  EELY
```

PUZZLE 26

```
SLAB  TOSS  FUMED
HOBO  ANTE  IRATE
APED  TEAM  ANNUL
DETECT  BIAS  ODE
ERS  OLD  SCORED
   TIEUP   COD
DRAWL  SUMO  DELI
ROLE  STRUT  EMIT
YELL  LYES  ASSES
   VIA   RIGHT
SOLEMN  COO  SET
TWO  AGOG  OYSTER
ALONG  GLOB  HERO
RESEE  ROPE  UNIT
STEWS  EWER  TOES
```

517

PUZZLE 27

```
CLAW  SILO  ESS
HOUR RENEWS BIT
INTO INFANT BRA
NEON ODOR ASSET
    GET  NEST
ENS REED WHISK
LOP ADMIRE FANS
KNOB ICE FREE
SOUR STEAMS GEL
STENO DRIP ELF
   WAYS  LYE
PRISM HARD ACRE
OAT ENAMEL TOOK
PIE REMEDY ELSE
ELM TENS NAYS
```

PUZZLE 28

```
SOAK SPA TABS
AIDE SLEDS AROW
GLEN CEASE LOSE
   OBOES ACCUSE
AWL ELK TWO SET
MAILED BREADED
PINUP FREELY
STEM BLOND EASY
PERIOD PRUNE
SKYLARK PISTOL
CAN SIT VAT OWL
ELOPED VINYL
DICE ELITE ATOM
ANKA DECAL WINE
REST GEL NEST
```

PUZZLE 29

```
FORGE LEIS FACT
LAIRS EACH ECHO
ATLAS ASEA MEAT
WHEN NECK ASPS
   DRAT REAL
CAMISOLE DENT
SALAMI LABS OWN
AGE DRAMA SEE
PER DEEM STREET
STAY TASTIEST
MESA TEED
SLAB TIRE TUTU
TOOL ALOE LAMAS
ACNE TEAR APPLE
TOED ERRS YESES
```

PUZZLE 30

```
SNOW EBBED NOVA
NODE CLARE ERAS
ERIE HALES ELLS
EMU LONE PROVE
SAMBA KRONA PET
   RIBS LUG
CALICO LITERARY
AXIS BLOOM ALOE
PEEKABOO EAGLET
BIB OGRE
SHE ANEAR ODEUM
CANIS ENOW DRY
ABUT CIGAR SIGN
TIRE UNITE OLEA
STEM ESSES BEDS
```

PUZZLE 31

```
EBBS MOSS MOST
ALIT SYRUP ETCH
TUTU ENEMY STAR
SEEN TAG WHERE
GNU AMMO RYE
RAG OPINION
ORALS SOLD GADS
BELIEFS DEMERIT
EASE LUTE ALIVE
BEESWAX DAM
EON RASH SIR
QUOTA IRK URGE
UNTO PUREE MEOW
ACES ASTER BARE
LESS DESK ADES
```

PUZZLE 32

```
SPAT ARID MARES
ARCH MICE APART
GOER AMEN ZEBRA
ASSORT RITE BOG
BEE SAW SIRE
OKS CUB LICK
REEF REF GUIDES
REMIT DUO DRIVE
SPIGOT RAW TREE
HOOF FIR END
BRAT TIC DAM
RUB JEER EMERGE
ERODE LEAN TOOK
WADER DELE ALOE
SLEEK SPED LEND
```

PUZZLE 33

```
NOSH FAT FACT
ALTO ALLOT LULU
PLAN LOINS IRON
SAGE TOE HOMAGE
YEARN IDS
CEDERS PRAYED
RIPENS KIT RID
AVOWS BEG SENOR
PIC PUG SPEEDY
CHOIRS SPARSE
BRO COATI
ASLEEP LAC NODE
CLOY EVOKE EBON
MANE LINED SOLD
EYED EER SETS
```

PUZZLE 34

```
ALAS STRAY LAMA
SOLO PROSE EGAD
POOL YELLS MAID
STEAM ALE HORNS
RAFT EBON
DAM LAY PAN FAT
ALINED REMADE
NOSE ODOR
CHEESE WATERS
EAR PRO ROW SEE
BEAU EELS
SOLID TAM SHOPS
ABUT ARMOR OGLE
POSE WAIVE TEEN
SETS ENDED SEAT
```

QUOTATION: It's better to be a lion for a day than a sheep all your life.

PUZZLE 35

```
ALE ALSO CLAP
SIR MUTE RICE
SEAFARER AMEN
USER TOSS
LACES ELSE
OVAL TOOK DAB
BONSAI LIKELY
EWE REEL OBIT
FERN CASTE
ARIA TOOL
MONK ARGUABLE
MATE HALL EEN
ODOR SPED DID
```

PUZZLE 36

```
APER TENS FRO
DOVE OMIT RAD
DEEP AUTO AND
STRAPS SMOG
IOTA PARKA
CHARMING RANG
OIL PETAL NEE
DRAB REROUTES
STROP SLAP
MAID ANSWER
POI NEON HIVE
URN CLAD ODES
BEG HITS TENT
```

PUZZLE 37

```
LAR GE    FA CA DE    SP AR
VA N ES    TE M PLE  AC ADE MY
   RE TI RE    TE DI UM
   MA IN TA IN    SP EN T
E LI TE   N EPT UN E  RAI SE
MI TER    S AGE   VE RSE  P ALE
R AT   PA R BO IL   MI SE R
   E SCO RT   NE ED LE SS
   R AN GE     AN I MUS
STO MA CH   NI C HE   ON S ET
OP T     AL AR M     EL UDE
```

PUZZLE 38

1. Robe/Probate, 2. Move/Improve, 3. Tale/Startle, 4. Halt/Asphalt, 5. Sage/Stagger, 6. Live/Believe, 7. Hike/Thicket, 8. Cite/Citizen.

PUZZLE 39

```
ODDS MART TEPEE
TAUT ICER IRATE
IDEA METE METAL
CALICO EBB ESS
DISC ARE
CAP NAHS RERAN
ATONE AUTO GNAT
STOA MORAN ONCE
TICS USER STORE
CHAFF ROMP YEN
LIT TURF
GAS NIP MYRIAD
UNPEG LAMB ORCA
STAGE AXEL CORM
TENOR NENE KNEE
```

PUZZLE 40

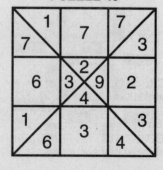

PUZZLE 41

```
SLAYS MIME  EBBS
COCOA EVIL  CLAP
AGENT SICK  RULE
MOD ETHER   CURSE
    PEA  SOSO  TAD
CHURNS      LODE
LINE  TAUPE  ODDS
ADDS  IRKED  GOOP
MEET  EMEND  TUNA
ROWS        IRATER
    ADS  ATOM  NAG
DECKS REIGN  CUR
ALOE  CALM  GOOSE
GARY  ATOP  ERRED
EYES  TENS  RENDS
```

PUZZLE 46

```
         FAD
         A E
       TACOSTS
       W A I T
     BLINDIGORGE
     U S E N A C
   MIDSTEPLIANTLER
   A D A T T G A E
 EARLYRICHIEFEATHERA
 L B N D O T R E L I
 FALLACYNICHEMISTORM
   E M L S E I T P
   GROWLITERANKALE
     O A R A E I
     RAGGEDROWSE
       E A E
       ROMPEAL
         E R
         ROY
```

PUZZLE 50

```
TYPE  GALA  BATCH
WORN  OWES  ALOHA
AGOG  REAL  LEGAL
SAFARI FEEL  ATE
     GAL   YEARN
  BEETLE   PROOFS
WON  ANY  SONATA
ERASE DOT  MORON
DECENT NOG  GUT
  STATUS  TEAPOT
     MINER  NIL
ASP  RACE  TRADES
WHALE OVAL  GIVE
LAPEL NUDE  UNIT
SHADY DEER  EELS
```

PUZZLE 51

```
ANI  GIST  AGENTS
WON  ACTA  MUSEUM
FIDDLERS   INSANE
USER  AKIN  PAW
LEXICON    LOBE
    FRUGAL  ARISE
LATTICED   TASTY
ORA THROUGH  LIE
OCTET   BLOTTERS
THANE   DETOUR
    DRAY INBOARD
SPY  HELM  TREE
TOUPEE   EARPHONE
ERRATA STOA  SAP
TETRAD TEED  ELS
```

PUZZLE 47

```
ORANG  TAT  QUAY
FOXIER ETA  URGE
FEEBLE ROC  ANON
   CAMPHOR
PAN  SOW  ATONE
ART ONESHOT AUK
SCHWA CUB  ERNE
  OPERATIVE
ROCK GUN  OLDIE
EVE CONTEST ERG
SALSA SUE  BEG
  PROWESS
AJAR RED  HAZARD
RANI ZIG  ISOMER
EMIT ORE  POPPY
```

1-L, 2-W, 3-H, 4-P, 5-J, 6-C, 7-Z, 8-O,
9-B, 10-Q, 11-F, 12-V, 13-Y, 14-S,
15-M, 16-K, 17-R, 18-U, 19-T, 20-E,
21-D, 22-N, 23-X, 24-I, 25-A, 26-G.

PUZZLE 42

1. V/is/it/or, Tr/ol/l/ey, Hu/b/ca/p, Pa/lom/i/no.
BONUS: V/ol/ca/no
2. K/not/t/y, Ema/n/a/te, En/de/av/or, R/ele/as/e.
BONUS: K/n/av/e

PUZZLE 43

```
AGRA  MESA  LADED
CLUB  ALAS  ISERE
TELEGRAMS  NOLAN
SEE  OTIS  GRIST
    COIN  REO
  PAR NEPAL  ADS
SAFARI  ENDICOTT
ALIVE ODA  CANOE
CORALSEA  SECOND
SET  ISLET  IRE
    ACE  VISA
ACORN JAPE  PSI
BARON  SIDEWALKS
IMBUE OVEN  VEIN
ESSEX NERD  EAST
```

PUZZLE 44

```
PINTO SPOT  PROS
ACORN LIVE  RAGE
RETAR ACED  OKRA
  CUSTARD  TEEM
DRIEST     LYRE
EEN HURRY  AIRS
ALB  PIE  NINETY
TOO PIGSKIN BOO
HORRID TIC  ARK
KNOT ASTER  TEE
  YAWL  SEVERS
GENA  APOSTLE
OPAL LIME  INANE
NEIL KNEE  CURES
EELY SEND  SECTS
```

PUZZLE 52

```
STIR  GAL   FLAP
PACE RAWER  LIKE
ACED EVADE  IRIS
TORE PER  TENANT
   FIELD  EGG
  TWIRLS  FLOSSES
THANKS AIL  CAP
URGES AIR  NOOSE
BEE  VIM  RAPPED
SEDUCED  PONIES
   NUN  GROAN
SCARED ROT  IOTA
LAME OLIVE  OBEY
ARMS RIPER  NONE
PLOT  DEN   SETS
```

PUZZLE 48

1. Reprisal, 2. Luckiest, 3. Tortoise,
4. Emporium, 5. Mustache, 6. Endeavor, 7. Raindrop, 8. Portable, 9.
Euphoric, 10. Computer.

PUZZLE 45

ACROSS: 1. Sweater, 2. Cassock, 3.
Cutoffs, 4. Chemise, 5. Slicker.

DOWN: 1. Tunic, 2. Dress, 3. Shawl,
4. Shirt, 5. Jeans, 6. Apron, 7. Frock.

QUOTATION: We are shaped and
fashioned by what we love. (Goethe)

PUZZLE 49

```
SMUG  SPAT  USAGE
PURL  NANA  RISEN
ALGA  APED  BESTS
SEEM  RAW  FAS
   OILY  INTRO
NOUN AMEN  AIMS
HURRAH OWES  VEE
ODD PATTERN ALE
AGE TWIT  YELLED
REAR KNOW  EAST
  SLICE  EARN
   PAD HAG  DOCK
EGRET NOVA  IRON
YEAST ABET  NAPE
EMPTY YORE  GLEE
```

PUZZLE 53

```
STAT  SICK  URBAN
LUGE  ECRU  NIECE
IBEX  READ  CASTS
TARTAR FURL  TAT
   SMART  YAM
MAS  ETA  PESETA
ARM NEWEL  PEELS
YEAH DEFAT  TROT
ONSET STIED  RHO
THROAT DAY  YAP
   BEG  ASSES
ASP  HOOD PRANCE
PIANO ROTO  BOOT
ORIEL TRIO  OTTO
DELED SEEN  TEEN
```

PUZZLE 54

```
TAFFY  RODE   ARTS
AFIRE  EXES   COAT
PREYS  HEAT   EDGY
EAR    KENNELS
SIC DAM  SEE    HOG
DECOR     MADAME
  HEARTH  PERIL
CAFE  TIEUP   LETS
AMUSE   DETECT
MORTAR    COAST
SKY SIS HAY   URN
  TYPHOON    DUE
ALTO  PENN  AIDES
PAID  LICE  CREST
TYPO  EKED  TENTS
```

PUZZLE 55

```
PAP    SHAH    SPAS
ERA    SWIPES  ARCH
ASS    PALEST  WARE
COT    ILLS  OBEYED
ENAMELS    CUED
  ADO    DATA   TWO
OKAY  WHIM   USHER
BELOW  ATE   STARE
INTRO  STOP   EWES
TOO   UNTO    IRE
  FLEE   DRIPPED
RESIDE  ORAL   AXE
EVER  DONATE   WIN
DIME  YELPED   ELS
SLID    RYES   DEE
```

PUZZLE 56

```
HAWK   COAST    ERR
ALEE   COPIER   COO
LOIN   AGENDA   HIP
THROWN     TADPOLE
SAD   HIES    NEE
  INLETS     SALT
JAM   PEEVE   TRIO
AREAS  VEE   HOIST
VANS   ENTRY   APE
ABUT    ANTHEM
  EAT   HEWN   SIS
SECRETS    ASLANT
IVE   READER  ALSO
DIE   ISSUED  USER
ELS   ETHER   DATE
```

PUZZLE 57

```
PLOD   LANCE    SGTS
LUNA   OCEAN    ELAS
ACID   TRANSCRIPT
TROOP  ORA    APSES
EEN   REBEL    RET
   EVAS     NEST
LIL   SETTO  ETNAS
ADO ELI  RDS   ETA
DOUBT  CADET   DER
ELIE     MIRE
  SEA   PANNE   SPA
TOITY  ADA   MANED
OPALESCENT    TATA
GENE   SAUCE   ORIG
ANAS   ESSEX   PETE
```

PUZZLE 58

```
REFER  SCAB   SCOW
AGILE  LULU   WIPE
DOGMA  APER   AVID
   SEW    EATING
ICEBOX  SOAR  LEE
RAVINE    CRUMB
OWED  CURB   SUNG
NERD  STEIN  SORT
DYER  TATA   HOER
  REHEM   SIESTA
ACT  AIRS  AGLEAM
SHIELD     FLU
PITY  IOTA  ALGAE
IDLE  NEON  NIECE
CEES  GROG  ADMEN
```

PUZZLE 59

```
JANET   ALMA   EDGAR
IRENES  LEAR   DIANE
BEWARE  LILI   INDIA
  SIAM    FIESTA
MAI  LOB  CSI   HARD
ELG  RETAKE  LASSIE
LEONI  ONE BEN  TNN
SCRIPT  NYLUND  AKA
  ATALE   ASTRO
ELL  OBERON  SOAPER
LIE RIN ADA   ITALY
SAVANT  AROUND  ALA
EMIR  HOP NEO   RAN
  AVALON   RONA
SHEBA  SLOB   SAILOR
PALIN  ELSA   ENDORA
ALIAS  NOEL   SAGET
```

PUZZLE 60

```
ALSO   APTS    SLEW
LAWN   ERROR   HIVE
ERAS   CROPS   AMEN
RIM   AHAS   APART
TAP  TOY   SIRE
  TYPO  SPADE  MAP
UMP   OWL    OIL
BLOB  ABUSE   ABLY
RAN   URN    RAM
AWE   ASIDE   UPON
  ITEM   YEN   POP
CLONE  HEAT   PIE
HAUL   HEELS   HOSE
ACRE   EERIE   USER
TEST   PLOD    MESS
```

PUZZLE 61

```
SPA    COMMA   NAPS
WAR    DEFEAT  ARIA
AYE    INFANT  TILL
TENANT  LIE   IDLE
SEAWEED     AMMO
  ARROW   PONCHO
BEAR   VISTA   HOW
EGRET  EPA    NOISE
TOE   RESET   ICED
ASSAIL     RERAN
  SPED    DARKEST
CROC  CON   COSTAR
LOVE  TWINES   HUE
OPEN  ENCORE   INN
PEND  DYERS    CAD
```

PUZZLE 62

```
PANDA  HILT   SLEW
AFOUL  OVER   TOGO
PANEL  METE   EDGE
ARE  OPE   OSPREYS
   EYE   ENSUE
BETA  YEA    ROOT
LEER  TESTER  FRO
ALP   ONION   FAN
BEE  INSERT  VEIL
DEAD   SEE    ARTY
  BLAST    RAT
ANALYST  ASP   BUN
MIME  CAST   ANISE
ICES  OLIO   CITES
DENT  TERM   EXERT
```

PUZZLE 63

```
DUST   CART    RETRO
INTO   OGEE    EARED
ATOP   NOTE    STEAD
NICEST  MOT    ADS
ELK   ARM    SNAGS
  MAUL    STRUMS
POSSESSED    EERIE
EMIT   TIGER   BENT
TAXES  CAFETERIA
ENTREE    LEVY
  YENTA   REP   SPA
OFF  DAD    REINED
ARISE  ANTE   RAND
FAVOR  MEAN   ERNE
STEPS  STUD   SEER
```

PUZZLE 64

```
ADAGE   GAIT  DAD  ARM
TOKEN   POUCH ODE  CUE
OMITS   LATER FLU  NIL
MENU  BOTH  EFFICIENT
  PELT  OPAL   BED
ATE  RUT  RATE   LOAM
COMPARED  REX   SWEATY
TRIO  TRAM  NEATH  TON
STRIFE  BAT  DIRE  SPA
   ODD  GAD   MAR
ADS  ROOT  REE  WELLED
SEA  TUTOR  BLAB  AIDE
PLIGHT  PEP  FREEREIN
SILL   IDEA  CRY   STY
  ESS   CHAT  AREA
RACEHORSE  TIDY  PROF
IVE  OWE  ACUTE  CRIME
SOD  EEL  DUNES  OILED
EWE  DRY  STEM   GLENS
```

PUZZLE 65

```
ASS    MELD    SLOT
VET    LILIES  TONE
ATE    ALKALI  ICES
STEIN   REENLIST
TOPMASTS    SOT
  PIKE    TSETSE
ERRS   INFRA   DRAW
BOO   TOO    UKE
BOAR   SHRUG   TEES
STRIPE     GALA
  SEC   PEROXIDE
BANKROLL    TIMID
ALAI   NOUGAT  ACE
ROPE   DOMINO  GEM
STAR   PENT    ERA
```

520

PUZZLE 66

```
P O I   V A S T   P A S S E
A N D   E N T E R   A R E A S
N E E   T I A R A   S C A L P
G R A B   M I N I   A R T Y
    L E A N   L E W D
  U S U A L   P R E H E A T S
A S T E R   L O O N Y   R O E
J A R S   K O L A S   S E N T
A G O   D I N E D   Z O N E S
R E P T I L E S   S E A T S
    I D O L   V E E P
M A A M   I C E R   Y A R D
A L T E R   E E R I E   T E E
I V O R Y   R E G A L   O P E
L A P S E   S E L L   M O P
```

PUZZLE 70

```
M I   M E   B R A W N   N
A N   T E S U   R   G E
M I N C   E S A   I L
  T E A   C H S E   A
M I   S H A   P A T E
O A T   H T E S   T E R
T   H R O N   E G   A B
  L U C I   D A L   L Y
H A P   P E   N E Y   E
C L E A   V E S   L O W
I   N G E   S T C A   N E
T E   N E T   N E E
E   D E   N Y E   A R
```

PUZZLE 75

```
S T A L K   B R A V O
U R B A N E   S L O W E D
D I E S E L   H O W L E D
S O D   E L F I N
    B L A R E D   S P A
W A G E   E L E C T O R
A C R E   K I D   R I N K
S H I N D I G   O R E S
H E P   E T H N I C
    U T T E R   L A B
S O U R C E   W A R I L Y
U N S E E N   S T O O G E
P E E P S   E T N A S
```

PUZZLE 67

```
A M P   O W E D   R A P T
C A R   S P I N E T   O G E E
E K E   T E R S E R   P O P E
R E V   O R E   R A T E
  A D V E R B   C I R C A
S T R E E T   A L E E   L E D
C H I T   T I L E   S H I R E
R A C E   A D L I B   E P I C
A W A R E   E A S E   S P A R
P E T   B E A D   W I S E L Y
  D E C O R   S P I D E R
  A N O N   A L L   S T Y
F R O M   D E L U D E   H U E
L A D E   E R A S E R   I N N
U P D O   D Y E R   P A S
```

PUZZLE 71

```
A C H E   G R A M   A G E   C A S T S
C O A X   R A R E   F U R   O P T I C
T A L C   A N T S   T A R A N T U L A
S L E E T S   S A D   R O W   D E B
    P E S O   A D D R E S S
C A T A L O G   I R I S   K O A L A
A L P   L A Z E   S E A   R I N S E D
S E E S   N E E R   A N T E   H I S
H A R M E D   S E E M   I C E R
E N S U E   G E R B I L S   R U D E R
  G L U E   O B E Y   C A M E R A
E R E   M E N U   R I C H   S C A M
G A L L O P   A T E   N O E L   A S P
O G L E D   S T E W   G I R A F F E
  D E S P I S E   L I M O
A S K   P R O   S O D   S P R E A D
M A I N T A I N S   P A T H   G A L E
I G L O O   G A P   A L O E   E V E N
D A N D Y   S L Y   L E N D   T E S T
```

PUZZLE 76

```
S I C   P H I   H I T   R A Y
T O O   R E C   A T E   A L E
E T A   I N K   I S M   B I N
M A X I M   Y A K   P R I N T
    L O W   S U N   I D E A
C A S K   O R T   O F F
A G A   B E E R   W A L L O P
F A N C Y   T O Y   W E A R Y
E R S A T Z   L O I N   M A R
    C E E   O U R   V A L E
H E F T   E G G   K O I
E Q U I P   A Y E   B A N J O
R U N   A D Z   U K E   O B I
B A N   R U E   R E S   V A N
S L Y   T O R   O N E   A R K
```

1-N, 2-L, 3-K, 4-W, 5-V, 6-C, 7-X, 8-R, 9-Q, 10-U, 11-Y, 12-E, 13-H, 14-S, 15-D, 16-J, 17-Z, 18-P, 19-I, 20-A, 21-F, 22-M, 23-G, 24-B, 25-O, 26-T.

PUZZLE 68

```
M A S E R   K I L O   S E C T
U L T R A   A C I D   A C H Y
S L A N G   N E R D   C L A P
T I R E   A G R E E D   I R E
S E C   A G A S   R O M P
  S H I N E R   D O S E D
  S Y N O D   F O R E G O
P I L L   C O A T I   O D O R
A V I A R Y   B R A E S
P E N N A   A S L E E P
  O D I C   L I C K   L A M
E E L   D O M I N O   F I L E
A C E R   M O V E   D U C A T
T R U E   E P E E   U N I T E
S U M S   T E N S   O T T E R
```

PUZZLE 72

PUZZLE 73

Greece, Denmark, Lithuania, Hungary, Latvia, Portugal, Finland, Sweden.

PUZZLE 77

1. COOKIE: Tollhouse, Oatmeal, Shortbread, Butter.
2. JACKET: Blazer, Mackinaw, Topcoat, Anorak.

PUZZLE 78

```
M A D C A P   E M U   P A S S
A M E L I A   N O N   A B U T
R E C O R D   D O C   S A G A
K N O T   D U D   T A R
  H E L D   R O B E R T
R E F E R E E   F L O E
E T E   R A B B I   R E N E E
A C T   F R A N C   E D D
P H A S E   I D A H O   A I D
  T W A S   L I B E R T Y
P R A Y E R   E M I T
R E D   R A M   H U L K
O B O E   B O O   B O N S A I
N E R O   I A N   O R I E N T
G L E N   A T E   D E C R E E
```

PUZZLE 69

```
L A C Y   C O O   H A Y S
O G R E   S H A R D   O R A L
A R O W   T A T E R   W I R E
N E W   G A S H   I S L A N D
S E N T R I E S   E K E
    H E R D   G R I D D L E
A R M I E S   G A S   O E R
L E A S T   P U B   S E V E R
S A X   C A N   L A Y E R S
O P I N I O N   F A R E
    E L L   S E P A R A T E
R E C A L L   M U S H   R A M
E V E R   A S I D E   D I K E
D E L L   R I L E D   U S E R
O N L Y   R E D   D E N Y
```

PUZZLE 74

```
S O W   B A S E   A R M S
O B I   O B E Y   C H I P
P O R T A B L E   T Y K E
S E E R   E L L S   T E D
    E S S   I T C H
B E R E T S   D R A M A S
A R E T E   A P I S H
G A L O R E   S T I C K Y
    A P E X   C A T
L A X   O I L Y   A L A S
A R I A   L I T T L E S T
H E N S   E C H O   T I E
R A G S   D E E M   S A P
```

PUZZLE 79

```
S T A B   O R C A S   H I M
C O L A   C H A L E T   A T E
A F A R   C O N T R A   L E T
B U R E A U   O U T C O M E
    S P E D   M A R
P A S   S A R A N   S U C H
A C T   E N A M O R   S L A B
T H R U S T S   V E S T I G E
H E A T   S E L E C T   M A T
    S W I M   D I N E R   B R A
    L I P   T A P E
C O M E D I C   T W I N E D
O B I   S C A M P I   M I L E
T I C   T O R E R O   A C M E
E T A   T E N O N   M E S S
```

PUZZLE 80

A: 1. Remit, 2. Irate, 3. Table, 4. Lease, 5. Scope, 6. Probe, 7. Brisk, 8. Swarm.

B: 1. Emit, 2. Rate, 3. Able, 4. Ease, 5. Cope, 6. Robe, 7. Risk, 8. Warm.

PUZZLE 85

```
SEE  SRI   MAAM
CAM  TECH  UNDO
ARM  ALOE  STIR
BLACKANDWHITE
    HEY  GAY
MAGI   RED  MEL
EBONYANDIVORY
TET  OVA  EDGE
    AGE  SHE
SALTANDPEPPER
LOOT  GRIN  ODE
ANNA  EARN  GIN
PEER  TEA   OTT
```

PUZZLE 89

```
     APT
     IRON
    ADAGIO
  CRAM  NUT
  LIMN  ECHO
DEITY    HANS
ERNE     TEEN
SAT       ROB
LEST     DIVE
LAIC    DEFAT
 DRUG  JAWS
  ERR  DUTY
   BANANA
    DIRT
    PEA
```

PUZZLE 81

```
AGAS  SHED   SLOP
INCH  AUTOS  LOGO
MAMA  LEAST  EARN
SWELLS    ELUDED
   LOATH  NAT
KABOB  RICOCHET
ELATE  ABASE  ARM
LAY    GAR    SEE
PRO  SLICE  ARENT
MUSTACHE  CELTS
   MOP  INERT
ENRAPT    REHASH
LIAR  ORANG  ISLE
SNIT  PATIO  NEAR
EENS   WEPT  KAYO
```

PUZZLE 86

```
SAT  AMES   ROPE
AGO  OREO   ARID
CHEERILY   TOGS
SADAT    SST
   TAPA  TASKS
MAPS  INTENTLY
ICI  ONION  EEN
DECENTLY   FREE
ISAAC    ESTE
   SEC   IMAGE
BALI  AMENABLY
ALEE  BABE   EEE
DEAR  SOBS   TED
```

PUZZLE 90

```
    9        5        2
7 C 7    7 F 1    1 G 8
    5        3        6
    5        3        6
1 E 8 8   X   4 4 D 8
    7        9        2
    7        9        2
4 A 6    6 H 7    7 B 9
    3        8        3
```

PUZZLE 82

1. Capsule, Asleep, Lapse, Soap, Sap; 2. Hoedown, Powder, Dwell, Dewy, Wed; 3. Tabloid, Absurd, Braid, Daub, Bad; 4. Adapter, Aspect, Tempo, Kept, Pet; 5. Romaine, Cinema, Mason, Amen, Man.

PUZZLE 87

```
HID   SKI   ASS
ONE   PIN   ILL
ELL   AND   SEE
RATS    IDLED
SWAN  EGRETS
    ANNOY
LEERED   EDGE
ORALS    REAL
COS   TAD   CUB
ADE   LIE   AGO
LED   ERE   YEW
```

PUZZLE 91

```
ACER         ETON
SHRUB      GLADE
PISTIL    ZEALOT
SPA  GAD  SETTERS
STY  CANOE  INS
ZIP  MIL   DOT
PEP   LATEN
RUB   RIM
RIPEN  CUR
AIL  SEA   REV
SIC  COEDS  CAT
ACROBAT  DUO  LEI
BAITER    MERINO
ARETE     RESEW
SERA       BETA
```

PUZZLE 83

```
BL  IMP  PRO SP ER     RE  CUR
AB  ET   F IN A  LE  IN SU  RE
    US EL ESS    AD JU ST ME NT
     D  OR ME R     PI E
BE H EST    DI ET  T  AD PO LE
CO AT    CH A RAC  T  ER    TI ER
ME CH AN IC   TE AL   CR ON Y
      CHO KE  D  ON AT E
E  ST RA N  GE      TE ST Y
LO UN GE  E  MI NE NT    AM BER
PE T        RE ST IVE    MER RY
```

PUZZLE 88

```
         ASP
        ANILE
       LITTER
      COOL  TAR
     PORT  LET
    ALOE  WAR
    PAT  FAN
   HEN  BAND
  BOX  HIRE
 ALA  SITE
CARTED
ENSUE
DEN
```

PUZZLE 84
NATIONAL

PUZZLE 92

Earth-Planet, Guardian-Angel, Gold-Rush, Play-Mate, Large-Enormous, Apple-Sauce, Nut-Acorn, Toe-Nail.

VEGETABLE DISH: Eggplant Parmesan

PUZZLE 93

```
    HAS       LEI
    ORAL      EARL
    TRUE     SMIRK
    TOTS      CUR
    AYES   GOO
  MEMOS  SOIL
VERA      COLDCASH
ANIL  READY  OREO
LUKEWARM      OGEE
    ATOP  SALON
   LES  PINE
   IRK   AMID
FOCUS     LIMO
IRON      OLAF
TEN       ELF
```

PUZZLE 97

```
             TEN
             ARAM
            MIAMI
          CALLED
ELD       COMO
LOAM      HEAR
FAVOR     LAD
FIRED  TONSIL
SALE  RUG  CAP
 LIE  CREASE  EKED
   ADE    DECOY
   CORE   SATES
   RUNS    NEAT
ATTARS      DRE
READS
TALL
LEE
```

PUZZLE 101

```
MUSIC   FRA  REPEL
ISERE   RUG  EVADE
RADAR  ONE  BINDS
EGG   EAT   OLEOS
DEEP  SHAVERS
     EGO  LION  SPA
MASTERPLAN  ALAI
ABEAM  EEN  EXERT
TEAL  LANDSLIDES
ELS  PARD  ADO
    NUCLEAR  MEAD
SHOOT   LAS  ODA
TAROT  WEB  ASSET
ERASE  EMU  GUILE
MINER  TOM  ABNER
```

PUZZLE 94

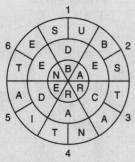

1. Buds, 2. Base, 3. Cart, 4. Rant, 5.
Idea, 6. Teen.
INNER RING: Barren
MIDDLE RING: Decade
OUTER RING: Substantiate

PUZZLE 98

1. DAY / ICE / GET
2. OAT / FIR / FLY
3. ART / VIA / EGG
4. CAM / ODE / WET

PUZZLE 102

```
LAM    LOAF   WHET
ONE  PEDDLE  HOAR
ATE   RIDDEN  ALGA
NITRO  SEDATELY
    EAST  CAR  YES
FESS  URGENT
AXLE  GAL  GYRATE
SPIN  AMUSE  ETAS
TOTTER  EAR  BORN
    SMUDGE  APSE
ADO  PAN  EDIT
BOBBYPIN   NEIGH
OGEE  LOOSEN  DUO
RISE  ENVOYS  ELM
TEEN   SANE   ALE
```

PUZZLE 99

```
    IMAGE
    BELLS     DRAFT
    ISAAC    PEOPLE
RAT  SANDALS  GUNBOAT
AXE     RATTAN  EDGE
FLEA   SPIRAL
TEND  ASH  RUPEE
   VALUE  NINON
   TILTED  GRANOLA
   ACT       NOD
 MEANDER  ELBOWS
   RAISE  LEASE
    PETIT  BIN  SWIM
    SONATA   TIDE
FALA  REPELS    PEN
ODORFUL  DEEPEST  EAU
REDEEM     TITLE
KNEAD      STOOD
           ESNES
```

PUZZLE 95

```
    BAG
   CARE
   FORCE
  IRON   SPAR
  IDOL  EAVES
 OLEG   YELL
GALS    RAY
BAT    YELPS
AGES    RILE
DARTS    MOW
   OUT   TRIP
   OPAL  FOOT
   PERIL  GOON
   REEL  WAIL
   AVAIL
   MAIN
   ANT
```

PUZZLE 103

```
SHRUB  FAIL  TRAM
NOOSE  UGLY  HULA
OBOES  ROLE  EMIT
WOK  TRY    MOVE
    BOO  ALTERED
FARAWAY  TIE
OPAL  MISTER  BOA
REVEL  EKE  MORNS
ERE  IDLING  KICK
    LED  DAMAGES
UPRISES    PAY
NEON      YEN  FOR
DEBT  FATE  GAUGE
EVER  IDOL  EYERS
REDO  REEL  RELET
```

PUZZLE 100

```
  THIS  BEAST
  HORA  ONWARD
 HARDER  LANYARD
 EGO  IVE  EMAIL
 RABBI  AROAR  PRO
  UNKNOWN  HEELS
PEND  STAT  LIEU  CLIFF
ENOUGH  YAPS  KNOT  NIL
ADIEU  CAGE  ETA  CRY
COS  SMOKER  FACE
EWE  TOR   ICE  ALP
   ROAN  FIESTA  LOO
APE  ERG  AMAH  SAGAS
ION  FAUN  SNAG  SESAME
RIATA  DUEL  GERM  KEYS
  LEVEE  REFEREE
  MOD  ARDOR  DWELL
  PRIOR  AYE   DOE
  SCANDAL  ACCEPT
  TRIAGE  REAM
  SEWED   SERA
```

PUZZLE 104

```
SARI   OBEY  ALERT
AXED   BARE  MELEE
ILKS   SNAP  MAUVE
LEI  WEDS  SODDEN
   NOISIEST  EELY
SADDEST  NOON
ELLEN   FILL  SPA
ATE  EVERTED  LID
MOD  REDO   SPEED
   USED  ATTENDS
SPAN  RYEBREAD
CRUSTS  TOUR  EBB
ROGUE  NUDE  TRIO
AVERS  ADES  WETS
PERES  PEST  ORES
```

PUZZLE 96

Advance, Caravan, Divan, Nirvana,
Savanna, Savant, Servant, Sylvan,
Vandal, Vane, Vanilla, Vanish, Vanity, Vantage.

523

PUZZLE 105

```
SIGHS DEBS  EGGS
EGRET OXEN  AURA
ALONE DIRE  REAR
ROW  ROOSTER SPA
SOLOED THREATEN
    BOOB SELL
BAGS RUT  DIMPLE
OWNER SAT  CARES
PLURAL MAR  NOGS
    VIES PITA
ARSENALS TICKLE
HEP STEPPED  NUN
EDIT HERO  INERT
MYNA EVER  EELER
SEER REEK  RETRY
```

PUZZLE 109

```
ASCOT CANS  WHIT
SCONE ANON  HOSE
SOUSA RISE  OLLA
ERR  PEP  EVADER
SET  OXIDIZE
  YETI EVER PSI
SLAP LOCI  YARNS
WARE EGRET  FOAM
ADDED REDO  ASPS
YES  ALEE  TARP
  MISDEAL  ELS
CEMENT ILK  RAW
LAIR AWED  AFIRE
ASEA NOTE  LUNGE
PENS YEAR  INGOT
```

PUZZLE 113

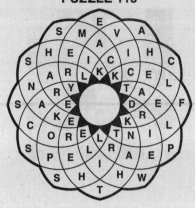

PUZZLE 106

```
CASE  SAKE  OGRE
APEX  CLAYS  DRIP
PERP  HAREM  DADO
ORAL  ISM  OUSTED
   IDS ARCS ERE
COXCOMB  UKE
UNRIG  LESS  SIS
STATE OAT  IDIOT
SOY  ANTI  DONNA
   POD CALMEST
ABS  AREA  LYE
REPORT GAL  SLIP
EVIL  ARGUE  TACO
NENE  SUING  ITEM
ALSO  METE  CEDE
```

PUZZLE 110

```
GRUMP  COMB  PYRE
RETIE  ALOE  REEF
UTTER  SLOG  EAST
FRANC  HAREMS
FOR  ALE  TOTEM
  PLOWED  NONOS
SPARED PARK  NUN
ALSO  GEODE  AURA
GUT  SEND  RACING
AMIDE  DELUDE
BROTH  AND  ASP
  WHINNY  ELITE
TEEN  ROOM  NODAL
OGEE  ESNE  DWELT
GOLD  SEEN  ASSES
```

PUZZLE 114

```
EPIC  WOVE  SMOG
NONO  BAKER  TAPE
TOMB  IRATE  EXAM
ERA  BONY  AILS
RETAR  ESTEEM
RECORD INN  ASH
   EWE GRAD PEA
IDES  DWEEB  STAG
RIG  DIET  LIP
KEG  YAP  EERIER
  BELTED  INNER
BALL  LIES  EGO
AREA  ABATE  BRAS
TINS  TUTOR  OGLE
HATE  EYER  AYES
```

PUZZLE 107

```
BAG  TOM  PAS  RES
ERA  OVA  ORT  EAT
FEZ  TERRIER  CRY
ONE  ROE  UTILE
GARB  DOFF  NAP
  EBON ROGUISH
MUSER  JAW  ETA
APT  AGROUND  NOR
MOA  NET  OCTAD
ANTIQUE  EDGE
EMU  FIVE  EXAM
TEMPO  COB  EGO
OPE  REVELRY  NAN
GIN  UKE  VIE  OPT
ACT  MET  ESS  NEE
```

1-Q, 2-E, 3-R, 4-K, 5-M, 6-J, 7-Y, 8-P,
9-D, 10-N, 11-H, 12-Z, 13-X, 14-I,
15-C, 16-S, 17-U, 18-T, 19-G, 20-L,
21-B, 22-W, 23-O, 24-F, 25-A, 26-V.

PUZZLE 111

```
POSSE  ERAL  ETAS
OAKEN  MACE  NEST
DRILL  BIRD  DELE
  LAREDO  PAP
ROE  CAD  BUS  ENS
ABASES  PARAPET
NOSE  PORTICO
GETUP  POI  SLOES
  SILENCE  ARIA
AUSTERE  TYRANT
INN  YEA  ANA  LES
DIK  TOWARD
AMID  DIVA  NONCE
HAND  AVER  ELIAS
OLDE  BEND  DELLS
```

PUZZLE 115

```
COGS  THANK  LACE
OVAL  RERUN  OPAL
DELI  ALIBI  GERM
ANACONDA  FJORDS
   ELS  SEA
GAS  DITCH  RUMBA
ROWS  ERROR  SIRS
IRON  NAIVE  EMUS
STOA  TIMED  SINE
TANGO  TELLS  COT
   WAS  EAT
TUBING  CITYHALL
APOD  ALLOT  OLIO
IDOL  ROUTE  NOES
LONE  SWEAR  GENT
```

PUZZLE 108

```
CIGAR  SHOP  TOFU
ARENA  HOUR  ADOS
POETS  ONTO  MERE
ENS  PAVE  CHASED
RYES  WED  EEL
  LIAR  CEREALS
BRAINY  ROD  TIE
LENDS  BAN  ALONE
OAT  PEP  ADOPTS
WRESTLE  CREW
  TOY  GOT  SALT
SORROW  HUSH  BAR
OBOE  ODOR  ELOPE
FEDS  OUST  ROUSE
AYES  DOTS  OPTED
```

PUZZLE 112

```
PARD  SIDE  LATH
ICER  CRAVE  ASEA
ERGO  HEMEN  ISMS
REIN  ESS  ACCEPT
SEED  ETCH  TOY
PET  BULLETIN
EER  BLEST  OHMS
ELAPSED  ROWBOAT
LYRE  GUAVA  UKE
  ATTENDED  SOW
ITS  WORD  RIFE
MATRON  ELS  AMER
BRAY  AGREE  VALE
URGE  LEGIT  OTIC
EYES  MOSS  READ
```

PUZZLE 116

```
SASS  SPLIT  ACTS
CLAP  TIARA  THOU
OILY  INTERSTATE
ONS  NEE  WIPER
TEABAGS  TWICE
  ICY  HARM  RAP
SPARE  TELESCOPE
LOUD  BARON  ANEW
OUTSPOKEN  SLEDS
PRO  ONES  VIM
MAKER  CORSAGE
ADAGE  MAT  LOG
LITERATURE  BOAR
AKIN  LOSER  ANTE
SECT  EWERS  NEST
```

PUZZLE 117

```
ADD   DAM   EMUS  COTS
FOE  SALES  LARK  OGRE
ADE  HYENA  EDGY  ALIT
ROMEO  SAG   CEE  REPS
  ODD   GENT   ESS
TERN  OWE  ARM  NEEDED
ACE  ICER  PIERCE  RAY
RHINO  BIO  CROON  ERE
SONATA  EAT  EAR  AWLS
   MARK  KIT  DEAL
GAME  SIS  NUN  SCORES
ERA  TELLS  GEE  NEIGH
LEI  INTENT  WERE  DOE
SALAMI  WOE  SLY  MESS
   REC   WASP   EKE
SOLO  GAB  CAT  ITCHY
LUAU  LIRA  APRON  HUE
ACTS  EVIL  BEING  ILL
THEE  TEAL  ROE  PAL
```

PUZZLE 121

```
TAN  EMIR   DOLES
UKE  LOGO   DIVIDE
TIE  FOUL   EMERGE
UNDO  SALSA  RAYS
   WHEN  IDOL
MANE  AIR  DYED
SERENE  DEED  RID
USER  SCENE  YOKE
PAN  ASEA  LEADEN
STOW  ALL  ACED
  BEDS  OATH
SLIT  RECON  TACT
PINATA  ASKS  HUE
AFFIRM  MELT  ORE
STONY  PREY  YEN
```

PUZZLE 125

```
SWIMS  RIBS  DATA
PATIO  ECRU  ALES
ENEMY  SOON  MONK
DEMO  DANISH  HOE
  SPEW  LEOPARD
ATTAIN  TOO
LAY  CIVIL  DIVER
ALP  MIRED  APE
SCOFF  MEDAL  MEN
  ION  RASPED
BARROOM  TEMP
AGO  DOUSED  ROBE
NIGH  DRIP  TAKEN
GLUE  LATE  AIRED
SEEM  ELSE  GNATS
```

PUZZLE 118

```
ALAS  CACHE  OWNS
GABE  OBOES  NAIL
IDEA  WORST  WINE
LET  ADD  ELATED
ENSNARE  BEER
  END  COMEDIAN
OWLET  GONER  ODE
GOER  POUND  STOW
LOG  LOONY  YEAST
ESSAYIST  PEN
  URGE  CAPTURE
FATTEN  EON  NOG
ECRU  AGATE  ODOR
DRUM  NAVEL  FUME
SEEN  TRESS  TEST
```

PUZZLE 122

```
ABED   OARS   ODD
LEVY  SPIELS  WEE
OGEE  PERMIT  ELF
HURRAH  SACREDLY
ANY  SIB  READ
  SNEAK  WEDGE
ADD  AXEL  MINE
REEDY  FEZ  BANAL
INFO  RITE  TRY
ATTIC  ATTAR
NULL  IVY  ACT
WINGTIPS  ELOPER
ORE  EVILER  BILE
RET  RENOWN  ONLY
ESS  RETE  EGOS
```

PUZZLE 126

```
LEI  LOBE  DADA
OWN  EGOS  OVEN
WESTERNS  LILT
  ORES  OLDIE
SORRY  ASP
EMUS  RITE  DAM
MIMOSA  ANGORA
ITS  ICER  REEL
  GEM  MURAL
GRAPH  PLAN
EASE  ALERTING
EVER  IONS  VIA
REAM  MYTH  ELL
```

PUZZLE 119

```
TWOS  ACID  DASH
HIDE  PURRS  ONTO
ATOM  PEKOE  STOP
THRILL  VET  IVE
  SEA  RETRACES
MET  DUPE  HAG
ICES  DAM  EPOCHS
THAWS  WOK  SNOOP
TOMATO  RIG  YOUR
MOW  SNUG  TRY
RESPONSE  MAI
ARC  DEW  DYNAMO
TEAS  RAZOR  AROW
ECRU  STENO  PEAL
STEM  SEEP  TANS
```

PUZZLE 123

```
GASH   APE   EAST
OBOE  AXELS  VIEW
WOOL  NEWLY  ALTO
NUTMEG   SIP
STY  LIDS  TOOTS
  MEET  ENRICH
GUMS  CALM  ALOE
CANE  SODAS  TERN
AVID  TRIP  FERN
RETIRE  USER
LETUP  MEMO  VAT
  AMP  EMPIRE
FIST  EDGER  ODES
ACHE  DINGY  LENT
REED  DUG  LOTS
```

PUZZLE 127

```
CUR  CHIC  HERE
OPE  REDO  AGES
ASH  APER  MOSS
CHASM  ANY  ICE
HOST  CENSUS
THUG  POLITE
  DURABLE
SAILOR  SCAR
CANOPY  EWES
ELK  SAT  ISAAC
DALI  LOCO  IDA
AMEN  TROT  TEN
RISK  YOGA  SRS
```

PUZZLE 120

```
SOLO  SWAT  BASE
APER  CANOE  AGOG
VEGETATION  PAIR
ENS  ARTS  TATTLE
ELF  EARLIEST
ACTRESS  REPS
BRYAN  ASEA  MEMO
LOP  TENANTS  RAW
EWER  FETA  HASTE
OAFS  SLANTED
ANECDOTE  IVY
BARKER  EAVE  SOB
HIRE  TURPENTINE
OVER  SPIEL  IDEA
REDS  SEXY  NERD
```

PUZZLE 124

```
SPED  VARY  CADRE
TALE  ALEE  ONION
ELAN  GAPS  BIPED
ALP  RUER  CAM
LESSEE  ISOLATES
TEAS  INERT  ASH
REENTER  ACNE
BIGGEST  SALUTED
IDLE  PEDALED
TOE  ARROW  GIST
ELECTING  NITERS
ROT  SWAT  SAP
ASPEN  ALIT  SAGA
LOUPE  TENT  OMIT
EBBED  EDDY  PECS
```

PUZZLE 128

```
CAPE  CLOPS  SLAMS
AGENA  HEART  PILOT
PORGY  ESTEE  ILONA
PRO  ROSS  SNIT  MER
ANGELS  ETON  DAYE
  USA  ONO  ACE
THAN  AMIN  HEATS
RING  EYED  PARTON
ELG  OVEN  BAIN  OLE
ADESTE  MELT  GNAR
TAROT  SOAP  LEND
  MOE  TNT  ARE
DACE  TARA  CHEERS
ALA  DONE  DRAB  AWL
VENUE  DELIA  EDDIE
IRONS  ITEMS  LUISE
STEAK  ESSES  BOSS
```

PUZZLE 129

```
RESEW VISA  CAPS
EATER IRIS  HULA
SCARE LESS  IRON
THY   ALL ESCAPE
     TEACART
 ALPHA ONTO PIG
PLEA SMOG  WEEDY
ROAR HELLO  PALM
ENDED LEEK  ICES
YES  EBBS  RACER
     BOATMAN
ADAPTS  ASK  SET
MOLE SPUN LATER
MEOW ELSE EXILE
ORES DYED TERSE
```

PUZZLE 134

```
SHIP  STIR  ACRE
LOLL PUMAS  CUED
ABLY EMPTY  CRAG
YOU MAUL  SPEEDY
   MEEKLY TOP
SKILLET  LETTER
TANKER GEM   VEE
ABASE VIA  BREAK
GOT  TIN  FIANCE
BEDLAM  ARTISTS
EAT   CLIENT
SESAME ALES  EGO
ICED ROSIN  AVOW
FREE SITED  CELL
TURN  LESS  ENDS
```

PUZZLE 139

```
LAGS  FEAT DAMP SPA
OGRE SINCE IDEA NAP
FREE OLDER SEND ONE
TEAMMATE MAT DRAWER
YET  AREAS  IRISES
   JERRY MET  HOOF
OFF ODE MASSED YORE
FLOUR DEBT SMOG ZEE
TUGS  GOT  SOONEST
    ESS OLIVE ROE
STEREOS ROW   AJAR
ERA AFAR EYED IRONY
MIST AGENDA ITS BYE
IOTA  ALE  GAVEL
UNISEX ELOPE   BIB
PATTED ATE PRESERVE
ICE WIGS TWICE VAIN
TIE TONE CONES EKED
ADD STUD HOED  REDS
```

PUZZLE 130

$$3258$$
$$+2525$$
$$\overline{5783}$$

PUZZLE 135

A C/LAM/ JAM

PUZZLE 131

```
BO AT  MO CHA  LO DE  CO DE
DY LAN RE L EV AN CE LO CAL
TIC K  LE AN   I RO NY
   AR RA NGE  IN VE ST
ES TI MA TE ED IT ER A TO
CA ME  CR UC IAL   MO OT
PE D AL   AT E W REC K ED
   MAN AG ER FAM ISH ED
   PRE AC H  SA IL E CHO
BRI M  AS SO C IA TE I RE
AR ISE  T AR  R EM CE NT
```

PUZZLE 136

```
   SOP PAP MAJOR
AQUA  AGO AROMAS
NUTS  GEE RETIRE
TIC BANTAM   TEA
ERR END LAY
MYNA AGILE   VEE
OUR  LEAN   ELK
FLIT EMEND AXLE
EAR  AMEN ELF
EWE  SALSA ATOP
HIE  FEZ  FED
HOB NEARBY  FLY
OKAYED LAB CITE
GRIEVE TIE ACES
ALTER ODD  WED
```

1-B, 2-R, 3-A, 4-L, 5-G, 6-H, 7-Q, 8-Z,
9-U, 10-V, 11-N, 12-X, 13-E, 14-M,
15-S, 16-C, 17-Y, 18-I, 19-F, 20-D,
21-T, 22-W, 23-J, 24-O, 25-K, 26-P.

PUZZLE 140

```
REAP  WHOA  SHIN
AXLE SEEPS  TACO
STOW PARES  ONES
PRO ERROR  ANGRY
SAFARI  NANNY
PANE  SIN   ACE
TRAP GAP  POLLEN
WORLD RAN  YIELD
OBEYED MAP  GELS
SEA  MOB  YEAH
BOGUS  ESTATE
LIKEN STARK  RUB
IDEA STALE  HOBO
FLED PLIED  OMEN
EELS YENS  EASY
```

PUZZLE 132

Scoff, Offend; Acrobat, Bathe; Origin, Ginger; Opera, Erase; Matinee, Needle; Armpit, Pitcher; Azalea, League; Stiffen, Fence; Divan, Vanish; Hippie, Pierce.

PUZZLE 137

1. Comic, 2. Veto, 3. Noah, 4. Agent, 5. Apple, 6. Sari, 7. Ness, 8. Eagle, 9. Riot.
RELATED WORDS: Vase, Chest.

PUZZLE 141

```
SCRAG  EBBS  SPAD
AROMA FLEA  AUTO
METER TEAL  UPON
BEINGS SKI  NAME
ADS  LIPS   VIA
SMELL CAM   SAP
THEE LAMA  POISE
HORN NIB   AXEL
ODIUM ELAN  STAT
USE  OTT  NEATH
GOO CART   SPA
DIAL WAR  DOTERS
INGA ALAR  NONOS
STUN RETE  ENSUE
COED DEEM  DEEDS
```

PUZZLE 133

```
DART EPOS  ROSES
APER SEPT  EVOKE
TONI PATE  VALET
ADAGIO  INFO
GNU  COLLIDE
FLENSE  ATTEND
SLUR ENVOY  STAR
TAP   OIL   ABA
EXIT DWELT  FILM
MENACE  AWHILE
NEGLECT  AIR
APAR  DEEJAY
SOLAR PARD  MINA
IRATE OVAL  AVOW
BEGET NENE  NEAP
```

PUZZLE 138

```
TOGA BUMP  FACTS
EGOS ASEA  APORT
ELLS TEAL  DECAY
DEFEAT TAME  OIL
RYE STY   CANE
LOTTERY  ETCH
AGO  YEW  HOARDS
TRUTH NIL  BROIL
HEROES TIP   SPA
OWED TIDIEST
DESK LET   OUR
ILL BLEW  NEIGHS
ASIDE JIBE  SOAP
LIMIT ACRE  EAVE
SEEMS YEAR  SLED
```

PUZZLE 142

```
PAWS EYES   DOSE
AROW MONEY  EGOS
LIRA UNCLE  GRIP
MANNA OFT   RELY
SCAR   ICE
POTHOLE  READ
VINE BISTRO  FAN
ENSNARE RECEIVE
EKE CANOED  ERIE
STEM BAYONET
PEP  STEP
HERO ERE  TRUST
EPIC NERVE  ANTI
MESH DEVIL  STUD
SEES LEAK  PONY
```

PUZZLE 143

```
STUNG   ALL   PICKS
PUREE   LIE   UNLIT
ANGELFOOD   SKATE
TEED   LENGTH   PEP
     YEA   SERUM
SIC   ASH   OPERA
ADE   SHIELD   NAGS
SILLY   FRO   FURRY
SOLO   FIASCO   EEN
MORAL   ERR   REC
     ELECT   ADD
IMP   TARIFF   AWLS
LEASE   EDITORIAL
LAGER   PAR   FENCE
STEWS   ELM   FREED
```

PUZZLE 147

```
AFAR   CITY   BOWS
RUDE   MOVIE   ANEW
KNOT   ADOPT   GLEE
   ASSERT   ASIDE
CHORUS   YOWL   NET
RUB   BEE   ERODED
AROW   DOT   YOU
BLEAT   NUN   FEVER
SAP   BOP   TIME
POPLAR   DOG   CUD
SIR   CLEF   UNLESS
   PLIES   VIRTUE
ALOE   MELEE   ALIT
ROLL   ARMED   PARE
EWES   DESK   TYKE
```

PUZZLE 151

```
AMPS   GIST   APPLE
BEET   ACNE   CORAL
USER   LEAN   ATOMS
THRILL   CARD   DEE
      CEE   KNEEL
BASTION   TAMALE
URN   NOT   LINENS
TRACT   GOB   CEASE
SORROW   POP   RUN
   WEIGHT   YEARNED
      BEERS   PIE
AFT   TWIT   PLANET
CLOTH   FARE   SOAR
EERIE   LIAR   ONTO
SANER   EDGY   NEST
```

PUZZLE 144

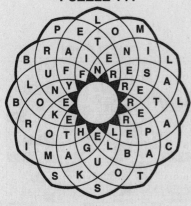

PUZZLE 148

```
APSE   OBOE   BARB
WRAP   AWARE   ERAL
LOWE   UNDERSCORE
SANEST   CAWED
   LOSE   PAL
ALOHA   ALDERMAN
CAROB   FORAY   LOP
EDIT   CAPER   GONE
DEE   LURID   DEUCE
SLEEPING   OLDEN
   FAS   GERM
CHAFF   EERIER
HONEYMOONS   EDGE
OBIT   AWAIT   AEON
POSE   PERT   PAST
```

PUZZLE 152

```
ACT   SLAM   SIP   PAST
LAY   TORO   STOOP   ALTO
ASK   USER   LITER   ROAM
SHEEP   EDUCATE   LETS
   VISA   IRKS   TOO
BOREDOM   SPY   YEARNED
ALE   SICK   CONK   AWE
RIG   DODO   EONS   GEE
EVADE   SLOGAN   EMU
RELIC   TOBACCO   EMERY
   GOB   GOPHER   SPREE
HEP   LONE   PISA   USA
UTE   JADE   ATOM   PET
GARLAND   RAN   LOCATES
   ARK   RENT   EGOS
POLS   EJECTED   OPERA
EDIT   TOTES   OPAL   GAM
TILE   SHINY   NOSE   AVE
ENID   NET   SPED   DEN
```

PUZZLE 145

```
ACID   FOAM   ASPS
SHOE   TIARA   FLAW
KITE   INTERSTATE
SCARAB   ASH   NIP
   WISPS   ARGOT
ELK   EACH   DYE
NAIAD   RANI   ACTS
DILL   AIRED   CLIP
SNOB   SPAR   SHALE
   UPS   OVAL   YEW
BLAME   RHYME
LIL   ODE   IDLEST
ASTONISHED   ARIA
SLOP   NOISE   PALM
TEST   EWES   SLOE
```

PUZZLE 149

```
FROM   STAT   GASPS
LIRA   WASH   ADMIT
APER   EXPO   ROUTE
BESIDE   RID   GAP
   NUT   ENTER
SCAMPER   SNIDE
BEE   PEDAL   MAXI
OWL   SAG   YEA   TIN
YELP   YARNS   ELK
DOUBT   MEASURE
   PLUMP   MEN
JOB   EGO   ETCHER
ABOVE   RAIL   LAMA
MOOED   ACNE   ALIT
BERTS   LEND   DOTE
```

PUZZLE 153

```
CHIPS   SOY   ACME
AERIAL   HUE   PRAY
PRONTO   ITS   ROLE
SON   BINS   LOPER
   SEEM   MAIN
PARKA   PSALM   FIT
AWHIRL   PROP   ONE
GAY   IRATE   OLD
ARM   ACED   SANDED
NEE   FIDEL   DUSTY
   MATE   ASST
ARDOR   EACH   TOW
LEAP   EMU   INSURE
MAZE   SET   PAINED
SPED   EDO   TRESS
```

PUZZLE 146

```
CHILI   RACY   OPAL
ROSIN   OBOE   VILE
INLET   TOWN   ELMS
BEE   EMIR   CRESS
   RUST   FAT
OPT   ELS   ARTISAN
CUR   SEEMLY   MAGI
CREPT   RUT   HEMAN
USER   MIMOSA   BIN
RESIDUE   GUN   ANY
   MID   NERD
CHORD   ITEM   DIM
LOGO   RICH   ABIDE
EARS   ACHE   DUELS
FREE   NEER   ESSES
```

PUZZLE 150

```
HEMS   SECT   ASCOT
AMEN   MOOR   PIANO
LIMO   INSISTENCE
TROWEL   TOO   SEES
   REVS   MET
CICADA   BEAST
FOCUS   GAMER   CAP
ACID   RUDER   SOUR
ROE   GUEST   CORNY
   ARSON   AMOUNT
   NOW   SLOW
AMMO   ASH   USABLE
COURTYARDS   CLOD
HATER   GUYS   RING
ENTRY   AGEE   EPEE
```

PUZZLE 154

```
SPRIG   MAKO   VOWS
ARENA   OINK   IDEA
ROAST   ODOR   NEED
IMP   HIS   WAVY
   LEVEE   ELMS
STORY   LOST   OPE
GOUGE   TANK   BAY
LAX   DRASTIC   IRE
ORE   AUTO   OILED
WED   ANTI   JANES
   DOER   CHURN
AMID   ITS   LIT
DAFT   TEMP   ELUDE
OGRE   CLAP   SABLE
GOON   HERO   TWEED
```

527

PUZZLE 155

```
SEEPS ORATOR BLACK
ATBAT DESIRED LITHO
CHESAPEAKEBAY VALID
CART END SPEED ARA
ONTO ASSAM EST TNPK
RUSE BIRD UNIT
CLARA BSA DENIM
DEALING ASIS EGGCUP
ILK STES INCAS SOTO
ALE OPOSSUM CAR
NICK SLAMS TORS ENC
ASHORE REIN SUNBATH
TAROT GPO MIENS
MEET CAPO AMPS
PAPA EDO INTRA TRAP
ELL TRAMS HAG RARE
AGAPE DELAWARERIVER
RAISE STAMINA IDEAS
LENIN SPINET DENSE
```

PUZZLE 159

```
DAD VAMP ALONE
EGO VENUE TOWEL
LAG ITEMS TALES
VIM LOW TOED
ENABLE UNSEW
EASE END BOY
TAME APACE BRA
ALE RETIRED ELK
FOR ELECT ODDS
TUG MAR HIFI
DEFAT RELATE
LIED HOW BIG
DIVAN OZONE BAG
ALIKE ROWER ORE
BLEED MOLD TAD
```

PUZZLE 163

```
RICH VAT ALIT
OOZE PILOT LORE
STAR RODEO UPON
YARDSALE MOMENT
TIER CAN
BREAST MARACA
BOOKIE JET INN
AUGER FUN CARGO
GNU PIT SOCCER
DEPORT SQUEAL
EWE SPUR
BEHALF CRITICAL
RAIN AGAIN TAXI
ECRU BURNT EVEN
WHET YET MELT
```

1-D, 2-C, 3-U, 4-F, 5-R, 6-M, 7-S, 8-Y, 9-T, 10-Q, 11-J, 12-O, 13-N, 14-B, 15-V, 16-W, 17-H, 18-X, 19-L, 20-I, 21-G, 22-Z, 23-A, 24-K, 25-E, 26-P.

PUZZLE 156

```
SILL DEMI ARTS
TREY HUMID GOOP
EAVE UNCLE LAIR
ATE FREED ONLY
MERGER ELBOW
LEAP YON FIR
SAGA HIM DEVICE
TIARA CUR SIREN
ADVERB GAP NERD
BEE COG PRAY
SHARP IDLEST
STOP OATES LIE
URGE BONUS CALM
NULL EVICT ATOP
KEEL DECK PEST
```

PUZZLE 160

```
EBB EAST MAILS
POI SPIEL OLDIE
ILK TEPEE DELVE
CLEO NAPE YEP
ABLE VOLT
OVERLOADED OPT
WEE ACRE SEERS
EER CONNECT DUE
DRINK STIR ACT
SEA SPECTACLES
BAKE HYPE
SAD BYTE EVIL
CLIMB ARENA IRE
AGREE LASER SON
BATTY SEEK END
```

PUZZLE 164

```
FOAM ODIC USED LETS
OLLA NOVA PURE OMIT
RETRIEVER GIRL ABBE
TOO OWE AORTA FREE
GNATS MASTIC ORR
APSE YAPPED ATARI
VOLTS IRONER ETUDES
EKE POLYP ISM SEGO
REDCAP PLEBE TROD
OTTO EEL MEWL
ALBS BADGE TIEPIN
BOAT FIX VOCAL ENE
SALAMI ENDEAR YOLKS
DROSS OINKED VEST
ABE THESIS SAUNA
CLAW SUSHI TEA TEE
RAGE SAGO SCULPTORS
ERLE IMAM LORE WRAP
SEED SERE EWER ONLY
```

PUZZLE 157

```
CLOT SIS ROLE
RACE SCRUB IDOL
ADES POKER PEGS
FLATTIRE ACE
TEN HEED ANTS
DADS FIN WHO
THIN LOVEBIRD
WHYS DIARY ICED
ERECTING PLED
DEN HES TAIL
WADE SALE ARC
INK PRODUCER
SAGA IMAGE NOVA
OXEN NUDES DRUM
DELE MET ONES
```

PUZZLE 161

```
SHAD CRAB RASPS
TOTO HARE UBOAT
EMIGRATED MEDIA
EEL ONSALE TANG
PYTHON SAXES
OMEN MIX CAP
HALL LAM TAMALE
ICILY BET MINOR
GRAYER NIT GEEK
HER TUG PATH
TIEUP RETEST
MOTH DREDGE ROE
OGRES GREENHORN
SLIME LILT ADES
TEPEE ELLS WERE
```

PUZZLE 165

```
CABS RES POSSE
HULA IVY VALLEY
EDIT PEN INDITE
AIM CONCEDE DAD
TOPMOST FALSE
ARTIST SPRAT
STAMPEDE HUGE
PERMS ELF MELEE
AMMO LABORERS
SPITS ESCAPE
SHAMS TRESTLE
APT PASTORS WAN
POISON ORE HIND
ENCORE GEL ONCE
REELS ADS WEED
```

PUZZLE 158

```
STUB TACO HEMAN
WIPE USER EXILE
EAST REAP PUREE
ERE SMASH DEER
TATTOO EAGLE
EXIT NAY DOG
PLEA LAD GRIEVE
RINSE RIM EMCEE
ARDENT POP PORK
YES VAT PEAL
MYNAS TRYING
AMMO COMIC MAR
WIELD KNIT LAMA
ESSAY LACE AGED
STARE ERAS BEDS
```

PUZZLE 162

```
SCAB MASH WHIP
HATE BASTE HARE
ANON RISER EVER
RON LINER REST
PEEKED TENSE
NEAR OAK WIG
VISA LUG PIRATE
EDICT BEA NAVEL
RECKON ETA GYMS
YAK WON ELSE
ANTIC LUSTER
STAN NYLON AGE
MAXI DECOY BURN
OILS ATLAS APED
GLEE DYED GETS
```

PUZZLE 166

1. Story, Store, Shore, Share, Shale, Whale.

2. Cheat, Chest, Crest, Crust, Crush, Brush.

3. Grand, Grant, Grunt, Brunt, Blunt, Blurt.

4. Stole, Stile, Still, Swill, Swirl, Twirl.

PUZZLE 167

```
APSE  ELMS   GUS  TEAM
CHIC  MEATS  ASH  RAVE
TILL  PICOT  MEA  IVES
   ATE   ARE   RIVERS
BESTIR  REAM   MINI
OWE  DODO  MIDI  TACKS
LEG  IRON  TEMPO  ONE
EROSE  WISP  PEAT  LIL
   ERAS  OUST  NODOFF
CPR  BEWITCHED   ERE
LOOFAH  ALTO  NAGS
ALP  SOPH  SWAN  OKRAS
BOP  TROOP  NUTS  ANO
SNAFU  WOOF  AIRS  STA
   ETAS  DISC  EITHER
ARGUER   FLO   APE
LOAD  BIG  TONED  DROP
LIVE  OVA  YODEL  DONE
SLED  REB  PANE  YEAR
```

PUZZLE 168

```
BOOST  DISCO  CLEAN   SKEET
THEN  SELL  ATTIRE  FLINCH
   TARANTULA   MISTAKE
MOTION  SIT  MESSAGE  SPAS
ONUS  N  NONCHALANT  REALTOR
   BEAT  SO  IREE  PRIMAL
FLABBERGAST  MELODE  ON
SPOOL   SAMBA   DIVE
EARRING  PERVERSITY  BALE
SING  PROVIDE  TEN  SLUDGE
   INSECT  BRACELETS
MUNDANE  ORCHARD  REIN  TRACE
CHEER   ARMOR   STING  DENT
```

PUZZLE 169

```
ALAR   SLAY   ERST
TALE  GEODE  SALE
TROD  EXPOSITION
AGE  ATE   SOLED
ROSEBUSH   ASP
   YUP  ILLUSION
BEGET  SMOTE  ROO
ABED  PESTO  DOZE
SON  BRAES  TONES
ENTHRALL   HOG
   AIM  FLAMENCO
ADLIB   ALB   ERG
REALESTATE  OVAL
MACE  AIDER  FIVE
SLED  DEER  FLED
```

PUZZLE 170

```
WIPE  HOST   SAY  MEAN
ADEN  ILIE  PLIE  AURA
REAL  FETA  IOTA  CROP
MALICIOUSNESS  PHONE
LEVI   EACH   MAI
   ERTE  BEE  ORNATE
FRANCESCA  SCREAMER
LAX  EXTOLS  RANTING
IRIS   ITEM   ASTI
TALC  CANADARMS  OGEE
ULAN   RENE   NODE
BOMBARD  RIPEST  OIL
AVIARIST  ASPIRANTS
HARDEN  ICE  ADAM
IDA  MARE   GARS
BRAVO  ROMANTICIZING
LIME  SITE  AIDA  IDOL
AVER  ECHO  CLEW  NERO
BESS  WHY  TESS  GREW
```

PUZZLE 171

```
OFFS   GELS    EFT
WARY  ENRAPT  PEA
ELAN  MURMUR  ILL
SKYCAP   MUSCLE
   SLIMMEST
COCKATOO   TOWS
GORY  NEAT  EMAIL
ADAPTER  TREADLE
RETRO  ABLE  TIKI
SEER  TRESPASS
   SPREADER
LESSEE   NYLONS
IRA  DEPEND  ABIE
MAN  OLIVES  DENT
OLD   STEW   DYES
```

PUZZLE 172

```
GAL  OBI  VENTED  FIANCE
ALA  RUN  IMBIBE  ANNEAL
GOKARTS  VICTORIAFALLS
SEEP  THOR  ANNA  RILKE
   LEGREE  ANI  MBAS
SAO  EMPATHY  TUBE  HAL
TAUTEN  RHEE  EMIT  PUNY
ORION  STUN  ACADEMIC
COSTA  WAS  EOS  ERASE
KNEE  PAC  UNDERLIE  NEE
   MARTHASVINEYARD
PSI  COHESION  ION  ESPY
OPRAH  PAY  CNN  STARE
SEESTARS  OAFS  KENYA
SANK  CHUB  NONO  CARTES
EKE  MUNI  THEREAT  ART
   ITEM  BAH  CAMERA
SOUSA  BEEN  ABET  ANKA
PORTCHARLOTTE  SURGING
AZALEA  GODSON  ANO  TEE
RELETS  STEPPE  TOM  AWE
```

PUZZLE 173

```
HEW   FETA   STEP
IMA   ICON   PURE
TURNDOWN   ERIN
   EELS   JANES
CATTLE   AUKS
OPUS   ELASTIC
AIR  MORAN   IRE
LANTERN   FLAN
   ORLE  TALENT
RIVET   BONO
ADEN  TURNPIKE
NERD  ASTO  NIL
TASS  WHEY  STY
```

PUZZLE 174

```
RED  SARA  ALTO
ELO  UPON  SOAR
PEW  DOWNSPOUT
SENTA   SALE
  SANK   ANEST
CLIP  ABET  ITO
HAZE  LON  ADAR
ARE  BEAD  VENT
RADAR   STIR
  CASE   ADDER
HUGHDOWNS  OVA
AMIE  FEET  WAY
LAND  TREE  NNE
```

PUZZLE 175

```
PLOW  I  MAJOR
L  RODEO  O  I
BLADE  L  LAYUP
AM  ARENA  R  E
YEAST   REIGN
O   HIFI   D
UNCLE  O  QUEUE
A   ZEBU   X
MORES   INGOT
O I  CIVIC  U O
TABOO  I  KNEEL
I  O  FENCE  S
FLUFF  E  NOSE
```

1-L, 2-H, 3-O, 4-Z, 5-B, 6-I, 7-E, 8-Q,
9-G, 10-U, 11-T, 12-D, 13-W, 14-P,
15-A, 16-S, 17-Y, 18-V, 19-C, 20-R,
21-X, 22-M, 23-F, 24-K, 25-J, 26-N.

PUZZLE 176

```
ASKEW   CAVEMEN
T H  H O  O  O  I
LIANA  MIDRIFF
A K  R  E K  R  T
SKIFF  TRAGEDY
A U  K  E A  O
EBON  USE  FUZZ
O  G D  D  F  E
OBLIQUE  RETRO
P A  U  P  A O R
TANGELO  JEWEL
I A  E  X  A E O
CHIMNEY  HERON
```

1-E, 2-C, 3-J, 4-F, 5-Z, 6-R, 7-Y, 8-I,
9-W, 10-B, 11-L, 12-P, 13-O, 14-G,
15-T, 16-H, 17-K, 18-U, 19-A, 20-V,
21-S, 22-D, 23-N, 24-M, 25-Q, 26-X.

PUZZLE 177

```
HART   WPA    FED
ALEE  VIAND  BATE
DOER  EERIE  ORAN
JULIENNE  STUMPS
   REE   POISE
APT  IER  TOOL
MERGER  CAT  LAD
PLEA   HOG   OLEO
FEZ  CAD  BANTER
  PART  SAD  IRE
GRACE   ONE
PLACED  CONSOMME
EACH  INANE  DOOR
OREO  TAPER  OVAL
NED   PER   RETE
```

PUZZLE 178

The only thing that goes as far as it
used to ten years ago is the dime
that rolled under the bed.

PUZZLE 179

```
SHOD  FIG  EGIS  SALT
HOLE  IDEA SODA  OBOE
ONELINERS  TWOTIMERS
EGO  RES  TEEN  IRATE
    BAD  RUDE  TROT
SATES RATE  CHINASET
KAHN SEVENSEAS  ILE
ARR  MUTE  PANT  AXLE
TEEMED  PHASE  UNFED
   EELS  BLADE  OTTO
TIRED GAUGE  RESORT
UNIT MUGS  LEES  TIE
TON  EIGHTBALL  NEVA
UNGAINLY ARIL  SORER
    WRIT  STIR  SOW
THAIS ATEE  AWN  BAA
FOURSCORE  FIVESTARS
BIRD URAL  SKIP  ORES
ILLS SALE  EST  EBON
```

PUZZLE 183

```
FLOP MARE  ELOPE NASAL
AIRY AMID  SOWER ANKLE
DEFLATION CONTRACTION
EFFECTS ABATES PHONED
    TEST  OPED  BOON
CAMPER ROWED  BOGS BOP
AVOID NAMES  RUNE SOAR
RENT WADED  PAYEE TOTE
PRE WOVEN  MATED POMES
STY ROADS  OVER MORASS
   STIFLE  TOE SHAKEN
SPURTS FRAN  SMILE DRU
NAPES PIERS  HARTS BIT
ASPS PECAN  BORES BUNT
GELS LAID  MARKS  PASSE
SOY LILT  BASTE MUTTER
   LAGS  SARA  TAIL
SMOOTH SHRILL INSIPID
COMPETITION AUSTERITY
ARIEL MANNA ISLE  KNEE
TOTSY ABYSS REED  SERS
```

PUZZLE 187

```
CASTS  OYSTER  FIN
AWARE  REPOSE  ADE
BOXINGGLOVES SLEDGE
IKE DEALT  CITY  IER
NESS ENS BOUTS  EVER
   LASS HOLES  BLISS
SCHEME  CAWED  JOIN
ALOES  BAILS  POI GAP
LOCK CACTI  SOWS  BRO
ASK FISHINGPOLE  ORO
DEE ALEE  GAILY  FAIR
STY LID ABUTS  NERVE
   SOSA  SLADE TRADER
LATHE  FOLLY  PAAR
IRIS VINYL  OOP  SHOP
SIC SAGA  SLIER  INA
TAKING TENNISRACKET
   TAU ALCOVE  TIERS
   OPE SLOWED  SASSY
```

PUZZLE 180

```
MISS  NEST  SAKS  LOMA
IDLE  OBOE  TUNE  EPIC
LEAN  ROOT  IRON  TACT
LAYDOWNTHELAW  ATLAS
    DAY  ELL  INGE
EASLEY ARM  STEERAGE
SILAS HIS  CHAT  OVAL
SNOW BED  COALS  FETA
OTTOMAN CHILL  STROM
    FOG  THANE  BAH
SPITE TEENS  DETENTE
TACH ERNST  CAT  LIRA
ALOE LAOS  MOM  OATER
BENJAMIN RIB  ALWAYS
    UPON  OIL  EGO
STINT LAWOFAVERAGES
LUNG CORN  OPEN  DADA
ABEL PANE  RIND  ALIT
GAZE ODOR  DATA  METE
```

PUZZLE 184

```
RABBI ELAN  RABB SHOUT
OCEAN RAGE  ERIE PASTA
BLACKARROW MALL OILER
SUMO LOG THEBLACKROSE
   NEARER  ADS  RED
DAB INS ENVY  ERA  OBOE
IDLERS EERO ADOBE  LIV
SHALE BLACKTIE  CRANE
BECK AMES  IRE  SHOCKS
ARK ACER  ATLI  SPOOK
REB BOSTONBLACKIE AHS
   ALORS STAS HAND CAT
AEGEAN SCI  CUTS  LAZY
MAJOR BLACKOUT  LOCAL
IVO DRIER  NUKE SATIRE
DEBS EDD GERE  PHI  ADD
    EON  SAL  SMOOTH
BLACKORWHITE ATV ALAS
RECUR ORAN INTHEBLACK
INTRA SANE  NOTE BLINI
MOSES APED  EWER CEDES
```

PUZZLE 188

```
WIDE  PREP  GROAN
ODES  RIPE  RADIO
REST  OBOE  APORT
MAKEUP XRAY  RYE
    ENEMY  TEE
TAMELY  ORBIT
RIDS STOMP  BRIM
AGO  HUE  ADO
WEBS ASTER  STEP
REPEL  TEPEES
   ASS ISLET
ODD  SOON  ATTEST
AROMA GLUT  LATE
TODAY LAKE  EVEN
SPOTS EYED  SEWS
```

PUZZLE 181

```
IMBED  UNCO  HANDY
SNEEZE ASHORE ALONE
IDLERS  SULLIVANSVAN
SULFA  CCR  LEARN
ACES SLOEGIN  CANS
LEN BOUT  LETS  HOURS
COOL SSE  SOD  STUD
PLAUDIT TAW  WIN  HIS
RIMS DARESAY  SIREN
EMPTY UNROBES  BARON
ISSUE SENATOR  BLUE
ETC MOM  OSS  BOMBAST
REAM NAB  SHE  MAIN
ADMAN CAPO  NIPS  DEB
PEAS TONSILS  ASTA
   CHAIN  AGO  TALUS
MITCHUMSCHUM  PARADE
IDAHO ITHACA  ATONED
TAPES AONE  TENDS
```

PUZZLE 185

```
CEASE  DAVE  EROS
ORDER  ALAN  REDO
UNDERSTAND  ASIA
TIER  OAR  EASTER
HERESY  MEAGER
    STAB AVERAGE
PASSE AUTO  SILK
EGO WESTERN  NEE
NEAT VEER  OPTED
DEPOSES  YEAR
STARTS THEMES
LITANY UFO  SEMI
IDOL DISINHERIT
NENE ARAB  ANGLE
TEED YENS  STEED
```

PUZZLE 189

```
VIOLA  SLID  ACHE
ACRES  PINE  DROP
TEENS  ANTE  DALE
   GEYSER  VEE
MATTE  OSPREYS
BOTH PIT  LEI
ACT  TOMATOES
THIS DENIM  TANS
ACADEMIC  TOP
FIB CAB  DEWY
ACCEPTS  EVERY
SHE  CREDIT
TILL PRAY  SAGAS
IDLE EAVE  TIARA
REST APED  ALLEY
```

PUZZLE 182

```
BLACKOUT  EGGING
A S  E N I U S E
RECITED  MONGREL
G E T E P M  A A
ANNUL  ROOSEVELT
I T E  S T L  I
NASH  AUSTRALIAN
  G T  E L
PIEDATERRE  LAUD
R N S N  P R E
ENGROSSED  LETUP
C L L I O A I O
INITIAL  ULYSSES
S S N S G E A I
ECHOED  WHODUNIT
```

PUZZLE 186

```
SHAD SPAS  ROOT  PLOY
TOGA PART  UNCUT CLOVE
UPON ONCE  METRO RUSES
BIGSHOTS POI  FOREMEN
    ENS  LARD  USE
GAMES FEN  ASCENT AYE
ILIAD DRAG  TARTS ROB
TORN BEADS  BALM  EGO
SAGA LINE  PEG ABSTAIN
   TUG ACCRUES  EAR
SNEEZE SNOOT  MADAMS
   RYE INTONES  IOU
DESSERT SOY  PORT NINA
RUE ADEN  ODORS  ENDS
ERR COCOA  ROSY  BREAK
WOE APOLLO  AGE  SISSY
    AVE  BATS  SAN
OFFICER LIE  KINGPINS
RIATA SEPAL  CASE UTAH
ALTER CARTE  ALAS BETA
YSER  REED  PELT  SMOG
```

PUZZLE 190

```
BARS  SARIS  PEW
ALIT  COVERT  OAR
BOOR  UNIVERSITY
YETI  BAD  SAT
    POET  NUDE
ASEA  AMENDMENT
FIESTA AYE  PATE
ESS  CATES  FEE
ALAS NIT  TAPERS
REMODELED  IONS
   SEAR  ERRS
KIT EGO  TROD
HORSEOPERA  MOVE
OWE STALER  ALEE
ELF TERSE  NERD
```

PUZZLE 191

```
ACED  USES   SPOT
WAVE  PAYEE  TAME
AMEN  SWEEP  OPEN
RENTS      ISLAND
DOS  OBSTACLE
   ABROAD  ANGRY
CLIP  UNREST  ROE
LAMEST   LEGION
AMP  PEARLY  OPTS
PASTA  GAYEST
   ETCETERA  GEM
SPLASH     GRIME
WAYS  ITCHY  OVEN
ACRE  PUREE  BEND
BEER   GYMS  ENDS
```

PUZZLE 195

```
HISS  RELET   LEST
ALOE  EXILE   AGIO
FISTICUFFS    DOLE
TAO  DELE  TRYSTS
   KEPT   LEAF
GARNET  BEDLINEN
LUAU  OVID  ENERO
ODIC  RIDGE  GROW
SINKS  BEEN  EDDA
STYLIZED   JERSEY
   EVAS  SODS
TEABAG  LIIII  MOA
OSSA  GREENTHUMB
ANIL  ENATE  ETAL
DEAL  DARED  MERE
```

PUZZLE 199

```
DOME  EXEC  BODE  HAM
AMEN  DIVA  TONED ETA
BIRDSOVER EASES   ELI
STEIN      OWES   DAN
   NOG  SLANTS  PASSE
OREGON  TINY   IRED
LEM  PATENT  FOREPAW
GAOL  RING  ALTO  RID
ARTICLE  VIA  FACETS
   IMP  DEPARTS  PAC
STOOLS  KIT  OSTRICH
KIN  OVEN  WHAT  SOYA
INSPIRE   HOORAY  UMP
RATE  MENS  BOSSES
BATON  SPENDS  SUP
ALI        ASSE  TODAY
SIR  CONDO  RACEHORSE
IKE  THORN  IVAN  NEIL
LES  SORE  FAME  SWAP
```

PUZZLE 192

```
GNAW   TUBA  SWIM
LAZE  BANAL  TIDE
OVAL  ABIDE  ELLS
SILT  TOO  SPADES
SEE  THONG   ELF
 SAFE    ACE   IMP
  LET  UPON   ROE
TOFU  HAREM  SEWN
ALL  NOUN   EAT
MEA  OUR    SYNC
  MID  ABACK  ERE
ASIDES  ERA  TEAS
VINE  HAVEN  ODDS
OLGA  AGENT  DELE
WOOL  MOLT   ODES
```

PUZZLE 196

```
GIFT  ANSEL   LEAR
IDLY  COPRA   ACRE
REUP  CRISP   THIN
LABOHEME    ABROAD
   OPAL   LEA
BILLET     CONVERT
AREAS  BOOM   IGOR
SWAG  LLAMA   AGUE
SISI  AARP   STOGY
INTOUCH     DIANES
   CPR   SLAV
ARIOSO   LAMANCHA
BONN  SLURS   ERIN
BIRD  SIEGE   SENT
ELIA  EDSEL   TETE
```

PUZZLE 200

```
BARGE  AWL  PATE  AMAT
ADORN  IRE  ONUS  NOVA
SAMUELMAVERICK    DIAN
EPEE  ASSERT   KINESIS
STOLES  SEAS  SMARTLY
    ATTEST    OPS
SHEARER  ORTS   SCREW
POEM  DIPS  OHIO  EURO
AGNES  GEORGEPULLMAN
   LOA  GLUEY   TIS
LOUISDAGUERRE    DIEGO
URSA  STET  SERF  USED
GRABS  EDEN  GRISTLE
   LES   ECHOED
OSBORNE  AWAY   SACHET
ACROBAT  PERSON  AONE
TRAM  CHARLESBOYCOTT
HAVE  KILO  TOE  ETHER
SPAR  SCAN  SPY  TIARA
```

PUZZLE 193

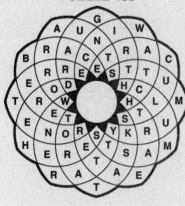

PUZZLE 197

```
CORD  PABA   EMAIL
ALOE  ELAL   LARVA
YELLOWBRICKROAD
SOLID  INSET   ONE
   ADDA   TOON
BID  MENSA  NIECE
ANIMAL  TIS  GAOL
BRAINHEARTNERVE
KENT  IVY   EILEEN
ADEEM  ESSES   DNA
   SOON   APSE
TDS  TOTES  APTER
WITCHOFTHENORTH
INURE  UTES   DATE
GABOR  LUST   EPEE
```

PUZZLE 201

```
BATT  PAC  BLOB  PGA
ELHI  ILO  LOBE  RIN
ETRE  TAPS  ISIT  SORT
FOURTHESTATE    RIFLE
   RAY   ADZ  APEX
RIVAL  JAGS  MANTRAS
ATO  LEONE  TOUR  HULA
SELF  THIRDBASE  SEAT
ARTISAN   ESTE  AERIE
   FIT  GRAPH  DON
PESTS  VEAL  IRKSOME
ITCH  FIRSTNAME  EMUS
ENOW  ROME  OLEIC  NOS
RAPHAEL  SNIT  OPINE
   EDDA  MAC  IDA
ASKED  SECONDNATURE
ITAL  ELLA  MORN  OPER
ROT  WAIT  ROE  ITEA
SAY  ESPY  APR  SOFT
```

PUZZLE 194

```
TOES  BETAS   URGE
WALE  ELATE   TARA
ITEA  LITER   TRET
THEGOLDENFLEECE
   RUSE    ERROR
ROGET   DALES
ABLE  PRIMER  SET
FOUNTAINOFYOUTH
TEE  ATTEST   VINE
   AMEER   SETAE
SCAPE    APAR
THEPROMISEDLAND
EIRE  MASSE   AREA
ELIA  ALIEN   PLOY
DEER  RENTS   SONS
```

PUZZLE 198

```
ALPS  ABET  PLOD  SLIP
SEAT  DOLE  RIDE  POLE
ISLE  MYFRIENDFLICKA
STORMED  ROSE   ARIAS
   EON  BANS   ERNE
STOOP  ACE  TREASURE
EARS  DARE  IRANI  REA
ALT  AILS  EDILE  TSPS
RESOLVE  ASEA   TOAST
   BLACKSTALLION
LAPIS  ONES  ACCEPTS
EMIT  NAPES  TREK  OHO
NAT  CORER  OAKS  DOUR
SHAMROCK  ERR  PURGE
   YENS  BRIE  PAS
SHARD  PESO  LETTERS
NATIONALVELVET   EDIT
ULNA  AGEE  EAVE  RACE
GOOD  PEAL  STIR  SMEW
```

PUZZLE 202

```
GERM  ADAGES  APT  LAW
ALOE  BANANA  URI  OHO
WALTERMITTY   FIERCER
KNEECAP   EER  GRAHAM
   OHM  HORRID  TIDY
ASTRO  WOW   DOMAIN
LOWS  BILLET  REMOVAL
ELI  ALLY  REVILE  ADO
CONTROL  CERIA  BIRDS
   ARGYLE   RANDOM
IMBUE  LEDGE  GRIPPED
DOE  APOGEE  BRAD  ALE
ANAGRAM  DEFEAT  RILL
UNSNAP  IVY   TONAL
OLGA  NOTARY   LIT
PIERCE  ERG  BONUSES
ENSLAVE  ELMERGANTRY
RET  PIN  SOIREE  DEAN
ARE  OLD  SWORDS  APSE
```

PUZZLE 203

```
ADDS LASTS SWARD LAVA
ROUE AWAIT PALER AGES
ANNA PAINE ALLAN PARK
BEER ERLAND LIMOUSINE
  BIBLE TERSE RENEW
SAUNA TROVE STAND
TUGGED AERIAL INS SAT
ERG ZEBRA CRUMMY METE
MAYA TOPPLE MAE NOLTE
  CLEO ASPEN HERMIT
SPACECRAFT STAGECOACH
COGENT RASPS OAKS
OMENS WAC STOWED EMIL
RENT NAMELY POSED OVA
EST MIN SOCCER DOTTED
  RILED SHINE LOOSE
ASTER RISEN ALTAR
STREETCAR DEFINE SHOP
TOOK HAYES MARIE TOTE
ROPE ARENA ARMOR EMIR
OPED WADED SEANS REST
```

PUZZLE 204

```
EIDER MARLO ARNE ANAT
CREPE OTHER COAX TORI
ROSSI STEAD COITTOWER
UNIONSQUARE MARINATE
MENU SNAGS DAD YES
ERG RAID SLATE SAC
MEOW PTAS SORTS LAMBS
INLET ORAD LATHS POOH
TIDBIT IRIS WEAN RUNE
ESTE NACHO MATINEE
TAN HAIGHTASHBURY TSP
REGRESS AFTER LIPS
IRAE EAST TINA SNOUTS
PITA SALAD ANIS GETAT
SEEDS COLES ANTE TRUE
YAO PINTS SERE OTT
ELF LUG ATRIA EIRE
MOLASSES EMBARCADERO
CHINATOWN TILDE SURER
EARN EDIE CLEAR ECLAT
ENTS DEMO HERDS REELS
```

PUZZLE 205

```
MILD PLEA BASAL ATTAR
OBIE REEL ADANO SHAPE
JINGLEALLTHEWAY HERON
OSTRICH IRA ATOP TORT
AMU AMEN LUNETTE
PREDATOR PAT TAMER
CONE RIA SATE PAMPA
SOD TEVYE TORSI ILLS
MOTTO AERO KILN NATO
HOTEL RIDE IGUANAS
MAENAD COLON MISTER
LAURELS ARES DERMO
URDU REAP DEMO OARED
GAIN ELLEN SIREN DEI
TONIC EDAM RID BEET
ICAME DAD COMMANDO
GRANULE DALE AIL
RANG LEVI TEA ATTAINS
ANIMA KINDERGARTENCOP
METAL EVANS ERIE CORE
SEANS RARAE STAR ENID
```

PUZZLE 206

```
APSE AMA TEC VIANDS
EXULT CALDERA ADHERE
LIKEABULLINACHINASHOP
YOKE OTT ATTAIN RIA
MATINEE SHOOTTHEBULL
BIRDS SOOTH
ALBEIT AWARD CHAINS
BULLDOGEDITION IGLOO
IXIA REARMOST SCALDS
DEPT SIR EST HULA
ESSENCE RALLIES
EAST ALT EGG ANNA
STREWN AMBIANCE MEAT
USURP BULLMOOSEPARTY
REGROW DETER TESTER
OREAD ASTER
BULLTERRIERS EERIEST
ENA VANLOO TEN ROUE
TAKETHEBULLBYTHEHORNS
APERCU REFEREE IDEAS
STROBE ENE SEE MESS
```

PUZZLE 207

```
DEE TWO LIT
ERA RAW ADO
MEG AXE DIN
OCEAN FLOG
STRICT LETS
  LEAVE
PATE PESTER
AMID RHINO
PUG DEB LEG
ASH YEA EMU
SET ELL RYE
```

PUZZLE 208

```
      ANO
MOM CAD ASAP
ERE ONE MADE
LATER HOMER
  SNIDE
STEP REMOTE
OAT PIN FED
STATUS ETES
  OTHER
ARGOT TRAMS
TBAR IOU BAA
TIRE NOD END
  APE
```

PUZZLE 209

```
  PACA
  RERAN
  LATENT
  SUITS
CANDY SAM
PANG WANED
WING TAILORING
AND WORST SEE
STOPWATCH SPAT
READS PEER
RYE CORAL
  LOGAN
  STARRY
  LEVEE
  YEAR
```

PUZZLE 210

1. Sage, Sale, Ague; 2. Sure, Surf, Sore; 3. Wolf, Wore, Oleo; 4. Tang, Tram, Gram; 5. Deep, Clap, Slap; 6. Nail, Nine, Aide; 7. Rear, Garb, Aria; 8. Late, Lute, Auto.

PUZZLE 211

```
TADS HAT AGA
OPEN SORA OTIC
MEMO WATERFRONT
BROUGHT ELLA
STOA FEEL
OMITTED
SCREW
OUT
ENERO
PASSAGE
FEET LYES
BANK KEENEST
BRIDESMAID TREY
ROTS KIND EVER
ASH ALT REPO
```

PUZZLE 212

SALAD: Cheese, Lettuce, Onion, Nuts, Eggs.

OCCUPATIONS: Carpenter, Librarian, Optometrist, Nurse, Engineer.

POETS: (Samuel Taylor) Coleridge, (Amy) Lowell, Ovid, (Pablo) Neruda, (T.S.) Eliot.

RIVERS: Congo, Loire, Orinoco, Nile, Euphrates.

PHOTOGRAPHY: Camera, Lens, Overdevelop, Negative, Exposure.

PUZZLE 213

```
      EBBS
OTIS SEAT
RUTA STRAW
ABET SARAH
LAREDO TREAT
DRIVE ALAR
OLEG ORALE
VITALSTATISTICS
ATALL DOCS
NERO SPOIL
MENDS NEARER
EATEN MOLE
MAMET PLEA
RIVE SEED
SLED
```

PUZZLE 214

```
HEW
OAR
PRAMS
POT
SEEPS
ARI
MOP
```

PUZZLE 215

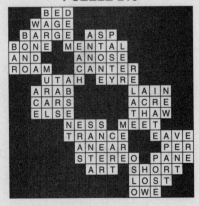

```
BED
WAGE
BARGE ASP
BONE MENTAL
AND ANOSE
ROAM CANTER
UTAH EYRE
ARAB LAIN
CARS ACRE
ELSE THAW
NESS MEET
TRANCE EAVE
ANEAR PER
STEREO PANE
ART SHORT
LOST
OWE
```

PUZZLE 216

FAMOUS LOUS OR LOUISES: (Lou) Piniella, (Louis) Gossett, (Jr.), (Lou) Costello, (Louis) Jourdan, (Louis) Braille.

HOOVED ANIMALS: Zebra, Goat, Buffalo, Pronghorn, Giraffe.

BROADWAY MUSICALS: Oklahoma!, Camelot, Chicago, Brigadoon, Annie.

LAND FORMATIONS: Mesa, Escarpment, Grotto, Canyon, Butte.

ASIAN CAPITALS: Manila, Beirut, Tokyo, Teheran, Singapore.

PUZZLE 220

PUZZLE 217

PUZZLE 218

MONOTONOUS

PUZZLE 219

PUZZLE 221

PUZZLE 222

PUZZLE 223

PUZZLE 224

PUZZLE 225

Aster, Format, Tirade, Battery, Reaction, Diameter, Terminate.

PUZZLE 226

PUZZLE 227

1. Room service, 2. Double occupancy, 3. Front desk, 4. Keyless entry, 5. Honeymoon suite, 6. Complimentary breakfast, 7. Airport shuttle, 8. Checkout time.

PUZZLE 228

533

PUZZLE 229

1. SCAT / HOLE / IRON / NEED
2. MICE / IDOL / LESS / DATE
3. DAMP / EVER / FETE / TREY

PUZZLE 230

```
SLOG  AWED  ADOBE
HOBO  POLO  BIKED
EBON  TOKE  ERRED
SEEDBED     NARY
   OURS  EKED
TALL  YODELLER
WASABI AGES  MIA
IRK  RATEL  CON
TOE  PILE  SAFETY
TREASONS  BEES
   ACHE  PALM
SASS     ROYALTY
EMAIL APER  LORE
CAGEY BRAT  EDIT
THERE SODA  SEMI
```

PUZZLE 231

```
FLUSH ACTS  URGE
AISLE IRON  PERM
SMEAR RULE  SCAB
TORI OMELET  APE
  NOVEL  ZIPPER
ANT  PEN  REPS
WOODEN RID  ASPS
ADORN JAM  PLEAT
YETI  HAG CAMERA
  FLUB  RAW  MET
BANTAM  HENNA
AWE DIGEST  NOVA
SAWS  DALE  AVOID
TREK  OMEN  SIZED
EELY  RENT  SLEDS
```

PUZZLE 232

```
SHOE  UPS   ALSO
WARS  DRIES LOAD
ARCS  INTRO ACID
BEHAVE  AEROSOLS
  EYE      NEW
BASSET  DARNERS
ACT  ICED  SLEPT
TURK  PALES MARE
STAID FIST  PEN
ESTATES  YAPPED
   TOT   ROE
CASTANET MENACE
OBOE  GRAPE CRAB
ALOE  SIREN HERB
LEND  ASP   ODES
```

PUZZLE 233

```
SPAS  SAD   AFAR
TILE  THROB LOBE
UNIT  RECUR TIED
DUB MOD  BEHOLDS
SPIRIT     TWO
  EXTRA  SOOTHE
SPOT  EAST  KNEEL
TAXI  DIKES CELL
OPERA LEAN  ASPS
PANELS  DRILL
  ALP    PILING
AEROSOL APT  GEL
RAIN  SINCE ALSO
ISLE  HEARD COTS
AYES  DYE   TOSS
```

PUZZLE 234

```
ERRS  BACK  EMBED
LEAK  OGLE  BEIGE
MAGI  NEON  BADGE
SLEDGE     DOMED
   ELK   ADOBE
PRETENDED   WERE
AREA  SEEN  HAW
PACT  SALAD EASE
EYE   DIME  EVES
REDO  ASSEMBLED
   RELAX  LAY
   DIETS  NEWEST
SPEED RAID  HATE
AROSE ONCE  EVEN
DONTS TEED  YEWS
```

PUZZLE 235

```
SPUD  LIP   ERIN
WINY  RICES LIVE
AKIN  EMOTE EVES
BETA  DIN  INVEST
  MEETS  ZEE
REMOVE     WETNESS
AXE   EMCEE TRAP
SATAN URN  WHALE
PLED  BATHE SON
STROBES    ORIENT
   RUM   ACRES
AFLAME  BAR  LAID
SLOB  RABBI ALTA
PEAL  YIELD NOEL
SANE  RYE   DEMI
```

PUZZLE 236

```
TORE  ADES  SWABS
AREA  SOLO  COBRA
LASS  STUD  RECAP
CLOTH     IDAHO
SSW   AONE  ALLOW
   STAG  ILLEGAL
BLOCK TNT   ALSO
COACH DOC   CREPT
PORK  HAT   BANDS
LEVELED    VATS
DATER PETE  APE
  SOBER  REDIP
OASIS LAST  DOLE
FLAKE ACED  ABLE
FEWER BEDS  MESS
```

PUZZLE 237

```
SCAM  APED  USES
TONE  DREAM PAVE
ACNE  DELTA SLAW
TOOTH FEEDS ODE
SAY   ICER CORNER
   FUR   SANE
RABBIT NAP  RAMS
IDOLS DOG   KAYAK
BODE  MUG  NINETY
   EKED  HOT
GOLDEN NEWT INS
RAY   GATOR YODEL
IRIS  CHIDE WIRE
MENU  EASEL LOVE
EDGE  WEDS  STEP
```

PUZZLE 238

```
ACME  SHAD  MELTS
COAX  TONE  AWAIT
TAMI  EPIC  PESTO
SLATER  SAD  SAP
  BENEFIT  INS
SAW  BOA   VASES
TWIGS     VOYAGE
YETI  CAPON MAID
LOLLED     WINCE
REDYE EYE   YEW
PEN  LABELED
ANT  RIM   ASSERT
GAILY NEWS  ALEE
EMCEE GNAT  GLEE
REEDS ODDS  ASKS
```

PUZZLE 239

```
SMELL ODDS  ACHE
MEDIA WRAP  NOOK
UNITY LIMA  NOSE
GUT  MUSES COSTS
  GAS    RETRY
BALONEY LEI  CAB
ODOR  REV  ASSAIL
TONED PIE  PURSE
CREDIT ARC  DALE
HER  NUT ROASTED
  DEBUT  PLY
SHRED REDYE ODE
TEEN  STAR  REPAY
ORES  ELSE  TWINE
POLE  WEED  SEEKS
```

PUZZLE 240

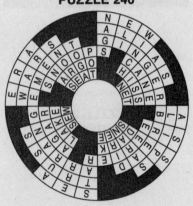

PUZZLE 241

```
HES  ALSO   TOMB
OAK  LATE   EVER
PRISONER   LAMA
   PEER   ALLOT
ESSES  ELMS
LOAN  ZOOM  TAD
SUNDAE     NOTICE
ERE  DRUG   WREN
   FOOT   SEEDY
STIRS  MOLE
CODE  TOGETHER
AGES  ISLE   ERA
NOAH  STEP   WRY
```

PUZZLE 242

A	M	A	S	S			H	U	S	K	S
P	I	N	T	O	S		H	A	M	L	E	T
E	X	T	E	N	T		A	L	P	I	N	E
			M	A	R	B	L	E		T	O	W
A	P	T		T	O	L	L	S			
B	R	A	V	A	D	O		T	A	S	T	E
L	I	C	E		E	W	E		S	L	O	P
E	M	O	T	E		O	N	S	H	O	R	E
			Y	O	U	T	H		W	E	E
H	A	S		E	S	T	E	E	M		
O	N	C	A	L	L		R	E	A	D	E	R
S	T	U	D	I	O		S	T	R	I	K	E
T	I	M	E	D			S	T	E	E	P

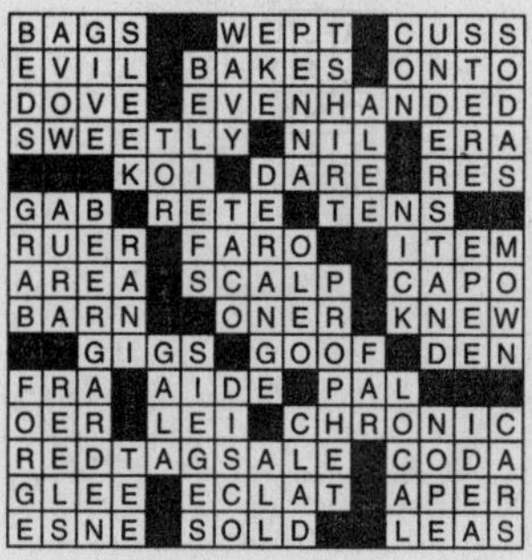

PUZZLE 246

1-f Pearl, 2-d Sowing, 3-a Finagle, 4-c Jaunt, 5-b Tray, 6-e Dumped.

6-LETTER WORD: Logjam

PUZZLE 247

H	E	M	P		A	L	G	A		A	S	P	S
A	C	E	R		D	I	A	L	S		P	L	I	E
T	R	I	O		I	D	Y	L	L		L	O	P	E
S	U	N	D	A	E		E	L	O	P	E	D
		U	S	U	R	P		D	A	M
E	P	O	C	H		E	L	I	G	I	B	L	E
R	O	P	E	Y		L	A	M	E	R		A	R	M
S	K	I		Y	I	P			S	U	E
T	E	N		C	L	O	N	E		S	L	E	P	T
D	E	T	A	I	N	E	D		T	O	R	T	E
		U	S	N		R	E	S	E	W
S	A	C	R	E	D		E	M	E	R	G	E
A	C	R	E		E	L	F	I	N		R	A	R	E
S	H	O	E		N	O	O	N	S		E	L	A	N
H	E	W	N		P	E	K	E		D	E	B	S

PUZZLE 243

(crossword grid)

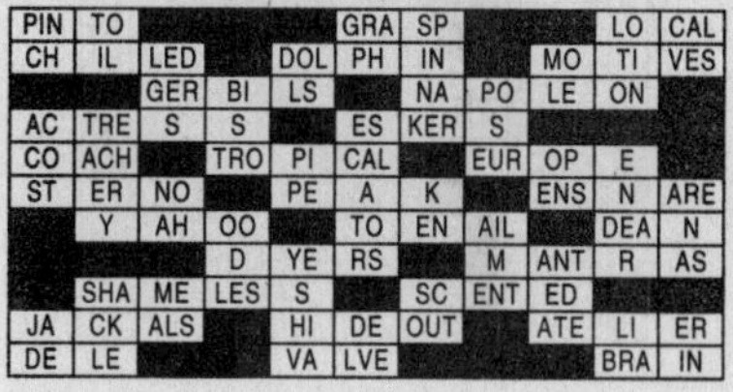

PUZZLE 244

Alert, Aloe, Alter, Alto, Earl, Late, Later, Lore, Oral, Orate, Rare, Rate, Real, Rear, Roar, Role, Rote, Tale, Tare, Taro, Teal, Tear, Tole, Tore.

PUZZLE 248

BOYS' NAMES: Robert, Peter, Bruce, Sean, David.

THINGS THAT FLY: Bat, Helicopter, Kite, Zeppelin, Bird.

POETS: (Robert) Frost, (Edward) Lear, (William) Shakespeare, (Emily) Dickinson, (Ezra) Pound.

DOG BREEDS: Whippet, Rottweiler, Beagle, Papillon, Greyhound.

BODIES OF WATER: Strait, River, Lake, Ocean, Pond.

PUZZLE 250

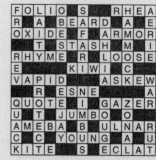

1-S, 2-W, 3-O, 4-Y, 5-V, 6-Z, 7-C, 8-I, 9-X, 10-A, 11-U, 12-N, 13-Q, 14-T, 15-P, 16-G, 17-F, 18-K, 19-B, 20-D, 21-E, 22-R, 23-J, 24-L, 25-H, 26-M.

PUZZLE 251

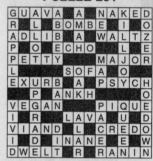

1-H, 2-O, 3-B, 4-N, 5-L, 6-M, 7-D, 8-Q, 9-S, 10-E, 11-P, 12-C, 13-G, 14-Y, 15-V, 16-Z, 17-J, 18-U, 19-A, 20-F, 21-R, 22-K, 23-I, 24-T, 25-W, 26-X.

PUZZLE 249

PUZZLE 245

B	A	G	S		W	E	P	T		C	U	S	S
E	V	I	L		B	A	K	E	S		O	N	T	O
D	O	V	E		E	V	E	N	H	A	N	D	E	D
S	W	E	E	T	L	Y		N	I	L		E	R	A
			K	O	I		D	A	R	E		R	E	S
G	A	B		R	E	T	E		T	E	N	S
R	U	E	R		F	A	R	O		I	T	E	M
A	R	E	A		S	C	A	L	P		C	A	P	O
B	A	R	N		O	N	E	R		K	N	E	W
		G	I	G	S		G	O	O	F		D	E	N
F	R	A		A	I	D	E		P	A	L
O	E	R		L	E	I		C	H	R	O	N	I	C
R	E	D	T	A	G	S	A	L	E		C	O	D	A
G	L	E	E		E	C	L	A	T		A	P	E	R
E	S	N	E		S	O	L	D		L	E	A	S

PUZZLE 252

W	H	E	N		A	G	E		B	L	A	H
E	A	V	E		S	C	R	A	P		A	I	D	E
B	R	I	G		T	I	A	R	A		I	T	E	M
S	E	L	L		A	D	D		P	O	L	E
		I	B	I	S		H	E	W		R	A	P
S	U	G	A	R		F	O	R	E		A	D	O
A	C	N	E	D		S	A	V	E	D		T	O	W
L	O	D	E		I	C	I	E	R		P	U	R	E
O	R	E		G	N	A	R	L		S	O	R	E	R
H	E	R		U	G	L	Y		H	I	R	E	D
A	R	M		F	R	Y		A	I	N	T
		I	N	F	O		I	N	K		A	L	S	O
B	O	N	E		W	R	O	T	E		B	O	O	K
A	P	E	X		N	O	T	E	D		L	A	N	A
T	E	S	T		W	A	S		E	D	G	Y

535

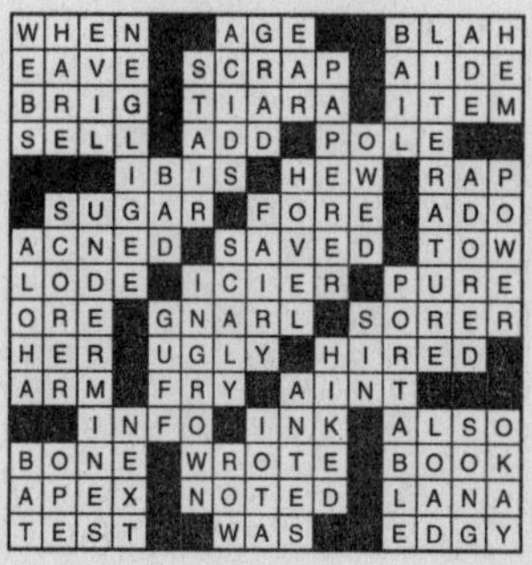

PUZZLE 253

```
VAST ASPS  SLOB
INTO FLEAS CONE
SNOW FORGE APED
OUR  TIP   MAR
RAM AXE DIG AWE
 LYNX SPINE RAT
   AIR ACADEMIC
MAAM ENDER MYTH
ANCESTOR  SKI
TEN OARED ATOM
EWE DIM OWL FOG
   CAN WOE FOR
PAPA EMBER LIRA
EYER REELS ACED
PEND NEST  WEDS
```

PUZZLE 257

```
ABET  FILM  INTO
DYER MANIA MEAN
DELI ANNEX PATS
   BITS DIG TEE
LAPEL    ALERT
UKE LAG ALIENS
BIN  DISPUTE
ENDS AREAS KEEL
  NEGLECT  AXE
CRAVES EYE  RIG
GROPE    AUNTS
LET RUT HARP
EATS NUKES PAPA
ASEA ITEMS EPIC
MEND TUGS  RENT
```

PUZZLE 261

```
RASPS SNOB  JOGS
ACORN HULA ALIT
MEDIA ODDS DIVA
   SPREE ELEVEN
SWAMPY SHE  END
ION  YET MIDI
TOGS ABUT  TIC
SELL PRODS CRIB
DEE AGOG  HAVE
  DIRE ELK TIE
STU CAT YODELS
OINKED  SPEAR
RATE IDOL LIVED
TRIP SAME AFIRE
SALT EYED STERN
```

PUZZLE 254

```
REPS COLA   CAT
ACRE SHIELD AWE
PROW HANDLE PAN
SUP  SUNK CHOKE
  EYING BARONET
ABLER ERASER
GULPED ORIENTED
ERE  ROUND  HAY
STRAYING ENDIVE
  MAPLES ERRED
SEVENTY CLAYS
CLINK DROP  TIP
RUG ECHOES AIDE
ADO DOUSES NEER
PER  TEEN  DRAM
```

PUZZLE 258

```
APERC RALO RAEL
MESAR OMAR ERNE
PRAYS EGSP IDSA
TASTIC UMPA AET
  BEAT OTARTE
ETRREAT EIRN
LEEPS RANSPTORT
PSAE ETRSE UTOS
TTAENDANT UREPE
  NAON RETENDP
EPASTR  AYER
ART ELET LMAOST
PAST EPRI OISNE
CIER NSEE ISLEA
ELSE TOSP LLEEN
```

PUZZLE 262

```
ROSY AMPS  LATH
ABLE WAITS ALOE
POINSETTIA SLOW
SET LIE RYES
   BUG   BOAS
FRIGHT HUB SOB
VEINS HOOP SUE
IMPS SEARS BURN
CAP IRKS CORED
ELL APE ECHOED
EELS   HAT
  AHOY WIT ARK
STAT ROTISSERIE
AIDE ELOPE LION
PEER KEEL  MATS
```

PUZZLE 263

```
TOAST SLAP STAT
IGLOO POPE AWRY
DRILY ROTS KICK
YETI BAN TSETSE
  DARN  WOK
AVE CIGAR IDEA
RINSED DEB ALGA
ONTO ARENA YELL
NEED LIP MASCOT
DRAB STABS TWO
   AUK TOSS
ALLEYS COO HEAL
MOOD IRON HELLO
ORIG NUKE OASES
RISE GEES GRASS
```

PUZZLE 255

```
TOTE PET  SLAB
IRON ALBUM LOCO
CAFE RABBI ECHO
SLUR ONE SPIKES
  GLUED  HOG
FRIEND FATHER
BLAZED MAP  DEW
RICER DAD SPICE
ARE CRY VIRTUE
TROPHY SANEST
  BOA TALKS
STEEPS ELL EGGS
AIRY ENSUE NANA
RENE RATTY CLAW
IRED BYE  EATS
```

PUZZLE 259

```
GUSTO ADOS  MAR
INTENT TRIO EGO
STEREO TILL DAB
TOWN SKIP ELATE
  SIC SMILED
DAPPLED DANK
ALLOYS BAY EWES
STOLE FED ENACT
HOPE AID SEETHE
  CRIB HARDTOP
ASSAIL  MOD
DITTO RIND PACK
ORE TWIT EDIBLE
BEE EAST REPLAY
END DYES  WEEDS
```

PUZZLE 256

```
PUMA ACHY  SKIM
ONES SLEEP UNDO
TINT POLAR BILL
STAIR SPRIG FED
  GRADES COMEDY
SHE CUR FETA
TERMED FLY CHIP
ARIAS YOU PHOTO
BEEN SEE IRONED
  NAHS ELI EMS
IMPAIR BAKERY
NIL LULUS DUMPS
ANEW BASIS MOLE
NEAR STENO BOOM
EDDY EDGY  ANTI
```

PUZZLE 260

```
ANTI STAY SIGHS
CORN URGE ALLOT
MOOS MAIL LLAMA
ENDED INPUT DEB
  RUING SIS
MOTOR VENEER
SIC KIWI EAVED
ORE ESTEEMS ADO
YEARN CEDE DIG
SNITCH LOPED
  DIE TITLE
RUM RETAR DOSED
APACE ALAS PLAY
VOCAL NOTE LOSE
ENEMY KNEW EWER
```

PUZZLE 264

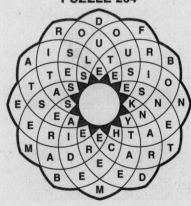

536

PUZZLE 265

```
OATS  GAS    GERM
FLEA BIRTH  ALEE
FEEL INTRO  LAMA
 EBB  SELF  PAN
APE ASP EEL  SIT
BRADY  EAT EVEN
 LAVISHED  OWE
EYER ERASE NOVA
 TON PARDONED
MAYO ITS EMCEE
BAG ZIG HOE  ESS
IRE EMUS URN
SING PATHS ACTS
ONTO SNOUT MOAT
NEST  AWE  EDGY
```

PUZZLE 266

```
CURB  RAP    FLAP
OBEY LITER  LAIR
MODE ADORE  AWRY
BAY STEP PET
STEEPER ALE  ELK
 NIX SCALLION
HEAT CHIC  OGRE
GARB ERODE THEE
ORAL NITS  BITS
ESSENCES  FRO
SHE OLD PIANIST
 TWO SIRS  SEW
TYPO SALES ISLE
HEAR EXACT MULE
YARN  EWE  PEST
```

PUZZLE 267

```
CLAP LASS  PEEPS
AURA ACHY  INLET
RAIN PEEN  AGATE
DUDE  CAN   NEW
 LAMBS  DOT
IFS LILIES  OFT
TOT INEPT KNEAD
AXE KIN HEN  ABE
LEAVE DUNCE SON
SKI ASPIRE  TRY
 ARF SCULL
APT ITS    INNS
RERAN TAME FAIL
MAILS ARIA ETNA
STOLE TENT REAM
```

PUZZLE 268

```
DOFF ECRU SPAS IOWA
ELLA BEEN HELP IDOL
LAOS SLAT AREA PERM
IVWHEELDRIVE NOISES
 INN JUNE  SIRE
OLMOS MUTT STACCATO
DION VISHOOTER EVEN
OVA FONT SURD  SOSO
REBIRTH DIANE AUNTS
 FOE HACKS CHI
CDROM MOCHA TOOTSIE
HEIR OATH AWRY  ORD
EMIT VYEARPLAN MOOD
FISHMEAL AILS NANNY
 ERRS KNEE  KEN
IBERIA IIIBLINDMICE
MILO LILT AUDI ARAL
ALIA LOST LIES DELL
MEAD SUEY DASH ESSE
```

PUZZLE 269

```
LASH ABEAM   DOG
ALEE TERRA  SODA
DOWNSTAIRS  TWIT
YEN HERS  TRANCE
 SONS  FEARS
SLOPED HART  TUG
POURS GUISE  RKO
ATTY URN    DEAR
CUR SMART  CEASE
ESE TORY  RAMMED
 AMEND  BORE
FACETS EASE  LOO
ASHE OUTLASTING
DIET OTTER  USER
SAD NEEDY  BASE
```

PUZZLE 270

```
LARA WATER  SHAM
ACAD ADORN  PACE
WHYDOFOOLS  ALMS
SEE MERLE  RILES
 MARE  LINE
SEVER LIT    BOB
AXIS LARENZ  ERA
DIVA ORATE  ARID
ALI ROCHON  FROG
TEC UPS    WAYNE
 AILS  BARR
CRANE LEASE  POT
LIFE FALLINLOVE
ATOP ATSEA  OPAL
NEXT YEARN  SELL
```

PUZZLE 271

```
ARAB  SIR    SHE
SITES ONE    WAX
HOODWINKS    III
 DOTS  CENTS
ALTERS  PUNDIT
HORDE  WHEEL
ANI HAD      EMU
 CUBED CARAT
ASKFOR HASSLE
BESOM  OURS
ANT BAMBOOZLE
TOE EWE  BROOK
ERR DEN   TOTE
```

PUZZLE 272

```
STOW ETA   PLAY
LASH SAL   RITE
ATLANTIS   EDEN
MAORI POMP
 FLEE  OASTS
LEA LILLIPUT
AZTECS  ODDITY
DROGHEDA   TUE
SAMOA EMIT
 IRAN  MANGO
SPAS STEPFORD
KILT EAR   FREE
YEAS ALE   YAWS
```

PUZZLE 273

```
PRUDENTCAFELAMP
RENEGERANIVAGUE
ODDEGRETELICITS
VEEROVERALLSLAO
ECRUDESERTEMEND
RANTEDIGNITEATE
BREEDINGITALIAN
STATENAILAPTDRY
PETOPENERNEEDED
OTHERDEWOILRITA
OATSECRETCARVED
FLAWSRILEDWEEKS
ALPISISLIESPREE
GEESEMEETLEAEEL
ERSEDENDELAYELF
```

PUZZLE 274

```
EVER TABOR  SCOW
DENY ADELE  COLA
ANTE RENES  ODIN
MIA ORANGOUTANG
 NAMELY  UNI
BEGGED  UNDATED
ELLEN WALDO  ANO
LEIS SALES  ONTO
INN AIRES  ALGER
EAGERLY SPEARS
 NEE  TAKEON
RECTANGULAR YES
ELIA CARAT  LIMA
ASTI ELITE  AKIN
PEEL DANES  GATE
```

PUZZLE 275

1. Elkhound, 2. Adjacent, 3. Skillful, 4. Chemical, 5. Scavenge, 6. Anywhere, 7. Backfire, 8. Juvenile, 9. Bachelor, 10. Diagonal.

PUZZLE 276

```
   AB LE   DE M IS E
SO BE R S EM O L L ENT
AP H ID S   DI ET  R EAR
S IN G   BR A SH  ALI E N
 D ES TR U CT STA GN AT ED
    A NT I DO TE
SE L FISH   V ES P ERS
R A LLY FO IST S  M OL E
F UR L IST     CH A IR
 A SHA M ED    IN CIT E
    D ER IVE  P ENT
```

PUZZLE 277

```
   554
x    3
 1662
```

PUZZLE 278

```
SWAM  TEN    ASEA
EAVE BUXOM  COBB
TIER UNITE  TUBE
STRIPS LESS  NET
 NOISE  ATODDS
ACCOUNT    YAP
GAL REAR  PETROL
EPOS STEER  HORA
RECESS FROM  OAK
 KEN  SHUFFLE
MAMMAL  STILL
ETA GASP  BEANED
ARKS SWAMI  MORE
LIEU TAROT  BONE
YARN  BED   EKED
```

PUZZLE 279

```
ALPS  SAKE   ROLE
PLEA  OPERA  OLAN
TARN  USERS  MEND
   MIDDLEPASSAGE
ASSE     STAIN
    LAG  AYE  ASP
OLEO  VEE   VILLA
MIDDLEOFTHEROAD
ADIEU   TRA  KEYS
RAT   RIP   ETE
     AIDES   NATE
  MIDDLEKINGDOM
GILD  ELATE  AREA
ELSE  DETER  MRED
MEAD  DEMO   SERA
```

PUZZLE 280

1. Speed reader, 2. Nacho business, 3. Mental gloss, 4. Dog-tired, 5. The Slice Is Right.

PUZZLE 281

```
LONG  MANA   SPA
EWER  AXEL   WEB
ANTI  GIST   AWL
    SPILT  KNEE
MUFTI     HIKER
EKE   QUOTED
WED   USHER  OAF
    DEEMED   FRO
CZARS      ESTER
LILY  CONDO
ELL   FUME  AJAR
ACE   IBEX  VOLE
THY   TENT  ETAS
```

1-K, 2-W, 3-T, 4-R, 5-Z, 6-V, 7-A, 8-C, 9-J, 10-B, 11-I, 12-O, 13-D, 14-G, 15-E, 16-S, 17-Y, 18-H, 19-M, 20-N, 21-X, 22-F, 23-Q, 24-U, 25-P, 26-L.

PUZZLE 282

```
PAR   ALBS   PILAF
AWE   LEAN   MANAGE
SAC   PILE   ICEMAN
HIT      SEEDER
ATOM  EARNS  TATA
   OFF   ITS  ZIP
JANITORS   PLUME
QUITE  PAL  OARED
UDDER   EYESORES
AGE   YEN   ELK
DESK  XENON  SAWN
    RAIDED   PIE
AVAILS  ADDS  APT
FILLET  PLIE  RET
TELLS   SYNC  TRY
```

1-Y, 2-H, 3-Q, 4-V, 5-X, 6-E, 7-F, 8-A, 9-O, 10-U, 11-C, 12-B, 13-W, 14-S, 15-G, 16-I, 17-L, 18-D, 19-N, 20-Z, 21-R, 22-P, 23-T, 24-K, 25-M, 26-J.

PUZZLE 283

```
CRATE  ARMS   ECHO
HIRES  LEAP   SLUG
OVENS  TAPE   CURL
MAN    PAL   LIABLE
PLATFORM    LOP
   ELLS  RENEWED
CEREAL  CUD   HAY
AXING  DAB   SIEVE
TAD    PAN  WETTER
  SMELLED  GAME
   OUR  ULTIMATE
SPRIGS  NOT   WAX
ALIT   IOTA  SNAKE
GAPE   SNIT  PARER
EYER   TEES  AGENT
```

PUZZLE 284

```
ERAS  SHARP  ATSEA  PAAR
LAME  MARIA  CHORD  ASTO
SHOWWINDOW  HORRORSHOW
   ALOE  EASES  ITEMS
MSS  REINS  DEE   EVE
ETHANS  TOGA   REALMS
DROPS  SHOWANDTELL  EPA
DEWS  SHOVER  ARMY  ADIT
LAB  HAVE  OLEO  ALINE
EMU  CINE  SALLE  SLICES
  SHAME  SURLY  AMATI
ALIENS  HENNA  AGES  NAT
CONES  HANS  ULNA  ESE
NOEL  MARS  LESSER  OSHA
ESS  VARIETYSHOW  COHOS
  ESTATE  ROTE  LAHORE
ALA  TEN  RAPID  WED
  AMASS  CROSS  TINE
HORSESHOWS  TALENTSHOW
ANNE  TEPEE  APACE  AIRE
BAAL  EWERS  BESET  WETS
```

PUZZLE 285

```
BOPS   RAMP   LIT
AVAIL  AGILE  IRE
SENSATIONAL  MOE
ENE  SYN  ICEMAN
  SLEEP   ANA
   BREATHTAKING
SLAB  ASHOE  ODOR
AUG   SIT   OVA
FLEE  GAELS  ALAS
  ELECTRIFYING
   TEA   SATES
GROANS  RAT  ROO
ORE  STIMULATING
LIS   EERIE  LOCAL
EDT   DENS   MARE
```

PUZZLE 286

```
SPAT  CPAS   CRAFT
HOLY  ARLO   HANOI
USES  MISO   ANTIC
THEOREGONTRAIL
   NOR    GEM
GAB   PARA  PSALMS
AGREE  OBOE  COOT
PAULREVERESRIDE
EVIL  TETE  TENET
SENECA  SOME  SSS
   APT   ENE
THENEWCOLOSSUS
ARENA  EAVE  TITO
PERIL  EPEE  OLEO
REEDS  DENS  POST
```

PUZZLE 287

```
OLEO  SWAT   EDGES
DELE  HOBO   NOONE
OVERTAKES   CREST
REG   EMS   STAYS
LYON  SEAM   UMA
  STARTSUP  NOR
AQUA  DEE   SADIE
PUNK  OVALS  MESA
PEDAL  LEI   ARTS
LEE   UPSTARTS
ERR   POOH   ESSE
  GRIEF  SEN  ERA
SWOON   TAKESOVER
PEEVE  EVIL  NECK
YESES  REPS  ORTS
```

PUZZLE 288

```
MICAS  SKIP   ICBM
APORT  EERO   DORY
YOUCANTGET   OPUS
NONETS   BYLINE
SIS  DEO  GOA  EEL
CLETE  SPOILEDIF
ASLEEP   OWLET
RASP  LAINE  ULLA
  INALL  REDIAL
YOUDOYOUR   NEONS
ARP  TET  EAT  NEO
BARRED   SABRAS
BLOT  OWNLAUNDRY
ELSE  FOAM  SNEER
RYES  FOPS  TENDS
```

PUZZLE 289

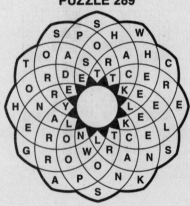

PUZZLE 290

```
STETS  ERST   IDEA
POPUP  NEAR   MULL
UTICA  TIMESPAST
DOCK  ERNE   AUDIO
   EDGE   CURSES
STORAGESPACE
COVEYS  EASY   UPS
ARID  HARSH  EPEE
ROD   SELF  MANTRA
  MILESPERHOUR
SCROLL   AREA
ALAMO  SORE  NORM
PIKESPEAK   ACHOO
OMEN  URSA  TEMPO
REST  GATS  ESSEN
```

PUZZLE 291

A. 25 (+1 +3 +5 +7 +9 +11 +13 +15)
B. 54 (+7 x2 +7 x2 +7 x2 +7 x2)
C. 47 (+4 -5 +6 -7 +4 -5 +6 -7)
D. 39 (-3 +9 -3 +9 -3 +9 -3 +9)
E. 71 (+2 +4 +6 +8 +2 +4 +6 +8)
F. 31 (-5 -4 +3 +2 -5 -4 +3 +2)
G. 28 (+9 -8 +7 -6 +5 -4 +3 -2)

PUZZLE 292

```
MOST ABLE BUGS OBOE
ETTA DRAT AFRO LOGE
STET MONO NOON DILL
HOMECOOKING  WAFFLES
      END LOOP ROO
POLLOI GENRES ELBOW
ARIA  SRA   TAD KENO
TEAS HOMEPLATE  SACK
HORSE CURIE ESTATES
  ISH TANGS KIT
POLECAT STALE  SHEEP
ALEC HOMEALONE ONTO
REDO AGO   PAM  MOTO
ROAMS APIECE  BREWER
    ERE ETTU TOO
SOPHIST HARVESTHOME
OMOO SERA SANS ABEL
FARM ERIC ERSE LIAM
TREE SAGA DYED LETS
```

PUZZLE 293

```
KRIS SCAR DULL CAMP
NODE CANE ESAU OBOE
OVER ARAB FERN YULE
BEAVERSTATE  SCOOTER
  IRE  TENT HAT
SPACE TREASON TENSE
TIDE CIA EPEE   SELL
ITA ELAINE SAL  TAIL
RAMBLE SONG REGATTA
    AMA ESTES MET
PANDORA HERO ENERGY
ORIG ESP RELENT EEE
LACE RIOT  INT DANA
ALERT ALAMODE SEDER
   SRI ENOS CON
SANTANA  GOPHERSTATE
AREA FREE RIVE ISAW
GILT ELAN EDIE SHOE
ELLE ROUT YELP TESS
```

PUZZLE 294

```
EBBS STAR AWL SPUME
REAP CODA LEA WATER
ASTI OWES IBM ARETE
THESUNSHINEBOYS
   LIT  EVER FEISTY
CATER DIRE RFD  TOE
AGAR TEN POUT TORA
TIP SINGININTHERAIN
CLERIC AGORA ELY
HERON   NRA   ASSET
  PER PITTS INTONE
GONEWITHTHEWIND NAN
OTIS AIDE ARN TACT
LOB OLE  DINE FORTS
DESERT OWEN  AIT
  SNOWBALLEXPRESS
SOUSA EIN ERMA BOAT
RESET REE TIER AURA
IRENE ESS SENT GRIN
```

PUZZLE 295

```
      LIEU DEMI
      OVEN ORAL
      BENCHMARK
         LEI
      PLANNED
MAS   BEAD OMEN   ROT
INA   BEAM UNIS   OBI
MOD   ANT  STA    COP
INDENT       SNAKES
   LED          DDE
CHEESE        THERES
HUB   AMP     SOO  AGE
ALA   WILD    SANG RAW
TAG   REIN    BUSS MDS
      BEEGEES
         WED
      CHAIRLADY
      EARS ASEA
      ETCH MEEK
```

PUZZLE 296

```
GAL  ACHY  SIAM
AGE  BLUE  UNDO
BOA  BURN  STEM
    FOYER  HOSS
SWIG   ANTI
TIER SHOE  LIE
UNSEEN ONWARD
BET GAWK IBID
    TOGA ROSY
CHAR  SHIER
RACE  SHED  ESS
AURA PEAL  RUT
BLED ARTY  SPY
```

PUZZLE 297

```
ADS  EPIC  STOP
PIP  MALL  HALO
TEE  ISLE  AXES
   CART ADVISE
SPIN AGREE
CAMEO REFRAIN
APE CREDO  WOO
MANATEE ELATE
   VESTS ERAS
INVITE  LAID
NEED RAID  ICY
FOAL VIED  NEE
ONLY ERRS  GET
```

PUZZLE 298

```
STOP  MAKE SLID
TINE  DUNES HERE
RASP  OCTET EGOS
IRE LIKENED INK
PATRON    ERAS
  EGGY SMELLED
OLIVE ILL WEAVE
KIN  EYE   TIE
RACES LED WIELD
ARRAYED SWAN
   ERNE  ORNATE
LOA CRATERS BOA
ALSO ICERS SONG
SEEP ERASE OVAL
HOST REST  DELE
```

PUZZLE 299

A.

```
LAPSE
ALIAS
PILLS
SALSA
ESSAY
```

B.

```
BALSA
ATOLL
LOCAL
SLAVE
ALLEY
```

PUZZLE 300

```
BALM PAST COLIN
ARIA ECHO ADOBE
REEL REEF MERIT
BANTAM USE  ESS
   PIC  TOW
PRICETAG  ASHES
LODE  COOL  AXED
OVEN STICK  LANE
PEAS PINE   ELSA
 SLOPE GANGSTER
   RON  NAN
 ILK ODD  MUSTER
MINOR ISLE CUKE
PRONE MAUL ABED
SABER EDGY TEDS
```

PUZZLE 301

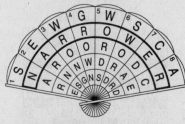

1. Snare, 2. Earns, 3. Wrong, 4. Grown, 5. Words, 6. Sword, 7. Cedar, 8. Arced.
8-LETTER WORD: Narrower

PUZZLE 302

```
WRAP  HAM  DIET
RATE WADED ONTO
ODOR AISLE GNAR
NIL ILK TIDIEST
  AYE EONS  TAR
HATS TACK  RULE
EMIT SWARM EBON
RIMS LUAU  DEED
ODE LASS SPY
  POEM ESTEEMED
RAILWAY TAP  EMU
AWED SATIN ADES
RACE SWING LINT
EYER  LET  PADS
```

PUZZLE 303

ROBERTO CLEMENTE

PUZZLE 304

```
COATI   HORDE
ORGANS SERIAL
PEEWEE ARBORS
    PRUNE  TEA
ADZ TENETS
FOIL  CLOUDED
ANTI PLY  LIVE
REISSUE   KNEE
   POMADE  END
ABS APNEA
RETAKE ARABLE
CLAWED DERAIL
SLYER  DENTS
```

539

PUZZLE 305

```
SKI ACME MOPS
PUT NEAP AURA
ADE NENE GROG
RUMBA TEAM
    ALAR CARAT
ONLY LAIR AMI
BEASTS DEACON
IVY OOZE CYST
TESTY EACH
    USER HYENA
OVAL DOLE CON
DELI GEES HUT
DEEP EDIT ONE
```

PUZZLE 306

```
TAP JAW EWE OPE
AGE ASH FIX BEE
BAGPIPE TRIVIAL
   ALERT ETA
LAIC NEWER QUAD
ANT TIL FURRY
DISC CONFERENCE
   ZOO NOR
NOMANSLAND ORZO
AWARE OVA YEP
YETI APORT BEET
   NAG WROTE
OCEANIC ANAGRAM
RHO OLA TAN ERA
BIN NEB ELK SKY
```

1-J, 2-G, 3-P, 4-X, 5-L, 6-E, 7-R, 8-A, 9-N, 10-O, 11-C, 12-T, 13-W, 14-Q, 15-U, 16-Z, 17-M, 18-K, 19-H, 20-F, 21-V, 22-D, 23-B, 24-Y, 25-S, 26-I.

PUZZLE 307

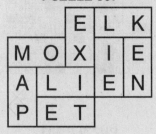

```
    ELK
MOXIE
ALIEN
PET
```

PUZZLE 308

```
AGES WEE ASHE
SILO HAL NEER
KNICKERS IVAN
   KIT STERE
ACHED PECAN
PLOT LOGO IRK
SAL CARAT RUE
EWE OWED LODE
   ICONS LINEN
PANEL SIT
EBON SANDTRAP
SENT EGO EAVE
ODES TAB REAP
```

PUZZLE 309

```
SHY LARA TADA
CEE ARAB ICED
ARA MISS ARES
NORMASHEARER
   USE NRA
AWLS ACE ARC
SHEEPSHEADBAY
POT ENS REND
   ARI SSA
RAMIFICATION
HALO FOOD ORE
OVAL ETUI WAX
DINE RARE ALT
```

PUZZLE 310

```
SCAM ALGA CHAFE
TOME ROAN HONOR
RUIN MELT ENNUI
ACTUP SLIME OLE
WHY ABS OKAY
   BRA COD BASH
HERO SIAM ONTO
AXEL SCREW ACED
WILE ERNE REMS
STAR FRY LED
   YOGI PLY FAB
MER ABATE EPOXY
OVALS LIKE ALIT
VICES ALOE NINE
ELEGY SEEK TOGS
```

PUZZLE 311

```
ELS BOTH WHAT
PIE AREA HERO
IRE YEAR INKY
CAMEO PET
   BULB DELIS
HERB YETI ATE
AXE TRAIT VEE
SPA HERD VAMP
HORSE SEMI
   LEG YACHT
AHOY ABUT HEY
LODE LASH IRK
PEER AGES CEE
```

PUZZLE 312

```
BID PANS JERK
ATE EMIT IRON
ICE ABLY BABE
THRONE RESEW
   BUREAU
SCOOT ELM YAM
POPE ERE MAXI
APT LEI BIKED
   ELEVEN
WRUNG IRISES
HOPE WOVE HAT
ODOR EDIT EVE
MEND BEDS DEW
```

PUZZLE 313

```
DAD EDGE BOSS
ICY XRAY ABUT
SHE TYPE TORO
CEDAR CHEEP
   PAGODA
MOST APER BUS
EWE STALE OPT
NET PELT EASY
   ASSAIL
BASIN SKULL
ARID ODES SUE
TILL LULU ERA
SAKE DOME DEN
```

PUZZLE 314

```
TATA CHIC TAD
ICER HERO ORE
NEAR AMEN FIN
   ASP GAUDY
VINYL BAD
ADE ALSO DABS
MET MAPLE ROE
PAST DADA ELL
   WAY SMALL
SPOON LEI
CAW GAME TWIT
AGE ERAS TOTO
BED LETS SOSO
```

PUZZLE 315

```
ARM DELI KITE
DUE AKIN NOEL
ESS REEF INNS
SHARE OAF
   ADS SECTS
SEMI ARCH HOE
OPEN FIR MIRE
BIN MEMO ICED
SCUBA CAT
   EGG STRAW
SPAR AMOK ERA
PAIR LORE AIL
AWRY APER RAT
```

PUZZLE 316

```
HEWS AWLS EGG
ALOE MOAT COO
SLED POGO HON
   ASS OZONE
RHINO SPA
ION RASH PLEA
POT TREAT URN
STOW MADE ART
   ICY AMUSE
PLANE SKI
RAW DEMO KITE
EVE AKIN EVIL
PAD REDS SEEM
```

PUZZLE 317

```
HAM SPAR LOAN
ALE TUNA UNTO
SEA OPTS MEET
HELLO HOP
   ELF DYERS
STAG RILE LAW
POP ERA SKI
AGE STEM SEEM
SARAH ASP
   SEE TYING
CHIC MADE DOE
AUTO ICER LOT
NEST TEEN ENS
```

PUZZLE 318

```
DELI WISP  JOB
ARID AREA  EMU
DATA REAR  SIS
     HEN   KITTY
STOOP SCAM
POP  IOTA  PETS
AGE  CURSE ARE
NANA SUET  SUE
     MUTT  CREEK
CREPT SHE
LAD  TALE  BIDE
EGG  EXIT  EVIL
FEE  REPS  LYES
```

PUZZLE 322

```
SPAT  PAW   OPUS
PAGE  BABES DINT
ITEM  UNLIT OTOE
TENPIN ERROR
END OIL DIM PAL
 TATTOOS PINATA
  RANCH STENOS
MENU  OAF  WEPT
AVENGE  FABLE
NICKEL  TRAILER
ELK MAD MUM DEN
  ASPIC BODICE
SARI  SNARL OBOE
OXEN  EERIE SLID
DEFT  DEB   EELS
```

PUZZLE 326

```
ALES  CLOG  SPLAT
BANK  RAIL  AROSE
ANTI  IDLE  TEPEE
SCENTS YEN  SEAM
HER UPS     OUT
  TAG TEASPOONS
AFAR  ENDED  COW
CLIMB ASH   OPERA
EON  UNDUE  RAMP
DESTROYER   SON
   AGO EMU  LAW
CADS NAB UNWISE
OBESE LEIS  ANTE
TUNER ITCH  KEEP
STYLE THEY  ERRS
```

PUZZLE 319

```
GALA  ASKS  WISPS
ACID  LINT  INLET
PROM  ASEA  SNARE
SENIOR ETCH VIE
   RAM LIZ  YELL
BRIEFER  CARE
OAT  DUD   REACTS
OCEAN NIT  CHORE
TEMPOS MUD  PEA
   EGOS GENTEEL
CARD  ROT  SIR
OWE  STOW  ELAPSE
LASSO TEAR COLA
TIEUP HALT ERAS
STEPS EKES DEWY
```

PUZZLE 323

```
AROW  ASH   GUSTO
MINI  ICY   TIPTOP
POLL  LAP   UNSAFE
STYLE MEAT  GUN
    OAK PUBS
CROWSNEST   OILS
HOP  TOWN   AGLOW
USER  WEIGH NANA
MERIT FOOD  MAR
 SAGE AFTERWARD
   SEMI DUE
HEW  ARMY  MACAW
EVILER OER SALE
RESULT BAY  EMIT
DREGS SHE   LETS
```

PUZZLE 327

```
AGOG  CON   FRAT
JEDI  TAROT LICE
ANDS  OPERA INRE
RESTED  LACKED
   WOOF ELK
ABATE BURNT MAP
RULE  SLATE ERE
CREAM ELF   RATER
ERR  ASSET  YANK
DOT  PASSE  DELAY
   OLD TRAY
LAGGED  WEEDER
OVAL  ELITE MAYO
COVE  RAVED ITEM
OWED  MEN   TARP
```

PUZZLE 320

```
CASE  FAT   BLAH
UGLY  ARRAY ROLE
TRUE  COMMA APER
EER  TINY  CRY
REPAINT  CHESTS
   KEG IOTA AWE
STIR  ACHED LOW
THAN  FRIAR MORE
IRK  LADEN  SEND
CUE  ODOR   RUM
GROCER  AEROBIC
 GOO ELSE  EGO
WELL  UNCLE SALE
ALEE  TAROT PROD
SKID  GUT   ADOS
```

PUZZLE 324

```
HATCH SAG   DOVE
ITALIC PIE  OVEN
POTATO  INNOCENT
SPAM  RANTED RUE
  PURSE ROSTER
SOB  MAS   HARE
PRO  PLURAL EYES
ACIDS MIL   SMOKE
TALE  MEMORY YEN
   LEES GIN ODD
DESIGN  FENCE
IRK  GAPING SHOW
TRICYCLE  ENSURE
TODO  EER  ROAMED
ORSO  DAY  TYPOS
```

PUZZLE 328

PUZZLE 321

```
BIB   BAWL  BREW
ADE  LINEUP RILE
LOG  ENDEAR ISLE
SLOWED DUO  DESK
ASTIR  PIE
   SEA SEER SOB
BLEEDS WALK AGO
LAY  TWIRL  ILL
ACE  WRAP   ERODED
BED  HOSE   REV
   HON TEARS
COVE  OWL  HORNET
LIAR  MOUSER ICE
ALSO  YOGURT SOW
DYED  FEND   ENS
```

PUZZLE 325

```
SNOB  VEAL  ACNE
LAMA  TALLY DOES
EVEN  ARMOR SNAP
DYNASTY HIS STY
   NUT VACANT
MACARONI  STEREO
ERE  FOALS RAMP
SENDS ILK  EDICT
ANTE  LAIRS NEE
STILES  IMITATED
PIGEON  FED
DIE  GAP  ELEVATE
ADDS  REDYE ICED
FLEE  CRIES CRAG
TEST  HAND  EELY
```

PUZZLE 329

```
ONE  PAST  CHAT
FIG  ECHO  RODE
FLOWERED   UPON
   IRE DRIEST
CALL   ALES
ACUTE  FEDERAL
VIA  RETRY  EWE
EDUCATE  EPEES
   USER  ODDS
DEARER  ELL
AVID  NOVELIST
TILL  AREA  VEE
ELSE  LEND  YEA
```

541

PUZZLE 330

```
ALS . ARIA . FELT
MET . CASS . ASEA
ATE . TILT . STEM
SURF . NERD . ARE
SPEAR . . IRATER
. SOLO . EDITED
. . CURRENT . .
. BOOTIE . KENO
PRUNES . SNORT
ROT . SKIP . DODO
OGLE . IDEA . DEN
DUES . ELKS . LAG
SETS . REEK . ELS
```

PUZZLE 331

```
PA STI ME . CA P TOR . ST RA P
NO R DIC . ST ER N . RE SP OND
RA RE . P ER CH . PI TCH
MA R IN ER . AN TI QUE . FA RE
. SE VER . CE LL . BUL LY
. CU RT SE Y . ER RO NE OUS
SO LVE . EA SE . B ARB
DA RT . WRE ST LE . BE Y ON D
. STU CK . C AR RY . COM ET
DE CA DE . RE TI RE . SP IN ACH
FER VE NT . IN VE ST . UR G ED
```

PUZZLE 332

1. Spoil, Regal, Apron, Singe.
2. Upend, Chart, Trade, Punch.
3. Count, Touch, Rinse, Shire.
4. Extra, Psalm, Split, Mixer.

PUZZLE 333

```
ATOP . SEAR . TATA
BIDE . VERGE . OWER
OBIS . ENGAGEMENT
DISOWN . TAP . STY
EAT . HOW . ERECT .
. EMIT . DEARTH
SWELL . ZAP . PURE
KAYAK . ERA . RECUR
IRED . NOD . IRKED
STOLID . TROD .
. PETER . EVE . FEZ
JOE . ETA . AROUSE
ORNAMENTAL . NETS
ICER . SCADS . CLOT
NARC . THUD . ESPY
```

PUZZLE 334

Pattern, Fashion, Custom, Practice, Habit, Wont, Tendency.
6TH COLUMN DOWN: Routine

PUZZLE 335

```
ANTI . ALB . IMAM
LOOM . SCALP . TELE
SOUP . ARMOR . SLID
OKRA . TEABAG . OBI
. SPY . IRONIC
ERASURES . RAP .
RAMEN . PLAINTIVE
RIM . CLEANED . CAW
SNOOTIEST . STOLE
. RUB . HEROINES
DISBAR . INN .
INK . LADLES . TOTE
GAIN . ROUGE . IBEX
INTO . YEGGS . NONE
TEST . RES . GETS
```

PUZZLE 336

Jumbo, River, Share, Erect, Hound, Raise, Melon, Tryst, Chart, Motel.

PUZZLE 337

```
SPACE . LIED . ACNE
PILAF . ENVY . BRAS
INEPT . GAIN . SUIT
NEST . DANCER . EVE
. OMELET . EELER
TERRACE . BAY .
ORE . WISP . IDEATE
MAP . BEATS . NOG
BLONDE . LACE . TUG
. AIL . NUGGETS
BEEPS . LOTION .
ADD . CRAVAT . OPTS
SUED . ONER . AMEBA
ACME . CARA . SISAL
LEAN . KITS . SCORE
```

PUZZLE 338

```
CAST . EGG . SILO
AREA . BROAD . ARID
LIES . AGORA . FOOD
FANTAN . FRY . ANNS
. ICE . SITAR .
TEEN . SILICA
PURSED . BOMB . LIT
TROT . INANE . WIDE
AND . FRAY . SHAMED
SELLER . ORBS .
. LUCRE . SOD .
SOFA . TAX . UPROAR
ALUM . ETUDE . OGRE
LIRA . DODOS . BLIP
TOYS . REN . EELS
```

PUZZLE 339

Batter, Double, Dugout, Inning, Lineup, Rookie, Second, Slider, Strike, Umpire.

PUZZLE 340

```
SWISHES . SELF . TAB
COMPARE . TREAD . ADO
REBATED . UNITE . MUG
AFIRE . ASPS . WHALE
PUBS . UNTO . ROYALTY
SLEEPS . ERRED . MESS
. REAM . OPENS .
TETHERS . LOO . ATTAR
OLIOS . SEEKS . PEACE
PLEAT . ERA . EMERGED
. GOONS . TSAR .
SARI . UTTER . SYNODS
PRIESTS . TART . ARIA
AROSE . PUMA . STIRS
DOT . WOOED . DELUGES
EYE . SPREE . AVARICE
SOD . TENS . REPENTS
```

PUZZLE 341

```
JACK . CON . AMID
ALOE . THROB . LOSE
BEST . RABBI . IAMB
. CHILI . SOB .
ALPHABET . QUICHE
SEE . RAT . JUT . OAF
KERNEL . FOE . NEWT
. JAM . FIT . VEX .
CHUG . BAN . PETITE
OUR . LOX . GAR . SAY
GEYSER . CASSETTE
. WIZ . ALTER .
SAKE . OWNER . GAGA
IDEA . IRONY . ODOR
CZAR . YEA . TOOK
```

1-N, 2-T, 3-K, 4-U, 5-Y, 6-G, 7-F, 8-Q, 9-E, 10-A, 11-I, 12-M, 13-B, 14-H, 15-D, 16-O, 17-X, 18-V, 19-P, 20-Z, 21-J, 22-L, 23-R, 24-S, 25-W, 26-C.

PUZZLE 342

1. Offspring, 2. Earthworm, 3. Plaything, 4. Caretaker, 5. Newshound, 6. Racehorse, 7. Archenemy, 8. Evergreen, 9. Nanny goat.
BONUS: Can opener

PUZZLE 343

```
STASH . HALO . NAG
HASHES . EVIL . OWL
ORIENT . MILD . TOO
OAF . APED . HUSKS
. RAYON . CANOES
SCHEMED . MATE .
PLACID . SEW . ALIT
RULED . CUT . PRONE
YETI . BUN . MATURE
. VIED . YACHTED
SERENE . MISTS .
CLODS . NONO . AFT
RUB . TWOS . NIBBLE
ADO . EAVE . STOLES
PET . PRAY . SWEET
```

PUZZLE 344

```
ARM . PLUG . SCOLD
CEE . ARENA . ARMOR
HEN . LOADS . WAIVE
ELUDE . PIKE . STEW
. ERR . DEPTH .
CACTUS . TIE . GNU
HOHO . THY . CANOES
OBEYS . EEL . SERVE
ERASED . WED . AGED
DAD . AIL . DEARER
. STAID . EBB .
COST . LARD . LYRIC
HULAS . BOOZE . ODE
ACUTE . LONER . MEN
THREW . ELSE . PAT
```

PUZZLE 345

```
PEST . FAZE . ISLES
OATH . AWAY . SWEEP
OVER . CAPE . SADLY
REMOTER . DAUB .
. WADER . BESET
ABET . EAR . NIP
SNORTS . GROG . ADO
EGO . ETHICAL . BIN
MET . ROAM . DIALED
IRE . LYE . DUES
SEIZE . NOSED
. CENT . RADICAL
CASES . OPAL . TACO
APART . MITE . OKRA
NEWSY . BEES . REEF
```

PUZZLE 346

```
ARMS  BABY   ACME
LION  EELER  PLAN
ONTO  GRATE  TENT
USER  ARISE  AGE
DELEGATE  TASTER
      ODE  GURU
DEPEND  HIP  SOAP
AMONG  WON  WHITE
MUDD  SEE  NAILER
      EPEE  RIG
SODDEN  TELEGRAM
PAY  ATTIC  RILE
ARIA  RETIE  EGOS
REND  YELPS  EONS
EDGE  DEES  TREY
```

PUZZLE 350

```
WASPS  LAVA   STOP
AGLOW  AMID   PUMA
CRUDE  GEMSTONES
KEG  EVEN  WRENS
YES  TAR  SLOT
     APT  SKY  YANK
COPIES  TIER  DOE
AROMA  LAM  EBONY
PAL  SMOG  CLOSES
ELLS  ARE  LAY
     EDGE  PET  ARC
STORY  HIFI  NOR
NONVERBAL  VAGUE
OGLE  YOYO  ELITE
WAYS  EAST  SLEEP
```

PUZZLE 354

```
DAME  SLIM   STEAL
RUIN  PONE   AWARE
URNS  RIND   NOTED
MAXI  INSIDE
      GIG  AERATE
BOND  BANG  FEND
GUT  EARL  ROTATE
ART  AVAILED  BIB
FEEBLE  EYED  ACT
FARE  NONE  EDGE
USEFUL  CRY
     LEDGER  EACH
CHINA  EAVE  ISLE
AIMER  SLEW  NEAR
TEPEE  TENS  GAPE
```

PUZZLE 347

```
ATOP  SCAM   THINS
SOAR  ALLY   AUDIT
SORE  RUES   DEITY
     SLIEST  OWL
PASTA  ITS  TIE
AXIOM  ITCHIEST
PET  ANNA  APE
ADES  UNION  REVS
EAR  LAKE  RAP
COARSEST  PHASE
PAR  KEY  EASED
URN  ELOPER
REARS  LOBE  PILE
SETUP  IRON  EVIL
ENEMY  DEED  DYES
```

PUZZLE 351

```
PASTA   ACT   DEBS
ACCORD  SHH   AREA
TRANCE  TOE   MERV
HEMS  STEREO  CEE
     SPARE  MITTS
GAB  EER  PER
AGO  TROT  ANKLET
GOT  ATWAR  EAR
AGHAST  OVAL  ARE
WEE  AGE  FLY
MODEM  SKIRT
ONE  IMPALA  LAVA
LILY  OIL  PRIMER
TOTE  VEE  HERMIT
SNAP  ELS  PEONY
```

PUZZLE 355

```
BETA   PICK   ACME
AMEN   AVOID  WHEN
RUNG   NEWLY  LITE
ESSES  HOES   LAM
     LAPSE  ICILY
MEASURER  FRO
UPS  NEEDLE  PARE
FEE  ASP  AID  JAY
FEAR  TSETSE  ACE
     EGO  LETTERED
HEAVE  DRYER
ENS  LOPE  RASPY
ASTI  BURRO  SALE
RUIN  INLAW  EVEN
TERN  TYPE  REDS
```

PUZZLE 348

```
FIB   PALM   OARS
ODE   COPIES PLOT
OLE   ATTEST TOGA
DEFER  SHAH  NUN
      APED  RAGGED
ACTS  ARCHERY
WHITESALE  AMASS
LAD  REPEATS  WHO
STEER  EAVESDROP
     ROOSTER  AYES
SAFARI  SNIT
AIR  SLOP  CEDAR
BLIP  ENRAGE  EKE
LEER  DEEDED  LID
EDDY  SPOT  INS
```

PUZZLE 352

```
MOATS  ABS   CHEFS
IDIOT  PIC   AISLE
DEMUR  EAR   TEPEE
     GEM  SAWN  YAK
MOHAIR  MAAM
SAP  KNOB  SPECS
IRE  SITED  SORES
RIND  SOBER  WANT
SNEER  ROPER  DIE
ADMIT  POPE  LOW
OVAL  TEMPER
APT  EGOS  LOU
BLEAT  FLU  TRESS
LUNGE  TOM  EERIE
ESTER  YEP  REACT
```

PUZZLE 356

```
LOAFS   TOT   URGE
ENTRAP  ADO   PALM
STOOGE  COW   SCAB
SOP  ADORN  HERE
     ALTO  HOSED
KHAKI  GARNET
EERIER  FAIR  HEM
GRIN  OWING  BEAU
SOD  EYER  HARASS
     POSTER  WARES
CHURN  UGLY
LONE  PROBE  WOO
ARCS  LAX  EBBING
IDLE  AGE  KEENER
MEET  YEN  GEESE
```

PUZZLE 349

```
THANK   IRK   PANE
ROWING  CUE   AVOW
ELOPER  EGG   PIPE
ELK  WORD  ADES
DYE  WIT  DAY
HENCE  UNABLE
LANES  HAPPY  RUN
APOSTLE  LEOPARD
REV  AISLE  NODES
DRAFTS  EASED
LET  ASP  JOG
TRUE  REAP  OWL
IONS  HON  DOMINO
LATH  AWE  ERASER
TROY  WED  ENTRY
```

PUZZLE 353

```
RITAS   TBS   EVAN
IRENES  WHALE GIGI
NADINE  AYRES ANTA
DENY  NEATNESS
NEMO  DANE  PIA
AVERY  TEPEE  GRAPE
MARCEAU  PARE  ENID
ANDRESS  ESCAPE
DEA  TEEN  EARP  SEN
RYDELL  GILLIAN
ARES  APER  FEDERAL
GESTE  ELMER  ELISE
VCR  AMEN  LOAN
SERGEANT  IDOL
ILER  PEARL  SOAPER
NINA  ELLIE  ENCINO
KATY  LEG  GEESE
```

PUZZLE 357

```
STAB   CHIN   NYC
TINY   GRADED YEA
RAGE   ROSIER RAN
ARE  ECHO  ABORT
WARILY  TRIO
NASAL  ANIMAL
MURKY  KIWI  LOBE
AGE  BISON  REV
SLAP  INTO  SEEDY
TYPIST  SLOPE
NOES  PANTED
PASTA  TOUT  WAY
ILL  PLEASE  RISE
TOE  YANKED  ICER
YEW  MOSS  GELS
```

543

PUZZLE 358

```
MAMBO ASS  MOSS  AGOG
EXILE SUP  IDEA  PAPA
ELMER HER  SEATBELTS
TEEN  ACT  LIE
   DRAG WORM NEPHEW
BASEBALLTEAMS   AIDE
RAN ALTO SAGA  UNFIT
EGG DYERS TIDES  ITS
AGED   DUB   CARED
PYRAMID MOB  MARINAS
   DOMES GUY GOSH
PUB OPALS TAKEN  ICE
ORALS TOTS RILE  SOD
OGRE  SHORTANDSWEET
LENTIL PAIR  SETS
   NOD  IRE   TREK
INTENTION NAP  HEAVE
NEER  HARE ALE EERIE
STAR  SLED SPA SMELL
```

PUZZLE 359

```
ACRE  BRAS  SAVER
DRUM  LULL  CRONE
SYNC OBOE  AMUSE
  EBB HEWN  CUD
TREE OATH  WHEY
FEE LAW  SOFA
AMP LYES    ISLE
SPA BESIEGE  ELF
TYPO  TOOL  AIR
  EYED NODSTY
SCAR ERAS  EPEE
TAM SNAG  PRO
EPOCH MIRE  PAST
VENUE ALOE  PLEA
EDGED SEER  YEAR
```

PUZZLE 360

```
AYES   FLED   TAR
SOLO FROLIC  ARE
HUFF LESSER  BRA
  ACUTE TAILED
TORSO    DRESS
AGO SPAS BLAST
PRO TALC LET
SETS PLATE ELKS
 PIE LEAD ONE
 PRIOR PETE FEE
CRIED    EATEN
LADDIE POOPS
AND NATURE TAGS
ICE EVILER IDEA
MEN  EELS  ROMP
```

PUZZLE 361

```
TICS  WEB  WISP
ACHE CARED ECHO
LOAN ORATE DIAL
ENTITY SANG ELK
  TOO   AORTA
CHERUB SMALL
OAR TASTED DUNE
ALE  TIRED LOW
TODO ELATED TOE
 DUSKY RESINS
ACIDS    AIM
URN EAST IDEALS
RIND FLINT STAT
ASEA TAMES TUTU
SPRY  WET  AMEN
```

PUZZLE 362

```
SCAR  SPAR  SPITS
TUTU URGE  TULIP
ARID BOLD  ANKLE
TOT ANEW WIT
  WAD RICOTTA
EDGING JUG POOP
MOANS TAN VAGUE
ISLE FOR WIZARD
REAPPLY CON
  TOO AHOY SAD
HAM SWORE LOTTO
ELECT IDEA GOOP
MELEE NEST ROLE
SEDER KNEE ELLS
```

PUZZLE 363

```
ATTIC  CAPE  VETO
LARVA OXEN  AMID
GREEN NERD  LURE
ASK ODD  IRISES
  HERO  AVID
 CREDO RUED  FRO
HOAX OPEN  POEM
ONCE PINTO AXLE
AGED  VEST DEAN
RAD AVOW HARDY
  GRIT MERE
CALICO  ORE  YAM
OWED LULU NIECE
DEAD AMEN ANTIS
ESPY SPIT SKIDS
```

PUZZLE 364

```
HAIR  COB  SLOT
ALOE OUI  TALE
MENU PROTRUDE
  STY  WIDEN
SHEER  TOP
CAP AMIE EAST
ARE MACAW RIO
BEEP DELI ELM
 ATE  PEAKS
POISE  YEN
OBSTACLE EMIT
ROLE OIL  MINI
KEEL GEL  YOKE
```

PUZZLE 365

```
SEMI  THAN  SOP  ASP
OPEN YETI MOORS  BOO
DIRT PREP UNZIP  LAD
ACCRUE  PAD EVADERS
 HOP JAIL DATA
BRA SAUCEPAN TUMBLE
EON CULTS LABEL  OER
APT ANY THINE AMBER
RESULT  OVAL  ASKS
 REST TIE TONY
PANG  ODES ROOTED
ARIES GOATS EBB IVY
PIG PSALM PERIL MAN
ADHERE ESCALATE ENE
 KICK  ARMS  SUP
PIMENTO INK STRIPS
ADE GIANT LATE BEAU
SEA SOLOS EXIT ACRE
SAT  NAG  DENS NEED
```

PUZZLE 366

```
SPAT  ACTS  URBAN
HEIR CHAP  LEASE
ARMY MICA  NIGHT
PIE PELT  RAG
ELDER LIVE  NAME
 ROT COLA CON
SAKE RASCAL ORE
TEA LOT ATE RAM
ERR EDIBLE ONLY
RIM IDLE DIN
NEAR ETCH CEASE
 OWN  LOPE  LEA
ADAGE FOAL EGIS
REVUE EURO LAZE
TWEED EDDY FEEL
```

QUOTATION: A friend might well be reckoned the masterpiece of nature.

PUZZLE 367

1. Clash, Clasp, Clamp, Clump, Slump, Stump.

2. Peony, Phony, Phone, Shone, Shore, Share.

3. Chimp, Chime, Crime, Grime, Gripe, Grape.

4. Bring, Brink, Brick, Crick, Chick, Check.

PUZZLE 368

```
OPALS   SCOWS
RODEOS UTOPIA
SIENNA  SITARS
  DARKEN  HES
DAB TOASTY
ELEGANT  AJAR
BOLA GYM KALE
STAG  DAISIES
  ARCING  LET
DRS IODINE
RATHER AIRBAG
ORIOLE STRATA
PERES   ESTER
```

PUZZLE 369

```
ALSO  REC PACA
DOTE OWE  REAP
EVER PERFORMS
PER FERAL APE
TREMOR MATTES
 SOAR WITHER
  DEBACLE
 CEASED AMMO
YAMMER SNEAKS
ERE EAVED RAT
ARRESTED MAYO
TOGA ETA ICER
STET SON  LADE
```

PUZZLE 370

```
RAJAH  SNAG  CEL
ADORE QUILL  AGO
MOTOR UNCLE  MOD
 SODA HEN  PIG
TORE ALTER  USE
IRE STIR GHOST
FAD PATE YAP
FLOUR YAW  REFER
 RIM DOME  APE
TANGO LOAM  TIE
ZEE  NEEDY PECK
ERR ASP MOVE
BRA LOOSE INANE
ROT TOXIN ENDOW
ARE ONYX  WEDGE
```

1-I, 2-U, 3-J, 4-X, 5-H, 6-L, 7-O, 8-W, 9-K, 10-Q, 11-M, 12-Y, 13-V, 14-P, 15-G, 16-N, 17-E, 18-B, 19-T, 20-F, 21-A, 22-C, 23-S, 24-Z, 25-D, 26-R.

544

PUZZLE 371

1. A handful of patience is worth more than a bushel of brains.

2. Shine like a light, but don't flash at people like lightning.

PUZZLE 372

E	R	A	L		H	E	R	O		A	L	A	S
B	O	L	A		A	T	O	L	L		G	I	R	T
B	U	S	Y	A	S	A	B	E	E		E	V	E	R
S	T	O	U	T			M	A	R	I	N	A	
			P	O	W	E	R	F	U	L		D	A	W
E	L	S		M	E	T	E	O	R	I	C	
G	O	A	T		V	E	T	O		N	I	C	H	E
O	F	F	I	C	E	R		T	O	E	N	A	I	L
S	T	E	E	L		N	A	A	N		E	R	G	S
	D	E	R	A	N	G	E	D		S	H	E	
B	E	D		F	I	L	T	E	R	E	D	
A	D	A	P	T	S			L	A	T	H	E	
S	E	R	A		K	E	T	T	L	E	D	R	U	M
S	M	E	W		Y	A	H	O	O		D	E	L	I
O	A	R	S		T	Y	R	O		Y	E	A	R

PUZZLE 373

A	N	T	I		M	A	E	S		C	H	A	T
T	O	R	N		T	I	B	E	T		H	O	M	E
O	R	A	L		E	N	U	R	E		A	P	E	X
M	A	N	E	G	E		T	I	P		P	E	R	T
			S	T	E	M		S	E	P	A	L	
A	R	C		M	E	T		R	E	C	A	P	S
N	O	R			D	U	D		S	H	I	E	L	D
O	M	I	T	S		G	U	M		E	N	J	O	Y
A	P	P	E	A	R		B	O	P		O	P	E	
	S	T	A	R	E	R		B	A	R		R	E	S
		M	I	L	A	N		I	O	T	A	
G	O	D	S		A	P	E		N	E	A	T	L	Y
O	B	I	T		P	I	V	O	T		L	I	E	U
L	O	V	E		S	E	E	R	S		O	V	A	L
F	E	A	R		E	R	R	S		N	E	N	E

PUZZLE 374

1. Hypnotic, 2. Solidify, 3. Wondrous, 4. Infinite, 5. Cardinal, 6. Thorough, 7. Cupboard, 8. Disclaim, 9. Granular.

PUZZLE 375

W	A	R	D		D	A	I	S		T	O	L	L
A	L	A	E		H	O	R	D	E		E	R	I	E
F	E	R	N		A	N	I	S	E		M	E	E	T
T	E	E	T	E	R	E	D		S	A	P	
			O	D	E		S	A	L	O	O	N
T	H	I	N	E		B	O	W	S		P	E	A
T	H	A	N		S	E	L	L		O	A	T	E	R
Y	O	L	K		T	R	U	E	D		S	I	D	E
P	R	E	Y	S		O	R	D	O		H	O	E	S
E	N	S		C	A	D	S		U	P	E	N	D
	S	T	R	O	D	E		O	B	I	
		A	W	E		T	A	T	T	O	O	E	D
E	L	M	S		P	R	O	S	E		W	A	R	E
S	O	A	P		T	I	G	E	R		E	S	N	E
P	O	N	Y		S	P	A	S		S	T	E	M

PUZZLE 376

1. Brocade, 2. Chiffon, 3. Chenille, 4. Corduroy, 5. Burlap, 6. Canvas.
BONUS: Velour

PUZZLE 377

C		A	L	L		D	E	C	A	D	E	S		A		B		B	A
A	R	E		L	A	T	E	N	T	L	Y		S	P		O	U	T	S
H	O	G	S		G	I	N	G	E	R		O	N		S
P	R	O	T	E	S	T	O	R		S	T	E	A	R	I	N	
		A	R	I	A			R	O	T	I	N	I
M	A	S	C	O	T		E	S	P	R	I	T		S	E	R	E	N	E
C	U	T	I	E		L	A	M	A
	M	E	T	A	L		L	I	T	E	R	A	T	U	R	E
G	R	A	S		S	O	P	H	I	S	M		M	A	N	G	L	E
O	U	T	E	R		E	R	R	A	T	A		B	O	A	S
T		R	O	U	T		S	E	N	D		A	T	E

PUZZLE 378

What common English verb becomes its own past tense simply by rearranging its letters?

Eat becomes ate.

PUZZLE 379

O	P	A	L		P	A	L	E		G	A	B
L	A	V	A		I	T	E	R		E	L	O
E	R	A	D	I	C	A	T	E		T	A	G
			L	O	T			A	S	I	S
O	F	T	E	N		C	H	O	I	R	
R	A	H	S		S	H	I	N	D	I	G
O	R	R		M	O	O	S	E		D	I	P
	M	O	H	A	I	R	S		C	O	V	E
	W	I	E	L	D		W	A	F	E	R
H	O	S	T			G	A	S	
A	D	O		P	O	L	I	S	H	O	F	F
L	O	U		A	R	A	L		E	D	I	E
O	R	T		N	E	W	T		W	E	N	D

PUZZLE 380

E	L	O	N		A	D	A	M		O	R	A
B	A	B	E		C	O	R	A		L	O	W
B	L	O	W	S	M	O	K	E		D	U	E
S	A	L	T	I	E	R		W	A	F	T	S
		O	P	S		H	E	E	L	
G	O	I	N		P	A	S	S	A	G	E
A	W	N		W	A	I	S	T		M	I	L
R	E	A	L	I	G	N		T	E	N	D
	F	I	N	E		E	Y	E	
P	I	L	E	D		T	R	A	M	P	L	E
O	D	A		S	P	A	R	K	P	L	U	G
L	E	S		O	R	D	O		T	A	N	G
A	S	H		R	E	A	R		S	T	A	Y

PUZZLE 381

A	R	E		H	E	S		S	P	A
B	O	X		A	G	E		T	O	W
S	W	A	L	L	O	W	T	A	I	L
		G	E	T		N	O	G	
M	A	G	I			Y	E	T	I
O	W	E					M	I	L
P	E	R	T			S	A	C	K
	A	I	D		W	I	N	
D	E	T	E	R	I	O	R	A	T	E
O	R	E		U	R	N		G	A	L
G	A	S		M	E	T		E	N	S

PUZZLE 382

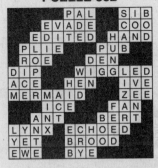

PUZZLE 383

PUZZLE 384

1. Pipe, 2. Here, 3. Oboe, 4. Tact, 5. Open, 6. Gust, 7. Risk, 8. Arid, 9. Pool, 10. Hone, 11. Elan, 12. Rely.
OUTER RING: Photographer
THIRD RING: Processional

PUZZLE 385

PUZZLE 386

1. Arch, Charm, Cram, Carom, Roam, Major.

2. Bowl, Elbow, Lobe, Noble, Lone, Novel.

3. Tray, Party, Pray, Raspy, Spar, Sharp.

4. Neon, Tenon, Tone, Onset, Sent, Stein.

5. Rock, Croak, Rack, Creak, Race, Carve.

6. Fast, Feast, Sate, Stage, Gate, Great.

545

PUZZLE 387

PUZZLE 391

PUZZLE 395

PUZZLE 388

OUT: 1. Netted, 3. Actor, 5. Racer, 7. Iterate, 9. Septa, 11. Ogre, 13. Fed.
IN: 14. Defer, 12. Goat, 10. Peseta, 8. Retire, 6. Carrot, 4. Cadet, 2. Ten.

PUZZLE 392

Best friends on Sesame Street
BERT AND ERNIE

PUZZLE 396

PUZZLE 393

PUZZLE 389

PUZZLE 397

PUZZLE 394

PUZZLE 390

1. Fore, Fare, Hare, Hard, Hand.

2. Foul, Fool, Food, Fond, Find, Fine, Line.

3. Sand, Band, Bend, Bead, Beam, Team, Tram, Trap.

4. Slam, Seam, Seat, Beat, Bent, Bunt, Bunk, Dunk.

PUZZLE 398

546

PUZZLE 399

```
CHIC WATTS AMMO
LOCH ALOHA FOUR
ALEE SITUP LODE
MERE GEM PONDS
    SCAN BOLA
  BREAD MYTHS
BOA RAFFLE OAF
ORB SPIRALS RYE
WEB TROWEL SEW
RIFLE TAMER
  JUDO ESPY
BEFOG AGE SNAG
EVER STORM EASE
TIED AERIE LIEN
ALLS GREET FLAT
```

PUZZLE 403

```
HOBO PAPA CAST
ANEW NASAL OILY
RYAN UNTIL WRAP
EXTENT IRON EVE
   RIM REWARDED
GRASPED DEMO
AIL GUM DESIRE
SPINS GOB DECAY
PETITE DEB ERE
   CART ELAPSED
SHOETREE OWL
TOT EARL CLAMPS
ARTS TRICK COAT
IDEA IOTAS EDGE
NERD CREW DEEM
```

PUZZLE 407

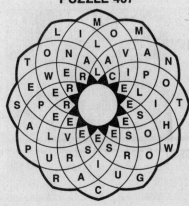

PUZZLE 400

```
ACME NASAL DOFF
BOOS AGILE ARIA
HUTS MANAGEMENT
OPE MET SIR SEE
RELEASE OAF
  BRA NONSENSE
LAMB KNEW EDENS
UKE SEAWEED RAP
BINGO PERM EDGY
ENDANGER PIE
  BAR STORAGE
OWN TOM TIN GUN
PRIVATEEYE ALIT
TACO TOLLS ROSE
SPEW OWLET EWER
```

PUZZLE 404

```
ACRE SAPS PITS
SOON AXLES ECHO
PSST TIARA GIRL
STEEL SNIFF CEE
   RIG EEL LAD
ODD CARPS USED
PRICKLES SEW
TYPO ADAPT ALOE
   WAS LEAPYEAR
VAST SMALL IRE
KIT OWN LOT
HOT POETS DRIFT
ALAS RERAN ASEA
KICK DROVE SLAB
INKY STEW HERS
```

PUZZLE 408

```
ITEM POET CHAT
CARA VALVE RICE
OPAL ENDER OGRE
NESTLE ENRICHED
   EAR REIN
GADGET REPAID
HAD DOG RUINED
EMOTE MOW TRACE
PERILS TEA PAW
RECITE BRATTY
   TANG DRY
UMBRELLA EMPIRE
POLE EATEN IDOL
OVEN SCOOT SEAM
NEWT TERN TADS
```

PUZZLE 401

```
ELF ESS YON BOP
BEE APT ANI EWE
BIZARRE KEN TEA
   BLEEP JAW
JAMB ALE SALIVA
AGEOLD RHO AXIL
MOTTO SIDESTEP
   DEPOSAL
SPACEMAN SLEPT
ARCH INN TEETHE
COQUET EGO VAIN
   UMP LARGE
KOI OFF ZEALOUS
EAR COO ERR ASK
ARE HEX ROB FEY
```

1-B, 2-N, 3-S, 4-Z, 5-P, 6-D, 7-X, 8-V,
9-K, 10-O, 11-U, 12-W, 13-T, 14-M,
15-Y, 16-F, 17-J, 18-H, 19-R, 20-G,
21-L, 22-E, 23-I, 24-Q, 25-A, 26-C.

PUZZLE 405

```
THAT SOSO JAVA
RICH SHUCK OVAL
ERNE TENOR GOLD
KEENER CLAN IVE
   COILED ODDER
ESSENCE SIDE
BOO STAT NECTAR
BULB ENACT KALE
SPOOFS BREW MOM
   NUTS ARRESTS
AMENS CAGIER
LAY EARN ONEWAY
UNIT WAGER COLA
MINE EPEES TRIP
SAGE DELL SETS
```

PUZZLE 409

```
OGRE LUGS PLAN
FLEW INLAW AONE
FACE BEIGE GATE
ERA BRAD ERODED
REPHRASE DID
   AIRY DEBATED
VALLEY OUR IVY
ICIER TWO EERIE
SEE OIL NAVELS
EDUCATE BARE
   ANT DETESTED
BLONDE RAID WAR
LOAN RHINO PITA
ONTO SEVEN ANEW
BEST REDS DENS
```

PUZZLE 402

```
CLOMP GERM CAST
HIKER AQUA ALLY
IRATE PUNT SOUP
PAY PAPA ADHERE
  LAPEL DUE
COLORED COBWEB
ABIDES FAR NOD
ROLES JUT RADIO
SEA BAN MEREST
  SCREAM DESIRES
   ART TIMID
TSHIRT AGOG BUD
AKIN LAKE NOISE
GIVE EXES EATEN
SPED DENT DRESS
```

PUZZLE 406

```
TBAR CASH AWARD
HOPE AXLE FAVOR
ORES REAR TRADE
UNROBE BOA SEA
   REF SIB ATOM
AMATEUR CLEF
WAG LET ELAPSE
ERODE DUB FROND
DEGREE GEL LUG
   ALSO GEOLOGY
CRAM PRO GAL
HUG YAP ERASER
ADAGE NEON MIDI
METAL GRAD ARID
PREYS EATS SETS
```

PUZZLE 410

```
ARCH SWAM WRAP
MARE WHOSE HERE
BRAN HONKS AMEN
LED SOW ABROAD
ELL PANIC AFT
YETI NARY EGG
   ANT SPAS SEE
PLUG RATES STEM
RAN SAGA HOE
OWE OPEN AWED
   AWL STUNT NET
SHREDS BUS GAY
CONE TALON WARP
ABED ARIAS OGLE
BODY BEET KEYS
```

PUZZLE 411

```
PAVE  ABLE  STEP   EBB
OPAL  GRIN  LIMIT  COY
DENS  LASTMINUTE   ONE
   EGO  PROD  AMENDS
PAS  OWN  IDEAL  PRO
OUTDO  ODE  GET  AMID
STAR  NOISY  ADHESIVE
TOGA  EKE  ORIGIN  CON
  PEW  TIDINESS  ART
   TIER   REC   UGLY
PIN  ASSAILED  HER
OAT  SPARSE  IVE  ACRE
PRESERVE  DRAIN  PREY
EARL  YEN  ELS  THINE
EEL  DARED  ADA  BED
WISDOM  ALES  INN
HOT  WATERMELON  URGE
ATE  STOVE  MARE  LOAN
TAD  HOER  SPED  LESS
```

PUZZLE 415

```
ATTIC  FUEL  AGED
CHINA  AMMO  CAVE
HUNKS  SPUN  CLEF
EGG  HATS  GREASY
   PEWS  SHIP
  DRAWL  PHANTOM
ORAL  FLUNG  LOW
WON  ERRANDS  DUE
LOG  NEONS  AINT
  PERSIST  AIRED
   AUNT  HIDE
BABIED  DALE  PRO
ARID  EYER  AVOID
WIRE  EONS  LASSO
LADD  RUSH  SNEER
```

PUZZLE 419

```
LABOR  SIT  MAMAS
AWARE  PLY  AWOKE
TAKEN  ALP  MEDIA
EYE  TIC  EBB  ENS
   WAGES  ION
DRILL  PAN  ATOP
DEAN  OPAL  TELE
AVID  OUTER  UNIT
MIDI  MUSE  REVS
ELSE  GAL  IRATE
   RAY  ANGEL
APT  UMP  AND  APE
MOURN  ADS  DARER
ORBIT  RAT  EXTRA
KEEPS  SPY  NESTS
```

PUZZLE 412

```
ATLAS  LIPS  YAWL
CREDO  ORAL  ARIA
HANDY  CITY  CENT
EGGS  SASH  SHAKE
SIT  AWL  APT
CHILI  ABRASIVE
  NOMADIC  FAS
ALINE  PAL  POSTS
NET  DEPLORE
DISTRUST  WARDS
  WEE  KEY  ROB
STRIP  POOR  SOLE
NOON  HARP  TONAL
IDLE  ONCE  ELECT
TOLD  TEAK  NODES
```

PUZZLE 416

```
SAGS  FAB  WEST
TRIO  GUILT  AXLE
ADDS  ORDER  SCAM
NODOFF  DYE  LIP
DRY  REAP  GRUNT
  AORTA  AGES
APED  ARCS  NICE
SILO  ALTOS  OVEN
HEIR  GLIB  WEED
  MEMO  ARSON
SLIDE  LAMA  LAD
CON  TUG  AFLAME
ROAD  PIPER  OPEN
UNTO  SNORT  BENS
BYES  SIR  ELSE
```

PUZZLE 420

```
CREW  SASH  FLO
LORE  IDEA  RIM
ACME  MEALTIME
SKI  FIST  REIN
PENCIL  SLANTS
  REHEAT  ANDS
   ARRESTS
SYNC  ETHICS
PLANET  RETOLD
LOPE  YVES  WAR
APPLEPIE  CAVE
ZEE  GENT  ORES
ADD  ODES  ODDS
```

PUZZLE 413

```
CRAB  PROP  CALMS
LAIR  ROLE  OCEAN
OKRA  OBIT  NEATO
DESIST  VAIN  PEW
   SUE  ELDER
STENCH  SECEDED
VOW  TOY  STARVE
ALIBI  NIB  SLAIN
SANEST  PIC  FLY
TRELLIS  BOASTS
   TAMPA  APT
HOW  NEER  REARED
AWARD  ERAS  POLO
REVUE  CARE  LOST
DRYER  HYMN  EKES
```

PUZZLE 417

```
ASEA  ATLAS  TALC
MAXI  RIATA  AFAR
PRAM  RENEW  LORE
SAME  ARK  GLOVE
  IRON  YAWN  TAP
CON  EGO  SOUP
EVE  REMOTE  EDGE
DARK  EAR  NEON
ELSE  ALTARS  TAD
  GALE  YUP  ELS
ASP  FETA  SYNC
CARET  MAT  ATOP
RUED  ATOLL  MIME
ICED  CAUSE  EVEN
DENY  ERROR  SEND
```

PUZZLE 421

```
GASH  HAND  HOP
ANTE  ICER  ALA
TOIL  SCRAMMED
EARL   EDGE
   OWLS  STATS
SAN  OUST  ECHO
PROBER  AGREED
ALOE  EIRE  SEA
TONIC  NORM
   GOAT  ODOR
DILEMMAS  NAPA
ARE  MIKE  EVEN
BED  ADEN  TENT
```

PUZZLE 414

```
SHAD  HOST  STARE
PUMA  ANTE  PUREE
ALIT  SEEM  EXCEL
RADIOS  EPIC  SLY
   NIL  ROCKY
EAGLET  SELECT
GAG  DUG  RELOAD
EVENT  GOB  SLICE
TENORS  ORE  NOW
  STREAM  ACCESS
   MAMAS  OUR
HEM  TENT  NEEDLE
ALIBI  TODO  CRAB
ISSUE  LOOM  TOMB
RESTS  EDGY  SPAS
```

PUZZLE 418

```
SCAM  RIGS  PEAKS
TODO  ECRU  ISLET
RUMP  FEARLESSLY
APIECE  SEA  OPE
YET  ARMS  BOB
   KEY  POPPA
TENCENTS  STOLEN
OVAL  CHIRP  TENT
REMADE  PURCHASE
ENEMY   DEE
PEP  MEAD  HAD
OFT  EWE  DEVISE
DRAWBRIDGE  IRKS
DECAY  LIAR  LEEK
STORE  DAYS  ERRS
```

PUZZLE 422

```
  CAN  PLATO  LIE
SALE  LASER  EVEN
CADES  ACHED  AYRES
AGE  MOZE  NERD  IVE
RAT  IDA  CARE  TEEM
   ATE  BAG  AMI
CATCH  MANE  ATEAM
UNIT  LISE  MARISKA
PET  REES  BANK  TIN
ITALIAN  SIRE  SEND
DANES  GETS  PUSSY
   SET  RAE  CON
ARAS  EVAN  BOW  DAM
LEN  SEEN  DUDE  IRE
ANDIE  GOREN  LLOYD
EYRE  ALIEN  LINE
SAD  SANDY  STE
```

548

PUZZLE 423

```
CONDO  ETAS  SAGA
ALIEN  NENE  ENOW
SILTS  GATE  RIAL
HOSE  OER  DWELLS
    CANNY  YIN
TATTED      PECS
TIN  EWER  RELATE
EAVE  AROSE  YUAN
CRISPY  OPTS  SIS
ALTO      RIOTER
    ERE  VIEWS
EGRETS  INS  ETCH
FROM  TICK  STOLE
TILE  OVAL  ASTIR
SPED  PYRE  PEEPS
```

PUZZLE 428

```
BASE  SODAS  ALAS
ICER  ANILE  PERM
THREATENED  SAGE
SEE  LIRA  USEFUL
    PAS  ACT  YET
ATTEST      OPERA
FARE  EMIT  AGORA
APORT  ALL  WAXER
RADII  KEYS  PENT
    EGGED  TRENDY
ATE  HER  DUO
FIESTA  DEFT  SIS
OLLA  RAINFOREST
REES  ERASE  OTTO
ERRS  DELED  WISP
```

PUZZLE 432

```
HAIR  RIOT  SPIRE
OGLE  ENVY  PALED
PELT  SNAP  IRKED
   ASH  LOIN  SLY
AORTAS      MAG
MIX  APT  SPLINT
ART  RERAN  LAID
ABASE  OWE  ELUDE
MAIL  LEERY  GIN
GLOBAL  ZEE  HES
    WED  EGRETS
HOG  ADES  ASS
EVANS  CHAR  SAME
RELET  HOLD  EXAM
BRATS  ODES  SETS
```

PUZZLE 424

Wag, Wan, Way, Web, Wee, Wet, Woe, Wok, Wow.

PUZZLE 429

1. Broil, 2. Memorabilia, 3. Mire, 4. Mare, 5. Realm.

PUZZLE 433

```
WAG  DEBT  BATS  REVS
EER  AVERS  ACHE  ARIA
ERA  MEDIA  GROW  NEAP
PITA  ARM  OUSTS
SEEN  BELIEFS  OOMPH
   TIRES  RASH  SMILE
MAGICAL  ERR  ESS  DIM
AROSE  COY  ARTERIES
SEA  RAVING  NOOSE
TALC  PERSONNEL  DUET
   ATTIC  RAISES  PLY
TORTILLA  OPE  CEDAR
AGE  LYE  DUE  ABALONE
CRAWL  DEAN  PRIDE
TEPEE  ENDURED  COPE
   ARDOR  SKI  TREY
LEAP  AKIN  EMOTE  ADE
ALTO  FREE  SERUM  TAR
GLEN  TART  REBS  ELS
```

PUZZLE 425

```
S CHE ME    SC AMP    HAR ROW
A SS ETS  TR UFF LE  LA BOR ED
GE M   DR EAD   ST AFF  S
  EN VI ABLE   IN SO FA R
  SO BER   CH AR ITY   S EAL
  CA RS   C OR KS  ACA CIA
BEG S   DO ODA DS   CRU DE
AN TE N NA   CA SH ME RES
  ES TE EM   BAR ES   PL USH
TRE STLE  BAR ON ET  SL END ER
MOR ALE      GO ES   ABS ENT S
```

PUZZLE 426

```
    AMPULE          LARGE
RAMP    EPOCH    MOLAR
SCRAM    CHARM    RIFLE
AMOEBA    ARMADA    LEAF
    BANDANA    ATOLL
    HUSBAND    ACROBAT
```

PUZZLE 430

```
OAT  TROD  SCRAP
ALE  RAZE  EQUATE
FLATIRON  GUTTER
   AMEN  BOA
WALL  EWE  BANJO
ASYLUM  ODD  POOR
SHE  KICKER  STYE
   KENO  COPE
SARI  CUCKOO  FRO
EXIT  ERA  LIQUID
TEPEE  SPA  URGE
   VIE  MAGI
POETIC  YULETIDE
ENLACE  ASEA  NOG
TEMPT  PEER  KEG
```

1-U, 2-S, 3-Z, 4-Q, 5-N, 6-Y, 7-L, 8-E, 9-T, 10-F, 11-I, 12-G, 13-D, 14-A, 15-K, 16-O, 17-M, 18-P, 19-W, 20-R, 21-B, 22-H, 23-C, 24-J, 25-X, 26-V.

PUZZLE 434

```
ODDS  BUST  SCALE
WEEP  UNTO  ELFIN
LAME  LIEN  RITES
SNOWPLOW  RUN
   EEN  HUMIDOR
CHART  GYM  CARE
SHAG  ISLE  GIN
ORSO  NEONS  AGED
NOT  GOAT  YENS
AMEN  RAM  AVERT
RENEWAL  FRO
   SOP  HOTWATER
PESTO  EARL  LODE
AGILE  BITE  GRIP
ROPER  BRED  ANTS
```

PUZZLE 427

```
ANTI  BATT  PASS
ROOM  AGORA  OLIO
TEMP  TENOR  WELD
SLEUTH  EWE  EELS
   RAT  DETER
OPENUP  LEASED
EVE  BOG  STAVES
REEDY  DAM  SWILL
ENVIES  BAT  CAY
SESAME  CRUSTY
   PHONY  ARK
ISLE  ODE  GEISHA
RUIN  TENSE  ICON
ELMS  HATED  NAME
DUPE  RACY  GREW
```

PUZZLE 431

1. Everybody laughs in the same language.
2. The sweetest of all sounds is praise.

PUZZLE 435

```
CHEF  WASP  SLUR
HULL  ARMED  AONE
ILLUSTRATE  FAIL
PAS  CEES  CRAFTY
   HARSH  OAR
CHALET  TYPISTS
THAWED  BUS  POP
RINKS  TAB  PLATE
OLD  DAY  SEARED
DISCARD  JESTER
   LIE  MONTH
CAMERA  AIDE  MAR
OVER  DINNERTIME
LINK  SKIER  ODES
ADDS  EARS  MINT
```

PUZZLE 436

```
RAVELS ARTS ASK
ITALIC DEAL BAN
DORMER MAXI IVE
SPY  EYELID DOE
  PREEN CEDERS
PATIENT  BARE
ALIGNS TUB ALOT
WORST TAD ADAGE
SEEK YEN ASPIRE
IDEA DREADED
TWINES WOMAN
RAN CHURCH AGE
OFT RISE OPTION
OER EVEN LOADED
PRO EARS EDGERS
```

PUZZLE 440

```
SOSO BLAST CARL
AVOW RATIO OBEY
RAINFOREST HEAR
ILL RIG  LADLE
   CELEB LOB
GLUE  IMAGINE
BEATS ZOOS TORN
ANT TOO WHO IRE
TIES WORN RESOW
EXTREME  DEER
RID BALER
CLAIM  BAR DUO
ROMP NOMANSLAND
ACME APACE AMID
GOOD PERKS PETS
```

PUZZLE 444

```
SOP TOGO PASTS
HUE APORT INERT
ERR STUDY EERIE
FAT REPS  WIFE
CLOSE DROOL ALL
AIRS  AISLE
REMAP HOOPLA
ENSUE ADE AMBER
LAWYER  CURVE
WATCH  RAID
WIG HOVER BAILS
REEF MINI LID
INNER ADAGE IVY
TEDDY LOTUS NEE
ERASE WAYS GET
```

PUZZLE 437

```
SCAT  FAME CRIB
POLE BLEAK RODE
ICON EERIE OBOE
TOO PLAIN WELT
SAFARI ELFIN
POEM YEN OPT
OKRA FIG ENTREE
PEARL LAD SECTS
UNITED GAL LAST
SON WAS BOWL
ADDED GEYSER
CURB SINGE IRE
ORAL CANOE FLOW
OGRE AMEND LODE
LEER PESO USED
```

PUZZLE 441

```
STRUM SHAD ARMS
TEASE TIDE BEAU
EAVES OPEN IDLE
ARE SHOP DOTS
MYNA APOSTLE
THY ERASERS
SPREE FEUD COO
TEA ADORNED HAM
OAR LEVY ERODE
WRESTLE DRY
THIRSTY EASY
AMMO POET LEI
FAIR EMIT ASIDE
ACRE LATE RIVAL
REED FEED TREND
```

PUZZLE 445

```
SWAB LEG FLOAT
NOVA ARE POODLE
AKIN PET EXPOSE
PEDALS SHE ROD
NOEL UPON
AFAR APT LAMB
ILL DANA EDGERS
CUE GENTS DIP
EMERGE DOSE ANY
STUN SAG ABLY
TUSK OGRE
HES TIC ANGLED
APIECE ROB GIVE
WILLOW OWL AMEN
SCOLD WEE ROSY
```

PUZZLE 438

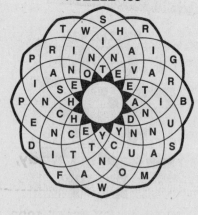

PUZZLE 442

```
RABBI  ROE WAFT
APIECE ERA ABLY
REDEEM OER SOAP
EXES CRISPY UKE
SEAL LASTED
ESS PEG SUMO
LOANED BIG LAMP
LURID FIR LINER
SPIN PIN MEDDLE
JOIN TEA STY
ESCAPE DEAF
RUE TRYING DELE
UGLY CON ERODED
PALE EGG RAVING
TROT DAY PETTY
```

PUZZLE 446

```
FLAT FILL BIOS BASH
AURA IDEA ACRE ORCA
RACK ROMP KEEN LIAR
MUSE SLOSHED ISLAND
NUT NEE TOOT
PER SPRY DREARY CAB
UKULELE GEAR EVADE
BETA APEMEN  ACME
DECADE EMS OCTET
LAP SEINE GAPED INS
ODORS RAT EXILED
DOLE IODINE OBOE
GRAVY ISNT EMOTING
EER ENOUGH STEP BEG
TANG EWE NET
HAWAII ABREAST HOBO
OMEN LIRA AREA UPON
PELT EVEN VEER MALL
ENDS REDS EDDY PLAY
```

PUZZLE 439

```
SCRAM BURB AMMO
CREDO ASEA COAX
RINDS SECT OOZE
AMT STIR HARDEN
PESO INS TIN
TENS PULSATE
LARIAT RIB KEG
EXIST HEN WRING
ALP SAD SOUNDS
DESTINY SUED
ONE MAR EASY
UNLIKE OFFS ROE
RAIL RATE OPERA
NICE EXIT DUNES
SLED DEFY APART
```

PUZZLE 443

```
ACTS MIDI BROS
CHAT LEMON OUST
HULA INPUT ISLE
EMERALD BELLHOP
VIA TRUE
FIERCE ERRED
HID AROSE LAW
ILL SCRIPTS ORE
SEE PANDA PET
DRIER LEERED
MAPS VEE
APPAREL BALDEST
CLOG TYPED DALE
NOSE ELITE EVES
EWES DYES NEWT
```

PUZZLE 447

```
SLOE ARISE FARM
PAPA RECON LUAU
UKES CLOUDBURST
RENEW ANNUL APE
ANY DRAT
JOB TART EBONY
EMU CHARTS DUET
DITCH CAW WORSE
ITCH SECEDE SEA
SHIFT KNEE ESS
NORM TEN
OFF REEDY YEAST
PLANTATION CLUE
TUTU MANNA RARE
SEEN SLEEP USES
```

PUZZLE 448

```
GLIB _ OAR _ MUSH
NINA SUMAC ANTE
ANTS TRUCE GLOW
TEETHE SILL IRE
_ REAR ENLISTED
OAF TEA GALA _
ALE OFF RAGING
TIRED TOM CANOE
STEERS GOB SUE
_ LIAR OAK INK
CHISELED KILN _
HER DAME ENACTS
ELKS DICER MERE
FLEE SNOWY BROW
SODA DYE SETS
```

PUZZLE 452

```
CLASP STUD PITS
HUMOR TIRE ACHE
ARENA ACNE TEEN
TEN YET PASSED
LINER DRY _
STAND EDIT SKY
SPRIG BLISS HOE
TAUT POACH DEAN
ARC WROTE WAILS
BEE HOSE PARKA
ROW DWELT _
ACTUAL IRK OFF
SHUN EVEN EAGLE
KING READ RILED
SPAS SETS SLEWS
```

PUZZLE 456

```
SHELF STOP TALL
AUDIO PAIR ARIA
FLIES ISLE LENT
EAT SANK VACATE
WIT SCAN _
TAILOR HIDING
MORN METAL MORE
EXIT CAP ASEA
WISE FATED GEAR
CEREAL LAMEST
GILA TIS
RESIGN LOAD JET
OVEN TWIN DROVE
SILK EAVE LIKEN
ALLY RYES EMEND
```

PUZZLE 449

```
BARS PTAS AMOS WEE
IGET ERIE RENTA ODD
NEAR WORLDCLASS RIG
DELAYED LIE SALTY
WIDE WOODS SEND
LYONS SOUR ENTRYWAY
OARS CARTA COAT ASA
ILL PURL MOONY BRAM
NED IRED AWN WASPS
UNLESS EDGARS
PAWNS ELF WARE FIR
AROD CAROL OVEN ROE
TAR SISI APRES PETE
SPLITTHE TELL AREAL
DERE SATED FLOW
SABRE DOL TIPTOED
ERE WORLDPOWER ERGO
AGA SATIE FORE GLAD
MOT FEND FOND EDDO
```

PUZZLE 453

```
SKULL SPA KIDS
PAPAYA ALP ECRU
ELOPED NET BEAM
DEN DYED WARTS
ALSO GAB
SILO USERS ACE
SPRIG PLOP BAY
TOOT SHREW JADE
EON ALEE OUTER
PLY LASER FRET
SAW IFFY
BOGUS LOPE AVE
ARES ROW LEADEN
NANA ARE LEGEND
GLEN WED LASTS
```

PUZZLE 457

```
SPA WAS OAF MOB
LIP ELK FLU EVE
ACE TOE TEN NEE
MAXI HEW GAUNT
RIATA SIS
SPAR LYE HEM
SKATES LEI VAN
HIDE TOPAZ VINE
ERR ERA ELICIT
TEA REP IOTA
DEN EASEL
JULEP RIM AQUA
ONE OFF SEA URN
ITS COO LAX AGE
NOT HEX ERE DEW
```

1-Y, 2-G, 3-F, 4-T, 5-V, 6-N, 7-A, 8-P,
9-Q, 10-H, 11-L, 12-D, 13-S, 14-M,
15-J, 16-K, 17-R, 18-W, 19-E, 20-B,
21-C, 22-O, 23-X, 24-Z, 25-I, 26-U.

PUZZLE 450

```
SLY SWAB FLASH
WOE EARL PRONTO
ACT TRIO OYSTER
MOIST ACHE ERN
LEI KITT
SHIRTS TIE BOA
EPIC SIR CLEATS
ROLES CUT LATHS
MOLDED BIO THEE
ALY NUT CAREER
DRUM FUR
OFF EXIT MYNAS
WRITES GRAB ILL
LEVELS HALL GOO
SEEDS TYPE HEP
```

PUZZLE 454

```
GAPS TARS LAS
RIOT AROUND IKE
IDLE BUREAU BRA
TELECAST TERROR
PASTA CLEANS
CHASTE SHEA
LOX STYE DRIPS
APES EON MOLE
PEDAL ANTI NIC
GABS CORSET
SALAMI SHINE
CRISES LICENSED
ASS STROLL ACME
LOP TRIPLE MAIN
ENS OBEY ERRS
```

PUZZLE 458

```
GASP ERLE STAG ATOP
AUTO NEER HALL ROVE
BREE SPAGHETTI GNAT
LAWMAN POI TODDY
ELS SAC GOO EELER
TRA THROB FELON
ODDBALL AWE AGE USA
PAIL CASAS KEA DEB
TYPO BULKY MINT ESS
BELLA ANISE
SEA NEAR FORGE PAPA
HUR JET VIBES IMAM
ORG ODE ILE OPACITY
WOODY DUSTY DAL
STEED NEE APE MAA
IDIOM ROE EXPAND
BERG TREASURER ANNO
AKIN KISS CITE STAR
GEMS AGHA HEAR SALE
```

PUZZLE 451

```
SPLIT FRAY AGOG
TIARA LOVE GAME
UPSET EDIT ALIT
BET TAXED DIETS
ROB OLDEN
BEHOLD YAP VET
ARMY YOU DOMINO
SEEMS CRY TOTER
PARENT NOW TAME
SKY AIM NOSILY
ARCED OAF
SLOPE READY AWL
LAMA HEMS IGLOO
ICER ALOE NOTED
DENT MYNA GOOSE
```

PUZZLE 455

```
BLAH SIR UPON
RAKE BASIC LAMA
AVID IGLOO TRIP
GANG AGE WRISTS
ESSES BUM
JAB WED TOTALS
UNLOAD RAY TICK
STERN RUG SUSAN
TEEN RIB TEMPLE
SPADED PAN SEE
MOM CASTS
DELETE LIT LOPS
OVEN DRONE ABUT
MEET YESES SOLO
ERRS FED HELP
```

PUZZLE 459

```
GLEAN MACE POOR
ROUTE AGOG ROVE
EGRET KINGSIZED
WOO WRONG OMENS
TOO GAFFE
ASSERTS LARVA
STARK PIKES ARM
PERM HATED PLEA
SAG MOSSY ALONG
KEBAB SAMURAI
ERODE MAG
DAMES INAPT EGO
ELEPHANTS EAVED
ROSE LEEK UPEND
NEAR ERRS RESTS
```

PUZZLE 460
1. Chalcedony, 2. Lapis lazuli, 3. Amethyst.

PUZZLE 464
```
SHIP SANS ODDS COST
TOOL CLEO PEAT ONTO
ANNA HOOF ELMO MIEN
BEANCOUNTER POMPOMS
     TOO  YEAH  LEAN
FRO ENOS ETON ASHES
EON DENTS ELON SEAT
EACH REALM EDAM ASA
TREES ALOOF SEEDER
   APPLEPOLISHER
MATTER ERASE TIGER
ELO DOLL SKEET ELSE
LAPS MOOT ERROR UTE
TIBIA WARP ESNE MAD
   ANTE FIRM ENE
TANGENT COUCHPOTATO
OVAL TASK THEO HURL
NONE EMIL EIRE ARIL
GNAT RENE SCAM NAPA
```

PUZZLE 468

```
GAL HINDU   MAD
ACE OREOS   EDO
STOPWATCH   TEE
    IAN    EER
OCHER  AIRPORT
RHO DOGS   ANOA
EAU SWALE   OBI
AFRO EVEN   MIL
DEGRADE   TEENS
   LET  HIE
ADA  TIMECLOCK
PAS ADORE   ROI
TDS ROBES   OWN
```

PUZZLE 461
```
AWAY HASP SHAD CPA
LOVE AROAR PATE OAR
GRINDSTONE ENSEMBLE
ANS OBIT SHAKE ABES
     NEE  ERSATZ
ADE NERD HAM EELS
SULTAN ICEPICKS AWE
SOLO MAR NEAT REP
   UKULELE TALE VEE
BURRITO LAT SERRATE
ENE NICE FINESSE
ALT GLAM TEA NOTE
SEI DELIVERS TETHER
DEMO GAR TERN MEG
   EMBERS  MAD
SUMS ELATE LOGO SPA
PROHIBIT WHITEWATER
INN ROTE EARED MISC
TSK SPED WARY PROS
```

PUZZLE 465
```
DAVIDCOPPERFIELD
ADITROARSCARSEER
ROMEUNTOALTOSLAY
ELSMINUSLAGGUILE
SPURDANEMIENEMIR
WHEELIMPARMORANT
EVEHOVELSUBTIGER
DIVANETASPRIGERE
GOOSLEETADOCAPON
ELKHORDEYAKEMEND
PIERTRIOSTEMEAST
INSETOFFNEVERATE
TWIGEMITABETIRAN
COLARICEROSECAGE
HOLLYTENEXTRABET
```

PUZZLE 469
```
FOCUS Z TOPIC
O Y CHINA I O
BONGO T LEMON
  I WHISK E
JACK    SINEW
A QUASH T I
BAYOU I OVOID
O A INLAW E
TOKEN   SHUN
  K EPOXY A
FRILL P ENVOY
A N LIANA O E
DOGMA L RECUT
```

1-T, 2-F, 3-J, 4-L, 5-R, 6-C, 7-I, 8-M, 9-Q, 10-S, 11-Z, 12-X, 13-U, 14-H, 15-A, 16-K, 17-O, 18-D, 19-V, 20-E, 21-N, 22-Y, 23-B, 24-G, 25-W, 26-P.

PUZZLE 462

```
AM A   B AN  ST UN  ST RA IN
ASS IM I LA TE RI DE EP I ST LE
   CI NCH TRA VE RSE SE IN E
   UN CLE PER IL GUE ST C RY
SK I CHI C  TA CO  A BET
E VER  LI EN  PE RSE VE RE
IN SE AM  T EN  NEAR T  T HE ME
   OU TRAGE OU S  MO PE  SI LO
MA NT EL  GH OUL  NI PPY  TA IN
RE ST LIS T  CRA ZE  ABA TE
PE ER S  AB RA SI VE  FO ND
AL M ON D  GO T  PE RS ON AB LE
IND IC ATE  UT TER  ST AKE  OVE NS
```

PUZZLE 466
```
ALF OPEN CREE HEAVEN
LEI VIVA HOED SURVIVE
BULLETINBOARD ABRADES
MORAL ORR YET ANENT
LILACS FLIER LEANTO
AMINO SOUNDEFFECT GEM
DAB APPOSE ALINE FARE
GRETEL DONS SUMMA
FIAT WILMA YES SPREAD
INRE CARNE DIAL
NEY SPECIALORDERS CUB
CHAR DWEEB OHNO
FUSION GAB ENLAI EAUX
ARENT WALL UTURNS
TETE MELEE DEACON NUT
SAC CABLESTITCH DREAR
HERETO SALUT REALLY
TRIBE OPS LED SHRUB
ROSEATE COMMERCIALART
AVERTED ARUM HANG COO
MELTED NADA OBOE KEY
```

PUZZLE 470
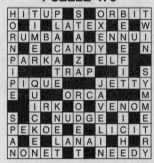
```
HITUP S ORBIT
O I LATEX E W
RUMBA A ENNUI
N E CANDY E N
PARKA Z ELF
I TRAP   I S
PIQUE   JETTY
E U ORCA   M
  IRK O VENOM
S C NUDGE I E
PEKOE E LICIT
A E LANAI H R
NONET T NEEDY
```

1-D, 2-H, 3-W, 4-Z, 5-V, 6-M, 7-Y, 8-U, 9-R, 10-G, 11-O, 12-S, 13-I, 14-K, 15-L, 16-C, 17-X, 18-T, 19-A, 20-N, 21-B, 22-P, 23-E, 24-F, 25-Q, 26-J.

PUZZLE 463
```
SHORN COMP  SLID
PAREU ABAS  HOBO
ATTIC BORICACID
RES LOSES  AVISO
    BED SHONE
  SERIAL BONUS
PUPA AGGIE SKA
AMONG MOA STAIN
LAC UPBOW UGLY
  CHAIR KERNEL
   BLOCS YEA
ERASE RISER MIL
LAKESHORE ARECA
AGIN OWER TINED
LENT EDNA EPODE
```

PUZZLE 467
```
TALC  FELT  RAP
OMAR  AGEE  ONE
PINE  LOISLANE
   ASTA   TIMER
FALSE MAYS
IRA ADAM ASAP
ZEN LODEN UFO
ZAGS DANE PAN
   ATOM WHERE
THOSE   STAR
SUPERMAN IBIS
ALE NOVA FOCI
RAN STEP AYES
```

PUZZLE 471
```
OLLA PERT  SALE
ROOD AXIOM IBEX
TRAM SCARE ELSE
SEMI ESNE  NETS
   RAMP AKIN
EMANATED OAST
STOLID TOWN HER
PHIS REUSE SEXY
AIR SEND IDEATE
CENT TERRIERS
   EYER ODES
SAPS WAFT  ALSO
EXIT ECLAT WILD
RETE STATE EKED
ALAR EPEE  DEWS
```

PUZZLE 472
1. Baste, 2. Print, 3. Aisle, 4. Nepal, 5. Contest.

PUZZLE 473
```
LIME SHAW DAMP AGAL
IDES TARA EVEL IRMA
MONT ERIN SETA REED
BLUERAIDERS STIPEND
   SAL REEL ETON
ALI NESS DRUM ERWIN
NET TRAPS TRIM TARE
KEEL SLATE KNOW VIA
ARMOR ATOLL DETEST
   GOLDENGOPHERS
CHOOSE EAGLE EASEL
OAR ESAU RAINS ROME
ALAS TART NEROS AMA
TENET AGRA DIRT PAD
   GLIB EIRE BUS
STELLAR CRIMSONTIDE
LAME TASK DOWN ASEA
ICER OVAL EVAN LENS
TONS NINE RENE KETT
```

PUZZLE 474
```
MADD STAN SCAM OSLO
ONER PIMA TACO PEEL
SORA IDAS EWES ETAL
TAMMANYHALL SHARONA
   ADS LOLA ELAN
AWL ATOP GAME ATHOS
SEA HERRS RICE EAVE
HADJ RIOTS DOSE LAW
ENDOW EMAIL STILLS
   HALLOFMIRRORS
STANCE FORAY ELMER
ERN ODOR NATAL EINE
TINA ARAB SINAI NIN
AMISS OMEN OSSA DDT
   ETON SLOE SGT
SCHOLAR ARSENIOHALL
HOAR MELT SLAT ABIE
ALLI EDIE AIDE TELE
GALA DODD YEAR STAR
```

PUZZLE 475
```
POLAR ESTATE SRI
AMIGO YEOMAN PAN
SALESMEETING ARCHER
SHA YOLKS LATE AVE
EACH DES SCANS SLIP
   IBET STUNT BILLS
   PAL MOOED RENO
WISPY PAWNS DUG FRY
HOHO MELEE HOPI FOE
ATO BAKERSDOZEN ASA
TAR ADOS TEPEE EMIT
SST IRE SHEER OMENS
   SITE FIRMS PUP
ANTES SOLOS DART
DOOR ARROW ARR YAMS
DAR ALOE BROKE LOU
SHYEST STORMWARNING
VIA TIDIES SANTA
EAR SPEEDY EMEER
```

PUZZLE 476
```
SLAVIC AMOUNTED
TGN AGEE E
IDEATE ANALYTIC
CNROIYHO
KIDNEYBEAN TEAR
YAPTTRA
DISAGREEMENT
CCDIUNDE
AULDLANGSYNE
UAYSIGR
LONE AFTERSHAVE
DKERTBPS
REINDEER TAHITI
ONIELNG
NEGATORY SLOGAN
```

PUZZLE 477
```
HOBO ADLER SLID SLASH
ACED TRIKE PINE TABOO
READYMADES LEGWARMERS
TAU OOPS THINE GABLES
ENTHUSE MOOT SWAYS
   ANT TARP STATE FLO
STUNG FOREIGN FEDERAL
WORD PINKS ROOTS VEND
ARAM ALAS LARKS PEACE
MOLEHILL CAPES HANKER
   DENY BASED TORI
ESCORT MALTS RIPENESS
GNAWS FALLS POLE GAPE
YARN SIDLE RAVED GREW
PRESUME ADHERED PONDS
TED SALAD ACTS SAW
   CURDS TRES CANNOLI
STUART SLITS AILS BAN
MONKEYSUIT SUNDAYBEST
UTTER ORAL ENTER USER
GOODS PERE DAIRY NERO
```

PUZZLE 478
```
LAMAR ELLS BALI SCROD
AGILE NEAP OMAN ALIBI
OUTOFPLACE OUST LATER
SEEN HIS CATCHONESEYE
   GHOSTS LEK IMP
CAD ANT OGEE JAN STOP
ACIDLY BUMP SUMAC OBI
SCANT HITTHEHAY OLSON
BEMA SOPH RAN PRESET
ADO OTTO CLAN DONNA
HEN WILDCATSTRIKE NCR
DOLLY RUDE AREA DIE
ALBEIT MAS RIGS ETNA
GEARS SAFEHOUSE TRUES
HOC HEART YULE THERMO
ASKS LYE SIRE ARE NAN
   PAS VAN REVAMP
BALLBEARINGS NOS ALIS
EMAIL ROOD PITCHBLACK
AMICE GALA IDEE ALLOY
TONER ORAL TART ASONE
```

PUZZLE 479
```
FLAMENCOMELET
LIMAPERSENIOR
AMORERICATONE
POUTEDEALENIN
JUNIPERRORAND
ASTRONAUTODAY
CIAODORSITEVE
KNOTETESEERAL
NESTAENIDROLL
ALIENSTAIRALE
VIEROWERAIDUD
EDGESARTREIRE
SEEDENSEYREEL
```

PUZZLE 480
```
LEDA ANGELA CAY EMIR
ALEC COATED ALIT LENA
PIER INLAID PAPERBACK
PAPERDOLL UFOS SOOTHE
   AILS SPAN STOW
SMOGGY LOUTS BAIT HUG
HONES VIDEO MAILS OBI
ACT CAMO MOLDY CLOD
RHO PAPERPLATE PLEAD
PAPERBOY LASER TOASTY
   LOIR SUITS SARI
AUTUMN SOMME PAPERCUP
BRADS PAPERTIGER ANE
ABBE DIRKS IVES TSP
SAL MYNAS ARDOR SLEEP
ENE ANDY QUIET SPARRY
   OKAY TUBA SHUN
SCARES BEAU PAPERCLIP
PAPERTHIN REALER EIRE
URSA YOKO NAGGER ROME
DYED GER STEADY SNAP
```

PUZZLE 481
```
EFT SRI ALSO WALL
REAP SCAN SUCH ALIA
STRETCHED SCROUNGED
TAPROOM YOURE READY
   ATOP GREETS
AMASS OHARE COASTED
MULCT ZONE WHO PUMA
POOR SEND PIE ELFIN
SNEAKED BEND COTTA
   TEE BEEPS ART
MERCY SORE SHUCKED
AMAHS QUA OPTS HIRE
LUTE BUT OBLA GENIE
ISADORE ADIEU UDDER
   PALACE ANTI
ASIDE CRISP CASSAVA
SCRUNCHED SCHLEPPED
POME HEAL SEEK YETI
SWAT IDLY TED DOT
```

PUZZLE 482
```
LAKES FADE STOW
OPERA AGES TRUE
RERAN URNS EAST
ERR IDLE EVENTS
   STATE NIPS
CREAMS ICE PEA
SHEARS WOE LAM
NIFTY PEN CHARM
ILL DUB PRONTO
PIE FIT WEALTH
   CLAN TRACE
ATTUNE WORK TUB
LAIR TWIN PAUSE
ALOE TANG OWNED
SEND EXES TEARS
```

PUZZLE 483
```
TACT MOAN SELF
IDLE ANDES OVAL
LIEN SLEET MEMO
TEA STY DEFENSE
SUNDAE MYNA
   AGREE CRAFTS
SLUR YAM HEROIC
CASES REC DRAMA
AVERTS NUT AMEN
BASSET TERRY
   PESO OUSTED
BANDSAW SUM WAY
AREA KEBAB RISE
RIOT SPOIL ICER
SANE TALE GELS
```

PUZZLE 484

```
BEARD APES  SHOP
RECUR SHOO  COVE
AROMA SANDPAPER
SIR BLISS  ALERT
HEN AGE OLD
  SHIN AWESOME
TAMPED PIN  WOK
OKAYS BID SOLVE
FIX  EAT BIASED
UNIFORM SACK
  OAR THY  BEE
SPORT GHOST RAY
NAUGHTIER ERASE
ANTE ELSE LOWER
PEST ADES LENDS
```

PUZZLE 488

```
LABEL PLEB  SLAT
OVULE AARE  COLE
FARFETCHED ONER
TIM CHER RANGER
SLATHER SORES
  REE SPLASHED
ARCED SHILL OTO
GILT CHINS STUN
ADO LOAMY ROSIN
RESPONDS FUR
  ELATE HOSTESS
DECADE PART ALA
ORAN NEARMISSES
RILE DARE EPEES
MELT STEM RASPY
```

PUZZLE 492

```
CHAP SWAP SCAM CLOT
HALE HOBO ROMA ROVE
OLAN ONUS ANON ABES
POINSETTIA SKIPPERS
AIL TRAP CEE
DOWNCAST TRIG AMPLE
ROOT CLAM ERIC YEAR
INK BEEPED ELL RASA
PASSE DETER TATTLES
CAB DAVIS NIL
BAHAMAS LIVED LEADS
AGER SAC LATEST NEA
GIRL SLOT LUMP STAN
SOOEY TMAN PIRATING
TOP POOR ORA
DISSUADE NASTURTIUM
ASEA GATE FLIT URGE
ZING AREA TAME ROLL
ETTE NEST SPED ENID
```

PUZZLE 485

```
SNIDE STAG  SPAN
WIRES LOBE  ALSO
ALOES UPON  PETS
BEND GRAVEL ARE
  SHY ZERO SAD
AWL AMP ALLEY
FOAMY LITTLE
TOGO CANOE EVEN
SKINNY DRIVE
VISIT SPY MET
GIN LYES LEG
ARC THEORY RAMS
STOW ARIA LAPEL
PUMA LILY OPERA
SEED LESS BERET
```

PUZZLE 489

```
HIS ALGA THROWN
UMP REAL HOODOO
SPA GERM EVADED
HARBORBARBER
ELTON EEL WOK
SEAL CHUGS BAKE
  IGUANA ARRAY
LEVITYBREVITY
SUDAN LADLED
EMIR TORSO GIGO
APT RAF TENON
  CASTLEVASSAL
DIDACT IDOL ELI
APOGEE OGLE TIN
NOTERS NETS SEE
```

PUZZLE 493

```
HOST ELIHU JIM HOPS
ALIA LEDON AGO OREL
DEAR OMENS BOX NERO
JONNYQUEST BRINGOUT
EUR HOME EEK
TROMPE SUPERB DOLED
RAMA NOW AJAR NORA
ORIG TWANG ASH GRIN
YETIS ETTU WHELPING
LAB HEP AAH
REALNESS SEAL SOUSA
ALVA ETC SAGAS ONAS
SMOG SOOT OPT ETCH
HONOR WOOING UNYOKE
ROW BONE ADA
UNLIKELY SPACEGHOST
POOL NOD TALON EVIE
TELL COO ALERT MARE
OLLA HMO LIENS SLED
```

PUZZLE 486

```
STRAW EKES  PAS
KOALAS LAMA  ERE
INGEST SLUG NOW
DEE TEPEE ANISE
  YETI ICED
SITE CAP ALI
TSETSE LIMB LYE
ALL PLATEAU LOW
GEE ALGA STRIKE
SUM ERR ONES
SACK ANEW
ALOES DEMON APE
LOP USED STOLEN
SUE MEAD HERALD
ADS OPRY RESTS
```

PUZZLE 490

```
AUDIO TIDY  YAMS
CRISP AREA  ALAI
RIGHTFLANK HAUL
ESS IRK SWELL
  ECO CNOTE
ASPS MINUTEHAND
MIAMI COTTA TAI
ANTENNA BOMBAST
SET KARMA SARAS
SWISSGUARD LILY
MISSY IRE
WAGON PSI USA
HULK COMICSTRIP
ATEE OVEN EAGLE
TOED PANG REEKS
```

PUZZLE 494

```
FUND PLAY MAAR BLAB
OLEO LUGE AIDE LENO
ANIL ELAN GRAS OTTO
LANCEBURTON REPOSES
EEE ARUM TAP
SET LIEU AMOK RERUN
CRISSANGEL DIATRIBE
AMEN NORA END TEX
RADIO ISTO TEACART
PRINCESSTENKO
SOMEONE SPAR ASTER
ODE GAS KATE TINE
REASSERT JAMESRANDI
EATEN SULU STOA TEN
SIS DENY TIA
TRISTAN DOUGHENNING
RANI LONG ROAR OMAN
ALTO ALEE TORI DELA
PEON DOOR SPEC ETAT
```

PUZZLE 495

```
RAM SCAM DAWG BATHE
ARE EURO ELEE ARIEL
GILBERTRAISIN NEPAL
ERS ENCORE GASPS
ALBEE KIR SAL
SOURSULTANAS SEVENS
IRR STEN GNASH AGEE
AILS INTO NEE NEAT
TAC DISTR BUSTS
THERAISINSOFWRATH
WRAPS DOEST RAT
HANS EEN SAFE USMC
OMOO SAIDA RASP AAA
SPINET CURRANTRANCH
MAN ETE OLSEN
BANDB AWNING EPA
AMOUR CONCORDRAISIN
SISSY REAL IRAN ADA
SEETO ESSE METE TAG
```

PUZZLE 487

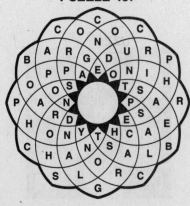

PUZZLE 496

```
MADAM APSE  CLOD  FEW
AGATE BEAN  AIDE  ANA
STRANGERTHANFICTION
   VAULT  ALIEN ERLE
DEPICT  ONES   STEAD
ERASE  WINCE   ASHE
FORM  TITLE  TRAY OWN
TSE CONEY MAIL  ACHE
     FORD  AIR  ASTIN
CHARITYBEGINSATHOME
RIVAL  IDA    WHEY
EVEN  ANTS  CREON BRA
WES  ODIE  SOUPY DEAN
    IRON  STINT COAST
PRINT  DIAN   CLOTHE
ROOT  ALIGN   SURER
OUTOFSIGHTOUTOFMIND
UTA  ASTI  OBIE  TAMER
DES  ANET  NITS  SNAGS
```

PUZZLE 497

```
DASH ACERB  UNIT  BASIN
EINE SOLAR  NANA  EROSE
FROMCTOSHININGC  THULE
YEW  ERLE  BOBCAT WATER
     ENOS  BEERY  SETH
PLANTS  ORSO  FETE  CSA
LACE  DORY  WOOLEN TOM
ERR  OCULI  ROAM  GAVE
ADE DEADCSCROLLS  OLIN
    MOLLS TEENS GREED
ESCORTS NACHO  ARRESTS
ALFAS  CILIA   ASIAN
SOON CARMELBYTHEC FRI
TAOS LIEU  ANELE  LAD
END REDDER  AMOS  PATE
REM  OREO  ECCE BROWSE
     AMOK  SPURN DUAD
CARET ARMORY  EARS SEE
ANKLE SHESELLSCSHELLS
SNEER TELE  IONIA TOOT
TOTES OATS  CLEAR APIA
```

PUZZLE 498

```
LIMP FEATS  SCATS STET
ODOR ALGAE  CAPRI THAR
BEHOLDYOURHORSES RASE
SASSIER  BUNSEN  SUITE
PARIAH  BEE   CRAM
CALEB AMOUR ASHEN YES
OVERLY BELITTLEBOPEEP
NAE EOS RUSH IRA  RARE
GIRL UPS  RAGS  MARIE
ALSO NAPE GUSH  RAINED
    BEGRUDGEMATCHES
MODELS RILE PLOY ELSE
ADELA  CREE  YUM  DEAR
MDII ALI ESTA PET  ALA
BEFALLINGSTARS SHARES
ORY OMEGA ENTER RINSE
    BRAN  SAR  STATER
STEAD TUTTED GOALIES
ERAS BELABORRELATIONS
CURE ELENA  AHEAD FLIT
TENS GEEKY  BONNY TADS
```

PUZZLE 499

```
WREN STROP  JAPAN BOLD
HALO CRAVE  ALAMO USER
EVAN RIVEN  RISER CIAO
WINEMAKER  DRESSMAKERS
    OPEN  TEEN  ACORNS
STATUE  BUND   WENT
KARAT STONY PAD  SHIMS
IRISH PAYS  MINGO OBOE
MOLT MAX  CANTER MEOW
     EKES SPLICE PLEASE
HOLMES SPOONED HEMMED
ALLAYS CASTER  BANA
LEAK ERODES  IAN  KELP
LAME SORER  MONK PETAL
SNARL DES  LORNE ARENA
     ACED  MARE RUSSET
SHASTA  VASE   NOEL
MATCHMAKERS LAWMAKERS
AUTO EXERT  RADIO INIT
STAN REEVE  EVENT TOLE
HERE ASPEN  BARGE SLEW
```

PUZZLE 500

```
MIND STRAP  CANT  GLOP
OREO PIETA  INURE RISE
LOWS INTERPRETER  EASE
ENS PEG ERICA  FEDERAL
    PARSES  OVER  LIT
EVADE  TOTO   COMICAL
DEPOT COAST  SWAN NAVE
GEE ENACT  STING GRIT
ERR RISK  CHORE  CRAG
     SIGHT CHOKED AERO
SMITH INHERES  SURLY
SHAG  ICIEST   EMEND
MORN SKEET  ROMP  MIN
EVIL ALECK  AVAIL ONO
LENA MARE  SPLIT ACRID
TRANSOM  TALC   CASTE
    GIN  FAYS  EFFETE
UPSURGE ARETE  LID COY
RATA SMOKESIGNAL POLO
GREG TURIN  MOORE EDDY
ESTE SERA  ESTER  PESO
```

PUZZLE 501

```
CAP   WHO   PAR
ALE   HEN   ERE
TOT   EYE   AIL
CHANT    WORSE
HALE     EAGLET
      VINYL
WIDENS    EDGE
HOERS     ADORN
ATE   ELL   ROE
LAD   RYE   MUM
ESS   TEE   SPY
```

PUZZLE 502

```
          PART
METE      EMIR
EASEL     PILAF
ATSEA     DEFEND
SCAMPI    FLEA
THY  SOLD  ITEM
      GENERIC
NOTE  EDIT  NAB
AIRS      PAGODA
GLITCH    LAMAS
PUREE     IMAGE
ROAD      CEDE
ECRU
```

PUZZLE 503

```
          CALF
     CAR  SONAR
     MALE NUTMEG
BONUS  SON  PERM
ATOM   PLOT  DAY
TIL   FLIP  MOST
FALLOUT   OOMPH
     AYES TOUT
MAUVE     CORRODE
ASTA  IAMB   INK
CHI  URNS   PATE
HELP  NOT  DOPEY
NIACIN    ONER
ZLOTY      EER
ESPY
```

PUZZLE 504

Since the first card on the left has a higher number than the second card, the second card must have a higher number than the third card, and so on through the eighth. This is only possible if the first card on the left has the number 8 or higher, and cards two through eight each have a number one lower than their neighbors to the left. It's given that the first card on the left is not 10. If it was 9, then the last two cards on the right would have to be 1 and 10, in some order. This is also not allowed. So the first card on the left is 8, the second card is 7, and so on until we reach the eighth card from the left, which has the number 1. The only two cards left have the numbers 9 and 10, so the second card from the right is 10, and the card on the right end is 9.

In summary, from left to right the cards are 8, 7, 6, 5, 4, 3, 2, 1, 10, 9.

PUZZLE 505

```
        AGO
     AREAS     ALB
ALBATROSS     SALS
CALM  LIP    ACUTE
TOE  TEDDY    ERG
     OLE      JAG
FAIRS        LEAP
PAS  SOP     ANY
SENT        DIANE
AWN          SRA
PEG  CITES   HOW
TAUNT ADO   HOWE
TINE  BALDEAGLE
NET   SEEMS
       INS
```

PUZZLE 506

LIGHT CREAM

PUZZLE 507

```
        TATA
MAR      ARIL
ALIT     LING
MASH   CATAMARAN
ASKEW      ALICE
RHO        SMART
AMINE     TOLE
SOMETIMES
MISS     AVERT
RECUT     YAP
AROMA    LLAMA
PENETRATE AXEL
EMIR     NINE
AMEN     SUE
LORE
```

PUZZLE 508
Tourism, Strudel, Stirrup, Culprit, Curtail, Leotard, Purport, Picture, Replica, Central, Romance, Treason, Mystery, Dormant.

PUZZLE 512
SINGER: Barbra Streisand

PUZZLE 516

R	Y	E		A	L	O	E		C	A	B	S
E	E	R		M	O	A	N		O	G	L	E
V	A	R	M	I	N	T	S		L	O	A	N
			A	D	E		N	A	U	G	H	T
L	A	D	Y			R	E	A	R	M		
A	F	O	O	T		G	R	I	N	D	E	R
M	A	D		E	A	G	L	E		O	P	E
B	R	O	W	N	I	E		L	O	V	E	D
		H	O	L	D	S		B	E	E	S	
I	N	F	O	R	M		T	I	E			
M	E	A	L		E	V	E	R	Y	O	N	E
P	A	I	L		N	O	N	E		W	O	K
S	P	R	Y		T	W	O	S		E	W	E

PUZZLE 509

PUZZLE 513

PUZZLE 517

PUZZLE 510
Acing, Acne, Agile, Alien, Align, Angel, Angle, Cage, Cane, Clan, Clang, Clean, Cling, Elan, Gain, Gale, Genial, Glace, Glance, Glean, Glen, Lace, Lacing, Lain, Lance, Lane, Lean, Lien, Line, Nail, Nice.

PUZZLE 514

PUZZLE 518

C	R	O	A	K		S	W	I	G		C	L	A	N
L	E	D	G	E		N	A	N	A		H	O	L	E
A	D	D	E	R		I	R	K	S		I	C	E	R
D	O	S		N	O	D			K	I	C	K	E	D
		D	E	F	E	N	D	E	D					
S	H	E	L	F		A	U	T	O		T	I	P	
M	A	A	M		E	L	S	E		L	L	A	M	A
A	L	T	O		R	A	T	T	Y		E	R	A	S
T	E	E	N	Y		R	I	S	E		T	O	G	S
E	S	S		E	A	V	E		A	C	U	T	E	
			T	E	A	R	D	R	O	P				
I	M	P	A	I	R		A	N	Y		B	A	D	
D	E	A	D		A	P	E	R		O	R	A	T	E
E	A	S	E		T	A	K	E		T	A	L	O	N
A	N	T	S		E	Y	E	R		E	N	E	M	Y

PUZZLE 511

PUZZLE 515

A	B	E	D		S	C	A	T		H	E	P
R	O	L	E		E	A	C	H		A	L	L
M	A	L	L		A	N	T	E		U	S	E
			T	A	L	C		I	D	L	E	D
M	A	D	A	M		A	C	R	E			
E	R	E		M	E	N	U		E	B	B	S
S	E	A	S	O	N		B	U	R	E	A	U
H	A	L	O		D	E	E	M		A	T	E
			B	A	S	S		P	A	T	H	S
C	O	A	S	T		C	U	S	S			
R	I	B		O	D	O	R		I	N	F	O
I	L	L		M	O	R	N		D	O	O	R
B	Y	E		S	E	T	S		E	D	G	E

PUZZLE 519
The art of being a good host consists of making guests feel at home even if you wish they were.

PUZZLE 520

```
ALOHA  BOA  POPS
MIMOSA URN  ALEE
PRINTS SEX  WEST
SAT ESPY  IDIOTS
   FREE  MOAN
ANTENNA  OUTGREW
LIAR TSETSE  IRE
TERN  ASH  ACRE
ACT SENSED  MEEK
RESPECT  RECORDS
   LESS  LEAK
ASLANT HYMN  GAL
CHUG APE  ENERGY
MENU SOW  DEWIER
EDGE YIN  DENSE
```

PUZZLE 525

```
OFFS  IDEA  RASPS
LULU  NULL  UNTIE
DRUM  SEMI  STATE
  ACT  VETERAN
RESCUE  KEG
ERA DADA  GLOVE
BOLA DOT  APING
EDICT GYM  STORE
LEVEE  DOC  SLOE
DARNS  IDOL  ELS
   KID NESTLE
JAVELIN  SIN
OLIVE GAVE  OGLE
HOSES OXEN  ROAD
NEARS TEXT  TOWS
```

PUZZLE 529

```
ARMS POGO  WREN
NEAT EARNS  HALE
TAXI GRATE  ODES
SLING  CODE  ACT
  GEESE ALERTS
LAP EAT  NOW
EMU RATS  PEARL
GEM ELLIPSE  GOO
SNAIL KNEE  ELS
   OIL ELF  DEE
PRONTO  IDLER
EEL EVEN  DISCS
REDS EXTRA  GLUE
IDEA DARES  HOLA
LYNX MOCK  TELL
```

PUZZLE 521

1. Happy, 2. Grand, 3. Horse.

PUZZLE 526

```
AMASS  FER  PATE
REGINA ERA  ACRE
GIRDED TON  REIN
ORA LATEST  ASPS
  ELMS  SOD
LAX HER  KEEP
MIDI TIMERS  PUG
EMIT IRONY  CONE
SIE SETTEE  ACNE
TUTU SEW  SHY
  INK  ALIT
UPON NOBLER  TOW
RANG APE  SALIVA
NICE VAN  STALER
SLED ELS  EMEND
```

PUZZLE 530

```
AMPS  HOBO  CHAT
DOLL CAGED  HERO
AWAY HIRED  RACE
PET SALE  BROTHS
TRESTLES  AIM
  TIED ALGEBRA
SPLINT NIL  RAG
ALERT CAD  SNAKE
FEE TOP  LAUDED
EARSHOT  BIRD
  WEB GINGERLY
CINEMA RAGE  HUE
ASEA CHASE  MYRA
SLOT COVER  AMES
TENS ODES  PEST
```

PUZZLE 522

```
MICA  APSE  DRAG
ODOR SPOIL  RAGE
DOME CHUCKWAGON
ELF GRIT  IMAGE
  OGLED  CODA
BORROW CAPE  HER
ACTUP CLIENTELE
STEM BOARD  HAUL
TARPAULIN  HEDDA
ELS BRIM  JERSEY
  SYNC  BERET
OASIS  BULB  RAD
RINGSABELL  TORE
CLAN TELLY  ANIL
ASPS EELY  UGLI
```

PUZZLE 527

```
SLY MERV  STALE
WOO ONION  ARRAY
ICY WASTE  VOICE
GOOD CEES  ODDER
  RAT STAR
ARGYLES  TYPED
FUR ADHERE  AXES
ALOES IVY  SLICE
REAR SPEECH  LOT
SNACK  SOARERS
  HISS  SHE
SPIKE PEAT  VEND
LONER ACRID  COO
ASTER STENO  HOT
PHONY SAGE  ONS
```

PUZZLE 531

```
PILAF FAME  SWAM
EVADE LOAN  TAME
NEWER ERRS  IVES
  RIATA  ARENA
VIDEO  ACED
DINETTE ARM  RAP
ROMP ART  SERENE
ALOOF EAR  NECKS
MISTED PUN  VOLT
ANT TUG  MATURES
  CORE  NEEDS
BATCH  ARRAS
ARIA ENNE  TAFFY
SELF AGED  EXILE
HATE TESS  DEBUT
```

PUZZLE 523

1. Post, Past, Cast, Cart, Card.

2. Miss, Moss, Toss, Tons, Ions.

3. Poke, Pone, Pond, Pend, Wend, Weed.

4. Shop, Shot, Soot, Sort, Wort, Worn.

PUZZLE 524

```
SPUD CASE  ERGO
WINY LLAMA  SOIL
ANTEBELLUM  PILE
POI RAYS  PHYLLO
STEPIN  ASEA
  ADS ERG  PHI
SPARE RECESSION
TAPE HURTS  OMEN
OVERCOMES  SCARS
WED LOB  AUK
  ORAL BROOCH
BELUGA ISLE  PRO
IRIS YESTERYEAR
OILS SOLES  URNS
SEAR NEWT  LAKE
```

PUZZLE 528

```
CLAD LAME  BLESS
LAIR OREM  REVUE
ACME TEAS  AGENT
MESA TAN  IRKS
  MIO TAROT
OTTER KID  DEE
PAIRED RIDE  ELM
ELL ORING  COB
ROE STAB  ESCAPE
AND HEN  OILER
  TEDDY INN
CHOW OLD  EMIL
HATED IDOL  MIDI
ALTAR MERE  ARES
PESKY PLED  SEAT
```

PUZZLE 532

```
LOB TOSS  TOGA
OLE AREA  AVER
OINTMENT  BALM
TOTE  DEAL
  NAB  SEIZE
LAM BASIS  LED
ONE SLICE  LAD
SET UDDER  SLY
SWEAR  STY
  IDES  ELSE
FANS DEVOTEES
EVIL GROW  NAP
DELE YAWL  TRY
```

558

PUZZLE 533

```
OAF  EASE  CADS
AGO  SPUR  AREA
KEROSENE  MILL
     CARD  EDIT
ABBEY  ALSO
GILA  PEAK  ANO
ATONER  NICKED
REB  MEEK  LIMO
     SUPS  HONOR
MEMO       TWAS
EVER  BARRETTE
WINE  ITEM  WAY
SLUR  DENS  OPE
```

PUZZLE 534

```
MOST  ANTE  PTA
INCH  BOOR  OAT
SCAR  OVERBITE
SEMI  LASSO
     LEI    TURK
ENCLASP  THREE
LOA  CHILI  GAP
BENCH  CONCERT
ALTO       AYE
     OFTEN  RASH
PRESERVE  EXPO
ROE  LEER  ALOE
OWL  LENS  LETS
```

PUZZLE 535

```
PEA  C  H   C  LA  IM   RA  P  ID
L  U  AU   EN  G  AGE   T  AL  ENT
SP  L  INT  ER   CUR  IO  S  ITY
        SPI  RAL   MO  LE
CA  SH  ME  RE    SA  ND  W  I  CH
P  A  RMA    A  FFR  AY   OD  ES  SA
PE  N  TA  G  ON    F  INE  S  T
      ST  AIN   TR  OLL
VEN  TU  R  E    F  ELL  OW  SHI  P
O  RR  IS   C  ACT  I    VE  R  GE
M  ET  ER   ON  ION  S    R  OA  M
```

PUZZLE 536

1. Only a mediocre writer is always at his best. (W. Somerset Maugham)
2. Status symbols are medals you buy yourself.

PUZZLE 537

```
BARON  SCAR  DAMP
ALONE  ARIA  ELIA
RIVER  BELT  CANS
GEE  OGLE  TWISTS
ENDS  EEL  LID
     TAM  BENEFIT
RADAR  OILS  ARE
ALERT  PRO  ROMAN
SEA  HEAT  AMEND
PENSION  SPA
     LON  SHE  ROLE
DEFINE  TONE  TOR
ARID  SLIT  ROTOR
RILE  TILE  OBESE
TEES  YELL  SIRED
```

PUZZLE 538

1. Cake, 2. Wall, 3. Work, 4. Boat, 5. House, 6. Wheel, 7. Wind, 8. Cat, 9. Trap, 10. Dust.

PUZZLE 539

```
MODEM  BLAB  PAIN
AWAKE  YORE  ONCE
CEDED  TAMS  STEW
ESS  ITEM  TSHIRT
     TAR  SON
CLINIC  TWO  GUY
BRUT  PAPA  BALSA
OATH  PEN  DOER
DWEEB  FAZE  LARD
ELS  EMU  ADMITS
     GEL  GAB
MIMOSA  TIER  ODE
ODOR  GOER  GAVEL
ALOE  EPEE  IDEAL
NETS  REDS  NERDS
```

PUZZLE 540

1. Careen, Thread, Parent; 2. Deduce, Endure, Unduly; 3. Recipe, Social, Pacify; 4. Dinghy, Single, Tongue.
BONUS WORD: Reducing

PUZZLE 541

```
WHI  T  ENPR   AWN
O   PE  R  A   AR   EA
NUD   GEAL   MOS   T
LE  ARNR  E  BEL
D  AIS   YABU   T
EA  VE  OSCUL  ATE
GLO  A  T   TEE   M
RESTIV   ESTA   IR
DR    EW  T   EE   N
M  ANSIO   NM   UM
E   LAPS  EACRE
BALAN   CER   IL  E
UN  T  ILKN  E   EL
     Y  EN  Y   EAST
TE  E    E  YE  LE  T
```

PUZZLE 542

```
ROD  APSE  JAIL
EGO  SLIM  UGLY
FEZ  PULP  LAKE
SEEP  MOOSE
     APE  REPAST
CHILI  FIX  JAW
RUT  SQUAT  AGO
ALE  TUN  OKRAS
BAMBOO  ANI
     UNTIL  NAVE
AUTO  IDOL  GEL
XRAY  NENE  ETA
ENDS  GAGA  DON
```

1-C, 2-K, 3-T, 4-H, 5-N, 6-W, 7-Y, 8-B, 9-J, 10-X, 11-S, 12-Q, 13-Z, 14-U, 15-P, 16-M, 17-G, 18-E, 19-F, 20-V, 21-D, 22-I, 23-O, 24-R, 25-L, 26-A.

PUZZLE 543

```
OFF  ERG  IRE  HIS
ALL  YOU  SIX  INN
SEA  EWE  LAC  PSI
TAXI  SPELL  PIP
     DELTA  ABIDE
AZALEA  RETIREE
SORELY  AROMA
HOE  MAKER  FIR
     SKATE  QUARTO
MATINEE  UPROSE
VINYL  THESE
EMS  LASSO  ALGA
NOW  JUT  VET  OIL
USE  ORE  ERR  OBI
EAR  YAW  RAY  NET
```

1-U, 2-I, 3-T, 4-C, 5-H, 6-B, 7-L, 8-W, 9-Y, 10-S, 11-A, 12-D, 13-J, 14-P, 15-X, 16-E, 17-F, 18-V, 19-N, 20-G, 21-R, 22-Z, 23-M, 24-K, 25-O, 26-Q.

PUZZLE 544

```
WAR  STUD  DROVE
HUE  CASE  NEARED
ITS  AXEL  INDEED
CHASM  DISCS  SPY
HOLE  EKES
     REAP  SPAN  TACH
     RETIE  AVENUE
SIN  SUPREME  YEN
POISON  CHEST
ANTI  NAHS  TUBE
     SEEP  NUNS
AMP  ALTER  BERTH
GALORE  VINE  LIE
ERODED  EDIT  ARE
SEWED  REPS  PEP
```

PUZZLE 545

```
SEWS  HIFI  BAGS
TRIO  BACON  ACRE
ROSY  EVILS  THIN
ADE  STEEL  TENT
PERMIT  ROWDY
     IRON  WEE  WIN
DISC  ROB  SECEDE
ADORE  TOO  RADON
FLOORS  ADS  ISLE
TEN  RIB  DOOR
     ESSES  INNING
PAWN  CABLE  GAL
USES  PAYEE  ALMA
BEAU  AMEND  GOER
SAKE  NERD  TORE
```

PUZZLE 546

```
SMEAR  EBBS  TACO
CELLO  RAIL  ATOP
ADDED  ABLY  TENT
LIE  SELECT
PARABLE  RIOTED
     LOUDLY  TORSO
MELON  LADY  ASP
HON  GRAPE  SEE
OUT  SEEM  BATHS
STENO  CALICO
THREAT  UTENSIL
     SKATER  PRO
SLAT  LEAK  SALAD
POPE  CASE  UNITE
AXED  SLED  BYTES
```

559

PUZZLE 547

```
ASPS  LIED   SPED
TOOT  ARROW  CLAY
ODOR  MIRTH  HOSE
MARINAS   OBEYED
   PAS  PSALM
  PREY  FAT  EELS
LOUD  PIRATE  ALP
ELM  TIE  ROD  BEE
DEB  INSERT  DEER
 SAGA  TOY  YELP
   URBAN  NOG
BUREAU   GOURMET
APES  LOVER  EAVE
BOAT  BUILT  EYES
ENDS  RASH   SORT
```

PUZZLE 551

```
SPUD  MAST   LOLA
TINE  APORT  OKAY
AXEL  STAIR  URGE
RIVER  POI   SASS
SEE  EELS  PIE
SNEAKY  SON  RIP
   EMERALDS  ORE
CHAR  ILE  ANEW
UAR  LECTURED
DYE  ASS  TUNDRA
  OPT  SHED  ATE
GOLF  AIL  SPITS
ABUT  TOUCH  USES
WORE  ENSUE  MINE
KEEN  SHES   ANDS
```

PUZZLE 555

```
AWE  SICS   LIMIT
LIV  AORTA  ERASE
ODE  KNEEL  VERSE
HENCE  SAGGY  RUN
ANTI  ASKER  RYES
   NAB  BARE
BLENDS   ORBITERS
REGAL  SRA  CANAL
ATOMIZER   FEISTY
   OBOE  URN
STUN  ORGAN  ELSE
WON  AMEND  BROWN
ATILT  SAMBA  VET
PATIO  STAIR  EAR
SLEEP  SNOB   DRY
```

PUZZLE 548

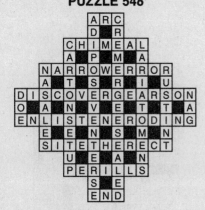

```
      ARC
      D R
    CHIMEAL
    A P M A
  NARROWERROR
  A T S R I U
DISCOVERGEARSON
O A N V E T T A
ENLISTENERODING
  E E N S M N
  SITETHERECT
    U E A N
    PERILLS
      S E
      END
```

PUZZLE 552

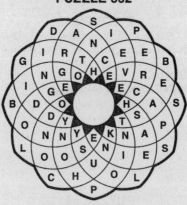

PUZZLE 556

```
ELUDE  FLAME  UKE  SUB
XENON  LOXES  LEX  ONO
INCUS  ARIAS  NYC  LOB
STAGNATION    WAPITI
TOPHAT  SMITH  ASHCAN
SSS  ROB  SERA  DERIVE
  REMAP  ETS  ITES
TORA  DAHS  SALIVA
OBEYED  SOPH  ROSETTE
GIA  RESTORATION  ION
SELLOUT  FAIR  MTHOOD
LUSTER  GRIM  INKS
NEON  MOC  ODEUM
ARCADE  WOES  AWN  OAS
TRACED  DONTS  ETERNE
TYPIFY   LACERATION
SKI  UTE  LIBRA  MUNRO
RIO  TOE  ISLET  EDGAR
INN  YRS  STEWS  DESKS
```

PUZZLE 557

```
YEW   ASPS   SKIN
AMI   WORE   TARE
PUN   ADIT   ALMS
   DAYAN  GREAT
PSST   SCONE
ROOM   ERA   BAH
ERR   SPORT  ALE
YES   ARF   SLOW
   CROWS  AMEN
TIARA  ALAMO
OSLO  ALAR  RUM
OLGA  METE  ASA
LEAK  ASEA  LET
```

PUZZLE 549

```
SAGE  CREW   SPRIG
TRUE  HOLE   OLIVE
ROLL  RULE   CADET
AMP  ROSS   BIN
PASTIME   PEEKED
  ICE  CULT  AWL
SHONE  SADLY  SEA
TOUT  BINGE  HELD
ANT  ARRAY  BADLY
BEE  NOEL  FLU
  DRAGON  GEOLOGY
  FED  BOUT  CUE
ASTIR  PLOD  TEAL
SPARE  ROSE  EARL
PAGED  OWED  ANDS
```

PUZZLE 553

```
COLA   WED   SPAS
AVID  BERET  KEEL
RENO  READY  YORE
PRESTO  SUP  PIE
  RAM  COG  LAP
OAF  ADOPT  NOEL
AIL  YETI  BUN
TRUE  SHAWL  EACH
  LOT  NEAT  FOE
BUFF  PORCH  TOW
LAM  FRO  EKE
ALP  ITS  TEMPLE
SLIP  BANJO  ORAL
TORE  STOOP  LENS
STEW  OWE   TYKE
```

PUZZLE 558

```
MESH  SIS   ARID
ARIA  TRI   DOOR
NIGHTOWL    DATA
YEN  OLIVE  DAY
   NINEVEH
SALTED   RENOWN
AGAR   OGEE
LAMINA   BASSET
  EMOTION
SOD  STRUT  SPA
PLUS  LONEWOLF
RICE  END  OMAR
YOKE  ESS  KENO
```

PUZZLE 550

```
STEM   TIS   HARP
ARMY  MANNA  ICER
PAIN  ANNUL  POLO
SPRAIN  BIB  RIB
  NODS  BOUNCE
COP  TRILLION
ORATE  NEO  KITES
ACTOR  NEW  STALL
TASTE  EVE  TERSE
  ESPRESSO  PEW
HEARTH   STAR
ARC  SOP  FEDORA
BOMB  NOBLE  AVID
IDEA  ERROR  VASE
TEST  EAT   ELKS
```

PUZZLE 554

```
CARED  SAND   CAPS
AWAKE  PRAY   OPAL
LAKES  AKIN   YETI
LYE  TAR  LABORED
   AIR  MAT
REINED   WISEST
MUMMY  EPICS  LAW
ORE  ART  AXE
MAR  PILOT  SATED
LYRICS   YIPPED
   ALE  ROT
PRECEDE  PEN  COP
LOVE  TACO  GRAVE
USER  ERAS  EASEL
MESS  ANTE  SPENT
```

PUZZLE 559

```
WET  ASSET   LAMA
CRAW  ICIER  EVEN
LOGO  DOLLY  TEST
ATE  SERE   CURSE
DERBY   ENTRAP
  END  COUP  OLE
CANDOR  ERE  KIP
ARE  DAB  EFT  ROE
VIA  WEE  URBANE
EAR  PENT  LYE
  GIRDER  STAND
LADLE  REST  TEE
OLEO  MANLY  BOWL
USER  AGAIN  ALEE
DORY  DOLCE   ALL
```

PUZZLE 560

```
COTTA ABBA ELSE
AREAS REAR NOEL
WEATHERTHESTORM
SORT DES   TIMES
    OTIS FAIR
 SHOOTTHEBREEZE
STEER  ALES  MOT
WILD DRILL CANE
ALL  WOOF  ARIES
 BLOWHOTANDCOLD
    RIMS EYES
ESSES  EWE  SHOW
RUNATEMPERATURE
OMIT LOIS WILTS
SOPH SECT LEAST
```

PUZZLE 566

Become, Bedazzle, Before, Befuddle, Beginning, Behavioral, Behemoth, Beholden, Believability, Benevolent.

HINT: BE

PUZZLE 570

```
TAPS ASTER LEFT
EURO PHASE AQUA
ARIL TORTS MUSS
SAVE  ROE  BEAST
EFT  SLAMMED
BREAKAGE ASPENS
BEEN CEDER ALOE
STRIPE INNOCENT
   ABRADED  MOA
ORB LOO ADDLE
PERIL TEN  ANKH
ELIS CADGE STOA
RIAL URGES TALL
ACRE DYERS SLAT
```

PUZZLE 561

1. Climate, 2. Cleanse, 3. Coterie, 4. Cyclone, 5. Capsize, 6. Cottage, 7. Chorale, 8. Cologne, 9. Carmine.

9-LETTER WORD: Maelstrom

PUZZLE 567

```
MOSS  QUAD  BAR
EVIL  UNDO  ALE
TAXI  AIDE  NOS
   DAIS    JET
OAF  BLOT  BOSS
HYENA  NULL
MENACE  BAITED
   RITZ  SPIRE
BEVY  AIMS  SEW
LEI   GOOF
ALL  ORZO  AWLS
ZEE  ROAN  KEEP
ERR  EDGY  EDDY
```

1-J, 2-W, 3-P, 4-O, 5-F, 6-I, 7-A, 8-S, 9-C, 10-V, 11-L, 12-Y, 13-U, 14-D, 15-R, 16-N, 17-X, 18-H, 19-K, 20-Z, 21-T, 22-G, 23-M, 24-Q, 25-E, 26-B.

PUZZLE 571

COTTONWOOD

PUZZLE 562

```
COM PLE TE   BAR RA GE        SH AW
P   AS TE    B   EIGE      M  ALL ARD
EL  AN    SP AR     R   HUB ARB
    T  REM END OUS      C  LE RIC
       OV ER    CAT N AP     KET CH
PRO DIG AL   CRO CH ET     SPR Y  EST
PER ES    PRE SS ING    SHO E
    T  RU ST        CHA RT  E  R
       P  IGE ON    R  AGE     HE W
MAR QU EE    GO  N  G      DOC TOR AL
SH  ACK      ING EST ED       K  IC KER
```

PUZZLE 563

A-5, B-4, C-3, D-7, E-1, F-6, G-8, H-2, I-9.

PUZZLE 572

```
ODDS ASTA  SEED
BRAT ALAMO APSE
IOTA HERON LINE
SPARE EASE ICED
   REV  SON
PROSPECT LEECH
PUERTO AWED LEI
IRIS XENON AIDE
TEN PYRE TINTED
YESES ARRESTED
   FIG  ARM
GAFF LAMB SCARE
OLEO ADOBE OVEN
AGAR DAVIT KIEV
DART METE  EDDY
```

PUZZLE 564

```
NILS ELSE  LIMO
OTIC NOONS OMAR
DEMO DOUGH APSE
EMBRYO SUES ESS
   EER ELATER
 PHRASE FREESIA
TIE  EGO SALONS
EXALT GNU MYNAH
AIRIER ORR ANY
RETREAD NETTLE
 TANGOS DOE
NAH  STOP NOSHER
EURO ADOBE TARO
ATOP GARYS ETAS
ROBE DEES  DELE
```

PUZZLE 568

```
NINJA HEAT HALF
OLEOS ONTO IDOL
BLESS OVER FOXY
 HUSKY  PHI
IMP RAY MOA BAY
FORGET SARI OWE
STOA  YAKS KRONA
 BURLESQUE
CLASS LIEU EPEE
OAR UPON ESKERS
GYM ALT BET WAS
 ALA AERIE
ACER ZING TUNER
SERF ALOE CRAVE
KEGS SKAT HONED
```

1-S, 2-M, 3-X, 4-W, 5-D, 6-K, 7-I, 8-E, 9-B, 10-Y, 11-A, 12-U, 13-F, 14-V, 15-L, 16-T, 17-N, 18-J, 19-Z, 20-O, 21-C, 22-P, 23-Q, 24-G, 25-R, 26-H.

PUZZLE 573

1. Tool, Toot, Tort, Tore, Tart, Tare, Tame, Tamp.

2. Wish, Wise, Wile, Will, Wale, Wall, Wail, Wait.

PUZZLE 574

```
INCUBATE EDITOR
N  A  A  I O R E A
DECRYPT CRIMSON
I H S I   T F T K
AGENT ABOUTFACE
N  A  N  P   M S
ADAPTS FIERCEST
   P E    E  N
PROTRACT CASTLE
O  C  H  A L   L
STRONGARM ISSUE
H  Y  O  L B S M C
EXPENSE LITHEST
S  H  E  T E I L O
TOASTY EDUCATOR
```

PUZZLE 565

```
CHAR  BATE  BUFF
LAVA  ARSON ETRE
AKIN  LASTS TEED
MEDIAL  ENCASES
   POSTMARK
 ABETTOR REELS
CHEF SPICES HAS
HEATS  OUR TEARY
AMC WARMUP TSAR
 SHOAL PELICAN
   BRIGHTER
OARSMAN  AKIMBO
BLUE  SOARS TIED
OTIS  EMCEE CLAD
EONS  SETS  HERS
```

PUZZLE 569

```
ACTS      LOSS   FETE
PHOTO     AREA   RACER
TIGER     COWCATCHER
CAMELBACK       VETO
   ARCH  AUTO
   SWORE BRING
JEAN WET ENS  OATS
ARIA         OHIO
WALKER    MUSSEL
   EVA    IKE
ASLEEP    DEEPER
CLAY      GREY
EYRE AMA ALP GONE
 SPRAY LUAUS
 EIRE  SNIP
 GNAW  TOADSTOOL
SHEEPSKINS  ARROW
OUNCE IDEA  MACRO
PEEK  DOOR  LANE
```

PUZZLE 575

```
CAPES ALIA  ASPS
AROSE LONG  SELA
FIRSTPLACE SCAN
EAT TOOTH RIOTS
   SLOTH SIGN
POTTER  SPINDLE
ACHED MATES BUM
CHIP LADED HARP
ERR BARON BESET
REDDEST  GREEDY
 PUTT FREUD
SEARS GLENS FEE
CURE FOURTHDOWN
ARTS ASTA  EARED
TOYS THEN  DYERS
```

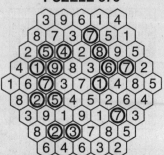

```
TWIT ACTS BALM DAMP
EIRE NOON ELEA ORAL
STAR NCAA DEAN WISE
SHERWOODFOREST NASA
    OAT UFO TIGE
OVERCAST TON SPRING
DEW OTTER MEG ASTER
DEEP EATER WAS GERE
SPREE GOMER SPARROW
  AMP NIGEL AGO
TRACTOR TALES EVENT
RUSH TIM LIMIT ELIE
ELIOT MAD CORED LPN
SEARCH HER NEAREAST
  CUES TIA BAN
BATH LAKEOFTHEWOODS
ASEA LUNN TIER UPON
CHAR EDIT EDER GILA
HERD RITE RELY HELP
```

```
PANE RAPA FORE ABLE
ASEA ELAN OLEG URAL
PARR LAID NEAR RACK
APOLLOCREED DEPOSES
    YAK AXLE TAR
FRAMED INTENT CABAL
LUGE ELM TAU BABA
ODER DIANAROSS ONUS
PESCI IMAGE SECRETE
  USA SHANT DEE
SUCROSE UTTER OATES
STAY HERMESPAN LAVA
TART ELA IWO IRAN
SHAHS SINBAD TISANE
  EAT LOAM NIT
CARACAS IRENECASTLE
ABET RAGS NEHI HOAX
DEAR OGEE DARN ANNE
IDLE TEES SLUG WEDS
```

```
BASSO HARP THEM TEPID
ALOUD ALAI RATE ALONE
HORNETPIPE ANTE HARTE
TUTU APE ROCKETBOTTOM
   PARENT LES REE
YEW RON ARMS SKA STAN
ENACTS ALEE FLING RIO
OGLE BOXCARET ELUDE
MILE MAIN LID ENAMEL
ANE SEND GAIA STROP
NET MANETOFBRONZE EDS
PAINE ALTI DEES TIO
STARRY FIE REEL SCAR
CAPEK BONMOTET GAPE
OLE SWEET AILS PETREL
TART ITS USMA TED DRY
    ESP ANI YARROW
BLANKETVERSE TAO EARN
LORNA RASE CABINETBOY
OCTET ENOS CLAN BELLE
WHERE KEPT EATS BREED
```

```
SENSE PLOD CLAM RAVES
PLOWS LATE AONE ABODE
AIRES AXIL NUTS BRIDE
RAIDERS CANADIANBACON
ESAI UTE YAP AIDE
    STRICT MEDICI ELKE
MACHO CHINESEWALL ENT
ALAMOS ORE COR ATSEA
TENANTS EERIE RECUSES
EPOS RIG URNS NER
SHES IRISHSETTER KEAN
AOK SOUS USO ISLA
TRIGGER LEEDS PLASTER
OILER EOE ATE SPHERE
ELL ENGLISHHORN ODETS
DEAR ADELIE PRAISE
  TESS TRA SSS LAPS
FRENCHWINDOWS TOPICAL
RIATA OLEO ALAI AGAPE
ASSET VIEW IONE SHREW
NEEDS EARN TEAR STIRS
```

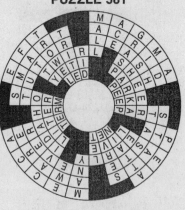

```
SPOT BLUR ENOS DEER
HIVE OISE LOPE ETNA
ALAS ALES AREA STIR
DELLASTREET CRUSADE
  ART TAIL STEP
CAB LEAK POEM ARLEN
ASA ORLON NEAP TALE
LEND SORES KEEP CIA
MADAM NEATO RESEAL
  MARGARETCOURT
BIPEDS SETON MANGE
ODE EVIL REMIT GOAD
RENT PLOT RECAP OLD
GENOA LOAD SELL NAY
  YANG TROT LAS
HOLSTER ZEBULONPIKE
ERAT NORA ELON ARAL
ANNE ROAN ANTE ROLL
PEER EMMA MASS KNEE
```

```
STIR SILO NAME DELL
TIDE CRIB IRON EDIE
ALOE HILL NEWT AGES
YELLOWSTONE NEATENS
   ERA NAPE RAH
PLACE BAGPIPE AVERT
LEFT CAW NIGH AREA
USA SENATE COO LIAM
GERMAN KANE SUNLAMP
  AFT ERASE SEE
HAMMERS SCAM TOYOTA
EXAM ATO TUCSON MAP
ALTO LUBE EON BAKE
TESTA NOVICES FIRED
   HOT LIRA EAT
CHOCKED DRYTORTUGAS
OONA PINE MODO MICE
AVIV IRAN ARID EVEN
TETE DEBT NENE NEST
```

```
SLIT ROMA SHED NYET
TODO AMEN TELE IOTA
AVER FIST RAIL GROG
YEAROFTHECAT ATHENS
   ELL NAP SWAT
MUD DEPEND TEATOWEL
ACRES AAA LEAR FIDO
ILAY FIT GENRE TRIS
LATERAL CRASS RHETT
   OAT BLASE TIE
ALOFT CLOTH GABFEST
MINT SHINE FIX OVER
INCH HOSE NIL EXILE
STEELERS PANAMA LAT
  TAPE FOR ACT
LAVISH HAIROFTHEDOG
AGOG EDAM OBIT ROPE
METE RIVE WORE SLUR
PEER DEED SEER ELSE
```

```
RATA DATA ODOR BED
IRAN ELAN CODA HULA
PERK LARK ACED ONLY
ESTATESALE TRIBUTES
   RAG EWER IRS
RUTABAGA EMIT AERIE
ALA STALE UNIT RICA
INC ELUDE ERE USER
LATHE AMEND ENDLESS
  OVA SNARE SUE
ELEMENT SCALP ESSAY
MOVE DOT TIDAL ERA
IDES SIRE NEVER AIM
RENTS LAGS REBOUNDS
  EOS MOAN ALP
ESCALLOP CABINFEVER
CHAD ILLS MORE NICE
HOGS PEEP ENOS DORA
ODE SORA DONE SLUR
```

DIAGRAMLESS STARTING BOXES

Puzzle 89 starts in box 6
Puzzle 91 starts in box 1
Puzzle 93 starts in box 4
Puzzle 95 starts in box 8
Puzzle 97 starts in box 13
Puzzle 99 starts in box 5
Puzzle 100 starts in box 5
Puzzle 209 starts in box 7
Puzzle 211 starts in box 1
Puzzle 213 starts in box 7
Puzzle 215 starts in box 4
Puzzle 217 starts in box 3
Puzzle 219 starts in box 9
Puzzle 220 starts in box 7
Puzzle 383 starts in box 6
Puzzle 385 starts in box 7
Puzzle 387 starts in box 1
Puzzle 389 starts in box 15
Puzzle 391 starts in box 3
Puzzle 393 starts in box 8
Puzzle 394 starts in box 4
Puzzle 503 starts in box 10
Puzzle 505 starts in box 4
Puzzle 507 starts in box 7
Puzzle 509 starts in box 12
Puzzle 511 starts in box 6
Puzzle 513 starts in box 5
Puzzle 514 starts in box 13